SHAKESPEARE SURVEY
77

Shakespeare's Poetry

SHAKESPEARE SURVEY
ADVISORY BOARD

JONATHAN BATE
DAVID STERLING BROWN
MARK THORNTON BURNETT
MARGRETA DE GRAZIA
CARLA DELLA GATTA
MICHAEL DOBSON
TON HOENSELAARS
PETER HOLLAND
JOHN JOWETT

HESTER LEES-JEFFRIES
VANESSA LIM
HARRY R. MCCARTHY
LUCY MUNRO
CLAUDIA OLK
LENA COWEN ORLIN
REIKO OYA
SIMON PALFREY
AYANNA THOMPSON

Assistant to the Editor KATIE MENNIS

(1) *Shakespeare and his Stage*
(2) *Shakespearian Production*
(3) *The Man and the Writer*
(4) *Interpretation*
(5) *Textual Criticism*
(6) *The Histories*
(7) *Style and Language*
(8) *The Comedies*
(9) *Hamlet*
(10) *The Roman Plays*
(11) *The Last Plays (with an index to Surveys 1–10)*
(12) *The Elizabethan Theatre*
(13) *King Lear*
(14) *Shakespeare and his Contemporaries*
(15) *The Poems and Music*
(16) *Shakespeare in the Modern World*
(17) *Shakespeare in his Own Age*
(18) *Shakespeare Then Till Now*
(19) *Macbeth*
(20) *Shakespearian and Other Tragedy*
(21) *Othello (with an index to Surveys 11–20)*
(22) *Aspects of Shakespearian Comedy*
(23) *Shakespeare's Language*
(24) *Shakespeare: Theatre Poet*
(25) *Shakespeare's Problem Plays*
(26) *Shakespeare's Jacobean Tragedies*
(27) *Shakespeare's Early Tragedies*
(28) *Shakespeare and the Ideas of his Time*
(29) *Shakespeare's Last Plays*
(30) *Henry IV to Hamlet*
(31) *Shakespeare and the Classical World (with an index to Surveys 21–30)*
(32) *The Middle Comedies*
(33) *King Lear*
(34) *Characterization in Shakespeare*
(35) *Shakespeare in the Nineteenth Century*
(36) *Shakespeare in the Twentieth Century*
(37) *Shakespeare's Earlier Comedies*
(38) *Shakespeare and History*
(39) *Shakespeare on Film and Television*
(40) *Current Approaches to Shakespeare through Language, Text and Theatre*
(41) *Shakespearian Stages and Staging (with an index to Surveys 31–40)*
(42) *Shakespeare and the Elizabethans*
(43) *The Tempest and After*
(44) *Shakespeare and Politics*
(45) *Hamlet and its Afterlife*
(46) *Shakespeare and Sexuality*
(47) *Playing Places for Shakespeare*
(48) *Shakespeare and Cultural Exchange*
(49) *Romeo and Juliet and its Afterlife*
(50) *Shakespeare and Language*
(51) *Shakespeare in the Eighteenth Century (with an index to Surveys 41–50)*
(52) *Shakespeare and the Globe*
(53) *Shakespeare and Narrative*
(54) *Shakespeare and Religions*
(55) *King Lear and its Afterlife*
(56) *Shakespeare and Comedy*
(57) *Macbeth and its Afterlife*
(58) *Writing About Shakespeare*
(59) *Editing Shakespeare*
(60) *Theatres for Shakespeare*
(61) *Shakespeare, Sound and Screen*
(62) *Close Encounters with Shakespeare's Text*
(63) *Shakespeare's English Histories and their Afterlives*
(64) *Shakespeare as Cultural Catalyst*
(65) *A Midsummer Night's Dream*
(66) *Working with Shakespeare*
(67) *Shakespeare's Collaborative Work*
(68) *Shakespeare, Origins and Originality*
(69) *Shakespeare and Rome*
(70) *Creating Shakespeare*
(71) *Re-Creating Shakespeare*
(72) *Shakespeare and War*
(73) *Shakespeare and the City*
(74) *Shakespeare and Education*
(75) *Othello*
(76) *Digital and Virtual Shakespeare*
(77) *Shakespeare's Poetry*

SHAKESPEARE SURVEY

77

Shakespeare's Poetry

EDITED BY
HANNAH CRAWFORTH
ELIZABETH SCOTT-BAUMANN
EMMA SMITH

Shaftesbury Road, Cambridge CB2 8EA, United Kingdom

One Liberty Plaza, 20th Floor, New York, NY 10006, USA

477 Williamstown Road, Port Melbourne, VIC 3207, Australia

314–321, 3rd Floor, Plot 3, Splendor Forum, Jasola District Centre,
New Delhi – 110025, India

103 Penang Road, #05–06/07, Visioncrest Commercial, Singapore 238467

Cambridge University Press is part of Cambridge University Press & Assessment,
a department of the University of Cambridge.

We share the University's mission to contribute to society through the pursuit of
education, learning and research at the highest international levels of excellence.

www.cambridge.org
Information on this title: www.cambridge.org/9781009531399

DOI: 10.1017/9781009531351

© Cambridge University Press & Assessment 2024

This publication is in copyright. Subject to statutory exception and to the provisions
of relevant collective licensing agreements, no reproduction of any part may take
place without the written permission of Cambridge University Press & Assessment.

When citing this work, please include a reference to the DOI 10.1017/9781009531351

First published 2024

Printed in the United Kingdom by TJ Books Limited, Padstow, Cornwall 2024

A catalogue record for this publication is available from the British Library

A Cataloging-in-Publication data record for this book is available from the Library of Congress

ISBN 978-1-009-53139-9 Hardback

Cambridge University Press & Assessment has no responsibility for the persistence
or accuracy of URLs for external or third-party internet websites referred to in this
publication and does not guarantee that any content on such websites is, or will
remain, accurate or appropriate.

EDITOR'S NOTE

Shakespeare Survey 77 has as its theme 'Shakespeare's Poetry', and is coedited with Hannah Crawforth and Elizabeth Scott-Baumann. I am also grateful to Li Lan Yong for coordinating the papers from the World Shakespeare Congress 2021 in Singapore, which form the second section of this volume. Our next issue, 78, will draw on the International Shakespeare Conference at Stratford-upon-Avon in summer 2024, and take as its theme 'Shakespeare and Communities'. Volume 79 will be on 'Late Shakespeare'. The editor and Advisory Board welcome submissions on these topics sent as email attachments to the editor at emma.smith@hertford.ox.ac.uk. The deadline is 1 September 2024 for volume 78, and 1 September 2025 for volume 79.

There is also space in each issue for articles not on the theme. The Advisory Board is particularly keen to encourage proposals for small clusters of 3–5 articles on a Shakespearian theme, topic or approach. These can be discussed with, or submitted to the editor at any time in the year. All submissions are screened for eligibility by the editor and then read by at least one member of the Advisory Board. We warmly welcome both early-career and more established scholars to consider *Survey* as a venue for their work.

Part of *Survey*'s distinctiveness is its reviews. Review copies, including article offprints, should be addressed to the editor at Hertford College, Oxford OX1 3BW: our reviewers inevitably have to exercise some selection about what they cover. On that note, I am grateful to Lois Potter, whose tenure as London theatre reviewer, across the most turbulent period in recent theatre history, has come to an end.

EMMA SMITH

CONTRIBUTORS

TIMOTHY BILLINGS, *Middlebury College*
JESSICA CHIBA, *Shakespeare Institute, University of Birmingham*
KATHARINE A. CRAIK, *Oxford Brookes University*
HANNAH CRAWFORTH, *King's College London*
EMMA DEPLEDGE, *University of Neuchâtel*
JEAN-MICHEL DÉPRATS, *Université de Paris Nanterre*
AMRITA DHAR, *The Ohio State University*
MICHAEL DOBSON, *Shakespeare Institute, University of Birmingham*
MIKA EGLINTON, *Kobe City University*
STEPHEN GUY-BRAY, *University of British Columbia*
KUMIKO HILBERDINK-SAKAMOTO, *Nihon University*
EZRA HORBURY, *University of York*
JUDY ICK, *University of the Philippines*
MIRIAM JACOBSON, *University of Georgia*
ALEXA ALICE JOUBIN, *The George Washington University*
SHOICHIRO KAWAI, *The University of Tokyo*
DENNIS KENNEDY, *Trinity College Dublin*
KIM TAI-WON, *Sogang University*
JANE KINGSLEY-SMITH, *University of Roehampton*
LEE HYON-U, *Soon Chun Hyang University, Korea*
BI-QI BEATRICE LEI, *Asian Shakespeare Association*
ALVIN ENG HUI LIM, *National University of Singapore*
JOYCE GREEN MACDONALD, *University of Kentucky*
TAMARA MAHADIN, *The Ohio State University*
MADHAVI MENON, *Ashoka University*
FEISAL G. MOHAMED, *Yale University*
ELEINE NG-GAGNEUX, *National University of Singapore*
LOIS POTTER, *University of Delaware*
AYESHA RAMACHANDRAN, *Yale University*
COLLEEN RUTH ROSENFELD, *Pomona College*
SARAH C. E. ROSS, *Victoria University of Wellington*
MARJORIE RUBRIGHT, *University of Massachusetts–Amherst*
ELEANOR RYCROFT, *University of Bristol*
ELIZABETH SCOTT-BAUMANN, *King's College London*
JAMES SHAW, *Bodleian Libraries Oxford*

LIST OF CONTRIBUTORS

SHEN LIN, *Central Academy of Drama, Beijing*
JYOTSNA G. SINGH, *Michigan State University*
ROBERT STAGG, *Shakespeare Institute / St Anne's College, Oxford*
PRETI TANEJA, *Newcastle University*
TANG SHU-WING, *Tang Shu-wing Theatre Studio, Hong Kong*
CHRISTOPHER THURMAN, *University of the Witwatersrand*
WILL TOSH, *Shakespeare's Globe*
VALERIE TRAUB, *University of Michigan*
YONG LI LAN, *National University of Singapore*

CONTENTS

List of Illustrations   page xi

JOYCE GREEN MACDONALD	Remembering Shakespeare's *Sonnets* in *Lucy Negro, Redux*	1
MIRIAM JACOBSON	The Poetics of Antiquarian Accumulation in *A Lover's Complaint*	12
STEPHEN GUY-BRAY	Different Samenesses	24
COLLEEN RUTH ROSENFELD	Shakespeare's Canvas	35
KATHARINE A. CRAIK	'Persuasion by Similitude': Finding Likeness in Shakespeare's *A Lover's Complaint*	51
JANE KINGSLEY-SMITH	'Nothing-to-be-Glossed-Here': Race in Shakespeare's *Sonnets*	62
MADHAVI MENON	Allegorical Desire, or, The Sufi 'Phoenix and the Turtle'	79
AYESHA RAMACHANDRAN	The Poetics of Shakespearian Erasure: Lyric Thinking with Bhanu Kapil and Preti Taneja	91
FEISAL G. MOHAMED	*Lucrece*, Letters and the Moment of Lipsius	104
ROBERT STAGG	Shakespeare's Arabic Sonnets	116
HANNAH CRAWFORTH AND ELIZABETH SCOTT-BAUMANN	How to Make a Formal Complaint: Sara Ahmed's *Complaint!* and William Shakespeare's *A Lover's Complaint*	130
AMRITA DHAR	They Also Serve Who Only Stand and Write, or, How Milton Read Shakespeare's *Sonnets*	147
WILL TOSH	Writing Delight with Beauty's Pen: Restoring Richard Barnfield's Lost Credit	158
TAMARA MAHADIN	Ocular Power and Female *Fascinum* in Shakespeare's *Venus and Adonis*	169
SARAH C. E. ROSS	Pretty Creatures: *A Lover's Complaint*, *The Rape of Lucrece* and Early Modern Women's Complaint Poetry	180
JYOTSNA G. SINGH	Lyric Voices and Cultural Encounters across Time and Space: The Poetry of William Shakespeare and Faiz Ahmed Faiz (1911–1984)	194

CONTENTS

XI World Shakespeare Congress: Shakespeare Circuits *edited by* Yong Li Lan

Preti Taneja	The Thing Itself or the Image of That Horror: Fictions, Fascisms and *We That Are Young*	205
Dennis Kennedy	Shakespeare's Refugees	217
Tang Shu-wing	Shakespeare as a Source of Dramaturgical Reconstruction	226
Jyotsna G. Singh, Jessica Chiba, Amrita Dhar and Christopher Thurman	Shakespeare, Race, Postcoloniality: The State of the Fields	235
Yong Li Lan, Michael Dobson, Mika Eglinton, Lee Hyon-u, Bi-qi Beatrice Lei, Alvin Eng Hui Lim and Eleine Ng-Gagneux	Asian Shakespeares Online from Singapore	244
Shoichiro Kawai, Timothy Billings, Jean-Michel Déprats, Kim Tai-Won and Shen Lin	Strange Shadows: Translating Shakespeare – The State of the Field	261
Marjorie Rubright and Valerie Traub, Kumiko Hilberdink-Sakamoto, Judy Ick, Alexa Alice Joubin and Madhavi Menon	Gender and Sexuality: The State of the Fields	270
	Shakespeare Performances in England, 2022–2023	
Lois Potter	*London Productions, 2023*	281
Eleanor Rycroft	*Productions Outside London, 2022–2023*	292
James Shaw	Professional Shakespeare Productions in the UK, January-December *2022*	312

The Year's Contribution to Shakespeare Studies — 320
1 Critical Studies *reviewed by* Ezra Horbury — 320
2 Editions and Textual Studies *reviewed by* Emma Depledge — 333

Abstracts of Articles in *Shakespeare Survey 77* — 345
Index — 350

ILLUSTRATIONS

1. Eric Zboya's version of Sonnet 30 © Nightboat Books. *page* 26
2. Daniel Tiffany's adaptation of Sonnet 43 © Nightboat Books 28
3. Pablo Picasso, *Las Meninas*. 17 August 1957. Oil on canvas, 194 × 260 cm. Museu Picasso, Barcelona. Photo: Fotogasull. © 2024 Estate of Pablo Picasso / Artists Rights Society (ARS), New York. 37
4. Pablo Picasso, *Las Meninas*. 4 September 1957. Oil on canvas, 35 × 27 cm. Museu Picasso, Barcelona. Photo: Fotogasull. © 2024 Estate of Pablo Picasso / Artists Rights Society (ARS), New York. 41
5. Pablo Picasso, *Las Meninas*. 15 September 1957. Oil and charcoal on canvas, 129 × 161 cm. Museu Picasso, Barcelona. Photo: Fotogasull. © 2024 Estate of Pablo Picasso / Artists Rights Society (ARS), New York. 46
6. Pablo Picasso, *The Piano*. 17 October 1957. Oil on canvas, 129.5 × 96.5 cm. Museu Picasso, Barcelona. Photo: Fotogasull. © 2024 Estate of Pablo Picasso / Artists Rights Society (ARS), New York. 47
7. Pablo Picasso, *Las Meninas [Nicolasito Pertusato]*. 24 October 1957. Oil on canvas, 61 × 50 cm. Museu Picasso, Barcelona. Photo: Fotogasull. © 2024 Estate of Pablo Picasso / Artists Rights Society (ARS), New York. 48
8. Gregory Betts, 'Shakespeare's Alphabet'. By permission of the author. 48
9. Title page of *Lucrece* (1594; Yale University, Eliz 179). By permission of The Elizabethan Club of Yale University. Full image set available at collections.library.yale.edu. 114
10. Title page of Justus Lipsius, *Six Bookes of Politickes or Civil Doctrine*, trans. William Jones (1594; Yale University, Ocg30 L669 589 g). By courtesy of the Beinecke Rare Book & Manuscript Library, Yale University. 114
11. *Titus Andronicus* performed in Cantonese by Tang Shu-wing Theatre Studio, Hong Kong Jockey Club Amphitheatre, The Hong Kong Academy for Performing Arts, 2012. 230
12. *Titus 2.0* performed in Cantonese by Tang Shu-wing Theatre Studio, Hong Kong City Hall Theatre, 2009. 230
13. *Titus Andronicus* performed in Cantonese by Tang Shu-wing Theatre Studio, Hong Kong Jockey Club Amphitheatre, The Hong Kong Academy for Performing Arts, 2012. 231
14. Act 5, scene 2 of *Titus 2.0* performed in Cantonese by Tang Shu-wing Theatre Studio, Hong Kong City Hall Theatre, 2009. 232
15. *Titus Andronicus* performed in Cantonese by Tang Shu-wing Theatre Studio, Hong Kong Jockey Club Amphitheatre, The Hong Kong Academy for Performing Arts, 2012. . 233

LIST OF ILLUSTRATIONS

16. Act 2, scene 4 of *Titus Andronicus 2.0* performed in Cantonese by Tang Shu-wing Theatre Studio, Hong Kong City Hall Theatre, 2009.   234
17. Lear and the Fools, Nine Years Theatre, *Lear Is Dead*, Singapore, 2018. Photo: The Pond Photography, courtesy of Nine Years Theatre.   247
18. Micari as the ghost of Desdemona, Shizuoka Performing Arts Center, *Miyagi Noh Othello ~Phantom Love~*, Shizuoka, 2018. Photo: K. Miura.   250
19. Wu Hsing-kuo as Prospero (right), with Shih Hung-Chun as Caliban (left), Contemporary Legend Theatre, *The Tempest*, National Theatre of Korea, Seoul, 2009. Photo: Kuo Cheng Chang.   252
20. Padmanabhan Nair as King Lear and Annette Leday as the dead Cordelia, Annette Leday / Keli Company, *Kathakali-King Lear*, Kerala Kalamandalam Institution, Cheruthuruthy, Kerala, 1989. Photo: Keli Paris.   253
21. Nakamura Kazutaro as Sandaime Richard (Richard III), *Sandaime Richard* (2016), written by Noda Hideki, directed by Ong Keng Sen. Image courtesy of Jun Ishikawa for World Theatre Festival Shizuoka, Singapore International Festival of Arts and Tokyo Metropolitan Theatre.   256
22. Nam Yoon-ho as young Pericles and Yoo In-chon as Gower, Yohangza Theatre Company, *Pericles*, Seoul, 2015. Photo: Park Gyeong-bok.   258
23. *Macbeth*, dir. Abigail Graham. Ben Caplan, Calum Callaghan and Ferdy Roberts as Witches, Max Bennett as Macbeth. Photo: Johan Persson / ArenaPAL. www.arenapal.com.   285
24. *As You Like It*, dir. Ellen McDougall. Nina Bowers as Rosalind and Macy-Jacob Seelochan as Celia. Photo: Ellie Kurttz / ArenaPAL. www.arenapal.com.   286
25. *As You Like It*, dir. Josie Rourke. Nathan Queeley-Dennis as Silvius, Tom Edden as Duke Frederick, Dickon Gough as Charles, Alfred Enoch as Orlando, Allie Daniel as Amiens, Michael Bruce as Pianist, Syakira Moeladi as Hisperia, and Martha Plimpton as Jaques. Photo: Johan Persson / ArenaPAL. www.arenapal.com.   291
26. Nicholas Woodeson as Prospero in *The Tempest*. Photo: Hugo Glendinning.   296
27. The betrothal masque as barn dance in *The Tempest*, dir. Elizabeth Freestone. Photo: Ikin Yum © RSC.   299
28. The Cockpit Theatre at The Shakespeare North Playhouse: Photo: Andrew P. Brooks.   300
29. Candlelight meets electric light in *A Midsummer Night's Dream* at Shakespeare North Playhouse, dir. Matthew Dunster and Jimmy Fairhurst. Photo: Patch Dolan.   303
30. Amber Sylvia Edwards, Dylan Reid and Eilidh Loan as the three witches in *Macbeth*, dir. Wils Wilson. Photo: Marc Brenner © RSC.   307
31. Kiren Kebaili-Dwyer as Hamlet and Claire Redcliffe as Gertrude in *Hamlet*, dir. Tinuke Craig (2022) and Ellie Hurt (2023). Photo: Harry Elletson.   311

REMEMBERING SHAKESPEARE'S *SONNETS* IN *LUCY NEGRO, REDUX*

JOYCE GREEN MACDONALD

'Memory', Derrida reminds us, 'is not just the opposite of forgetting.'[1] Since, as he argued, the ancient archives where public memory was stored were the property of the state, knowledge of the past was controlled by gatekeepers who held a vested interest in what could become known and in how citizens who managed to achieve access to it could use this knowledge. To remember, then, is at least potentially to engage in acts of subterfuge, rebellion, stealing away.

For the purposes of this article, the difficulty of retrieving embargoed memory – much less of recirculating it and living in its light in the present – is only exacerbated by the trauma of the transatlantic slave trade, beginning to gather its dreadful force during Shakespeare's lifetime. The sheer scope of what Saidiya Hartman calls 'the catastrophe that was our past'[2] – for millions to have been abducted and violently transformed from human beings into objects – might seem to form an unnavigable dead zone between what may once have been and what survives now, in catastrophe's wake. But I say 'might' because of what we know about the power of the yearning of the enslaved to recover the past, and about the will of the descendants of the enslaved not only to remember, but to reanimate. The remembrance and reanimation I discuss here is Caroline Randall Williams's 2019 poetry collection *Lucy Negro, Redux*, which meditates on critical claims that the Renaissance London bawd known as Lucy Negro was the inspiration for the 'Dark Lady' of Shakespeare's Sonnets 127–154. Randall Williams's collection asks us to imagine what we cannot know about the time and space between Hartman's 'catastrophe' and our own contemporary vantage point on that past, and to fill in details of an autonomous creative power that escaped and defied bondage.

Randall Williams's poems imitate the sonnets, absorbing and reproducing them for the present. Her poetic imitation also accepts the larger mission of confronting black Atlantic subjects' dispossession. Thus, her collection must play with time, moving back and forth from the present to the Renaissance to US slave culture, as it imagines a life for Lucy Negro and a point of origin for all the black women subsumed into slavery's wake. Indeed, Randall Williams's imaginative play is enabled by the blank spaces in the records of Lucy Negro's historical presence, as well as by Africans' disappearance into the gulf of transatlantic time. Her project was inspired by the research of Shakespearian Duncan Salkeld into the minutes of London's Bridewell Hospital, which was not a place for treating the sick, but rather a combination of a criminal court and a prison for those convicted for crimes connected to the city's sex trade.[3] She notes that the only one of the Bridewell Minute Books that did not survive

---

[1] Peter Krapp, 'Derrida online', *Oxford Literary Review* 18 (1996), 159–74, quotes a 1995 interview transcription on p. 164.
[2] Saidiya Hartman, *Lose Your Mother: A Journey along the Atlantic Slave Route* (New York, 2007), p. 4.
[3] Duncan Salkeld's *Shakespeare among the Courtesans: Prostitution, Literature, and Drama, 1500–1650* (London, 2012) reviews the Lucy Negro materials in the Minute Books, pp. 128–34.

London's Great Fire of 1666 was the volume covering 1579–1597, which would have included any arrests or prosecutions arising from the wild night when Lucy Negro first comes into historical view. As the fire raged, people inside the hospital threw the books down to barges on the Thames below to save the history they contained, but 'that one volume missed its mark, and lies from that day to this at the bottom of the river'.[4] Randall Williams resurrects and reads from the drowned book of state memory. In her hands, absence and loss generate possibility.

Gesta Grayorum is the chronicle of the Christmas revels put on by Gray's Inn on the Feast of the Innocents, 28 December 1594. According to its mock-heroic narrative of the occasion, Lucy Negro and some of the prostitutes she ran were invited to perform: 'Lucy Negro, Abbess de *Clerkenwell*' held her title 'by Night-Service in *Cauda*' to the Prince of Purpoole, the imaginary patron of the law school, and had been charged 'to find a Choir of Nuns, with burning Lamps, to chaunt *Placebo* to the Gentlemen of the Prince's Privy-Chamber'.[5] 'In *Cauda*' is an abbreviation of the Latin phrase *in cauda venenum*, meaning 'the poison is in the tail'. '*Placebo*' means 'I will please.' Lucy Negro's choir of nuns who will please the gathered audience with what is in their (poisoned?) tails points to her ill fame as a madam in Renaissance London. Apparently, the night got so out of hand that the planned entertainment devolved into 'a disordered Tumult and Crowd upon the Stage', with some of the well-connected audience members even leaving their places to join Lucy's 'nuns'.[6]

The image of Lucy Negro in motion is dazzling, one of the few descriptions that survive of a black woman in Renaissance performance.[7] Perhaps inspired by it, G. B. Harrison proposed her as Shakespeare's lover and the inspiration for the so-called 'Dark Lady' sonnets in 1933.[8] He hung much of his conjecture, which he put in an endnote (where he doesn't use her name) rather than in his main text, on *Gesta Grayorum*'s account that another part of the entertainment that night was a play called 'a Comedy of Errors', which from its description was probably Shakespeare's *The Comedy of Errors*. But its description of the evening's festivities doesn't mention Shakespeare's name, as it does Lucy Negro's, nor does it describe anything about the play, while it enthusiastically details the performance of Lucy and her girls. Shakespeare might well have been there, as a young playwright eager for the kind of recognition a successful holiday performance for the well-connected lawyers at Gray's Inn could have brought him, but there is no absolute evidence that he was, or that he even knew her, much less fell disastrously in love with her. As with the lost minute book, this absence of proof one way or the other is one of the factors enabling Randall Williams's invention.

As I've written elsewhere, I'm not particularly interested in whether Shakespeare and Lucy Negro were lovers or if the 'Dark Lady' sonnets are inspired by their relationship; the poetic flows of time, memory and absence – my real subject here – don't necessarily require material facts to manifest in the present.[9] Shakespeare's biographers no longer work under the assumption that his works directly reflect events in his

---

[4] Randall Williams's poems first appeared as her MFA thesis in 2015. They were republished as *Lucy Negro, Redux: The Bard, a Book, and a Ballet* (Nashville, 2019), in a volume that also includes the transcript of a conversation between Randall Williams and Paul Vasterling, the artistic director of the Nashville Ballet, who based his 2019 ballet *Lucy Negro, Redux* on Randall Williams's poems, as well as the ballet's libretto and some rehearsal photographs. In this article, I cite this 2019 volume; here, p. 18.

[5] *Gesta Grayorum: Or, the History of the High and Mighty Prince, Henry Prince of Purpoole* (London, 1688), p. 12.

[6] *Gesta Grayorum*, p. 22.

[7] Peter Fryer, *Staying Power: The History of Black People in Britain* [1984] (London, 2010), p. 3, describes the participation of a young female 'More' at a tournament of a black knight and a black lady staged at the court of King James IV of Scotland in 1507 and 1508.

[8] Harrison's *Shakespeare at Work, 1592–1603* (London, 1933) doesn't use a proper name, calling her only the 'Black Woman' (p. 64, pp. 310–11).

[9] See Joyce Green MacDonald, 'The legend of Lucy Negro', in *The Routledge Companion to Black Women's Cultural Histories*, ed. Janell Hobson (Abingdon, 2021), 66–74. I cite some of the material on Rollins and Hotson here.

life. And yet, in the decades after Harrison, the very idea that Shakespeare and Lucy Negro *could* have been sexually connected was firmly rejected. Hyder Rollins, editor of the 1944 New Variorum *Sonnets*, doubted that enough evidence existed to assign Shakespeare 'a negro mistress', but, referring to a suggestion by a nineteenth-century German scholar that the poet had been her lover and that she may have been 'a mulatto or a quadroon', was not surprised that Shakespeare's 'eyes ... in her "a thousand errors" noted'.[10] Twenty years later, in a book published during the quadricentennial of Shakespeare's birth, Leslie Hotson is even more racially explicit. For him, Harrison's advancement of Lucy Negro as the 'Dark Lady' was a 'dark ... misapprehension'. It was a 'discredit' to Shakespeare to imagine that he could have fallen so desperately in love with 'a blackamoor'.[11]

More recently, Miranda Kauffmann has expanded doubt about a sexual relationship on occupational, evidential or racial grounds to doubt about the possibility that Lucy Negro existed at all. *Gesta Grayorum* 'does not provide straightforward evidence of a real woman named Lucy Negro', she writes. '[I]n creating the character of Lucy Negro', the author of the description of the 1594 Christmas revels may have been referring to one of two known bawds in the city who were forenamed Lucy, but there is no evidence that either of these women 'were of African origin'.[12]

There are actually two claims here – one, that Lucy Negro wasn't a real person; and two, that even if she were, there is no proof that she was black. Both claims, I would argue, fit into this article's framing within a conviction of the memory void imposed on the history of racial relations shadowed by African slavery and on those subsumed within that void. Proof of black people's existence in Renaissance Britain is increasingly a matter of recovered historical fact, and yet still we can't always immediately recognize what we're seeing when we look into the racial archive of a period that was still figuring out everything it meant by the term 'race'. Kim Hall pointed us to the racial valence that familiar Renaissance poetic vocabularies of fair and black accumulated in a period of colonialism that would be underwritten by race-based slavery.[13] Attentively searching British archives, Imtiaz Habib found traces of black lives that he used to create a compelling narrative of emerging premodern black urban existence, despite incomplete and inconsistent parish documentation, eccentric spelling and naming, and 'the pressures of the conversion process, whereby ethnic identities disappear under Christian names'.[14] More recently, Urvashi Chakravarty has drawn our attention to the role of the domestic in shaping ideologies of service which in their turn invisibly shaped ideologies of slavery, linking their origins to the household.[15] Intimate household circumstance is necessarily at least partially hidden from public view, making the generation and administration of race in many respects a private family matter. Historian Jennifer L. Morgan, noting the degree to which black women and the children they bore to white men were denied civil status in Britain's North American colonies, describes the entanglement of rules of kinship, inheritance and disinheritance, and slavery as a mechanism that would make 'African women ... particularly illegible – both historically and archivally'.[16] Thus, in London, to read the remaining Minute Books, Randall Williams was obligated to 'dig and root about and trawl and query and wildly surmise until there is a place for you, Lucy. And it will be my place for having carved yours out, and altogether earned by you for us, and proved by me for us' (p. 19).

Of course, transported and enslaved Africans could not be entirely erased from public memory, even if

---

[10] *New Variorum Edition of Shakespeare: The Sonnets*, ed. Hyder Rollins, vol. 2 (Philadelphia, 1944), p. 272, p. 243, n. 1.
[11] Leslie Hotson, *Mr. W. H.* (New York, 1964), p. 244.
[12] Miranda Kauffmann, '"Making the beast with two backs": interracial relationships in early modern England', *Literature Compass* 12 (2015), 22–37; p. 30.
[13] Kim F. Hall, *Things of Darkness: Economies of Race and Gender in Early Modern England* (Ithaca, 1995).
[14] Imtiaz Habib, *Black Lives in the British Archives: Imprints of the Invisible* (Aldershot, 2008), p. 7.
[15] Urvashi Chakravarty, *Fictions of Consent: Slavery, Servitude, and Free Service in Early Modern England* (Philadelphia, 2022).
[16] Jennifer L. Morgan, *Reckoning with Slavery: Gender, Kinship, and Capitalism in the Early Black Atlantic* (Durham, NC, 2021), p. 5.

the conventions of silence might have preferred it. The magnitude and horror of the slave trade were simply too great. In the spring of 1769, residents of Charleston, South Carolina, would complain that slavers' crews were throwing so many dead captives into the Cooper River as it emptied into the city's harbour that the stench from their decomposing bodies was creating a public health hazard: the sophisticated, prosperous city reeked of death.[17] As Randall Williams imitates Shakespeare in order to bring one shadowy black female subject into full presence, she works to fashion a way across the drowned horrors of the Middle Passage and reimagine a place of origin. Together, the knowledge of slavery and a yearning for times before it frame Randall Williams's project.

The yearning for a generative and nurturing place of origin that *Lucy Negro, Redux* demonstrates is itself a product of the early modern. What we now know as nostalgia was first given a name in 1688 by Swiss medical student Johannes Hofer, based on his clinical studies of people we would now recognize as having been politically or economically alienated from their homes: young men from powerful and oligarchic Bern studying in Basel, natives of Germany and France working abroad as household servants, Swiss soldiers who had been fighting abroad. Those afflicted with this disease would 'easily become sad, continually think about the Fatherland, and because of the perpetual desire of returning there ... finally fall into this illness'.[18] The only cure was to return home, and if patients could not, they remained dangerously vulnerable to being 'snatched up' at any time by 'grief for the lost charm of the Native Land'.[19] When 'the use of native liberty is prohibited', as it was prohibited for those effectively exiled by the unforgiving conditions of life under Bern's system of inherited economic and political power, the 'melancholy delirium' of nostalgia was the inevitable and tragic result.[20]

The links Hofer establishes between nostalgia, melancholy and distance – distance dictated by circumstances beyond the sufferer's control – resonate powerfully in the suffering of those caught in the period's slave trade. Captured, transported across a vast ocean, enslaved and permanently barred from 'the use of native liberty', the enslaved were subjected to a variety of Hofer's diagnosis that was effectively terminal because it could not be cured by going home.

Yearning attachment to the place of one's birth survived into the social practices of the West Africans who were brought as slaves to Georgia and its barrier islands. Trapped among strangers, far away from West Africa, in 1803 captured members of the Ibo tribe newly transported to St Simons Island walked together into the waters of Dunbar Creek and drowned in what was either a mass suicide, or an action undertaken in the belief that they could return home.[21] Throughout small towns in the Georgia sea islands, stories of Africans who did find a way to escape bondage and satisfy their 'perpetual desire' to go back home survived into the 1930s, as these slaves' descendants reported that some of their ancestors either turned themselves into birds, or flew away in their human bodies. According to Wallace Quarterman, who was born as the property of Roswell King – the manager of the plantation on St Simons where the Ibos walked into the water – the slaves on the plantation who had come directly from Africa were troublesome: no one could understand their language, and they either didn't know how or refused to learn to work the fields. Finally, they simply decided that they 'ain't stay down here'. One day, when the frustrated overseer set out to whip them, they all downed their hoes, 'then say "quack, quack, quack," and they riz up in the sky and turned themselves into buzzards and fly right back to Africa'.[22] The grandmother of Rosa Grant from Possum Point had been brought from Africa with

---

[17] Peter McCandless, *Slavery, Disease, and Suffering in the Southern Lowcountry* (Cambridge, 2011), p. 47.
[18] Carolyn Kiser Anspach, trans., 'Medical dissertation on nostalgia by Johannes Hofer, 1688', *Bulletin of the Institute of the History of Medicine* 2 (1934), 376–91; p. 385.
[19] Hofer, 'Medical dissertation', p. 380.
[20] Hofer, 'Medical dissertation', pp. 384, 381.
[21] See the *New Georgia Encyclopedia*: www.georgiaencyclopedia.org/articles/history-archaeology/ebos-landing.
[22] Wallace Quarterman, quoted in Savannah Unit of the Georgia Writers Project, Works Project Administration, *Drums and Shadows: Survival Studies among the Georgia Coastal Negroes* (Athens, Georgia, 1940), pp. 150 and 151.

her own mother, called Theresa, when she was just a little girl, and Grant remembered her grandmother Ryna telling her how Theresa got to the point where she just couldn't stand her American life any longer: '[S]he wanna go back to Africa. One day my gran Ryna was standing with her in the fiel'. Theresa turn 'roun' ... She stretch her arms out – so – an rise straight up and fly right back to Africa.'[23]

The myth of flying Africans in Georgia and South Carolina percolated through the decades, finding its imaginative way into texts as different as Lionel Hampton's 1939 swing tune 'Flying Home' (which in its turn generated Billy Eckstine and Gerald Valentine's 'Second Balcony Jump'), Toni Morrison's 1977 novel *Song of Solomon*, and documentary filmmaker Sophia Nahli Allison's 2019 short *Dreaming Gave Us Wings*.[24] Robert Hayden's 1943 poem 'O Daedalus, Fly Away Home' layers the imagination of Africans' return to their origins in freedom and sovereignty over the Greek myth of the designer of the labyrinth who was imprisoned there, and whose son Icarus fell to his death when he mismanaged the wings Daedalus created to help them escape:

> Night is an African juju man
> weaving a wish and a weariness together
> to make two wings.[25]

For Hayden, Daedalus' labour and creativity – disrespected and suppressed by the evil power confining it, but still surviving – echoes in the work of a slave longing to '*cleave the air fly away home*'.[26] Flowing through its classical foundation, the 'wish and a weariness' of Hayden's poem invoke a kind of remembering that does not so much recall what has happened as it conjures the circumstances under which something *could* happen, if the 'weariness' of the poem's present hadn't quashed the possibility of flight.[27]

If access to memory is policed and nostalgia for lost homeplaces which is not treated by a return home will eventually disable knowledge of oneself, the problem of imagining how to heal nostalgic loss and act in light of the remembered power of return to a time and place before is perhaps particularly acute in representing black women, who have been so deliberately absented from the historical record. 'No one archived your existence', Sophia Nahli Allison remarks in her narration for *Dreaming Gave Us Wings*, and so poets and historians have had to learn to find traces of these women's lives in the stories others told about them, and in the ways these stories were recorded.[28] Just as Hayden used classical myth as a tool for recalling the myth of flying Africans, thus borrowing the outline of an existing story to bring into being one that had been suppressed but that nevertheless told of the existence of a rich life that predated and escaped the confinements of slavery in the Americas, Caroline Randall Williams turns to another part of the Western canon – Shakespeare's Sonnets – in order to conjure the traces of autonomous power left by the lost black subject we know as Lucy Negro.

Given the vagaries of archival recording for black women in the early modern period, it is not surprising, and perhaps even appropriate, that Lucy Negro – also sometimes known as Black Luce or Luce Baynham – both is and is not present in the surviving Bridewell Minute Books. There is no record of her arrest, conviction or imprisonment, but other, less lucky arrestees do bring up her name, perhaps in an

---

[23] Quarterman, quoted in Savannah Unit of the Georgia Writers Project, *Drums and Shadows*, p. 145.

[24] Allison includes a clip of her film and discusses the legend in 'Revisiting the legend of flying Africans', www.newyorker.com/culture/culture-desk/revisiting-the-legend-of-flying-africans.

[25] I cite the poem 'O Daedalus, Fly Away Home' as it appears in Hayden's *Collected Poems*, ed. Frederick Glaysher (New York, 1985), p. 55.

[26] Hayden, 'O Daedalus, Fly Away Home'.

[27] See Wendy W. Walters, '"One of dese mornings, bright and fair, take my wings and cleave de air": the legend of the flying Africans and diasporic consciousness', *MELUS* 22 (1997), 3–29.

[28] On black women's invisibility in the archive and on the methods required for recovering their presence, see Jennifer L. Morgan, *Laboring Women: Reproduction and Gender in New World Slavery* (Philadelphia, 2004); Jessica Marie Johnson, *Wicked Flesh: Black Women, Intimacy, and Freedom in the Atlantic World* (Philadelphia, 2020); and Marisa Fuentes, *Dispossessed Lives: Enslaved Women, Violence, and the Archive* (Philadelphia, 2016).

effort to deflect some of the state's punishing power away from themselves. It's clear that Black Luce – whoever she was – ran a brothel that moved through various locations in Clerkenwell, north-west of the city. A pander named William Mekyns testified that the prostitute Margaret Goldsmyth 'laye at Black Luces a great while and greate companye resorted to her and black luce has much gayne by kepyng of her and was lewde to her and knewe yt well that she was noughte'.[29] A prostitute named Elizabeth Kirkman who worked for the pimp Gilbert East testified before the court that Black Luce and East were partners: they agreed 'that when Blacke Luce had any great geste' that either Kirkman or another of East's prostitutes should go over to Luce's house to serve the prominent customer, 'and Luce Bayntham should have thone halfe of the money and East thother halfe'. Kirkman insisted to the court that 'Black Luce is a vilde bawde and lyveth by it', and that she, East, and his wife Margaret 'agree together and devide the monye that is geven to the harlots and helpe to tryme them up with swete water … and cotes and things for the purpose fitt for the degree of them that use them'.[30]

Randall Williams partly remembers and partly imagines Lucy Negro as she plots to recover what is not there:

My exiat sayeth that

If Black Luce alias Luce Baynham alias Lucy Negro alias lewis eeaste might have been Shakespeare's Dark Lady then she is indeed the Dark Lady and is me also.

. . .

My exaiat sayeth that

Her black wires are where the World began, and all of it pouring out from atwixt her thighs. Enough to make any man write that harder Hallelujah:

Exhibit A	Exhibit B	Exhibit C
Thy black is fairest in my judgement's place	And this, also, has been one of the dark places of the earth	Justlikeablackgirl-howcomeyou-tastesogood

('Black Luce', in *Lucy Negro*, p. 19)

'Exiat' is one of the Minute Books' abbreviations for 'examinat', the record of witnesses' examinations by the hospital authorities. As she first reports on the Minute Books' records and then fills in the blanks they contain, the blanks where she acts to create a kind of history for black women's agency and sexuality, Randall Williams adopts their fluid lingo: 'My exiat', 'My exaiate', 'My exaiat'. This poem, 'Black Luce', renders its final findings as a table, as if to invest her reconstructed 'wildly surmise[d]' history with a certain technical rigor. Her newly excavated line of historical descent flows from line 10 of Shakespeare's Sonnet 131 – 'Thy black is fairest in my judgment's place' (12) – through a phrase from Conrad's *Heart of Darkness* that identifies London, the imperial centre, as 'one of the dark places of the earth'.[31] 'Her black wires are where the World began', Randall Williams writes, affirming Sonnet 130's rejection of a Petrarchan vocabulary for women's beauty. Conrad's 'dark' heart of empire becomes the dark space between Lucy Negro's legs, adorned with textured black pubic hair. Randall Williams goes on to invoke this vulvar space again in the poem 'Sublimating Lucy. Considering Courbet':

> It's the beginning of the world,
> That endless human vessel,
> And what is mightier?
>
> (p. 22)[32]

For Randall Williams, Lucy Negro's blackness – her hair, her skin, the unseeable spaces inside her body – generates light and knowledge. 'There is beauty in the dark / Lucy', she observes early in her sequence ('BlackLucyNegro III', p. 14).

---

[29] Quoted in Salkeld, *Shakespeare among the Courtesans*, p. 141.
[30] Quoted in Salkeld, *Shakespeare among the Courtesans*, p. 136.
[31] Joseph Conrad, *Heart of Darkness*, ed. Timothy S. Hayes, with introduction by Adam Hochschild and afterword by Maya Jasanoff (London, 2017), p. 5.
[32] The poem's subtitle, 'after *L'origine du monde*', refers to the title of Gustave Courbet's 1866 painting of a nude woman, shown reclining on a bed from the breasts downward, her legs splayed wide to display her thick dark pubic hair.

REMEMBERING SHAKESPEARE'S *SONNETS* IN *LUCY NEGRO, REDUX*

Shakespearians have observed that even though Shakespeare's characters spend a lot of time talking about black people and about blackness, very few black people actually appear onstage in his plays. That is one of the things that makes the 'Dark Lady' sonnets so striking. They obsess over the speaker's obsessive love for a woman who is clearly not white, at least as whiteness was understood in the period. The final couplet of Sonnet 132 serves as the epigraph for Randall Williams's collection: 'Then will I swear that beauty herself is black, / And all they foul that thy complexion lack' (13–14). 'Complexion' could refer to character or personality as well as to skin colour, so that the 'Dark Lady's' blackness – or a traditional sonnet lady's fairness – was about more than her physical appearance. Williams's Lucy Negro knows this well:

> Say she wild, that she live by it,
>   that she like it,
> like that money, like that witness,
>   like that grotesque, and his *yes, yes* –
>   and she dazzle him, when she monkey shine,
> 'causa how *she* know and *he* know
>   his people shamed
> of how he go
>   for them darker juices, her darkness using
>   him up
> like ain't nobody watching.
>   ('Then Will I Declare That Beauty
>   Herself is Black V', p. 50)

In this poem the only shame surrounding the sexual connection between Lucy Negro and the poet is the shame of 'his people', embarrassed by his helpless desire for someone he should not want. Her wildness, her 'monkey shine', her characterological darkness calls him out and into her orbit. He is a devoutly helpless object and not the discerning, disciplined subject that Rollins and Hotson insist he must have been.

Although their physical and sexual and reproductive labours sustained the distorted domestic intimacies of slave culture, the stories enslaved women might have told remain unvoiced; no life story told by a female survivor of the Middle Passage survives. Thinking of the women who lived and died in slavery without being able to record their own histories, Hartman wonders how we, as descendants and survivors, can uncover those lost lives without merely 'reiterating [the] violent speech' and the 'rituals of torture' that swallowed them.[33] As she discovered the traces of Lucy Negro that Duncan Salkeld outlined in his study of the Bridewell Minute Books, and as she reread the 'Dark Lady' sonnets in light of her imagined presence, Randall Williams creates an opportunity to speak with and through one of these lost female ancestors, to fly away home to her and revive her in the present. Through her presence in Shakespeare's sonnets and through the poet's claiming of her as a historical ancestor, the poem 'Black Luce' declares that, finally, 'Lucy Negro is a seat at the table' (19). Not only Randall Williams, but Lucy Negro herself, emerges from historical silence.

Lines and phrases from more than a dozen of the sonnets mark Randall Williams's collection: it is made in light of Shakespeare's. But *Lucy Negro, Redux* is equally animated by its liberating lack of a critical or creative archive. For Randall Williams, the gap in the Bridewell Minute Books' evidence of Lucy Negro's presence becomes an invitation to freely imagine how she might fit into the historical record if it were whole. One poem, 'From Volume IV of the Bridewell Prison Records. London. 1579–1597', records 'exiats' referring to a scandalous triangle between Black Luce, a lawyer named William Hatclyffe, and one 'William Shaxberd'. Randall Williams's 'Shaxberd' gets into 'a grete disturbance' with a lawyer from Gray's Inn in the street in front of Black Luce's house, apparently because he thought the lawyer was visiting Luce too often, and the entries end with Hatclyffe's accusation that 'William Shakepere' performed 'lewde acts' on her 'in the curtain playhouse' and that while

---

[33] Saidiya Hartman, 'Venus in two acts', *Small Axe* 12 (2008), 1–14; p. 4.

she left the playhouse singing, 'Mstr Shakespeare never came again to the stage that nyghte' (27).

The historical William Hatclyffe played the Prince of Purpoole at the 1594 Gray's Inn Christmas celebrations and was advanced by Leslie Hotson as the mysterious 'Mr. W. H.' to whom the 1609 first edition of the *Sonnets* is dedicated. When she invents this scandalous brawl over Lucy's affections, however, Randall Williams deliberately outdoes Hotson by not only putting Hatclyffe into Shakespeare's orbit, but also putting Lucy Negro between them; her Hatclyffe is as obsessed with her as her Shakespeare is, as we see in 'In Which the Fair Youth Loves Black Luce' (p. 31). She thus engages in a second kind of remembering and re-evaluation, of materials from the thriving Shakespeare biography industry as well as of the *Sonnets* themselves. Randall Williams's play with Hotson's William Hatclyffe story opens that industry to the same kind of imaginative rereading she conducts on the sonnets themselves, a playfully documented reversal of Hotson's certainty that Shakespeare could not or would not have had sex with 'a blackamoor'.

While both Randall Williams and Hotson might be accused of writing the kind of Shakespeare fan-fiction that foregrounds autobiographical readings of the sonnets, Randall Williams joyfully scandalizes the poetic archive in a way that Hotson's book explicitly refused to do.[34] Hotson even advances another (white) candidate for the role of the real-life 'Dark Lady', a disgraced royal maid of honour named Mary Fitton, whom he believed fell into prostitution.[35] For him, there was no scandal – or, if there had been, it only involved white people. Shakespeare's disastrous love affair was only conventionally scandalous, and not interracial to boot. But in the absence of the life records that might have confirmed or denied the possibility of an intimate connection, Randall Williams is as free to assert or intuit a historical narrative as Hotson was to deny one: 'Lucy Negro / I am you / Lucy Negro / You can become anything I say', she writes in 'BlackLucyNegro III' (p. 14). This poem is subtitled 'after Jack Spicer', indicating some inspiration by the work of the San Francisco Renaissance poet (1925–1965) who described his own work as being 'dictated', in the conviction that poets acted as receptors to language and ideas rather than creating entirely of their own will. Is she thus positing herself as a receiver and transmitter of what was true but obscured about Lucy Negro – what she would have said herself if her words had been recorded?

This claiming of Lucy Negro's standing – a claim Randall Williams can make through her own determined creative labours over historical records that only partially exist ('I will dig and root about and trawl and query and wildly surmise') – in its turn enables the speaker's claiming of her own beauty and sexuality. '[W]hat would you think of my body?' she asks in 'Nude Study Or, Shortly Before Meeting Lucy. A White Boy':

> Had you ever negotiated such coarse hair,
> Seen nipples dark and darker in their tensing,
> Breasts swaying sideways with the weight
> Of them? Did you know how much it was to ask,
> To be the first glimpse of a naked black body?
>
> (p. 20)

Part of what these poems' speaker is unquestionably drawn to in Lucy Negro is what the existing records portray as her successful commandeering of a sexual economy in which women had been designated objects for men's consumption: Randall Williams's Lucy walks away 'singing' from the Curtain Theatre while jealous Hatclyffe rages and Shakespeare tries to gather his wits. But if the poems begin with the delighted establishment of a connection between their speaker and their confabulated Lucy Negro, the collection's second section more deeply historicizes the notion of specifically miscegenous scandal as object of erasure and denial as they begin to engage with the sexual oppression of black women in US slavery. In

---

[34] My notion of the sonnets' miscegenous scandal comes from Margreta De Grazia, 'The scandal of Shakespeare's Sonnets', in *Shakespeare Survey 46* (Cambridge, 1993), 35–49.

[35] Hotson, *Mr. W. H.*, pp. 245–9.

'Field Holler', the bag for harvesting picked cotton becomes

> a whitish exclamation mark
> pointing
> back to the house.
> Baby girl
>   the anchor
>   to this earth,
>   this house,
> the accidental crop,
> the unwanted harvest yield.
>
> (p. 38)

Following the Caribbean children's rhyme 'Brown Girl in the Ring', 'Brown Girl, Red Bone' sings:

> There's a red bone in the field, oh lord, oh lord, oh lord
> There's a red bone in the field, oh lord, oh lord, oh lord
> There's a red bone in the field, oh lord, oh lord, oh lord
> And she looks like the house girl in the house. His house.
>
> (p. 40)

This secret, yet open, history of white men forcing sex on black women in slavery and the unacknowledged biracial babies such rapes produced is a constant presence in this second section of *Lucy Negro, Redux*. At its 2019 Nashville premiere, the ballet Paul Vasterling choreographed around Randall Williams's book includes several poems from the collection, many theatrically delivered onstage by Randall Williams herself, but this second group of poems was instead represented by Rhiannon Giddens's live performance of her song 'At the Purchaser's Option', from her 2017 album *Freedom Highway*.[36] The song's title comes from a phrase in an 1822 notice advertising a young 'Negro Wench' for sale in New York's Hudson Valley. She was used to both house and field work, the notice said, and she had a nine-month-old baby who could be included in the sale – or not – 'at the purchaser's option'. The song's speaker is that young mother, facing the possibility of separation from her baby, who was probably the result of rape by the man who owned her.

Giddens's performance of the song served as the score for a solo by dancer Kayla Rowser in the role of Lucy, so that the music and the dance together articulated the backstory of concealed and denied sexual violence against enslaved black women. In one way, of course, the cruel story Giddens's song tells is not applicable to who the historical Lucy could have been; Lucy Negro disappears from the historical record in the early seventeenth century, long before the slave trade was fully established in North America, and no surviving mention of her ever connects her to any place but London. But in the gulf of absence in which women's memories of the Middle Passage have been drowned, and in the unproven but tantalizing possibility that Shakespeare and Lucy Negro knew each other, Randall Williams works with the tools she has to recover the past unspoken scandal of enslaved black women's sexual abuse by white men – a scandal that permeated life in Atlantic slave cultures but that was rarely publicly acknowledged by the white people who witnessed and perpetrated it. Randall Williams herself is a descendant of Edmund Pettus, the Confederate general and Grand Dragon of the Ku Klux Klan for whom the Edmund Pettus Bridge in Selma, Alabama is named. 'I have rape-colored skin', she wrote. '[A]s modern DNA testing has allowed me to confirm, I am the descendant of black women who were domestic servants and white men who raped their help.'[37] The sexual secret of miscegenous desire her poems imagine resonates within the later rapes of enslaved women and those rapes' reproductive consequences. In Randall Williams's recounting of this tale, only Shakespeare's desire is scandalous; Lucy is neither abused nor abandoned. Nor does Randall Williams romanticize Lucy Negro's prostitution: 'The skin rubbed raw / Behind the cry in the night' ('BlackLucyNegro II', p. 9). But the placement of this second section of the collection nevertheless identifies them both, I think, with that 'accidental crop', grown now in the collection's

---

[36] Giddens composed and performed the rest of the ballet's score with Italian musician Francesco Turrisi.

[37] Caroline Randall Williams, 'You want a Confederate monument? My body is a Confederate monument', *New York Times*, 26 June 2020: www.nytimes.com/2020/06/26/opinion/confederate-monuments-racism.html.

leaps back and forth across time, inflicting a version of the emotional pain they were born into on a white man, and then walking away singing. Time blurs as Randall Williams supplies a lineage that history has denied.

The 'accidental crop', the 'red bone in the field', live in the shadows of their mothers' exploitation – a sexual inevitability that the narrators in some of this section's poems accept and attempt to turn to their own purposes. Here, for example, is 'Knowing Thy Heart Torment Me with Disdain':

> The way my body   *I don't want you*
>   Is my body
> *to be true*   and nobody else's,
>   and how I do I
>   what I want to do
> without seeming selfish,
>   that's the why and the how
> *I just wanna*   come I divide myself:
> my heart from my head
>   from my snatch from his stuff,
> *make love to you*   so when I get it together
>   *love to you*   with him, or whoever,
> I stay belonging to me.
>
> (p. 53)

The title of this poem comes from Sonnet 132:

> Thine eyes I love, and they, as pitying me –
> Knowing thy heart torment me with disdain –
> Have put on black, and loving mourners be,
> Looking with pretty ruth upon my pain
>
> (1–4)

Here, Randall Williams intersperses her poem with lines from the sonnet and lines from Willie Dixon's 'I Just Want to Make Love to You', best known from its 1960 recording by Etta James. She does make one significant change to the quoted lyrics, though: James recorded 'But I want you to be true'. Lucy Negro does not. Her sexual prerogative, and not the gratitude for a man's fidelity that we hear in James's version, is the new subject. Building out an enunciative authority for Lucy Negro requires mixing Shakespeare with her own composition and with lines (almost) sung by the woman known as 'The Matriarch of the Blues': there is no single, clear line from the poem's present back to its pasts. Each of these pasts lives in the others.

Not knowing the truth about any relationship between Shakespeare and Lucy Negro clears space for Randall Williams's fictions, although we do know that the paths of sex workers and theatre workers could often cross in Renaissance London. Philip Henslowe, owner of the Rose Theatre and obsessive record-keeper, noted in his *Diary* that he had dinner with former pimp Gilbert East, professionally associated with Lucy Negro, thirty times in 1600. By 1604, Lucy Negro and Gilbert East were apparently sharing rooms in the Boar's Head buildings that Henslowe owned on Bankside, where big public theatres like the Rose, the Swan and the Globe were also located. Working on such hints, the last part of the collection keeps pressing what evidence there is – evidence which for Randall Williams includes the *Sonnets* themselves – in order to excavate Lucy as ancestor, and herself as a contemporary black woman, from the shadows: 'And it will be my place for having carved yours out, and altogether earned by you for us, and proved by me for us' (19). Not only will she make 'a seat at the table' for Lucy Negro by writing her into history and literature and by imagining a voice and agency – perhaps especially sexual agency – for black women even within their embedment in sexual shame during their enslavement, but she will find herself there, too. The last column of the formal table Randall Williams constructs in 'Black Luce' puts a line from the Rolling Stones' 'Brown Sugar' – 'Justlikeablackgirlhowcomeyoutastesogood' – next to the quotation from Conrad and the line from Sonnet 131. Randall Williams thus implies that she herself lies somewhere at the end of this chronological progression that moves from Shakespeare's original statement of blackness's allure, through Conrad's uneasy recognition of the earth's 'dark places' as the source of imperium, to a final reiteration of black women's erotic power. 'Mick. Bob. Bowie. All my favorite rock stars have black babies', a poem in this last section observes ('This Exiat Sayeth That', 73).

REMEMBERING SHAKESPEARE'S *SONNETS* IN *LUCY NEGRO, REDUX*

In line with the collection's interest in recovering black women's subjectivity, some of its last poems imagine Black Luce as a member of the audience at the Globe – dismissing the romantic effervescence of *Much Ado About Nothing* ('Some People Don't Have Enough Real Things to Worry About'), resenting *Othello*, thrilling to *Henry V*. This section details Shakespeare's sexual approach to Black Luce and, more importantly, her reactions to him. She even writes her own, uneven sonnet about their connection:

> Once he bent him down to me,
> he bent and
>   his words came
> with him. His blood
>   word –
> *his. beauty. black.*
>   His writ word,
> all breathing between us
> all doing that old
> that old
> that old thing between us.
>   Never made him pay,
> never after the words came
>   first, held ransom sin.
>
> (p. 70)

The power of his words moves her to give herself to him without demanding payment, to hold captive the knowledge of the 'sin' of his lust for her. It is she who refuses to release this erotic knowledge into the public domain until and unless it can receive its just due in the world's 'false esteem'.

Lucy Negro, Redux dislocates time, blurs place, and blends multiple speakers into a single story. Its refusal of linearity is suited to its project of bringing to voice a character whose very existence has been denied, and to speaking out loud a story whose materiality uncomfortably contradicts the stories that white supremacy has chosen to tell about itself. Merely speaking a truth out loud is its own kind of achievement in the face of denial, refusal and loss. Flying home in order to begin again, Randall Williams exhorts us at the beginning of her sequence to

> run and tell everything,
> every truth you ever knew
> about BlackLucyNegro.
> Say she is the loose light.
> Say she is the root.
> Say she ate at his table.
> Say she ate at all. Say she.
> Say she. Say she.
>
> (p. 7)

THE POETICS OF ANTIQUARIAN ACCUMULATION IN *A LOVER'S COMPLAINT*

MIRIAM JACOBSON

INTRODUCTION: AN ARCHAIC ANOMALY

Critics have long puzzled over *A Lover's Complaint* (*LC*), the long lyric poem that appears at the end of Thomas Thorpe's 1609 quarto edition *Shake-speares Sonnets*. Recalling an earlier tradition of sixteenth-century complaint poems and written in an intricate and obscure style embedded with complicated metaphors and multiple voices, it has caused some scholars to call into question its Shakespearian authorship,[1] and others to puzzle over its uniqueness while attempting to make sense of its deliberately archaic structure – whether in conjunction with or against other early modern sonnet sequences that end in complaints in the so-called 'Delian Structure', or in relation to the 1609 edition of the preceding sonnets as a whole volume.[2] Does it expose the Petrarchan love that inspired earlier sonnet sequences as derivative mimicry, or does it offer a more sinister and sarcastic perspective on the uses to which love sonnets can be put? *A Lover's Complaint* has been labelled an anomaly, an enigma, an archaism.[3] Its enfolded narration of a tale of anticipated seduction and deceit by way of sonnets encourages readers to imagine it in dialogue with the *Sonnets*, whether, as Margreta de Grazia contends, as the culmination of a continued argument about the cyclical nature of Time, or as an alternative perspective that challenges the sonnet sequence – one that simultaneously gives voice to women and depicts their downfall. To Catherine Bates, the poem's enigmatic difficulty is its point; however, 'there is clearly something about this poem that nags, troubles, and complains – that piques and irritates but that clearly refuses to go away', to the point that, for Bates, the poem *itself* stages its own authorship debate, and is in fact directly asking to be simultaneously marginalized and singled out, 'more motivated than accidental, more defensive than benign'.[4]

Published only once in the seventeenth century, the publication history of *A Lover's Complaint* has turned the poem itself into an antiquarian artefact, detached from the sonnet sequence it originally annexed, missing in action for centuries. Stephen Booth's scholarly edition of the *Sonnets*, which places a strong emphasis on the material text of the 1609 quarto to the point of reproducing it in

---

[1] Brian Vickers, *Shakespeare, 'A Lover's Complaint', and John Davies of Hereford* (Cambridge, 2011) and 'A rum "do": the likely authorship of "A Lover's Complaint"', *Times Literary Supplement*, 5 December 2004, 13–15.

[2] See, for example, Heather Dubrow, '"Dressing old words new"? Re-evaluating the Delian Structure', in *A Companion to Shakespeare's Sonnets*, ed. Michael Schoenfeldt (Newark, NJ, 2006), 90–103, and Margreta de Grazia, 'Revolution in Shake-speares Sonnets', in the same volume, 57–69.

[3] De Grazia reads it as medieval archaism that, like the 'ancient' classicism of the final two sonnets – or epigrams – that precede it, directs the reader to travel back in time, imitating the 'revolutionary' time-scape of the sonnets. See de Grazia, 'Revolution', p. 59.

[4] Catherine Bates, 'The enigma of *A Lover's Complaint*', in *A Companion to Shakespeare's Sonnets*, ed. Schoenfeldt, p. 427.

facsimile, does not include *A Lover's Complaint* (the poem is only mentioned in Booth's endnotes),[5] and *Shakespeare Survey*'s style guide neglects to include the poem's title in its list of Shakespeare's works abbreviations (though with four authors addressing the poem in this volume alone, the list will likely be updated soon). Even in Thorpe's 1609 first edition of *Shake-speares Sonnets*, the poem's title is absent from the title page, suggesting a text and author already in the process of creating its status as a hidden curiosity, an 'Easter egg' for readers to excavate.

Rather than debate whether *A Lover's Complaint* works against or in conversation with the *Sonnets*, I want to argue in what follows that it is the poem's anomalous nature itself – its status as an oddity, a throwback and an archaism, and its self-awareness of that positionality – that allows *A Lover's Complaint* to depict and investigate a newly emergent early modern mode of history invested in the study and recovery of anomalies, oddities and ancient artefacts, or what John Donne in a short epigram called 'old strange things': antiquarianism.[6] *A Lover's Complaint* is not only an artificially constructed antiquarian poetic artefact that calls attention to its weirdness, its out-of-placedness in its present. It is also a poem invested in depicting and interrogating the early modern antiquarian impulse to amass the fragments of the past with the purposes of reenacting and recovering that past. And this reenactment and act of recovery, the poem's many voices seem to say, is a dangerous and unending cyclical enterprise, doomed to failure yet inescapable. I am not suggesting that we read *A Lover's Complaint* as an allegory for and caveat against the antiquarian version of history. I want instead to draw attention to the way the poem's many echoes, borrowings and recurrent rhetorical motifs and poetic conceits model two different versions of early modern antiquarianism: the weeping maiden and her broken love tokens as antiquarian objects and interpreters, and her unfaithful male lover as a dangerous form of antiquarian accumulation and reenactment. By drawing attention to the dual material practices of antiquarian history – legible material artefacts and embodied reenactment – the poem reminds its readers that early modern love sonnets, too, can be artefacts and reenactments, actors in an endless cycle of seduction, accumulation, capitulation and reinterpretation.

ANTIQUARIANISM AND ITS CONTENTS

Early modern English antiquarianism positioned itself as a more material and sensory form of historical analysis than traditional documentary history. Antiquarians dug up, poked around, excavated and *tasted* the past. Antiquarians also reenacted the past, whether through staged tournaments, triumphs and banquets or in literary depictions of lost cities and architecture. Which past? Any past – prehistoric, Roman, medieval, British, Egyptian, it was all ripe material for antiquarian excavation, collection and reenactment. Thomas Browne writes in *Urn Burial* that the perfumed and spiced oils buried with ancient Roman corpses in small vials called *unguentaria* tasted even better after centuries of curing:

> Some find sepulchrall Vessels containing Liquors, which time hath incrassated into gellies. For beside these Lachrymatories, notable Lamps, with Vessels of Oyles and Aromaticall Liquors attended noble Ossuaries. And some yet retaining a Vinosity and spirit in them, which if any have tasted they have farre exceeded the Palats of Antiquity.[7]

In early modern English, the word 'antiquary' (which gave way to 'antiquarian' by the eighteenth century and was conceptually adapted into 'archaeologist' and 'anthropologist' by the late nineteenth) meant someone preoccupied with studying the past through its material remains. With sixteenth-century cognates in French, Italian and Spanish, 'antiquary' spawned a number of early modern

---

[5] *Shakespeare's Sonnets*, ed. Stephen Booth (New Haven, 1977 and 2000).
[6] John Donne, 'Antiquary', in *John Donne: The Major Works*, ed. John Carey (Oxford, 2008), p. 34.
[7] Thomas Browne, *Hydriotaphia, Urne Burial, or a Discourse of the Sepulchrall Urnes Lately Found in Norfolk* (London, 1658), p. 33.

related words, as the *Oxford English Dictionary* reveals: 'antiquarium', for example, indicated a collection of antiquities or an architectural temple built according to an ancient design, whereas William Warner refers to the cartographer and chronicler '[John] Stow's *antiquarious* pen' in 1606 to suggest a scholarly penchant for the ancient past.[8] As scholars such as Stuart Piggott, William Stenhouse, Anthony Grafton and Lisa Schwab have shown,[9] European antiquarians were consulted by monarchs and state officials, from Pompanio Leto and John Leland in the late fifteenth and early sixteenth centuries, to William Camden in the late sixteenth, and Fortunio Liceti, Anthony Wood and John Aubrey in the second half of the seventeenth century. Distinguished from historians' text-based, documentary study, antiquarian work was 'hands-on', materialist, centred on objects and three-dimensional matter – already a more sensory and tactile examination of the past than textual history alone.

Early modern antiquaries were some of the first sensory historians and material culture scholars, and their influence over the vast literary output of the late sixteenth and seventeenth centuries has been underestimated. For this reason, as Piggott has demonstrated, antiquaries were mocked and reviled in English literature by writers such as Thomas Nashe, John Donne and John Earle.[10] Francis Bacon described the materialist bent of antiquarian activities in *The Advancement of Learning* (1605) as 'unperfect histories'.[11] The principal criticism, it seems, is that they muck around in the dirt with ruinous old, dead things to add to their curious collections. This motif of digging is also used by scholars of premodern sensory history, most recently by the scent historian William Tullett in his 2021 'State of the field' essay: 'an increasing number of historians are taking up a sensory "habit", mining the sources of the past for information about past ways of sensing'.[12] Like sensory historians, antiquaries did more than unearth and collect the artefacts of the past; they also reconstructed and reenacted it, and such reconstructions could be found in printed books, poetry and even plays. Literary antiquarian reenactments both gave the past a voice and provided a critical metacommentary on the act of recreation. Just as Browne's description of ancient, jellied unguents highlights the impossibility of fully immersing oneself in the past (we can never taste fresh unguents), early modern antiquarian reenactments attempted to revive the past while simultaneously articulating its inaccessibility in improbable and revelatory ways.

Reenactment is where antiquarianism and sensory history meet. And this meeting occurred in the past as well as the present, as William Stenhouse's accounts of the inventiveness of Renaissance Italian antiquarian ritual reveal: Italian antiquaries held banquets and triumphs, they built replicas of Roman temples, they wrote letters to dead Romans, they changed their names, and they even *gardened* based on classical treatises.[13] According to the authors and editors of the *Routledge Handbook of Reenactment* (2021), reenactment is an immersive 'attempt to copy the past', activated by the imagination and sustained by affect. It is also primarily a sensory experience: '[m]ost reenactments began with the aim not of *knowing* what history was like but rather *feeling* what it was like.'[14] As the editors observe, reenactment

---

[8] *OED Online*, 'antiquarium, n.'; 'antiquarious, adj.' (emphasis mine).

[9] Stuart Piggott, *Ancient Britons and the Antiquarian Imagination: Ideas from the Renaissance to the Regency* (London, 1989); William Stenhouse, 'Imagination and the remains of Roman antiquity', in *The Routledge History of the Renaissance*, ed. William Caferro (London, 2017),125–39; Maren Elizabeth Schwab and Anthony Grafton, *The Art of Discovery: Digging into the Past in Renaissance Europe* (Princeton, 2022).

[10] Piggott, *Ancient Britons*, pp. 15–17.

[11] Francis Bacon, *The Oxford Francis Bacon*, vol. 4: *The Advancement of Learning*, ed. Michael Kiernan (Oxford, 2000), p. 66.

[12] William Tullett, 'State of the field: sensory history', *History* 106 (2021), 804–20; p. 804.

[13] Stenhouse, 'Imagination', pp. 127–31.

[14] Vanessa Agnew, Jonathan Lamb and Juliane Tomann, 'Introduction: what is reenactment studies?', in *The Routledge Handbook of Reenactment Studies: Key Terms in the*

has never been modern. It is present in religious and cultural rituals with long and layered histories such as the Eucharist and the Passover Seder.[15]

Dependent upon the imagination, reenactment functions similarly to Philip Sidney's early modern definition of poetry as a conditional mode of possibility, the only art able to consider 'what may be and should be': '[r]eenactment erodes the boundaries between the real and the simulated, between the world as it is, and the world as we would like it to be.'[16] This is because, as Rebecca Schneider has elucidated, in what seems like perfect harmony with Leonard Barkan writing about the Renaissance view of the classical past in fragments, the past is 'never complete, never completely finished, but incomplete: cast into the future as a matter for ritual negotiation and as yet undecided interpretive acts of *reworking*'.[17]

Reenactments take multiple forms, from staged battles to pedagogical role-playing games, to experimental archaeology and forensic architecture. Reenactment is always embodied, but not always enacted. In Julie Park's essay on 'heritage', reenactment takes the form of eighteenth-century extra-illustrated antiquarian books.[18] In my reading of *A Lover's Complaint*, reenactment appears both in the poem's framework and in its narrative. It involves literary appropriation and ventriloquism: Shakespeare quotes and references Spenserian complaint and the 'ghost complaints' of the 1590s, and inside the story the lover courts the so-called 'fickle maid' with indecipherable old artefacts.[19] These objects form a cabinet of curiosities made up of gemstones, inscribed rings, hair lace bracelets, and poetry composed by his female ex-lovers. The maid reproduces his voice and his courtship as a complaint embedded in her own, an early modern Echo whose Narcissus' desirability is constructed solely from the desire of his former lovers. This poem is obsessed with reenacting the past materially, sensorially, poetically and performatively, though its male and female protagonists go about it in different ways: the maid is an expert reader of the past, whereas the male lover perverts the past by appropriating it and binds himself to it (like a complaint to a sonnet sequence), in order to seduce the maid through the voices of others. In representing these two forms of antiquarianism – reader and writer – the poem is also able to explore the ethical implications of early modern poetry's obsession with the past.

SPENSERIAN ECHOES

Edmund Malone wondered whether in *A Lover's Complaint* Shakespeare 'perhaps meant to break a lance with Spenser'.[20] Echoing those Shakespearian poetry critics interested in uncovering an early modern intratextual conversation between *A Lover's Complaint* and other complaint authors, I want to begin my exploration of antiquarianism in the poem by emphasizing how much this poem shares with one of Spenser's *Complaints*, and how it deliberately alludes to and then departs from that comparison, in order to demonstrate how *A Lover's Complaint* embraces and critiques the early modern antiquarian impulse as a way of recycling and reenacting the past.

Field, ed. Agnew, Lamb and Tomann (London, 2021), 1–10; p. 5.

[15] The Seder reenacts at least three historical periods (and not two as Stephen Greenblatt has argued): a culinary and gustatory reenactment of the Exodus, a reenactment of scholarly commentary on the Exodus, and reenactment of the Hellenistic Jewish (i.e. Roman) banquet modelled on Plutarch's rules for a proper symposium.

[16] Agnew, Lamb and Tomann, 'Introduction', pp. 8–9.

[17] Rebecca Schneider, *Performing Remains: Art and War in Times of Theatrical Reenactment* (London, 2011), p. 33; Leonard Barkan, *Unearthing the Past: Archeology and Aesthetics in the Making of Renaissance Culture* (New Haven, 1999).

[18] Julie Park, 'Heritage', in *Handbook of Reenactment Studies*, ed. Agnew, Lamb and Tomann, pp. 100–5.

[19] On the genre of 'ghost complaint', see Donald Jellerson, 'Haunted history and the birth of the republic in Middleton's Ghost of Lucrece', *Criticism* 53 (2011), 53–82; p. 54; 'The spectral historiopoetics of the *Mirror for Magistrates*', *Journal of the Northern Renaissance* 2 (2010), 54–71; and his dissertation 'Ghost complaint: historiography, gender, and the return of the dead in Elizabethan literature' (Vanderbilt University, 2009).

[20] Quoted in Colin Burrow, 'Introduction', in *William Shakespeare: The Complete Sonnets and Poems*, ed. Burrow (Oxford, 2002; 2008), 1–158; p. 139.

In the 1609 sonnet sequence, Shakespeare's complaint, like Spenser's 'Epithalamium' and *Amoretti*, is appended to the rest of the text; however, it is closer to Spenser's poem *The Ruines of Time* (*RT*), which opens his 1591 collection of *Complaints*, and which I will argue Shakespeare's poem directly references and reframes in its opening lines, setting and conversation.

The opening setting and soundscape of *A Lover's Complaint* directly references the opening of Spenser's poem. At the outset of *The Ruines of Time*, the speaker finds himself in an impossible place, talking to an impossible woman. Sitting on the banks of the river Thames, which according to legend, once flowed through the Roman city of Verulamium in ancient Britain – but now no longer does (and in fact never did) – the poet encounters a weeping woman who, it turns out, is not a human woman but the spirit or ghost of that ruined and forgotten city, noble Verlame herself:

There on the other side, I did behold
A Woman sitting sorrowfullie wailing,
Rending her yeolow locks, like wyrie golde,
About her shoulder carelesslie downe trailing,
And streames of teares from her faire eyes forth railing
In her right hand a broken rod she held,
Which towards heaven shee seemd on high to weld.[21]

This is the scene: a woman who is the ghost of a ruined city sitting on the banks of a river, weeping profusely, wailing loudly and waving a broken staff, observed from afar by a poet who empathizes and wishes to console her. Shakespeare's poem opens by echoing and remixing Spenser's scene, announcing that it is both in imitation of and a departure from Spenser. Though no longer occupying an explicitly untimely and impossible space, the opening lines of *A Lover's Complaint* when read alongside Spenser's complaint seem to reverberate with the voices of previous poetic complainers including Spenser, a hint at the poem's recurring motifs of multivocality, repetition, and accumulation:

From off a hill whose concave womb re-worded
A plaintful story from a sist'ring vale,
My spirits t'attend this double voice accorded,
And down I laid to list the sad-tuned tale;
Ere long espied a fickle maid full pale,
Tearing of papers, breaking rings a-twain,
Storming her world with sorrow's wind and rain.
(*LC*, 1–7)

Here we have another woman in an outdoor setting on the banks or 'weeping margin' (*LC*, 39) of 'a river' (*LC*, 38), also with loose yellow hair, also accessorized with broken objects, though she is actively breaking and tearing rather than brandishing them. And although the poem does not tell us until six stanzas in that she is, exactly like Verlame, sitting on the bank of a stream, the poem first describes her profuse weeping and tears as prolific enough to be their own stream or pond, with which she is able to sit 'Laund'ring' (*LC*, 17) her silken embroidered handkerchief and other love tokens.

The riverbank setting is important: for Spenser, it indicates a site of former commerce in a flourishing city that has fallen to such ruin over time that it has left no trace of itself – even the river that supposedly once flowed there has dried up and moved away. That Spenser meets Verlame on the Thames suggests that either the river or the city is outside of space and time; perhaps the river in that poem is a ghost as well. Spenser's Verlame and its placeless river Thames are thus representations of untimely matter. I take this concept from Jonathan Gil Harris, who identifies several early modern palimpsestic spaces and texts as 'untimely' where the layered past pushes back against the present.[22] Though Harris rejects Derrida's description of 'untimely as ghostly revenant' in pursuit of a more material-based argument,[23] I want to suggest that Spenser's Verlame and the two resurrected ghost-like complainants in *A Lover's*

---

[21] Edmund Spenser, *The Ruines of Time*, in *The Yale Edition of the Shorter Poems of Edmund Spenser*, ed. William A. Oram, Einar Bjorvand and Ronald Bond (New Haven, 1989), lines 8–14. All further quotations from this poem are from this edition.
[22] Jonathan Gil Harris, *Untimely Matter in the Time of Shakespeare* (Philadelphia, 2011).
[23] Gil Harris, *Untimely Matter*, p. 12.

Complaint are untimely in both a spectral Derridean and material Gil Harrisian way – they are both textual palimpsests and poetic revenants.

In Shakespeare's poem, the river is less an untimely or impossible space than it is a flowing and growing textual palimpsest and commentary. Its presence serves to amplify the already profuse tears that the maid is weeping and with which she is attempting to wash away her love tokens, 'applying wet to wet' (*LC*, 40). The stream is also – like all the objects mentioned in Shakespeare's poem, including the maid, the love tokens and her male seducer – presented as a text in need of interpretation, with the maid positioned as a gloss to that text, situated on the 'weeping margin' of its page (*LC*, 39), pouring out her sorrow like inky comments from a pen.[24] Both Verlame and Shakespeare's plaintive maid sit on the edges of the river, in a space of limits, where, if we follow Alberto Pérez-Gómez's reading of Aristotle and the *Hypnerotomachia Poliphili* (another antiquarian reenactment),[25] negotiations with time and desire take place. Spenser's river in *The Ruines of Time* constitutes untimely matter, a resurrected past that lives in lyric alone, whereas Shakespeare's river is a textual margin of copious tears. The river setting that opens both poems also recalls Ovid's Pythagoras of Book 15 of the *Metamorphoses*, who famously describes time as similar to a river, an image that both Shakespeare and Spenser adapted in other writings (Shakespeare in Sonnet 60 and Spenser in *Amoretti* 75 and the Mutability cantos of *The Faerie Queene*). As Ovid's Pythagoras informs us, 'ipsa quoque adsiduo labuntur tempora motu, non secus ac flumen'[26] ('time is constantly slipping away, not unlike a river'). Both heroines are sitting on the banks of a river that is not unlike time. Verulame's river is a ghostly one from the past, and the maiden's river seems to run in a circle, as the poem's self-description as a reworded echo, its many repetitions and borrowings, and the maid's conclusion that she would fall all over again indicate.

In an even further Ovidian–Spenserian repetition, the opening three lines of Shakespeare's complaint self-reflexively describe the sounds of the weeping woman that reach the narrator as echoes: the tale reverberates 're-worded' (*LC*, 1) from the valley of a hill, described as a 'concave womb' (*LC*, 1), and echo all the way across to a second valley, the 'sist'ring vale' (*LC*, 2), where the speaker is situated to receive them as a 'double voice' (*LC*, 3). As scholars have already noted, this landscape is encoded as female and generative; the valley is a womb that generates sound to a sister valley.[27] Though this clearly hints at the community of female lovers that it later transpires have lent their voices and hands to boosting the signal of the attractiveness and courtship of the male lover, which Bates identifies as a model of feminine homosocial exchange,[28] I want to draw attention to the way this poem also invokes Ovid's myth of Echo and Narcissus. In Ovid's *Metamorphoses*, Echo, an overly chatty nymph, is cursed by Juno (for delaying Juno on her way to discover Jove's conquests of other women) to repeat only the final words of others.[29] When she falls for Narcissus she wastes away, transforming not just into a disembodied repetitious voice, but also into the craggy valley that reverberates her voice: 'vox tantum atque ossa supersunt: / vox manet, ossa ferunt lapidis traxisse figuram' – only the voice and bones remain, and the bones are said to have been shaped into stone.[30] Not only does the maid's complaint reach the ear of the narrator only via echo across two valleys, it is also already described in the first

---

[24] Both Catherine Bates and Mary Floyd-Wilson draw attention to the love tokens that the male seducer gives to the maid and she then attempts to destroy as legible, interpretable texts, though for Floyd-Wilson they are also vibrant, natural matter. See Bates, 'Enigma', 430, and Mary Floyd-Wilson, 'The preternatural ecology of "A Lover's Complaint"', *Shakespeare Studies* 39 (2011), 43–53.

[25] Alberto Pérez-Gómez, *Poliphilo, or the Dark Forest Revisited* (Cambridge, MA, 1992), p. 37.

[26] Publius Ovidius Naso, *Metamorphoses*, ed. R. J. Tarrant (Oxford, 2004), 15.179–80 (all further Latin quotations are from this edition, and the translations in the current article are my own, unless otherwise indicated).

[27] See Burrow, 'Introduction', and Bates, 'Enigma', p. 434.

[28] Bates, 'Enigma', pp. 434–5.

[29] Ovid, *Metamorphoses*, 3.359–405.

[30] Ovid, *Metamorphoses*, 3.398–9.

line as 're-worded' (*LC*, 1), suggesting that the story has been told before and both the maid's song and Shakespeare's poem are merely echoes of the original tale, as well as rewordings of Spenser and of Ovid. Like the nymph Echo, Shakespeare's 'fickle maid full pale' falls for a man attractive to many, whose attractiveness is defined by their desire, and who remains uninterested in any of them. And as Anthony Archdeacon has intriguingly suggested, we have early modern English sonnet sequences' (including Spenser's) critique of Petrarchan love to thank for developing the idea of pathological Narcissism.[31]

Though Archdeacon does not mention the tradition of following sonnet sequences with complaints, and thus neglects to address Daniel's *Complaint of Rosamond* and Shakespeare's *A Lover's Complaint*, he nevertheless points out that Arthur Golding's translation of the Echo and Narcissus myth inserts the English word 'fickle' into the text to reprimand Narcissus: 'why dost though raught the fickle image so?'[32] In the original Latin, Narcissus rebukes his own reflection, but does not give it any adjectival attributes. Golding changes this speech to an omniscient narrator rebuking Narcissus for following a 'fickle' and unstable reflection. For Archdeacon, this usage reveals how self-love grew into an illness. But I think it also draws attention to the liquid instability and inconstancy of Narcissus' desire for his mirror-image, which early modern poets in turn incorporate into descriptions of unfaithful lovers such as the young man in *A Lover's Complaint*, the Narcissus to the pale maiden's Echo. Ironically, Ovid's Narcissus is not unfaithful to his love for his own reflection: even in the underworld, he finds a pool into which to gaze.[33] His 'fickle' quality and the fickleness of the inconstant male lover in Shakespeare's complaint are characterized by their joint ability to enchant others (and to encourage that enchantment) without reciprocating.

Yet it is Shakespeare's maid, and not her inconstant male lover, who is described as 'a fickle maid full pale' (*LC*, 5), thus connecting her and her watery activities (weeping, washing, 'adding wet to wet') through Golding's translation with Narcissus' unstable reflection.[34] This attribution seems deliberately confusing: editors puzzle over why the maid herself should be described as unfaithful, rather than her inconstant lover. Many gloss this as describing the maid as emotionally unstable, with Colin Burrow concluding that the narrator mistakenly assumes she is breaking her vows at first.[35] But, as Burrow notes, the *OED* also defines 'fickle' in this era as 'uncertain, unreliable', and I would add it also describes the verb form of 'fickle' as 'to puzzle'.[36] This 'fickle maid' who is not fickle herself, but rather hyper-aware of the fickleness of her male lover, is also an inscrutable curiosity for both narrator and audience to puzzle out, an antiquarian artefact or text awaiting further excavation and interpretation, similar to the inscrutable artefactual love tokens that are described three times in the poem, first by the narrator and then twice by the male lover (*LC*, 15–21; 43–56; 197–21). Later on in the poem, when the maid reproduces her lover's argument (the complaint within a complaint), we learn that the male lover has harnessed his own tears to the tears of his previous female lovers to add emotion to his persuasive force, linking him both to Narcissus and to Echo's refrains.

Spenser's Verlame and Shakespeare's 'fickle maid' resemble other Elizabethan wronged

---

[31] Anthony Archdeacon, 'Ovid's Echo and Narcissus myth in English Petrarchan poetry', *Early Modern Literary Studies* 20 (2018): https://extra.shu.ac.uk/emls/journal/index.php/emls/article/view/372. See also Archdeacon, *From Narcissism to Nihilism: Self-Love and Self-Negation in Early Modern Literature* (London, 2022).

[32] *Ovid's Metamorphoses: The Arthur Golding Translation of 1567*, ed. John Frederick Nims (Philadelphia, 2000), 3.543.

[33] 'postquam est inferna sede receptus, / in Stygia spectabat aqua' (Ovid, *Metamorphoses*, 3.504–5); or, 'after he was taken to Hell, he was always gazing in the Stygian waters'.

[34] Several other authors in this volume of *Shakespeare Survey* also pay special attention to the watery forces at work in the poem, particularly Katharine A. Craik, Elizabeth Scott-Baumann and Hannah Crawforth.

[35] *LC*, in *The Complete Poems*, ed. Burrow, p. 695, n. 5.

[36] *LC*, in *The Complete Poems*, ed. Burrow, p. 695, n. 5; *OED Online*, 'fickle, v.²'.

women in the literary complaint tradition such as Daniel's Rosamond and Middleton's ghost of Lucrece – both weep profusely, both ghostly, though unlike Rosamond or Lucrece they are not summoned or conjured from the afterlife by their poets but rather encountered by them. Yet *The Ruines of Time* and *A Lover's Complaint* are unique in that both narrators encounter their wailing, weeping protagonists on the banks of a river, describe these women as wearing carelessly loosened, melancholic yellow hair, and holding broken objects (Verlame), or engaged in actively breaking them (the maid). More spirits than revenants, more ghostly than ghosts. Verlame's broken staff suggests the ancient past in fragmentary form – she is literally a ruin. And although Shakespeare's maid is not the ghost of a historical ancient ruined city, she describes herself as a besieged city in Petrarchan fashion: 'And long upon these terms I held my city, / Till thus he gan besiege me' (*LC*, 177–8).

If we read Shakespeare's plangent maid as an echo of Verlame, she is actively engaged in accelerating the passage of time by turning her immediate present into the fragmented ruins of the past. Both women are ghosts or ghostly. Spenser refers to Verlame as a spirit, characterized as 'th'auncient *Genius* of that Citie brent' (*RT*, 19), and Verlame announces her ghostly identity as a dead, lost city: '[I] have in mine owne bowels made my grave' (*RT*, 26). Shakespeare's maid is more ghost-like than ghost: she does not seem to have died or risen from the grave, yet she is 'full pale' (*LC*, 5) and prematurely aged, poetically a corpse: 'The carcass of a beauty spent and done ... Some beauty peeped through lattice of seared age' (*LC*, 11–14). A liminal figure situated between life and death, youth and old age, the maid later explains that her experience of betrayed love over time has caused her only to *seem* ruined and old:

> ... 'though in me you behold
> The injury of many a blasting hour,
> Let it not tell your judgement I am old;
> Not age, but sorrow over me hath power.
> I might as yet have been a spreading flower,
> Fresh to myself, if I had self-applied
> Love to myself, and to no love beside.
> (*LC*, 71–7)

Not only has her poor judgement in love and the inconstancy of her lover caused the maid to age prematurely through sorrow, she also compares herself to Narcissus suggesting that his fate (self-love transformed into 'a spreading flower') would have been far better than the ruin she has suffered. To loosely paraphrase Ovid's Pythagoras: there are no ghosts in the *Metamorphoses*, only transformations. Departing from Spenser and the tradition of the ghost complaint, Shakespeare has his maid appear ghostly and wasted away, but inserts her mentality instead into an older Ovidian ethos of regenerative transformation, a move that Lisa Starks might refer to as Ovidian appropriation and allusion, and I would modify to describe as Ovidian reenactment.[37] Shakespeare yet again links not the lover but the maid to Narcissus, inverting both the gender and the punishment in Ovid's myth, suggesting it as more innocent and 'fresh', and a more generative ('spreading') alternative to what the maid has suffered. Like Echo, she has wasted away and can only repeat her song of betrayal, wishing instead for an isolated, flowery fate more like Narcissus'. The maid's legacy, like the complaint itself, as we learn, is one of accumulation, repetition and cyclicality, but here she explicitly categorizes contained self-love as self-generating and harmless, whereas the relationship she has with the suitor is in a sense polyamorous (he courts her through and with the words of his previous female lovers), grotesque and uncontainable.

LEGIBLE AND ILLEGIBLE ARTEFACTS

Unlike *A Lover's Complaint*, the temporal mode of Spenser's *The Ruines of Time* is explicitly pro-antiquarian. Announcing itself as a complaint sung by an ancient, ruined and forgotten city, the poem turns to this embodied fragment of antiquity

---

[37] Lisa Starks, 'Ovidian appropriations, metamorphic allusion, and theatrical practice on the Shakespearean stage', in *The Routledge Handbook of Shakespeare and Global Appropriation*, ed. Christy Desmet, Sujata Iyengar and Miriam Jacobson (New York, 2019), 398–408.

to catalyse a double literary memorial to the departed Leicester and Philip Sidney. Verlame makes this clear when she invokes William Camden, one of the first English historians to call himself an antiquary, to articulate a desire to preserve and study the remains of the past:

> Cambden the nourice of antiquitie
> ...
> To see the light of simple veritie,
> Buried in ruines ...
> Cambden, though time all moniments obscure,
> Yet thy just labours ever shall endure.
>
> (RT, 169–75)

Verlame mentions Camden because he is the exception to the rule: the only historian around who can gently, maternally (he is a 'nourice' or nurse) shed light on Britain's ancient past. The monuments Camden might bring out of obscurity reappear in the subsequent stanza as Verlame longs for a similar Camden to restore her 'antique moniments defaced' (RT, 179). With a play on the early modern double meaning of 'monument' as both architectural edifice and text Spenser speaks through Verlame to insist that he, Spenser, is the poetic equivalent to the historian Camden, and that through multivocality poetry can achieve the same kind of excavations and reenactments that preserve and memorialize cities, statesmen and poets.

For Shakespeare, on the other hand, it is the instability between text and artefact that illustrates both the allure and futility of the antiquarian desire to recover, interpret and reenact the material past. This artefactual instability is embodied in the poem in the plethora of love tokens from other women that the maid destroys at the outset of the poem, and that the male lover later in the text and earlier in the maid's history recasts as 'tributes' and the foundation of his courtship. When we first see them from the voyeuristic narrator's perspective, they are inscribed and indecipherable. Her handkerchief is embroidered with 'conceited characters ... silken figures' (LC, 16–17) that she reads aloud as 'undistinguished woe' (LC, 20). We cannot decipher or hear what she is reading, neither on the handkerchief nor on the 'folded schedules' (LC, 43), nor the inscriptions on the 'many a ring of posied gold and bone' (LC, 45) she cracks, nor any of the words in the 'letters sadly penned in blood' (LC, 47) whose contents remain obscured 'With sleided silk feat and affectedly / Enswathed and sealed to curious secrecy' (LC, 48–9). Bound in silk so as to be impenetrable, both the phrases on the handkerchief and in the letters are inaccessible to the poet and the poem's audience. These are materials of the past that call out for antiquarian illumination, clarification initially denied.

Both Bates and Floyd-Wilson attend to the signifying quality of the amassed love tokens in their readings of the poem. For Bates, they are important because they are all women-authored textual artefacts, 'objects that signify'.[38] Even the jewelled favours of amber and jet have early modern lapidary significance and symbolic meaning, as Bates notes.[39] Floyd-Wilson is more interested in the stones, beads and gemstones' significance as vibrant, transformative recycled matter – including a reference to Ovid's myth of amber deriving from Niobe's tears. For Floyd-Wilson, textual matter is less important in the poem than the 'effervescent' and metamorphic stones the female lovers exchange with the male seducer.[40] Bates's and Floyd-Wilson's readings are accurate: the love tokens function both as metamorphic, elemental charms operating in their own economy of recycled use and meaning, and as texts. But these texts are obscured, unread and indecipherable, and these recycled beads, stones, rings and hair lace bracelets are part of a larger economy of reuse and accumulation in the poem that describes a deeper critique of how poets recycle and reappropriate the relics of the past.

As we learn in the young man's embedded speech, these tokens do not initially derive from him, but are gifts fashioned and given to him by other women's careful effort. They include objects

---

[38] Bates, 'Enigma', p. 429. [39] Bates, 'Enigma', p. 429.
[40] Floyd-Wilson, 'Preternatural ecology', p. 48.

fashioned exclusively by women, such as hair lace bracelets: 'behold, these talents of their hair, / With twisted metal amorously impleached' (*LC*, 204–5). Hair bracelets were lacework in early modern England, a craft that was practised solely by women. Based on the few examples of early modern hair lacework that survive, these are unlikely to have been interwoven with real metal. Therefore, in what may be a reference to Shakespeare's own anti-Petrarchism in Sonnet 130 ('If hair be wires, black wires grow on her head' (4)), the male seducer further indicates his rhetorical insincerity. When we first encounter these objects saturated in tears, they are conceited but concealed. But according to the youth, they are more legible, and their quantity and power is accumulative. Each gem contains its own interpretive text: 'deep-brained sonnets that did amplify / Each stone's dear nature' (*LC*, 209–10), and each gemstone vocalizes in Petrarchan verse: 'With wit well blazoned, smiled or made some moan' (*LC*, 217). Intriguingly and frustratingly, we do not have access to these women's sonnets, but the complaint seems to ask us to reread and interpret the preceding sonnets in the 1609 quarto as if they were part of this ancient hoard of past female lovers.

The youth styles his amassed love tokens as 'tributes' (*LC*, 197). His seductive power depends upon accumulating, reappropriating and reusing these past loves' gifts. Tellingly, he calls them 'tributes', not only gifts of gratitude, but periodic payments made to a conquering nation by a lesser nation to acknowledge dependence and maintain peaceful relations. The male lover positions himself as conqueror of these women's hearts, but more important here is the role tributes play in maintaining the status quo. By conceiving of the gifts as tributes, the lover *maintains* the endless cycle of gift-giving, seduction and reuse. And it is no accident that the gifts continue to accumulate as jewelled 'annexions' and poetic creations that 'did amplify / Each stone's dear nature, worth, and quality' (*LC*, 208–10), as this viciously repetitive temporal cycle is defined by its copious amplification. Yet even as the youth reads his love tokens as building blocks of text to amplify his seductive power, he presents the maid as a blank page to be written upon, a 'phraseless hand' (*LC*, 225), offering her the chance to write her own love poem out of the past lovers' texts of love, like an early modern version of refrigerator poetry: 'Take all these similes to your own command' (*LC*, 227), he entreats, and fashion your own Petrarchan reenactment – which is what the maid does, despite her attempts to tear and shatter them in the opening, by reenacting his seduction in her tale.

Unlike the indecipherable and reinterpreted love tokens and the pathologically narcissistic, Petrarchan love-bomber, the maid clocks her male seducer as false from the start. In direct opposition to Shakespeare's Lucrece, who is illiterate to Tarquin's sinister, flirtatious winks metaphorized as marginal glosses, 'the subtle shining secrecies / Writ in the glassy margins of such books' (*Lucrece* 101–2), this maid describes her seducer as a 'false jewel' (*LC*, 154) in direct opposition to the symbolic gemstone treasures he has accumulated and given to her. She also elides his past conquests with their pile of tokens in the same line as 'amorous spoil' (*LC*, 154). In what seems like an allusion to his earlier poem that focuses on Lucrece's post-rape rhetorical literacy, Shakespeare has the maid interpret and gloss her seducer from the outset:

> For further I could say this man's untrue,
> And knew the patterns of his foul beguiling;
> . . .
> Saw how deceits were gilded in his smiling,
> Knew vows were ever brokers to defiling,
> Thought characters and words merely but art,
> And bastards of his foul adulterate heart.
> (*LC*, 169–75)

Both Lucrece and the maid are confronted with a man's face and seductive intent as a glossed text. Unlike Lucrece, who gains literacy with loss of chastity, the maid not only can read the 'patterns', the 'gilded ... smiling' and the 'characters and words merely but art', she also willingly enters into a relationship with this inconstant man despite expertly interpreting his texts, and at the poem's conclusion (such that it is), she says she would do it again. Part of being a good antiquarian interpreter of the past is knowing how to read and interpret its texts and objects, even if one becomes a ruined text in the process. The male lover, as we will see, represents a more threatening version of antiquarianism, a form of appropriation and reenactment that creates ruins in its wake.

AMPLIFICATION AND REENACTMENT

A Lover's Complaint critiques the antiquarian desire to accumulate and reenact the past through the poetic motif of amplification and the language of refashioning and reenactment ('re-worded' appears in the poem's first line). Critics have noted the poem's rhetorical motifs of copiousness, cyclical repetition and surrogacy. For Bates, the poem's rhetorical copiousness, the 'sheer quantity' of women who have loved the male wooer, the love tokens that number in the thousands, create a sense of 'collective frenzy'.[41] And for Heather Dubrow, substitution and surrogacy are what distinguish early modern complaints from other forms of poetry, seen in the poem's emphasis on speaking in another's voice, a pattern she connects to the *Sonnets*' treatment of jealousy and same-sex love.[42] In my reading, images of accumulation and amplification instigate and maintain this cycle of collective frenzy and continuous substitution, creating the poem's unending temporal circuitry.

The force of the male lover's seductive cycle depends upon amplifying his power through the accumulation of the past in the form of love sonnets 'that did amplify' (*LC*, 209), collected tears, and hearts from his past female lovers, one of whom – a nun – is also a representative figure of a lost medieval English past (*LC*, 232–63). The amplifying force of the youth's amorous power culminates in his reappropriation and reenactment of their accumulated tears, which he mixes with his own and the maid's:

> The broken bosoms that to me belong
> Have emptied all their fountains in my well,
> And mine I pour your ocean all among.
> (*LC*, 254–6)

This is a powerful image of accumulated increasing aqueous force, from fountain to well to ocean. And he continues to reenact this act of weeping, with 'wat'ry eyes ... / Each cheek a river running from a fount / With brinish current downward flowed apace' (*LC*, 281–4). Buoyed with others' tears, the youth transforms himself into a monstrous lachrymatory, a giant vessel of tears collected from multiple mourners. Though archaeologists agree today that lachrymatories did not exist in ancient Rome and people buried their dead only with *unguentaria* (bottles of scented oils), the idea was a potent one for early modern antiquarians and poets alike. The youth also compares himself to a grotesque assemblage of hearts, a giant heart beating with the many hearts of his past lovers, who 'extend' their sighs through him to pursue the maid:

> Now all these hearts that do on mine depend,
> Feeling it break, with bleeding groans they pine,
> And supplicant their sighs to you extend
> (*LC*, 274–6)

Mirroring – or perhaps reenacting – the youth's rhetorical accumulation, the poem's formal structure, too, gathers and amplifies voices. Both Spenser's and Shakespeare's complaint poems involve a male narrator as witness to the woman's despairing vocalizations – one character in Spenser's poem, two in Shakespeare's. Shakespeare amplifies the number of voices from Spenser's complaint, and attaches this trope of multivocal amplification to the rhetorical power of the reenacted male lover. In Spenser's poem, the speaker calls out to Verlame and is moved to pity, compelled to produce his own tears at seeing hers: 'I (to her calling) askt what her so vexed' (*RT*, 21); 'Much was I mooved at her piteous plaint ... That shedding teares a while I still did rest' (*RT*, 29–32). This is how complaints are supposed to work: they effect affective piety in the audience, allowing wrongs to be righted. But Shakespeare's

---

[41] Bates, 'Enigma', p. 434.
[42] Dubrow, 'Re-evaluating the "Delian Structure"', pp. 98–101.

complaint doesn't work that way. The maid's sorrows are not transferred onto either the narrator or the old rustic man who tries to console her. Further, she embeds a second complaint within her own speech when she relates her lover's plaintive seduction act by speaking in his voice. The two characters who weep in *A Lover's Complaint* are the rejected maid and her no longer present lover, whose suit is presented as a performance by the maid. Shakespeare's poem inverts the sympathetic response a complaint is supposed to produce by retroactively reproducing the initial (and ill-willed) complaint of the lover that led the maid to weep herself, which is mirrored in the way the youth's charm inverts the sequence of persuasion, bewitching people into giving consent to him before he desires it (*LC*, 131).

This confusing amplification and retroactive enfolding of characters and voices highlights *A Lover's Complaint*'s distinctive use of poetic doubling, echoes, rhetorical *copia* and images of accumulation throughout the poem. The poem reenacts the maid's complaint, inside of which the maid reenacts her lover's seductive complaint, which is constructed out of the female complaints of love for him that came before. Spenser's poem, by contrast, has only two narrators, and takes pains to show it: at one point in the complaint, Verlame rails against the lack of poets who will memorialize Leicester's death, wittily calling out Colin Clout, Spenser's pastoral alter ego, for remaining silent: 'Wake shepheards boy, at length awake for shame' (*RT*, 231). Colin keeps his mouth shut, and Verlame complains for another 200 lines. After that, the narrator silently observes six 'tragicke Pageants' (*RT*, 490) of vanity and speaks only in the concluding two stanzas of envoi.

Spenser's complaint's envoi puts Verlame, Leicester and Sidney to rest. But nothing is put to rest in Shakespeare's complaint; instead, the act of seduction and betrayal exists in what Burrow calls 'temporal looping', continually replicated, reenacted and resurrected.[43] The false youth dubs the maid his 'origin and ender' (*LC*, 222) and she, in turn, describes their tears as currency in a reciprocal death and resurrection: 'His poisoned me, and mine did him restore' (*LC*, 301), calling to mind the opening of the poem where she launders his collection of love tokens in her tears, along with her subsequent restoration of his voice.[44] This loop is furthered through the poem's opened frame: the narrator never returns, and there is no envoi. It ends with the maid concluding that she would most likely fall all over again for the unfaithful lover, that the 'borrowed motion' (*LC*, 327) of the lover, like a puppet or automaton clumsily reenacting other women's expressions of love, nonetheless 'Would yet again betray the fore-betrayed, / And new pervert a reconcilèd maid' (*LC*, 328–9).[45] Instead, as de Grazia posits, the complaint's ending invites us to open the 1609 quarto of sonnets to the beginning and start the 'program of return' again as indicated by the printer's decorative vignette.[46] If we did this, we would turn to the first sonnet in the sequence, with the narrator desiring 'increase' from 'fairest creatures, / That thereby beauty's rose might never die' (Sonnet 1.1–2), which reread ('re-worded') in this order appears to echo both the complaint's accumulative rhetoric and the maid's sadness at her beauty's ruin. Fast forwarding through the sonnets to the complaint at the end shows us beauty's rose in a prolonged circuit of dying and resurrection, of excavation and reenactment.

---

[43] Burrow, 'Introduction', p. 143.

[44] The maid speaks for 105 lines (*LC*, 71–176), embeds her suitor's monologue in her speech for 103 lines (*LC*, 177–280), giving her own conclusion for the final 48 lines (*LC*, 281–329).

[45] I am reading 'motion' here in line 327's 'borrowed motion' as an allusion to early modern puppet shows, which were called 'motions'. I am indebted to Tiffany Stern and Richard Preiss for this information. By the 1600s (*A Lover's Complaint* first appeared in 1609), 'motion' could also describe clockwork and automata. See also *OED Online*, 'motion, n.', senses I.5 and I.8.

[46] De Grazia, 'Revolution', p. 68.

DIFFERENT SAMENESSES

STEPHEN GUY-BRAY

In 2012, Sharmila Cohen and Paul Legault published a book called *The Sonnets: Translating and Rewriting Shakespeare*, in which each of Shakespeare's sonnets appears in a version by a contemporary poet. There are several other contemporary rewritings of the sonnets, both in book form and published independently in journals, such as *On Shakespeare's Sonnets: A Poets' Celebration,* edited by Hannah Crawforth and Elizabeth Scott-Baumann (2016), and *Out of Sequence: The Sonnets Remixed,* edited by Duane Gilson (2015); I have chosen Cohen and Legault's version because a number of the poets make interesting uses of the original words of the poems. The emphasis in adaptation studies – and this has certainly been the case with discussions of adaptations of Shakespeare's plays – has typically been on the differences between the original and the new version. When scholars have stressed the similarities between a text by Shakespeare and an adaptation, they have chiefly been interested in the persistence of themes or narrative elements.[1] In contrast, in this article I will be concerned with some of the poems in which the contemporary authors have chosen to incorporate words from the original sonnets. This incorporation takes various forms: sometimes the letters are present but not divided into words, sometimes the words are present but are ordered differently, sometimes the original sonnet is reproduced but with altered typography, and sometimes the original rhymes are used but the words that lead up to those rhymes are different. I want to look at how some of the poets in this collection use sameness and differences in the versions they create in order to complicate the readers' sense of the relationship between the earlier and later poems. The poets I discuss seek to complicate the movement from the Renaissance text to the contemporary one: their poems pull us back as well as push us forward.

I propose that we think of the poets who chose to incorporate Shakespeare's words in their own versions as choosing to operate under writing constraints. Although writing constraints of various kinds have been used for a couple of millennia in a number of languages, they are now usually associated with the OuLiPo movement (*Ouvroir de littérature potentielle*) that began in France in the 1960s and that has continued to be popular among avant-garde poets both in France and in the anglophone world. These constraints can take a number of forms: one, for instance, is S+7 (N+7 in English), in which each noun is replaced by the seventh noun after it in a dictionary. Probably the most famous constraint is the lipogram, however. In this scheme, the challenge is to write a text without using a certain letter; the best-known example is Georges Perec's *La Disparition*, in which Perec gave himself the extremely difficult task of writing an entire novel without the letter 'e', the most frequently used letter in French. As I see it, the poets I discuss in this article are writing according to a constraint that is the opposite of the lipogram: they require themselves to leave things in

---

[1] See, for instance, my discussion of a poem from this collection: '"Remembering to forget": Shakespeare's "Sonnet 35" and Sigo's "XXXV"', in *Sexuality and Memory in Early Modern England: Literature and the Erotics of Recollection*, ed. John S. Garrison and Kyle Pivetti (New York, 2015), 43–50.

their poems rather than to leave them out. To describe this, I have invented the term 'menogram', from the Ancient Greek *menein*, meaning 'to remain'.

The first menogram I want to look at is by Jen Bervin. In a sense, it is a double menogram, both in that it uses Shakespeare's words and in that she previously published this poem in her collection *Nets* in 2004: she thus reproduces the original sonnet and her own previous publication of it. *Nets* consists of between one-third and one-half of Shakespeare's *Sonnets*. Each sonnet Bervin presents is complete, but she uses two shades of greyscale in reproducing the poems. Most of each sonnet is printed in pale greyscale while certain phrases or words or even parts of words are printed in darker greyscale. Thus, for each sonnet Bervin chooses, we get two poems: the original sonnet and the new poem she has fashioned out of it. The sonnet she includes in the Cohen and Legault volume is Sonnet 2. In effect, she reduces it to three lines:

> a weed of small worth
> asked ...
> to be new made.[2]

Rather than write an independent poem inspired by Shakespeare's, Bervin's insists that we see the relationship between the texts. Even if her three-line poem had been published as a free-standing poem, the phrase 'a weed of small worth' is famous enough to send readers back to Shakespeare (Sonnet 2), or at least to Google. Bervin's poem hovers between being a reproduction of the original and being a new poem. It forces us to consider what is at stake in adaptation and how much of the original has to be changed in order for the new text to count as an adaptation. Bervin's method here and in her other adaptations of the sonnets focuses our attention on the work of adaptation. We could even say that it provides us a template to create adaptations of our own.

We might consider Bervin's decision to include 'a weed of small worth' as an assessment of Sonnet 2, which is certainly not one of the best sonnets, although suggesting that it is 'of small worth' seems rather harsh. We might also consider that, just as weeds grow everywhere and proliferate rapidly, so too did sonnets and sonnet sequences proliferate rapidly throughout Europe during Shakespeare's life. We could thus see Bervin's poem as a comment on Shakespeare's, if not exactly an interpretation of it. It is also a comment on textual production, on the labour that went into the sonnet sequences of the past, and that goes into her poem and into a volume of new versions of the sonnets as a whole: rather than just giving us a finished poem, Bervin shows us adaptation at work. Her poem has a curious status: it is somewhere between being an agent – insofar as it asks something – and being a patient – insofar as it is remade. In the original, it is the young man's beauty that is remade in being reproduced in his child; here, the tattered garment that his beauty will become as he ages is remade as a poem. In its shifting of the means of preserving beauty from human reproduction to textual production, Bervin's poem anticipates Shakespeare's own shift from one to the other several sonnets later in his sequence. Bervin's decision to emphasize 'to be new made' can also be seen as an allusion to Ezra Pound's famous exhortation to 'Make It New', often seen as the unofficial motto of modernism. For Bervin – and, by extension, for all the other poets who contributed to the volume – to make it new is also to remake something that already exists.

Bervin gives us both the original and the new version of her chosen Shakespearian sonnet; I want now to look at three other versions that also present the original poems, but in very different ways. The most extreme of these is Eric Zboya's version of Sonnet 30 (p. 48): he gives us a black rectangle dotted with what most readers – or, perhaps more accurately, viewers in this case – would take to be stars, and then strewn with letters (Figure 1). The picture contains all the letters used in the original, but in no order at all, some pointing one way, some

---

[2] Jen Bervin, 'Sonnet 2', in *The Sonnets: Translating and Rewriting Shakespeare*, ed. Sharmila Cohen and Paul Legault (Brooklyn, 2012), p. 2; lines 4, 5 and 12. Subsequent quotations from this volume will appear in the body of the text.

Eric Zboya   SONNET 30

1 Eric Zboya's version of Sonnet 30 © Nightboat Books.

against their black background – a visual analogue to the original's mention of 'death's dateless night' (6) – are not necessarily bound to Shakespeare's sonnet. In his discussion of materiality and avant-garde poetics, Craig Dworkin points out that 'The self-evident materiality of language somehow induces a chronic amnesia.'[3] In reducing Sonnet 30 to its components, Zboya fights against this amnesia: these letters could give rise to many different texts.

Like Zboya, Laynie Browne gives the entire Shakespeare sonnet rearranged, but while he reduces Sonnet 30 to its constituent letters, she retains the original words of Sonnet 26. She does change their order, however: as she writes in the headnote, this is 'An Abecedarian Translation Using only Text From the Original'. Browne divides her version into four stanzas – three quatrains followed by a couplet, her unrhymed lines following the rhyme scheme invented by the Earl of Surrey and used by Shakespeare. The original sonnet is more easily recognizable in her version than Sonnet 30 was in Zboya's, but the poem she creates resists understanding as a whole, or rather it moves in and out of being understandable. The first line is 'All apparel as aspect bestows bare conceit', which has at least the form of a statement that we might understand, and the lines

> Love mayst make me
>   Merit moving
> Naked
>
> (p. 33; lines 6–8)

another, some bigger, some smaller. The capital letters that begin each of the sonnet's lines are still capitalized, but they appear at random, unconnected to the lower-case letters that originally followed them. The dots that we originally took to be stars are perhaps better understood as marks of punctuation, scattered across the rectangle. Zboya's picture/poem works by getting us to remember the subject of the original, which is, of course, a poem about memory, as the first two lines make clear: 'When to the sessions of sweet silent thought / I summon up remembrance of things past'. Without the context of the volume in which it appears and the listing of the poet's name beside Sonnet 30, our memories of the sonnet could not be activated and the picture would not be recognizable as a poem. Zboya gives us the letters for the poem while requiring us to rewrite the poem ourselves. Or possibly to write a new one, as the letters

work fairly well, but the lines 'That thine thought till vassalage / Wanting words where' (lines 11–12), resist even the simplest paraphrase altogether. Her final couplet – 'Wit will witness / Worthy will' (lines 13–14) – works very well as an ending. The heavy alliteration and the breaking of the alphabetical scheme at the very end (emphasized by the extra spaces she puts before the final word) create a chiasmus that makes a strong conclusion, if not one that is particularly clear.

---

[3] Craig Dworkin, *Radium of the Word* (Chicago, 2020), p. 8.

To say that both Zboya and Browne present us with the original poems is true, but the statement obscures the differing extent to which they preserve Shakespeare's sonnets. Zboya's treatment seems more extreme, as he reduces the words of the sonnet to individual letters. As I have pointed out, if his poem had not appeared in Cohen and Legault's collection, it would not be possible to identify it as an adaptation of Sonnet 30. His retention of the poem's original capital letters demonstrates, however, that he, as the writer, and we, as the readers, are still dealing with a poem, however unrecoverable it may seem. Our recognition is further impeded by the fact that the letters are also of different sizes and thickness; nevertheless, he preserves the capitalization of the first letters of the words that begin the lines of Shakespeare's sonnets. In contrast, Browne's poem is seemingly more conventional: as an abecedarian, her poem consistently echoes the original's alliterative beginning – 'Lord of my love' (1) – and its *mise en page* is recognizably that of a poem, with each of her fourteen lines beginning with a capital letter. But none of the words capitalized in Shakespeare's sonnet is capitalized in hers: that is, part of the effect of Browne's decision to use the traditional form of a printed poem is to demonstrate that her poem is organized according to her own purposes. Considered together, these two poems show that what might look like total fidelity to the text – especially compared to most of the adapted sonnets in the collection – might also look like deviation from the text.

I turn now to two poems that reproduce the words of the original sonnet in the order of the original sonnet, to quite different effect. The first is Dara Wier's version of Sonnet 106. Not only does she give us the original words in their original order, but she does so twice. For example, here are the first four lines of her poem:

> When in the chronicles of wasted time
> When in the chronicles of wasted time
> I see description of the fairest wrights
> I see description of the fairest wrights.
> (p. 174; lines 1–4)

Wier's only change in all 28 lines of her poem is to substitute 'wrights' for the original 'wights' (twice).

This is conceivably a typographical error, but I choose rather to think that she wanted to use a word that suggests manual labour. She gives us a picture of textual production as a repetitive form of work, something that may certainly seem true of sonnets and sonnet sequences and that is also true of the printing process. To some extent, this is also Shakespeare's point in Sonnet 106: he makes clear that the 'antique pen' (7) of those writers of long ago depicted the same beauty that he sees in the young man and 'all their praises are but prophecies / Of this our time, all you prefiguring' (9–10). The redundancy of 'prophecies' and 'prefiguring' – the last three words of line 10 effectively repeat the phrase that has just ended – is thus logically connected to the repetition that is the most striking feature of Wier's poem. Her creation of a poem that repeats itself while repeating Shakespeare is true both to Shakespeare's words and to the point he makes in Sonnet 106.

Like Wier, Daniel Tiffany's adaptation of Sonnet 43 reproduces the original sonnet (p. 63). On the one hand, this hardly qualifies as an adaptation as the entire sonnet is given in its original order: of all the poems in the Cohen and Legault volume, this is obviously the one closest to the original sonnet. On the other hand, it does qualify as an adaptation as it – unlike the other poems in the collection (with the very different exception of Zboya's poem) and the vast majority of texts ever printed or indeed written – is not black type on a white background but rather white type on a black background (Figure 2). Tiffany's poem evokes the photographic negative, which is to say the material from which the photograph we look at is produced. In that respect, we might see the poem as a comment on the nature of adaptation itself: the poet requires a first stage before writing the adaptation that we read. We might infer that Tiffany presents his version as the finished product, the one we really want. Tiffany is thus arguably more candid than the other contributors, as he shows us exactly what he is adapting. His poem resembles Zboya's in that both poets use white letters on a black background. As I have suggested, both poets also get us to think about the material nature

> **Daniel Tiffany** SONNET 43
>
> When most I wink, then do mine eyes best see,
>
> For all the day they view things unrespected;
>
> But when I sleep, in dreams they look on thee,
>
> And darkly bright are bright in dark directed.
>
> Then thou, whose shadow shadows doth make bright,
>
> How would thy shadow's form form happy show
>
> To the clear day with thy much clearer light,
>
> When to unseeing eyes thy shade shines so!
>
> How would, I say, mine eyes be blessed made
>
> By looking on thee in the living day,
>
> When in dead night thy fair imperfect shade
>
> Through heavy sleep on sightless eyes doth stay!
>
> All days are nights to see till I see thee,
>
> And nights bright days when dreams do show thee me.

2 Daniel Tiffany's adaptation of Sonnet 43 © Nightboat Books.

of poetry. As I see it, one of the crucial differences between them is that, while Zboya's adaptation appears like a work of visual art, and could have an independent existence as a picture, Tiffany's still looks like a poem. In reversing the basic colours of the printed text, Tiffany leads us to consider the extent to which a poem is also always a visual object: in the case of a sonnet, for instance, a primarily rectangular and primarily black object on a white page.

In making black the chief colour of the page on which his poem appears, then, Tiffany draws attention to printing conventions; he also suggests an inverted relation between the original sonnet and his rendition of it. If, as I have argued, we see his version as resembling a photographic negative, we might even wonder which of the two versions of Sonnet 43 is the original. His change is also in keeping with Sonnet 43 itself, which focuses on looking, on doubling, on seeing versus imagining, and on dreams versus reality. This focus is often expressed in ways that make the sonnet difficult to parse at first, as for instance in these lines: 'Then thou, whose shadow shadows doth make bright, / How would thy shadow's form form happy show' (5–6). Tiffany's repetitious practice in this poem as well as his inversion of the standard ratio of black to white in a printed page reminds us of Shakespeare's own repetitions in Sonnet 43. The phrase 'shadow's form' is especially noteworthy in this regard. If a shadow has a form, that form can only be the original object or person that casts it. Sonnet 43 is in many ways a meditation on representation – most saliently on the representation provided by dreams but also of course (and as so often in the sonnets) on the representation provided by poetry. In changing white to black and black to white, Tiffany produces a poem that is very much in keeping with the sonnet he adapts and with the sonnets as a whole.

We could also see Tiffany's inversion of black and white in Sonnet 43 as a comment on blackness and whiteness in the entire sequence. The racism of the sonnets is most obviously connected to the so-called 'Dark Lady' of the last poems of the sequence and to speculation about her racial identity, but throughout the poems Shakespeare relies on the ubiquitous discourse of whiteness (or fairness) and blackness (or darkness) in Renaissance literature. In her monograph on blackness and Renaissance literature, for instance, Kim F. Hall argues that Renaissance lyric poetry employs 'a poetics of color in which whiteness is established as a valued goal'.[4] Most recent work on race and Shakespeare has looked at his plays, but much of this work is also relevant to his poetry and to the poetry of the period more generally. Tiffany's reversal of this binary – his decision to make black the dominant colour of his page – could prompt us to reconsider the 'poetics of color' in Shakespeare's sonnets, which rely on an association between whiteness and goodness on the one hand, and blackness and badness on the other. Returning to my comparison of his poem to a photographic negative, we could say that what we might develop from it is a fresh perspective on any supposed black/white binary, presenting us with a world in which blackness is the rule and whiteness the exception. In an excellent article, Farah Karim-Cooper argues that, '[i]n this period, whiteness and blackness are constructed as not just colors or complexions but also entire systems of value codified to produce a dubious but enduring sense of difference.'[5] Tiffany's poem makes this difference different.

In her adaptation of Sonnet 20 (p. 26), Vanessa Place also intervenes in an important contemporary discourse – in this case, the discourse of gender and sexuality. This sonnet is one of the most hotly contested of all the sonnets. Many conservative critics have argued that Shakespeare's couplet – 'But since she pricked thee out for women's pleasure, / Mine be thy love and thy love's use their treasure' (13–14) – means that the relationship between the speaker of the poems and the man to whom they are addressed cannot be seen as sexual. Much recent work, especially in queer studies, has questioned that reading and proposed new ones, pointing out, for instance, that in early modern English 'nothing' was a slang term for the vagina and as a consequence what appears to be a disavowal is instead ambiguous. Most recently, Colby Gordon has argued that the initial description of the man having a face 'with nature's own hand painted' (1) 'raises suspicions about whether the features are natural or artificial'.[6] In his brilliant reading of the sonnet, Gordon goes on to show that Shakespeare consistently emphasizes artistic practice rather than supposedly natural development. He points out that the poem 'does not actually present us with the prick but rather

---

[4] Kim F. Hall, *Things of Darkness: Economies of Race and Gender in Early Modern England* (Ithaca, 1995), p. 66. See also Sujata Iyengar, *Shades of Difference: Mythologies of Skin Color in Early Modern England* (Philadelphia, 2013), pp. 166–9.

[5] Farah Karim-Cooper, 'The materials of race: staging the black and white binary in the early modern theatre', in *The Cambridge Companion to Shakespeare and Race*, ed. Ayanna Thompson (Cambridge, 2021), 17–29; p. 18.

[6] Colby Gordon, 'A woman's prick: trans technogenesis in Sonnet 20', in *Shakespeare/Sex: Contemporary Readings in Gender and Sexuality*, ed. Jennifer Drouin (London, 2020), 268–89; p. 273.

with *pricking*, an activity that opens onto yet another scene of technical fabrication'.[7] Sonnet 20 gives us two binaries – male and female; art and nature – and blurs the distinctions between them while it seems to uphold them, in ways that Place picks up on in her version of the poem.

I have summarized this critical discourse to give a sense of just how important Sonnet 20 has been to queer studies in the last few decades. Place presents most of the sonnet as it is, but she makes a crucial change. Here are the first two lines of her version: 'A man's face, with nature's own hand painted, / Hast thou, the master-mister of my pleasure' (lines 1–2). Place replaces the original 'woman' of line 1 and the original 'mistress' of line 2 with their masculine equivalents. In the rest of the sonnet, Shakespeare writes 'woman' or 'women' five more times (lines 3, 4, 8, 9 and 11); Place changes each to 'man' or 'men'. As well, the two instances of 'she' (lines 10 and 13), which refer to nature personified as female, are changed to 'he'. Her changes have the important effect of giving us a world without women. Her poem takes place in the absence of the gender binary on which Shakespeare depends so heavily throughout his sonnet (and, of course, throughout all his works). In this sonnet, he draws on the standard misogynistic tropes about women's faithlessness, for instance, but in Place's version this becomes men's faithlessness and, as the first phrase indicates, it is now male beauty that is the standard. As well, Shakespeare tells us that the subject of his poem was originally supposed to be a woman until nature provided a penis, the 'one thing' of line 12. In Place's poem, it is not clear what this thing is. If there are only men, then what distinguishes the subject of her poem must be something else: a true and faithful nature, perhaps. Place removes both the gender binary and the phallus from her poem. As a result, her poem cannot be recuperated for the traditional gender discourse that Shakespeare echoes in his sonnet.

Although Place's changes are relatively minor in terms of word count, as she changes only 9 of the poem's 114 words, it is fair to say that her version is striking. What was already a quite complex (if clearly articulated) poem has become opaque. To some extent, I think this was Place's aim. In changing female nouns and pronouns to male ones, she rids the poem of its misogyny: Sonnet 20 shores up misogynistic ideas about women's behaviour and reaffirms the belief that a very beautiful face is feminine, but in Place's poem these attributes – both the beauty and the falsity – are said to be typical of men. And it is not only the real women towards whom Shakespeare's sonnet gestures that cease to exist; nature itself is now masculine. But another way to think about what Place has done is to say that, rather than make a fundamental change to the original poem, she has instead demonstrated a truth about the poem and, I would argue, about most literature in general: Place's version is also a critique. The women who appear in most sonnets are not real women any more than the goddess Nature is a real woman. Feminist critiques of male-authored lyric have argued that female characters tend to be based on stereotypes and are important chiefly to provide something for the poet to love and for readers to gaze at. The inaugural work in this critical tradition is probably Nancy J. Vickers's 'Diana described'; many critics have built on her analysis, and I think Place does as well.[8] In the place of the relations between men and women that are the subject of so much literature, Place presents us with a solely male homosocial world. In being untrue to Shakespeare's words, she reveals the network of relations among men that underpin the poems.

The final two poems that I wish to discuss in this article are by Paul Hoover and Randall Mann. Both Hoover, in his adaptation of Sonnet 5, and Mann, in his adaptation of Sonnet 124, retain the line-ends of the original sonnets in their menograms, a strategy that recalls the formerly popular game of *bouts-rimés*, in which a person would be given a list of end words and have to write a poem that used them.[9] One result of this decision is, obviously, that both new

---

[7] Gordon, 'A woman's prick', p. 277.
[8] Nancy J. Vickers, 'Diana described: scattered woman and scattered rhyme', *Critical Inquiry* 8 (1981), 265–79.
[9] In their adaptation of Sonnet 17, Timothy Liu and Jimmie Cumbie use the same end words in twelve of the lines with substitutions in the other two. I decided not to discuss this poem.

versions are rhyming poems and conform to the English sonnet structure used by Shakespeare. This familiar form stands out in the collection, chiefly composed of non-rhyming poems, as well as of letters strewn across the page and of illustrations. The form also stands out in the context of contemporary poetry as a whole. The use of traditional form is especially noteworthy in the case of Hoover, who typically writes free verse and in this case writes lines that are generally in recognizable metres. Mann, however, uses a number of traditional forms, many of his poems are in rhyme, and in this poem the lines are iambic pentameter. The rest of each of the lines of Hoover's and Mann's poems here is largely new. The experience of reading these poems is that the lines head inexorably towards the established end words that have been waiting for over 400 years. Adaptation works by bringing something old into the present and – as I wrote at the beginning of this article – in our discussions of it, our tendency is to focus on the newness. In performing in each line a movement backwards in time, Hoover's and Mann's poems might usefully complicate the ways in which we think about adaptations and can be seen as parallel to the idea of Tiffany's poem as a photographic negative. In their different ways, all three poets want readers to think about the extent to which adaptation can be as much a return to the original as a departure from it.

Like Sonnet 20, Sonnet 5 is a poem in which Shakespeare gives human agency to nonhuman things. In the case of Sonnet 5, it is time itself. Shakespeare begins by referring to 'Those hours that with gentle work did frame / The lovely gaze' (1–2). Hoover takes this prompt to create a poem about art: 'If you must make a picture, paint within the frame. / Our gaze within two perfect eyes must dwell' (p. 8; lines 1–2). Shakespeare uses 'gaze' in the unusual sense of 'something to be gazed at' – 'The lovely gaze where every eye doth dwell'. Hoover preserves this sense while also using it in the more familiar way: in Shakespeare, the gazing is unidirectional, but in Hoover it is mutual. As his use of 'gaze' suggests, Hoover retains many words of the original as well as the end words. For instance, Shakespeare's 'For never-resting time leads summer on / To hideous winter, and confounds him there' (5–6) becomes in Hoover 'such restless vision leads infinity on / to hideous zero, and confounds it there' (ll. 5–6). Shakespeare focuses on the man's beauty and on how it will change, but Hoover focuses on the act of looking itself. The picture he mentions in his first line is like a mirror image, which recalls my idea that Tiffany's poem can be seen as a photographic negative, at once the same and not the same as what it represents; as a result, we can also read it as a depiction of the process of adapting an old poem.

Over the course of Hoover's sonnet, the vision blurs or, as he writes, it is confounded: 'all that's left / is a pair of liquid scissors, paper thin glass' (ll. 9–10). The original is 'Then were not summer's distillation left / A liquid prisoner pent in walls of glass' (9–10). Hoover's change is crucial. For Shakespeare, the distillation – the attar of roses from which perfume can be made – is, as he writes at the end of the poem, the 'substance' (14) of the flowers. The implication is clearly that Shakespeare's poetry will transmit the young man's beauty, free from the ravages of time. This is one of Shakespeare's main themes in his sequence, perhaps most notably in Sonnet 15 and Sonnet 55. In Hoover's poem, however, what remains is not the sweet-smelling liquid but rather the glass that encloses the picture and acts as a mirror: his focus is on the container rather than on the thing contained. The glass is like paper in being very thin, but it is also like paper in that it provides the medium for artistic representation. The surreal image of the 'pair of liquid scissors' is, I think, impossible to paraphrase, although to some extent in being two things that are one thing, the pair of scissors figures the couple formed of two people as well as the couple formed of a person and their reflection. At this point in Hoover's poem, the representation itself is lost, but the tools that created it persist in some form. Similarly, Shakespeare's poem has disappeared into Hoover's adaptation of it and his equivalent to the 'liquid prisoner' is the poem itself, held not in a vial like the attar but in the structuring end words of the sonnet: Shakespeare's 'walls of glass' become, in effect, walls of rhymes.

The last three lines of Hoover's poem form a memorable unit:

> Neither it, nor I, remember what an image was:
> in a grandstand of mirrors, eyes multiplied meet
> in one of light's car crashes, short but sweet.
>
> (lines 12–14)

In some ways, these lines are the most Shakespearian of the poem as a whole. As he does in so many of the sonnets (and, especially, the early sonnets), Shakespeare has sought to find out ways to preserve fast-fleeting beauty: children, visual art and poetry, eventually settling on poetry, which he sees as immortal, in the way that poets often do. His desire is to ensure that the young man's beauty and the poetry that celebrates it are remembered even after the beauty itself has gone. By contrast, in Hoover's poem, even what an image is has been forgotten. Instead, the eyes that he has presented as both gazing at and being gazed upon are multiplied in a kind of *mise en abyme*.[10] Instead of the everlasting poetry that Shakespeare boasts of writing, Hoover gives us 'light's car crashes', collisions – of eyes, of bodies, of poems and of rhymes – that are 'short but sweet'. Shakespeare's ambition is to write poetry that will last forever; in contrast, and although the rhyme scheme remains, Hoover gives us the temporary pleasures of accidents.

In Sonnet 124, Shakespeare likewise grandly proclaims the permanence of his love. But here he praises this miraculous and everlasting love chiefly in a negative mode. He begins with the subjunctive mood – 'If my dear love were but the child of state' (1) – and goes on to say all the things his love is not: for instance, it is not affected by politics or the moods of the court and 'it nor grows with heat, nor drowns with showers' (12). It ends with a somewhat enigmatic appeal: 'To this I witness call the fools of time, / Which die for goodness, who have lived for crime' (13–14). The negative expression of this sonnet recalls the much more famous Sonnet 116, in which Shakespeare again expresses his love mainly by saying what it is not; perhaps most memorably, he uses enjambment to isolate the statement that 'Love is not love' (2). That sonnet is easier to recuperate as a romantic statement, however. For me, at least, Sonnet 124 is hard to read positively. While it certainly contains much praise of his love – although the initial ambiguity of 'my dear love' (1), with 'dear' conceivably meaning either or both treasured and expensive, is never resolved – the sonnet gives us the familiar Elizabethan rhetoric of the falseness of the court and the transitory nature of human relationships. In this sonnet, writing about love has become a way to write about politics.

In his adaptation, Mann focuses on the more troubling side of this sonnet, starting with a concentration on his contemporary political situation. His first quatrain gives us a picture of the difficulties of life in San Francisco, a city that could certainly be described as dear in both senses:

> So much has gone to shit. My hair. The state.
> The addicts lie on Ellis Street, unfathered.
> Reporters scribble synonyms for hate:
> the men in blue have billy-clubbed the gathered.
>
> (p. 197; lines 1–4)

Mann elaborates his opening sentence by listing things that have 'gone to shit'. Beginning with the personal – the speaker's hair – he proceeds to the large scale – the government – before supplying some specific details about what has gone wrong: drug addicts sleep in the street with no one to care for them, reporters promulgate bigotry through euphemisms, and state order is enforced through police brutality. This dystopian picture of urban life in the United States was familiar when the poem was first published and has depressingly become even better known in the decade since. Shakespeare begins Sonnet 124 by writing about love – although, as I have noted, in the subjunctive mood – before placing it against the backdrop of state corruption. In Mann's poem, this backdrop has apparently become the foreground and the focus for the poem, rather than merely its setting.

Love enters the poem in the second quatrain, but not, as one might have thought, as a relief from the

---

[10] See also Tamara Mahadin, 'Ocular Power and Female *Fascinum* in Shakespeare's *Venus and Adonis*', later in this volume.

problems of urban life: 'And then, as grisly as an accident, / Comes love, what feels like love' (ll. 5–6). In Sonnet 124, I think that our sense of the speaker's love is vitiated by his negative definitions and by his emphasis on the corrupt world that surrounds him. In Mann, the speaker himself vitiates his love: he cannot even say with confidence that he is in love. It seems that the grand romantic love that is the typical subject of sonnets is no longer attainable in the contemporary world, nor is whatever love the speaker has found a consolation:

> Befalls
> the best of us, as if the discontent of days
> were not enough.
>
> (lines 6–8)

The effect of these lines is to place love among the problems mentioned in the first quatrain. As I remarked, that quatrain moves from the personal – 'my hair' – to the general – 'the state' – and then to the public, which we should see as being situated somewhere between the first two. The second quatrain suggests that these are ultimately not different spheres and that private life is an inadequate refuge from public troubles. Mann has kept Shakespeare's rhymes, but he has greatly increased the unsettling implications of Shakespeare's presentation of his love.

Mann's second quatrain ends with the speaker telling us that 'I make the calls' (line 8), a statement of confidence that is immediately qualified:

> or so I think: Desire, that heretic,
> is stealing, spider-fingered, all the hours.
> The years.
>
> (lines 9–11)

Mann treats the ninth line of his sonnet as a volta in the Petrarchan manner and changes direction somewhat, revealing the extent to which the speaker is not in control. It is desire that controls him and that fills up his time. The speaker seems like Shakespeare or Petrarch, hemmed in by the ever-increasing number of poems his love – if in fact it is love – generates. In the context of this poem, the speaker resembles the addicts mentioned in the poem's second line: like them, he is in thrall to something that hurts him and, also like them, no one will come to help him. There is no real sense in Mann's poem that love has given him access to a private world that might provide some solace. Shakespeare proclaims that his love is separate from the state, but for Mann there is no such possibility.

The last three lines of Mann's poem reinforce our sense of love as part of everyday life rather than a utopian alternative to it by indicating that the love that burst in like an accident in the second quatrain is now completely domesticated:

> I peck him on the cheek, then hit the showers.
> – Soapy, erect, I'll conjure up a time
> When love was just a fecal, furtive time.
>
> (lines 12–14)

The implicit opposition in line 12 is between a love that is no longer passionate – the 'peck on the cheek' has replaced the ardent kisses that we associate with the beginnings of love – and a desire that seeks other objects, one not found within the home (since Mann writes of showers in the plural, we can assume he means the communal showers of a gym rather than the singular shower of a home). In the showers, he stands showing his hard penis and waiting for strangers. What Mann presents here is the familiar scenario of the power of queerness tamed by the respectability of much gay male life today and depressingly recuperated by the state. The word 'fecal' in the last line echoes the 'shit' in the first line, but while the word was meant metaphorically then, at the end of the poem it refers to the always potentially messy and dangerous pleasures of anal sex. There is perhaps some limited possibility of a transgressive sexuality, one that is not simply 'the child of state'.

I chose to end this article by discussing the two poems that reproduce the original end words of the sonnets as I think they most clearly demonstrate the tension between the sameness that comes from the retention of parts of the original poems and the difference that comes from poems written by 21st-century poets with their own ideas about what a poem should be. Both Hoover's and Mann's poems present, in every line and in their different ways, both the new and the old. As we read each line of their poems, we are faced again and again with the new words that they have written and with the old rhyme-words provided by Shakespeare. As menograms, all the poems I discuss here clearly do that to some extent, but while this tension between old and new is necessarily built into all the poems, the fact that Hoover and Mann present us with the rhyming words that structure Shakespeare's sonnets brings us back – literally and metaphorically – to the original sonnets. We can see their poems as demonstrating one important model for adaptation, which is always balanced between old and new, and also demonstrating how we should experience new versions of old works in whatever medium we may find them. The poems I discuss here – and, to one extent or another, all the poems in Cohen and Legault's collection – should remind us that an adaptation is always also a work about adaptation. The poems I've discussed all focus attention on the work of writing poetry.

SHAKESPEARE'S CANVAS

COLLEEN RUTH ROSENFELD

Piano keys, like human teeth, are buried in the gums. When ripped out, they have roots: slender rails of soft, blonde wood, often at a slight angle. I discovered early on that the flesh of a key received ink gladly, yielding under pressure. On a whim, I inscribed one key with a quotation, before carving the name of the author into the ivory with a screwdriver. I decided I would do this with all the keys. I developed a suite of formal constraints.[1]

I

Michel Foucault begins his description of Diego Velázquez's *Las Meninas* (1656) in *The Order of Things* (1966) with the painter 'standing a little back from his canvas'. We cannot know if the painter 'is considering whether to add some finishing touch' or if 'the first stroke has not yet been made' because we cannot see the surface of the canvas. 'The painter's gaze, addressed to the void confronting him outside the picture, accepts as many models as there are spectators', because the invisibility of his canvas extends pictorial space into a 'precise but neutral place' where 'the observer and the observed take part in a ceaseless exchange'; 'stubbornly invisible', the reversed canvas 'prevents the relation of these gazes from ever being discoverable' and 'the opaque fixity that it establishes on one side renders forever unstable the play of metamorphoses established in the centre'.[2] The reversal of Velázquez's canvas is a sustaining inaccessibility in *Las Meninas*. For Foucault, the act of interpretation does not aim to see the other side of the canvas by, for example, analysing the actual proportions of the depicted room.[3] Interpretation aims, instead, to describe the predication of the painting on the act of withholding of which the reversed canvas is both emblem and cause.

Velázquez's reversed canvas renders what is 'withdrawn' from the painting 'in an essential invisibility': the sovereign 'centre around which the entire representation is ordered'.[4] 'The tall, monotonous rectangle occupying the whole left portion of the real picture, and representing the back of the canvas within the picture, reconstitutes in the form of a surface', Foucault writes, 'the invisibility in depth of what the artist is observing.'[5] The inaccessibility of the canvas defines the vantage point of *Las Meninas* as 'a place' that 'from moment to moment, never ceases to change its content, its form, its face, its identity'.[6] In other words: the inaccessibility of the canvas permits this 'place' to be occupied by more than

---

[1] Andrea Long Chu, *Females* (London, 2019), p. 17. Reproduced with permission of Verso through PLSclear. Readers of the printed journal will find colour images in the electronic edition.
[2] Michel Foucault, *The Order of Things: An Archaeology of the Human Sciences* (New York, 1970), p. 3.
[3] See Jonathan Brown, *Images and Ideas in Seventeenth-Century Spanish Painting* (Princeton, 1979), pp. 89–90; Gary Shapiro, *Archaeologies of Vision* (Chicago, 2003), pp. 227–8. For a critique more generally of 'our interest in sleuthing the "ideal geometry"', see James Elkins, *The Poetics of Perspective* (Ithaca, 1996), pp. 219–27.
[4] Foucault, *Order of Things*, p. 14.
[5] Foucault, *Order of Things*, p. 4.
[6] Foucault, *Order of Things*, p. 5.

one person; at its most extreme, Foucault suggests that the inaccessibility of the canvas permits for the historical diversity of the sovereign subject.

What is the imperative of this 'ceaseless exchange', or 'play of metamorphoses', for the work of interpretation? How can criticism account for the work of art when the fact of withholding means that the work of art is never just one thing? In a 2009 special issue of *Representations*, Sharon Marcus and Stephen Best offer the term 'surface reading' to designate criticism that aims to 'attend to the surfaces of texts rather than plumb their depths', presenting a methodological and ethical counter to 'symptomatic reading' that seeks to name what is withheld and to render visible what is otherwise invisible.[7] Modelling a full submission to the work of art as it 'is', surface reading proceeds from Susan Sontag's call for a criticism of the art object that can 'show *how it is what it is*, even *that it is what it is*, rather than to show *what it means*' and its central discursive practice is description.[8] The 'play of metamorphoses' sustained by Velázquez's reversed canvas requires us, however, to consider the work of art within a modal ontology where *what it might be* vibrates alongside *what it is*. Which discursive practices are adequate to a criticism that seeks to value potentiality alongside actuality, to render depth, as Foucault wrote, in 'the form of a surface'?

II

In 1957, Pablo Picasso painted fifty-eight variations on Velázquez's *Las Meninas*.[9] In Variation 1, two shafts of light fall at irregular angles from windows that line the right side of the painting (Figure 3). One line of light twists in on itself in a strangled double helix; it rests on the head of a foregrounded figure like a party hat. Another line of light intersects with the centre of that same figure's back but illuminates the entirety of his torso and, impossibly, the dog that lies beneath his raised foot. Unlike the other figures in the painting, illuminated man and dog appear exclusively in outline as mere contours, barest abstraction of the representations to which they refer: in *Las Meninas*, the dwarf identified as Nicolas Pertusato rouses a sleeping dog with his foot.[10] Susan Grace Galassi has described Variation 1 as 'unfinished'.[11] The lines that shape dwarf and dog encircle what otherwise remains blank canvas.

Picasso's 'unfinished' figures and the lines of light with which they coincide reveal what we cannot see in *Las Meninas*: the reversed side of the canvas. In the lower, right-hand corner of his composition, Picasso flips Velázquez's canvas by displaying depth as a visible and blank surface. In Variation 1, dwarf and dog combine two features held in perpetual tension by the original: 'the invisible canvas' and 'the window' – as Foucault describes it, 'a pure aperture' that 'establish[es] a space as manifest as the other is hidden'.[12] Picasso's fusion of window to canvas suggests that when the hidden is made manifest, it reveals precisely nothing. Picasso shines a glaring light on what Velázquez's painting withholds. Insofar as they enclose visible, blank canvas, dwarf and dog

---

[7] Stephen Best and Sharon Marcus, 'Surface reading: an introduction', *Representations* 108 (2009), 1–21; pp. 1–2. For a survey of metaphors of surface and depth in literary criticism, see Rita Felski, *The Limits of Critique* (Chicago, 2015), pp. 52–89. For a recent critique of surface reading in the discipline, see Bruce Robbins, *Criticism and Politics* (Stanford, 2022), pp. 73–100, esp. pp. 81–4.

[8] Susan Sontag, *Against Interpretation* (New York, 1978), p. 14; quoted by Best and Marcus, 'Surface reading', p. 10. On Foucault's reading of 'the oscillating coincidence' of model, painter and spectator as 'strengthen[ing] Foucault's idea that there is an essential gap or absence in this painting, one that can be read symptomatically', see Shapiro, *Archaeologies of Vision*, p. 227. On descriptive techniques, see Heather Love, 'Close but not deep: literary ethics and the descriptive turn', *New Literary History* 41 (2010), 371–91.

[9] See Claustre Rafart i Planas, *Picasso's Las Meninas*, trans. Valerie Collins (Barcelona, 2001); Susan Grace Galassi, *Picasso's Variations on the Masters: Confrontations with the Past* (New York, 1996), pp. 148–84. The full suite of paintings is accessible at https://museupicassobcn.cat/en/whats-on/discover-online/chronology-las-meninas-picasso. For ease of reference, I number Picasso's variations in chronological order of composition.

[10] Subjects of *Las Meninas* were identified by Antonio Palomino in 1724 (discussed by Brown, *Images and Ideas*, p. 88).

[11] Galassi, *Picasso's Variations*, p. 154.

[12] Foucault, *Order of Things*, p. 6.

3 Pablo Picasso, *Las Meninas*. 17 August 1957. Oil on canvas, 194 × 260 cm. Museu Picasso, Barcelona. Photo: Fotogasull. © 2024 Estate of Pablo Picasso / Artists Rights Society (ARS), New York.

become quasi-allegorical embodiments of potentiality as such.

If dwarf and dog are 'unfinished', it is because they withdraw the completion of the masterpiece and endlessly defer perfection to a future moment that is, paradoxically, prior to the variations. The fifty-eight paintings that make up Picasso's *Las Meninas (after Velázquez)* articulate a metamorphic aesthetic that turns on formal variation. Picasso's variations model a critical practice that approaches form not in terms of the necessity of the work of art, where the perfection of a poem entails the idea that it could not have been otherwise, but the contingency of the work of art: the idea that the poem shelters its own variations as a dimension of its ontology.

III

In this article, I track the transformation of dwarf and dog across Picasso's series, and I suggest that these variations allow me to understand why critics have described Shakespeare's *Sonnets* as 'vague' and 'uncertain' and 'ambiguous'.[13] Practising what Valerie Rohy calls 'anamorphic' reading, I suggest that, from the perspective of Picasso's variations, the aesthetic feature of Shakespeare's *Sonnets* traditionally described as their 'vagueness' snaps into focus as a capacity for transformation.[14] I read

---

[13] On Shakespeare's 'vagueness', see, for example: John Crowe Ransom, 'Shakespeare at Sonnets', in *Discussions of Shakespeare's Sonnets*, ed. Barbara Hernstein (Boston, 1964), 87–105; p. 92; Yvor Winters, 'Poetic style in Shakespeare's Sonnets', in *Discussions*, ed. Hernstein, 106–15; p. 109, p. 111. See *Shakespeare's Sonnets*, ed. Stephen Booth (New Haven, 1977) for 'constructive vagueness' (e.g. p. 138, p. 419). On 'uncertainty', see Winters, 'Poetic style', p. 107. For 'ambiguity', see William Empson, *Seven Types of Ambiguity*, 2nd ed. (London, 1947), p. 3. See also Heather Dubrow's critique of assumptions about gendered address in sonnets that leave uncertain, or indeterminate, pronominal reference ('"Incertainties now crown themselves assur'd": the politics of plotting Shakespeare's Sonnets', reprinted in *Shakespeare's Sonnets*, ed. James Schiffer (New York, 2000), 113–33).

[14] Valerie Rohy, 'Ahistorical', *GLQ* 12 (2006), 61–83. Suggesting that 'perverse effects of the text appear when observed from the wrong time', Rohy argues that anamorphic reading can 'untether meaning from intent' in order to 'foreground instead the relational contingent' and 'to make visible a textual shading not available to the direct

Quarto and manuscript variations of Shakespeare's Sonnet 128 alongside formal translations and contemporary rewritings in order to value potentiality alongside actuality – what the poem may be alongside what the poem is. In conclusion, I propose variation as not only an object of study but a method of study and a vibrant form of creative-critical practice.

Shakespeare's Sonnet 128 participates in the genre of Ovidian love poems featuring a poet who desires to transform into an object in order to get closer to his mistress.[15] Like the poet of Sonnet 63 in Barnabe Barnes's *Parthenophil and Parthenophe* (1596) wishing to become his mistress's 'sweet wine' so that he might 'Runne through her vaynes',[16] the poet of Sonnet 128 desires the access transformation might afford:

> How oft, when thou my music music play'st
> Upon that blessèd wood whose motion sounds
> With thy sweet fingers when thou gently sway'st
> The wiry concord that mine ear confounds,
> Do I envý those jacks that nimble leap
> To kiss the tender inward of thy hand,
> Whilst my poor lips, which should that harvest reap,
> At the wood's boldness by thee blushing stand.
> To be so tickled they would change their state
> And situation with those dancing chips,
> O'er whom thy fingers walk with gentle gait,
> Making dead wood more blest than living lips.
>   Since saucy jacks so happy are in this,
>   Give them thy fingers, me thy lips to kiss.[17]

The poet's music is itself capable of making more music; the poet wishes to become the instrument that she plays. The aesthetic product seems beside the fact. Is a 'wiry concord' nice sounding? Does one take pleasure in music that the 'ear confounds'? Pleasure in Sonnet 128 resides not in the value of the aesthetic product but in the value of the aesthetic process, here described as 'so tickled'. But even as Sonnet 128 signals its participation in this Ovidian tradition, it holds the metamorphosis it proposes at a distance. It is the poet's 'poor lips' that desire to 'change their state / And situation with those dancing chips'. Unlike Parthenophil's 'Would I were chang'd', the speaker of Sonnet 128 relegates desire for transformation to a single part; the designation of the part as 'poor' suggests that pity might be one measure of the distance between the speaker and what of him desires.

The fantasy of transformation at play in Sonnet 128 deals in the relation of parts to wholes. The speaker's lips would undergo a metamorphosis in order that they might be 'so tickled'. Tickled how? 'So' loosely gestures to the preceding octave. What the poet wants is to be 'tickled' *in that way*. In this fantasy of transformation, the speaker would lose his lips. At the most literal level, to 'change their state / And situation' suggests that the poet's 'lips' would transform into the 'chips' that his mistress handles. The poet would now wear 'chips' on his face and his 'lips' would join a community of lovers. Shakespeare's Sonnets 60 and 64 draw on Pythagoras' speech from Book 15 of the *Metamorphoses* to generalize this redistribution of

---

gaze' (p. 74). Jennifer Nelson similarly writes in *Disharmony of the Spheres: The Europe of Holbein's 'Ambassadors'* that anamorphosis 'ironizes perspective': whereas 'perspective techniques' often suggest 'unified space that extends the real', anamorphosis uses those same techniques to suggest 'disjunctive space that interrupts the real', thereby encouraging our apprehension of 'transreality', or 'the acknowledgment of multiple possible worlds or worldviews' ((University Park, PA, 2019), p. 17). In separate studies of *Hamlet* and *King Lear*, Heather James and Nan Z. Da describe their transhistorical readings of Shakespeare as critical acts of historical anamorphosis. James describes 'a nontriumphal tradition associated with art, in which the most arresting literary and artistic allusions . . . create *anamorphoses of history*: they vigorously shift the reader's perspective on the features of a text that may be taken for granted, or even diminished as purely artistic flourishes, and thus not interpreted' ('The graveyard and the frontier: Hamlet among the buffaloes', *Representations* 159 (2022), 58–89; p. 82). Da argues that the accelerated causality characteristic of *Lear* becomes newly comprehensible within the context of Maoism in her unpublished manuscript 'The Chinese Tragedy of *King Lear*' (forthcoming, Princeton University Press).

[15] See *Shakespeare's Sonnets*, ed. Booth, p. 438. Gordon Braden discusses this subgenre in 'Ovid, Petrarch, and Shakespeare's Sonnets', in *Shakespeare's Ovid: The 'Metamorphoses' in the Plays and Poems*, ed. A. B. Taylor (Cambridge, 2000), 96–112; pp. 101–3.

[16] Barnabe Barnes, *Parthenophil and Parthenophe* (London, 1593), p. 43, lines 12–14.

[17] Quotations from the *Sonnets* are from *Shakespeare's Sonnets*, ed. Booth, unless otherwise stated.

matter as 'such interchange of state' (64).[18] The poet formerly known as 'Will' would become just another Jack. One Jack among many.

IV

Picasso's variations constitute what Jacques Rancière calls in *Aisthesis* (2013) a 'scene of thought': an 'optical machine that shows us thought busy weaving together perceptions, affects, names and ideas'.[19] Within such a scene, 'a mutilated statue' like the *Belvedere Torso* 'can become a perfect work' precisely because 'it is mutilated, forced, by its missing head and limbs, to proliferate into a multiplicity of unknown bodies'.[20] Such 'metamorphoses' are not, Rancière insists, 'individual fantasies' particular to a critic; they are instead determined by 'the logic of the regime of perception, affection and thought' that he calls '"the aesthetic regime of art"'.[21] Criticism, for Rancière, does not represent the art object *as it is*, but neither does criticism define the art object by *what it excludes*. Criticism, instead, participates in the art object by describing the 'multiplicity' of its being as a range of possibilities. The logic within which criticism takes place is itself an expression of the aesthetic.[22]

This is one way to understand the abiding power of Stephen Booth's 1977 edition of Shakespeare's *Sonnets* and his sense that, even as 'the language of the sonnets ordinarily limits its reader's mind to the terms of specific assertions', that language is 'at the same time suggesting room and direction for vast and multidirectional expansion'.[23] Booth documents the weird presence of 'unharnessed' potential across a range of lexical, logical, syntactical and contextual axes,[24] such as, for example, the 'syntactically causal potential' of a preposition; the 'fleeting potential' of a pronoun; a 'potential but unexploited pun'; a 'potentially complete assertion'; a 'potential oxymoron' that 'is not quite realizable'.[25] Booth describes 'momentary potential', 'unrealized and previously irrelevant potential', and 'inoperative potential'.[26] At the level of word, clause and line, as well as their coordination, Booth suggests that Shakespeare's sonnets retain, as a constitutive property of their being, the potential to be otherwise.

As a genre of criticism, 'commentary' allows Booth to describe Shakespeare's 'unharnessed' potential without treating poetry as evidence in the service of an argument; it allows him to value 'elements in poems that are demonstrably present but just as demonstrably doing nothing that can be harnessed in a critical exposition of what a poem says'.[27] 'Unharnessed' potential is Booth's name for

---

[18] On Sonnet 64 and Pythagoras' speech, see: Braden, 'Ovid, Petrarch', p. 98, pp. 107–8; on 60 and 64, see Raphael Lyne, 'Ovid, Golding and the "rough magic" of *The Tempest*', in *Shakespeare's Ovid*, ed. Taylor, 150–64; pp. 152–3; *Shakespeare's Sonnets*, ed. Booth, p. 245; Jonathan Bate, *Shakespeare and Ovid* (Oxford, 1993), pp. 90–4.

[19] Jacques Rancière, *Aisthesis*, trans. Zakir Paul (London, 2011), p. xi.

[20] Rancière, *Aisthesis*, pp. xi–xii, p. 20.

[21] Rancière, *Aisthesis*, p. xii. For the metamorphic aesthetic that underwrites Rancière's 'scenes of thought', see also p. xiv.

[22] The codetermination of 'two heterogeneous kinds of logic – the concept that art implements, and the beautiful without a concept' creates 'the power, which remains obscure to the artist, of doing something other than what he does, of producing something other than what he wants to produce, and thus giving the reader ... the opportunity to recognize and differently combine many surfaces in one, many languages in one sentence, and many bodies in a simple movement' (Rancière, *Aisthesis*, p. 11).

[23] *Shakespeare's Sonnets*, ed. Booth, p. 371.

[24] For example, *Shakespeare's Sonnets*, ed. Booth: 'unharnessed suggestions' (p. 188), 'logically unharnessed' (p. 209), 'logically unharnessed pertinence' (p. 301), 'syntactically unharnessed' (p. 324), 'vague, unharnessed, and substantively irrelevant overtones' (p. 363), 'syntactically unharnessed overtones' (p. 373), 'syntactically unharnessed literal meanings' (p. 435), 'logically and syntactically unharnessed by-reference' (p. 440) and 'complex reverberations of logically unharnessed senses' (p. 518).

[25] *Shakespeare's Sonnets*, ed. Booth, pp. 440, 137, 169, 186, 266.

[26] *Shakespeare's Sonnets*, ed. Booth, pp. 294, 329, 358.

[27] *Shakespeare's Sonnets*, ed. Booth, p. 370. Foucault described the parasitism of criticism as the paradox that literary commentary must 'say for the first time what had, nonetheless, already been said, and must tirelessly repeat what had, however, never been said' ('The order of discourse', trans. Ian Mcleod, in *Untying the Text: A Post-Structuralist Reader*, ed. Robert J. C. Young (Boston, 1981), 48–78; p. 58). See Robbins, *Criticism and Politics*, pp. 73–84.

what Shakespeare's *Sonnets* include but do not mean. When Sonnet 128, for example, places the mistress's hands 'Upon that blessèd wood', the clause 'carries accidental overtones of the crucifixion of Christ';[28] associative force pulls a religious allegory the sonnet does not tell into the orbit of the poem. Such 'accidental overtones' lend Shakespeare's sonnets an epistemological and ontological expansiveness.[29] Except, Booth explains, for Sonnet 112. Reading line after line, entertaining one emendation after another, Booth determines that Sonnet 112 is the single instance in which Shakespeare's 'unharnessed' potential runs away with the poem. He concludes that it must be 'unfinished'.[30]

V

Like outlines of dwarf and dog in Picasso's Variation 1, the two empty parentheses at the close of Sonnet 126 render potentiality by actualizing only blank space. Clearing out room for the couplet that might have concluded this otherwise twelve-line poem, the 1609 quarto typographically renders potentiality as such:

(   )
(   )[31]

Jessica Rosenberg argues that 'the dramatic emptiness of these typographical markers' participates in what Rayna Kalas describes as Shakespeare's '"non-proprietary" poetics', one that includes a 'formal detachability of couplets' emphasized by the blank space of indentation throughout the sequence. 'The movement across this white space', Rosenberg argues, 'performs the work of speculation': 'as a formal invitation to dispersal, the couplet opens to the reader and to its own future recirculation – leaving us, perhaps, to read the curved brackets as a pair of empty quotation marks from which a sentence has already been removed'.[32] If those brackets capture a poetry that was (but is not), it is equally possible that they capture a poetry that never was (but might have been). In so far as those brackets stretch the canvas of the page across two lines of equal length: a poetry that might yet be. Taking our cue from Kalas, we might describe the empty parentheses of 126 as oscillating between both a modern definition of 'frame' as 'the frame of a painting' and the older sense of 'the material realization of a thing *in potentia*'.[33]

The closing couplet of Sonnet 128 hinges on an explanation: 'Since saucy jacks so happy are in this' (line 13). 'Since' lacks the tight adversative turn of the ubiquitous 'But', or the syllogistic tension of the rare 'Therefore'; what little pressure 'Since' exerts loses steam as the line extends across a series of sibilant sounds, idling finally on the vague deixis of 'this'. The line break cuts the engine. The subsequent command is surprising: 'Give them thy fingers, me thy lips to kiss' (line 14). The Ovidian fantasy of transformation in 128 is a pretence. Rather than requiring an exchange of 'state / And situation' between those 'chips' and these 'lips', the addressee might simply gift the poet her lips. This fantasy would restore the speaker to himself, not as the desiring subject of Barnes's poem 'Would I were', but as the recipient of an action he commands: *Gimme*.[34]

According to this second fantasy, the mistress would lose her lips and the speaker would gain an extra set. The spectre of mutilation shadows the line as the poet has her giving her fingers

---

[28] *Shakespeare's Sonnets*, ed. Booth, p. 439.
[29] For example, *Shakespeare's Sonnets*, ed. Booth, p. 439. He explains elsewhere: 'incidental verbal patterning can enrich poems by making them feel as though they encompassed the broad range of attitudes and topics that any word, sentence, or paragraph is designed to exclude' (p. 372).
[30] *Shakespeare's Sonnets*, ed. Booth, p. 369.
[31] *Shake-speares Sonnets*, ed. Thomas Thorpe (London, 1609), sig. H3r.
[32] Jessica Rosenberg, *Botanical Poetics* (Philadelphia, 2022), esp. pp. 252–3. See also Rayna Kalas, *Frame, Glass, Verse: The Technology of Poetic Invention in Renaissance Verse* (Ithaca, 2007), pp. 166–98.
[33] Kalas, *Frame, Glass, Verse*, p. 166.
[34] On Shakespeare's imperatives, especially in the couplets, see John Roe, 'Unfulfilled imperatives in Shakespeare's *Sonnets*', in *The Sonnets: The State of Play*, ed. Hannah Crawforth, Elizabeth Scott-Baumann and Clare Whitehead (London, 2017), 77–94.

to one kind of lover and her lips to another. The strong syntactical parallel implies the repetition of what it elides, leaving unspecified the logical relation between the two parts. Is it permissive? *Give them your fingers so that I might have your lips.* Is it concessive? *They can have your fingers so long as I can have your lips.*

In the 1609 quarto, however, the poet gifts the Jacks only what is already theirs:

> Since sausie Iackes so happy are in this,
> Giue them their fingers, me thy lips to kisse.³⁵

It is probable that 'their' is the error of a compositor. By one account, the final line of the poem originally read 'your', was written over with 'thy', and subsequently misread as 'their'.³⁶ In other examples of this error in the Quarto, there is no possible referent for the third person pronoun in the poem.³⁷ In 128, by contrast, the 'sausie Iackes' are an obvious referent and compel us to imagine that an envious poet withdraws his gift at the moment in which he commands it bestowed. 'Giue them their fingers' is another way of saying, *Give them not even your fingers.* Such a command effectively severs the Jacks' fingers from their hands because the poet's mistress has the capacity to give them away.

VI

Is the fact that the 'unfinished' figure from Picasso's Variation 1 is a dwarf a permitting condition for Picasso's formal variations? Sara van den Berg has argued that the dwarf of Renaissance courts 'challenged humanist ideals of perspective, proportion, and stable form in art and politics'; as 'a surrogate for and critique of the subject, the self, and the artist as well as the ruler', the dwarf inhabited an aesthetic at once 'playful and contradictory, decorative and enigmatic, pure and transgressive, powerless and powerful'.³⁸ Like the artist, the dwarf enjoyed privileged access to the court where his value, Van den Berg writes, was that of the 'ornament'.³⁹ Picasso's iterative attention to this pair, dwarf and dog – always in proximity to one another, never identical – also suggests the status of the dwarf as 'pet' in the Renaissance court.⁴⁰

4 Pablo Picasso, *Las Meninas*. 4 September 1957. Oil on canvas, 35 × 27 cm. Museu Picasso, Barcelona. Photo: Fotogasull. © 2024 Estate of Pablo Picasso / Artists Rights Society (ARS), New York.

In Variation 13, the dwarf's foot rests on the haunches of a black dog with elongated body, as if pushing down on his perpetually perky tail (Figure 4). But in this variation, Picasso's composition cuts the dwarf off just above the bend in his knee. He is an autonomous, severed leg. The abbreviation of the figure's body presses the dwarf's presence to a point of contact. By reducing this figure to the bend of his knee, the angle of his leg,

---

³⁵ *Shake-speares Sonnets*, sig. H3v.
³⁶ See *Oxford Shakespeare: The Complete Sonnets and Poems*, ed. Colin Burrow (Oxford, 2002), p. 432.
³⁷ See Booth's discussion of 26.12 (*Shakespeare's Sonnets*, p. 176).
³⁸ Sara van den Berg, 'Dwarf aesthetics in Spenser's *Faerie Queene* and the early modern court', in *Recovering Disability in Early Modern England*, ed. Alison P. Hobgood and David Houston Wood (Columbus, 2013), 23–42; pp. 25, 23, 25.
³⁹ Van den Berg, 'Dwarf aesthetics', p. 26.
⁴⁰ Van den Berg, 'Dwarf aesthetics', pp. 28–30.

and the pressure of his foot, Picasso focuses our attention on the question of the relation of figure to dog. Picasso restores the full body of the dwarf in Variation 14 where his knee now bends at an impossible angle, as if he might unhook his own joint to double the frame of the painting in which he is represented.[41] With one leg roundly curved to set the foot on the back of the dog, the figure's inverted bend at the knee is a frame within the frame.

In writing this article, I find myself revising clauses in which I refer to 'his dog', withdrawing my assertion of a logic of possession. Possession is merely my interpretation of the figure's physical domination of the dog, which sometimes doubles as his footstool.[42] By resting my foot on the hind haunches of a dog, I activate that dog in his capacity to double as my footstool. Do I possess a dog or a footstool? In Variation 13, the figure's foot does not stand on the back of the dog. He is not asking the dog to bear his weight. His foot rests rather than stands but it remains tense, full of energy. It is not at rest.

VII

Contributing to the confusion of parts and wholes in Sonnet 128, subtending the question – made explicit by the compositor's error in the 1609 quarto – of whose fingers belong to whom, is the materialist problem described by Booth as 'the physics of keyboard instruments'.[43] In reality, the 'Jacks' never touch a player's hand. 'Jacks' in Sonnet 128 is a linguistic measure of the distance between the material instrument and the fictive conceit.[44] Thus, this seventeenth-century transcription renames 'Jacks' 'kies' or 'keyes':

how oft when thow, deere deerist musick plaiest,
vpon that blesed wood whose mocions sounds,
with thy sweet fingers when thow gently swaies,
the wiry concord that myne eare consoundes,
o how i enuy those kies that nimble leapes,
to kisse the tender inward of thy hand,
whilst my poore lippes wich should that haruest reped,
at the wood bouldnes by thee blushinge stand,
to bee so tuched the faine would change there state,
and situacion with those dancinge chippes,
ouer whome youre fingers walke with gentle gate,
makeing deed wood more blest than liuinge lipes,
Since then those keyes soe happy are in this,
giue them youre fingers mee youre lipes to kisse.[45]

'Jacks' must have felt like a catachresis in need of correction. But what the substitution of 'keyes' for 'Jacks' makes explicit is that the poet's fantasy of transformation relies on a metamorphic aesthetic that is not unique to his desire. The poet inhabits a world in which the instrument on which his mistress plays is already a community of lovers. Transformation would not require an act of innovation in that world. The fact that the part, the poet's 'lips', is at least two suggests that his desire operates within a metamorphic aesthetic in which transformation entails amplification. In desiring to transform into a 'Jack', the poet wants to make more of what already is.

The substitution of 'keyes' for 'Jacks' witnesses one reader's impatience with the poem's conspicuous misalignment of historical and fictional worlds. We can see another kind of impatience at work in the emendation of the first line, which transforms the admittedly awkward 'How oft, when thou my music music play'st' into 'how oft when thow,

---

[41] See Pablo Picasso, *Las Meninas*. 4 September 1957. Oil on canvas, 46 × 37.5 cm. Museu Picasso, Barcelona. MPB 70.446.
[42] On early modern footstools and human furniture, see Aaron Kunin, *Character as Form* (London, 2019), pp. 181–213.
[43] See Regula Hohl Trillini's important corrective to criticism of Shakespeare's 'mixed metaphor': 'Shakespeare explores the popular derogatory tropes associated with the mechanism of the virginals for a dense and purposeful enactment of fundamental ambiguities about female sexuality and music' ('The gaze of the listener: Shakespeare's Sonnet 128 and early modern discourses of music and gender', *Music & Letters* 89 (2008), 1–17; p. 17).
[44] *Shakespeare's Sonnets*, ed. Booth, p. 438.
[45] For the MS transcription, see *Shakespeare's Sonnets*, ed. Katherine Duncan-Jones (London, 1997), p. 466. For a reproduction, see Bruce R. Smith, 'Shakespeare's Sonnets and the history of sexuality: a reception history', in *A Companion to Shakespeare's Works*, vol. 4: *The Poems, Problem Comedies, Late Plays*, ed. Bruce R. Smith, Richard Dutton and Jean E. Howard (Oxford, 2003), 4–26; p. 8. See also R. H. A. Robbins, 'A seventeenth-century manuscript of Shakespeare's Sonnet 128', *Notes & Queries* 14 (1967), 137–8.

deere deerist musick plaiest'. The seventeenth-century transcription substitutes the more familiar term of endearment and varies repetition with the superlative, thereby straightening out the syntax. The addressee shares her own dearness with the music she plays; perhaps she even lends some of her own dearness to the music in order to render it the superlative instance. But she is not herself music. The poet neither makes nor possesses her.

VIII

Robert Tofte's Ovidian poem begins and ends with the poet's desire to become Proteus:

> Oh that I were sly *Proteus*, for to take
> On mee that forme, which most I like or wish;
> Then would I change my selfe into the shape
> Of that thy little whelpe, thy ioy and blisse,
> Into that little worme thou so doost like,
> And dallying plaist with him both day and night.
> Those sauerie smacks, those busses, sweet which be,
> Which thou to him doost giue, should all be mine;
> And I would make my hart to leap for glee,
> Whilst I did licke that bosome faire of thine:
> But since I to despaire of this am brought,
> My wish shall *Proteus* be, thy Dog my thought.[46]

As with Barnes's sonnet, the poet desires access to his mistress. And, as in Barnes's sonnet, the fantasy of access seems like a pretence for the desire to transform into now this, now that, and still this other creature. When the poet moves from 'thy little whelpe' to 'that little worme', he begins to generate a list. 'Worme' disparages the dog, but it also allows the poet to imagine becoming an altogether different creature.

Tofte's poet does not desire to assume an alternate form. He desires ceaseless alternation. By transforming into Proteus, the speaker might retain the capacity to 'take / On mee that forme, which most I like or wish'; brought 'to despaire' without explanation, the poem concludes by distinguishing potentiality from particularity. The particularity of 'thy Dog', a single form, belongs to 'thought'. The 'wish', by contrast, is for the capacity to assume whatever 'shape'. 'Oh that I were sly Proteus' produces a tautology. 'My wish shall Proteus be' is like wishing for more wishes. For Picasso, the desire for continuous metamorphosis is a matter of aesthetic practice. Speaking of *Tête de Taureau* (*Bull's Head*, 1943) in an interview with André Warnod, he imagines a possible future for his piece:

> You remember that bull's head I exhibited recently? Out of the handle bars and the bicycle seat I made a bull's head which everybody recognized as a bull's head. Thus a metamorphosis was completed; and now I would like to see another metamorphosis take place in the opposite direction. Suppose my bull's head is thrown on the scrap heap. Perhaps some day a fellow will come along and say: 'Why there's something that would come in very handy for the handlebars of my bicycle...' And so a double metamorphosis would have been achieved.[47]

Picasso's imagined future returns the displayed piece to an earlier function. Metamorphosis might look like rewinding the tape. But Picasso's supposition also amplifies the act of metamorphosis from one to two. In order for the bull's head to undergo 'a double metamorphosis', the work of art must experience a shift in context, a move from exhibition space to 'scrap heap'. The 'scrap heap' is a scene of potentiality in which the transformation of head into handle is merely one possibility among many.

IX

In 1931, Picasso provided thirty illustrations for *Les Métamorphoses de Ovide* (ed. Skira).[48] In *Myth and Metamorphosis* (2000), Lisa Florman argues that Rubens's oil sketches and paintings illustrating Ovid's poem served as Picasso's primary interlocutor. In *The Fall of Phaethon*, for example, Picasso takes Rubens's diagonal composition and 'condensed the already compact, chaotic arrangement into an utter tangle of limbs'.[49] The lines of

---

[46] Robert Tofte, *Laura The Toyes of a Traueller* (London, 1597), sig. C7r.
[47] Translated by Alfred H. Barr Jr in *Picasso: Fifty Years of His Art* (New York, 1946), p. 241.
[48] Ovid, *Les Métamorphoses*, ed. Albert Skira (Lausanne, 1931).
[49] Lisa Florman, *Myth and Metamorphosis: Picasso's Classical Prints of the 1930s* (Cambridge, 2000), pp. 49–52.

Phaethon's body become indistinguishable from the mess of horse below him; it is not always clear whether you are looking at the heel of Phaethon's foot or the bent knee of a horse's leg.

Reduced to a series of entangled contours, Picasso's compositions attribute a versatile value to the line and draw a relation among abstraction, violence and metamorphosis. Picasso revisits this idea in an early sketch for *Guernica* (1937) where a problem of perspectival depth momentarily fuses the body of a grieving mother to the hind quarters of a brutalized horse. As T. J. Clark describes the sketch, '[l]ogically, she is back in an undefined middle ground, on the far side of the horse's splayed hindquarters; but visually, one part of us registers the horse's haunches as belonging to *her*.'[50] Booth describes the syntactical equivalent in Shakespeare's Sonnet 50, 'His rider loved not speed, being made from thee. / The bloody spur cannot provoke him on' (8–9): 'common sense says that *him* refers to the horse, but the grammatical antecedent is *His rider*'.[51] Rider and horse momentarily fuse by way of vague reference. A single line doubles for the body of man and horse.[52]

The oscillation of the viewer's eye across multiple possible forms is one example of what Florman describes as the viewer's complicity in Picasso's Ovidian illustrations. Picasso's representation of Orpheus, for example, is a 'spatial amphiboly': '[a]lternating between frontal and dorsal readings, we seem to be in collusion with Orpheus's attackers, effectively wringing him out like a rag with each visual reorientation.'[53] Picasso's illustrations interpellate the viewer into the scene as well as the aesthetic of transformation prepared for by dismemberment, rape, the carnage of the crushing heap.[54] In the fantasy of Shakespeare's closing, 'Give them thy fingers, me thy lips to kiss', the capacious imperative extends to the reader: *you have fingers; you have lips; give them to me.*

'In effect', Florman concludes, 'the *Metamorphoses* illustrations take *possession* of their audience (every bit as much as vice versa), compelling involvement – that is, compelling the viewer, for a change, to enter the picture.'[55] What does 'for a change' mean here? That in the traditional configuration, the picture enters the viewer but, in this instance, Picasso's composition requires the viewer to enter the picture? Or that, 'for a change', in search of a change (any change), the viewer might enter the picture? Or 'for a change' as in a transaction: for the small price of 'a change', just change, a little transformation, the viewer may be permitted to enter the picture? Catherine M. Soussloff has written that '[f]or Foucault, paintings and their history demonstrated how an observing subject could be transformed through art and what such a transformation might offer for a politics of the present.'[56] Foucault understood, finally, criticism in terms of 'the arts of existence' with which a person might 'seek to transform themselves, to change themselves in their singular being, and to make their life into an oeuvre that carries certain aesthetic values and meets certain stylistic criteria'.[57] *For mere change.*

X

Suppose you were to rewrite Shakespeare's Sonnet 128 as a Petrarchan sonnet. Just to see what it might look like. Among the formal alterations required – open to closed quatrains, interlaced sestet, the consolidated closure of the final imperative attendant on the dissolution of the couplet, etc. – you might

---

[50] T. J. Clark, *Picasso and Truth* (Princeton, 2013), p. 258.
[51] *Shakespeare's Sonnets*, ed. Booth, p. 217.
[52] See also Kalas's 'anamorphic' reading of Sonnet 24, line 4 in *Frame, Glass, Verse*, p. 181.
[53] Florman, *Myth and Metamorphosis*, pp. 33–4. This is nowhere more explicit than in his sequence depicting Tereus' rape of Philomela, climaxing with 'contours in the final etching ... broken or plural, as if intermittently registering a transient form'. Comparing Picasso's lines to 'futurist "force-lines"', Florman argues that our attempts to look animate the violence they depict (p. 28).
[54] See Colin Burrow, 'Original fictions: metamorphoses in *The Faerie Queene*', in *Ovid Renewed: Ovidian Influences on Literature and Art from the Middle Ages to the Twentieth Century* (Cambridge, 1988), 99–119.
[55] Florman, *Myth and Metamorphosis*, p. 42.
[56] Catherine M. Soussloff, *Foucault on Painting* (Minneapolis, 2017), p. 4.
[57] Foucault, *The Use of Pleasure*, in *The History of Sexuality*, trans. Robert Hurley, vol. 2 (New York, 1985), 10–11. Quoted in Soussloff, *Foucault on Painting*, p. 19.

tighten the volta at line 9.⁵⁸ In Sonnet 128, the volta turns on a sound: the 'wood whose motion sounds / With thy sweet fingers', the 'wood' that the poet envies for its 'boldness', the very material into which the poet's 'lips' wish to transform, also names the desire for transformation, what the poet 'would'. 'To be so tickled', the poet's lips 'would change their state' into wood. But they do not.

Our seventeenth-century reader amplified the fictiveness of 'would' with the lexical addition of desire: 'to bee so tuched the faine would change there state'. Call 'tickled' 'tuched', and rename the aesthetic process described in the octave. Call 'tickled' 'tuched', and clear out the metrical space to explicate a desire implicit to 'would' with 'faine'. This reader emphasizes that 'would' is an expression of desire; the word with which they do so pulls the homonym, 'feign', into the linguistic orbit of the poem. 'Faine/feign' renders the fantasy itself an object of desire even as it also names the act of fiction-making. Maybe the poet's lips do not actually want transformation. Maybe they are just pretending.

Is that why what the poet 'would' never takes place? The volta picks up the material cause of the musical instrument and casts it into the realm of potentiality. Following Joel Fineman's central insight in *Shakespeare's Perjured Eye* (1986), we might pair 128 with a sonnet from the first subsequence to consider how repetition performs 'a deliberately parodic quotation' or an 'inverted imitation' to produce 'a kind of mimic version'.⁵⁹ In Sonnet 29, the poet measures his envious desire by similitude rather than transformation, 'Wishing me like to one more rich in hope, / Featured like him, like him with friends possessed' (lines 5–6), until the poet puts a halt to accumulation with 'Yet' (line 9). What prohibits the poet from 'myself almost despising' is that 'Haply I think on thee' (lines 9–10). 'Haply' means: *I think on thee, but I might not have. I think on thee, but I might have thought on someone else*. Like the 'How oft' that opens 128, 'When in disgrace' is a pattern into which the poet falls. Each time, he thinks on 'thee', and each time, he might not have. By landing on 'thee', a particular object of thought puts a stop to the poet's intrusive spiral; his 'state' instead

'sings hymns at heaven's gate'. Because of this singing, the poet possesses a certain kind of wealth: 'such wealth'. The characteristic quality of this wealth brings about the conditions under which 'I scorn to change my state with kings.' What kind of wealth? 'Such wealth': vague in that we do not know the kind to which 'such' refers but precise in that it is this wealth and not that wealth (or some other kind of wealth) that prohibits the poet's desire for change.

Is Sonnet 128 what happens when the poet's thought lands on someone other than 'thee'? The problem with envy in 128 is that it makes parts of the poet wish that he were something other than what he is. But is the 'scorn' of 29 still there, prohibiting the lips of the poet from changing into what they 'would/wood'? The closing command of Sonnet 128 sets transformation to the side. *Let's not disappoint the Jacks. There is more than enough of you to go around.* The poet trades in the fantasy of transformation for the fantasy of possession: *I can have your lips and my lips as lips.*

XI

Suppose you were to rewrite Shakespeare's Sonnet 128 in the form of a Spenserian sonnet. Suppose you treated its interlocking quatrains as a form of research. Your opening quatrain would require no change. But to easily carry Shakespeare's rhyme into the second quatrain, you might find yourself confronting the problem of the one and the many:

How oft, when thou my music music play'st
Upon that blessèd wood whose motion sounds

---

⁵⁸ Writing of *Venus and Adonis* and *Lucrece*, Elizabeth Scott-Baumann and Ben Burton argue that, 'If we wish to understand poetic form historically, we must trace the multiple genealogies behind a stanza, revealing the other legacies that lie behind its most famous usage. In order to fully appreciate Shakespeare's manipulation of his stanzas, we need to let go of the idea that they are Shakespearean stanzas at all' ('Shakespearean stanzas? *Venus and Adonis, Lucrece*, and complaint', *ELH* 88 (2021), 1–26; p. 21).

⁵⁹ Joel Fineman, *Shakespeare's Perjured Eye* (Berkeley, 1986), pp. 66–7.

With thy sweet fingers when thou gently sway'st
The wiry concord that mine ear confounds,
Do I envý that Jack that nimbly rounds
To kiss the tender inward of thy hands,
Whilst my poor lip, which ere that harvest bounds,
At the wood's boldness by thee blushing stands.

Formal translation explicates a problem already implicit to Shakespeare's Sonnet 128. Does the poet have one rival or many? There is one instrument, but it is composed of many parts. The poet has several particular rivals, but those rivals share a common name and are of one kind. Is he also her type? Or is the problem that he is not her type? The addressee is willing to entertain several instances of a kind. The singular 'wood whose motion sounds' is both a whole and a metonymy from the part: the 'wood' that is an erection. The part as activated by desire: 'the wood's boldness'. The poet's refusal to transform into 'wood' is also his refusal to undergo the metonymic translation required to join this sexual community.

Perhaps the poet turns away from the fantasy of transformation in Sonnet 128 because he is disinclined to accept all variations on his name. Sonnet 128 might plausibly be included among the 'Will' sonnets and their notorious alignment of the many meanings of 'will' with an equal number of lovers. As Melissa Sanchez writes, 'the argument of both 135 and 136 can be summed up, more or less, as: "C'mon, you'll hardly know I'm here."'[60] Or, 128 might plausibly *almost* be included. The possible variation on Shakespeare's name, the move from the future indicative 'Will' to the modal auxiliary 'Would', is a potential that Sonnet 128 leaves 'unharnessed' at the volta, even as the form of the sonnet, like the 'so' with which it syntactically sums up the octave, relies on the existence of this potential.

The closing command of a Spenserian Sonnet 128 that writes of a single 'Jack' would have to read 'him': 'Give him thy fingers.' There is something true to the poem about an allegorical consolidation of the 'dancing chips' into a single Jack who oscillates between positions of rival and kind. But, as we saw, allegorical excess has always been a problem in Sonnet 128 with 'the blessèd wood'. Clauses that 'carr[y] accidental overtones' suggest that the poem may be an instrument capable of playing music other than the tune for which it was originally designed.[61]

XII

Pertusato is one of two dwarfs depicted in Velázquez's *Las Meninas*. The other, Maribárbola, stands at the threshold between the cluster of characters at the centre of the composition and foregrounded figures of dwarf and dog. Sometimes, Picasso removes the female dwarf entirely from the composition, as in Variation 28 where she is replaced by the twisted shape of negative space (Figure 5). In this variation, dwarf and dog are exclusive occupants of a diagonal strip in a composition that trades in the depth of *Las Meninas* for the layered feel more familiar from collage. The focused contact between foot and dog from Variation 13 is here inverted: a thick and twisting black shape marks out the space between the two figures. The black shape resembles a shadow, but it is not cast; it separates dwarf and dog from the Infanta

5 Pablo Picasso, *Las Meninas*. 15 September 1957. Oil and charcoal on canvas, 129 × 161 cm. Museu Picasso, Barcelona. Photo: Fotogasull. © 2024 Estate of Pablo Picasso / Artists Rights Society (ARS), New York.

---

[60] Melissa E. Sanchez, 'The poetics of feminine subjectivity in Shakespeare's Sonnets and "A Lover's Complaint"', in *The Oxford Handbook of Shakespeare's Poetry*, ed. Jonathan Post (Oxford, 2013), 505–21; p. 518. See also Eve Kosofsky Sedgwick, *Between Men* (New York, 1985), p. 37.
[61] *Shakespeare's Sonnets*, ed. Booth, p. 439.

and her attendants, as well as from one another, curving with the gentle bend of a knee. In Variation 28, the male dwarf's hands reach out as if to touch the shadow.

In Variation 40, Picasso places a piano beneath the dwarf's hands (Figure 6). His raised fingers appear to bang away at the keys and his leg lifts, hovering just above the prone body of the dog, moving in the direction of the piano's pedals. Picasso retains the dwarf's gestures in *Las Meninas*: the raised foot and the distribution of space between two active hands, wrists bent. The insertion of a piano that is decidedly not in *Las Meninas* reveals something nonetheless about the posture of this figure. He looks exactly as though he could be playing a piano. (Don't you think? Can't you see it, now? Will you ever be able to look at *Las Meninas* and not see it? Has Picasso's variation ruined *Las Meninas* for you?)

At the opening of *Monstrous Kinds* (2019), Elizabeth Bearden tells the story of her first encounter with *Las Meninas* when her mother 'had determined, in light of my degenerating vision, that she would take me to Europe to go look at art and architecture'.[62] 'All the times I heard descriptions of this painting in the Prado', she continues, 'there was something important missing: the two dwarfs on the right.'[63] Bearden asks:

How should we interpret these figures who are visually contrapuntal to the artist? As illustrations of the oscillation of illusion and disillusion of which the Spanish baroque was so fond? The power of art to render perspective juxtaposed with nature's own variations of scale? ... Can we theorize their representation, and does this theorization give us new insights into what is one of the greatest works of Western art?[64]

Picasso's variations provide a set of answers to Bearden's questions. In Variation 40, the piano occupies the space cleared out by removing Maribarbola in Variation 28. The piano is the actualization of a potential immanent to the negative space of her absence. In Variation 41 (Figure 7), Picasso paints a portrait of Pertusato, reduced in profile to sharp angles and with the keys of a piano lining his elongated neck. Picasso isolates a part of the instrument that is composed of many parts and renders it a part of his body.

Each variation, a twist of the kaleidoscope: a rearrangement of parts into a new whole; sometimes, parts removed to make room for new parts appended.

XIII

In his variation, Gregory Betts begins by discovering 'Shakespeare's Alphabet' from within Sonnet 128, as if reducing that poem to a set of components at the level of the letter (Figure 8).[65]

6 Pablo Picasso, *The Piano*. 17 October 1957. Oil on canvas, 129.5 × 96.5 cm. Museu Picasso, Barcelona. Photo: Fotogasull. © 2024 Estate of Pablo Picasso / Artists Rights Society (ARS), New York.

[62] Elizabeth Bearden, *Monstrous Kinds: Body, Space, and Narrative in Renaissance Representations of Disability* (Ann Arbor, 2019), p. 1.
[63] Bearden, *Monstrous Kinds*, pp. 2–3.
[64] Bearden, *Monstrous Kinds*, pp. 3–4.
[65] Gregory Betts, 'Shakespeare's alphabet', in *The Sonnets: Translating and Rewriting Shakespeare*, ed. Sharmila Cohen and Paul Legault (Brooklyn, 2012), p. 201. In my turn to

7 Pablo Picasso. *Las Meninas [Nicolasito Pertusato]*. 24 October 1957. Oil on canvas, 61 × 50 cm. Museu Picasso, Barcelona. Photo: Fotogasull. © 2024 Estate of Pablo Picasso / Artists Rights Society (ARS), New York.

Shakespeare's Alphabet

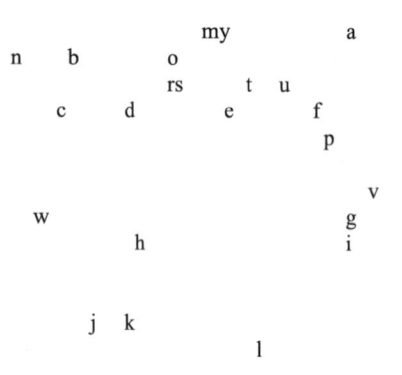

```
                        my          a
        n     b     o
                       rs      t    u
              c     d      e        f
                                    p
                                              v
              w
                         h                g
                                          i


                      j   k
                              l
```

8 Gregory Betts, 'Shakespeare's Alphabet'. By permission of the author.

Replacing everything but these letters with the blank page, 'Shakespeare's Alphabet' resembles a linguistic 'scrap heap'. Then, a 'double metamorphosis' takes place.[66] Betts entitles it 'Fold In, Freely':

> Howl on my muse, play it
> up in sound
> while I sweet and gently sway
> to the work my mind unfounds.

Do I silence a mental leap
to kiss wordy hands?
Will stunned lips arrest a rape
and at the boldness shining stand?

To be the air, its state
in situ with singing hips singing
of fingers walking gentle
as kings adorned upon living alps.

Sin is a happy art in this.
I've found and met lips to kiss.[67]

Out of Shakespeare's Sonnet 128, Betts makes another poem. He finds, for example, in the closing command to 'Give', the first-person pronoun and contracted possessive 'I've'; his variation fulfils the couplet's command by wresting future action into the past. Betts hears, in the entitlement of the obligatory 'should that harvest reap', the threat of rape; or in 'Making', the 'kings' with whom the poet 'scorn[s] to change [his] state' in Sonnet 29.

Suppose we treat this variation as a metamorphosis from the 'scrap heap' of alphabetic reduction? Suppose we read this variation as the actualization of a potential immanent to 128 and akin to Picasso's representation of the distributed energy of Pertusato's body across a piano. As a 'scene of thought', Betts's poem does not make an argument about Shakespeare's sonnet. Insofar as it treats 128 as the material out of which it builds another poem, it proceeds from the admission, as Booth describes it, 'that everything in a sonnet is there'.[68] But instead of 'harnessing' the homonyms it hears into evidence and

---

contemporary verse to think about Sonnet 128, I am indebted to Hannah Crawforth's challenge to the 'strongly periodized lines' of 'our professional infrastructures and pedagogical obligations' in 'Queer echoes: reading "The Faerie Queene" with Evie Shockley', *Spenser Review* 51 (2021): www.english.cam.ac.uk/spenseronline/review/volume-51/512/queer-echoes-reading-the-faerie-queene-with-evie-shockley-1.

[66] See Barr, *Picasso: Fifty Years of His Art*, p. 241.
[67] Gregory Betts, 'Fold In Freely', in *The Sonnets*, ed. Cohen and Legault, p. 202.
[68] *Shakespeare's Sonnets*, ed. Booth, p. xiv. See Kim F. Hall's important critique of Booth's 'strangely recalcitrant' refusal to read 'black' as 'black' in *Things of Darkness: Economies of Race and Gender in Early Modern England* (Ithaca, 1995), p. 69.

argumentation, it treats them as the elements of a composition that vibrates alongside 128, the actualization of a potential sheltered within its words.[69] When Betts transforms 'reap' into 'rape', he renders what Sonnet 128 does not say but nonetheless includes by transposing the poem's letters across a surface.

The first quatrain of Shakespeare's Sonnet 128 laboriously extends its opening clause beyond the first line where it is, as Booth writes, 'potentially complete' and 'syntactically ready for *Do I envý*'; the opening clause is 'again potentially complete' at the end of the second line,[70] but continues again, now with a prepositional phrase, now with a direct object, again delaying the introduction of the sentence's main verb until, finally, the second quatrain delivers with, 'Do I envý those jacks that nimble leap'. It is difficult not to hear a question in the inverted syntax of 'Do I envý'. The question is a form that Shakespeare's line holds in potential but does not actualize. Betts's poem offers a 'scene of thought' that actualizes this potential. His question describes the difficulties of an art object that 'my mind unfounds': 'Do I silence a mental leap / to kiss wordy hands?'[71] Do I?

XIV

The blank surface of Betts's 'Shakespeare's Alphabet' is a charged field, as if the poem from which this alphabet derives continues to exert a conceptual force, especially apparent in the proximity of 'm' and 'y'; 'my', held tight by its aural resonance with 'I'.[72] As Best and Marcus maintain, a strong tradition of *Sonnets* criticism, including that by Fineman, Aaron Kunin and Kalas, turns on the idea that 'depth is continuous with surface and is thus an effect of immanence'.[73] If criticism is an expression of the aesthetic object it seeks to describe, then variation is one practice by which the critic can actualize a potential immanent to the art object. Such an approach attributes a modal ontology to the poem, one that values what Booth described as the 'unharnessed' potential of Shakespeare's sonnets.

Variation values potential by raising it to the level of actuality. If description seeks to render the art object as it 'is', a means of affirming that '*it is what it is*', variation seeks to render the art object as it 'may be', in the process affirming that it might yet be something else.[74] Bruce Robbins's critique of surface reading might equally apply to the practice of variation in criticism: it 'will ... seem less valuable, and perhaps not valuable at all'.[75] Why practise a criticism that turns on making a lesser poem? ('I can appreciate', my friend said as she joined me in the Picasso Museum in Barcelona, 'the obsession.') What is the value of a criticism that prioritizes process over product? What are the criteria by which we might evaluate such criticism?

In *Life Destroying Diagrams* (2022), Eugenie Brinkema argues that a 'radical formalism' proceeds by taking 'contingent formal givenness' as our object of study: we are therefore only ever reading 'a particular variation set against the general potential for any other formal variation against which every form and every distortion of form is *possible*'.[76] 'Radical formalism' is not 'strategic', nor is it an example of

---

[69] Describing Jen Bervin's *Nets*, Toby Altman argues that 'Bervin marshals her poetics of queer fragmentation, nonprocreative pleasure, and textual error from within the resources that the *Sonnets* themselves – in all their multiplicity – offer', such that Bervin's Sonnet 19, for example, 'is not so much a critique of Shakespeare's as a consummation of the implicit direction of his poetics' ('"What beauty was": Jen Bervin's untimely sonnets', *ELH* 89 (2022), 489–522; p. 501, p. 503).
[70] *Shakespeare's Sonnets*, ed. Booth, p. 439.
[71] Betts, 'Shakespeare's alphabet'.
[72] Altman argues that 'erasure' is the wrong term for Bervin's *Nets*, reading the co-presence of black letters, grey letters and white page as 'compressing multiple kinds of time into the surface of its pages' (Altman, 'Jen Bervin's untimely sonnets', p. 516).
[73] Best and Marcus, 'Surface reading', p. 11. Kalas argues that Sonnet 24 'consolidates these surfaces of steely resemblance and reflective transparency and challenges its readers to consider the instrumentality of the surface' (*Frame, Glass, Verse*, p. 185).
[74] Sontag, *Against Interpretation*, p. 14.
[75] Robbins, *Criticism and Politics*, p. 82.
[76] Eugenie Brinkema, *Life Destroying Diagrams* (Durham, 2022), p. 272. 'For radical formalism – not a formalism in thrall to radical politics but radical as in *radix*, to return to the speculative *ground* or *roots* of what thinking can claim – involves reading without guarantee' (pp. 20–1).

'affirmative instrumentality' as Caroline Levine has described it, though 'radical formalism' shares with Levine's account of 'formal affordances' an attention to the agility and versatility of forms, the capacity for latent possibilities to be activated in new contexts like that of the 'scrap heap'.[77] By 'thinking *from* form', however, Brinkema suggests that it becomes possible to think what has not yet been thought, except insofar as that thinking exists in the radical contingency of the art object itself.[78] The practice of 'radical formalism' suggests that a criticism attentive to the 'unharnessed' potential of Shakespeare's *Sonnets* might take the form of the 'riff': '[t]o say that someone is *riffing* in writing or speech', Emily Ogden writes, 'is to say that they are constructing their utterance by starting with a single idea and putting it through a series of changes.'[79] Those changes do not resemble progression because they require return. But they may, as with Shakespeare's belaboured syntax, allow an assertion to transform into a question.

---

[77] For 'affirmative instrumentality', see Caroline Levine, 'The long lure of anti-instrumentality: politics, aesthetics, and sustainability', *Modern Fiction Studies* 27 (2021), 225–46; p. 235. For the 'affordances' of form, see *Forms* (Princeton, 2015) esp. pp. 1-23.

[78] Brinkema, *Life Destroying Diagrams*, p. 259.

[79] Emily Ogden, *On Not Knowing* (Chicago, 2022), p. 50. Mark Doty's account of description, of the writer's attempt to translate what he sees into what he says, sounds also like a kind of riffing, though his word for it, in a linguistic mash-up of Hart Crane and Shakespeare is 'transmemberment'. Bypassing the adequacy of word to the world, 'transmemberment' produces 'a kind of fusion between the word and the world, one becoming', he concludes, 'a part of the other' (*The Art of Description* (Minneapolis, 2009), p. 10).

'PERSUASION BY SIMILITUDE': FINDING LIKENESS IN SHAKESPEARE'S *A LOVER'S COMPLAINT*

KATHARINE A. CRAIK

A Lover's Complaint opens in the aftermath of an unnamed young woman's calamitous entanglement with an unscrupulous young man. Much of the poem deals with the abusive use of language which plays an important role in the young man's adeptness, amongst women, to 'Consents bewitch' (131). At the poem's key moment, the loss of the young woman's chastity is registered through an elaborate image involving her transformation from stone to water. The beautiful young man is already weeping, and the young woman eventually melts sympathetically into tears:

> But with the inundation of the eyes
> What rocky heart to water will not wear?
>
> (290–1)

The image of a marble- or flinty-hearted woman is familiar from Petrarchan poetry but here Shakespeare blends the vocabulary of courtly love with the language of spiritual devotion. The young woman envisages her earlier resistance before the young man's 'altar' (224) as a kind of irreligiosity which now gives way to soft-hearted grace.[1] Her question in the passage above however suggests uncertainty and, a few lines later, the significance – and peril – of this liquid softening becomes clear. She takes on the likeness of the tearful young man in order that she may (as she believes) 'Appear to him as he to me appears, / All melting' (299–300). Both are weeping now, and both seem unguarded. This article explores problems of desire and consent in *A Lover's Complaint* by considering the unpredictable processes of likening which are revealed through stones, water and other elemental things. According to a popular Renaissance proverb, *similis simili gaudet* ('like takes pleasure in like').[2] In this unusual and disturbing poem, however, Shakespeare's theories of resemblance reveal erotic force, uncertainty and dissonance.

Early modern poets used a variety of literary techniques to sketch out resemblance. George Puttenham offers a detailed account of the 'figure of similitude' in chapter 19 of book 3 ('Of Ornament') in *The Art of English Poesy* (1589). Puttenham begins with general examples comparing one person or thing to another, arguing that the ability to identify and express likeness is an essential feature of good writing: 'the Figure of Similitude is very necessary, by which we not only beautify our tale but also very much enforce and enlarge it. I say enforce because no one thing more prevaileth with all ordinary judgments than persuasion by similitude.'[3] Puttenham's theory is capacious enough to include a range of comparative techniques, including but not limited to what are now

---

[1] These lines recall Ezekiel 36.26: 'I will take away the stony heart out of your flesh, and I will give you an heart of flesh.' See Tiffany Jo Werth, 'A heart of stone: the ungodly in early modern England', in *The Indistinct Human in Renaissance Literature*, ed. Jean E. Feerick and Vin Nardizzi (New York, 2012), 181–203; p. 181.

[2] See Colleen Ruth Rosenfeld's discussion of simile in *Indecorous Thinking: Figures of Speech in Early Modern Poetics* (New York, 2018), p. 104. This article is deeply indebted to Rosenfeld's work in this area.

[3] *The Art of English Poesy by George Puttenham: A Critical Edition*, ed. Frank Whigham and Wayne A. Rebhorn (Ithaca and London, 2007), p. 326.

called 'simile' and 'metaphor'. Noting that the expression of resemblance makes writing more pleasing, he introduces a distinctive vocabulary of 'enforcing' to suggest that such figures are also useful tools for compelling readers' judgement. Carefully chosen words effect profound 'alteration in man' through the power of persuasion: 'what else is man but his mind? Which, whosoever have skill to compass and make yielding and flexible, what may not he command the body to perform?'[4] The mind is 'assailable' by words, and this in turn determines actions. Puttenham emphasizes that skilfully constructed figures assert authority over others, making them flex and yield. Resemblance is an important part of this work, and Puttenham deploys his own 'figure of similitude' to drive home the point that many words are better than few: 'one or two drops of water pierce not the flint stone, but many and often droppings do'.[5] His account of the careful arrangement of words overwhelming others' resistance is disquieting in the context of Puttenham's own life. Court records confirm that he was a sexual predator and serial abuser, and his recent editors offer him as 'a limit case of Renaissance misogyny'.[6] The present discussion does not pursue a biographical angle, but neither does it regard Puttenham's character as coincidental. He knew, as Shakespeare did, that 'figures of similitude' were more than technical exercises, and that likening one thing or person to another could powerfully influence people's judgements and actions. Shakespeare's poem, like Puttenham's *Art*, recognizes the operations of similitude as a means towards asserting power. Unlike the *Art*, however, *A Lover's Complaint* is equivocal in its treatment of such figures. While this equivocation reveals the force of literary figures which express resemblance, it is also sensitive to the complex and sometimes ruinous feelings, including desire, which draw people into one another's likeness.

A Lover's Complaint has long been considered 'among the most bafflingly beautiful poems in English', and readers have found the language of its 329 rhyme royal lines (ababbcc) strange and elusive.[7] Together with 'The Phoenix and the Turtle', it tends to be regarded as an outlier in the Shakespearian canon. Part of the problem lies in long-standing doubts about authorship, and the conviction among some scholars that its quality is insufficiently Shakespearian. Many readers wish the poem away, or wish it was something other than it is.[8] A clear thematic and structural relationship is, however, well established between *A Lover's Complaint* and the preceding poems which together comprise the 1609 volume entitled *Shake-speares Sonnets*. The sonnets delve into love's agonies and complexities, whilst *A Lover's Complaint* deals with a disastrous and duplex erotic entanglement. The pairing of these two texts is aligned with Elizabethan tradition where sonnet sequences were conventionally followed by a narrative complaint in a woman's voice.[9] Recent critical responses tend to cluster around questions of this sort, attending to origin, form and structure rather than pursuing interpretive approaches. This reluctance surely stems, in part, from the difficulty of the poem's subject: the portrayal of an abusive sexual relationship, and the persistence of confused desire.[10] This article takes *A Lover's Complaint* seriously on its own terms, proposing that Shakespeare brought the formidable and equivocating capabilities of 'figures of

---

[4] Puttenham, *Art*, p. 281. [5] Puttenham, *Art*, p. 281.
[6] See Whigham and Rebhorn's introduction to Puttenham, *Art*, p. 8.
[7] Jonathan Post, *Shakespeare's Sonnets and Poems: A Very Short Introduction* (Oxford, 2017), p. 108.
[8] On the 'authorship question', see Brian Vickers, *Shakespeare, A Lover's Complaint and John Davies of Hereford* (Cambridge, 2007), and Hugh Craig, 'George Chapman, John Davies of Hereford, William Shakespeare, and *A Lover's Complaint*', *Shakespeare Quarterly* 63 (2012), 147–74. Post helpfully summarizes this debate in *Introduction*, p. 106.
[9] Colin Burrow, 'Shakespeare the poet', in *The Cambridge Companion to Shakespeare*, ed. Margreta de Grazia and Stanley Wells (Cambridge, 2010), 91–104; p. 101.
[10] Stephen Whitworth has aptly described complaint as 'that mode that forever presences a traumatic and seductive past'. See '"Where excess begs all": Shakespeare, Freud, and the diacritics of melancholy', in *Critical Essays on Shakespeare's A Lover's Complaint*, ed. Shirley Sharon-Zisser (Aldershot, 2006), 165–77; p. 165.

similitude' to a singularly challenging subject. As Colleen Rosenfeld has argued, '*simile* builds hesitation, negotiation, and even accommodation into its own syntax – in English, its *as* and its *so*'.[11] Far from folding one thing into another – such as a hard heart into a stone, or a softened heart into water – the hesitation in simile, and in other related 'figures of similitude', offered Shakespeare a way of expressing the consequences of emotional manipulation. As the young woman knows by the end of the poem, the awfulness of abuse exposes the abused to disturbed feeling. If the processes through which such similes emerge in *A Lover's Complaint* sometimes seem strained, this is part of the poem's enquiry into 'likening' – and, relatedly, its anatomization of what it means to be forcibly 'lovered' (320).[12]

A Lover's Complaint relays a series of overlapping stories in which stones and gemstones feature prominently, together with material detritus such as twisted metal, melted wax, salt crystals and silk threads. Despite the poem's thorough attention to 'objects manifold' (216), it has seldom caught the attention of readers interested in materialities. A lively strand of scholarship on early modern literature and culture has recently revealed diverse and often unexpected connections between people and things, not least seemingly inert substances. Scholarship on Renaissance aliveness has shown that the early modern world of elemental stuff such as stones, metal and water cannot be neatly separated out from human agency, affectivity and embodiment. Shakespeare's works often explore the relationship between people and material things, as Jean E. Feerick and Vin Nardizzi have shown, finding 'the lively presence of dirt, earth, wood, and stones imagined as states and substances embedded within and alongside "the human"'.[13] This article considers from a new angle the relationship between objects and affective personhood, focusing on resemblance rather than correspondence. It is argued here that the embedding of elemental matter within and alongside people in *A Lover's Complaint* addresses specifically gendered questions around control and consent. Working through patterns of likeness rather than sameness or signification, Shakespeare explores the chilling risks involved for women when they – or their lovers – resemble material stuff.

Part of the poem's oft-cited difficulty lies in its structural complexity. The young man's voice is heard only when it is spoken by the young woman, and she describes him perplexingly as 'maiden-tongued' (100). His voice resembles hers, and her voice resembles his. It is therefore unclear which lover's complaint we are reading, making even the poem's title feel uneasy. The young woman is speaking to a 'reverend man' (57) and their conversation is overheard and reported, in turn, by an anonymous narrator. Unlike most narrators in early modern complaint poems, however, this one does not return in the closing lines. The poem tells a story about deception which is left open in that the victim seems willing, at the end, to repeat the violation which has been perpetrated against her. *A Lover's Complaint* has a legal flavour, in keeping with its interwoven and sometimes competing testimonies, and deals centrally with evidence, witnesses and verdicts.[14] The recalcitrance of what the poet-lawyer Abraham Fraunce calls 'fayned similitudes' makes clear the difficulty of determining who, if anyone, is telling the truth.[15] It is a difficulty which works in this poem to the

---

[11] Rosenfeld, *Indecorous Thinking*, p. 97.

[12] This thinking is indebted to Elizabeth Scott-Baumann and Hannah Crawforth's original reading of *A Lover's Complaint* in the present volume, which explores, through the work of Sara Ahmed, the ways in which 'the object of the complaint enforces his (usually his) will upon the complainant'.

[13] See the introduction to Feerick and Nardizzi, eds., *Indistinct Human*, 1–12; p. 4; and, relatedly, the essays in two important collections on early modern ideas of 'the human': Wendy Beth Hyman, ed., *The Automaton in English Renaissance Literature* (London, 2016), and Kevin Curran, ed., *Renaissance Personhood: Materiality, Taxonomy, Process* (Edinburgh, 2020).

[14] For the poem's legal context, see Katharine A. Craik, 'Shakespeare's *A Lover's Complaint* and early modern criminal confession', *Shakespeare Quarterly* 53 (2002), 437–59, and John Kerrigan, *Motives of Woe: Shakespeare and 'Female Complaint' – An Anthology* (Oxford, 1991), p. 29.

[15] Abraham Fraunce, *The Lawiers Logike* (1588), sig. U1v; quoted in Rosenfeld, *Indecorous Thinking*, p. 102.

young man's advantage, and to the young woman's detriment. Arguments *ex similitudine* are a notably weak form of proof since they depend, by their very nature, on approximation rather than precision. Shakespeare does not resolve this problem in *A Lover's Complaint*, which focuses determinedly on what people are like, rather than who or what they are. 'Figures of similitude' dwell on inexactness, qualification and provisionality rather than any fixed capacity to determine who or what is real. While this inexactness demonstrates the richness of likeness as a way of approaching early modern personhood, and expresses elegantly the dereliction of apparent affinity into remoteness, it also registers the doubts which make it so demanding to voice, or to believe, a lover's complaint.

I

A Lover's Complaint introduces the theme of erotic desolation through the language of gemstones (rubies, pearls, diamonds, emeralds, sapphires, opals) familiar from epideictic poetry. Towards the start of the poem, but after her abandonment, the young woman casts an array of stony love-tokens into a river:

> A thousand favours from a maund she drew
> Of amber, crystal, and of beaded jet,
> Which one by one she in a river threw
> Upon whose weeping margin she was set;
> Like usury applying wet to wet,
> Or monarch's hands that lets not bounty fall
> Where want cries some, but where excess begs all.
> (36–42)

The young woman rescinds these mementos in a highly dramatic and stylized manner whilst 'breaking rings a-twain' (6) and tearing up letters and sonnets. There is something luxurious in the young woman's persona which the poem's narrator will later call 'suffering ecstasy' (69). Her acts of destruction against symbolic objects, and therefore against the young man, seem like performative acts of self-destruction as she sets about 'Storming her world with sorrow's wind and rain' (7). Margreta de Grazia has argued, in an essay on *King Lear*, that 'if having is tantamount to being, *not* having is tantamount to *non*-being – to being nothing'.[16] And yet the gemstones, or the young woman's act of destroying them, seem to function productively 'like usury' – a simile which suggests their lawless multiplication as they generate more weeping water, and more excess, which together intimate the course of devastation which will follow.

Gemstones are locked into an interpretive system which maps their appearance onto female virtues of beauty and restraint through the well-worn tradition of *blason*.[17] The significance of gems in *blason* generally works through uncomplicated logic, their colours and lustre matching women's bodily, emotional or moral complexions. According to this precisely calibrated affective register, 'pallid pearls' signify grief while 'rubies red as blood' encode either passion or the modesty of a blush (198). It is a register with which the young man is clearly familiar. To him, however, 'fair gems' (208) have a qualitative economic frame as well as a visual and affective one. Their beauty and lustre are, he claims, guarantors of their giver's 'nature, worth, and quality' (210). The young man is not referring only to his own credentials, for the stones which the young woman casts into the water are the same ones which he had received from women whom he had previously deceived:

> ... they their passions likewise lent me
> Of grief and blushes, aptly understood
> In bloodless white and the encrimsoned mood –
> Effects of terror and dear modesty,
> Encamped in hearts, but fighting outwardly.
> (199–203)

The passion, grief and modesty encoded by the gemstones does not originally belong to either of the

---

[16] Margreta de Grazia, 'The ideology of superfluous things', in *Subject and Object in Renaissance Tragedy*, ed. Margreta de Grazia, Maureen Quilligan and Peter Stallybrass (Cambridge, 1996), 17–42; 21–2.

[17] Catherine Bates argues that these gems are keyed into 'a long history of lapidary symbolism and are to be treated as signifiers loaded with meaning'. See 'Feminine identifications in *A Lover's Complaint*', in *Masculinity, Gender and Identity in the English Renaissance Lyric* (Cambridge, 2007), 174–215; p. 185.

lovers, then, but to the 'many a several fair' (206) whom the young man has earlier courted and likewise abused. Still their meanings are not in doubt because they are, he insists, 'aptly understood'. Women and gemstones are precisely aligned, and the human is seamlessly folded into the natural world. In the young man's imagination, these are objects which 'surround ... inhabit ... even constitute' the discarded women they refer to.[18] In this respect, *A Lover's Complaint* engages with what Wendy Beth Hyman has described as the 'long and often troubling poetic tradition wherein the female addressee is featured as an object – specifically, an object made by poetry'.[19] The young man's account of his conquests, and the precious materials which are their expression and residue, draws from this masculinist tradition. In what follows, however, women look *like* objects but no longer feature *as* them.

The young man claims that the 'wounded fancies' of his former lovers prompted them to offer him further material stuff:

> And, lo, behold these talents of their hair,
> With twisted mettle amorously impleached,
> I have received from many a several fair,
> Their kind acceptance weepingly beseeched,
> With th'annexations of fair gems enriched,
> And deep-brained sonnets that did amplify
> Each stone's dear nature, worth, and quality.
> (204–10)

A troupe of already abandoned women offered 'talents' of their own hair, plaited into metal ornaments. Talents are coins, or plates of precious metal, suggesting again that the enrichment expressed by such gifts is literal as well as affective. In the young man's estimation, women's suffering subjecthood is twisted or plaited ('impleached') into these objects:

> The diamond? – why, 'twas beautiful and hard,
> Whereto his invised properties did tend;
> The deep-green em'rald, in whose fresh regard
> Weak sights their sickly radiance do amend;
> The heaven-hued sapphire and the opal blend
> With objects manifold; each several stone,
> With wit well blazoned, smiled or made some moan.
> (211–17)

The male-seeming diamond expresses 'his invised properties' of beauty and hardness, which sound like the young man's own. Shakespeare often evokes stones to suggest men's lack of human feeling.[20] Here, however, the young man self-regardingly affirms, through stoniness, his own beautiful and remote desirability. Meanwhile, the fresh green hue of the emerald soothes 'weak sights', in accordance with contemporary medical belief, while the blueness of the sapphire suggests heaven.[21] These stones, too, 'smiled or made some moan' on behalf of the forsaken women who willingly gave them. To the young man, the women's agonized desire, however, seems readily transferable to a new lover-in-waiting. Shakespeare here reflects on *blason*'s rigorous and cold codework, but also hints at the cost to women when the human fuses unproblematically with the natural world. As John Kerrigan writes of the young woman in *A Lover's Complaint*, '[a] bundle of suasive metaphors – made up of gemstones and "deep-brained sonnets" – is her undoing'.[22]

Puttenham regards *blason* as part of the '*Icon*, or Resemblance by Imagery', offering examples from his own work *Partheniades*, which compares Queen Elizabeth to a clutch of precious stones: her forehead is silver, her brows are ebony, her hair is gold, her lips are 'ruby rock', her breasts are alabaster. Puttenham explains that *blason* works in this way to 'resemble every part of her body to some natural thing of excellent perfection'.[23] As Nancy Vickers

---

[18] Feerick and Nardizzi, eds., *Indistinct Human*, p. 4.
[19] Wendy Beth Hyman, *Impossible Desire and the Limits of Knowledge in Renaissance Poetry* (Oxford, 2019), p. 28.
[20] For example, Cordelia's murderers are 'men of stones' (*King Lear* 5.3.232) and Murellus addresses the commoners as stones or 'senseless things' (*Julius Caesar* 1.1.35).
[21] For a discussion of *materia medica*, see Marcia Pointon, *Brilliant Effects: A Cultural History of Gem Stones and Jewellery* (New Haven and London, 2009), esp. pp. 2 and 108.
[22] *The Sonnets; and A Lover's Complaint*, ed. John Kerrigan (London, 1986), p. 18.
[23] Puttenham, *Art*, pp. 329–30. Lisa Gim discusses Puttenham's departure from conventional *blason*; see 'Blasoning "The princesse paragon": the workings of George Puttenham's false semblant in his *Partheniades* to Queen Elizabeth', *Modern Language Studies* 28 (1998), 75–92; p. 82.

has observed, *blason* tends, however, to disassemble women by breaking them up into constituent parts. An elaborate imaginative projection of the male speaker's desire, *blason* sets out to praise the uniqueness of the female beloved. But through an accumulation of similitudes, the effect is to suggest that – as the narrative attributed to the young man in *A Lover's Complaint* affirms – all women are the same.[24] The capriciousness of such comparisons is, famously, the subject of Shakespeare's Sonnet 130:

> My mistress' eyes are nothing like the sun;
> Coral is far more red than her lips' red.
> If snow be white, why then her breasts are dun;
> If hairs be wires, black wires grow on her head.
> I have seen roses damasked, red and white,
> But no such roses see I in her cheeks
>
> (1–6)

This sonnet draws attention to the artificiality, and indeed mendacity, involved in comparison, and sticks resolutely instead to what is real. 'Figures of similitude' conventionally register women's beauty by mapping their features onto natural properties. The poem insists, however, that the beloved is 'nothing like' coral, snow or roses, and indeed like nothing else. Similes cannot do her justice because she is not similar to anything. Sonnet 21 also suggests that comparisons are cheap, including any 'couplement of proud compare / ... with earth, and sea's rich gems' (5–6). Such couplement only devalues the beloved's singular uniqueness. Shakespeare returns to the futility of comparison in *A Lover's Complaint*, which thoroughly explores, through the unscrupulous young man's (reported) words, the consequences of likening women to things. Now the 'aptness' of the comparison expressed by *blason* looks like a strict sameness akin to coercion, while unwarranted likenesses are rhetorical ploys which contribute to a considered strategy of sexual predation.[25] *A Lover's Complaint* is still more sceptical than the *Sonnets* about the role of comparison in gendered relationship, particularly the traditions of love poetry in which men tag female beauty into a pre-existing set of correspondences. In other parts of this poem, however, 'figures of similitude' encompass less familiar, less predictable and therefore less readily dismissed patterns of likening.

The narrator observes of the young woman that 'Some beauty peeped through lattice of seared age' (14). Old before her time, her youth is nevertheless still discernible through her lattice-work wrinkles. This strange comparison grows stranger when the narrator describes how the young woman's 'seasoned woe had pelleted in tears' (18). A pellet is a gunstone, shot or projectile, a jarring image which the next stanza develops further:

> Sometimes her levelled eyes their carriage ride
> As they did batt'ry to the spheres intend;
> Sometime diverted their poor balls are tied
> To th'orbèd earth; sometimes they do extend
> Their view right on; anon their gazes lend
> To every place at once, and nowhere fixed,
> The mind and sight distractedly commixed.
>
> (22–8)

Rather than resembling rich gems, or stars, the young woman's rolling 'eyes their carriage ride' as though they are on wheels. Her face becomes a careering cannon poised on a gun-carriage which takes aim, randomly, at larger 'spheres' in the sky and at 'th'orbèd earth'.[26] This comparison is sufficiently discordant to render the young woman not quite human, developing a sense of her deathlike aspect which elaborates the narrator's early impression that her body is 'The carcass of beauty spent and done' (11).[27] The comparison is unexpected, but is nevertheless in keeping with Puttenham's account in *The Art of English Poesy* of

---

[24] See Nancy Vickers's influential discussion of 'the limits – indeed the dangers – of that inherited, insufficient, descriptive rhetoric' in '"The blazon of sweet beauty's best": Shakespeare's *Lucrece*', in *Shakespeare and the Question of Theory*, ed. Patricia Parker and Geoffrey Hartman (New York and London, 1985), 95–115; p. 96.

[25] For an account of competitive similitude, see *Sonnets*, ed. Kerrigan, pp. 18–23. Kerrigan points out that 'Similarity depends on difference; for without difference there is identity, not similitude' (p. 23).

[26] This discussion is indebted to Kerrigan's perceptive notes to this passage in *Sonnets*, pp. 398–9.

[27] The young woman is described as 'a living ghost' by Rosalind Smith, Michelle O'Callaghan and Sarah C. E. Ross in 'Complaint', in *A Companion to Renaissance Poetry*, ed. Catherine Bates (Chichester, 2018), 339–52; p. 345.

certain 'figures of similitude' which are capable of finding 'resemblance in a kind of dissimilitude'.[28] This kind of likening involves drawing attention not only to what someone is like, but also to what they are ordinarily *not* like. Other examples arise in Shakespeare's plays when Othello imagines an immaculate world, free from the threat of sexual abandonment and infidelity, as 'one entire and perfect chrysolite' (*Othello*, 5.2.152),[29] and when Lartius describes the bloodied Coriolanus as a bright red 'carbuncle entire' (*Coriolanus* 1.5.26). It is the *in*exactness of the resemblance between a colossal green gemstone and a chaste world, or between a small glistening garnet and a military colossus, which is striking. Rather than the sameness and correspondence expressed by *blason*, these comparisons between people and material stuff keep the possibility of difference in play. Such surprising and dissonant 'figures of similitude' are well equipped, as we will see, to express the young woman's intractable desire which betokens the gravity and incommensurability of the young man's actions against her.

The presence of difference in similitude is particularly important in the stanza where we began. Here the young woman turns her 'reason into tears' (296):

> But with the inundation of the eyes
> What rocky heart to water will not wear?
> What breast so cold that is not warmèd here?
> O cleft effect!
>
> (290–3)

Stones were sometimes connected to constancy and stability through ideas of Stoic stoutheartedness. One of the young man's previous conquests, after all, was a nun who resolved to be 'immured' (251), or fastened into rock, in order to avoid further temptation. Here the young woman's rocky resistance dissolves into warm aliveness. And yet she is no Niobe for whom 'An objective, stony "it" becomes a weeping, stony "I"', and in whom subject and object slide smoothly together. In an essay on mineral emotions in Shakespeare, Lara Bovilsky argues that 'emotional distinction between stones and men is not an absolute'. For Bovilsky, this indistinctiveness creates a new 'mineral identity' which facilitates the expression of emotional extremity such as grief or despair.[30] While *A Lover's Complaint* uses stones and stoniness to express strong feeling, the phasing of stones and people into one another does not permit new ways of being or doing. The young woman enters into likeness with the tearful young man, but also recognizes their resemblance as a 'cleft effect' which involves difference as well as sameness. 'To cleave' means to split apart, but also to stick fast or adhere. The word is an apt description of those 'figures of similitude' which express, through resemblance, both togetherness and apartness. The technical work of literary figures also, however, betokens a wider dynamic of 'likening' which suggests the terrible risks involved for women in prospecting for similitude. The young man and the young woman had seemed to share a moment of tearful preparedness, but this seeming sameness is short lived. For as the young woman realizes, in her stark retrospective commentary, they were never really together or even proximate: 'our drops this diff'rence bore: / His poisoned me, and mine did him restore' (300–1).

II

Puttenham's description of *Omiosis*, or Resemblance, forms part of his account 'Of figures sententious, otherwise called rhetorical'. His theory of 'general Resemblance, or bare Similitude' is followed by three specific examples which together make a poet

---

[28] Puttenham, *Art*, p. 328. Kerrigan notes in *Sonnets* that 'Shakespeare writes with a keen sense of the difference in similitude' (p. 23).

[29] The imagined chrysolite is surely connected to jealousy's 'green-eyed monster' (3.3.170).

[30] Lara Bovilsky, 'Shakespeare's mineral emotions', in *Renaissance Posthumanism*, ed. Joseph Campana and Scott Maisano (New York, 2016), 253–82; pp. 266 and 260. Jane Bennett outlines her related theory of 'the vitality of matter and the lively powers of material formations' in *Vibrant Matter: A Political Ecology of Things* (Durham, NC, 2010), p. vii.

'an excellent persuader'. The first operates, as we have already seen, through visual imagery (*icon*), while the second offers moral lessons (*parabola*), and the third aligns past with present examples (*paradigma*). The first, resemblance through visual imagery, 'is not only performed by likening of lively creatures one to another, but also of any other natural thing bearing a proportion of similitude, as to liken yellow to gold, white to silver, red to the rose, soft to silk, hard to the stone'.[31] Resemblances which engage the reader's perceptions, particularly the senses of sight and touch, may be convincing enough to 'alter and affect the ear and also the mind'. The aim is to bring about, as Puttenham describes in his account of metaphor, 'an inversion of sense by transport'.[32] The sketching out of resemblance not only enchants the reader, but also inverts their judgement – and perhaps transports them altogether. Jenny Mann has recently argued that early modern literature and rhetoric had absorbed ancient Greek theories of the rhetorical sublime in which skilful orators sought to overwhelm listeners, overcoming resistance through height and magnitude of eloquence. As Mann points out, there is a strongly gendered aspect to this vocabulary of violent forcing and vanquishing.[33] The young man in *A Lover's Complaint* is an accomplished speaker who deploys many persuasive 'figures of similitude', including all three of Puttenham's strategies detailed above. As the young woman says, he has at his fingertips 'the dialect and different skill, / Catching all passions in his craft of will' (125–6). She recognizes that his arguments are moreover designed with an aggressive purpose to 'besiege' (177) or to 'maim' (312). The young man himself makes clear, speaking of his former lovers, 'Harm have I done to them' (194). The young woman has been manipulated by the young man's rhetoric, like many others before her, and her 'white stole of chastity' (297) has been seized without her consent. But while *A Lover's Complaint* deals with predatory abuse, it is not only the story of an offence perpetrated against a hapless victim. The poem ends with the victim wishing it would happen again, so that the young man's falseness might 'yet again betray the fore-betrayed, / And new pervert a reconcilèd maid' (328–9). How to interpret these concluding lines? It seems important to acknowledge their ambiguity, which resists straightforward judgement or condemnation. Attention to the dynamics of similitude reveals the depth of the young man's betrayal, but also the disturbing effects on the young woman of the calumny perpetrated against her.

This moral complexity arises, in part, from Shakespeare's attention to Puttenham's first 'figure of resemblance': the *icon* which compares people to any 'natural thing bearing a proportion of similitude'. When Puttenham discusses visual likeness, he borrows 'the painter's term, who yieldeth to the eye a visible representation'. Poets, too, can achieve 'Resemblance by Imagery or Portrait', creating a picture by likening a person to someone or something.[34] In *A Lover's Complaint*, it is the young woman's words (reported by the narrator) which picture the young man's beauty by comparing him to material stuff. Like the 'silken figures' (17) embroidered on her own handkerchief, his downy chin is 'unshorn velvet' (94). He is a soft, desirable thing whose 'browny locks … hang in crookèd curls' (85) like 'silken parcels' (87). She goes on to describe the young man's belongings as not simply accoutrements, but ways of conceiving and experiencing his aliveness:

> His real habitude gave life and grace
> To appertainings and to ornament,
> Accomplished in himself, not in his case.
> All aids, themselves made fairer by their place,
> Came for additions; yet their purposed trim
> Pieced not his grace, but were all graced by him.
> (114–19)

The young man's 'real habitude', or way of being, gives 'life and grace / To appertainings and to ornament'. Whilst he carries with him many lovely and expensive things designed to supplement his beauty, these do not confer grace upon his person. Instead, it is the youth's lovely-seeming person

---

[31] Puttenham, *Art*, p. 329. [32] Puttenham, *Art*, pp. 282, 238.
[33] Jenny Mann, *The Trials of Orpheus: Poetry, Science and the Early Modern Sublime* (Princeton, 2021); see ch. 4, 'Softening', 128–56; p. 136.
[34] Puttenham, *Art*, p. 329.

which gives grace to his things, making these trimmings appear not only graceful but also as nobly alive as he is. Like a still-life *vanitas* painting, subject and object seem for a moment not only interchangeable but also mutually constitutive: 'The subject passes into the object, the object slides into the subject, in the activity by which each becomes itself.'[35] In the young woman's account, however, such processes of passing or sliding do not happen smoothly or seamlessly. There is no straightforward levelling of humans with the natural things which surround them as Shakespeare keeps dwelling on the kinds of difference created and maintained by expressions of resemblance.

The young woman reflects not only on the young man's likeness *to* objects, but on his likeness *as* an object. Just as the unthinking multitude in *Hamlet* longs for a 'picture in little' (2.2.367) of the villainous Claudius, everyone wants a copy of this unscrupulous young man:

> Many there were that did his picture get
> To serve their eyes, and in it put their mind,
> Like fools that in th'imagination set
> The goodly objects which abroad they find
> Of lands and mansions, theirs in thought assigned
>
> (134–8)

This resemblance has a volatile effect on those who encounter it. The young man is irresistible, but so is his pictured likeness. People treasure the picture as a highly desirable thing, and this makes them believe that they possess the young man himself. Rather than harbouring his image in their minds, as one might expect, besotted viewers bestow their minds upon his image. Those who contemplate his likeness believe – erroneously – that the young man's person becomes 'theirs in thought assigned', as though his features and qualities are 'goodly objects' which can be purchased. Shakespeare offers a similar account of the caprices of devoted perception in Sonnet 113, where all 'quick objects' (7) take on the likeness of the absent beloved. Here the sense of sight is distorted by the mind's loosening grip on reality: 'My most true mind thus makes mine eye untrue' (Sonnet 113.14). The stakes are higher in *A Lover's Complaint*, where seeing likenesses of people in objects, or objects in people, involves a similar sense of alienation but also proves perversely impossible to resist.

Such vagaries of perception are central to *A Lover's Complaint*. The poem is set in a 'concave womb' (1) which functions like an eerie echo chamber. The narrative emerges through a series of reported speeches in which the same story is heard and then 'reworded' several times. The young woman ventriloquizes her assailant; and her voice is, in turn, re-worded by the poem's narrator. As Bruce R. Smith has written, 'The maiden's voice is "double" not only because it echoes across the vale but because the spectator-listener makes *her* voice *his* voice'.[36] A series of metaphors conveys the young man's ruthless strategy:

> O then advance of yours that phraseless hand,
> Whose white weighs down the airy scale of praise.
> Take all these similes to your own command,
> Hallowed with sighs that burning lungs did raise.
> What me, your minister for you, obeys
>
> (225–9)

Despite this cluster of resemblances (hand/language, comparing/weighing, breath/fire, lover/priest), the young woman's 'phraseless' hand seems beyond comparison, and beyond the usual literary formulae exemplified by *blason*. Her hand is whiter than anything registered by a familiar 'scale of praise' which might make reference, say, to alabaster. In a culminating gesture which heightens the significance in *A Lover's Complaint* of 'figures of similitude', the young man invites the young woman to '[t]ake all these similes to your own command'. Given the forcibleness of simile in the young man's hands, it seems a radical move.

---

[35] See the introduction to de Grazia, Quilligan and Stallybrass, eds., *Subject and Object*, 1–13; p. 2.

[36] Bruce R. Smith, *The Key of Green: Passion and Perception in Renaissance Culture* (Chicago and London, 2009), ch. 5, 'Listening for green', pp. 168–207; p. 175.

When the young woman's (reported) voice takes over from the young man's, she does indeed command simile by painting her seducer into an elaborate *ekphrasis*:

> This said, his wat'ry eyes he did dismount,
> Whose sights till then were levelled on my face.
> Each cheek a river running from a fount
> With brinish current downward flowed apace.
> O, how the channel to the stream gave grace,
> Who glazed with crystal gate the glowing roses
> That flame through water which their hue encloses.
>
> (281–7)

This stanza returns to the image of tears as bullets: when the young man casts his eyes downwards, the 'dismount' resembles an act of removing guns from a carriage. The word 'levelled' confirms again that his gaze has taken aggressive aim. And yet the young man resembles a fountain, and his tears are a stream. In Desdemona's Willow Song in *Othello*, an abandoned lover's 'salt tears fell from her and softened the stones' (4.3.44). In *A Lover's Complaint*, however, it is the treacherous abuser who weeps while his stony fabric remains unsoftened. A 'false fire' glows in his blushing cheeks like a precious stone emanating glowing light, or a wet ornament enclosed in glass.[37] Reflecting and refracting the poem's opening tableau, the young man is a 'false jewel' (154) who resembles the stony favours which the young woman casts into the river at the start of the poem, 'applying wet to wet' (40). Hyman points out in her discussion of Renaissance *carpe diem* poetry that, 'as these poems relegate their love objects to inert matter, they exile themselves from the successful consummation of desire'.[38] In *A Lover's Complaint*, however, neither the young man nor the young woman are relegated to inert matter but instead persistently likened to it. And in keeping with this poem's complexities, these acts of likening intimate rather than hindering sex whilst also prolonging the equivocation of desire.

The poem's ending portrays the young woman as an abused but still ardent lover, and it is this unfashionably ambiguous conclusion which has hardened the poem's reputation as 'the most abjected part of the Shakespeare canon'.[39]

Complaint poetry usually leaves women in a state of repentant abjection, but in the closing stanzas of *A Lover's Complaint* the young woman describes her loss of chastity as more or less inevitable:

> Who, young and simple, would not be so lovered?
> Ay me, I fell, and yet do question make
> What I should do again for such a sake.
>
> O that infected moisture of his eye,
> O that false fire which in his cheek so glowed,
> O that forced thunder from his heart did fly,
> O that sad breath his spongy lungs bestowed,
> O all that borrowed motion seeming owed
> Would yet again betray the fore-betrayed,
> And new pervert a reconcilèd maid.
>
> (320–9)

The young woman now recognizes all of the young man's resemblances – false tears, blushes, words – as adjunct or not quite real: 'this man's untrue' (169). He has presented a simulacrum of himself full of borrowed 'motion' or emotion. Suspended between what is and what is not, he is a consummate performer who 'takes and leaves, / In either's aptness, as it best deceives' (305–6). *A Lover's Complaint* resembles Shakespeare's other poems, especially the *Sonnets*, in its attention to the ways in which people can fashion themselves, misleadingly, into a variety of unreal personae for their own ends. It is, however, different from the *Sonnets* in its insistence that the reader bear witness to the skilful planning of naked sexual abuse. Less easily still, however, Shakespeare requires that the reader look unflinchingly at one particularly problematic legacy of abuse: the persistence of desire. It is significant in this regard that the young woman expresses intractable yearning not for the young man, but instead for his treachery against her ('Would yet again betray the fore-betrayed'). The feeling looks perverse, even to the young woman herself. But the fact that her longing is not readily erased by her recognition of the young man's perfidy

---

[37] See Kerrigan's notes in *Sonnets*, pp. 420–1.
[38] Hyman, *Impossible Desire*, p. 28.
[39] Bates, 'Feminine identifications', p. 174.

underlines the efficacy of the abuse – and the sheer difficulty of answering or escaping from it.

While many readers have found the language of *A Lover's Complaint* artificial and ornate, this article has considered its stylistic technicity as an important aspect of its achievement. Shakespeare scrutinizes what Puttenham and other literary theorists regarded, with more or less relish, as the capacity of 'figures of similitude' to persuade, manipulate and overwhelm. Puttenham's rough and unruly nature suggests that he, in particular, knew that words could become agents of control against women, making their minds and bodies 'yielding and flexible'. In his *Apology for Poetry* (1579?), Philip Sidney is unimpressed by writers who labour with the blunt instruments which he calls *'similiter cadences'*. Resemblances are weak proofs that achieve nothing on their own terms, he argues, only nudging the listener in a direction they were already pursuing: 'the force of a similitude not being to prove anything to a contrary disputer, but only to explain to a willing hearer'.[40] Similes persuade only those who are already a 'soft audience' (278). *A Lover's Complaint* explores the forcible operations of simile by showcasing the young man's shifty fluency with *blason* which blends vulnerable women and natural objects seamlessly together. *Blason* fixes women into stone, and presses home their featureless indistinguishability. The poem's other 'figures of resemblance' move beyond such transparently coercive efforts of same-making, however, and explore instead the inexactness and hesitancy involved in comparison. Similes were never intended to offer resolution, as Sidney makes clear, for readers are directed 'by similitudes not to be satisfied'.[41] *A Lover's Complaint* explores how such equivocation can be deployed to unscrupulous ends, but also how and why these ends can be so difficult to identify, recognize and expose.

A Lover's Complaint pays particularly close attention to imprecise resemblances between people and natural or elemental objects. Recent criticism on Shakespeare's plays has focused on 'the coextensive nature of human and nonhuman living things' which look and act like one another, and which share the same environment.[42] In his comedies, as Mary Floyd-Wilson has argued, Shakespeare uses metal and stone to express the mysteries of desire: 'The same force that draws metals to stones can also activate extraordinary bonds between people.'[43] In particular, the lodestone (or magnet) makes visible the secret attraction of one entity to another. *A Lover's Complaint* does not, however, deal with pleasurably mutual attraction, where like hearkens inexorably to like, but instead with a disastrously unbalanced connection. Accordingly, *A Lover's Complaint* does not make humans into objects, but into likenesses of objects which keep registering their difference from one another. Shakespeare shows how a skilful abuser of language can captivate the imagination through creating seeming sameness. In its closing lines, however, the poem concentrates on desire's capacity to bend the will, and its disturbance of how and what people feel – and who or what people are. Catherine Bates is correct to argue that 'the poem presents a view of human motivation and desire that is profoundly at odds with all that might seem logical or reasonable, let alone ethical'.[44] *A Lover's Complaint* is nevertheless truthful and therefore ethical in its account of the messiness and trickery involved in encountering (and assuming) others' likenesses, but also in its clear-sighted picture of the disturbed feelings which register grievous injury. The poem's engagement with equivocating 'figures of similitude' is inseparable from its attention to the devastating end of a devastating encounter, and its wider exploration, through likening, of the ominous unknowability of the other.

---

[40] Philip Sidney, *An Apology for Poetry*, ed. Geoffrey Shepherd (Manchester, 1973), p. 139.
[41] Sidney, *Apology*, p. 139.
[42] Feerick and Nardizzi, eds., *Indistinct Human*, p. 5.
[43] Mary Floyd-Wilson, 'The nature of attraction in *Twelfth Night*', in *Occult Knowledge, Science, and Gender on the Shakespearean Stage* (Cambridge, 2013), 73–90; pp. 73–4.
[44] Bates, 'Feminine identifications', p. 195. For a Lacanian reading, see Shirley Sharon-Zisser, '"True to bondage": the rhetorical forms of female masochism in *A Lover's Complaint*', in *Critical Essays*, ed. Sharon-Zisser, 179–90. Sharon-Zisser finds in the poem 'a poetic theorization of the psychic condition which psychoanalysis came to call female masochism' (p. 179).

'NOTHING-TO-BE-GLOSSED-HERE': RACE IN SHAKESPEARE'S *SONNETS*

JANE KINGSLEY-SMITH

In Ayanna Thompson's introductory essay to *The Cambridge Companion to Shakespeare and Race* (2021), she describes how editions of Shakespeare's plays she read as an undergraduate 'routinely fell silent at certain moments':

Romeo's remark that Juliet's beauty 'hangs upon the cheek of night / As a rich jewel in an Ethiope's ear' (1.5.44–45), is not explained by the editor of the 1980 Arden edition. Instead, the editor notes the similarity of the phrase to one used by Christopher Marlowe in *Hero and Leander*: 'Rich iewels in the darke are soonest spide.' The implicit message of [this] and other observances was that race did not exist in Shakespeare's cultural and creative imagination. That there was no difference between Marlowe's 'dark' and Shakespeare's 'Ethiope' – that Shakespeare's employment of 'Ethiope' was not a reflection of a growing awareness of Africans.[1]

Despite all the work that has been done subsequently to articulate the racecraft operative in Shakespeare's plays, this silence – the sense of 'nothing-to-be-glossed-here'[2] – is still largely the case in editions of the *Sonnets*.[3] Take, for example, the phrase 'woman coloured ill' (4) in Sonnet 144, which sits in opposition to the 'man right fair' (3). There is very little variation in how this has been glossed by editors in the last twenty-five years:

4 coloured ill of an unpleasing or ugly complexion; but like the 'fairness' of the man, the bad colouring of the woman may be as much emotional as literal, especially given the sense of *coloured* as 'specious' or 'falsely glossed over' (*OED* 3a, b). (1997, 2010)

4 coloured ill dark, with a suggestion of evil. The idea that one had a good and a bad angel who argued over one's soul is common in the drama of the period, as in *Dr Faustus* (A Text), 2.3.12 ff. Drayton's *Idea* (1599) 22 provides an analogue in the sonnet tradition. The convention here is transformed into a seduction and corruption of one angel by the other. (2002, 2008)

4 coloured ill of dark complexion; see Sonnets 127, 130. (2018)

4 coloured ill of unpleasing colour, dark (and in appearance); also morally corrupt. (2020)[4]

Whilst these notes demonstrate the religious, moral and rhetorical meanings of 'coloured ill',

---

[1] Ayanna Thompson, 'Did the concept of race exist for Shakespeare and his contemporaries? An introduction', in *The Cambridge Companion to Shakespeare and Race*, ed. Thompson (Cambridge, 2021), 1–16; p. 1.
[2] Thompson, 'Concept of race', p. 5. I use the term 'racecraft' as defined by Karen E. Fields and Barbara J. Fields in their seminal study *Racecraft: The Soul of Inequality in American Life* (London, 2012).
[3] In 1995, Kim F. Hall noted how '[e]ven critics who purport to be open-minded in their interpretations of the sonnets become strangely recalcitrant when faced with the possibilities of racial difference in the "blackness" of the dark lady' (*Things of Darkness: Economies of Race and Gender in Early Modern England* (Ithaca, 1995), p. 69).
[4] These are from the following editions respectively: *Shakespeare's Sonnets*, ed. Katherine Duncan-Jones (London, 1997), p. 402; *Oxford Shakespeare: The Complete Sonnets and Poems*, ed. Colin Burrow (Oxford, 2002, 2008), p. 668; *The Complete Poems of Shakespeare*, ed. Cathy Shrank and Raphael Lyne (Abingdon, 2018), p. 597; and *All the Sonnets of Shakespeare*, ed. Stanley Wells and Paul Edmondson (Cambridge, 2020), p. 74. The new Arden 4 edition of the *Sonnets* by Lukas Erne was not published at the time of writing but will hopefully address this issue more directly.

they draw back from acknowledging any explicit racial connotation, just as the language they use to gloss the phrase – 'dark' – perpetuates the obscurantism inherent in the problematic term 'Dark Lady'. But for most readers in the early 2020s, not least in the wake of the Black Lives Matter movement, the term 'coloured ill' looks immediately and explicitly racist. And for Shakespeare scholars, informed by Critical Race and Critical White scholarship on the early modern period and more recently by Anti-Racist Shakespeare, a refusal to engage with this phrase as a racialist term on the basis of historical anachronism is increasingly difficult to defend.[5] As I will argue, 'coloured ill' in Sonnet 144 could have directed Shakespeare's readers both to the assumption that Black Africans were 'coloured', i.e. bearing a darker 'tincture' on top of their 'originary' whiteness, and to the practice of the fallen angel blacking up on the early modern stage. In either case, the racial implications of this phrase are readily apparent and highly troubling in a way that editors have tended to obscure.

There are several reasons why we have been slower to acknowledge the race-making of the *Sonnets* than of the plays. The latter are more explicit about the otherness of their Black characters, through terms such as 'Ethiope' and 'Moor', and they explore the construction of race materially on stage through costumes, wigs and other prostheses, features which are often alluded to in the text.[6] By contrast, the Blackness of the *Sonnets*' female protagonist is unsupported by ethnic or geographical markers, and the parts to which blackness might apply are more elusive: the mistress's 'complexion' could mean her face or '"the combination of the four 'humours' of the body in a certain proportion" (*OED* 1a)'.[7] This means that she could be black psychologically – in the sense of being melancholy and constant – or somatically, depending on how we interpret this word.[8] Of course, the fact that we read the *Sonnets* rather than see them performed on stage means that definitive judgements do not have to be made, an element of their reception which has allowed the figure of the 'Dark Lady' to endure for so long. It is worth stating from the outset that I believe rejecting this nineteenth-century euphemism in favour of Black Mistress or Black Woman is one of the first steps we must take towards acknowledging the importance of race in the *Sonnets*.[9]

Another feature of the sonnets that has inhibited discussion of their racecraft is bibliographic: the belief that a sonnet's position in the 1609 Quarto sequence determines its addressee and therefore its meaning.[10]

---

[5] On the different meanings of the term 'race' in early modern culture, see Ania Loomba, *Shakespeare, Race and Colonialism* (Oxford, 2002), ch. 1. Addressing this question of anachronism in *Race in Early Modern England: A Documentary Companion* (New York, 2007), Loomba and Jonathan Burton argue that 'it makes less sense to try to settle upon a precise definition or indeed to locate a precise moment of origin for racial ideologies than to delineate the ways in which they order and delimit human possibilities through a wide range of conjoined discourses and practices' (p. 2). See also Thompson, 'Did the concept of race exist?' p. 8.

[6] See Morwenna Carr, 'Material/blackness: race and its material constructions on the seventeenth-century stage', *Early Theatre* 20 (2017), 77–95; and Ian Smith, 'White skin, black masks: racial cross-dressing on the early modern stage', *Renaissance Drama* 32 (2003), 33–67.

[7] *Complete Poems*, ed. Burrow, p. 644. It is notable that when glossing this word, editors almost without exception avoid the term 'skin', although this is what most modern readers of the poems will think of. One exception is Wells and Edmondson, whose gloss for 'Thy black' in Sonnet 131 is 'blackness (of features or skin)' (*All the Sonnets*, p. 59).

[8] For further discussion, see Elizabeth D. Harvey, 'Flesh colors and Shakespeare's sonnets', in *A Companion to Shakespeare's Sonnets*, ed. Michael Schoenfeldt (Oxford, 2007), 314–28, and Elizabeth Spiller, *Reading and the History of Race in the Renaissance* (Leiden, 2011), especially the chapter on Pamphilia's black humour, pp. 153–201.

[9] Most recently, Imtiaz Habib has opted for 'Black Woman', in his essay '"Two loves I have of comfort and despair": the circle of whiteness in the *Sonnets*', in *White People in Shakespeare: Essays on Race, Culture and the Elite*, ed. Arthur L. Little Jr (London, 2023), 29–43. I prefer 'Black Mistress' because it reminds us that the blackness of this protagonist is partly a function of her erotic relationship with the male speaker. It is also the term Margreta de Grazia used in her ground-breaking essay, 'The scandal of Shakespeare's sonnets', in *Shakespeare Survey 46* (Cambridge, 1993), 35–50, to which I am much indebted.

[10] This approach persists despite Heather Dubrow's observation that 'we do not definitively know the direction of address of many sonnets' and should 'entertain the possibility that not only Sonnets 40 to 42 but also a number of the others in the first 126 poems describe the Dark Lady' (*Echoes of Desire: English Petrarchism and its Counter-Discourses* (Ithaca and London, 1995), p. 123).

Such an approach dictates that allusions to blackness in any sonnet in the 'Fair Youth' sequence (1–126) cannot address racial blackness because such allusions are confined (if they are acknowledged at all) to the 'subsequence' (127–54). One of the consequences of Malone's binary division of the *Sonnets* has been to fence off the relationship between Shakespeare and a Black Mistress: to make it marginal to the main body of the *Sonnets* and something that might be ignored.[11] Indeed, we might go further and argue that *any* issues of race in the *Sonnets* have tended to be confined here.[12] Furthermore, when critics do engage with the sonnets' racecraft, their arguments tend to be defined by whether they are following the Quarto order, in which case the Black Mistress sonnets come last, or the supposed date of composition, which makes them among the earliest sonnets Shakespeare wrote.[13] Thus, for Carol Mejia La Perle, who reads in the Quarto order, the Black Mistress interrupts and disrupts an existing white male friendship, and shifts the sequence 'from amity to promiscuity, from counsel to corruption, from selflessness to the mockery of such sentiments'.[14] But for Imtiaz Habib, Sonnets 127–54, 'written as a group by themselves in the late 1580s to early 1590', reveal Shakespeare's 'traumatic encounter ... with an unnamed historical black woman upon his arrival in London', so that 'the self-expostulatory sonnets of fairness are accordingly the after-effects of the blackness sonnets ... composed after the writing of the black woman sonnets, and an attempt to thematically eclipse them'.[15] Compelling as these readings are, neither fully accounts for the construction of race in the *Sonnets*, which seems to me more troubled and inconsistent, so that poems 127 and 130–3, for example, include both a self-critical questioning of the black/white binary and a leaning-in to racist stereotypes. Furthermore, although the *Sonnets*' delineation of their protagonists is important to how they think about race, this does not limit us to unique historical persons: it seems highly likely that the Fair Youth is a conflation of at least two young men Shakespeare knew, and the language of blackening which the sonnets deploy might have been aimed at a Black and a white woman.[16] We also need to bear in mind

Helen Vendler's warning that '[t]he true "actors" in the lyric are words not "dramatic persons"; and the drama of any lyric is constituted by the successive entrances of new sets of words'.[17] Hence, we need to pay attention to the racialist discourse that lurks in phrases such as 'beauteous niggard' (4.5) and 'gross painting' (82.13), whilst being sensitive to the fact that the racecraft of the sonnets is imbricated in the act of writing itself.

The following article is divided into three sections. The first focuses on the Black Mistress, and how our increased awareness of the presence of Black people in Shakespeare's England can and should illuminate our reading of the *Sonnets*. The second thinks about the Fair Youth as a white man whose praise advances a discourse of white superiority, but one that is distinctly vulnerable. The final section draws upon the race-ing of praise in the *Sonnets* and the anxiety of the not-white-enough poet when he memorializes his love/Love in black ink.

---

[11] See Robert Matz's discussion of the lack of attention given to these poems before the mid twentieth century in 'The scandals of Shakespeare's *Sonnets*', *ELH* 77 (2010), 477–508; pp. 499–500.

[12] An important sole exception for a long time was Kim F. Hall's discussion of the Young Man's whiteness in '"These bastard signs of fair": literary whiteness in Shakespeare's sonnets', in *Post-Colonial Shakespeares*, ed. Ania Loomba and Martin Orkin (London, 1998), 64–82.

[13] On the dating of the sonnets, see A. Kent Hieatt, Charles W. Hieatt and Anne Lake Prescott, 'When did Shakespeare write "Sonnets 1609"?' *Studies in Philology* 88 (1991), 69–109.

[14] Carol Mejia LaPerle, 'The racialized affects of ill-will in the Dark Lady sonnets', in *Race and Affect in Early Modern English Literature*, ed. LaPerle (Tempe, AZ, 2022), 205–21; p. 209.

[15] Habib, '"Two loves I have"', p. 29, p. 37, p. 36.

[16] For further discussion of the sonnets' multiple addressees, see Paul Edmondson and Stanley Wells, 'The plurality of Shakespeare's sonnets', in *Shakespeare Survey* 65 (Cambridge, 2012), 211–20. The argument that more than one female beloved is implied dates back to at least the mid nineteenth century. See *A New Variorum Edition of Shakespeare: The Sonnets*, ed. Hyder Edward Rollins, 2 vols. (Philadelphia and London, 1944), vol. 2, p. 247.

[17] Helen Vendler, *The Art of Shakespeare's Sonnets* (Cambridge, MA, and London, 1997), p. 3.

THE SONNETS' BLACK AND BLACKENED MISTRESS

The stubbornly persistent term 'Dark Lady', which dates from at least the mid nineteenth century,[18] misrepresents the female antagonist described in Shakespeare's *Sonnets* in a number of ways. As Paul Hammond points out, 'we do not know that she is, in any accepted social (or even moral) sense, a "lady"; the word "lady" is never used in the poems, and "dark" when applied to a person occurs only in one poem (147:14) which is not self-evidently about the Woman at all'.[19] The term has historically directed attention away from issues of racial difference towards a more familiar Western *femme fatale*, whose darkness is seductive, adulterous and 'brunette'.[20] Even Kim F. Hall's brilliant, racially engaged discussion of the 'dark lady' as a figure in early modern sonnets – white Caucasian women with 'dark' features, allowing aristocratic poets to 'negotiate involvement with the sexual, racial and "linguistic" difference brought about by increased travel abroad' – does not quite describe Shakespeare's mistress.[21] These 'dark ladies' are dark so that they can be transformed to fair, 'represent[ing] not their seductive power but the poet's power in bringing them to light'.[22] Shakespeare's *Sonnets* may allude to this kind of rhetorical conversion, 'For I have sworn thee fair and thought thee bright, / Who art as black as hell, as dark as night' (147.13–14), but they do so in order to demonstrate that this power has failed. The speaker repeatedly blames his own judgement in desiring this woman, repudiates the poetical conventions by which she might be made whiter, and threatens to use language that will make her (and the Fair Youth and even himself) blacker.

One of the many important legacies of Hall's work is the critical understanding of 'black' as a racialized linguistic weapon, used against the women in Shakespeare's plays. Drawing on the 'tawny Tartar' reference in *A Midsummer Night's Dream*, Hall notes that '"black" women – real or rhetorical – are coded as the ultimate in undesirability and thus are not suitable objects of social exchange ... the evocation of blackness serves to racialize whiteness and make it visible'.[23] Subsequent critics have taken up this insight to powerful effect. Wendy Wall observes how, in *As You Like It*, Phoebe's transgressive pursuit of her desire is castigated by references to her physical darkness – her 'inky brows' and 'cheek of cream' (3.5.47, 48) – reaching a climax in her letter, which Rosalind condemns as 'Ethiop words, blacker in their effect / Than in their countenance' (4.3.36–7). Hence, Phoebe 'becomes blackfaced rhetorically ... [her] "Ethiop" text becomes a sign of her own difference and unruliness, conveniently coded in terms of the text's color'.[24] In *Othello*, white Desdemona is blackened as a consequence of Othello's suspicions of her infidelity: 'Her name, that was as fresh / As Dian's visage, is now begrimed and black / As mine own face' (3.3.389–91).[25] Lara Bovilsky has noted Desdemona's 'progressive and virulent racialization in the play' and argues more generally that 'the links between ideologies of race and gender operating on the early modern English stage and elsewhere [are] far more literal and materialist than has been generally believed'.[26] Such insights have not often been

---

[18] Gerald Massey uses the phrase 'The "Dark" Lady' in one of his chapter headings in *Shakespeare's Sonnets Never Before Interpreted* (London, 1866), p. 323, and it was picked up by subsequent reviewers, though 'dark woman' tended to be more common until the beginning of the twentieth century. The championing of the term by George Bernard Shaw in his play *The Dark Lady of the Sonnets*, performed at the National Theatre in 1910, seems to have considerably increased its usage.

[19] *Shakespeare's Sonnets: An Original-Spelling Text*, ed. Paul Hammond (Oxford and New York, 2012), p. 4.

[20] For further discussion, see Marvin Hunt, 'Be Dark but not too Dark: Shakespeare's Dark Lady as sign of color', in *Shakespeare's Sonnets: Critical Essays*, ed. James Schiffer (New York, 1999), 369–90.

[21] Hall, *Things of Darkness*, p. 64.

[22] Hall, *Things of Darkness*, p. 67.

[23] Hall, *Things of Darkness*, p. 22.

[24] Wendy Wall, 'Reading for the blot: textual desire in early modern English literature', in *Reading and Writing in Shakespeare*, ed. David M. Bergeron (Newark and London, 1996), 131–59; p. 143.

[25] See also David Schalkwyk's discussion of black and white in terms of female chastity in 'Race, body and language in Shakespeare's sonnets and plays', *English Studies in Africa* 47 (2009), 5–23.

[26] Lara Bovilsky, *Barbarous Play: Race on the English Renaissance Stage* (Minneapolis, 2008), p. 39, p. 51.

applied to Shakespeare's *Sonnets*, but I would argue that, just as the possibility of a 'real' Black woman as the addressee opens up important new readings of the *Sonnets*, the language of blackness as slander coexists with this perception. In his essay, 'Is it possible to read Shakespeare through Critical White Studies?', Arthur L. Little Jr avers the commitment of Shakespearian critical race scholarship to:

> understanding the *raison d'être* of the black (and blackened) others who grace the pages of Shakespeare: Aaron, Aaron's son, 'Blackamoors with music', Caliban, Cleopatra, the Dark Lady (perhaps Lucy Negro), the Indian Changeling, the 'Negro' impregnated by Lancelot, Othello and the Prince of Morocco. It is imperative that we continue to address these impersonations, since such raced embodiments in Shakespeare's works and afterlives continue to affect the *real* lives – the experiential and existential beingness – of peoples of color.[27]

Enfolded within our conception of Shakespeare's Black mistress, we find both the historical Black woman, here indicated by the reference to 'Lucy Negro', and the 'blackened' mistress, whose slander is an invention of the men who talk about her. This continues to do harm, especially to 'the *real* lives' of peoples of colour today. But how might we read specific sonnets differently with an awareness of this Black and blackened mistress?

Through the work of Imtiaz Habib, Miranda Kaufmann and Duncan Salkeld, we have become aware of the names, locations and sometimes the professions of a small number of Black women living in early modern London. Salkeld has demonstrated that Shakespeare likely knew Luce Baynam, described in legal and literary documents as 'Black Luce' or 'Lucy Negro', who was a brothel owner in Clerkenwell, and who may have attended a performance by the Gray's Inn students during the Christmas festivities of 1594. This would have been just over a week before *The Comedy of Errors* was performed there, with its reference to a character called 'swart' Luce (3.2.102).[28] Shakespeare might also have been aware of the silkweaver John Reson(able), described as a 'blackmor' or 'blacman' in parish records, living in Southwark between 1578 and 1594, whose widow and son, Edward, might still have been living in the area when Shakespeare was writing in the 1590s.[29] In *The Merchant of Venice*, where Lorenzo tells Lancelot that 'The Moor is with child by you', the latter replies: 'It is much that the Moor should be more than reason, but if she be less than an honest woman, she is indeed more than I took her for' (3.5.37–40). Salkeld has brilliantly identified 'more than reason' as an allusion to Resonable's widow, who appears in the token book for St Saviour's parish in 1595 as 'being brought a bed', which might be a reference to her pregnancy at around the same time that *The Merchant of Venice* was being performed. It is even possible that the actor playing Lancelot, Will Kemp, had fathered her child.[30]

This connection between Black lives in the archives and Shakespeare's playwriting throws into relief a pun in Sonnet 40:

> Take all my loves, my love, yea, take them all:
> What hast thou then more than thou hadst before?
> No love, my love, that thou mayst true love call –
> All mine was thine before thou hadst this more.
>
> (1–4)

---

[27] Arthur L. Little Jr, 'Is it possible to read Shakespeare through Critical White Studies?' in *The Cambridge Companion to Shakespeare and Race*, ed. Thompson, 268–80; p. 268.

[28] See Duncan Salkeld, *Shakespeare among the Courtesans: Prostitution, Literature and Drama, 1500–1650* (Ashgate, 2012), pp. 128–34, pp. 139–42, and 'Black Luce in Sonnets 127–54', in *Shakespeare's Global Sonnets: Translation, Appropriation, Performance*, ed. Jane Kingsley-Smith and W. Reginald Rampone Jr (Cham, 2023), 335–51. For a blistering poetic response to Shakespeare's *Sonnets*, which draws directly on Salkeld's research, see Caroline Randall Williams, *Lucy Negro, Redux: The Bard, a Book, and a Ballet* (Nashville, 2019).

[29] See Imtiaz Habib and Duncan Salkeld, 'The Resonables of Boroughside, Southwark: an Elizabethan Black family near the Rose Theatre', *Shakespeare* 11 (2015), 135–56, and also Matthew Steggle's discussion of Edward Resonable as a potential member of the audience for *Othello* in 'Othello, the Moor of London: Shakespeare's Black Britons', in *Othello: A Critical Reader* ed. Robert C. Evans (London, 2015), 103–24.

[30] Salkeld, 'Alienating laughter in *The Merchant of Venice*: a reply to Imtiaz Habib', *Shakespeare* 11 (2015), 148–56; pp. 153–4.

In the notes to this poem in her Arden edition, Katherine Duncan-Jones observed: 'It is tempting to find a pun on "Moor" (note also l. 2), and detect here an anticipation of the sonnet alluding to "a woman coloured ill" (144); but nothing else in this part of the sequence supports such a reference.'[31] Perhaps because of Duncan-Jones's caution, this reading has not been taken up by subsequent editors. And yet, to insist on the authority of the 1609 Quarto sequence to the extent that it limits how individual sonnets might resonate is, as I have argued elsewhere, unnecessarily reductive and ahistorical.[32] We would probably hesitate to describe it as 'tempting' to engage in biographical speculation about the name 'Will' in the sonnets, but something of this judgement is applied here, despite the fact that 'the Moor' is a standard speech prefix for Shakespeare in, for example, *Titus Andronicus*, and that the pun has a Shakespearian precedent.[33] To overlook it is to overlook a rare example of the *Sonnets* identifying their black mistress as Black.

More broadly, an understanding of what the lives of early modern Black women might have been like requires us to engage sympathetically with the *Sonnets*' depiction of their Mistress, and to engage more critically with her vilification. Some time ago now, Ilona Bell warned against taking the account of her promiscuity at face value, citing derogatory comments by Samuel Schoenbaum ('About her sexual appetite and promiscuity ... there is no question' (1980)) and Stephen Greenblatt (she 'is everything which should inspire revulsion' (2004)) as evidence of the way in which the *Sonnets*' self-serving vitriol is taken as moral truth.[34] But accusations such as those in Sonnet 137, that the mistress is 'the bay where all men ride' (6), or the expectation that if she will take one Will, she must indiscriminately take another, in Sonnet 135, whilst being overtly misogynist, look even more suspect in light of the contemporary hyper-sexualization of Black women. As Joyce Green MacDonald has shown, this supposed characteristic began to appear in the travel narratives produced by white Western merchants and colonizers in the late sixteenth century, where it would become 'deeply useful in producing and justifying notions of Europeans' right to exploit the physical and reproductive labor of African women'.[35] Closer to home, we find it in the dramatic representations of Black women as sexually voracious servants on the early seventeenth century stage (see, for example, Zanche in Webster's *The White Devil* (1612) and Zanthia in Fletcher's *The Knight of Malta* (1616–19)), acting not just as a foil to the chastity of white women, but as a deflection of the sexual abuse which many Black English servants must have suffered at the hands of white masters, and partly accounting for the number of illegitimate children born to them.[36] Furthermore, if the *Sonnets*' condemnation of the Mistress's sexual indiscriminacy alludes to her involvement in prostitution, as some editors have suggested,[37] then this is likely to reflect the economic necessity to which we know many Black women were driven far more than their 'sexual appetite[s]'. Habib draws our attention to a letter of 28 May 1599, from Dennis Edwards to Thomas Lankford, the Earl of Hertford's secretary: 'Pray enquire and secure my negress; she is certainly at

---

[31] *Shakespeare's Sonnets*, ed. Duncan-Jones, p. 190.
[32] See Jane Kingsley-Smith, *The Afterlife of Shakespeare's Sonnets* (Cambridge, 2019), 'Introduction'.
[33] On the self-consciousness about puns evident in Shakespeare's own work, and the venerable biblical tradition of punning, see Michael Silk, 'Puns and prose: reflections on Shakespeare's usage', in *Shakespeare Survey 69* (Cambridge, 2016), 17–29.
[34] Ilona Bell, 'Rethinking Shakespeare's Dark Lady', in *A Companion to Shakespeare's Sonnets*, ed. Schoenfeldt, 293–313.
[35] Joyce Green MacDonald, 'The legend of Lucy Negro', in *The Routledge Companion to Black Women's Cultural Histories*, ed. Janell Hobson (Abingdon, 2021), 66–74; p. 68.
[36] See Iman Sheeha, '"A maid called Barbary": Othello, Moorish maidservants and the Black presence in Early Modern England', in *Shakespeare Survey 75* (Cambridge, 2022), 89–102; pp. 91–2, p. 100.
[37] This reading is often prompted by Sonnet 137, wherein the speaker rages that what he thought a 'several plot' is actually 'the wide world's common place' (9–10). See *Complete Poems*, ed. Burrow, p. 654, n. 10.

the Swan, at the Dane's beershop, Turnbull Street, Clerkenwell'. As Habib explains:

> The 'stews' of Clerkenwell in northwest London ... was at this time one of the most notorious brothels of the city, particularly along Turnbull or Turnmill street, as it is sometimes called ... If the 'negress' is not the infamous prostitute Lucy Negro that I have elsewhere proposed she is, she is certainly one of her colleagues, and Dennis Edwards's proprietary addressing of her illuminates the sexual bondage within [sic] she is cast. Her sexual exploitation as a prostitute is the most vicious form of the performance of a negative pathology for black people, particularly young black women, in which the only use that destitute enslaved black females can have is as casual sexual conveniences for the male public at large.[38]

The degree to which distinctions between servitude, prostitution and enslavement are blurred in early modern England might also lead us to a re-examination of Sonnet 133,[39] where the speaker berates his mistress:

> Beshrew that heart that makes my heart to groan
> For that deep wound it gives my friend and me!
> Is't not enough to torture me alone,
> But slave to slavery my sweet'st friend must be?
> (1–4)

Line 4 recalls the familiar Petrarchan designation of the male lover as a slave to his cruel tyrant mistress, but it might also refer to the mistress's own personal experience of enslavement, so that the two men become 'slaves of a slave'.[40] Although slavery was illegal in Shakespeare's England, this does not mean that some of the Black women there had not formerly been slaves on the Continent, or that the practice did not continue in an unlawful but unobtrusive fashion within English aristocratic and mercantile households.[41]

Even the seemingly positive responses to black beauty that we find in Sonnets 127–52 demand re-examination in light of the possibility that they represent a Black African rather than a dark Caucasian beloved. I quote Sonnet 127 in full here because of its importance for any discussion of race in the *Sonnets*.

> In the old age black was not counted fair,
> Or if it were it bore not beauty's name:
> But now is black beauty's successive heir,
> And Beauty slandered with a bastard shame,
> For since each hand hath put on Nature's power,
> Fairing the foul with Art's false borrow'd face,
> Sweet beauty hath no name no holy bower,
> But is profan'd, if not lives in disgrace.
> Therefore my Mistress' eyes are Raven black,
> Her eyes so suited, and they mourners seem,
> At such who not born fair no beauty lack,
> Sland'ring Creation with a false esteem.
>   Yet so they mourn becoming of their woe,
>   That every tongue says beauty should look so.[42]

For Hall, this sonnet is consistent with the trope she identifies, whereby '[t]he whitening of the dark lady becomes crucial for the exercise of male poetic power', but she also finds in it something more positive: 'a sense of something new – if not a literal Second Coming, then certainly a new age of poetry: "But now is black beauty's successive heir" (3). Blackness seems to replace a degenerate old language/beauty, truer than "whiteness".'[43] MacDonald takes this further. Building on Hall's work, she describes how, '[a]s Petrarchan lyric

---

[38] Imtiaz Habib, *Black Lives in the English Archives, 1500–1677: Imprints of the Invisible* (London and New York, 2008), p. 107. See also Hannah Crawforth's discussion of the way in which Caroline Randall Williams, in her collection *Lucy Negro Redux*, writes back both to the English archive and to Shakespeare's *Sonnets* in 'Imtiaz Habib and "Lucy Negro, Redux"', https://manyheadedmonster.com/2023/05/25/imtiaz-habib-and-lucy-negro-redux/#_ftn6. I am extremely grateful to Dr Crawforth for her comments on a draft of this article.

[39] See Urvashi Chakravarty's *Fictions of Consent: Slavery, Servitude and Free Service in Early Modern England* (Philadelphia, 2022), in which she argues that 'before the development of a transatlantic trade in slaves, slavery ... informed the languages, literatures, and learned conduct of English men, women and children', and that 'the long ideological history of slavery was rooted in a set of everyday relations and sites of service' (p. 2).

[40] See Hunt, 'Be Dark but not too Dark', pp. 385–6, and MacDonald, 'The legend of Lucy Negro', p. 70.

[41] Miranda Kaufmann, *Black Tudors: The Untold Story* (London, 2017), pp. 48–50.

[42] The text is given here as in the 1609 quarto (*Shake-speares sonnets Never before imprinted* (London, 1609)), with modernized spelling.

[43] Hall, *Things of Darkness*, pp. 115–16.

participated in the large-scale cultural production of feminine beauty in terms of whiteness, it also indirectly invoked the Black female object of early modern racial discourse, an object against which values of white female beauty and virtue could become more visible'.[44] This is the case not only in portraiture of aristocratic white women in the late seventeenth century, where the figure of the Black servant conventionally functions to enhance white beauty,[45] but also in early modern literary tropes, such as the image of the 'jewel in an Ethiope's ear' in *Romeo and Juliet* (1.5.45) and in Sonnet 27, where the beloved 'like a jewel hung in ghastly night / Makes black night beauteous' (11–12).[46] In Sonnets 127–52, however, MacDonald finds a radical challenge to this familiar binary, underpinned partly by the new archival knowledge that we have of Shakespeare's likely encounter with Black women: beginning with 127, they 'simply refuse the equation between whiteness, beauty, and virtue'.[47]

But whilst there is disagreement about whether Sonnet 127 represents Black beauty or merely anticipates it, this debate is once again not something that we find in contemporary editions of the *Sonnets* where the opening line is not glossed as though it could have any racial meaning:

1 black ... fair a dark (complexion) was not adjudged to be blonde (beautiful): the paradoxical assertion that what is black (dark) is now regarded as fair (light) identifies this sonnet, like 130 and 132, as a conceited exercise in mock-encomium.   (1997, 2010)

1 black ... fair Dark colouring (dark hair and dark eyes) was not considered beautiful (with a pun on 'fair' meaning 'blonde')   (2002, 2008)

1 black ... fair 'Black was not formerly regarded as beautiful' (see headnote to this sonnet);[48] 'fair' puns on blonde. The assertion in Sonnet 127 that black is beautiful is reminiscent of Berowne's description of the dark-haired Rosaline in *Love's Labour's Lost*   (2018)

1 black ... fair   (no gloss, 2020)[49]

Editors cannot agree how extensive the dark features of the Mistress are – Is it just hair? Hair and eyes? Complexion? – and they avoid acknowledging the implications of their choices, as though the reader is not likely to make assumptions about race from these somatic markers. But what makes Sonnet 127 a particularly fascinating example of the way in which editorial practice can obscure Blackness is how this obfuscation extends beyond the notes and into the text itself. As reproduced above from the 1609 Quarto, lines 9–10 repeat the term 'eyes': 'Therefore my Mistress' eyes are Raven black, / Her eyes so suited ...'. Uncomfortable with this 'lame repetition',[50] and frustrated at the suspension of the *blazon* which usually moves down or across the body, as implied here by the notion of something being 'suited' or matched *to* something else, some editors have changed the second 'eyes' to 'hairs', 'brows' or even 'brow', in a way that also has implications for the woman's racial identity, though again this is rarely acknowledged.[51] I am not suggesting

---

[44] MacDonald, 'The legend of Lucy Negro', pp. 68–9.
[45] See Hall, *Things of Darkness*, pp. 211–53.
[46] Both Robert Fleissner and Duncan Salkeld have noted the recurrence of this trope of the jewel in the Ethiope's ear in Shakespeare's work as potentially suggestive of Shakespeare's own encounter with a Black woman. See Robert F. Fleissner, '"That cheek of night": toward the Dark Lady', *CLA Journal* 16 (1973), 312–23, and Salkeld, 'Black Luce and Sonnets 127–54'.
[47] MacDonald, 'The legend of Lucy Negro', p. 72.
[48] The headnote explains that this sonnet is 'the first sonnet, in Q's sequence, addressed to a dark-haired, dark-eyed mistress' (*Complete Poems*, ed. Shrank and Lyne, p. 556).
[49] *Shakespeare's Sonnets*, ed. Duncan-Jones, p. 368; *Complete Poems*, ed. Burrow, p. 634; *Complete Poems*, ed. Shrank and Lyne, p. 556; and *All the Sonnets*, ed. Wells and Edmondson, p. 55. The fact that Wells and Edmondson don't gloss 'black' here, but explain in the one-line paraphrase for this sonnet that '[a]lthough black used not to be considered beautiful, my mistress is now making it so, and better than any fair beauty enhanced by cosmetics', leaves it up to the reader to supply the racial implications. As in Shrank and Lyne above, the dramatic analogy of *Love's Labour's Lost* potentially steers it away from a racialized reading.
[50] See *Shakespeare's Sonnets*, ed. W. G. Ingram and Theodore Redpath (New York, 1964, 1978), p. 290.
[51] Duncan-Jones (*Shakespeare's Sonnets*, p. 368) and Stephen Booth (*Shakespeare's Sonnets*, ed. Booth (New Haven and London, 1977), pp. 436–7) stick to the authorized reading of Q. Kerrigan (*The Sonnets and A Lover's Complaint*, ed. John Kerrigan (Harmondsworth, 1987), p. 354) and

that the decision to retain 'eyes' is necessarily intended to keep the sonnet at a distance from racial Blackness – Duncan-Jones justifies the deliberate repetition, and it is in this form that the poem was reprinted by John Benson in 1640 – but the choice *not* to amend may subconsciously respond to the pull of Sir Philip Sidney's *Astrophil and Stella* 7:

> When nature made her chief work, Stella's eyes,
> In colour black why wrapped she beams so bright?
> Would she in beamy black, like painter wise,
> Frame daintiest lustre, mixed of shades and light?
> Or did she else that sober hue devise,
> In object best to knit and strength our sight,
> Lest, if no veil these brave gleams did disguise,
> They, sun-like, should more dazzle than delight?
> Or would she her miraculous power show,
> That, whereas black seems beauty's contrary,
> She even in black doth make all beauties flow?
> Both so, and thus: she, minding love should be
> Placed ever there, gave him this mourning weed
> To honour all their deaths, who for her bleed.[52]

This poem does seem likely to have been Shakespeare's model when he composed Sonnet 127,[53] but the difference of tone is rarely remarked on. In Sidney's poem, Nature makes Stella's eyes black to demonstrate Nature's power to create beauty, despite 'black seem[ing] beauty's contrary', and to acknowledge Stella's power to make men die for love by placing Cupid in mourning. By contrast, Shakespeare dispenses with Nature entirely, and replaces this positive image of female artistic power with a negative one, introducing a misogynistic anti-cosmetics argument which sees his mistress mourning other women's transgressions rather than their destructive beauty.[54] 'In the old days' is more often used as a term of nostalgia in Shakespeare, and it is in this context that blackness has displaced 'Sweet beauty', clearly coded as white, which now lives in 'disgrace', meaning shame and ill repute and also ill-favouredness or disfigurement.[55] Having dismissed the possibility that white beauty can be redeemed, the sonnet moves on to a limited praise of his mistress's Black beauty, though she herself continues to 'mourn' and to express 'woe' at the loss of a white ideal. This is far from a positive recommendation of Black beauty and reads more as an elaborate defence of the speaker's own 'aberrant' taste. As Vendler notes, this is a 'myth of origin' sonnet: 'How did a black-haired, black-eyed woman come to be the reigning heir of beauty? ... the speaker finds himself attracted not to a conventionally beautiful fair woman, but to a dark-eyed woman, and must explain this aesthetically anomalous choice.'[56] A sense that Shakespeare's speaker is racially transgressive in his preferences, that he is not attracted to 'fair' in the way that he should be, also potentially resonates through other poems, for example Sonnet 137, which begins 'Thou blind fool Love, what dost thou to mine eyes ... ?' or 148, which ends with Cupid keeping the speaker blind, 'Lest eyes, well seeing, thy foul faults should find!'

Rather than allow its Sidneyan progenitor to pull Sonnet 127 back to Caucasian darkness, we

---

Burrow (*Complete Poems*, p. 634) choose 'brows', partly on the basis of the similarity between this sonnet and the passage in *Love's Labour's Lost*, where Berowne muses:

> O, if in black my lady's brows be decked,
> It mourns that painting and usurping hair
> Should ravish doters with a false aspect
>
> (4.3.256–8)

Ingram and Redpath choose 'brow' which opens up the possibility of the 'whole countenance' and therefore of Black skin (*Shakespeare's Sonnets*, 264–5).

[52] *Sir Philip Sidney: The Major Works*, ed. Katherine Duncan-Jones (Oxford, 2002), p. 155.
[53] See *The Sonnets*, ed. Kerrigan, pp. 352–3.
[54] See Frances E. Dolan's discussion of the limitations on female creativity and social position expressed through the cosmetics debate in 'Taking the pencil out of God's hand: art, nature and the face-painting debate in early modern England', *PMLA* 108 (1993), 224–39; and Farah Karim-Cooper, *Cosmetics in Shakespearean and Renaissance Drama* (Edinburgh, 2006), pp. 13–15, pp. 132–75.
[55] *Sonnets*, ed. Booth, p. 435. Without wishing to place any weight on the traditional bipartite division, I find it notable that the only uses of 'sweet' as an adjective occur in Sonnets 1–80 and, where the addressee is gendered, they are only identified with the Fair Young Man: in Sonnets 1 and 4, the speaker refers to 'thy sweet self' (8, 10); in Sonnet 63, 'My sweet love's beauty' (12).

might look ahead to the later seventeenth-century defences of Blackness in lyric poetry. Line 13, 'Yet so they mourn becoming of their woe', not only resonates with the conventional humoral and Petrarchan association of Blackness with grief, but also anticipates the use of mourning to describe Blackness in, for example, George Herbert's Latin poem 'Aethiopissa', where the Black female protagonist explains her colour by the prospect of imminent rejection: 'Lo, Grief's prophetic hue my cheek imbues'.[57] But I would argue that a neglected – though richer (and earlier) – source of analogues for Sonnet 127 can be found in early modern drama's fascination with Black characters. In *Titus Andronicus*, for example, Aaron extols the virtues of his skin colour:

> Coal-black is better than another hue
> In that it scorns to bear another hue;
> For all the water in the ocean
> Can never turn the swan's black legs to white
>
> (4.2.98–101)

This insistence on the authenticity and permanence of Black skin also recurs in Ben Jonson's *The Masque of Blackness* (performed 1605, printed 1608), where Niger explains that the sun originally burned his daughters' skin to draw 'in their firm [i.e. constant] hues'

> Signs of his fervent'st love; and thereby shows
> That in their black the perfect'st beauty grows;
> Since the fixed colour of their curlèd hair
> (Which is the highest grace of dames most fair)
> No cares, no age can change, or there display
> The fearful tincture of abhorrèd grey;
> Since Death herself (herself being pale and blue)
> Can never alter their most faithful hue[.][58]

Here, Black beauty seems to defy the ravages of Time, a power denied the Fair Young Man of the *Sonnets*, whose physical decay is repeatedly foretold. Moreover, where Death produces pallor in her victims (she herself being 'pale and blue'), she has no power over Black beauty, implying the daughters' immortality as well as their resistance to physical change. It is only because of the prejudices of 'brain-sick men', i.e. poets, who prefer

'The painted beauties other empires sprung',[59] that Niger's daughters now seek to be whitened. Finally, we might compare Sonnet 127 with Nathan Field, Philip Massinger and John Fletcher's tragicomedy, *The Knight of Malta* (c.1616–19), which post-dates the publication of the *Sonnets* but extends their opposition of Black female beauty and white cosmetic deception. Here, Zanthia, the 'Moore Servant to Oriana', is described as 'My Pearl, that scornes a stain' by her white lover, Mountferrat. She refuses to flatter him in return:

> My tongue Sir, cannot lisp to meet you so,
> Nor my black cheek put on a feigned blush,
> To make this seem more modest than I am.
> This ground-work,[60] will not bear adulterate red,
> Nor artificial white, to cozen love.
> These dark locks are not purchas'd, nor these teeth,
> For every night, they are my bed-fellows;
> No bath, no blanching water; smoothing oyles,
> Doth mend me up[61]

Whilst this passage tacitly invokes the much quoted premodern proverb about the impossibility of washing the Ethiope white,[62] it also foregrounds cosmetic treatments: the 'adulterate red',

---

[57] Reprinted and discussed in Hall, *Things of Darkness*, p. 117.
[58] Ben Jonson, *The Masque of Blackness*, ed. David Lindley, in *The Cambridge Edition of the Works of Ben Jonson*, ed. David Bevington, Martin Butler and Ian Donaldson, 7 vols. (Cambridge, 2012), vol. 2, lines 103–10. On the connection between blackness and constancy, see Mary Floyd-Wilson, 'Temperature, temperance and racial difference in Ben Jonson's *The Masque of Blackness*', *ELR* 28 (1998), 183–209; pp. 205–6, and Spiller, *Reading and the History of Race in the Renaissance*, ch. 4.
[59] Jonson, *Masque of Blackness*, line 118.
[60] 'Ground-work' refers to the basis of both a painting and a cosmeticised face that takes on other colours, though it could also be 'that portion of a surface, which is not coloured, decorated or operated upon' (*OED Online*, sense 6b).
[61] Nathan Field, Philip Massinger and John Fletcher, *The Knight of Malta*, in *The Works of Francis Beaumont and John Fletcher*, ed. A. R. Waller, 10 vols. (Cambridge, 1909), vol. 7, pp. 83, 84.
[62] See Hall, *Things of Darkness*, pp. 66–9, and Anu Kornohen, 'Washing the Ethiopian white: conceptualising black skin in Renaissance England', in *Black Africans in Renaissance Europe*,

'artificial white' and 'blanching water' used to produce false beauty in white women. It is also notable that the Black woman is now the pearl, rather than being the backdrop that sets off a pearl.

In all three cases, there is an irony at play, given that the performance of Blackness is itself cosmetic. This is implied by Aaron's reference to being 'Coal-black', with coal dust a common material used to produce Blackness on the stage.[63] In the *Masque of Blackness*, the 'tincture' of white women ironically reminds the audience of the make-up used to create the more authentic hue, and in *The Knight of Malta*, Zanthia's 'dark locks', which cannot be 'purchas'd', are very likely a theatrical wig. This might also be a paradox that underpins Sonnet 127. Ian Smith has brilliantly suggested a pun on 'sooted' in 'Her eyes so suited', i.e. made black by the application of soot.[64] Since soot was used to blacken the skin rather than the eyes, it might reinforce the argument that 'eyes' in line 10 should be replaced by something like 'brows' or 'brow', but as a form of theatrical artifice it might also undermine any potentially positive associations of Black beauty in the sonnets. Andrea Stevens explores how *The Masque of Blackness* undercuts the authenticity it claims for Blackness: 'Exploiting the connection between paint and theatricality helps [Jonson] discredit the more positive significations of black skin and confirm whiteness as a temperate norm.'[65] The 'suit'/'soot' pun in Sonnet 127 might equally draw attention to the deceptiveness of the Mistress who only 'seems' to mourn.[66]

This debate over which colour is most 'authentic' – most resistant to artifice or deception or contamination – naturally shapes the representation not only of Blackness in the sonnets but also of whiteness, expressed not only through the 'characters' of the Fair Young Man and the Poet-Lover, but also the language and materiality of the *Sonnets* themselves, and it is to this that we must now turn.

THE NOT-SO-WHITE OR FAIR YOUNG MAN

We are familiar now with readings of the opening statement of Sonnet 1, 'From fairest creatures we desire increase', as being as much a eugenic argument as a moral or aesthetic one. In '"These bastard signs of fair"', Hall indicts fairness as 'an emergent ideology of white supremacy',[67] and editors are increasingly alert to the privileging of whiteness which is implicit in the *Sonnets*, although there is still work to be done. In 1997, the line 'A man in hue, all hues in his controlling' in Sonnet 20 (7) did not require an explanation that included 'colour': 'denot[ing] either "form, aspect", or "external appearance of the face" (*OED* 1a and 2)';[68] by 2008, the gloss included 'able by nature to adopt the perfect colouring of any

---

ed. Thomas F. Earle and Kate J. P. Lowe (Cambridge, 2005), 94–112.
[63] On the history of blackface performance, see Ayanna Thompson, *Blackface* (London, 2021), and Miles P. Grier, *Inkface: Othello and White Authority in the Era of Atlantic Slavery* (Charlottesville, VA, 2023).
[64] Smith, 'White skin, black masks', p. 52.
[65] Andrea Stevens, 'Mastering masques of Blackness: Jonson's *Masque of Blackness*, the Windsor text of *The Gypsies Metamorphosed*, and Brome's *The English Moor*', ELR 39 (2009), 396–426; p. 408.
[66] The pun on 'suit'/'soot' is even clearer in Sonnet 132, in which the speaker implores the mistress to put on mourning:

> And suit thy pity like in every part.
> Then will I swear beauty herself is black,
> And all they foul that thy complexion lack.
>
> (12–14)

The mistress should mourn with her heart, as well as with her skin, and should 'suit thy pity like in every part', i.e. make that emotional response black in the way that the rest of her body is. If she does this, the speaker will produce a poem like Sonnet 127, in which he de-thrones Beauty and replaces it with blackness.
[67] Hall, '"These bastard signs of fair"', p. 67. See also Ian Smith, *Black Shakespeare: Reading and Misreading Race* (Cambridge, 2022); Little Jr, ed., *White People*; and David Sterling Brown, *Shakespeare's White Others* (Cambridge, 2023).
[68] This is Duncan-Jones's annotation to Sonnet 20 (*Shakespeare's Sonnets*, p. 150), although she does refer to colour in the note to Sonnet 82, line 5, 'Thou art as fair in knowledge as in hue', which is glossed as: 'external appearance, colour (*OED* 1, 2, 3a)' (p. 274).

complexion, including that of a woman ... so comely that all complexions (blushing or turning pale) lie in his power'.[69] In 2023, we might want to go further and call this out as whiteness, not least because of Francesca T. Royster's work on *Titus Andronicus*, in which she shows Shakespeare repeatedly using the term 'hue' to describe extreme whiteness, as when he has Saturninus observe of Tamora: 'A goodly lady ... of the hue / That I would choose, were I to choose anew' (1.1.261–2).[70] As Royster notes: 'The critical assumption that a reference to skin color can mean only "black" or "colored" seems based on a belief that white is not a hue, that whiteness is not "racial".'[71] I would suggest that the line 'A man in hue, all hues in his controlling' should be glossed to reflect not only the fact that white light contains all the other colours, but that whiteness is the privileged complexion in early modern culture, and hence confers both power and control.[72]

Elsewhere in the *Sonnets*, however, the supremacy of whiteness is less secure and in its failure it becomes more visible. This is partly because the immorality of the Young Man puts his own whiteness metaphorically, if not literally, at risk, as in Sonnet 35 which begins with numerous examples of discoloration:

No more be grieved at that which thou hast done:
Roses have thorns, and silver fountains mud.
Clouds and eclipses stain both moon and sun,
And loathsome canker lives in sweetest bud.

(1–4)

Although 'canker' in line 4 has sometimes been glossed as the 'caterpillar or cankerworm (*OED* 4)' which eats the rosebud from within,[73] it could equally be the disease ('canker', *OED* 5a) which produces black spots on the leaves and stems of roses.[74] Whilst syphilis produced literal dark patches on the skin, this staining is also a consequence of the moral corruption which the speaker perceives in him. Indeed, it has been argued that the couplet of Sonnet 147 is equally as appropriate to the Fair Young Man as it is to the Black Mistress: 'For I have sworn thee fair and thought thee bright, / Who art as black as hell, as dark as night' (13–14).[75] I would argue that this increasing resemblance between the Black Mistress and the Young Man fundamentally informs Sonnet 144, whose racecraft emerges as an attempt to create difference.

The first four lines of the Sonnet suggest a fundamental opposition:

Two loves I have, of comfort and despair,
Which, like two spirits, do suggest me still.
The better angel is a man right fair,
The worser spirit a woman coloured ill.

(144.1–4)

As we have seen, this juxtaposition is not usually identified as a racial one. When the phrases 'coloured ill' and 'ill coloured' occur elsewhere in the literature of the period, they do so overwhelmingly in medical tracts, particularly as symptoms of lovesickness and pregnancy.[76] They also appear in the

---

[69] *Complete Poems*, ed. Burrow, p. 420.
[70] Francesca T. Royster, 'White-limed walls: whiteness and Gothic extremism in Shakespeare's *Titus Andronicus*', *Shakespeare Quarterly* 51 (2000), 432–55; p. 433.
[71] Royster, 'White-limed walls', p. 434.
[72] See also Smith's argument: 'Devised as a non-color because it consists of all colors, whiteness can evade responsibility for attending to race, since blackness bears the burden of high visibility, racial attribution, and cultural embodiment of the thing itself. That is, this silent, invisible racial majority can suspend direct, responsible involvement, rely on the privileges of being merely human and redirect all things racial elsewhere' (*Black Shakespeare*, p. 85).
[73] *Shakespeare's Sonnets*, ed. Duncan-Jones, p. 180.
[74] See also the Young Man's beauty being 'spot[ted]' by canker in Sonnet 95. For further discussion of the moral, spiritual and creative resonance of spots in Shakespeare's work, see Sophie Chiari, 'Shakespeare's poetics of impurity: spots, stains, and slime', *Études Épistémè*, 33 (2018), https://doi.org/10.4000/episteme.2164.
[75] Heather Dubrow, '"Incertainties now crown themselves assur'd": the politics of plotting Shakespeare's Sonnets', *Shakespeare Quarterly* 47 (1996), 291–305; p. 295. See also Schalkwyk ('Race, body and language', p. 19), who argues that '[f]ar from being the dark foil by which the fair friend's fairness may shine ever more brightly, the woman reveals the *darkness* of both her player-poet and his Dark Lord'.
[76] See, for example, *The Whole Aphorismes of great Hippocrates* (London, 1610), translated into English by S. H.: 'If a woman conceiued with childe doe beare a manchilde shee is well and fresh coloured: if shee beare a maide childe, she is ill coloured' (p. 96, no. 42).

anti-cosmetic debate. In the poem 'To painted women', affixed to Thomas Tuke's *A Discourse Against Painting and Tincturing of Women* (1616), Edward Tylman suggests that women will not necessarily be praised by men for their use of cosmetics, for 'who would willingly her beauty saint, / Whose face ill-colour'd is clouded o're with paint?'.[77] The fact that Sonnet 144 first appeared in print in William Jaggard's collection *The Passionate Pilgrim* (1599) probably encouraged readers to interpret 'coloured ill' as referring to pallor, brought on by sickness or love, rather than Blackness, because the poem does not sit within any sustained discussion of the properties of black and fair, as it does in the Quarto.

And yet, one of the early modern explanations for how Black Africans came to have their complexion was that they had painted colour onto their skin, which then became permanent. So John Bulwer notes in 1653 that 'divers affectations of painting' led the Moors to become permanently Black by an 'artificiall way of denigration'.[78] And as Sonnet 144 evolves from the version in *The Passionate Pilgrim* to that in the Quarto, a change is made which reinforces an opposition between the man and woman based on colour. Where line 8 in *The Passionate Pilgrim* reads, 'Wooing his purity with her faire pride', Q revises the line: 'Wooing his purity with her fowle pride'.[79] 'Foul' has a variety of derogatory meanings in Shakespeare's work, but it is often coupled with Black imagery, for example in Sonnet 132: 'Then will I swear beauty herself is black, / And all they foul that thy complexion lack' (13–14).[80] The decision to take 'fair' away from the woman and identify it solely with the man increases the racial polarity between the protagonists, and reinforces the association of Blackness with immorality. If this was Shakespeare's work, then he may have done something similar with *Othello* where, as Leah Marcus has observed, the Folio contains markedly more racial pejoratives than the Quarto, and accordingly sharpens the contrast between Black Othello and Fair Desdemona.

What *Othello* does, and much more explicitly and powerfully in F than in Q, is enact a process by which skin color comes to be associated even by Othello himself with innate differences that demand his subordination or exclusion on ethical grounds ... If Shakespeare was the reviser who turned Q into F, then he revised in the direction of racial virulence.[81]

Elsewhere in Sonnet 144, I would argue that there are hints of a material, racial difference between the Young Man and the Black Mistress, which simultaneously reveal how tenuous is their moral difference. The poet raises his anxiety about not being able to judge whether the Young Man is corrupted or not:

And whether that my angel be turned fiend
Suspect I may, yet not directly tell;
But being both from me, both to each friend,
I guess one angel in another's hell.
  Yet this shall I ne'er know, but live in doubt
  Till my bad angel fire my good one out.
          (144.9–14)

'Fire my good one out' probably does primarily refer to the burning of venereal infection, which the poet will discover if he is himself infected by the woman, as most editors note. However, stage tradition also had a more literal answer to the question of how to tell if one's

---

[77] Edward Tylman, 'To painted women', in Thomas Tuke, *A Discourse Against Painting and Tincturing of Women* (London, 1616), n.p.

[78] John Bulwer, *Anthropometamorphosis: Man Transform'd: or The Artificiall Changling* (London, 1653), pp. 468–9. For further discussion of the contemporary idea of Blackness as 'defined by an anterior whiteness' so that 'black finds itself expressed as ornament, as an overlay of whiteness', see Dympna Callaghan, *Shakespeare without Women: Representing Gender and Race on the Renaissance Stage* (London and New York, 2000), p. 79.

[79] William Shakespeare, *The Passionate Pilgrime* (London, 1599); for the Quarto, see n. 42.

[80] See also David Sterling Brown's argument about *Macbeth*'s 'Fair is foul and foul is fair', in *Shakespeare's White Others*, though here 'whiteness polices blackness to negotiate its own meaning in the absence of Black people' (pp. 37–8).

[81] Leah Marcus, 'Constructions of race and gender in the two texts of *Othello*', in *Rethinking Feminism in Early Modern Studies: Gender, Race and Sexuality*, ed. Ania Loomba and Melissa E. Sanchez (London, 2016), 113–32; p. 123.

'angel be turned fiend'. Devils and damned souls were frequently depicted with darkened skin in medieval painting and subsequently in mystery cycles and guild pageants. Virginia Mason Vaughan notes that, in the late fifteenth-century Coventry *Creation*, Lucifer states after the fall, 'I am a devyl ful derke / that was An Aungell bryht', and, more recently for Shakespeare, a stage direction in Thomas Lupton's moral interlude *All for Money* (1578) reads: '*Iudas commeth in like a damned soule, in blacke*'.[82] Sonnet 144 might well suggest that the man will only know his male lover has been in hell (with a play on the Mistress's genitals),[83] when he appears blackened by her, thinking of the stage practice of signifying damnation in this way, with a visceral link between soot and the fires of hell. Black skin was represented through the same sooty cosmetics as that used to signify fallen characters and, as Morwenna Carr observes: 'Soot and coal render the person who has been crudely smeared with them unreadable; the application of these flat cosmetics renders the planes of the face stiff and without depth from reflections, thus obliterating both the features and delicate facial movements of anyone to whom they are applied.'[84] If the Fair Young Man is blackened by physical contact with the Mistress, he is also rendered less easy to read.

And yet, the Poet is hardly an innocent participant in the conversion of the beloved from white to black, and an increasingly notorious case in point is Sonnet 4. Here, the speaker addresses the Young Man as 'beauteous niggard', and in Sonnet 1 he uses the term 'niggarding' (12). The *OED* and subsequent editors of this poem tell us that the etymology of 'niggard' and the highly offensive racial slur are different.[85] If we look at the use of the former as it appears in Sonnet 4, the immediate parallel does not imply any racial significance: 'Unthrifty loveliness' ('wasteful beauty') is inverted in the phrase 'beauteous niggard' ('lovely miser'). The supposed race-innocence of the phrase might be strengthened by the fact that Thomas Heywood, who has clearly been reading the *Sonnets*, uses it in his Cupid and Psyche play, *Love's Mistress* (1636), when he has Psyche uncover the form of her sleeping lover as Cupid and exclaim: 'Churle beauty, beautious nigard, thus Ile chide, / Why did'st thou from mine eyes this glory hide?'[86] Yet we cannot discount the possibility of a racist subtext, given Shakespeare's habit elsewhere of juxtaposing blackness and beauty, and it seems unlikely that he would have been oblivious to the similarity of 'niggard' and 'neigar', 'nigor', 'negar', 'nyger', all terms used to signify Black men and women in early modern parish records.[87] As Habib notes,

if 'niger', meaning black in Latin, becomes 'negro' meaning a black person in Spanish-Portuguese, and 'negre' in middle French and 'neger' in early modern English evolve with the same meaning – that is a racialization process because it essentializes a physical attribute; a color becomes an essential determinant of a person which then is made to signify the entirety of the individual (without the same happening to white people in that moment). The word cannot be neutral, irrespective of whether the negative, racializing connotations show up obviously in it.[88]

In this context, 'beauteous niggard' becomes a threat to the white beloved, warning that he will incur a slander that is intensified by being racialized.[89]

---

[82] Virginia Mason Vaughan, *Performing Blackness on English Stages, 1500–1800* (Cambridge, 2005), p. 21, p. 23.

[83] See *Shakespeare's Sonnets*, ed. Duncan-Jones, pp. 403–4, n. 12.

[84] Carr, 'Material/blackness', p. 83.

[85] The *OED* identifies 'niggard' as a derivation of 'nig', a Middle English word based on old Scandinavian, meaning a miserly person, whilst the highly offensive racial slur derives from various terms for 'black'.

[86] Thomas Heywood, *Loves Maistresse* (London, 1636), sig. F3v.

[87] I am indebted to Lynne Magnusson, who recently described her experience of teaching the *Sonnets* and the distress it had caused one of her students when they had come in late and overheard the reading aloud of Sonnet 4, specifically the phrase 'Beauteous niggard'. Even if this had been carefully glossed in the text (which it isn't), this student would not have benefitted from that explanation. Instead, they were confronted with a lecturer reading Shakespeare using a term that they found triggering in a way that they hadn't been prepared for, and which many of us wouldn't have thought we needed to prepare them for, because for us it means something else.

[88] Habib, *Black Lives in the English Archives*, p. 12.

[89] Although editors do not approach the phrase in this way, at least one recent critic, Carol Mejia LaPerle, describes this and 'profitless usurer' as 'Racial slurs that evoke anti-Semitism and anti-Blackness ... deployed to emphasize that the fair friend is neither of these identities' (n.p.).

THE RACE-ING OF PRAISE

This brings us finally to the racial identity of the Poet himself, and his project of celebrating the Fair Young Man through writing. In his essay 'Is it possible to read Shakespeare through Critical White Studies?', Little asks:

> Who are Shakespeare's white characters? Are some of Shakespeare's characters that we may uncritically think of as white not actually white? How white are Shakespeare's more explicitly non-white characters, given the fact they were created by a white playwright? How white are Shakespeare's works? How white is Shakespeare?[90]

There are some subtle suggestions in the *Sonnets* that the speaker does not consider himself 'fair' enough.[91] If Sonnet 1 places emphasis on 'fairness' as an attribute which 'we', i.e. white people, wish to see perpetuated, 'From fairest creatures we desire increase' excludes the speaker from that category of the 'fairest', which we might expand to mean not only the most socially elevated and beautiful but also the whitest. In Sonnet 135, the speaker tries to persuade the mistress to satisfy his desires by emphasizing his similarity to the other 'Will' who has been accepted: 'Shall will in others seem right gracious, / And in my will no fair acceptance shine?' (7–8). Although the 'fair acceptance' should presumably be identified with the mistress, its absence implies that the speaker himself is less (or even not) 'fair'. Similarly, the final couplet reads: 'Let no unkind no fair beseechers kill; / Think all but one, and me in that one Will' (13–14). If this particular beseecher is being denied, does that imply he is not 'fair'? Elsewhere, there is a suggestion that the speaker's profession has blackened him. In Sonnet 111, he deplores the necessity to make his fortune by public means:

> Thence comes it that my name receives a brand,
> And almost thence my nature is subdued
> To what it works in, like the dyer's hand
> (5–7)

If to be dyed is a professional hazard for the inky poet, then it is not only he who bears the stain. One of the recurrent paradoxes around blackness in the *Sonnets* is the use of black ink to immortalize fair beauty.[92] This is tacit in the conclusion of Sonnet 65, where the speaker despairs at the possibility of preserving the beloved from the ravages of time: 'unless this miracle have might: / That in black ink my love may still shine bright' (13–14). The penultimate line of Sonnet 63 also contemplates the paradox that 'His beauty shall in these black lines be seen'. But, as Farah Karim-Cooper notes, 'Textual production is racially charged when looked at from a material perspective. Ink is black and the same materials used to make black ink (galls and alums) were used in some cosmetic preparations as well.'[93] Ink was imagined as an equivalent means of blacking-up in *Mr Moore's Revels* (1636), a masque performed at Oxford, in which four boys came on stage to impersonate adult 'moores', with one holding 'an inkehorne in his hand to blacke themselves'.[94] But this identification of racial Blackness with ink was more than skin deep. In his attempt to understand the causes of Blackness, Thomas Browne argues that chemicals worked within the body to produce blackness in much the same way as one produces ink: so that 'bodies become blacke' through 'an Atramentous ['black as ink', *OED*] condition or mixture, that is a vitriolate [of vitriol] or copperose [of copperas][95] quality

---

[90] Little, 'Is it possible?' p. 275.
[91] See also Brown's work on the creation of the white other, 'a figure like Richard III, Tamora, or Macbeth who is not "white enough" or who registers as less-than-ideal', in *Shakespeare's White Others* (p. 5). Brown does not extend this argument to the *Sonnets*, but it is very suggestive in relation to them.
[92] See Mitchell M. Harris, 'The expense of ink and wastes of shame: poetic generation, black ink and material waste in Shakespeare's Sonnets', in *The Materiality of Color: The Production, Circulation, and Application of Dyes and Pigments, 1400–1800*, ed. Andrea Feeser, Maureen Daly Goggin and Beth Fowkes Tobin (Farnham, 2012), 65–80.
[93] Karim-Cooper, *Cosmetics*, p. 167.
[94] John R. Elliott, 'Mr Moores Revels: a "lost" Oxford masque', *Renaissance Quarterly* 37 (1989), 411–20; p. 417.
[95] See the *OED* definition of 'copperose' (noun): 'A name given from early times to the protosulphates of copper, iron, and zinc … it has always been most commonly, and is now exclusively, applied to *green* copperas, the proto-sulphate of iron or ferrous sulphate … used in dyeing, tanning, and making ink.'

conjoyning with a terrestrious and astringent humidity, for so is *Atramentum scriptorium*, or writing Inke commonly made, by copperose cast upon a decoction or infusion of galls'.[96] However, the operation of ink to make men and women Black also operated at an ideological level, if we consider the impact of the printing trade. In a fascinating article on the impact of switching from a range of chromatic inks in manuscript to the black and white of the printing press, Averyl Dieterling explores 'how print illustrations of blackness were deployed to foster the growth of a white English identity that defined itself in opposition to blackness'.[97] She demonstrates, for example, how the techniques for creating black bodies on the page obscured the facial features and therefore the psychological depth of those illustrated in this way, thereby creating and perpetuating a set of racist assumptions about Black people:

> Such illustrations signal to the white English reader that they need not be concerned about the fact that it is difficult to read detail or emotion in black bodies. After all, these black bodies are not really imagined as individuals: just as they lack visual dimensionality, they also lack affective dimensionality. Because they lack individuality and affective dimensionality, they are not human beings like the white bodies; they do not have access to that ontological status.[98]

Whilst there are obviously no visual illustrations of the Fair Young Man in Shakespeare's sonnets (there are, in fact, very few details of his appearance), we might find this fear of misrepresentation imagined through the spectre of 'gross painting' in Sonnet 82. Here we find the speaker contrasting his poetic technique with that of his rivals. Where they rely on the 'strainèd touches' of rhetoric (10),

> Thou, truly fair, wert truly sympathized
> In true plain words by thy true-telling friend;
>   And their gross painting might be better used
>   Where cheeks need blood: in thee it is abused.
>   (82.11–14)

This sonnet has ostensibly nothing to do with race. And yet its concern with literary and rhetorical colouring, and with the representation of the beloved, creates a particular charge around the word 'gross'. This term, which occurs sixty-eight times in Shakespeare with a rich array of meanings, brings together a sense of something that is palpable or obvious, with something crude, rough, unrefined, impure. It bears specific references to paint and painting: paint was created by a process of repeated refinement, whereby 'the grosser body' of the materials is left at the bottom of a basin and discarded.[99] It is also an adverb used to describe the efforts of the unskilful or untalented painter (here a metaphor for the rhetorician), 'that hath pourtraied those things coursly and grosely, which shoulde haue beene painted with fair and fresh colours'.[100] But it is probably most familiar to Shakespearians from *Othello*, where its racial charge becomes clear, as in Roderigo's description of 'fair' Desdemona transported 'To the gross clasps of a lascivious Moor' (1.1.128). Here, the materiality signified by grossness, which also stands in for sexual appetite, contaminates Desdemona, who takes on the epithet when she is later accused of a 'gross revolt' (136). For Bovilsky, the gross/fair opposition represents one of the ways in which Othello's blackness is used to intensify 'the racialized association of marriage and adultery' in the play: 'As long as female desire is identified with "gross" transformation and female chastity with unmatchable purity, all the possibilities imagined for marriage in *Othello* are interracial or racially compromising ones.'[101] If we apply a similar logic to Sonnet 82, the poet's claim to distinguish his

---

[96] Thomas Browne, *Pseudodoxia Epidemica* (London, 1646), p. 527.
[97] Averyl Dieterling, 'Black ink, white feelings: early modern print technology and anti-black racism', in *Race and Affect*, ed. LaPerle, n.p.
[98] Dieterling, 'Black ink, white feelings', n.p. See also Miles P. Grier's important discussion of what it meant to be a 'creature of ink' at this time in 'Inkface: the slave stigma in England's early imperial imagination', in *Scripturalizing the Human: The Written as Political*, ed. Vincent L. Wimbush (London, 2015), 193–220.
[99] See, for example, Alexander Browne's *Ars Pictoria or, An Academy Treating of Drawing, Painting, Limning, and Etching* (London, 1669).
[100] See Robert Wolcomb, *The State of the Godly Both in this Life, and in the Life to Come* (London, 1606), p. 83.
[101] Bovilsky, *Barbarous Play*, p. 59, p. 64.

poetic representations of the beloved from the 'gross painting' of others extends beyond the metaphor of cosmetic or artistic misrepresentation to a notion of racial misrepresentation: not only an impure, corporeal blurring of his fineness, but a darkening of his fairness. This is a kind of racial painting which 'denigrates' the beloved, in the full sense of that word, extending the inky blots and stains of the writer to the person he is trying to describe and, indeed, to praise.

CONCLUSION

This article has argued that we still have more work to do to understand the racial implications of both blackness and whiteness in the *Sonnets*, and that editors have a responsibility to open this up for readers more than they have done so far. As Colin Burrow points out, '[e]diting a text is part of a conversation about that text, and it is an act of accommodating a text to a particular audience.'[102] Attention to the racial aspects of Shakespeare's *Sonnets*, in terms of verbal imagery and materiality as well as characterization, is something that readers today bring to the text, and if editors believe it to be anachronistic they should at least try to explain why and how it is so to their readers. One thing that might emerge from paying more attention to the racecraft of the *Sonnets* is an understanding of the extent to which the speaker is often aware that he constructs the colour of the mistress depending on his own desires. In Sonnet 131, he attests: 'Thy black is fairest in my judgement's place' (12). The same sonnet also shows an awareness that Blackness as a somatic feature may be subject to moral and aesthetic judgements, but also eludes them: 'In nothing art thou black save in thy deeds, / And thence this slander, as I think, proceeds' (13–14). The recognition that blackness is a form of verbal slander, created by the poet, rather than an intrinsic quality possessed by the beloved, is amply demonstrated by the ways in which Black Mistress, Fair Youth and Poet-Lover are all 'blackened' by the sonnets themselves. Indeed, we might come to see the sonnets as a space in which Shakespeare was working out a bigger question whose racist consequences he seems intermittently aware of: what does it take to become black and how does one become fair?

---

[102] Colin Burrow, 'Editing the Sonnets', in *A Companion to Shakespeare's Sonnets*, ed. Schoenfeldt, 145–62; p. 158.

ALLEGORICAL DESIRE, OR, THE SUFI 'PHOENIX AND THE TURTLE'

MADHAVI MENON

Don't mend what's torn, what's sewn together tear!
(Farid ud-din Attar, *Mantiq-al-Tayr* (1177 CE))[1]

Sewn into centuries of brilliant Shakespeare scholarship is a robust thread of European provincialism: scholars tend not to consider texts from outside Europe as interlocutors for Shakespeare's poetry and plays.[2] Non-European texts are welcome if they illuminate plot points (about shipwrecks in the Americas, for instance), or if they are adaptations of an English master (such as Akira Kurosawa's *Throne of Blood*). But other than these two categories of source and consequence, Shakespeare scholarship is squarely European in matters of intellectual engagement. The Norton Shakespeare's introduction to 'The Phoenix and the Turtle' – an allegorical poem about two birds, published in 1601 – is instructive in this regard. Discussing the paradoxes that riddle Shakespeare's poem, the introduction notes that '[b]ehind the emphasis on the paradoxical unity of two separate beings lies the mystery of the Christian Trinity as understood in Scholastic theology.'[3] This emphasis on Christianity occurs despite the opening lines of the poem, which announce:

> Let the bird of loudest lay
> On the sole Arabian tree
> Herald sad and trumpet be,
> To whose sound chaste wings obey.
>
> (1–4)

As the line about the Arabian tree makes clear, even though the poem is written in (Christian) England, it is set in (Islamic) Arabia. 'The Phoenix and the Turtle' might thus be more closely related to Sufi poetry than to the *Divine Comedy*.[4] This relationship is, as I will suggest, both analogical – Sufi poetry and 'The Phoenix and the Turtle' address similar ideas – and genealogical – both sets of poetic traditions drink from the same well of allegorical mystical thought.

It is in the spirit of allegory that 'The Phoenix and the Turtle' is both self and other; its setting is both here and not here. If we follow the poem's lead to Arabia, and provincialize Europe, then we might be able to stake out other directions in which to move, other interlocutors to tap, and other theories to investigate.[5] This would involve taking

---

[1] Farid ud-din Attar, *The Conference of the Birds (Mantiq al-Tayr)*, trans. Afkham Darbandi and Dick Davis (London, 1984), line 2542.
[2] Martin Lings is an exception to this general rule; in addition to being a Shakespeare scholar, he is also the author of such texts as *What Is Sufism?* (Cambridge, 1993). William Empson too is another great exception in this regard; he has not only thought about *King Lear* in relation to Buddhism (in *The Structure of Complex Words* (Oxford, 1951), pp. 125–57), but also worked authoritatively on Andrew Marvell's poem 'The Garden' in light of Buddhist thought (*Some Versions of Pastoral* (New York, 2020), pp. 119–48).
[3] Walter Cohen, introductory note to the poem in *The Norton Shakespeare*, 3rd ed., gen. ed. Stephen Greenblatt (New York, 2016),1973–5; p. 1973.
[4] Glossing line 2, the footnote in the Norton Shakespeare says that the Arabian tree is '[s]upposedly, a unique tree on which sits the phoenix, which is similarly unique: only one exists at any given time' (p. 1977).
[5] See Dipesh Chakrabarty, *Provincializing Europe: Postcolonial Thought and Historical Difference* (Princeton, 2007).

the other – the *allos* of allegory – more seriously than we have done. I suggest that thinking about 'The Phoenix and the Turtle' exclusively in relation to the Christianity of Dante, Petrarch and Chaucer, or the paganism of Ovid – the scholarly progenitors of choice for Shakespeare scholarship – would be to ignore the poem itself.

ALGEBRAIC INEQUATIONS: 'NUMBER THERE IN LOVE WAS SLAIN'

The tradition of avian allegory trades on 'the idea, common since time immemorial in many different cultural traditions, that the soul is a bird'.[6] Annemarie Schimmel is speaking here not of Chaucer or even of Shakespeare, but of Sufi poetry. The characters in avian poems both are and are not human – both one and not one. The inevitability of overflowing the category of the one in order to inhabit the more-than-one is the hallmark of allegory. 'The Phoenix and the Turtle' inhabits this overflow from the very beginning as it cross-genders its protagonists: the traditionally male phoenix is here gendered female, and the traditionally female turtledove is here gendered male. Combined with the poem's early and repeated insistence on chastity – 'To whose sound chaste wings obey' (4), 'It was married chastity' (61) – this cross-gendering suggests a complex relationship between a cross-dressing allegory that is both human and avian, and a cross-gendered desire that is both male and female.

These allegorical relationships, in which Male (seems to) = Female, and Marriage (seems to) = Chastity, are at the heart of the poem. As though to clarify the contours of these equations, the narrator describes the love between the phoenix and the turtle in algebraic terms:

> So they loved as love in twain
> Had the essence but in one,
> Two distincts, division none.
> Number there in love was slain.
>
> (25–8)

These lines are temporally intriguing. They begin post facto as a gesture to an account that has already been detailed: '*So* they loved' suggests a postscript rather than a present moment. And then it moves into ever more unclear commentary on this already described love, the upshot of which is that the phoenix and the turtle are both separate and conjoined, both apart and a part of a single entity. If allegory is based in a relationship between two entities, then it is crucial for its functioning that the reader be able to recognize the distinctness of self and other. But equally, and in order to keep its movement alive, allegory encourages us to lose sight of this distinction, allowing each entity to slide into the other. This tension between needing to count and losing track of the count is one of the movements that 'The Phoenix and the Turtle' repeats in a bravura display of its allegorical form.

On the one hand, the simultaneous ability and inability of things to add up is a common paradox – love is understood to join *two* separate entities into *one* single unit.[7] Lovers are both two and one at once. But, on the other hand, this equivalence of one and two poses a serious algebraic problem. The phoenix and the turtle are both distinct from one another, and also not divided from one another.[8] They belong both on the same side of the equation and on opposite sides. Taking cognisance of this dilemma, the poem acknowledges the horror to which the problem potentially leads:

> Property was thus appalled
> That the self was not the same.
> Single nature's double name
> Neither two nor one was called.
>
> (37–40)

---

[6] Annemarie Schimmel, *A Two-Colored Brocade: The Imagery of Persian Poetry* (Durham, 1992), p. 178. The closest English parallel is Geoffrey Chaucer's *Parliament of Fowls* (1382) but, despite its setting on Valentine's Day, the poem is not particularly interested in the question of desire.

[7] See Madhavi Menon, 'Zero', in *Infinite Variety: A History of Desire in India* (New Delhi, 2018), 60–9.

[8] Karl Steel, 'The phoenix and the turtle / Number there in love was slain', in *Shakesqueer*, ed. Madhavi Menon (Durham, 2011), 271–8.

There is something improper about this confusion of identity. After all, identity (from the Latin *idem*, or 'same' – the quality of being the same) etymologically insists on oneness. But the poem suggests, allegorically, that oneness is a twosome. If the self is not identical to itself, then that opens up space for otherness within what passes for the self. Or, to put it another way – and to underscore the irony – the hetero of identity (which depends on the self-sameness of two different beings) threatens to become the homo of allegory (which points to the difference within the seemingly self-same thing).

Perhaps picking up on this threat posed by allegory, Walter Cohen suggests that 'the heterosexual love praised in this self-contradictory fashion parallels the celebration of homoerotic love in the sonnets to the young man: "Let me confess that we two must be twain, / Although our undivided loves are one" (36.1–2)'.[9] The allegorical 'Phoenix and the Turtle', while still harping on numbers, suggests that love has 'slain' the very idea of number. The property of numbers – to be the building blocks on the basis of which things add up – has been evacuated by the love of the phoenix and the turtle. What this leads to is the evisceration of identity itself – the self can no longer be owned or bought or sold like property. Or, rather, the self is also immediately other-than-self, and, therefore, lacks the title to its own self. This is why Property is appalled – it can no longer access the paperwork needed to execute identity. In the poem, the love of the phoenix and the turtle undoes ownership of the self by undermining the reign of numbers. And undoing rationality itself:

> How true a twain
> Seemeth this concordant one!
> Love hath reason, reason none,
> If what parts can so remain.
>
> (45–8)

In the battle between Reason and Love, Love wins by undermining Reason's deputy, Number. The being of one mind ('con-cordant') is actually twain. But the twain only 'seemeth' to be true and actually each is in accord with the other. As this allegorical statement suggests, the poem's play with the one and the two is not invested in making each number add up to something *else*. Rather, each of the two numbers circulates within the other so that there is no duality: the two are one.

The etymology of 'algebra' – from Ibn Musa al-Khwarizmi's ninth-century book, *'ilm al-jabr wa'l-muqābala* – suggests it is 'the science of restoring what is missing, and equating like with like'.[10] The desire to match like with like makes algebra the science, and patron god, of identity. As such, algebra is in direct conflict with allegory since the latter is the muse of the other – the otherness of what seems like the self, the propertylessness of what should be propertied, the alien, the *allos* rather than the *idem*. The failure of algebra in 'The Phoenix and the Turtle' to make two numbers add up to a different number, is responsible for the success of the allegorical mystery in the poem and its defiance of the normative. The poem's attempt to assure us that what seems to be allegory is really algebra cannot be sustained in the face of Reason's failure. The phoenix is not equal to the turtle; rather, the two birds challenge discreteness itself. After all, if one is meant to be understood as being equal to two, then we are no longer in the realm of an algebra in which separate numbers add up to a different conclusion. We are instead in an arena in which a battle is under way about what

---

[9] Cohen, in *The Norton Shakespeare*, p. 1974.
[10] See www.google.com/search?q=etymology+of+algebra&oq=etymology+of+algebra&aqs=chrome.0.69i59j0i22i30l2j0i15i22i30l2j0i390i65ol3.3546j0j4&sourceid=chrome&ie=UTF-8. The *OED*'s etymology notes the 'restoration (of anything which is missing, lost, out of place, or lacking), reunion of broken parts', but does not include the phrase 'like with like' (*OED Online*, 'algebra', etymology). In '"Thou wilt single prove none": counting, succession and identity in Shakespeare's Sonnets', Shankar Raman 'pursue[s] the arithmetical underpinnings of Shakespeare's poetics, to propose that the distinctive conjunction of repetition, identity and difference so evident in Sonnet 2 expresses (and indeed repeats) at its deepest stratum persistent issues in mathematical thought concerning the nature of numbers' (in *The Sonnets: The State of Play*, ed. Hannah Crawforth, Elizabeth Scott-Baumann and Clare Whitehead (London, 2017),157–82; p. 162).

counts as like and unlike, self and other. We are in the register of what the poem calls 'love'.[11] In this register, the self is both like and unlike itself; the other is both like and unlike the self. It is love that complicates an understanding of the self, and allows allegory victory over algebra. In love, things do not add up, and the self is not easily equitable, even – and especially – to itself.

Continuing the Shakespearian charge of allegory against algebra – or perhaps initiating it? – is another poem from a different part of the world. Growing away from al-Khwarzimi (780–847), though blossoming in the same Persianate soil, is the allegorist Farid ud-din Attar (1145–1212), whose masterpiece, *Mantiq-al-Tayr* (translated as *The Conference of the Birds*) presents us with many of the same ideas (and the same birds) as Shakespeare's 'Phoenix and the Turtle'. Led by the hoopoe, the *Mantiq-al-Tayr* stages a pilgrimage of a group of birds to find their leader, the legendary Simorgh. The travel is long and arduous, and it is punctuated by several allegorical tales told by the hoopoe in order to keep his congregation engaged. One of these tales, 'The world compared to a wax toy', ends with the dervish (a Sufi holy man) saying: 'All things are one – there isn't any two; / It isn't me who speaks, it isn't you'.[12]

Like all Sufi poetry, the *Mantiq-al-Tayr* is written in the mode of allegory. The significance of this mode is made clear in the introduction itself:

Mysticism tells us emphatically that the meaning of things does not lie on their surface, but must be searched for; it is the search that gives purpose and direction to the Sufi's life ... Allegory is therefore the perfect form for a mystical poem, because the form exemplifies what the content is telling us. In allegory, the meaning does not lie on the surface but must be dug for; the surface is merely a symbol of the meaning and can in fact be a veil to it.[13]

Allegory makes us work to understand it, perhaps because understanding (algebraic equations) might not be the primary purpose of allegory. And so, the *Mantiq-al-Tayr* insistently plays with puns that deflect away from meaning. Perhaps the most important example of such wordplay is the pun that both enables and disables the ground on which the pilgrimage is built. The birds – tattered, torn, disaffected, exhausted – have travelled for many years in search of their king. But when they finally reach their destination (the meaning of their quest), this is what they encounter:

> There in the Simorgh's radiant face they saw
> Themselves, the Simorgh of the world – with awe
> They gazed, and dared at last to comprehend
> They were the Simorgh and the journey's end.
>
> ...
>
> They ask (but inwardly; they make no sound)
> The meaning of these mysteries that confound
> Their puzzled ignorance – how is it true
> That 'we' is not distinguished here from 'you'?
> And silently their shining Lord replies:
> 'I am a mirror set before your eyes ... '
>
> ...
>
> And since you came as thirty birds, you see
> These thirty birds when you discover Me[14]

The thirty birds discover thirty – 'si' – birds – 'morgh' – at the end of their quest. The start of their quest is also its end. The pun on 'simorgh' seemingly collapses the temporal extension that is characteristic of allegory by making the end the same as the beginning: the thirty birds find the thirty birds. Finding another is the same as finding yourself, and, even better, finding your self is to find another. A pun, after all, is the other contained within the seemingly self-same. But the collapse of temporal extension in terms of plot – the questers are the goal of their own quest – is counterbalanced by the proliferation within in the form of extended narrative detours. In one such detour, a slave says ecstatically, 'I know not whether You are I, I You; / I lose myself in You; there is no two', while in another, a lover replies, when asked why he

---

[11] I am using 'desire' and 'love' interchangeably in this article to refer to a state of passionate attachment that is not governed or explained by reason.
[12] Attar, *Conference of the Birds*, lines 3705–6, trans. Darbandi and Davis.
[13] Dick Davis, in Attar, *Conference of the Birds*, p. xiv.
[14] Attar, *Conference of the Birds*, lines 4230–2, 4240–3, 4257–8, trans. Darbandi and Davis.

dived into a river to near certain death after his beloved: 'I dived because the difference / Of "I" and "you" to lovers makes no sense'.[15]

These many instances of algebraic confusion – how is one different from two? – echo Shakespeare's insistence that love slays the very rational idea of number ('Love hath reason, reason none' (47)). The Sufi poem's certainty that 'there is no two' points in the direction of a single and singular truth – a celebration of One God at the heart of a monotheistic religion. But the aesthetics of punning complicates such an understanding of singularity. The pun too looks like one but is always more-than-one. Indeed, this is the reason why allegory likes wordplay: while novices can be duped into thinking there is a straightforward meaning to the narrative, the initiates can enjoy the text's more-than-oneness. The simorgh is always more than one; it is, at one and the same time, both one bird and thirty birds, and all the birds in-between. What seems to have been a collapse of allegory's temporal extension in the *Mantiq-al-Tayr* turns miraculously into a dilation of number. This increased roster of numbers continues to upstage algebraic equivalence. One both is and is not the same as thirty. Dick Davis, the English translator of the *Mantiq-al-Tayr*, notes that 'the love Attar chooses to celebrate … is of a particular kind; it is always love that flies in the face of either social or sexual or religious convention. … In each case the love celebrated is seen by the world as, in some sense, scandalous.'[16] The scandal of love is that love is scandalous. It never adds up to one, and one never counts in relation to love. Indeed, as we shall see, if allegory always trumps algebra in love, then it does so by replacing the addition or equal signs by that of subtraction.

'BULLEH! I KNOW NOT WHO I AM!' / 'AY NO, NO, AY'

But why think of Shakespeare in relation to Sufi poetry? This is not a historical relationship: my claim is not – it cannot be – that Shakespeare read Sufi texts before writing his poem about a gathering of birds. Rather, we can think of it as an analogical relationship – I suggest that both Sufi poetry and Shakespeare explore strikingly similar questions about the relation of poetry and the self, the self and desire, and desire and annihilation. The rhetoric of paradox that is at the heart of Sufi poetry – the mutually intertwined relationship between beloved and Beloved, profane and sacred, imprisonment and freedom, comfort and pain – also marks the Petrarchan sonnet tradition that Shakespeare mined so obviously in the sonnets, *Romeo and Juliet* and, more subtly and effectively, in *Richard II*. Whether it is Bulleh Shah's exemplary announcement in the eighteenth century, 'Bullha, what do I know about who I am',[17] or Richard, stating in his sixteenth-century play, 'Ay no; no, ay' (*Richard II*, 4.1.191), the echoes between Shakespearian texts and Sufi poetic tropes are deafening. These echoes open up Shakespeare for us in ways that have hitherto not been considered.[18]

As Davis notes, Sufi poetry celebrates a love that defies convention. These conventions are as much poetic as they are sexual: 'His tongue is Turkish, and I don't know Turkish – / how nice it would be if his tongue were in my mouth', says the famous

---

[15] Attar, *Conference of the Birds*, lines 3748–9, 3756–7, trans. Darbandi and Davis.
[16] Davis, in Attar, *Conference of the Birds*, p. xviii.
[17] *Bullhe Shah: Sufi Lyrics*, trans. and ed. Christopher Shackle (Cambridge, MA, 2015), *Kafi* 106, l. 1.
[18] Historically, the poetic/spiritual/sexual traditions of Sufi poetry made their way into Europe via the French troubadour poets and then the Petrarchan sonnet. In his forthcoming book on 'The Jewish Silk Road', Jonathan Gil Harris suggests that 'Multifaith associations like these were responsible for rescuing classical Greek writing from oblivion. Arabic translations of Aristotle and Plato from the Bayt al-Hikma would then migrate to Moorish Spain, where similar dialogues between Muslim, Jew and Christian would transform the intellectual landscape of Europe. The so-called European Renaissance – the era of intellectual and artistic "rebirth" that drew its energies from the rediscovery of classical literature, and that produced figures like Leonardo da Vinci in Italy, Michel de Montaigne in France, and William Shakespeare in England – could never have happened without the translation projects of the Bayt al-Hikma' (MS shared by the author, p. 144).

Sufi poet of Delhi, Amir Khusrau.[19] By writing allegorical poetry about desire, Sufism extends poetic licence to a realm that is usually strictly policed.[20] If allegory suggests that love does not add up to a knowable self and other, then the specifically Sufi dimension of allegory insists that love requires an annihilation rather than a reinforcement of the self – 'don't know' is a more popular phrase than 'know' (except in its punning negation as 'no'). Negation rather than addition negates the very sanctity of the lover's self.

The *Mantiq-al-Tayr* is clear in this regard: '"A lover," said the hoopoe, now their guide, / "Is one in whom all thoughts of Self have died".'[21] Davis notes that '[t]wo themes in particular are diffused throughout almost the entire poem – the necessity for destroying the Self, and the importance of passionate love.'[22] True to his Sufi lineage, Attar juxtaposes passion and death. The death of the Ego is considered to be necessary for unification with God, and the Sufis take this relation to its ecstatic limit. This is why, as Schimmel points out, 'the soul regains its spiritual freedom by following the old Sufi advice – "Die before ye die"'.[23] The death of the Self is considered to be far more important than physical death. Perhaps this Sufi understanding can help shed some light on the otherwise puzzling decision Shakespeare makes to kill the phoenix with finality in his poem.

'The Phoenix and the Turtle' was printed in 1601 as one poem in a collection titled *Love's Martyr: or, Rosalin's Complaint*. Every other poem in the volume – by John Marston, George Chapman and Ben Jonson, among others – tows the traditional line and describes the phoenix as the bird that miraculously rises from its own ashes. But Shakespeare's poem kills the phoenix without talking about its resurrection:

All of the poems with which 'The Phoenix and the Turtle' were printed are on the subject of the phoenix and turtle, and all but Shakespeare's deny the finality of the phoenix's death. 'The Phoenix and the Turtle' alone forgoes the possibility of exploiting the standard treatment of the phoenix as the intersection of the temporal and the timeless.[24]

It is almost as though the phoenix's physical death is of little consequence to Shakespeare. And before the Christian explanation of the-soul-remaining-alive-after-the-body-has-died can be wheeled in, let me hasten to add that the poem is not about the transcendence of the soul. If anything, physical death is uninteresting to an author who seems far more fascinated by the desire that death has in its maw. The poem insists that the death of the phoenix and the turtle is a desirable thing in and of itself. Not only because that death stands as a testament to the intensity of their (cross-gendered) love, but also because life and the self are not the poem's concern – it is death that keeps its narrative engine charged.

'The Phoenix and the Turtle' insists on this:

> Death is now the Phoenix' nest,
> And the Turtle's loyal breast
> To eternity doth rest.
>
> Leaving no posterity,
> 'Twas not their infirmity:
> It was married chastity.
>
> (56–61)

Not only do the phoenix and the turtle die without being reborn, but they have also refused to give birth, thereby resisting any future versions of themselves; Shakespeare's birds are *sui generis*.[25] The poem's scrambling of space – 'The Phoenix and the Turtle' is written in England and set in Arabia – is also

---

[19] Quoted by Schimmel in *Two-Colored Brocade*, p. 138.
[20] The debate around whether Sufi poetry is 'really' about sexuality or not demonstrates one aspect of this policing. See, for instance, https://scroll.in/article/810007/from-bulleh-shah-and-shah-hussain-to-amir-khusro-same-sex-references-abound-in-islamic-sufi-poetry.
[21] Attar, *Conference of the Birds*, lines 1164–5, trans. Darbandi and Davis.
[22] Davis, in Attar, *Conference of the Birds*, p. xviii.
[23] Schimmel, *Two-Colored Brocade*, p. 183.
[24] Cohen, in *The Norton Shakespeare*, p. 1974.
[25] Does 'married chastity' suggest the two birds did not have sex, or that they did not have penetrative sex, or that they took precautions? Given the passion celebrated in the poem, it doesn't seem to me that this 'chastity' was devoid of pleasure.

a complication of time: the poem is sung posthumously by the titular phoenix about himself. What should come before – the Phoenix's song when alive – comes after: the Phoenix sings about himself after his death. This is one of the many difficulties in the notoriously dense poem: we are never quite sure who is singing about whom, where and when. This resistance to reproduction is also an active embrace of death in Attar; as the mentor of the moths in the *Mantiq-al-Tayr* says approvingly after one of his mentees has immolated himself: 'No creature's Self can be admitted here, / Where all identity must disappear'.[26] Death becomes the companion of passion rather than an opponent to be overcome. The Sufi embrace of passion is laced with scorn for identity and disregard for the sanctity of the self. Sufism frequently urges its adherents to 'break this bond [of the self], / And as it shatters you are worthy of / Oblivion, the Nothingness of love'.[27] The love of the phoenix and the turtle celebrated in Shakespeare's poem echoes the destruction necessary for, and necessitated by, passion. With a self, there can be no love. With identity, there can be no passion. Instead, love needs to be self-less, subtracting identitarian ontology rather than asserting it.

In the Sufi worldview, this destruction of the self – the immolation of the birds – is called *fana*. Translated from the Arabic as 'annihilation', *fana* is the bedrock of Sufi desire. It is not only the goal of desire, but also the reason for, and the form of, desire. No desire without annihilation. In terms of allegorical content, Sufi poetry describes the quest undertaken by the human for the divine. But as a *template* of desire, it moulds our understanding of love itself. Sufi poetry challenges the future-orientation of romance and the ego-centred version of psychology that frame contemporary narratives of love. This is perhaps why Shakespeare's phoenix and turtle, in keeping with their Sufi lineage, have to die without hope of a future – their death best exemplifies what it means to be burned by desire, to go up in flames for love.

This drama of an immolating desire pivots on the belief that: 'A true Sufi is he who is not.'[28] Speaking about Richard II's relation both to the self and to theatricality, Scot McMillin notes that at 'the heart of loss, there is nothing for the theatrical eye to see, and "I" and "no" are one'.[29] McMillin is commenting on Richard's flustered response to Bolingbroke's question about whether or not he is contented to resign the crown: 'Ay, no; no, ay; for I must nothing be' (4.1.201). Richard's punning abnegation of selfhood – I know no I – echoes Sufi poetry's pervasive investment in puns and wordplay (one scholar suggests that 'the ambiguity of [allegory's] ultimate meaning has become an essential feature of the genre').[30] But, more specifically, it echoes the way in which puns are put in the service of an eviscerated self. The simorgh (originally a female bird, like the phoenix) is punningly reflected in the si-morgh – the thirty birds – that undertake the quest to find their leader. The moment at which they find the simorgh is also the moment at which they lose themselves. Or, rather, the fulfilment of their desire is simultaneous with the annihilation of their selves. For Richard too, caught on the horns of a dilemma, an assertion of the self has to be accompanied by a negation of the self. This simultaneity is a compulsion – 'I *must* nothing be' (emphasis mine). For the Sufis, the 'I' is always never 'one'.

In both Sufi and Shakespearian poetry, the I is no one because the I never belongs to the self: 'The Ṣufi is he that has nothing in his possession nor is himself possessed by anything.'[31] Equally, the I is always and only a reflection of an other. The thirty birds in the *Mantiq-al-Tayr* see themselves in the

---

[26] Attar, *Conference of the Birds*, lines 4001–2, trans. Darbandi and Davis.
[27] Attar, *Conference of the Birds*, lines 4012–13, trans. Darbandi and Davis.
[28] Annemarie Schimmel, *Mystical Dimensions of Islam* (Durham, 1975), p. 16.
[29] Scott McMillin, 'Richard II: eyes of sorrow, eyes of desire', *Shakespeare Quarterly* 35 (1984), 40–52; p. 52. Richard is a complex character in an often allegorical play written entirely in verse.
[30] J. T. P. De Bruijn, *Persian Sufi Poetry: An Introduction to the Mystical Use of Classical Poems* (New York, 1997), p. 56.
[31] 'Ali b. Uthman al-Jullabi al-Hujwiri, *The Kashf-al-Mahjub* ('The Revelation of the Veiled'), trans. Reynold A. Nicholson (Edinburgh, 2000), p. 41.

simorgh in the same way as Narcissus sees himself in the pool of water: they are both self and other. For the Sufis, this otherness of the self is the condition of *fana*: the annihilation enacted by desire. And the annihilation of the self is simultaneous with discovering the self in and as the other. Without the other, there is no self. Which is to say, the self can only ever exist allegorically:

> So between them love did shine
> That the Turtle saw his right
> Flaming in the Phoenix' sight;
> Either was the other's mine.
>
> (33–6)

The turtle might have been a turtle even before he saw his reflection in the phoenix, but he was not *this* turtle. This turtle sees himself only in the eyes of the phoenix. The phoenix gives the turtle to himself, and vice versa. Each bird gets a sense of self ('mine') only from the lover; the 'mine' of the self is mined from the other, making two mines where we want only one. Here, 'The Phoenix and the Turtle' can easily be retitled 'The Phoenix in the Turtle', and vice versa. Since we know the 'in' cannot be penetratively sexual – the birds are chaste – we can only focus on the interpenetration of identity in the condition of love. Their identities are continually 'between them' rather than belonging individually to either. The sameness (*idem*) of identity is *allos*, and the self is always a reflection of and from the other.

In fact, Sufism emphasizes the idea that the heart must be a 'polished mirror' that can reflect God.[32] This reflection is what makes a Sufi a Sufi, and the mirror is always a mirror of desire. In this allegorical register of the image in the mirror, a glance is enough to bring the self into being. A glance is also sufficient to transport the self to heights of ecstasy. It is this ecstasy that Amir Khusrau (1253–1325) describes in relation to his teacher, Nizamuddin Auliya: *chap tilak sab chheeni re, mosey naina milayke*. Paul E. Losensky and Sunil Sharma translate this phrase variously as 'you left me breathless / when our eyes met', and 'you made me a married woman / when our eyes met', each line testifying to the power of the glance to bestow and to take away.[33] According to Khusrau, Nizamuddin's look has ravished him as a bride; Khusrau's sexuality is entirely tied up with Nizamuddin's glance. In the *Mantiq-al-Tayr*, the hoopoe ontologizes this trope: 'Great Solomon / Once looked at me – it is that glance alone / Which gave me what I know'; and again: 'Consume your life with prayer, till Solomon / Bestows his glance, and ignorance is gone'.[34]

The glance of the other – what the Sufis call a *nazariya* – turns the self from a subject with agency to an object that is created and acted upon. In Sufi poetry, this switch from the register of subject to object comes in the face of desire. The passionate self is not, and can never be, an agential self. If the glance is vivifying of the object, then it is simultaneously destructive of the individual subject. The self gets created and destroyed in a relation between self and other ('So *between them* love did shine'). Joel Fineman has noted that '[a]llegory becomes, for literature as for theology, a vivifying archaeology of occulted origins and a promissory eschatology of postponed ends'.[35] Both beginning and end are unknown and unknowable in the allegorical mode. In Sufism, desire is allegorical, and in Sufi poetry, the narrative runs in more than one direction and operates at more than one level. The beloved is a placeholder, not an actual or finite person, but this is not (only) because the beloved is god. In an allegory, everything is more than one thing. Even as Shakespeare may not have god as his ideal (Shakespeare's poem does not participate in a theological longing, and this is perhaps the single biggest difference between the two texts), the Sufis too do not fix on any one being for their desire. The beloved is not only god

---

[32] See, for instance, the chapter on 'What Is Sufism?' in Schimmel, *Mystical Dimensions of Islam*, pp. 3–22.
[33] *In the Bazaar of Love: The Selected Poetry of Amir Khusrau*, trans. and ed. Paul E. Losensky and Sunil Sharma (Gurgaon, 2013), p. 109.
[34] Attar, *Conference of the Birds*, lines 1664, 1665, trans. Darbandi and Davis.
[35] Joel Fineman, 'The structure of allegorical desire', *October* 12 (1980), 46–66; p. 49.

and not only an actual person because desire is not, and cannot be, tethered by just one object. As J. T. P. De Bruijn points out, 'This kind of ambiguity, in which the beloved (*ma'shuq*) not only seems to reflect the Divine (*ma'bud*) but also the person of a worldly patron (*mamduh*)', is par for the course.³⁶ Sufi desire is not fixed by an object, and object-choice — as we understand that psychoanalytical term today — is changeable in the Sufi worldview. This means that in Sufi poetry, desire does not add up to being an ontology, and desire does not bestow us with identity and life — instead, it trades in death.

NEVER-ENDING DESIRE: 'DEATH IS NOW THE PHOENIX' NEST'

Both Christian and Islamic mysticism have been connected to the Neoplatonism that was resurgent in Europe from the eleventh century onwards. But, as Mark Sedgwick notes, what is less often thought about is the relation between the two mystical strands:

> The teachings of the great Christian mystic Meister Eckhart, who was born in Thuringia, Germany in about 1260, show remarkable similarities to the teachings of the great Sufi mystic Ibn Arabi, who died in Damascus, Syria in 1240, twenty years before Eckhart's birth ... [T]he key explanation is that Eckhart and Ibn Arabi both built much of their theology around emanationism, an aspect of the Neoplatonic philosophy that was developed in late antiquity on classical Greek foundations ... Neoplatonism passed into Arab philosophy, and one early consequence of this was the rise of Sufism.³⁷

Emanationism believes that human beings emanate from the divine and can and should return to it. The story of that return is of central importance to Sufi philosophers, and is the cornerstone of *wahdat al-wujud* — the philosophy that promulgates the oneness of being. However, as Sufis such as Ibn Arabi firmly believed, that journey back to the One can never in fact be concluded, the goal cannot be reached. The journey back 'leads first to love and then to passion (*ishq*) ... [I]t is also a preparation for death.'³⁸ Passion and death exist in close proximity to one another, which is why the self cannot be united with the Self. The self must die as it approaches the Self, otherwise it cannot be admitted into its company. But equally, unification with the One (through death) is impossible because 'it is impossible to unite with that which one is already part of'.³⁹ Unification can only be said to take place between two separate and separated entities. But if, according to the principle of *wahdat al-wujud*, all entities partake in and emanate from the One, thus making it more-than-one, then 'unification' is the wrong term to use since there has been no separation. A necessary nerve in Sufi poetry thus maintains that union (*wasl*), though desirable, is impossible. Allegorical desire depends on distance, even — and especially — when it seems to aim for union.

In Sufi poetry, the yearned-for sexual union allegorically mimics a spiritual union with god. In itself, this may seem unremarkable, but what is fascinating is that the desire in Sufi poetry is strong *because* an ultimate union is impossible. Unlike what Plato espouses in *The Symposium*, Sufi poetry does not *convert* sexual longing into spiritual fulfilment.⁴⁰ Allegory is never about conversion; it is always about keeping in tension multiple strands that circulate among themselves. Sufi desire seeks not solutions, but delays; twists and turns keep it alive. The yearning for union is followed by ... more yearning. As Imam Bakhsh Nasikh puts it: *Tamam umr yuun hi gaee basar apni / Shab-e-firaq gaee roz-e-intizar aaya* ('My entire life has been spent this way / The night of separation followed by the day of waiting').⁴¹ Thwarted desire is not the opposite of desire — it is its very

---

36 De Bruijn, *Persian Sufi Poetry*, p. 56.
37 Mark Sedgwick, *Western Sufism: from the Abbasids to the New Age* (Oxford, 2017), p. 15.
38 Sedgwick, *Western Sufism*, p. 45.
39 Sedgwick, *Western Sufism*, p. 45.
40 See Plato, *The Symposium* (London, 2003), especially his argument about the 'ladder of love'.
41 Imam Bakhsh Nasikh, in *Love, Longing, Loss in Urdu Poetry*, ed. Sanjiv Saraf (Noida, 2021), p. 203.

condition. In his work on allegory, Angus Fletcher argues that the trope seems to be premised on incompletion,[42] never able to achieve its lofty goals. Sufi poetry suggests that this 'failure' is what makes for the success of allegory.[43]

This endlessness of allegory conduces not only to epic poetry, but also to a theorization of death that echoes 'the Freudian view that what desire seeks is always the restitution of a prior state'.[44] Sedgwick spells it out for us while discussing the principles of the earliest Sufis: 'He [al-Junayd] defined the goal of Sufi practice as being the loss of individuality in order to reach *homoioisis*, which he called *fana* (literally, extinction), and which we will call "union". He saw this as a return to a primordial state of relations between the soul and the One.'[45]

A return to a primordial state. Let us turn to a particularly allegorical part of *Richard II*, where the deposed king, in the throes of self-pity and from the depths of a labyrinthine prison, lays out a structure for his thoughts:

> My brain I'll prove the female to my soul,
> My soul the father, and these two beget
> A generation of still-breeding thoughts
>
> (5.5.6–8)

A few lines after setting up this hermeneutical framework, the king observes:

> whate'er I be,
> Nor I, nor any man that but man is,
> With nothing shall be pleased till he be eased
> With being nothing.
>
> (5.5.38–41)

Scott McMillin notes that by the time he reaches the end of his play, Richard has discovered 'that the experience of loss is more interesting to him than the experience of command'. And even further: 'Containing birth ["still-breeding thoughts"] within himself allows Richard a stifled pleasure, the pleasure of knowing that the imagined world of his own mind continually dissolves into the ease of being nothing. All men, Richard supposes, desire this condition.'[46] Moving from pregnancy ('breeding') to abortion ('still-breeding'), the deposed king traces an inexorable trajectory towards nothingness.

This desire to 'be nothing' is what Freud calls the death drive and the Sufis term *fana*.[47] This is not necessarily physical death, but, rather, the desire not to be, not to have a self that can be defined, to be polymorphously perverse. If '[d]isappearance is the direction of Richard's role', then, equally, 'Phoenix and the Turtle fled / In a mutual flame from hence' (23–4).[48] But this disappearance is not a one-time occurrence; it is ongoing. The paradox of the death drive is that it is an active (though not necessarily conscious) movement towards stasis. It is an energetic pursuit of stillness. It repeats itself in an ongoing quest for a conclusion. This repetition is also a compulsion, and defies the boundaries of reason:

> Reason in itself confounded
> Saw division grow together
> To themselves, yet either neither,
> Simple were so well compounded
>
> That it cried, 'How true a twain
> Seemeth this concordant one!
> Love hath reason, reason none,
> If what parts can so remain.'
>
> (41–8)

Division multiplying ('Saw division grow together'), ontology evacuated ('To themselves yet either neither') and reason confounded ('Love hath reason, reason none'), all paint an image of the end of the world. Or *fana*.

---

[42] Angus Fletcher, *Allegory: The Theory of a Symbolic Mode* (Ithaca, 1964), pp. 174–80.

[43] Karl Steel has noted of 'The Phoenix and the Turtle' that 'because the two birds are lost to the world; they can be experienced only as an absence to be longed for' ('Number there in love was slain', p. 273) and, as Joel Fineman has reminded us, 'desire originates in and as the loss of structure' ('Allegorical desire', p. 61).

[44] Robert D. Cottrell, 'Allegories of desire in Lemaire's *Concorde des deux langages*', *French Forum* 23 (1998), 261–300; p. 275.

[45] Sedgwick, *Western Sufism*, p. 40.

[46] McMillin, 'Eyes of sorrow', pp. 43, 47.

[47] See Sigmund Freud, *Beyond the Pleasure Principle*, trans. and ed. James Strachey (New York, 1961).

[48] McMillin, 'Eyes of sorrow', p. 49.

At the end of the world, desire remains. Unfulfilled, since that is the only way to continue as desire. While physical death can spell the end of the individual, the death *drive* destroys the very idea of the self. When the edifice of the self is misinterpreted as ontology, then desire gets deflected away from the death drive and put on the path of self-fulfilment, where no allegory dares to tread. For Sufism, the desire of the death drive (what *Romeo and Juliet* calls 'death-marked love', Prologue 9) is not tethered to an object and does not provide an identity for the self. If tropes generally obscure their origins, hiding from where they arrive, then allegory is perhaps unique in also obscuring its destination, treating arrival (or identity) as a loss. The end of 'The Phoenix and the Turtle' is classic in this regard:

> Truth may seem, but cannot be;
> Beauty brag, but 'tis not she:
> Truth and beauty buried be.
>
> To this urn let those repair
> That are either true or fair:
> For these dead birds sigh a prayer.
>
> (62–7)

The poem begins its end by announcing the end of Truth and Beauty. With the death of the phoenix and the turtle, both beauty and truth, true beauty, have disappeared from this world. Not only that. But they are never again to be found, since the phoenix and turtledove are not resurrected and have left behind no progeny. Immediately after this gloomy exordium, the poem exhorts all those that 'are either true or fair' to pray for the dead birds.

Except that there is no one left in the world who is either true or fair – we have just been told that. So even as the poem has narratively come to an end, it can allegorically only end on a note of the impossibility of endings. The premise and promise of allegorical desire are that its end is death, never fulfilment. Robert D. Cottrell argues that 'it is not within the logic of desire to conclude. Propelling the subject forward through time, desire ends only when the subject perishes.'[49] And if, as Paul de Man notes, 'desire is organized around the moment that separates possession from its opposite', then 'The Phoenix and the Turtle' and *Mantiq-al-Tayr* assert the desirability of non-possession, an immersion in desire.[50]

The discourse that would see desire as the basis of an identity will find no comfort in Sufism. All we get here is arid, wild, untamed, poetry. As Oludamini Ogunnaike observes, 'In Islamic contexts, the art of poetry is [itself] often referred to by the Qur'anic term "the language of the birds" (*manṭiq al-ṭayr*) from verse 27:16, in which Solomon says, "O people, we have been taught the language of the birds, and we have been given of all things."'[51] All things here lead to one end: 'I have no need of my identity – / I long for death; what use is "I" to me'.[52] The relation between allegory and desire, and the resistance of allegory and desire to knowable identity, are central to both Sufi poetry and 'The Phoenix and the Turtle'. Allegorical poetry is perhaps the only medium in which such desire can be theorized since it allows for a mirroring of form and content such that both poetry and desire never refer only to one object, never attach to identitarian markers, and never arrive at finality. Rather than a 'One' who waits at the end of the allegory – which suggests a strictly monotheistic theology – Sufi poetry is, willy-nilly, immersed in the more-than-one. *Plus ultra*. There is always more that lies beyond. But this beyond is always just out of our reach because 'we' cannot exist there as our selves.

Sufism's absolute goal is desire, and desire's absolute condition is death. '[W]here love thrives, there pain is always found', says Attar.[53] Sufi poetry – in

---

[49] Cottrell, 'Allegories of desire in Lemaire', p. 274.
[50] Paul de Man, *Allegories of Reading: Figural Language in Rousseau, Nietzsche, Rilke, and Proust* (New Haven, 1979), p. 215.
[51] Oludamini Ogunnaike, 'The logic of the birds', *Renovatio: The Journal of Zaytuna College* (6 May 2022), https://renovatio.zaytuna.edu/article/the-logic-of-the-birds.
[52] Attar, *Conference of the Birds*, lines 3971–2, trans. Darbandi and Davis.
[53] Attar, *Conference of the Birds*, line 1172, trans. Darbandi and Davis.

whose ranks, unlike all extant scholarship on the poem, I include Shakespeare's 'The Phoenix and the Turtle' – theorizes allegory as the necessary mode of desire. The immersion of both 'The Phoenix and the Turtle' and *Mantiq-al-Tayr* in Neoplatonic thought, their commitment to connecting desire with death, and their resistance to ontologizing desire make them kissing cousins of one another. This relation is not only analogical, which is the mode of allegory. It is also genealogical – both texts reflect their light from similar allegorical mirrors of desire.

THE POETICS OF SHAKESPEARIAN ERASURE: LYRIC THINKING WITH BHANU KAPIL AND PRETI TANEJA

AYESHA RAMACHANDRAN

In her recently published essay-lament, *Aftermath*, the British-Asian writer Preti Taneja turns to poetry — especially that of Black American women — who, she writes, 'distil scales of violence and degradation into bare lines'.[1] Searching for coherence in the face of terror and grief, and seeking to situate the pain of individual lives against crushing institutional structures of exclusion with their long histories of violence, Taneja adopts the language of lyric. This may come as a surprising claim for a book that won the Gordon Burn Prize, which focuses on fiction and non-fiction.[2] Her book may be read as an extended prose poem, a meditation — alternately raging, tragic, hallucinatory, exhorting, indignant — on the recognition of subjection and subjectivity. The work opens with the following lines:

It is a bright morning when the call comes. Everything becomes brighter: like a vision of a nuclear blast in a film. It is as if everything solid has broken into pieces. As if the world has cracked. It is a shivering, unshakeable sickness. It feels like concrete in the stomach. Shattered and stark as ice on deep water, struck with a blade … The repetitive rhythm is not a *glitch*. It is an artefact of pain   repeating. It feels like being constantly watched. It is an assault: it is a wailing … Like a hand around the throat. Forced deeper into the wreck of it. A rage. Like raging. This is the core of the atro-city. The outside world turned inwards.[3]

Taneja's words enact the repetition of trauma, the unfolding of a grief so overwhelming that there is no outside, no beyond. What form, what language can capture this place? Refusing the chronological and propositional order of prose, whether expository or narrative, Taneja breaks into prose poetry, allowing her style to shatter and crack. If the opening sentence is complete grammatically, each subsequent line gradually unravels into sentence-shards. The cascade of images, culminating in fragments of nouns and verbs ('A rage. Like raging.'), the alliteration (*shivering … sickness … stomach … shattered … stark … struck*), the visual gaps ('pain   repeating') and the intertextual allusion ('deeper into the wreck' recalls Adrienne Rich's influential 'Diving into the Wreck') are tell-tale markers. They point towards the province of lyric poetry. As the 'outside world turn[s] inwards', subject and object blur, and the first-person self is consumed by the world. *Aftermath* plunges us into the vortex of this terrible interpenetration.

But what kind of lyric poetry is this? Recent debates over lyricization have alerted us to the dangers of flattening all poetic forms and devices

---

[1] Preti Taneja, *Aftermath* (Sheffield, 2021), p. 107.
[2] 'The Gordon Burn Prize recognises literature that is forward-thinking and fearless in its ambition and execution, often playing with style, pushing boundaries, crossing genres or challenging readers' expectations … The judges seek work that shows an affinity with the spirit and sensibility of Gordon's literary methods: novels which dare to enter history and interrogate the past; writers of non-fiction brave enough to recast characters and historical events to create a new and vivid reality.' See https://newwritingnorth.com/gordon-burn-prize.
[3] Taneja, *Aftermath*, p. 11.

into 'lyric'.[4] But Taneja is self-conscious in her gestures towards multiple lyric traditions. She imagines herself as a 21st-century successor of Adrienne Rich, diving into the wreckage of colonial histories, inspired by Claudia Rankine's chronicle of aggressions, a fellow traveller with M. NourbeSe Philip. She writes about social erasure through the techniques of aesthetic erasure, addition and remaking. The book's epigraph comes from the twelfth-century Persian poet Jalāl al-Din Rūmī, and the final section on 'Radical Hope' opens with a citation of the early twentieth-century South Asian poet Faiz Ahmed Faiz. At its centre is a chapter simply entitled 'Poetry'. Conspicuously absent from this rich choir of voices from across the world, given Taneja's previous work, is the poetry of William Shakespeare.

For Taneja, this omission is strategic. Her first novel, *We That Are Young*, a reimagining of *King Lear* set in contemporary India, won the Desmond Elliott Prize. Even before the novel's publication, she undertook a postdoctoral project on 'Shakespeare and Human Rights' which chronicled the 'production, performance and reception of Shakespeare ... by practitioners making work to mediate their own conflict and post conflict zones'.[5] In 2020, the year she completed *Aftermath*, she was Writer in Residence as part of the Travel, Transculturality and Identity in England (TIDE) project at Oxford, where she curated a digital TIDE Salon which once again returned to Shakespeare through creative remaking. For this project, she wrote a series of fragmentary prose-poems which framed a set of video vignettes by British-Asian artists who were asked to respond in a contemporary poetic idiom to three keywords from the TIDE lexicon – 'alien', 'traveller' and 'savage' – words which are bound up with English poetry's own long histories of linguistic violence and exclusion.[6] Writing in the voice of 'Aliena', Taneja evokes Celia's pseudonym in *As You Like It* only to explore the racial dialectics of Aliena/Celia: 'You come to me and are restless: you call me *Aliena* in your sleep. My name is Celia in my white-girl dreams. My whisper-name is Pṛthvī I am transparent in your arms, I am naked, brown and soft.'[7] Celia, a Latinate name derived from *caelum* ('heaven, sky'), is here given an alter ego who is 'brown', 'soft', associated with the earth (*Pṛthvī*, in Sanskrit, signifies the earth as a mother goddess). She is the opposite – elementally, somatically, politically – of Shakespeare's heroine, and yet is irrevocably bound to her. Weaving together a fiction of archival rediscovery with contemporary poetic re-enactment, Taneja invites us to confront the racialized materialities of embodiment. Her writing stretches time from the early modern past to a fictional future of science fiction as she returns critically to Shakespeare through nodal keywords that activate and continue transhistorical poetic networks.

Why then is Shakespeare absent in *Aftermath*, an essay saturated in poetry through form, style, allusion? To be fair, Shakespeare does feature in *Aftermath*, but he does so through a broken lens. Ruminating on representations of prison education, Taneja turns to Margaret Atwood's *Hagseed*, a reimagining of *The Tempest* (not unlike her own project in *We That Are Young*) set in a prison. Noting the racial blind spots of Atwood's novel, Taneja remarks:

To set *The Tempest* in a prison in contemporary times and not have it be about racial justice in some profound ways – instead to offer it as a kind of antidote of

---

[4] See, most notably, Virginia Jackson, 'Historical poetics and the dream of interpretation: a response to Paul Fry', *Modern Language Quarterly* 81 (2020), 289–318, and *Dickinson's Misery: A Theory of Lyric Reading* (Princeton, 2005). For an alternative view, see Jonathan D. Culler, *Theory of the Lyric* (Cambridge, MA, 2015). For an assessment of the two positions, see Stephen Burt, 'What is this thing called lyric?' *Modern Philology* 113 (2016), 422–40. My own position on the question of lyric is most closely aligned with Jahan Ramazani, *Poetry in a Global Age* (Chicago, 2020).

[5] Personal communication with author. See www.shakespeareandhumanrights.org.

[6] For details on the project, see www.tideproject.uk/2020/12/03/tide-salon-a-voyage-through-our-new-digital-project.

[7] I cite from the transcript of the TIDE Salon available here: www.tideproject.uk/wp-content/uploads/2020/11/tidesalon.pdf. Page numbers refer to this transcript and will be cited as 'TIDE Salon transcript' followed by page number, thus: 'TIDE Salon transcript', p. 52.

rehabilitative whiteness to that interpretation [of the *Tempest* as a play about race and coloniality] – is as disappointing (if unsurprising) as the book being commissioned and published in the Hogarth Series of Shakespeare re-tellings, named for the Bloomsbury group, neither of which include writers of colour, though in their work dark bodies are often imagined, and written onto and about.[8]

The distances Taneja measures here are not just from Shakespeare to Atwood via Virginia Woolf and the new Hogarth series, but also across different kinds of prison settings, literal and metaphorical – from the colonial and postcolonial interpretations of *The Tempest*, to black and brown colonial subjection, to those non-white bodies reading Shakespeare in prisons, to the continuing exclusion of black and brown writers from white canons and structures of justice.

In choosing to critique Atwood and invoking *The Tempest* aslant, Taneja calls attention – albeit through absence and erasure – to that play's postcolonial poetic aftermath. *The Tempest* is arguably Shakespeare's most musical play, permeated by 'sounds and sweet airs', filled with song, featuring a masque, and dense with lyrical soliloquies. It is also a play that has inspired a wide range of poets from the seventeenth century to the present, notably the Caribbean poets Aimé Césaire, Kamau Brathwaite and, most recently, Safiya Sinclair. More important, this tradition reflects on precisely the racial and colonial dilemmas with which Taneja wrestles in her book. Why this determined refusal to engage with Shakespeare's poetry? And, paradoxically, what might this absent-presence tell us about Shakespeare's poetry – both in the context of contemporary South Asian anglophone diasporic poetry, and in a long, continuing history of lyric?

Recent approaches to Shakespeare's poetry – whether the verse forms of the plays, the long epyllic poems such as *Venus and Adonis*, or the *Sonnets* – have typically unfolded along three distinct trajectories: formalist interpretations that consider local poetic effects and meanings; historicist interpretations within topical, political or generic contexts; and reception studies that follow the poetic and performance afterlives of images, phrases, forms. Typically, these strands have been kept relatively discrete, occasionally borrowing from other methods to heighten their own stakes, and much criticism has focused on the relative merits of each approach. In contrast, however, this article proposes a counter-intuitive method that begins from absence, erasure and fragmentation. What might we learn about Shakespeare's poetry – and our own critical expectations – if we focus on the places where it seemingly should be – but is not? Or where its fragmentary and passing appearance alerts us to looping transhistorical dialogues that do not follow the logic of reception history?

Such questions emerge, for me, out of my interest in the forms of thinking made possible by lyric poetry: particularly lyric's capacity to hold multiple histories in the balance, to bear witness to particular events, lives and subjectivities. Cutting against the grain of rhetorical and historical-poetic accounts of the lyric as an object in the world, I explore what it means to engage with lyric as a process of thinking *in* and *about* the world.[9] In this view, lyric is not defined by a specific formal mode or set of generic conventions, but, rather, the lyric poem becomes an instrument, a technology for making sense about various kinds of relation. Indeed, it offers a distinctive ontology that *frames* a world.[10] At the heart of my claim for the significance of lyric thinking is an embrace of the poem's partial, fragmentary, ephemeral first-person standpoint – one that is inevitably historically located, but which also,

---

[8] Taneja, *Aftermath*, p. 153.
[9] Ayesha Ramachandran, 'Lyric thinking: towards a global poetics', unpublished MS.
[10] I draw here on anthropological work on the 'ontological turn' and explore its affordances for literary study. For explanatory frameworks that lay out this approach, see Joe Moshenska and Ayesha Ramachandran, 'Faerieland's cannibal metaphysics: Spenser with Eduardo Viveiros de Castro', *Spenser Studies* 37 (2023), 119–44, and Carina L. Johnson and Ayesha Ramachandran, 'Introduction – the jaguar's beer: critical approaches to multiplicity in the early modern world', *Modern Philology* 119 (2021), 1–12.

paradoxically, seeks to transcend time and place through poetic unfolding. Defined in these terms, lyric becomes a capacious category as easily including soliloquies and songs from Shakespeare's plays as it does sonnets. Thus defined, lyric also includes works such as Taneja's *Aftermath*, ostensibly written in prose, but which draw on the phenomenological and ontological force of lyric. To put these various modalities of lyric thinking in conversation is to open up new ways of charting the continuing, if fraught, meanings of Shakespeare's poetry in our own time.

I come to these questions inspired by two very different interpretive exhortations: Sheldon Pollock's assertion of philology's continuing importance, and Sandeep Parmar's meditations on the British lyric inheritance for poets of colour.[11] Pollock has identified 'three dimensions of philology', that is, the tensions between emplacements of the text in its own time (historicism), traditions of its reception (traditionism) and attention to the particular interpreter's own subjectivity (presentism). For Pollock, successful acts of philological interpretation (understood in a Nietzschean sense of 'slow reading') are self-reflexive, involving a delicate balancing act between these dimensions.[12] Such a 'state of heightened self-awareness about what exactly we are doing when we are reading', he argues, 'arises in direct proportion to the time-space distance that separates us from the origins of the text. The closer the text is, the less conscious we are of the processes by which we make sense of it.' Philology is at its best, in other words, when the philologist is multiply removed from her object of study: '[w]hen we read forms of literature that are maximally distant in time and space', he argues, 'when modern Westerners read non-modern non-Western texts, for example – philology becomes maximally present.'[13] Though Pollock, as a white male Sanskrit scholar, speaks from a particular critical subject position, inverting the terms of his claim produces a useful perspective: what if philology becomes maximally present when modern *non-Western* readers read *non-modern Western texts*? Leaving aside the difficult ontological question of how we might differentiate Western and non-Western readers and texts, Pollock's assertion highlights the ways in which embracing our maximal removal from the source or original text – that fetishized grail of literary critics – might in fact be far more instructive than interpretive efforts to bridge the gaps. I therefore take Pollock's insight about philology and interpretive distance as a model for an alternate lyric theory: one that embraces variously distanced and different subject positions as an effective means towards poetic interpretation. In practical terms, this means allowing contemporary 'non-Western' readers and writers to lead our way back to Shakespeare.

Just such a critical experiment leads me to Sandeep Parmar's powerful analysis of race, colonialism and lyric, first in *Threads* (co-written with Bhanu Kapil and Nisha Ramayya) and then in her long essay, 'Still not a British subject'. In these essays, she confronts the ways in which British Asians – poets like herself, Kapil and Taneja – are still not considered British, and thus 'Western', subjects because their South Asian heritage, diasporic connections and religious difference have been racialized into a space of 'non-Western' alterity. Presented as a dialogue with Bhanu Kapil, captured in the hybrid idiom of the scholarly essay, autobiographic meditation and lyrical (yes, lyric!) email exchange, *Threads* opens by confronting the legacy of the lyric I in British poetry:

The lyric subject, the lyric 'I', was largely invisible to me until I crossed a border. To put it more accurately, it became noticeable only when I returned to England, where I was born, and into the sovereignty of its dominant poetic mode. Accustomed to a broader range in American poetry, my first encounter with the contemporary British lyric placed me where I felt I had no

---

[11] Sheldon Pollock, 'Philology in three dimensions', *postmedieval: A Journal of Medieval Cultural Studies* 5 (2014), 398–413; Bhanu Kapil, Sandeep Parmar and Nisha Ramayya, *Threads* (London, 2018); Sandeep Parmar, 'Still not a British subject: race and UK poetry', *Journal of British and Irish Innovative Poetry* 12 (2020), 1–44.

[12] Pollock himself makes the comparison to Nietzsche, referring to *Morgenröthe* ['Daybreak'] which contains a long critique of practices of biblical exegesis: see 'Philology in three dimensions', p. 400. For Pollock, Nietzsche is an exemplar of the force of philological interpretation.

[13] Pollock, 'Philology in three dimensions', p. 400.

natural place. Its 'I' spoke from within a kind of integrated knowingness and belonging, even if anxious, transcending the self in favour of coherence. I, on the other hand, transformed into a curio of voice, an embodied other, vitrined like an artefact alongside those with whom I shared a passing resemblance or some common history ... Yet the lyric, of course, has a complex historical relationship with subjectivity and individual voice, both within and beyond Britain's borders ... To my mind, it is impossible to consider the lyric without fully interrogating its inherent premise of universality, its coded whiteness ... Like the exoticised subject, the absence of referentiality, of the lyric 'I', is an enactment of violence. But how do poets of colour embody the 'I'? How does it come to embody us? Is it no more than the dead metaphor of our universality, our being as other?[14]

Parmar is not the first to critique the assumed universality of the lyric first-person and its implicit reliance on humanism's desire to transcend the local differences of 'culture', which is often code for race, religion and language.[15] Here, she interrogates how the lyric subject comes into being – a process that requires self-recognition and is necessarily mediated through external signs of belonging or foreignness. Not to be recognized as a fellow-subject is to be objectified, literally rendered into a 'curio ... vitrined like an artefact'. The difference recognition and reception make, as Parmar articulates it, is reminiscent of Frantz Fanon's much discussed coming-to-consciousness of his racial difference as a colonial subject in Paris.[16] Parmar's encounter with objectification through third-person consciousness when she returns to Britain from the United States also reveals the radically different poetic ontologies that can underlie theories of lyric – that is, the assumptions and predications about what poetry *is* and thus what it can do.[17] What kind of thing is the lyric – and what is its relation to the shaping of subjectivity and subjection?

Parmar's logic depends on a frequent slippage between the poem understood as a mode of being in the world (a phenomenological and existential account of lyric) and the poem as an object in the world (an aesthetic account of lyric). If lyric universalism is premised on a coded whiteness, it does not need to engage with human particularities and can simply become an aesthetic artefact of an implicitly shared 'culture'. But such a position necessarily erases the subjectivities of those who do not share in – or who are perceived not to share in – that culture. When the lyric 'I' is evacuated of particular markers so that it can transcend the person, thereby becoming a floating signifier occupied by a myriad of similar bodies, lyric loses its ethical force, becoming, in Parmar's words, 'an enactment of violence'.

The problem Parmar diagnoses here is exacerbated when the shared culture in question is a literary inheritance: is Shakespeare, for instance, a marker of British or South Asian culture? Is he a Western or Eastern writer? In 2023, given the continuing legacies of British colonialism and the thriving afterlives of Shakespeare in Asia, these boundaries are blurry.[18] When Taneja's *We That Are Young* was published many critics saw its setting of *Lear* in contemporary India as a cultural displacement; and yet, for Taneja, a British citizen whose mother moved to the United Kingdom after Partition, Shakespeare was the means through which she came to better understand her diasporic heritage.[19] Parmar's demand to know how poets of colour can embody that universal lyric 'I' without allowing the tacit desire for universal legibility

---

[14] Kapil, Parmar and Ramayya, *Threads*, pp. 9–10.
[15] See, for instance, Dorothy J. Wang, *Thinking Its Presence: Form, Race, and Subjectivity in Contemporary Asian American Poetry* (Stanford, 2013).
[16] Frantz Fanon, *Peau noire, masques blancs* (Paris, 1995).
[17] I am drawing here on Philippe Descola, 'Modes of being and forms of predication', *HAU: Journal of Ethnographic Theory* 4 (2014), 271–80.
[18] See, for example, Alexa Alice Joubin, *Shakespeare and East Asia* (Oxford, 2021); Dennis Kennedy and Yong Li Lan, *Shakespeare in Asia: Contemporary Performance* (Cambridge, 2010); Poonam Trivedi and Minami Ryuta, eds., *Re-Playing Shakespeare in Asia* (New York, 2010).
[19] See the interview with Taneja: Joseph Campana, Ayesha Ramachandran, and Preti Taneja, 'Shakespeare and the ethics of the global', *SEL: Studies in English Literature 1500–1800* 62 (2022), 123–50.

either to erase their particular personhood or to transform them into mere emblems of otherness touches on fundamental questions of how we stake out the bounds of poetic traditions – who or what we include and exclude.

My article is, consequently, as much a meditation on the challenge of discussing Shakespeare's poetry through the lens of a poetic corpus that self-consciously resists the time-honoured technique of clearly recognizable imitation and allusion, as it is a charting of Shakespeare's continuing presence in the lyrics of contemporary British poets from the formerly colonized diaspora. I prefer not to use the term 'postcolonial', so frequently deployed to categorize and name minority writers in the Anglo-European sphere, to describe writers such as Parmar, Taneja and Bhanu Kapil because they are all British citizens who have showcased the subversive racism entailed in their separation from the mainstream British literary establishment. Terms such as 'postcolonial' and 'anglophone', while useful and transformative at particular critical and political junctures, have now become charged terms of exclusion, particularly when referring to writers born in (or who have emigrated to) the United Kingdom, the United States or Europe. Kapil's *How to Wash a Heart* (2020) and *Schizophrene* (2011) explicitly consider the tensions of trauma, migration and belonging, while Taneja's *Aftermath* is a confrontation with the structural conditions that precipitate domestic 'terrorism' in Britain. Usman Khan, a former creative writing student of Taneja's in a prison education programme, attacked and killed Jack Merritt (Taneja's Learning Together colleague) and Saskia Jones (who was volunteering on the day of the attack), after his release from prison. This double murder happened at a celebration for the very prison education programme in which he had participated. It is an event that Taneja's essay-lament struggles to reckon with and move through. Poetry's place – particularly Shakespeare's place – in these explicitly political works that resist genre and form is itself uncertain.

In an interview with Gina Apostol following the publication of *Aftermath,* Taneja identifies *Threads* as 'a lyrical work I turn to often – three of the most important voices in the UK today thinking about the ties that bind us to each other, to home, and to language itself'.[20] *Threads* opens with a citation from Bhanu Kapil's *Ban en banlieue* (2015), a collection of prose poems on racial and sexual violence that emerged from performances in Britain, the United States and India. It closes with 'Avert the Icy Feeling', Kapil's 'prose sonnet' comprised of fourteen fragments or 'notes on race and creative writing'.[21] This final movement of *Threads* is also a suggestive Shakespearian absence/erasure for it is perhaps impossible to craft an English sonnet without some acknowledgement of the shadow of Shakespeare. Kapil had in fact participated in Sharmila Cohen and Paul Legault's experiment of English-to-English 'translations' of Shakespeare's *Sonnets,* published in 2012 as *The Sonnets: Translating and Rewriting Shakespeare.*[22] There, she takes on Sonnet 91, the first of a mini-series of three sonnets in which the poet struggles with his desire and the beloved's imagined infidelity. Instead of continuing a venerable Renaissance tradition of poetic imitation, or 'translating' the poet's early modern verse into the idiom of contemporary English (as so many contributors to the volume do), Kapil fractures the poem and the form itself.

Kapil's entry – which I read as a metapoetic statement of her craft – opens with a truncated citation of Shakespeare's sonnet (only the sestet) followed by a series of prose fragments that meditate on 'the breakdown of a great love' and the therapeutic functions of poetry and writing. The Shakespearian text and Kapil's after-text are carefully bound together by techniques of recursion and reprise that are characteristic of the *Sonnets* (and of lyric more generally). The entry is divided into three distinct parts whose images recall each other: 'SONNET 91: an excerpt' (the citation of the poem's sestet only); 'SONNET 91: the last two

---

[20] Gina Apostol, 'Toward a radical hope and a world-changing rage: a conversation with Preti Taneja', *LARB,* 4 January 2022: https://lareviewofbooks.org/article/toward-a-radical-hope-and-a-world-changing-rage-a-conversation-with-preti-taneja.
[21] Kapil, Parmar and Ramayya, *Threads,* pp. 49–64.
[22] Paul Legault and Sharmila Cohen, eds., *The Sonnets: Translating and Rewriting Shakespeare* (Brooklyn, 2012).

THE POETICS OF SHAKESPEARIAN ERASURE

lines' (a lyrically inflected paragraph by Kapil describing her waking by loud birdsong); and 'HOW FRAGMENTS ATTRACT: Ecstatic pilgrimage, dismemberment, and the recombinant text' (three paragraphs that weave theoretical considerations about poetics with a personal tale of love and loss). Kapil's 'translation' of Shakespeare begins with an erasure of the sonnet's octave to produce a fragment, which becomes an occasion for the poet to grapple with the poetic and personal aftermaths that are so often thematized in her work. Writing about the significance of fragments, Kapil observes:

In writing about bodies on the point of, or just after, dispersal: what happens to the parts of the body just before they touch the ground? These are notes towards a diasporic or immigrant poetics, with a close look at non-Western models of recombinance and futurity. How can experimental writing bring an attentive, ritual approach – an adequate form – to the question of bodies and violence? And at the moment that the body 'reappears' – in time – in a different form – how might a 'recombinant text' avoid the fantasy of re-integration? In my writing, I want to think about fragments. I want to think about a fragment as vibration: as both sound and light.[23]

Though Kapil often writes of violated physical bodies, zooming in unflinchingly on their broken fragments, the 'bodies' that are dispersed here are also, in a metaphoric sleight of hand, poetic corpora. Shakespeare's poetic corpus – represented by the fragmented Sonnet 91 – is one obvious case. The *Sonnets* themselves were scattered across the British Empire through colonial educational curricula, providing a model and cultural idiom for writers from the Americas to South Asia to Australia. Kapil explicitly turns away from this (Western) model of colonial, patriarchal poetic lineage forged through assimilation, imitation and exemplarity. In 'non-Western models of recombinance and futurity' that she associates with an 'attentive, ritual approach', she hopes to find an alternative which avoids fantasies of re-integration. What she envisions is a poetics of the fragment – not a metonymic poetics gesturing back to a (lost) whole, but rather a poetics of resonance predicated on vibration, an echo ringing forward. Such a poetics is also, crucially, a poetics of erasure and transmission, a deconstruction (and destruction) of textual bodies into fragments to pass them down in new forms.

Sonnet 91 is especially suited to such a poetic vision because it celebrates the power of relation, while also capturing the consequent subjunctives of hope and despair:

> Thy love is better than high birth to me,
> Richer than wealth, prouder than garments' cost,
> Of more delight than hawks or horses be;
> And having thee, of all men's pride I boast.
>   Wretched in this alone, that thou mayst take
>   All this away, and me most wretched make.[24]

By excising the octave, Kapil removes the abstracting opening of Shakespeare's poem ('Some glory in their birth . . . '). She creates a fragment, a volta lacking its original proposition. The sonnet opens by listing various loci of self-love (birth, wealth, garments, hawks, horses) valued by unnamed others before turning to emphasize, in the sestet, the poet's desire for 'thy love'. Unlike those who care about social status as an index of self-value, the only thing the poet cares about is his relationship with the beloved – the final couplet reveals the precariousness of the poet's sense of self, utterly reliant as it is on someone else for recognition and stability. The chiastic repetition of *wretched . . . wretched*, which hinges so momentously on the 'mayst' of the penultimate line, highlights how 'all this' – everything meaningful in the poet's world – depends on the beloved's attention and regard.

For Kapil, who writes frequently of belonging and exclusion, of the desire to be recognized, and of the fragility of intimate relations that can be unmade too easily, 'it is possible to survive the last line of Sonnet 91'. This survival of an abyss of precarity comes through writing, which affords freedom and control: 'like a hawk, or horse, loosened from its dynamic tether'.[25] The loss of 'all this' in the sonnet's last line stands for the loss of a love

---

[23] Bhanu Kapil, 'Sonnet 91', in *The Sonnets*, ed. Cohen and Legault, 139–40.
[24] Kapil, 'Sonnet 91'. [25] Kapil, 'Sonnet 91'.

that is self-constituting and socially sustaining – here, Kapil refers to the end of a love affair, but the images she uses resonate with the traumatic losses she records in *Humanimal* (2009), *Schizophrene* and *How to Wash a Heart*. In Sonnet 91, the hawks and horses are symbols of aristocratic status; they are also creatures turned into objects for human consumption, restrained, domesticated and forced into docility through violent modes of training. To be untethered through writing is to break away from restraint and assimilation in terms of both social convention and literary form.

An experimental poet and striking performer, Kapil has carefully eschewed lyric's familiar habits of intertextual allusion and formal reprise in her volumes of poetry, except in strategically distanced ways. In *How to Wash a Heart*, a volume that shares close affinities with her reworking of Sonnet 91 and the 'prose sonnet' 'Avert the Icy Feeling', Shakespeare returns amid a list of prized possessions that are lost in the violence of migration:

> Silk, rubies, scripture
> Written from right
> To left.
> A shirt made from raw cotton.
> Earrings
> Torn from the ears
> In one gesture.
> A Raleigh bicycle.
> All the Arden Shakespeares.
> ...
> Either we dumped it off
> Or it was taken from us
> In a great boiling wave
> Of human gain.[26]

The 'Shakespeares' crown a rising crescendo that begins with the colonial commodities of silk and gemstones and the alterity of the Qur'an, whose verse flows in the opposite direction from English. These editions are doubly implicated in colonialism's legacies – though once imposed through colonial educational systems, they are now beloved objects, a precious part of the exile's own lost heritage. Shakespeare here signals violence, loss, complicity, desire. The poet's inability to keep the Shakespeares, like the silks and rubies, like her religion and British-made bicycle, ironically underlines her double exclusion from the places both of origin and of arrival. Stripped of all her valuables, from indigenous resources (silk, rubies) to acquired cultural capital (the Shakespeares), she is rendered unrecognizable as anything more than a refugee forced to seek the hospitality of strangers. The looting of these objects, captured in the violence of the earrings 'Torn from the ears', stands as a figure for varieties of erasure – of persons, relationships, histories – that can never be re-integrated or recombined. The unending assault of those erasures can only be held in fragments.

Kapil is not in any obvious sense a poet who can be assimilated easily into a tradition of Shakespearian reception. Yet she certainly writes 'after' Shakespeare: her metaphors and stark turns of phrase remake English poetry with a knowingness that comes from engaging with 'All the Arden Shakespeares', with having digested and remade them. *How to Wash a Heart* ends on a brilliantly Shakespearian note: as the poet-guest is taken away by an officer from the Department of Repatriation, she 'clock[s] the look / that passes between you' and understands that 'This is your revenge'.[27] Like the hero in the closing beats of a revenge tragedy, Kapil's poet-guest is consumed from both the inside and outside:

> There's a knock on the door.
> There's a hand on my arm.
> Your daughter is screaming.
> My eyes are on fire.
> There's a knock on my eye.
> There's a hand on my fire.
> There's a break in the scream.
> The scream is mine.
> My scream is at hand.[28]

In the rhythmic, staccato repetitions, scrambled and recomposed in rapid succession, Kapil captures trauma, anxiety and despair. The swift, supple shifts of words through different meanings and parts of

---

[26] Bhanu Kapil, *How to Wash a Heart* (Liverpool, 2020), p. 35.
[27] Kapil, *How to Wash a Heart*, p. 44.
[28] Kapil, *How to Wash a Heart*, p. 44.

speech is a Shakespearian poetic inheritance. There is no mention of Shakespeare, of course, but in this stripping away of the guest's place of refuge the host re-enacts the cycle of systematic erasure – the cycle of revenge itself, explored so knowingly in tragedies such as *Hamlet*, *Othello* and *The Tempest*.

Kapil's example thus offers a model for reading Taneja's glancing allusions to Shakespeare's poetry in *Aftermath*. Taneja's strategic refusal to perform familiar Shakespearian imitations, even though she draws liberally on the poetics of many other non-white poets, is also an exhortation to consider the dilemma of belonging. She too practises a poetics of Shakespeare erasure – one that she develops, arguably, in the interstices between the digital installation that she helped to co-curate and collaborated on as a Writer in Residence for the TIDE project at Oxford in 2019–20 and the subsequent writing of *Aftermath* (2021).

Imagined as a 'salon' – an intimate gathering of scholars, poets and artists, usually in a house, and familiar across both European and South Asian cultural contexts – the TIDE Salon was initially planned as a live performance event. The advent of the COVID-19 pandemic in 2020 forced its relocation into a digital venue, transforming it in the process into a 'radical new archive' and 'a groundbreaking, interactive multimedia collaboration' between the scholars of the TIDE project – funded by the European Research Council – Preti Taneja and six sound and spoken-word artists (Steve Chandra Savale, Sarathy Korwar, Shama Rahman, Ms Mohammed, Sanah Ahsan and Zia Ahmed); the ensemble was brought together by curator and creative producer Sweety Kapoor, and made into an online video installation by filmmaker Ben Crowe (ERA Films). In its final form, the TIDE Salon is a metapoetic and critical exploration of the links between early modern and contemporary language, poetry, art; it figures the making of culture as an ongoing process of curation and preservation. Taneja contributed the poetic fragments that shape the narrative conceit of the digital installation, which opens multiple itineraries. From the embarkation page, visitors click the journey map and choose their own voyages through keywords, soundbites, video clips, images, poetry and literary fragments. These interconnections, the project notes assert, 'are meant to replicate the messy, eclectic process of historical research itself, where different ways into source material can influence the stories we tell, and where archives often invite self-reflection and creative expression'.[29]

Taneja's poetic fragments are presented as having been found by an archivist and translator working a century on from now, who seeks to make sense of them as part of a deep cultural past. Taking the name of her poetic alter ego, Aliena, from Shakespeare, Taneja builds a poetics of estrangement through the fiction of the fragmentary archive, itself a figure for historical erasure. Aliena's poems and writing fold back on a literary history of lyric from Sappho to Shakespeare to Agha Shahid Ali, punctuated by critical reflections on translation and reception from Walter Benjamin. Writing of this experiment, Taneja explains:

The fragments are in a unique form: part translation, part diary of desire ... Working in oral puns, overheard lyrics, canonical texts, original ideas, and found phrases, the fragments can be read in any order ... They allow the researcher to discover them in their own time and space of longing for unity beyond hierarchy, reversing through the installation itself the divisive project begun by Empire, allowing the researcher through interacting with the fragments and the installation to embrace and celebrate hybridity in all forms.[30]

What Taneja articulates here is akin to Kapil's emphasis on 'non-Western models of recombinance and futurity'. To reverse the divisive legacies of Empire is not to reconstitute some imagined pre-imperial whole, but rather to work with and through the fragments produced by imperial wreckage, to recombine them in new ways that produce newly hybrid forms and ways of being in the world. What might it mean to describe such a vision as a poetics of erasure? To do so, I would argue, is to

---

[29] From the online description of the TIDE Salon: www.tideproject.uk/2020/12/03/tide-salon-a-voyage-through-our-new-digital-project.
[30] From online description of the TIDE Salon (see note 29).

understand Taneja's artistic process as historically alert and future-oriented, not a shoring up of fragments so much as a gathering, a reckoning, aimed towards forging different futures that can embrace multiplicity.

The final section of the TIDE Salon project, 'Savage', which contains the most extended of Taneja's poetic fragments, illustrates these aims most clearly. The installation opens with an abstracted quote:

> But you are more intemperate in your blood
> Than Venus, or those pampred animals
> That rage in savage sensualitie.[31]

Taken from act 4, scene 1 of Shakespeare's *Much Ado About Nothing,* these are the words with which Claudio shames the innocent Hero, whom he believes has sexually betrayed him with another man. Hero, in these lines, loses her humanity – she is either divinely intemperate (like Venus) or, more likely, subhuman, like 'those pampred animalls / That rage in savage sensualitie' (*Much Ado* 4.1.60–1).[32] This opening frame proves to be a double citation – for the TIDE keyword entry for 'Savage' uses the Shakespeare quotation to illustrate the word's lexical origin as signalling 'a liminal space between the human and the animal'.[33] As Taneja and her collaborators highlight, already in Shakespeare's play, 'savage' also has a distinctly gendered dimension – it suggests a straying from a tempered masculine and patriarchal norm, a wandering impelled by desire whose consequences are dehumanization, a loss of personhood and, in Hero's case, symbolic death.

This dehumanizing language of sexual depravity is, moreover, not far from the *Sonnets*, where 'savage' appears only once, but tellingly, in Sonnet 129:

> Th'expense of spirit in a waste of shame
> Is lust in action; and till action, lust
> Is perjured, murd'rous, bloody, full of blame,
> *Savage,* extreme, rude, cruel, not to trust
> (1–4; emphasis mine)

If Hero is wrongly accused of promiscuity, the 'Dark Lady' of the *Sonnets* is unswerving in the pursuit of her desire, unabashed in her sexual agency – she evokes the lust that 'Is … Savage' in Sonnet 129, and though never directly applied to her, it is a word that captures the phenomenology of the poems associated with her. To enter into the furious energy of the 'Dark Lady' sonnets is to encounter the disintegration of syntax and meaning, the breakdown of the subject into repetitive phonemes: 'Will will fulfill the treasure of thy love, / Ay, fill it full with wills, and my will one', spits out the angry poet in Sonnet 136 (5–6). This breakdown already unfolds in Sonnet 129 as the 'savage sensualitie' of *Much Ado* is rephrased more directly as 'lust in action' which is also 'murd'rous, bloody' – the stripping away of personhood which allows the savage to emerge is here, too, figured as a patriarchal accusation.

This savage conjunction between the 'Dark Lady' of the *Sonnets* and Hero in *Much Ado* discloses a thematic nexus between sexuality, personhood and poetic subjection that feminist poets after Shakespeare have exploited to reconfigure both the history of lyric and the politics of subjectivity. For a British writer of South Asian heritage like Taneja, the racializing dimensions of the word 'savage' and its use within the Shakespearian corpus to signal both racial and gendered alterity are unmistakable. Lyric rewriting across time preserves the memory of this linguistic violence on the person, bearing witness repeatedly and, eventually, redirecting its energies into self-conscious political reflection. It is only by voicing a reimagined subject *in and through* lyric that Taneja both reveals and strips away the savagery of the *Sonnets*. In her fragmentary ghazal that concludes the TIDE Salon, Taneja, through her poetic alter ego, Aliena, ruminates on the nature of savagery and

---

[31] 'TIDE Salon transcript', p. 88.
[32] I follow the quotation here from the 'TIDE Salon transcript', but have provided the reference to the 2005 *Oxford Shakespeare.*
[33] Nandini Das, Lauren Working, Haig Smith and João Vicente Melo, *Keywords of Identity, Race, and Human Mobility in Early Modern England* (Amsterdam, 2021), p. 217.

speech, and on lyric traditions that spill over the boundaries of cultural norms:

They say the savage is almost a human who longs for something lost
Has forgotten their father, who cannot spell son, whose name is lost.

They say the savage came over here crawling, legs wide open, whose body is hair,
Who has never known laughter, who cannot spell daughter, whose shame is lost.

In the Middle French 'savage' were the spaces beyond human control: ships set out
Now in line, column, in row, rank, file a 'great game' being played (as clerks, we lost).

The English were afraid their language was the savage (compared to the Italian)
They turn tide on us, the sounds we make, our children weep as bame are lost.

Savage is unnatural and inhuman, shakespeare means woman, and dark matter
Inhuman needs punishment for the fall: so says the religion that came with the lost.
. . .

The origin of this ghazal was a ghazal: this is not a true ghazal the poet protests
The form is corrupted, the form is savage, is the form love? The train is lost –

. . .

] don't you recognise me?
] I will admit it, I like my mangoes juicy and sweet: in you, Shahid, the rain, I am lost.[34]

The choice of the ghazal form here itself signals a slanted displacement and rewriting of the sonnet tradition: as Agha Shahid Ali notes in his celebrated foreword to *Ravishing DisUnities,* the groundbreaking collection of 'real ghazals in English', sonnets are *not* the 'oldest poetic form still in wide popular use' – that privilege belongs to the ghazal.[35] Though the ghazal and the sonnet have been repeatedly analogized, such comparisons, Ali notes, are arbitrary and geared towards familiarizing and domesticating the foreignness of this Perso-Arabic form within Anglo-European poetic traditions. I would argue, moreover, that the familiarizing gesture of juxtaposing ghazal and sonnet must be understood itself as a poetics of erasure – a desire to overcome difference through assimilation rather than an exploration of that difference on its own terms (as Ali insists in *Ravishing DisUnities*). The fictional 'archivist's notes' that follow Aliena's ghazal in the TIDE Salon (also authored by Taneja) observe that

This fragment is one of the most complete of Aliena's works to survive the final years. As an example of Aliena's style it can be considered classic – with themes of love, longing, sexual desire and speaking as if from a submissive position in history.[36]

By making Aliena's longest surviving fragment a ghazal rather than a sonnet, though both share themes and subject positions, Taneja makes Shakespeare a part of the ghazal tradition rather than vice versa. She thereby enacts both a poetic erasure and a displacement.

In Aliena's savage ghazal, Taneja draws together Shakespearian preoccupations with desire and personhood (language, naming, laughter, race, relation) – the images of the colonizer – with Agha Shahid Ali's meditations on the poetic filiation and the grafting of multiple lyric traditions. The poem opens anthropologically by probing the line between human and animal through the figure of the 'savage', but within the first two couplets, 'savage' becomes identified with a resistance to patriarchy and an assertion of sexual agency ('Has forgotten their father, who cannot spell son', 'whose shame is lost'). Shifting from evolutionary histories to linguistic ones, Taneja then connects the English language itself to the racialized primitivism that it denigrates as 'savage': the word originates in Middle French ('sauvage' signifies wild, uncultivated space), and the development of vernacular English literature in the sixteenth century was itself indebted to Italian borrowings, then considered more

---

[34] 'TIDE Salon transcript', p. 109; square brackets indicate missing material.
[35] *Ravishing DisUnities: Real Ghazals in English*, ed. Agha Shahid Ali (Middletown, 2000), p. 1.
[36] 'TIDE Salon transcript', p. 109.

cultivated and elite. The sonnet is one of these Italianate inheritances, an effort to 'civilize' an unruly English idiom and give it an elegant form. Connecting this early modern moment of linguistic cultivation and hybridity to the contemporary world, however, Taneja notes how, contrary to English's own multilingual histories, language is used in the United Kingdom as a tool of exclusion: 'They turn tide on us, the sounds we make, our children weep as bame are lost.' 'BAME', the acronym for Black, Asian and Minority Ethnic, is used to denote non-white British subjects; but the implicit pun here on 'bane' suggests an attitude of hostility towards these supposedly more savage immigrants from the colonial diaspora.

Thus, in the following couplet, at the centre of the ghazal, 'savage' becomes a synonym for 'unnatural' and 'inhuman', as Taneja alludes to the sensual, sexually agentive 'Dark Lady' of the *Sonnets*, the 'dark matter' of Shakespeare-as-woman that now becomes identified with BAME poets such as Aliena/Taneja. *The Tempest* is of course another crucial intertext here. 'Savage' appears twice in that play, long associated with the dynamics of colonialism and with the use of language to discipline colonized subjects. Miranda famously tells Caliban:

> I pitied thee,
> Took pains to make thee speak, taught thee each hour
> One thing or other. When thou didst not, savage,
> Know thine own meaning, but wouldst gabble like
> A thing most brutish, I endowed thy purposes
> With words that made them known.
>
> (*Tempest* 1.2.355–60)

To be 'savage' here is to lack language and, thus, self-understanding – to not 'Know thine own meaning'. 'Gabble', a Shakespearian coinage, is the sound of BAME children, marking them as 'most brutish'. Even more tellingly, the only other use of the word 'savage' later in the play, is when Stephano encounters Caliban: 'What's the matter? Have we devils here? Do you put tricks upon's with savages and men of Ind, ha?' (*Tempest*, 2.2.57–9). There is no ambiguity here about the genealogy of colonial savagery that connects Shakespeare's Caliban to contemporary British South Asians ('men of Ind') like Taneja.

The final movement of the poem, however, takes a self-reflexively poetic turn. If the ghazal has supplanted the sonnet – or, perhaps, has engulfed the sonnet and Shakespeare – it too is a 'savage' form. Taneja's ghazal is not quite a ghazal, since it lacks the formally precise repetition of the *qafiya* (monorhyme scheme) and the *radif* (refrain).[37] But in this self-conscious falling away from Persianate poetics, the poem alludes to another ghazal about the poetics of writing across multiple literary traditions – Agha Shahid Ali's early ghazal, 'In Arabic'. The celebrated *maqta* to this poem is cited as part of the fictional 'archivist's notes' that accompany Aliena's ghazal:

> They ask me to tell them what 'Shahid' means –
> Listen: it means 'The Beloved' in Persian, 'Witness' in Arabic.

The final fragmentary lines of Aliena/Taneja's poem demands an act of poetic recognition and re-thinking through the lyric encounter, here unfolded across three languages: 'don't you recognise me? /] I will admit it, I like my mangoes juicy and sweet: in you, Shahid, the rain, I am lost.' 'Shahid', here an allusion not only to the poet, but also to the meanings of his name in Persian and Arabic, points to an elliptical, allusive exfoliation of pasts that are both personal and poetic: the entwinement of Shakespeare and Shahid, of poetic personae that blur into the etymologies of naming. Ali himself had famously and wryly written of the spectre of Shakespeare looming over postcolonial South Asian writers in various contexts. In his ironic essay, 'A darkly defense of dead white males', he notes: '[w]e who write in English are often in a bind of anger that we take out on Shakespeare and others.'[38] In 'Ghalib's ghazal',

---

[37] On the poetics and prosody of the ghazal, see *Ravishing DisUnities*, ed. Ali, pp. 3–4, which is of particular relevance for Taneja given her allusion to Shahid in her ghazal.

[38] Agha Shahid Ali, 'A darkly defense of dead white males', in *Poet's Work, Poet's Play: Essays on the Practice and the Art*, ed. Daniel Tobin and Pimone Triplett (Ann Arbor, 2008), 144–60; p. 159.

however, Ali draws on Shakespeare as a critical trope to describe the nineteenth-century poet ('He is to Urdu what Shakespeare is to English').[39] And in 'The editor revisited', Ali bitterly reflects on the ambivalences of writing in English and within an English literary tradition:

> Now collecting a degree in English,
> will I embrace my hungry country
> with an armful of soliloquies?
> This trade in words continues however as
> Shakespeare feeds my alienation.[40]

Shakespeare is omnipresent even when he needs to be erased. Even erasure, however, is a palimpsestic form of presence. Taneja emphasizes the significance of these fraught recognitions – of poets, of subjectivities, of canons – through time and across linguistic and cultural boundaries.

Aftermath, too, returns to Shakespeare, savagery and *The Tempest* in its closing movement. As 'creative work keeps going alongside grief', the writer goes to the coast. There, she makes 'spirals in sand, aware of the difference between doing this and capturing it in writing'.[41] How can writing, art, creativity respond to and transform 'this world', asks Taneja, fiercely attempting to make sense of the gaps between the quotidian dramas of grief, violence, exclusion and 'attempting to live with clarity in the struggle'. The answer she offers, perhaps not surprisingly, is a return to Shakespeare and lyric. Her essay-lament becomes 'the words that keep [us] in this world'; she leaves them, she writes, 'for everyone who falls to violent harms, out from the wreck towards some imagined new future'. This wreck is now that of Shakespeare's *Tempest* merged with Rich's unconscious: 'Light changes under water, and through the refraction, the wreck might disappear. We do not want to make it anew. We need a different kind of ship to sail on a collective breath, taken and exhaled.'[42] *The Tempest* opens with a shipwreck. That shipwreck is at once real and fictional, orchestrated by Prospero, controlled by Ariel, designed to precipitate a reckoning with the past. But the shipwreck is also a metaphor – for personal culpabilities, for long grief and incurable suffering. And yet what begins as a gesture towards revenge, a cycle of remaining in thrall to past wrongs, turns almost unexpectedly into forgiveness and a future-oriented healing (for the younger generation at least). For *The Tempest* is not a tragedy but a romance whose logic is fuelled by lyric. Its most memorable character, Caliban, gains a powerful literary afterlife beyond and outside Shakespeare.

Taneja's gesture towards Shakespeare in this closing is both glancing and profound. She becomes an ambivalent mix of Prospero and Caliban. One of the teachers whose student turned against her (civilizing?) mission, she also remains, nevertheless, a Caliban in contemporary Britain. By erasing Shakespeare – and being erased by the Shakespeare industry (instantiated by Atwood's *Tempest*) – Taneja cannot help but engage in a counter-intuitive call and response, a practice that I have been calling a poetics of erasure. Such a poetics draws on lyric thinking through layers of poetic tradition to see and make visible the ambivalences of reception, canon-formation and creative rejuvenation – while also refusing the erasure of voices which might otherwise be reduced to savagery. Seen in these terms, poetry itself becomes an integral part of a transhistorical critical-interpretive tradition. Lyric, I argue, is also a self-reflexive agent of literary critique, not only of other poems, styles or cultural inheritances, but also of theories of lyric as they have developed in dialogue with poetic praxis over time. Taneja's *Aftermath*, a self-proclaimed lament, simultaneously inhabits the positions of poet, critic and teacher. And in so doing it begins to open up and shape alternate lyric canons – where Shakespeare and Shahid, Faiz and Rankine can speak to each other despite time, despite difference.

---

[39] Agha Shahid Ali, *The Veiled Suite: The Collected Poems* (New York, 2009), p. 270.
[40] Agha Shahid Ali, *In Memory of Begum Akhtar* (Kolkata, 1979).
[41] Taneja, *Aftermath*, p. 222. [42] Taneja, *Aftermath*, p. 224.

LUCRECE, LETTERS AND THE MOMENT OF LIPSIUS

FEISAL G. MOHAMED

Letters, we already know, matter a good deal in Shakespeare's plays. In his book-length account of the topic, Alan Stewart estimates that 111 letters appear on stage in the plays of the First Folio. In fact, there are only four plays in which letters do not appear: *A Midsummer Night's Dream*, *The Taming of the Shrew*, *The Tempest* and *Henry V*. Shakespeare goes well beyond his sources in this respect; Stewart associates this tendency with an early modern culture of letter-writing, a culture that has been well documented by several scholars, including Roger Chartier, Gary Schneider and James Daybell.[1] Lynne Magnusson has drawn our attention to the significance of letter-writing to the social and discursive environment of late Elizabethan and Jacobean drama.[2] Yet despite all of this critical attention, and in a way significant to the focus of this special issue, there is a notable, if also typical, absence in Stewart's observation that letters 'run through all the genres and [Shakespeare's] entire career – early plays and late plays, comedies, tragedies, tragicomedies, and histories'.[3] Missing from the list is poetry. That absence is striking given that 'letters sadly penned in blood' make a brief but memorable appearance in *A Lover's Complaint* (line 47),[4] and, more significantly, that the climax of *Lucrece* hinges on a letter: the missive Lucrece writes on the morning after being raped by Prince Tarquin, summoning her husband and her father to Collatia. Lucrece's not only adds to our catalogue of Shakespeare's letters, but is also quite unique in offering us a moment of composition. Letters tend to arrive on stage fully formed: sitting down with pen and paper to struggle over one's sentences demands too many props and yields meagre dramatic dividends (imagine a performance of *King Lear* in which the writing of every one of its letters was staged). Turning to poetry allows Shakespeare to linger on Lucrece's act of writing, heightening our awareness of the many ways in which it is extremely fraught and remarkably strategic.

In so presenting Lucrece, Shakespeare stands apart from his sources: we do not find a writing Lucretia in Livy or Ovid. After being raped by Tarquinius, Livy's Lucretia

grieving at her great disaster, dispatched the same message to her father in Rome and to her husband at Ardea: that they should each take a trusty friend and come; that they must do this and do it quickly, for a frightful thing had happened.

('Lucretia maesta tanto malo nuntium Romam eundem ad patrem Ardeamque ad virum mittit, ut cum singulis fidelibus amicis veniant; ita facto maturatoque opus esse; rem atrocem incidisse')[5]

---

[1] Alan Stewart, *Shakespeare's Letters* (Oxford, 2008), pp. 4–5; Roger Chartier, *La correspondence: Les usages de la lettre au XIXe siècle* (Paris, 1991) [three chapters translated as *Correspondence: Models of Letter-Writing from the Middle Ages to the Nineteenth Century* (Princeton, 1997)]; Gary Schneider, *The Culture of Epistolarity: Vernacular Letters and Letter Writing in Early Modern England* (Newark, DE, 2005); James Daybell, *Women Letter-Writers in Tudor England* (Oxford, 2006) and *The Material Letter in Early Modern England* (Houndmills, 2012).
[2] Lynne Magnusson, *Shakespeare and Social Dialogue: Dramatic Language and Elizabethan Letters* (Cambridge, 1999).
[3] Stewart, *Shakespeare's Letters*, p. 4.
[4] See the article by Hannah Crawforth and Elizabeth Scott-Baumann in this volume.
[5] Livy, *History of Rome, Volume I: Books 1–2*, trans. B. O. Foster (Cambridge, MA, 1919), pp. 200–3 [book 1, ch. 58].

LUCRECE, LETTERS AND THE MOMENT OF LIPSIUS

The *nuntium* in the Latin original is usually applied to a message delivered orally, as when Livy himself uses the term elsewhere in his *History of Rome*. When Philip learns of the fall of Chalcis, 'news was brought to him of the disaster that had befallen his allied city' ('esset nuntiata clades sociae urbis').[6] The noun that is a cognate of this verb, *nuntius*, is also associated with oral delivery of messages, referring either to the messenger or the message, as when Horace describes Mercury in the *Odes* as 'messenger of mighty Jove and of the gods' ('magni Iovis et deorum / nuntium').[7] In the *Fasti*, Ovid offers even less detail than Livy does, simply telling us that Lucretia 'summoned' ('evocat') Collatinus and Lucretius. While he emphasizes Lucretia's deep emotional distress – 'She sat with her hair dishevelled, like a mother who must attend the funeral pyre of her son' ('passis sedet illa capillis, / ut solet ad nati mater itura rogum') – she does not pause to contemplate how the summons itself might best be phrased. It is clear that when they arrive, her father and husband do not know exactly what has happened, and are left wondering 'why she mourned' ('quae luctus causa') and 'what ill had befallen her' ('quove sit icta malo').[8]

Shakespeare develops this moment significantly, and in ways befitting his poem's emphasis on internal conflict and moments of decision. Livy and Ovid have Lucretia send for her father and husband without fully revealing Tarquinius' crime. Shakespeare turns that non-revelation into a moment of writerly self-questioning. His Lucrece composes a letter and struggles to achieve just the right tone: she wants to produce something neither 'too curious-good' nor 'blunt and ill' (line 1300). We are aware not just of her withholding information for strategic effect, as in Shakespeare's Roman sources, but of questions of style: how her letter might come across to its recipient, and how that recipient then views and responds to the letter and its author.

Thomas Heywood seems to have picked up on this in his terrible play *The Rape of Lucrece*, likely written shortly after the 1594 publication of Shakespeare's poem. Here Lucrece sends her husband Colatinus a letter that is then read aloud by her close ally Brutus:

> Deere Lord, if ever thou will see thy *Lucrece*
> Choose of the friends which thou affectest best,
> And all important businesse set apart,
> Repaire to *Rome*: commend me to Lord *Brutus*,
> *Valerius, Mutius, Horatius*.
> Say I treat in their presence, where my Father
> *Lucretius* shall attend them, farewell sweet,
> Th'affaires are great, then doe not faile to meet.[9]

Heywood stays within his sources in not having Lucrece reveal the reason for her summons. But in staging the reading of the letter in front of Colatinus and his associates, its opacity becomes the subject of curiosity and speculation. Valerius sniffs an opportunity for revenge against the house of Tarquin. And the clown who has delivered the letter reveals that Tarquin's son has paid Lucrece a visit, but 'my Lady swore me, that whatsoever I suspected I should say nothing'.[10] He, Valerius and Horatius then break into a merry song imagining the progress of the prince's sexual advances: '*Did he take the Lady by the thigh man / Thigh man / I man / Ha ha ha ha man.*'[11] It is an oddly timed moment of levity, given that we have just witnessed young Tarquin's assault on Lucrece and are about to return our attention to her in the next scene, in which she declares herself to have 'the

---

[6] Livy, *History of Rome, Volume IX: Books 31–34*, trans. J. C. Yardley (Cambridge, MA, 2017), pp. 68–9 [book 32, ch. 24].

[7] Horace, *Odes and Epodes*, trans. C. E. Bennett (Cambridge, MA, 1914), pp. 30–1 [1.10.5–6].

[8] Ovid, *Fasti*, trans. James D. Frazer, rev. G. P. Goold (Cambridge, MA, 1931), pp. 116–17 [2.814–18].

[9] Thomas Heywood, *The Rape of Lucrece*, ed. Allan Holaday, *Illinois Studies in Language and Literature* 34 (1950); lines 2246–53; italics in original. On this play, and larger questions of the performance of rape on the early modern stage, see Jean E. Howard, 'Interrupting the Lucrece effect? The performance of rape on the early modern stage', in *The Oxford Handbook of Shakespeare and Embodiment: Gender, Sexuality, and Race*, ed. Valerie Traub (Oxford, 2016), 657–72.

[10] Heywood, *Rape of Lucrece*, lines 2280–1.

[11] Heywood, *Rape of Lucrece*, lines 2329–32.

truest grief of heart, / That ever entered any Matrons brest'.[12]

The comparison to Heywood shows just how tightly Shakespeare's Lucrece is able to control events following young Tarquin's attack, through her letter and her careful dramaturgy of her suicide. Perhaps this is a natural consequence of the difference in genre between a poem and a play, a difference releasing Shakespeare from the temptation to lighten the mood for a moment with songs and clowning. But there may be other reasons, too. Shakespeare makes his Lucrece a conspicuously canny political operator, and, I will argue, her moment of letter-writing highlights that canniness in a way consistent with the vogue for *raison d'état*.[13]

We shall explore these aspects of the poem in the context of sixteenth-century humanist interest in letter-writing, and especially of Justus Lipsius's rising influence in the 1590s, centred on his landmark work of political theory, the *Politicorum sive civilis doctrinae libri sex* (1589), and his manual on letter-writing, the *Epistolica institutio* (1591). The *Epistolica* especially makes more visible the complex ways in which stylistic choices ought to be made according to a letter's aims and audience, qualities at play in Lucrece's brief letter, which treats a matter of public and private concern, and which must head off any potential questions about consensual coupling with young Tarquin. The letter as genre impresses upon us other dynamics of the poem, and of *Lucrece* as a material text, as well. Uncertainty and vulnerability haunt every stage in the life of a letter: composition, circulation, interpretation. It is a genre especially prone to unintended consequences. Much as Lucrece exerts remarkable mastery over the actions and emotions of the audience she gathers to her suicide, her corpse then becomes an important artefact that enters public circulation. This letter-like quality is reproduced in the first edition of the poem, with its title page offering the work simply as *Lucrece*, with no indication of authorship, and with an 'anchora spei' device – a sort of seal that may signal associations with other works published by Richard Field.

* * *

The first name that comes to mind in a history of early modern letter-writing is Desiderius Erasmus, whose manual on the subject and whose vast corpus of letters fix the genre as central to humanist circulation of ideas and concern with style. For Erasmus, Cicero both is and is not a foundational figure. On the one hand, he is the classical apostle of rhetorical arts whose own letters offer a model for early modern writers. Erasmus points to Cicero as a pattern of elevated style in the letter, and of length should occasion demand:

Those who would never have the diction of a letter rise above the commonplace, but maintain that it should stay close to everyday speech, will easily be confuted by a single letter of Cicero: I mean, of course, the letter he wrote to Octavian, which, far from creeping along the ground, rises to storms of oratory and even ends on a note of tragedy.[14]

Addressed to Octavian in the final weeks of Cicero's life, and in the days before the inauguration of the Triumvirate of Octavian, Mark Antony and Lepidus, sixteenth-century editions of Cicero included the letter to which Erasmus refers, though it is now considered spurious. Notably, even as Erasmus points to Cicero as a model in this moment, he does so with frequent reference to Horace. In telling us that this letter is 'far from creeping along the ground', Erasmus quotes Horace's modest remark in the *Epistles*, in which he distinguishes between his own crawling verse and the soaring achievements of Virgil and Varius.[15] In saying that this letter builds itself up to a tragic outburst and makes use of 'bombast and

---

[12] Heywood, *Rape of Lucrece*, lines 2352–3.
[13] I have previously explored the relevance of *raison d'état* to *Lucrece* in 'Raison d'état, religion, and the body in The Rape of Lucrece', *Religions* 10, Special Issue: Religions in Shakespeare's Writings, ed. David V. Urban (2019); available at mdpi.com.
[14] Erasmus, *On the Writing of Letters*, in *Collected Works of Erasmus*, vols. 25–6, ed. J. K. Sowards (Toronto, 1985), vol. 25, p. 15.
[15] Horace, *Epistles*, in *Satires, Epistles, The Art of Poetry*, trans. H. Rushton Fairclough (Cambridge, MA, 1926),416–17 [2.1.251–2]; see Erasmus, *On the Writing of Letters*, p. 15, n. 3.

sesquipedalian words', Erasmus quotes Horace's *Ars poetica*.¹⁶ Erasmus cites Cicero, or thinks he is citing Cicero, as a touchstone, but his use of Horace highlights the literariness of the epistolary form as much as its debts to conventions of oratory.

The letter receives renewed attention, and renewed interest as a political art, in the 1590s through the work of Justus Lipsius. In his brief treatise on letters, the *Epistolica institutio* (1591), Lipsius also advertises his debts to Cicero while going further than Erasmus in distancing letter-writing from the conventions of oratory. Though Lipsius recommends reading Cicero, and in fact reading only Cicero, as an important phase in a young humanist's development, he is emphatic that the many conventions surrounding orations should not be duplicated in letters. Even for what he calls a 'serious' letter, which is to say a letter 'which pertains to public or private matters, but also treats them fully and carefully', one should arrange one's writing with studied carelessness: serious letters require most 'in the way of arrangement; but in such a way that you stop short of the diligence of oratory, and take it as a model, not copy it. Why bind yourself with rules? ... [O]rganize according to discretion and topic.'¹⁷ For Erasmus, and especially for Lipsius, then, letters are a key means of following Cicero while putting Ciceronianism in its place, delimiting its utility and querying the extent to which it comprises the height of eloquence in all places and at all times.

For Lipsius this delimiting of Ciceronian style is part of a larger embrace, stylistic and intellectual, of Tacitus and Seneca. Much of his career is focused on these two authors. He publishes an edition of Tacitus in 1575 and his 1589 *Politicorum libri sex* – or, to use the title of its English translation, *Sixe Bookes of Politickes* – is widely regarded as a major source in the period on the subject of Tacitist *prudentia*. Its appearance builds on several key *raison d'état* texts of the latter half of the sixteenth century: Francesco Guicciardini's history of Italy first appears in English translation in 1579, and Giovanni Botero's *Della ragion di stato* is first published in Venice in 1589, quickly to become something of a sensation, with further editions in 1590, 1596 and 1598.

Contributing to this interest is Henry Savile's 1591 translation of Tacitus' *Agricola* and the first four books of the *Histories*, the first English translation of any of the Roman historian's works.¹⁸ Lipsius's *Politicorum* rides this trend, first appearing on the Continent in 1589, published in London in 1590, and translated into English by William Jones in 1594. This is the same year as the first publication of *Lucrece*, with both texts being printed by Richard Field, a point to which we shall return. There is evidence that *raison d'état* had currency in circles important to Shakespeare in the 1590s: Richard Tuck has framed the politics of the Essex circle in terms of revived interest in Tacitus, in which light he views the famous performance of *Richard II* on the eve of Essex's ill-fated rebellion. As Andrew Hadfield has emphasized, Southampton, the dedicatee of *Venus and Adonis* and *Lucrece*, as a member of the Essex circle, likely shared its political and intellectual affinities.¹⁹ If we believe Ben Jonson's remark to William Drummond of Hawthornden, it was Essex who wrote the epistle prefacing the Savile translation. But we probably should not believe Jonson. Jan Waszink has unpacked the several reasons why this is likely a post facto association of Essex with the Savile translation's supposed promotion of rebellion, though he also confirms the importance of Tacitist thought in the Essex circle: while Savile's 1591 translation was not likely a product of Essex's patronage, it is likely a text that led Essex to take an interest in Savile in the years that followed.²⁰ Tuck suggests as

---

¹⁶ Horace, *Ars poetica*, in *Satires, Epistles, The Art of Poetry*, trans. Fairclough, pp. 458–9 [line 97]; see Erasmus, *On the Writing of Letters*, p. 15, n. 10.
¹⁷ Justus Lipsius, *Principles of Letter-Writing [Epistolica institutio]*, trans. and ed. R. V. Young and Thomas Hester (Carbondale and Edwardsville, IL, 1996), pp. 21–3. Further references to this text are indicated in parentheses by the abbreviation *EI*.
¹⁸ *The ende of Nero and Beginning of Galba. Fower Bookes of the Histories of Cornelius Tacitus. The Life of Agricola*, trans. Sir Henry Savile (Oxford, 1591) [STC 23642].
¹⁹ Andrew Hadfield, *Shakespeare and Republicanism* (Cambridge, 2005), p. 139.
²⁰ Jan H. Waszink, 'Henry Savile's Tacitus and the English role on the Continent: Leicester, Hotman, Lipsius', *History of European Ideas*, 42 (2016), 317–18. On Lipsius and Tacitism,

a potential author of the epistle Anthony Bacon, brother of Francis and member of the Essex circle.[21] All of this makes Lipsius's manual on letter-writing deserving of our notice, though it has been ignored in scholarship on letters in Shakespeare, in which Erasmus may be given more credit than is due.[22]

A deep investment in Tacitus, and in practical politics more generally, inflects Lipsius's brief manual on letter-writing. Although he recommends that an early reader focus exclusively on Cicero, and that a mature one read Cicero nightly, he also makes clear that others are better models for the mature letter writer:

in *adult* imitation, I permit him to go forth freely and wander through every type of writer. Read, examine, and gather flowers from every meadow for this garland of eloquence. But especially I would urge the reading of Sallust, Seneca, Tacitus, and that kind of concise and subtle writer by whose sharp pruning hook the luxuriance is cut back for a little while, and the discourse is made terse, strong, and truly masculine.

(*EI*, 38–41; italics in original)

Experienced readers may close their Cicero for a moment so that they might promiscuously wander and gather in the meadows of eloquence. But in the next breath Lipsius whisks away this image of openness and fecundity: Sallust, Seneca and Tacitus are ruthless gardeners whose carefully pruned writings provide a model of 'masculine' style. We do best to gather not the lushest flowers, but those which have been artfully stripped of excess.

So, at its best, a letter is not Ciceronian oratory. It affects a greater carelessness of style, adopting a tone of familiarity with its reader by imitating the rhythms, and the tendency towards brevity of expression, typical of conversation. Cicero is enlisted as supporting this principle, as he describes one of his letters as woven 'from everyday words' (*EI*, 31). Seneca equally likens letters to everyday conversation, saying that both should be as 'if we were sitting and walking together, unlabored and easy' (*EI*, 31). 'Just as women are said to adorn in order not to seem adorned', Lipsius tells us, 'for the same purpose only should ornament accompany a letter, and not be affected in it or by it' (*EI*, 31). Here the gendered terms of cutting back luxuriance are reversed: not masculine exercise of the pruning hook, but feminine allure through restrained adornment. The letter writer would also do well to study drama, as a mode of writing in which authors achieve stylistic virtuosity while also imitating everyday speech. And if it is everyday speech that we are after, then the particular kind of drama that ought to be imitated is comedy. Lipsius urges as 'especially suitable for the letter' the careful study of Terence and Plautus, the latter especially being praised for his 'charm, loveliness, and graciousness' (*EI*, 39). The *Epistolica* also makes visible the physical resemblance of books and letters. Several Roman authorities are cited likening letters to 'a kind of compact little book'. Suetonius tells us that Julius Caesar was the first 'to have changed letters to the Senate into pages with the format of a small notebook', and Isidore likewise describes 'poems and letters' as a 'briefer form' of book (*EI*, 7). These remarks, according to Lipsius, explain Seneca's statement that 'a letter ought not to fill up the reader's left hand' (*EI*, 7). Letters are a kind of book, then, but on a small scale.

---

see Waszink, 'Lipsius and Grotius: Tacitism', *History of European Ideas* 39 (2013), 158–62.

[21] See Richard Tuck, *Philosophy and Government 1572–1651* (Cambridge, 1993), pp. 104–8. For further accounts of the rise of Tacitism and *raison d'état* in the late sixteenth century, see Peter Burke, 'Tacitism, scepticism, and reason of state', in *The Cambridge History of Political Thought 1450–1700*, ed. J. H. Burns and Mark Goldie (Cambridge, 1991), 479–98, and Maurizio Viroli, *From Politics to Reason of State* (Cambridge, 1992).

[22] Stewart refers to Erasmus as the scholar who 'most fully realized the possibilities of the letter form', though he also persuasively argues that late sixteenth-century influence of Erasmus's manual on letter-writing has been overstated (*Shakespeare's Letters*, pp. 12–15). Neither Stewart nor Magnusson mentions Lipsius's significance in the 1590s; Schneider offers only a brief mention (*Culture of Epistolarity*, p. 49). Curtis Perry rightly notes that Lipsius is a key figure in late humanist interest in Tacitus and Seneca; see his *Shakespeare and Senecan Tragedy* (Cambridge, 2021), pp. 156–60.

LUCRECE, LETTERS AND THE MOMENT OF LIPSIUS

Lipsius's influence on *Lucrece* has already been discerned in the language of 'mixed prudence' deployed by Prince Tarquin during his brief attempt at seduction. Answering the question as to whether the pure wine of prudence may be mixed with deceit, Lipsius remarks that, while outright mischief is to be avoided, virtuous aims might sometimes be followed by 'indirect courses': 'Wine, although it be somewhat tempered with water, continueth to be wine: so doth prudence not change her name, albeit a fewe drops of deceit bee mingled therewith.'[23] Young Tarquin offers a perverse application of the principle:

> A little harm done to a great good end
> For lawful policy remains enacted.
> The poisonous simple sometime is compacted
>   In a pure compound; being so applied,
>   His venom in effect is purified.
>   (528–32)

As András Kiséry observes, these lines are marked with gnomic pointing in the 1594 edition. This offers a further visual cue signalling their status as political *sententiae*, and suggests that the Lucrece story is being offered to readers in part as a case study in *raison d'état*.[24]

While Kiséry suggests that placing Lipsian maxims in the mouth of Prince Tarquin ultimately calls the discourse of political prudence into question, we must recognize that Tarquin is clearly offering a corruption of Lipsian principles, aimed at satisfying his own base impulses rather than preserving the state – and in fact, as every reader enters knowing, in a way that will cause major disruption in the state. There are countervailing examples of Lipsianism in the poem. Strategically restrained letter-writing signals the way in which Lucrece is also a Lipsian actor, even if not, as we will see, to the same extent as Brutus is at the poem's conclusion: her actions may have political consequences, but in their immediate aims they are limited to the sphere of domestic honour. Lucrece faces letter-writing challenges that Lipsius associated with those typical of playwrighting: how to produce polished prose that also imitates the ease of everyday speech, how to treat serious matters while also maintaining a tone of familiar address. And letters are a sort of published dramatic monologue. They can circulate beyond one's intended audience, as we see in Heywood's play, and can fall into hostile hands, adding another reason for care and caution – or prudence, to use the Tacitist keyword – in their composition. Much work on the material history of Shakespeare's plays has drawn our attention to the ways in which performance and print interact with one another.[25] The letter adds to that conversation by suggesting that interactions between drama, letter-writing and the circulation of material texts are suggested not only by the market concerns of the playhouse and the bookstall, but also by intellectual interest in the practical political arts, which are also practical humanistic arts, made visible in Lipsius.

* * *

With all of these concerns of style and occasion, of circulation and effect, in mind, we can turn to the scene of Lucrece's letter-writing in Shakespeare's poem. In her bedchamber on the morning after being attacked by young Tarquin, Lucrece is weeping with her maid, though her maid's sympathetic tears are shed without fully knowing the cause of her mistress's distress. At this point Lucrece sends for 'paper, ink, and pen', before immediately realizing she already has these things at hand: 'Yet save that labour, / For I have them here' (1289–90). She is, apparently, a habitual letter writer. Nonetheless, the challenges of writing at this particular moment are made clear: 'What should I say? ... The cause craves haste, and it

---

[23] Justus Lipsius, *Six Bookes of Politickes or Civil Doctrine*, trans. William Jones (London, 1594) [STC 15701], p. 114. On *Lucrece* and Lipsius, and the importance of *raison d'état* in the Essex circle, see Martin Dzelzainis, 'Shakespeare and political thought', in *A Companion to Shakespeare*, ed. David Scott Kastan (Oxford, 1999), 106–7.
[24] András Kiséry, *Hamlet's Moment: Drama and Political Knowledge in Early Modern England* (Oxford, 2016), pp. 74–7.
[25] For a recent, book-length study of the interaction between print and performance, see Claire M. L. Bourne, *Typographies of Performance in Early Modern England* (Oxford, 2020).

will soon be writ' (1291, 1295). We are thrust into the middle of a situation demanding extreme care in writing while also demanding celerity. The maid leaves and Lucrece 'prepares to write, / First hovering o'er the paper with her quill' (1296–7). It is a moment of writerly hesitation and decision-making unique to Shakespeare's interpretation of this oft-told story:

> Conceit and grief an eager combat fight;
> What wit sets down is blotted straight with will;
> This is too curious-good, this blunt and ill.
>   Much like a press of people at a door
>   Throng her inventions, which shall go before.
>
> At last she thus begins: 'Thou worthy lord
> Of that unworthy wife that greeteth thee,
> Health to thy person! Next, vouchsafe t'afford –
> If ever, love, thy Lucrece thou wilt see –
> Some present speed to come and visit me.
>   So I commend me, from our house in grief;
>   My woes are tedious, though my words are brief.'
>   (1298–1309)

At this point, Lucrece 'folds . . . up the tenor of her woe' (1310), indicating that we are seeing the letter in its entirety, summoning the image of a folded sheet and recalling Lipsius's remarks on the letter as resembling a little book. Foregrounding 'inventions' thronging for inclusion in the letter brings conventions of rhetoric to the fore – these are the focus of Cicero's *De inventione* and the second book of *De oratore*. 'Inventions' will also bring to mind the conventional topoi whereby ideas are persuasively organized and expressed. And in the same stroke we are further distanced, though the distance has been made clear already, from any account of Lucrece's letter as a spontaneous outpouring of grief.

So Cicero is summoned. But the adjustments to Ciceronian conventions that Lipsius has identified as necessary to effective letter-writing are visible, too. Lucrece has certainly been brief, and she has written to an intimate in intimate terms. Her letter is highly personal: though 'inventions' crowd at her door, she balances formality – 'Thou worthy lord' – with affectionate familiarity – 'If ever, love, thy Lucrece thou wilt see'. The latter, interjected phrase achieves what Lipsius has described as an affected unaffectedness of style resembling natural speech, or at least dramatic speech, more than oratory. Coming to this letter with Lipsius in mind also draws our attention to some of the particular challenges that Lucrece is facing. This is a letter on a matter both public and personal. As Lucrece made clear in her impassioned appeals to Prince Tarquin during his attack, his crime has political ramifications and will tarnish his father's reputation as king. Part of the stylistic challenge Lucrece faces is whether to adopt the tone of a serious letter or a familiar one: she has news to report of major consequence to her household, to Collatia, and to Rome, but she is also an injured wife making an appeal to her husband. Erasmus tells us that a letter's 'best style' is that suited to the topic.[26] What does *that* mean in Lucrece's situation? She has several potential causes to pursue, as a wronged subject objecting to a tyrannical prince, a noble who has been assaulted by a member of the royal household, a violated woman seeking justice, a wife anxious to defend her honour. After her hesitation, she opts for a brief, familiar letter summoning her husband to 'our house in grief', a letter that significantly opens with the language of a dutiful and modest wife.

That opening is but one of the letter's strategic manoeuvres. Her letter engages in a purposeful ambiguity – 'Her certain sorrow writ uncertainly' (1311) – so that 'Collatine may know / Her grief, but not her grief's true quality' (1312–13). And the reason is that the distance of a letter might give Collatine time and space to wonder about his wife's virtue: 'She dares not thereof make discovery, / Lest he should hold it her own gross abuse' (1314–15). Here we see that the page, even if informed by conventions of drama, is no replacement for drama itself, as Shakespeare must have felt keenly in this poem written with the theatres closed due to plague. Lucrece is already planning her suicide, to stain with 'blood' her 'stain's

---

[26] Erasmus, *On the Writing of Letters*, p. 19.

excuse', and she knows that her letter must not steal the thunder of that spectacle:

> the life and feeling of her passion
> She hoards, to spend when he is by to hear her,
> When sighs and groans and tears may grace the fashion
> Of her disgrace, the better so to clear her
> From that suspicion which the world might bear her.
>   To shun this blot she would not blot the letter
>   With words, till action might become them better.
>   (1317–23)

Seeing sorrow has more impact than hearing about it, for 'the eye interprets to the ear / The heavy motion that it doth behold' (1325–6). Language is most effective when supplemented by visible, bodily signs of sincerity. Attempts to achieve the same effect with a profusion of words can be counter-productive: 'Deep sounds make lesser noise than shallow fords, / And sorrow ebbs, being blown with wind of words' (1329–30). Surfaces matter, and shallow communication is an important tool, especially when one is after an intense emotional response in one's audience rather than reflection and scepticism.

And so we learn that Lucrece is a masterful letter writer not because of what she has written, but because of what she has not written. She does not go on at length and give the full details of her grief. In her very brief missive, she strikes a chord of intimacy and wifely dutifulness on which she can then draw in summoning Collatine away from the battlefield to attend to the calamity with which their household has been stricken. She is clear-sighted on what letters do well and what they do less well. A good letter will stir concern and prompt her husband's return home; it will not divulge information that might ultimately be used in ways contrary to Lucrece's interests. The letter does not stand alone, but is carefully limited in scope so that it more effectively prepares the conditions of a final performance advancing the ends of clearing her honour and securing a pledge of vengeance from her husband and his associates.

Other dynamics are visible in Lucrece's contemplation of her letter, signalled by the repetition of 'blot'. As we have seen in the passages quoted already, her 'will' blots out passages of her letter crafted by her 'wit' (1299), suggesting that an effective, final letter strikes a balance between emotion and craft. And to shun the potential blot to her honour, she blots out words that might reveal too much about the source of her grief (1322). She also will not 'blot the letter with words' in order to avoid the 'blot' of suspicion (1321–3). Lucrece's honour is metonymic with her letter: to avoid staining the former, she must avoid staining the page with excessive explanation. The effect is to heighten our sense of her vulnerability at this moment when her reputation can be reduced to tatters at a moment's notice, like a sheet of paper sent into a rough world. Shakespeare uses a similar trope in *The Merchant of Venice*, when Bassanio opens the letter containing news of Antonio's failed ventures:

> Here are a few of the unpleasant'st words
> That ever blotted paper . . .
>   Here is a letter, lady,
> The paper as the body of my friend,
> And every word in it a gaping wound
> Issuing life-blood.
>   (3.2.250–1, 262–5)

The several appearances of 'blot' in *Lucrece* similarly work to render Lucrece's letter a stand-in for her body. Hesitating before his attack on Lucrece, Prince Tarquin tries to dismiss 'unhallowed thoughts' before he 'blot[s] / With [his] uncleanness that which is divine' (192–3). Later seeking to persuade Lucrece, he declares that if she yields willingly he will keep it a secret, and so she can avoid a shame 'Worse than a slavish wipe, or birth-hour's blot', the mark of a slave or a disfiguring birthmark (537). Reading the Troy tapestry, Lucrece sees it as a sign of the workman's art that Sinon is represented in such a way 'jealousy itself' would not suspect his motives, or suspect that 'False creeping craft and perjury' could 'blot with hell-born sin such saint-like forms' (1517–19). 'Blot' is a keyword in *Lucrece*, and its several usages draw together moral stain, the defiled body and the written page.

It does not seem so large a step, then, when in the final stanzas of the poem Lucrece's body is itself placed in circulation as a galvanizing political message. Here we will be reminded of work on letters as an important form of women's writing in the period, one reaching well beyond the private and domestic in cultivating broad social and intellectual circles, and, as Daybell observes, one that is politically significant via participation in news and intelligence networks.[27] Shakespeare's *Lucrece*, however, evokes the potential power of women as letter writers only to limit it in significant ways. Even as Lucrece proves herself to be a skilled tactician in securing a vow of revenge from her husband and her father, and does so without them raising questions about her honour, her motives remain just below the political – a hair's breadth below, but a significant distance nonetheless. In securing a commitment from the men present to 'venge this wrong of mine', Lucrece speaks a romance language of gallantry, honour and chivalric service:

For 'tis a meritorious fair design
To chase injustice with revengeful arms.
Knights, by their oaths, should right poor ladies' harms.
(1692–4)

It is after securing a pledge of vengeance in these terms, and hearing the men present declare that 'Her body's stain her mind untainted clears' (1710), that Lucrece reveals the identity of her attacker and commits suicide. Her final actions certainly have political consequences, and she has worked assiduously to bring those consequences to pass, but they do not directly promote the revolution in Roman government that is to come: she remains a wife who has been wronged, and one who values the honour attached to chastity more than life itself. It is Brutus who seizes the political moment, and who is immediately described in terms invoking *raison d'état*:

[Brutus] Began to clothe his wit in state and pride . . .
But now he throws that shallow habit by,
Wherein deep policy did him disguise
(1807, 1814–15)

Lucrece adroitly balances wit and will, and withholds key details, in crafting a letter setting in motion events allowing her to retain her honour and to effect retribution on young Tarquin. In parallel, if also fundamentally different, ways, Brutus hides his full abilities until such time as revealing them can allow him to overthrow the house of Tarquin and effect a revolution in Roman political order. And in that process of hiding and revealing, he displays a political prudence that immediately vaults him above Collatinus, whose imprudent boasting started all the trouble in the first place and who, at this moment pregnant with political opportunity, is a weepy mess. Brutus does not shy away from pointing this out: 'Let my unsounded self, supposed a fool, / Now set thy long-experienced wit to school' (1819–20). Much as Lucrece is able subtly to direct her husband's actions, she does not deviate from her role, as the poem emphasizes, as her husband's property. In the closing parallel between Lucrece and Brutus, the poem shows that it has heightened our awareness of the agency Lucrece exercises while constraining its scope.[28] The metonymy of letters and bodies in the poem prepares us for Lucrece's transition from letter writer to something like a letter herself: in seizing her final writing implement, the knife, from her side, Brutus seizes control of

---

[27] See Daybell, *Women Letter-Writers*, esp. pp. 3–4 and 152–7; *The Letters of Lady Arbella Stuart*, ed. Sara Jayne Steen (Oxford, 1994); Sister Mary Humiliata, 'Standards of taste advocated for feminine letter writing, 1640–1797', *Huntington Library Quarterly* 13 (1949–50), 261–77; and Linda C. Mitchell, 'Entertainment and instruction: women's roles in the English epistolary tradition', *Huntington Library Quarterly* 66 (2003), 331–47. See Stewart (*Shakespeare's Letters*, pp. 243–4) on the motif of the woman letter writer in Dutch painting.

[28] On gender issues in the poem, see Coppélia Kahn, 'The rape in Shakespeare's *Lucrece*', *Shakespeare Studies* 9 (1976), 45–72; Joyce Green MacDonald, 'Speech, silence, and history in *The Rape of Lucrece*', *Shakespeare Studies* 22 (1994), 77–103; Sara E. Quay, '"Lucrece the chaste": the construction of rape in Shakespeare's *The Rape of Lucrece*', *Modern Language Studies* 25 (1995), 3–17; and Nancy Vickers, '"The blazon of sweet beauty's best": Shakespeare's Lucrece', in *Shakespeare and the Question of Theory*, ed. Patricia Parker and Geoffrey Hartman (New York and London, 1985), 95–115.

Lucrece's body and puts it into circulation to serve his own aims.

In its first publication, the text prepares us from the start for this circulation of Lucrece as text: the 1594 title page offers the title as *Lucrece*, with no indication of authorship. We encounter an object named 'Lucrece', a name suggesting that, like a letter, the object stands in for a particular subjectivity. The *New Oxford Shakespeare* follows this title, where most editors opt for *The Rape of Lucrece*, which appears at the head of the poem and in the running head of the 1594 text.[29] The circulation of this *Lucrece* in its own way reenacts the circulation of the body of Lucrece with which the poem ends. And, like a letter, the text bears a seal: the 'anchora spei' printer's device adorning the title page, which allows a printer, in this case Richard Field, to place a readily identifiable mark on the text, making it immediately recognizable as authentically his. That device also creates a set of associations with other texts, poetic, theological and political. Also authorial: the 1593 *Venus and Adonis* also bears the 'anchora spei'.[30] Edmund Spenser's *Fowre Hymnes*, first printed in 1596, bears the 'anchora spei', as does the 1589 edition of George Puttenham's *Arte of English Poesie*.[31] As Adam Hooks has shown, anchor devices have several iterations in the period.[32] Thomas Vautrollier had used a different 'anchora spei' on the 1574 edition of the Protestant martyr Peter Ramus's *Logic*, and on his 1575 edition of Martin Luther's commentary on Paul's epistle to the Galatians.[33] A new and more ornate version of the 'anchora spei' first appears on the 1577 *Auncient Ecclesiasticall Histories*, a landmark translation and compilation of Eusebius Pamphilus, Socrates Scholasticus and Evagrius Scholasticus.[34] This newer iteration makes more obvious its Reformed values: the hand of grace emerges from a cloud to draw the anchor heavenward. Field, who inherits Vautrollier's printing business, continues using this cloud and anchor device on Reformed texts, such as the 1589 edition of Jean de Frégeville's *The Reformed Politicke, That is, An Apologie for the Generall Cause of Reformation*.[35] Within a year of running the shop, he appears to have had made a fresh version of the same device, slightly more intricate in design and with subtle differences of detail, most obviously that the laurel branches now cross in front of the anchor (compare Figures 9 and 10).[36] The two versions of the cloud and anchor device remain simultaneously in use, and their frequent appearance makes them a mark of Field's offerings, and register continuity with the prominent, cosmopolitan printer Vautrollier.

We might see Protestant impulses at work in at least some of the poetry bearing the device. That is certainly true of Spenser's *Fowre Hymnes*, especially in its stated impulse of offering heavenly hymns that are a 'retractation' and 'reforme' of its earthly ones, and in the dutifully Christocentric *Hymne of Heavenly Love*.[37] On the title page of *Lucrece*, such

---

[29] See William Shakespeare, *Lucrece* (London, 1594) [STC 22345], t.p., sig. B1r and running head.

[30] Shakespeare, *Venus and Adonis* (London, 1593) [STC 22354], t.p.

[31] Edmund Spenser, *Fowre Hymnes* (London, 1596) [STC 23086], t.p.; George Puttenham, *The Arte of English Poesie* (London, 1589) [STC 20519.5], t.p.

[32] Adam G. Hooks, 'Reading devices', *Anchora* [blog], 2018, available at adamghooks.net; on the relationship between Shakespeare and Field, see his *Selling Shakespeare* (Cambridge, 2016), pp. 35–49.

[33] *The Logike of the Moste Excellent Philosopher P. Ramus Martyr*, trans. Rollo MacIlmaine (London, 1574) [STC 15246], t.p.; Martin Luther, *A Commentarie of M. Doctor Martin Luther upon the Epistle of S. Paul to the Galatians* (London, 1575) [STC 16965], t.p.

[34] Eusebius Pamphilus, Socrates Scholasticus and Evagrius Scholasticus, *The Auncient Ecclesiasticall Histories of the First Six Hundred Yeares after Christ* (London, 1577) [STC 10572], t.p.

[35] Jean de Frégeville, *The Reformed Politicke* (London, 1589) [STC 11372], t.p.

[36] The earliest text that I have been able to find bearing this updated version of the cloud and anchor device is *The Copie of a Letter Sent from Sea by a Gentleman* (London, 1589) [STC 10653]. Other differences between the two devices include the patterns in the cloud, the addition of a rosette beneath the bottom scroll, the addition of a bow and ribbon at the centre of the top scroll, a longer and more curled moustache for the figure on the left, a flatter stomach for the figure on the right, and a changed motif in the ring around the central image. For their assistance in spotting differences between the two designs, I am indebted to Chloe and Kate Mohamed.

[37] Edmund Spenser, dedication to *Fowre Hymnes*, in *The Yale Edition of the Shorter Poems of Edmund Spenser*, ed. William A. Oram, Einar Bjorvand and Ronald Bond (New Haven, 1989), p. 690.

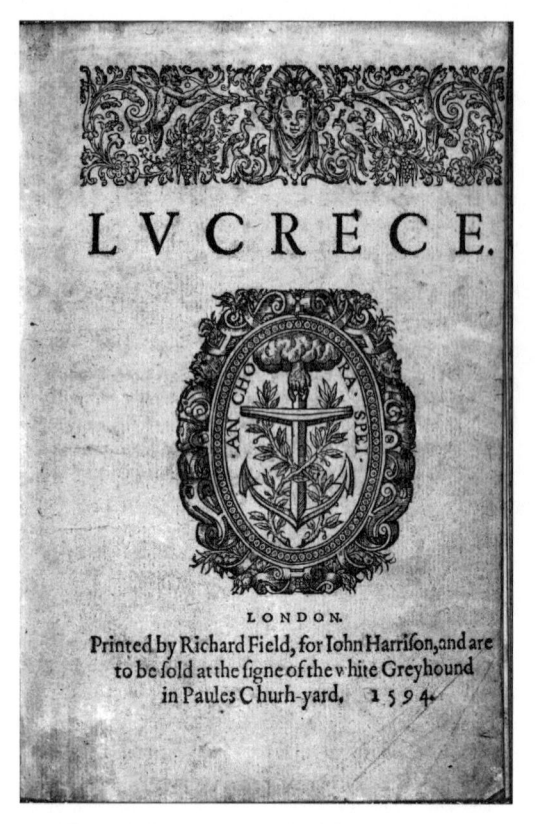

9 Title page of *Lucrece* (1594; Yale University, Eliz 179). By permission of The Elizabethan Club of Yale University. Full image set available at collections.library.yale.edu.

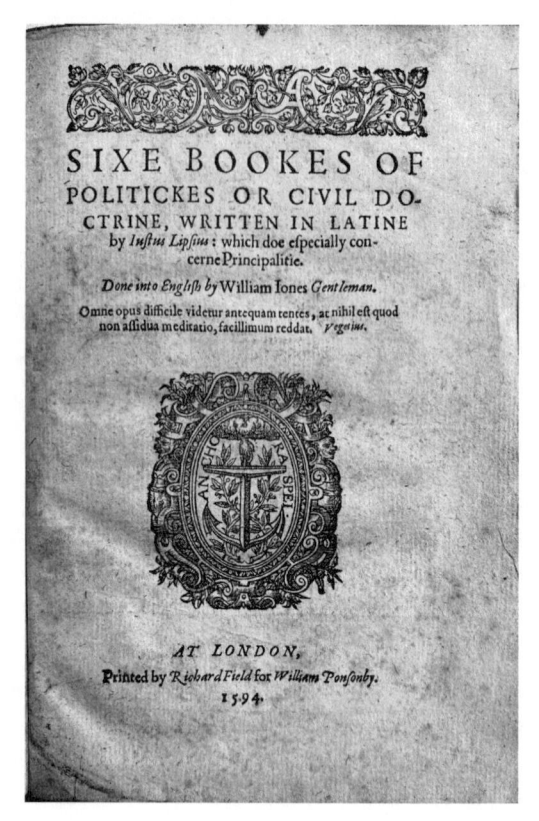

10 Title page of Justus Lipsius, *Sixe Bookes of Politickes or Civil Doctrine*, trans. William Jones (1594; Yale University, Ocg30 L669 589 g). By courtesy of the Beinecke Rare Book & Manuscript Library, Yale University.

an association highlights core concerns of the text that are indebted to Saint Augustine's remarks on Lucretia in *De civitate Dei* – namely, whether Lucretia retains spiritual innocence after her body has been defiled, a possibility disallowed by Roman religion.[38] In a way more difficult to parse from the design itself, though especially relevant to present discussion, the 'anchora spei' also becomes a device repeatedly appearing on *raison d'état* texts. The 1594 Jones translation of Lipsius, the *Sixe Bookes of Politickes*, bears the 'anchora spei'. So do two *raison d'état* texts published by Vautrollier: Sir Geoffrey Fenton's 1579 translation of Guicciardini's *History*, and Charles Merbury's 1581 *Discourse of Royall Monarchie*, an advice-to-princes text that includes a 'collection of Italian proverbs' indebted to Guicciardini.[39] When Field reprints Guicciardini's *Historie*, the re-set title page includes the device.[40] *Lucrece* as a material text thus comes to resemble a letter in its sociality, which is to say that, rather

---

[38] See Augustine of Hippo, *City of God [De civitate Dei]*, vol. 1: *Books 1–3*, trans. George E. McCracken (Cambridge, MA, 1957), pp. 84–7 [book 1, ch. 19].

[39] Lipsius, *Sixe Bookes of Politickes*, t.p.; Francesco Guicciardini, *The Historie of Guicciardin*, trans. Sir Geoffrey Fenton (London, 1579) [STC 12458a], t.p.; Charles Merbury, *A Briefe Discourse of Royall Monarchie* (London, 1581) [STC 17823.5], t.p. On Field's printing of texts on statecraft, see Dzelzainis, 'Shakespeare and political thought', p. 107.

[40] Francesco Guicciardini, *The Historie of Guicciardin*, trans. Sir Geoffrey Fenton (London, 1599) [STC 12459], t.p. Not all copies of this text bear the cloud and anchor device: compare STC 12458 to 12458a and 12459.

than standing alone, it summons various chains of associated texts: its surface creates an association with other objects informing an alert and knowing reader's approach to the text. Or at least it might. We should be reluctant to paint too tidy a picture of similar texts sharing a printer's device on the title page. *Venus and Adonis*, after all, also bears the 'anchora spei', and does not have anything to do with Reformed theology or *raison d'état*, and the satirical *Pope's Parliament* (1591), which promises an account of 'the paltry trash and trumperies of him and his pelting prelats', is not a text asserting its place in the highest echelon of Renaissance culture.[41] Given everything discussed here, the association that this device forms between *Lucrece* and Lipsius is certainly suggestive, though not entirely dispositive.

We might nonetheless think of Shakespeare's *Lucrece* as something of a supplement to Lipsius's *Epistolica*. We can see it as consistent in many ways with this brief manual, and also as extending some of its principles to show that a form of writing resembling drama is no replacement for drama itself, an insight on which the fate of marriages and kingdoms can depend. We find here letter-writing as a significant form of women's writing, as has been explored previously – which is even at its most superlative subordinated to a masculine realm of politics. In its concern with the political effects of speech and performance, Shakespeare's *Lucrece* thus also extends the timeline of a culture of 'political competence' that András Kiséry has associated with Hamlet's moment.[42] Here too, in the mid-1590s, we find such concerns present themselves, and in a way consistent with that decade's fascination with *raison d'état*.

---

[41] [John Mayo,] *The Pope's Parliament* (London, 1591) [STC 17752], t.p.
[42] Kiséry, *Hamlet's Moment*, 9.

SHAKESPEARE'S ARABIC SONNETS

ROBERT STAGG[1]

During the eighteenth century Shakespeare became 'the national poet'; from the nineteenth century onwards he has become the international poet.[2] He is what Bengalis (on the model of Rabindranath Tagore) refer to as a *biswakabi*, a world poet, having been elevated to 'almost the status of a world language'.[3] Yet scholarship about a 'Global Shakespeare' has said little about his status and practice as a 'poet', worldly or otherwise, whether that be with regard to the sonnets, the narrative poems, 'The Phoenix and the Turtle', or the sometime versification of his drama. Historicist and New Historicist scholarship of Shakespeare's place in the early modern world has largely concerned itself with the plays. Other scholarship about a 'Global Shakespeare' has been oriented by the study of translation, adaptation, appropriation and performance – a constellation of critical terms by which Shakespeare's poems come to look belated and marginal, since, as Jane Kingsley-Smith writes:

if the first Shakespeare play is translated into French in 1731, the first few sonnets do not appear until 1821 in Amedée Pichot's translation, and the full 154 must wait for François-Victor Hugo in 1857. The first Russian Shakespeare play is *Hamlet* in 1748, but the Sonnets do not follow in printed translation until 1859 (with a complete edition in 1880). In India, Bengali translations of the plays began in the mid-nineteenth century, but the complete sonnets would not be translated into Bengali until the twentieth, most notably in the 1950s work of Manindranath Roy and Sudhanshu Ranjan Ghosh[.][4]

Moreover, Shakespeare's poems were not included in the Lambs' *Tales from Shakespeare* (1807), the book that first transmitted his works to many countries around the world, and they clearly do not sport the extensive performance history of the plays. If Philip Sidney was right to defend poetry as a 'passport', Shakespeare's does not appear to have many stamps.[5]

The 'global' character of Shakespeare's poems has thereby been obscured – such that the persistent terminological elision of the 'Shakespearian sonnet' with the 'English sonnet' has seemed apt, figuring Shakespeare's poetry as somehow nationalist, or as a metonym for Englishness, or as merely provincial in its attention. The 'Shakespearian'

---

[1] I would like to thank Peter McCullough, Henry Woudhuysen, Samantha Brown and Lindsay McCormack for their advice about Richard Brett and Lincoln College; Abdulhamit Arvas, Yasmine Seale and Murat Öğütcü for helping with Turkish translation; Timothy Harrison, Walter Cohen and Ladan Niayesh for allowing me to read some of their unpublished work; and Hannah Crawforth, Elizabeth Scott-Baumann and Jyotsna Singh for reading and commenting on my article in draft.
[2] Michael Dobson, *The Making of the National Poet: Shakespeare, Adaptation and Authorship, 1660–1769* (Oxford, 1992).
[3] Shawkat Toorawa, 'Translating *The Tempest*', in *African Theatre: Playwrights and Politics*, ed. Martin Banham, James Gibbs and Femi Osofisan (Johannesburg, 2001), 125–38; p. 128.
[4] Jane Kingsley-Smith '"Mine is another voyage": global encounters with Shakespeare's Sonnets', in *Shakespeare's Global Sonnets: Translation, Appropriation, Performance*, ed. Jane Kingsley-Smith and W. Reginald Rampone Jr (Cham, 2023), 17–33; p. 22.
[5] Philip Sidney, *The Defence of Poesie* (London, 1595), sig. B3r. All quotations from early modern texts have been modernized.

sonnet form is anyhow quite different from that of the first tranche of 'English' sonnets. Those by Thomas Wyatt mostly preserved the 'Italian' ABBAABBA octave, and about a third of the extant sonnets by Henry Howard, the Earl of Surrey, do not adopt the ABABCDCDEFEFGG rhyme scheme that is now considered constitutively 'Shakespearian'. In any case, the first 'English' sonnets had a 'mixed' quality, 'caught somewhere between the Italian and the English forms': as John Harington noted in a preface to his translation of *Orlando Furioso* (1591), the first English sonneteers were 'translators out of Italian' as much as they were poets of an 'English' form.[6] To the extent that Shakespeare was writing in an originally and vestigially Italian verse structure, he was, in this and other respects, a 'product of' world literature as well as being a 'producer of' it.[7]

However, this well-worn argument about the Italian origins of the 'Shakespearian' sonnet only goes so far. Now, like the Doctor in Richard Brome's play *The Antipodes* (1640), 'Of Europe I'll not speak, 'tis too near home'[8]– because the origins of sonnet form lie outside the Italian mainland, on the island of Sicily, in the midst of the Mediterranean, within sight of Africa, on a host of Middle Eastern trading routes, and with a long history of Arab settlement. In properly understanding this, we can recover the true internationalism of 'Shakespearian' sonnet form as well as develop an appreciation of how literary form travels across space and time. We might also wonder whether Shakespeare could have known the global origins of the lyric poetry he was writing, given that those origins were couched in a language very few of his compatriots could understand. We may be surprised by the answer.

***

Although most histories of the sonnet begin with Petrarch, the very first sonnets pre-dated him by almost a century and emanated from the island of Sicily, not the Italian mainland. They were poems of fourteen lines with a volta between their octave and sestet and mostly bore the rhyme scheme ABABABABCDECDE, a considerably different arrangement from that in what we now call the 'Italian' sonnet. They were written by the early thirteenth-century 'Scuola Siciliana' of poets loosely grouped around the court of the king of Sicily, Frederick II. About thirty-five 'Sicilian' sonnets have survived, about twenty-five of which are by the court notary Giacomo da Lentini. In the critical literature on these earliest sonnets, two principal explanations have been given as to how and why they emerged: (1) that the sonnet 'sprung fully formed from Giacomo's pen';[9] or (2) that Giacomo and his fellow poets built the sonnet from sections of the Occitan or Provençal *canso*, refashioned in Sicily as the canzone, or from the more local form of the strambotto.[10] The second of these arguments is bolstered by the manuscript survival of twenty-two canzoni (pre-dating or contemporaneous with the Sicilian sonnet) that begin with a *fronte* or opening section cross-rhymed ABAB in the manner of the Sicilian sonnet's octave.[11] Thus Giacomo's sonnets could be a 'recombinative' form, 'an imitative innovation'.[12]

Scholars have also wondered 'whether the dawn of Italian poetry in Sicily was somehow linked to the twilight of the local Arabic literature' (the influence of Arabic culture in Sicily began to

---

[6] Stephen Guy-Bray, 'Notes on the couplet in the sonnet', *Shakespeare* 18 (2022), 322–31; p. 323; John Harington, 'A Preface, Or Rather A Briefe Apologie of Poetrie', to *Orlando Furioso In English Heroical Verse* (London, 1591), n.p.

[7] Walter Cohen, 'Afterword: around the world in 154 poems, or, how to do things with Shakespeare's Sonnets', in *Shakespeare's Global Sonnets*, ed. Kingsley-Smith and Rampone Jr, 381–98; p. 383.

[8] Richard Brome, *The Antipodes* (London, 1640), n.p. [1.3.63].

[9] Karla Mallette, *The Kingdom of Sicily, 1100–1250: A Literary History* (Philadelphia, 2011), p. 76.

[10] A version of this argument dates back in English criticism to Ernest H. Wilkins, 'The invention of the sonnet', *Modern Philology* 13 (1915), 463–94.

[11] Michael R. G. Spiller, *The Development of the Sonnet* (London, 1992), p. 14. The manuscripts in question are MS Vaticano Latino 3793, MS Laurenziana Red.9 and MS Laurenziana Pal.418.

[12] Christopher Kleinhenz, *The Early Italian Sonnet: The First Century (1220–1321)* (Lecce, 1986), pp. 26, 33.

decline around the accession of Frederick II at the very end of the twelfth century).[13] From the ninth century, when the Aghlabid dynasty conquered the island, Sicily was home to a large Arab population; even after the twelfth-century Norman conquest, Sicily was a 'hybrid culture', an island 'where three worlds met' – the Arab, the Christian/Latin and the Greek.[14] In a treatise, *Dell'origine della poesia rimata*, written in the sixteenth century but not published until 1790, Giammaria Barbieri argued that rhyme as a whole came into Sicilian poetry 'dal modo della nazione degli arabi' ('by way of the Arab peoples') since the saj', or rhymed prose of the Qur'an, 'precede in tempo ad ogni Scrittura rimata così Latina come volgare, della quale noi abbiamo memoria' ('precedes in any way rhymed writing, either Latin or vulgar, of which we have any memory or knowledge').[15] Michele Amari developed this argument with respect to the Sicilian sonnet in his *Storia dei musulmani di Sicilia* (1854), and it has been pursued again in the twentieth and early twenty-first centuries (most recently by Kamal Abu-Deeb and Hassanaly Ladha).[16]

On its face, the hypothesis of Arabic influence upon the first sonnets is plausible. One need only look at the architectural constructions of the Norman kings to see the importance of Arab culture in Sicily. The dome of La Cubula and the rounded arches of La Zisa in Palermo are redolent of Fatimid design; the latter even has Arabic (in Naskh script) impressed above its entrance. Seventy-three of the ceiling panels in Palermo's Cappella Palatina feature Arabic inscriptions, and the architectural historian Jeremy Johns has argued that an 'Arabic inscriptional programme' would have originally decorated doors, caskets, textiles, lamps and liturgical vestments in the chapel (the mantle of the Norman King Roger II, now in the Viennese Schatzkammer, is likewise fringed with Arabic saj').[17] Three of the surviving inscriptions on the ceiling refer to the ceremonies of the hajj, while a trilingual psalter now in the British Library implies the presence of Arabic in the chapel's liturgy.[18] Some of the ceiling is in the muqarnas style, 'a compact arrangement of niches, convexities, concavities and stalactites' typical of a mosque and highly unusual in church design of any region or period.[19] On the walls of the chapel are 'thoroughly Fatimid' depictions of Arab musicians, dancers, scribes and possibly poets (one image features the word 'nazm' or 'poetry').[20]

Numerous Arabic poems survive from medieval Sicily. Although the largest anthology of Siculo-Arabic poetry (collated by Ibn al-Qatta') has been lost, fragments survive in seventeen volumes gathered by Imad ad-Din al-Isfahani – including Ibn Qalaqis's dedicatory ode to William III and a paean to the gardens of the Palazzo della Favara by al-Atrabanishi. Best known are the poems of Ibn Hamdis who was born in Syracuse but who wrote the majority of his verse in Al-Andalus and at the Zirid court in what is now Tunisia.

The accession of Frederick II, the Hohenstaufen emperor whom Giacomo da Lentini served as notary while writing the first 'Sicilian' sonnets, is sometimes read as a 'cultural interregnum' for Sicily's Arab residents.[21] This is now most visible

---

[13] Francesco Gabrieli, 'Arabic poetry in Sicily', *East and West* 2 (1951), 13–16; p. 16.

[14] Mallette, *Kingdom of Sicily*, p. 5; Sarah Davis Secord, *Where Three Worlds Met: Sicily in the Early Medieval Mediterranean* (Ithaca, 2017).

[15] Giammaria Barbieri, *Dell'origine della poesia rimata* (Modena, 1790), pp. 41, 44.

[16] Michele Amari, *Storia dei musulmani di Sicilia* (Florence, 1854); Kamal Abu-Deeb, 'The quest for the sonnet: the origins of the sonnet in Arabic poetry', *Critical Survey* 28 (2016), 33–157; Hassanaly Ladha, 'From bayt to stanza: Arabic khayal and the advent of Italian vernacular poetry', *Exemplaria* 32 (2020), 1–32.

[17] Jeremy Johns, 'Arabic inscriptions in the Cappella Palatina: performativity, audience, legibility and illegibility', in *Viewing Inscriptions in the Late Antique and Medieval World*, ed. Antony Eastmond (Cambridge, 2015), 124–47; p. 144.

[18] British Library Harley MS 5786.

[19] Giovanni Fatta, Tiziana Campisi, Mario Li Castri and Giuseppe Costa, 'The Muqarnas ceiling of the Palatina Chapel in Palermo', *Conservation Science in Cultural Heritage* 17 (2017), 65–85; p. 65.

[20] Lev A. Kapitaikin, 'David's dancers in Palermo: Islamic dance imagery and its Christian recontextualization in the ceilings of the Cappella Palatina', *Early Music* 47 (2019), 3–23; pp. 16, 9.

[21] Mallette, *Kingdom of Sicily*, p. 49.

in Frederick's removal of the *'alama*, the Arabic royal honorific, from the island's coinage and was most profound in his removal of many of his Arab subjects to a ghetto at Lucera. But the argument for such a 'cultural interregnum' has been overstressed. Like his Norman predecessors, Frederick spoke fluent Arabic, having grown up in Palermo. He carried out an extended correspondence with Arab scholars such as the philosopher Ibn Sab'in, who used Frederick's 'Sicilian questions' ('al-masa'il al-Siqilliyya') as the prompt for one of his treatises.[22] Thus a linguistic and cultural 'Arabic residue' remained at the royal court even as the likes of Giacomo da Lentini replaced the so-called 'palace Saracens', the Arab bureaucrats who previously attended on the Normans.[23]

In an article about 'The quest for the sonnet', Kamal Abu-Deeb has gingerly proposed 'the origins of the sonnet in Arabic poetry' in Sicily.[24] In a complementary article, Hassanaly Ladha has argued that 'the [Sicilian] sonnet evinces literary and epistemological contact' with Arabic lyric.[25] As Ladha observes, if the canzone and strambotto provide suitable models for the Sicilian sonnet, then the same can be said of various Arabic lyric forms. Rather as the canzone turned from *fronte* to *piedi*, the rough equivalents of octave and sestet, so the Arabic *qasida* (such as those Sicilian poems preserved in Imad ad-Din's anthology) formally shifts from the *nasib*, its erotic prelude, to the *rahil*, a litany of complaints about the journey the poem will ultimately depict. Adam Talib has described the *qasida* as 'the tree trunk from which a number of boughs of Arabic poetic genres sprouted'.[26] One of those poetic 'genres' or forms, which appears to have emerged in Andalusia in the ninth century, was the *muwashshah* (named after the *wishah*, a belt or girdle with a double band, because of its involved rhyme schemes). Like the canzone, we have numerous extant *muwashshahat* that commence with something like an ABAB rhyme scheme; in fact, some chart exactly the ABAB pattern that would inform Giacomo's 'Sicilian' sonnet octaves.[27] None of these *muwashshahat* survive in Siculo-Arabic, although a few Andalusian-Hebrew *muwashshahat* are extant from late twelfth-century Palermo and we know that *muwashshahat* with these sonnet-like rhyme patterns travelled across the Mediterranean as far as Egypt, Syria and Yemen.[28] The aforementioned Ibn Hamdis is tantalizingly recorded as a *washshah*, a writer of *muwashshahat*, in *al-Wafi-bi-l-wafayat*, a miscellany or anthology of Arabic lyric by the Mamluk historian Al-Safadi, although none of Ibn Hamdis's *muwashshahat* have yet been located or recognized.[29]

We know that Giacomo da Lentini had some contact with the Arabic language, if not its poetry, through his canzone 'Amor non vole'. It turns on two descriptions of gemstones, one an 'oriental' sapphire and the other a historic turquoise ('li scolosmini / di quel tempo ricordato'). Until a 1953 article by the scholar Antonino Pagliaro, readers were unsure of the second gemstone thanks to the obscurity of Giacomo's word 'scolosmini'. Pagliaro demonstrated how the word had been translated and transliterated via Arabic, and ventured that Giacomo's depiction of the degenerating turquoise ('invilute') may owe something to Arabic lapidary tradition.[30]

Clive Scott has observed that '[t]he sonnet is able to deal with so many different kinds of subject because it has, in its own structure, access to so many different poetic modes.'[31] From its inception in Sicily, the sonnet had access to the peregrine forms of the *qasida*

---

[22] Bodleian MS Huntington 534, fols. 298v–346r.
[23] Aziz Ahmad, *A History of Islamic Sicily* (Edinburgh, 1975), p. 82.
[24] See note 16. [25] Ladha, 'From bayt to stanza', p. 17.
[26] Adam Talib, *How Do You Say Epigram in Arabic? Literary History at the Limits of Comparison* (Leiden, 2017), p. 5.
[27] Abu-Deeb gives various examples of the ABAB rhyme in the *muwashshahat* of the early thirteenth-century Ayyubid poet Ibn Sana' al-Mulk ('Quest for the sonnet', pp. 146–8). More germanely, Samuel Miklos Stern gives a host of Andalusian instances of the ABAB *muwashshah* pattern in *Hispano-Arabic Strophic Poetry*, ed. L. P. Harvey (Oxford, 1974),19–25.
[28] For the Sicilian Hebrew *muwashshahat*, see Samuel Stern, 'A twelfth century circle of Hebrew poets in Sicily', *Journal of Jewish Studies* 5 (1954), 60–79 and 110–13.
[29] Stern, *Hispano-Arabic Strophic Poetry*, ed. Harvey, p. 106.
[30] Antonino Pagliaro, 'Invilute sono li scolosmini', in *Nuovi saggi di critica semantica* (Messina, 1953), 199–212. See the discussion of George Puttenham later in this article.
[31] Clive Scott, 'The limits of the sonnet: towards a proper contemporary approach', *Revue de Littérature Comparée* 50 (1976), 237–50; p. 244.

and *muwashshah* as well as the canzone and strambotto. Both the Romance and Arabic forms evince in embryo the sonnet's volta and its initial ABAB rhyme template. Medieval Sicily was rich with 'contact zones', Mary Louise Pratt's term for 'social spaces where cultures meet, clash, and grapple with each other', through which the first sonneteers could encounter Arabic as well as Troubadour lyric.[32] Or perhaps, following Karen Laura Thornber's revision of Pratt, we should refer to these zones as '*contact nebulae*', '[c]onsidering their frequent ambiguity and constantly changing internal dynamics, as well as their hazy edges'.[33] Whatever critical language we prefer, Hassanaly Ladha is right to argue that the 'continuities' between the sonnet and its Arabic precursors not only 'subvert narrative accounts of the spontaneous origin of the sonnet' but also 'by extension, the myth of Italian and "Western" cultural authenticity and self-invention'.[34] The 'deeply ingrained belief in the utter separability of the Arabic and Romance traditions', what Maria Rosa Menocal has dubbed 'the myth of Westernness in medieval literary historiography', is disturbed by Sicily's 'poetic geography' and the sonnet's loose, capacious and sometimes obscure genealogy.[35]

This 'myth of Westernness' becomes yet harder to sustain when we consider that the 'English' sonnet form is closer than the 'Italian' sonnet form to its 'Sicilian' original. On the Italian mainland, the sonnet octave gradually changed from an ABABABAB to an ABBAABBA rhyme scheme. The 'English' sonnet reverts to the 'Sicilian' rhymes, vexing any literary-historical attempt to construct pure, clean lines of formal genealogical descent. If the 'Sicilian' opening to the sonnet was partly motivated by the *muwashshah* or other Arabic lyric, as is likely, we might even hear the Shakespearian sonnet's acoustic and structural debt to Arabic verse. Our entry to the Shakespearian sonnet, its opening ABAB quatrain, is probably partly Arabic by design.

With our ears attuned to an Arabic rhyme scheme at the beginning of a Shakespearian sonnet, it is tempting to hear echoes of Arabic poetry elsewhere in the 1609 *Sonnets*. Are those 'festivals' of wordplay on Shakespeare's name in Sonnets 135–6 and 143 somehow indebted to the Arabic ghazal and its customary play upon the poet's name (*takhallus*) in its final *maqta'a*?[36] Is there any significance to each of Shakespeare's sonnets being headed with Arabic rather than Roman numerals in the 1609 quarto, which was a relatively new development in the printing of English sonnet sequences?[37] Or do such questions tip the critic into the lamentable position of the nineteenth-century scholar Pietro Valerga who, struck by the poetic similarities between Petrarch and the thirteenth-century mystic Ibn al-Farid, came to believe that the former was literally a reincarnation of the latter? (As Robert Irwin has drily noted, 'the reincarnation theory is not now a fashionable tool of literary criticism'.)[38]

It is nevertheless worth asking why 'cultural circulation' should be the sole warrant for a comparative literary criticism.[39] The 'almost automatic equation between the literary and the territorial' and the understanding of 'points of origin ... as belonging to geographically or culturally contiguous areas' may be less applicable in understanding the development and distribution of literary form.[40] Form can lie dormant or latent for long periods of time. Consider the sonnet's relatively quiescent state in eighteenth-century

---

[32] Mary Louise Pratt, 'Arts of the contact zone', *Profession* (1991), 33–40; p. 34.

[33] Karen Laura Thornber, 'Rethinking the world in world literature: East Asia and literary contact nebulae' [2009], reprinted in *World Literature in Theory*, ed. David Damrosch (Oxford, 2014), 460–79; p. 463.

[34] Ladha, 'From bayt to stanza', p. 15.

[35] Maria Rosa Menocal, *The Arabic Role in Medieval Literary History: A Forgotten Heritage* (Philadelphia, 1990), p. 119, title of c.h.1; John Gillies, *Shakespeare and the Geography of Difference* (Cambridge, 1994), p. 6.

[36] *Shakespeare's Sonnets*, ed. Stephen Booth (New Haven, 1977), p. 466.

[37] The earliest English collection of sonnets to be headed with Arabic numerals is the anonymous sequence *Zepheria* (1594).

[38] Robert Irwin, 'Petrarch and "that mad dog Averroes"', in *Re-Orienting the Renaissance: Cultural Exchanges with the East*, ed. Gerald MacLean (Houndmills, 2005), 108–25; p. 118.

[39] Timothy M. Harrison and Jane Mikkelson, 'What was early modern world literature?' *Modern Philology* 119 (2021), 166–88; p. 168.

[40] Wai Chee Dimock, 'Literature for the planet', *PMLA* 116 (2001), 173–88; p. 175; Harrison and Mikkelson, 'What was early modern world literature?' p. 188.

England before its recrudescence in Romantic versification. Or consider Daniel Sawyer's account of a mid fifteenth-century poem that assumes the profile of what we would later call an 'English sonnet', which he describes as having an 'accidental form' that appeared 'before its time'.[41] Perhaps the initial quatrain of the 'Shakespearian' sonnet is an instance of form appearing *after* its time, of the medieval Siculo-Arabic *muwashshah* surfacing in early modern English verse. For literary form is a 'long-memoried' thing, a 'panchronic' property.[42] Literary critics have dwelt upon the phenomenon of 'lyric time', that 'intensified awareness' of 'temporal condensation' that seems particular to the creation and experience of lyric poems.[43] Literary historians may need to think of a lyric timelessness, or a lyric 'deep time' with still 'older, slower stories of making and unmaking', or some synonymous vocabulary to detail the ways in which lyric forms sunder to and from each other across long, unpredictable stretches of history.[44]

Literary form can almost invisibly cross borders. It can be arrived at quite coincidentally, and can be invented independently in more than one place, such that 'geographies of style' cannot be easily plotted.[45] Moreover, as Nandini Das has argued about the incipient early modern relations between England and Japan, encounters between peoples and their literature do not always take the shape of 'an individual event' or 'a series of closely connected events'; they can happen through 'cumulative and collective means'.[46] And lest we replace the 'myth of Westernness' that regards the sonnet as emerging from Troubadour lyric with a similarly straightforward myth of Easternness that regards the sonnet as emerging from Arabic lyric, it is worth knowing that 'in almost 10% of cases' we find Ibero-Romance language in the *kharja*, the final couplet, of the extant Andalusian *muwashshahat*.[47] Romance and Arabic forms were themselves mingled together, long before they could have had any influence upon the Sicilian sonnet. Such lyric forms are finely, finally inextricable from one another, and obdurate to any literary-historical quest for plain, transparent geographies and chronologies.

***

Some readers may by now be raising a sceptical eyebrow. Even if Shakespeare's sonnets possess an Arabic lyric history, could he really have known anything of it? And doesn't such authorial knowledge (or ignorance) matter, or have some significance, and require some degree of attention? On the first point, at least, sceptically raised eyebrows would seem to be in order. G. J. Toomer summarizes the state of Arabic learning in England at the start of the seventeenth century, around the time of the publication of Shakespeare's sonnets:

Not only was there no provision for teaching Arabic in universities, but even those who wished to study it privately faced formidable difficulties. Printed grammars were few and miserable, and there was no dictionary worth the name. Indeed there were very few printed books in Arabic at all, and those that existed were hard to obtain in England. Access to Arabic manuscripts, apart from stray copies of the Koran, was virtually impossible.[48]

We could add that the library of Cambridge University did not own a single Arabic text until the appearance of Thomas Erpenius's Arabic New Testament in 1626 (albeit the Bodleian Library was slightly better stocked in this regard).[49] The first

---

[41] Daniel Sawyer, 'Form, time, and the "first English sonnet"', *The Chaucer Review* 56 (2021), 193–224; pp. 202, 223.

[42] Jahan Ramazani, *A Transnational Poetics* (Chicago, 2009), p. 13; Boris Maslow, 'Lyric universality', in *The Cambridge Companion to World Literature*, ed. Ben Etherington and Jarad Zimbler (Cambridge, 2018),133–48; p.135.

[43] Howell Chickering, 'Lyric time in "Beowulf"', *The Journal of English and Germanic Philology* 91 (1992), 489–509; p. 493; David Nowell Smith, 'Parsing time in the lyric', *Critical Quarterly* 64 (2022), 138–54; p. 139.

[44] Robert Macfarlane, *Underland: A Deep Time Journey* (New York, 2019), p. 5.

[45] Alexander Beecroft, *An Ecology of World Literature: from Antiquity to the Present Day* (London, 2015), p. 134.

[46] Nandini Das, 'Encounter as process: England and Japan in the late sixteenth century', *Renaissance Quarterly* 69 (2016), 1343–68; pp. 1345–6.

[47] Walter Cohen, *A History of European Literature: The West and the World from Antiquity to the Present* (Oxford, 2017), p. 156.

[48] G. J. Toomer, *Eastern Wisedome and Learning: The Study of Arabic in Seventeenth-Century England* (Oxford, 1996), p. 53.

[49] Alastair Hamilton, *William Bedwell, the Arabist, 1563–1632* (Leiden, 1985), p. 26.

English university chair in Arabic, the Adams professorship, was not established in Cambridge until 1632, followed by the Laudian professorship at Oxford in 1636 (which was informally preceded by the arrival of the Copt Yusuf Abu Dhaqn in Oxford in 1610, where he seems to have offered some rudimentary instruction in Egyptian dialect Arabic).[50]

'Not until later in the seventeenth century', writes Irwin, 'did a few scholars make a serious start at translating the great Arab poets.'[51] The first English translation of the Qur'an would have to wait until 1649, and even then it was translated via French. The 'first instance of any work of Arabic poetry being put into print' (in the original) is by Erpenius's student Jacobus Golius, who gathered a miscellany of Arabic verse, proverbs and sermons in Leiden in 1629.[52] The first critical treatise about Arabic poetry to be printed in Europe is an essay, 'Coronis de poësi aut metrica ratione in genere, et arabicae linguae propria' by the German scholar Johann Fabricius in his *Specimen arabicum* of 1638.[53] The inaugural occupant of the Laudian chair at Oxford, Edward Pococke, used Golius's miscellany in his lectures (as a number of surviving manuscript notes attest) and printed the first Arabic poetry in England in the *Carmen Tograi* (1661) which also included a 'Tractatus de prosodia arabica' by his student Samuel Clarke.[54] In other words, it ought to be impossible for Shakespeare to have known anything of the Arabic history of his sonnet form.

However, there were some intense flickerings of interest in Arabic poetry within Shakespeare's lifetime. For example, in a remarkable manuscript of original poems about the Gunpowder Plot, dated 1605, the Oxford scholar and translator Richard Brett included one poem in Arabic (alongside poems in Hebrew, Chaldaic and Syriac).[55] The poem does not appear to be attempting any established Arabic form, but must be the earliest original poem in Arabic by an Englishman (composed about the same time Shakespeare was writing *Macbeth*, another text stirred by the events of 5 November 1605). Eight years earlier, this time on a printed sheet, Brett had attempted a translation of a Latin stanza into Arabic – but the lack of any Arabic type forced him to enter the script by hand under the heading 'In eadem Arabica'.[56]

Shakespeare is unlikely to have been privy to such obscure learning, but the poetry of the Middle East had attained an almost proverbial quality in the circles among which he moved and read. In al-Hasan ibn Muhammad al-Wazzan's / Leo Africanus's *Geographical Historie of Africa*, perhaps originally written in Arabic before being translated into English by John Pory in 1600, the author is introduced as the nephew of a 'poet', to have been 'trained up at the University of Fez' in poetry, and to have written 'divers excellent poems ... which are not come to light'.[57] In the history proper, al-Wazzan informs us that the 'Arabians which inhabit Africa' take 'great delight in poetry, and will pen most excellent verses ... done for the most part in rhyme' (Erpenius treated this passage to a rhapsodic commentary in his 'Oration on the value of the Arabic language' in Leiden in 1620).[58] In the Moroccan city of Hadecchis (since destroyed), al-Wazzan claims to have been 'entertained by a certain courteous and liberal-minded

---

[50] Toomer, *Eastern Wisedome*, pp. 44–5.
[51] Irwin, 'Petrarch and "that mad dog Averroes"', p. 116.
[52] Jan Loop, 'Arabic poetry as teaching material in early modern grammars and textbooks', in *The Teaching and Learning of Arabic in Early Modern Europe*, ed. Jan Loop, Alastair Hamilton and Charles Burnett (Leiden, 2017), 230–51; p. 233.
[53] Leo Africanus's treatise *De arte metrica* existed only in manuscript and was very little referenced until its rediscovery in the 1950s.
[54] Bodleian MS Pococke 427, fols.110, 227–32; Bodleian MS Pococke 428, fols. 1–2.
[55] Bodleian MS Selden supra 84. The Arabic poem appears on fol. 8v.
[56] Richard Brett, *Theses Mri Bret respondentis in comitiis*. Oxon (Oxford, 1597). Surviving copy held in the University College Library, Oxford.
[57] Leo Africanus, 'To the reader', in *A Geographical Historie of Africa*, trans. John Pory (London, 1600), n.p.
[58] Africanus, *Geographical Historie*, pp. 23–4; Robert Jones, 'Thomas Erpenius (1584–1624) on the value of the Arabic language', *Manuscripts of the Middle East* 1 (1986), 15–25; p. 19.

[imam] who was exceedingly delighted with Arabian poetry'.[59] In Fez, al-Wazzan relates, 'there are divers many excellent poets' who 'entreat of love'.[60]

Other histories and accounts of travel in the Middle East and North Africa mention poetry – especially Turkish poetry. Narrating the life of the Ottoman Sultan Selim I in his *Historie of the Turkes* (1603), Richard Knolles mentions three epitaphs 'in the Greek, Turkish and Sclavonian [sic] tongues' affixed to the sultan's tomb in Istanbul.[61] He translates the epitaphs into Latin verse and English fourteener couplets.[62] Since no epitaph corresponding to these lines remains at the sultan's tomb at the Yavuz Sultan Selim Mosque today, it is difficult to know whether Knolles (who never visited Istanbul) was accurately representing whatever Turkish epitaph may once have existed. There is no mention of these epitaphs in the German historian Johannes Leunclavius's *Historiae Musulmanae Turcorum* (1591), the adverted source for Knolles's life of Selim, and Knolles supplies yet more fourteener couplets under engraved images of sultans throughout the *Historie* such that long-lined couplets may simply have been his preferred mode of poetic composition rather than a translational effort at anything in a supposed source text.

In the *Defence of Poesie* (1595), Philip Sidney writes of how 'In Turkey, besides their lawgiving divines they have no other writers but poets', a state of affairs with which the Turks are 'delighted'.[63] In an account of his *Voyage into the Levant* (1636), Henry Blount, for whom 'the Ottomans became like a language', describes the Ottoman Empire as having been home to 'the greatest divines, philosophers and poets in the world' and recounts how he has 'often seen copies of love verses … pass amongst them with much applause', including 'two or three sonnets' at a feast in Ottoman-controlled Hungary (with the word 'sonnets' here probably meaning 'short poems').[64] Indeed, Ottoman merchants and diplomats were one of the primary conduits through which Middle Eastern poetry acceded into European libraries – for example, in a letter dated 8 October 1608, the Arabist Étienne Hubert writes to Joseph Scaliger of 'Hussinus noster Turca' ('our Turkish friend Husseyn') as a go-between for acquiring 'libros 10 aut 12 Arabicos, Persicos, Turcicos' ('ten or twelve Arabic, Persian and Turkish books') containing verse by the fifteenth-century Sufi poet Jami.[65] Thomas Blount's epigram in the *Glossographia* of 1656 rings true: 'as with merchandise, with terms it fares, / Nations do traffic words, as well as wares'.[66]

Among these histories, anthropologies and travel narratives, Shakespeare may have read Leo Africanus / al-Wazzan and certainly read (at least parts of) Knolles around the time he was writing *Othello*.[67] Perhaps more germanely to Shakespeare's sonneteering, early modern English treatises on poetics also displayed an interest in the Middle East and its versification. At one point in his *Certayne Notes of Instruction Concerning the Making of Verse or Ryme in English* (1575), George Gascoigne goes so far as to identify 'poetical licence' with the 'turkeneth' of 'all things at pleasure', as though there is something of the 'turk' about the very operations of poetry.[68] It is clear from the surrounding examples – 'it maketh words longer, shorter, of more syllables, of fewer, newer, older, truer, falser' – that Gascoigne's highly unusual word 'turkeneth' is

---

[59] Africanus, *Geographical Historie*, p. 50.
[60] Africanus, *Geographical Historie*, p. 146.
[61] Richard Knolles, *The Generall Historie of the Turkes* (London, 1603), p. 562.
[62] Knolles, *Generall Historie*, p. 562.
[63] Sidney, *Defence*, sig. B3r, G3r.
[64] Eva Johanna Holmberg, 'Avoiding conflict in the early modern Levant: Henry Blount's adaptations in Ottoman lands', in *Travel and Conflict in the Early Modern World*, ed. Gábor Gelléri and Rachel Willie (New York, 2021), 127–38; p. 138; Henry Blount, *A Voyage into the Levant* (London, 1636), p. 84.
[65] Étienne Hubert to Joseph Scaliger, 8 October 1608, in *The Correspondence of Joseph Justus Scaliger*, ed. Paul Botley and Dirk van Miert, 8 vols. (Geneva, 2012), vol. 7, p. 642.
[66] Thomas Blount, *Glossographia* (London, 1656), sig. A7v.
[67] Virginia Mason Vaughan has argued that 'Shakespeare read Knolles carefully and at length' – see 'Supersubtle Venetians: Richard Knolles and the geopolitics of Shakespeare's *Othello*', in *Visions of Venice in Shakespeare*, ed. Shaul Bassi and Laura Tosi (Farnham, 2011), 19–33; p. 31.
[68] George Gascoigne, 'Certayne notes of Instruction …', in *The Poesies of George Gascoigne Esquire* (London, 1575), n.p.

a loose synonym for 'turneth', presumably drawing on an imagined association between Turks and 'turning' (a trope that included 'the shifting of political, religious, sexual, and moral identities').[69] The *OED* suggests a relationship to an earlier word 'turkesse', meaning 'to transform or alter'.[70] Yet readers have heard in Gascoigne's 'witty phrasing' – or is it a parapraxis? – 'a larger conversation' about 'the link between the foreign and the poetic', specifically between the Middle East and English poetry.[71]

That 'conversation' is continued elsewhere in more detail. In the *Art of English Poesy* (1589), George Puttenham describes being 'conversant with a certain gentleman' in Italy 'who had long travelled the oriental parts of the world, and seen the courts of the great princes of China and Tartary' (A. L. Korn reckoned Puttenham's 'Tartary' corresponded to 'the region east of the Caspian ... encompassing parts of northeastern Persia and western Turkestan').[72] Puttenham supposedly discovers from his interlocutor that the peoples of this region or regions

> have the use of poesy or rhyming, but do not delight so much as we do in long tedious descriptions, and therefore when they will utter any pretty conceit, they reduce it into metrical feet, and put it in form of a lozenge or square, or such other figure, and so engraven in gold, silver or ivory, and sometimes with letters of amethyst, ruby, emerald or topaz curiously cemented and pieced together, they send them in chains, bracelets, collars and girdles to their mistresses to wear for a remembrance.[73]

Puttenham claims to have been given '[s]ome few measures composed in this sort' which he translates 'word for word', first rendering them in diagram and then offering examples and ostensible translations fenced around by commentary.[74] The first two examples of this 'oriental' *carmina figurata* are reply poems by 'Timur Cutlu' (probably Tamburlaine) and 'the Lady Kersemine', both in the shape of a 'lozenge' made in 'letters' of 'intermingled' jewels.[75]

These poems have been variously described as 'fake', 'invented' and 'an elaborate sixteenth-century hoax', because no pre-1589 Middle Eastern engraved pattern poetry has ever been found (the nearest equivalent proposed by Miriam Jacobson is the so-called Timur Ruby, decorated with the ownership inscriptions of several Mughal emperors and Persian shahs).[76] However, Puttenham's history of pattern poetry may not be as spurious or fanciful as it first appears. Numerous examples of *hui-wen*, Chinese palindromes arranged in different shapes, have survived from the decades antedating Puttenham's treatise, although very few of these are obviously in verse.[77] More germanely, the Indian *citrakavya* – pattern poems in which the verse was first presented stanzaically and then in a visual shape, known as a *bandha* – were being written in substantial quantities in the sixteenth century, often with Sanskrit scripts set into a lotus flower design, rather in the manner of the engraved or inset poetry that Puttenham describes.[78] Berta Cano-Echevarría has argued that Puttenham's bejewelled pattern poetry might have 'a source of inspiration' in an evocation of the Persian shah's calligraphy in

---

[69] Daniel Vitkus, *Turning Turk: English Theater and the Multicultural Mediterranean, 1570–1630* (New York, 2003), p. 107.

[70] *OED Online*, 'turken' and 'turkess', sense 1.

[71] Catherine Nicholson, *Uncommon Tongues: Eloquence and Eccentricity in the English Renaissance* (Philadelphia, 2014), p. 70.

[72] George Puttenham, *Art of English Poesy* (London, 1589), p. 75; A. L. Korn, 'Puttenham and the Oriental pattern-poem', *Comparative Literature* 6 (1954), 289–303; p. 300.

[73] Puttenham, *Art*, p. 75. [74] Puttenham, *Art*, p. 75.

[75] Puttenham, *Art*, p. 77.

[76] Berta Cano-Echevarría, 'Puttenham's failed design: the fake genealogy of English pattern poetry', *Cahiers Élisabéthains* 94 (2017), 57–73; p. 64; Korn, 'Puttenham', p. 302; Miriam Jacobson, *Barbarous Antiquity: Reorienting the Past in the Poetry of Early Modern England* (Philadelphia, 2014), p. 222.

[77] For a helpful summary of the history and practice of *hui-wen*, see Herbert Franke, 'Chinese patterned texts', in Dick Higgins, *Pattern Poetry: Guide to an Unknown Literature* (Albany, 1987), 210–19.

[78] For a helpful account of the history and practice of *citrakavya*, see Kalanath Jha, *Figurative Poetry in Sanskrit Literature* (Delhi, 1975).

Richard Willes's *History of Travayle* (1577).[79] If Puttenham was acquainted with Willes's writing, he may have also known the pattern poetry in Willes's *Poematum Liber* (1573) – including one poem confected in Ancient Egyptian hieroglyphics, which may have been enough to spur Puttenham's notion that technopaegnia was a Middle Eastern preoccupation.[80]

Moreover, when Puttenham mentions pattern poetry 'by the Greek or Latin poets', he focuses on one Ancient Greek pattern poem with a Middle Eastern point of origin: 'I find not of this proportion used by any of the Greek or Latin poets, or in any vulgar writer, saving of that form which they call Anacreon's egg' (this figure poem, 'eccentrically versified in the form of an egg', is actually by Simias of Rhodes not Anacreon).[81] Anacreon was widely known to hail from Teos on the coast of Turkey, and Simias was associated with the famously cosmopolitan 'Alexandrian school' of Egypt. Thus, Puttenham's somewhat offhand dismissal of classical technopaegnia bolsters his argument for what he calls the 'oriental' (here Turkish and Egyptian) quality of the verse form. As Margaret Church had it, if the 'pattern poem probably originated in Asia Minor or even farther East and came into the Greek Empire' via 'Oriental influence at the school in Alexandria', then Puttenham's putative 'contact with oriental patterns' might be 'the first direct contact since the original impetus from the East in the time of Simias of Rhodes'.[82] Whether through Anacreon and Simias, or through Richard Willes, or even through the genuine testimony of an Italian traveller, the pattern poem could have looked an intriguingly Middle Eastern verse form to Puttenham and other of Shakespeare's contemporaries.

The 1609 quarto of Shakespeare's sonnets can reasonably be said to contain two pattern poems, although (to my knowledge) no critic has said so in those terms. One is Sonnet 126, one of the collection's 'formally aberrational' poems.[83] The sonnet is laid out in couplets, not the usual cross-rhymed quatrains, and ends with two pairs of curved brackets arranged where the final couplet would normally appear. These brackets have been severally interpreted as forming the image of an hourglass; as the publisher Thomas Thorpe's intervention to spare the blushes of the sonnet's named addressee or to identify missing lines; as marking a deliberate irresolution; as lunular lunulae; and even as a distorted 'S' for 'Shakespeare'.[84] One way of gathering together some of these interpretations would be to describe Sonnet 126 as a pattern poem, or at least partly a pattern poem. After all, it is far from implausible to think that Shakespeare may have known some pattern poems – especially given that the final two sonnets in the 1609 quarto are versions of an epigram in the *Greek Anthology*, the collection that contained the very first technopaegnia (including some examples by Simias).

The brackets of Sonnet 126 may have been fashioned by Thorpe not Shakespeare, and the other possible pattern poem in the 1609 quarto is the 'magniloquent' prefatory paratext beginning 'TO.THE.ONLIE.BEGETTER' and appended with Thorpe's initials.[85] This is usually interpreted as being 'set out like a lapidary inscription' or a 'monumental brass', or as emulating 'the style of a Roman monumental inscription', and as being in prose.[86] Yet the tapering *mise-en-page* of Thorpe's

---

[79] Cano-Echevarría, 'Puttenham's failed design', p. 68.
[80] Richard Willes, *Poematum Liber* (London, 1573), p. 43.
[81] Puttenham, *Art*, p. 75; Elena L. Ermolaeva, 'The figure poem egg by Simias of Rhodes and metrical terminology', *Philologia Classica* 12 (2017), 122–9; p. 122.
[82] Margaret Church, 'The First English pattern poems', *PMLA* 61 (1946), 636–50; pp. 636, 648.
[83] Roy Neil Graves, 'Shakespeare's Sonnet 126', *The Explicator* 54 (1996), 203–7; p. 203.
[84] A summary of criticism is provided in Rayna Kalas, 'Fickle glass', in *A Companion to Shakespeare's Sonnets*, ed. Michael Schoenfeldt (Oxford, 2007), 261–76.
[85] Leona Rostenberg, 'Thomas Thorpe, publisher of "Shake-Speares Sonnets"', *The Papers of the Bibliographical Society of America* 54 (1960), 16–37; p. 32.
[86] Katherine Duncan-Jones, 'Was the 1609 *Shake-Speares Sonnets* really unauthorized?' *The Review of English Studies* 34 (1983), 151–71; p. 159; Donald W. Foster, 'Master W.H. R.I.P.', *PMLA* 102 (1987), 42–54; p. 43; Lynne Magnusson, 'Thomas Thorpe's Shakespeare: "The only begetter"', in *The Sonnets: The State of Play*, ed. Hannah Crawforth, Elizabeth Scott-Baumann and Clare Whitehead (London, 2017), 33–54; p. 48.

dedication also assumes a shape akin to what Puttenham calls 'The Tricquet reversed' or 'The Taper reversed', a concrete poem in the form of a downward-pointing arrow.[87] (In his history of technopaegnia, Dick Higgins has anyway described lapidary inscriptions or 'texts which are made as if they were to be so carved' as 'analogous forms' to the pattern poem.)[88] In addition, the brackets of Shakespeare's Sonnet 126 look akin to what Puttenham calls a 'Lozenge', the same technopaegnic structure as the bejewelled verses purportedly by Tamburlaine and Kersemine.[89] Thorpe and/or Shakespeare may have read some of Puttenham's *Art* and been inspired by his pattern poems but, even if not, an early modern book buyer might have been inclined to read parts of the 1609 *Sonnets* under the interpretive aegis of pattern poetry and to have recognized that genre or verse form as having a faintly Middle Eastern air – because of the 'oriental' history supplied by Puttenham, or the Turkish and Alexandrian origins of the classical technopaegnia, or the 'Ancient Egyptian' concrete poetry of Richard Willes.[90]

Puttenham's 'predilection for the outlandish over the normative classical models for poetry' was shared by a writer much closer to Shakespeare.[91] In his *Defence of Rhyme* (1603), Samuel Daniel evinced rhyme's ubiquity in its favour: '[t]he universality [of rhyme] argues the general power of it, for if the barbarian use it then it shows that it sways the affection of the barbarian'.[92] Daniel was responding to the neoclassical, 'quantitative' arguments of Thomas Campion's *Observations in the Art of English Poesie* (1602), which preferred the relative rhymelessness of Ancient Greek and Latin verse. Campion portrayed rhyme as a 'barbarian' accretion, only to be found in Latin verse thanks to Vandal invasions at the fall of the Roman Empire.[93] Instead of challenging Campion on the veracity of his literary history, Daniel took another tack. In a daring passage of the *Defence*, he eschews the classical tradition altogether and gestures instead to some 'barbarian' histories of rhyme. He begins with an alternative history of 'feminine' rhyme (that is, rhyme that occurs on an extra, unstressed syllable at the end of the line or, in another contemporary definition, that also happens on the immediately precedent stressed syllable, as a species of 'double' rhyme). Daniel thinks feminine rhyme 'never begotten I am persuaded by any example in Europe, but born no doubt in Scythia':

The Slavonian and Arabian tongues acquaint a great part of Asia and Africa with it, the Muscovite, Polish, Hungarian, German, Italian, French, and Spaniard use no other harmony of words. The Irish, Briton, Scot, Dane, Saxon, English, and all the inhabitants of this island either have hither brought, or here found the same in use.... [T]his harmonical cadence ... made the most learned of all nations labour with exceeding travail to bring those numbers likewise unto it[.][94]

Daniel's history of feminine rhyme pictures the 'learned' European languages as altogether belated – importing the 'harmonical cadence' of feminine rhyme from 'Scythia', originally, via the 'Slavonian and Arabian tongues' and the 'great part of Asia and Africa'. Where Campion attacked rhyme as 'barbarian' and 'barbarous', Daniel reclaims it as such.

Daniel gives an example of the 'barbarian' aptitude for feminine rhyme: '*Georgievez de Turcarum moribus* hath an example of the Turkish rhymes just of the measure of our verse of eleven syllables, in feminine rhyme.'[95] Daniel is referring to a captivity memoir written in Latin by the Croatian soldier Bartholomaeus Georgievitz who was sold into slavery by the Ottomans after defeat at the Battle of Mohács in 1526. A decade after his capture, Georgievitz escaped and made his way to

---

[87] Puttenham, *Art*, p. 76. [88] Higgins, *Pattern Poetry*, p. 173.
[89] Puttenham, *Art*, especially p. 76.
[90] Puttenham's most recent editors have suggested that the art/nature debate in 4.4 of *The Winter's Tale* may borrow from a passage in book 3 – see George Puttenham, *The Art of English Poesy: A Critical Edition*, ed. Frank Whigham and Wayne A. Rebhorn (Ithaca, 2011), p. 383.
[91] Jacobson, *Barbarous Antiquity*, p. 81.
[92] Samuel Daniel, *A Defence of Ryme* (London, 1603), sig. F3r.
[93] Thomas Campion, *Observations in the Art of English Poesie* (London, 1602), p. 2.
[94] Daniel, *A Defence of Ryme*, sigs. F3r–v. [95] Daniel, sig. F3r.

Antwerp where he published his ethnographic chronicle in 1553. Sure enough, on page 26 of *De Turcarum Moribus* we find a song or poem (*carmina*). It is a quatrain in romanized Turkish:

> Birechen bes on eiledum derdumì
> Iaràdandan istemiseem iardumì
> Terch eiledum Zahmanumì gurdumì
> Ne ileim ieniemezum glunglumì.[96]

Georgievitz glosses the quatrain as amorous verses spoken by a love goddess ('Sunt enim carmina amatoria, Deae ipsorum lingua ASSICH vocatae, id est, Deae amoris') and provides a 'verbo ad verbum' ('word for word') translation into Latin.[97] Georgievitz 'carried the singular authority of one who had travelled and lived long enough among the Turks to claim familiarity with their language' but his explanation of the Turkish quatrain has a rather 'feigned authoritativeness'.[98] 'ASSICH' or, properly, *aşık* does not mean a goddess of love but a lover, or even a troubadour, and Georgievitz's word-for-word translation does a disservice to the nature of the Turkish language.[99]

Daniel, however, was right to detect feminine rhyme in this Turkish quatrain – both in its transliterated version and in the Turkish original (which can be reconstructed quite straightforwardly from Georgievitz's romanized version). The quatrain is indeed hendecasyllabic, or a 'verse of eleven syllables' as Daniel has it. It is a typical example of a *murabba müzdeviç*, a common four-line stanza with the same rhyming sound in every line. As befits a popular form encountered in straitened circumstances, the Turkish in this example is closer to *kaba Türkçe*, 'raw' or vulgar Turkish, than the high Ottoman one would expect to find at court. 'An expansion on the traditional Islamic monorhyme patterns' of the *qasida*, the *murabba* ends with a *redif* (or *radif* as it is known in Arabic).[100] The *redif* is a diffuse rhyme structure that extends across the length of each verse line as well as proceeding vertically down the ends of the lines; it encompasses both the rhyming syllable at the line end and the rhyming syllables that occur immediately beforehand. In the case of this quatrain, we have the unstressed rhyming syllable at the end of the line, 'mì', and the stressed syllable immediately beforehand, 'du' (or, in the final line, 'lu'). The rhymes in this *murabba* therefore satisfy all the early modern English definitions of feminine rhyme. If the Ottomans were sometimes construed as 'a form of antimatter ... a huge anti-Europe', as Leeds Barroll argued, then on this occasion Daniel contrarily forges a precise literary connection between Turkish and English versification.[101] At this moment in the *Defence* the Ottomans are 'not only in but also of Europe', sharing a prosodic kinship with English modes of versification.[102] Decades earlier than we might expect, we can see and hear a detailed prosodic involvement with Middle Eastern poetic form – one that has until now attracted no critical or editorial comment.

Later in the *Defence*, Daniel recoils from his initial enthusiasm for feminine rhyme. He relates a conversation with Hugh Sanford in which Sanford warned him 'of that deformity' which is induced when poets 'mix uncertainly feminine rhyme with masculine'.[103] Daniel revised his verse in this spirit of 'metrical insecurity'.[104] He deleted twelve feminine rhymes from the 1592 edition of his sonnet sequence *Delia* and another

---

[96] Bartholomaeus Georgievitz, *De Turcarum Moribus Epitome* (Lyon, 1558), p. 26. The 1553 text is identical in this respect.
[97] Georgievitz, *De Turcarum*, pp. 26–7.
[98] Gerald MacLean, 'Early modern travel writing (1): print and early modern European travel writing', in *The Cambridge History of Travel Writing*, ed. Nandini Das and Tim Youngs (Cambridge, 2019), 62–76; p. 74; Nil Ö. Palabıyık, *Silent Teachers: Turkish Books and Oriental Learning in Early Modern Europe, 1544–1669* (New York, 2023), p. 24.
[99] Palabıyık, *Silent Teachers*, pp. 24–6.
[100] Walter G. Andrews Jr, *Ottoman Poetry* (Minneapolis, 1976), p. 159.
[101] Leeds Barroll, 'Mythologizing the Ottoman: *The Jew of Malta* and *The Battle of Alcazar*', in *Remapping the Mediterranean World in Early Modern English Writings*, ed. Goran Stanivukovic (Houndmills, 2007), 117–30; p. 119.
[102] Abdulhamit Arvas, 'The Ottomans in and of Europe', in *England's Asian Renaissance*, ed. Carmen Nocentelli and Su Fang Ng (Newark, 2022), 31–54; p. 47.
[103] Daniel, *Defence*, sig. Ir.
[104] Edward Haviland Miller, 'Samuel Daniel's revisions in *Delia*', *The Journal of English and Germanic Philology* 53 (1954), 58–68; p. 65.

twenty-five from the 1594 edition.[105] Having 'turned Turk', as it were, by writing 'barbarian' feminine rhymes into his sonnets, Daniel would ultimately turn on this 'harmonical cadence' and attempt to purge it from his verse.

Yet Shakespeare had his ears on Daniel's feminine rhymes, however quickly they were disappearing from print. Shakespeare's Sonnet 20 is not only about the feminine comportments of its 'master-mistress' (2); it is also about the feminine comportments of the sonnet itself, in which every rhyme is feminine. (The same is true of Sonnet 87, barring lines 2 and 4.) Sonnet 20's feminine rhymes help to fashion the paradoxical effect of the poem. In extending one syllable beyond the normal length of the pentameter, they might suggest, as the sonnet does, 'the queerness of desire' with its 'passionate, illicit excess'; the very words 'passion' (2) and 'pleasure' (13) seem to tremble off the edge of their verse lines.[106] Yet in being so clearly gendered themselves, the feminine rhymes also regulate any excess. They 'recognise and concede the definitions, the contents, of the terms of gender', rather as the sonnet ultimately seems to resolve (at least some of) its gender ambiguity 'By adding one thing' (12), the 'prick' of the couplet (13), to 'nothing' (12), an early modern English slang word for the vagina.[107]

Shakespeare probably filched the prosodic conceit of ending every line of a sonnet with a feminine rhyme from Sonnet 17 of Daniel's *Delia* (Daniel's sonnet was the first in English in which every rhyme was feminine). Ever since Edmond Malone's eighteenth-century argument that 'Daniel's sonnets ... appear to me to have been the model that Shakespeare followed', scholars have established the close connections between *Delia* and *Shake-speares Sonnets*.[108] Shakespeare's 1609 quarto follows the broad structure of *Delia*, whether in appending a lover's complaint poem to the sonnets proper or in concluding with Anacreontic verse. In addition, scholars have detected a plethora of direct allusions to Daniel's sonnets within Shakespeare's, locating the poems of the 1609 quarto in a 'Delian tradition', with Daniel's sequence proving 'a decisive document' for Shakespeare's poems.[109] If the feminine rhymes of *Delia* were an inspiration for Shakespeare's Sonnet 20, as seems likely, then Shakespeare was indirectly importing – only at one remove – a supposedly 'Turkish' or 'barbarian' cadence into the structure of his verse form.

***

John Keats wrote of Shakespeare's sonnets that they 'seem to be full of fine things said unintentionally'.[110] Are the feminine rhymes of Sonnet 20 'unintentionally' Turkish? Did Shakespeare know Daniel's 'barbarian' lineage of feminine rhyme in the *Defence*, or Daniel's opinions on the subject in the early-to-mid 1590s at the time he was probably writing Sonnet 20?[111] Although the *Defence* wasn't printed until 1603, the volume's title page describes it as 'heretofore written'. It may therefore have been available to read, in some form, at a substantially earlier date. We know that Shakespeare read, often ransacked, 'almost all of Daniel's work' (Daniel's biographer John Pitcher has noted that this is 'especially' the case 'for his narrative poems and sonnets').[112] As

---

[105] Miller, 'Samuel Daniel's revisions'.
[106] Natasha Distiller, 'Shakespeare's perversion: a reading of Sonnet 20', *Shakespeare* 8 (2012), 137–53; p. 143; Alan Sinfield, 'Coming on to Shakespeare: offstage action and Sonnet 20', *Shakespeare* 3 (2007), 108–25; p. 113.
[107] Distiller, 'Shakespeare's perversion', p. 150. The term 'feminine rhyme' was in vogue at the time of this sonnet's writing – see Robert Stagg, 'Rhyme's voices: hearing gender in *The Taming of the Shrew*', *Studies in Philology* 119 (2022), 323–46.
[108] *The Plays and Poems of William Shakespeare*, ed. Edmond Malone, vol. 16 (Dublin, 1794), p. 5.
[109] Brian Vickers, *Shakespeare, A Lover's Complaint, and John Davies of Hereford* (Cambridge, 2007), p. 76; *The Sonnets, and A Lover's Complaint*, ed. John Kerrigan (Harmondsworth, 1987), pp. 14, 13.
[110] John Keats to J. H. Reynolds, 22 November 1817, in *Selected Letters of John Keats*, ed. Grant F. Scott (Cambridge, 2002).
[111] See A. Kent Hieatt, Charles W. Hieatt and Anne Lake Prescott, 'When did Shakespeare write "Sonnets 1609"?' *Studies in Philology* 88 (1991), 69–109.
[112] Stuart Gillespie, *Shakespeare's Books: A Dictionary of Shakespeare's Sources* (London, 2016 [2001]), p. 103;

J. M. R. Baker has put it, 'Shakespeare followed Daniel's literary output with particular keenness' and was 'notably interested' in Daniel's 'thought'.[113] Moreover, Shakespeare's Stratford friend Richard Field (the 'Richard du Champ' of *Cymbeline* (4.2.379)) had printed Campion's *Observations*, the precipitating text for Daniel's *Defence* (and, intriguingly, Field also served as the printer of choice for the Arabist scholar William Bedwell (1561–1632)). The *Defence* itself was printed by Edward Blount, the man who also published some of Shakespeare's poetry (in *Love's Martyr*), who entered *Antony and Cleopatra* and *Pericles* in the Stationers' Register, and who eventually worked to publish the First Folio.

Nor would it be surprising for Shakespeare to have shown an interest, however rudimentary, in Turkish (and, more generally, Middle Eastern) poetry: John W. Draper observes that 'Shakespeare's Turkish allusions are almost twice as numerous as his Spanish; and he mentions [the sultans] Solyman and Amurath but never Philip II.'[114] If Shakespeare's adoption of a feminine rhyme scheme for Sonnet 20 was knowingly indebted to Daniel's 'Turkish' history of the rhyme, then the ostentatious 'pricking out' of the final couplet, in which the ambiguously gendered 'master-mistress' is afforded a penis, may even be a somewhat puerile inversion of the notorious practices at the Ottoman sultan's court, which lavishly celebrated the circumcisions of its male children and which was staffed by a fleet of eunuchs.

If; perhaps; maybe. The argumentative mode of this article has inevitably been strung somewhere between the suppositional and the speculative. Yet, as Touchstone has it, there can be 'much virtue in "if"' (*As You Like It*, 5.4.100–1). It is possible that Shakespeare, like some of his contemporaries, had a nascent, elementary understanding of and/or interest in Middle Eastern poetic forms, and probable that his 'English' sonnets had long ago been moulded by Arabic lyric conventions. Granted, the influence of Middle Eastern verse on Shakespeare's sonnets is more likely to be indirect and inadvertent, perhaps mediated through Daniel and his 'Turkish' reading material, or through Puttenham's 'oriental' concrete poetry, as well as emerging almost geologically through centuries of development in sonnet form. There are nonetheless glimmers of another possibility, even if those glimmers are too like the 'orient' sun in Sonnet 7 which 'Lifts up his burning head' (2) only to 'reel' (10) into a 'low tract' (12). Shakespeare's sonnets are undoubtedly 'worldly' poems, made so by the long international and interlingual history of their form. But is Shakespeare a 'worldly' writer not only in the sense given above, but with the meaning supplied by the *OED*'s entry for 'worldly', adj. 5: 'Sophisticated, experienced, cosmopolitan, worldly-wise'? Perhaps those fine things that Keats treasured in Shakespeare's sonnets were said intentionally, after all.

John Pitcher, 'Daniel, Samuel (1562/3–1619)', *Oxford Dictionary of National Biography*, published online 23 September 2004.

[113] J. M. R. Baker, '"Mutuall render": A study of Samuel Daniel, and some aspects of Shakespeare's debt to his work', unpublished D.Phil. thesis (University of Oxford, 1990).

[114] John W. Draper, 'Shakespeare and the Turk', *The Journal of English and Germanic Philology* 55 (1956), 523–32; p. 532.

HOW TO MAKE A FORMAL COMPLAINT: SARA AHMED'S *COMPLAINT!* AND WILLIAM SHAKESPEARE'S *A LOVER'S COMPLAINT*

HANNAH CRAWFORTH AND ELIZABETH SCOTT-BAUMANN[1]

A young woman in evident distress finds someone to whom she will tell her story. We do not know how long she has been holding it within herself. We do not know what it has cost her not to tell it. We do not know what it will cost her to tell it now. We do not know the other costs she has borne because of what has happened to her, but we can assume they are significant. She everywhere bears the signs of its impact, even while she has remained silent. She has evidence. Papers. Gifts she has been given. Damage wrought upon her body. But nobody, so far as we can tell, has yet listened to her. The letters she holds are hers on condition of secrecy. Somebody doesn't want her to tell.

When she does begin to speak, the story that unfolds is (perhaps we have already recognized the signs) one of abuse. A man's attentions have fallen upon her though she considers herself too young for this – it is too soon. He is young, too, he is attractive to her. But she is not ready. He begins his attempts to persuade her. People would later talk about this as if she was a willing accomplice; the word they will often use to describe his behaviour is 'seduction'. But it is not that. It is an effort to force her consent. His tongue works to subdue her, as she will describe it. He will take any argument she offers, any reason she deploys, and turn it against her. He is manipulative. He tries to manipulate her. And he has done it before, as he delights in telling her. Many times. Even a nun once found him so irresistible she succumbed to his desires, he says. If all these other women were prevailed upon, surely she can see her way to doing the same? He makes her feel like her agreement is inevitable, predestined. Like she has already consented.

But she, of course, is different from those other women, he says, with a smile. They were just ... (something). It's her he really loves. He shows her the relics offered up by these women. The jewels, the poems, the locks of their hair. He wants to give them to her. He wants her to touch them. The coercion steps up a gear here; a refusal now means a rejection of all these women, too. A compounding of their pain. Haven't they suffered enough? Does she think herself so much better than them? Better than him? At this point he squeezes out some tears, and stops speaking. He leaves his words, and his beautiful, weeping face, to do his work for him.

As she will later tell it, when she finally tells someone, it was the tears that did it. She knew, really, that his words were well practised. She didn't really believe them. She knew he had the power to hurt her, as he had hurt all those other women. But then he cried.

***

'To be heard as complaining is not to be heard', Sara Ahmed's *Complaint!* begins.[2] Ahmed goes on to recount the numerous ways in which those who complain about institutionalized abuse are not listened to: 'To hear someone as complaining is an

---

[1] With thanks to Sara Ahmed for her work and her interest in ours. We are grateful for feedback on this article from Farah Karim-Cooper, Hannah Dawson and Emma Smith.
[2] Sara Ahmed, *Complaint!* (Durham, NC, 2021), p. 1. All further citations appear parenthetically in the text.

effective way of dismissing someone' (1). This is especially true when women complain, particularly women of colour: 'We learn how only some ideas are heard if they are deemed to come from the right people; right can be white' (4). But to truly hear someone complaining is to listen to the distinct patterns of their pain. 'To hear complaint is to become attuned to the different forms of its expression', Ahmed writes (4), coining the term 'complaint biography' to describe one form it can take.[3] The 'complaint biography' with which this article began is that of the Young Woman whose story is told in Shakespeare's poem *A Lover's Complaint* (1609).[4] Shakespeare's Young Woman is enshrined in an institution – a poetic form, and a literary critical history – constructed by white men, she exists within the genre of the complaint poem which early modern women were working collectively to reclaim and make their own.[5] Within its strictures, her labours to convey her story are often in vain; her suffering is dismissed, her pain unheard. We want to ask here what it would mean to listen – to really listen – to the Young Woman's complaint, to hear her story with what Ahmed elsewhere calls an explicitly 'feminist ear'.[6] We also want to listen with a feminist ear to Ahmed, to express our indebtedness to all we continue to learn from her work, and to follow her lead in a feminist movement that seeks solidarity across and through difference, and that foregrounds the inextricability of racism from patriarchal ideology. As Carol Mejia LaPerle – drawing upon the foundational work of Margo Hendricks – observes, Premodern Critical Race Studies shows the need to continually question '[w]hich subject positions are privileged and which are, by violent design, erased or distorted?'[7] We want to acknowledge from the beginning of this article our own white privilege and that of the Young Woman of *A Lover's Complaint* (who is explicitly racialized as white, and created by a white, relatively middle-class, man). At the same time, we want to explore what it means to take seriously the Young Woman of Shakespeare's complaint poem and her experiences of sexual violence and misogyny. To hear her testimony as that of a survivor of abuse. To believe her.[8]

Following the lead of bell hooks, we are not seeking to demonstrate a 'common oppression' experienced by both the Young Woman and the young women of colour whom Ahmed interviews. Instead of eliding difference, this article aims rather to seek a solidarity founded in difference of the kind hooks advocates: 'Rather than bond on the basis of shared victimization or in response to a false sense of a common enemy, we can bond on the basis of our political commitment to a feminist movement that aims to end sexist oppression.'[9] In grateful acknowledgement of Ahmed's work, we seek to uncover the ways in which the Young Woman of the poem has been shaped by a racist patriarchal system that

---

[3] Ahmed coins the term 'complaint biography' in response to one of the many interviews she conducted when researching her book. It is through this conversation with a 'woman of color academic' – and the specific experiences of racism and sexism articulated by this interviewee – that Ahmed arrives at this key term. 'If the term was mine, the inspiration for it came from her' (19–20).

[4] On our designation of the female character in *A Lover's Complaint* as the 'Young Woman', see below. All citations to the text refer to *Oxford Shakespeare: The Complete Sonnets and Poems*, ed. Colin Burrow (Oxford, 2002).

[5] See Sarah C. E. Ross and Rosalind Smith, eds., *Early Modern Women's Complaint: Gender, Form, and Politics* (Cham, 2020). See also Sarah C. E. Ross, 'Pretty Creatures: *A Lover's Complaint*, *The Rape of Lucrece* and Early Modern Women's Complaint Poetry' in this volume.

[6] Ahmed coins this term in *Living a Feminist Life* (Durham, NC, 2017), pp. 202–4.

[7] Carol Mejia LaPerle, 'Introduction', to *Race and Affect in Early Modern English Literature*, ed. Carol Mejia LaPerle (Tempe, AZ, 2021), ebook freely available under Creative Commons License: https://doi.org/10.54027/AOGZ4936.

[8] Informed by a recent special issue of *Spenser Studies*, we seek to practise 'companionable thinking' in juxtaposing Shakespeare with Ahmed, an approach that seeks to 'dislodge some wonted habits of thought' and to practise radically 'ambivalent forms of openness' that lie not in eliding the differences between the texts under scrutiny here but instead in valuing their disparateness and divergence, 'keeping the potential for discomfort in play' in a dialogic relation that can be 'by turns, collaborative, sympathetic, recuperative, frustrating, undermining, and antagonistic'. See David Hillman, Joe Moshenska and Namratha Rao, 'Preface', *Spenser Studies* 37 (2003), 1–9; pp. 3, 2.

[9] bell hooks, 'Sisterhood: political solidarity between women', *Feminist Review* 23 (1986), 125–38; p. 129.

depends upon both her abuse and her chastity, as a condition of the white supremacist logic of the society in which her story has been written. As one instance of the ways in which we seek to show our allyship – to work as what David Sterling Brown, quoting Mikki Kendall, calls 'accomplice feminists' – we have throughout this article rejected the objectification of the central female character in Shakespeare's poem as a 'Maid', a title imposed upon her by generations of (white, male) critics which we resist here because of its sexist and sexually judgemental connotations and ideological investment in the notion of white chastity. Instead, we use the term 'Young Woman', in parity with the 'Young Man' conventionally referred to in denoting the abuser whose acts are described in the poem. (We have likewise avoided any reference to the 'seduction' that many other critics refer to.) Following Ahmed, and out of respect for her own powerful and inspirational ways of working, we have also sought to make other conscious choices in writing and structuring this article. In the hope of building feminist solidarity founded in anti-racist commitments and – in hooks's words – 'not irrevocably tainted by politics of domination', we have adopted the non-hierarchical structure that characterizes the argument of *Complaint!* (and other works by Ahmed).[10] We have sought to centre Ahmed's voice and that of the young women she interviews (as well as the Young Woman of Shakespeare's poem, as the victim of a very different kind of abuse, but abuse that nonetheless depends upon – and exposes – racist patriarchal structures). This article is co-written in a spirit of collectivity as championed by Ahmed; the 'we' of this article represents the authors' perspectives, and is not meant to imply or coerce readers' agreement.[11] This is, however, a collectivity founded in what Audre Lorde influentially terms 'the creative function of difference in our lives', a form of solidarity that both resists the eliding of difference (such as the gulf between the Young Woman of the poem and the young women Ahmed interviews) and at the same time acknowledges that the dismantling of hierarchies of oppression depends upon recognizing that difference.[12] To read the misogyny, abuse and racist thought structures underpinning *A Lover's Complaint* only in relation to a (predominantly) white, male, literary critical canon is to deny the possibility of a radical 'accomplice feminism'. In Lorde's memorable formulation: 'What does it mean when the tools of a racist patriarchy are used to examine the fruits of that same patriarchy? It means that only the most narrow perimeters of change are possible and allowable.'[13] Reading *A Lover's Complaint* with *Complaint!* is our attempt to seek a bigger, and more enduring, form of change.

***

Shakespeare's poem begins when an old 'reverend man' decides, finally, to listen.

> So slides he down upon his grainèd bat,
> And comely distant sits he by her side,
> When he again desires her, being sat,
> Her grievance with his hearing to divide
> (*LC*, 64–7)

Even this moment, so long coming, is complicated by the suggestion that this man finds something erotic in the Young Woman's suffering. Shakespeare allows the glancing possibility that he 'desires her' here, the subclause intervening between the sexually charged verb and its subject for just long enough to ensure that the implication that he takes some pleasure from her pain resounds through the ensuing complaint (which will be figured as 'her suffering ecstasy' (69)). And that other

---

[10] hooks, 'Sisterhood', p. 125. We discuss Ahmed's prose style and structure below.
[11] On what Lehua Yim describes as the 'arrogance of assumption' embedded in the inclusive 'we', see Margo Hendricks, 'Coloring the past, rewriting our future: RaceB4Race', transcript available at www.folger.edu/research/featured-research-projects-and-initiatives/race-and-periodization.
[12] The absence of consideration of 'difference of race, sexuality, class, and age ... weakens any feminist discussion of the personal and the political', Lorde writes. It is a form of 'particular academic arrogance to assume any discussion of feminist theory without examining our many differences': Audre Lorde, 'The master's tools will never dismantle the master's house', in *The Selected Works of Audre Lorde*, ed. Roxane Gay (New York, 2020), 39–43; pp. 40, 39.
[13] Lorde, 'The master's tools', p. 40.

strange verb choice, 'divide' does not help. While this moment is often interpreted as the Old Man seeking to lessen her pain by sharing it, taking some of it away from her by taking it on himself, the verb is perhaps more troubling than such an account of the poem allows. To 'divide' is to break up, to fragment – suggesting a failure to comprehend the full meaning of what she has to say. Shakespeare's poem hints that this 'hearing' will not heal or restore the Young Woman, will not make her whole after the violent schism brought about by the act that has led to this moment, but will rather leave her divided; this complaint will splinter her, leaving her broken. 'A complaint can be shattering', Ahmed writes, 'we can be left in pieces' (15). The Young Woman's first words to the Old Man register this fact: 'in me you behold / The injury of many a blasting hour' (LC, 71–2). One of Ahmed's interviewees likens her complaint biography to having experienced 'fifteen car crashes'. Tracing the roots of the word *complaint* to the Old French *complaindre*, 'to lament', and thence to the Latin *lamentum*, 'wailing, moaning; weeping', Ahmed observes that the word *complaint* itself 'can sound like a crash, a collision, the loud sound of something breaking into pieces' (17).[14]

In keeping with this commitment to acknowledging the cataclysmic nature of the breaks a complaint instigates within the person who makes it, this article takes the form not of a cohesive whole, a single narrative (nor, for that matter, does Shakespeare's poem, the infamously incomplete framing of which has long been taken as a sign of its brokenness). Rather – and in tribute to the method by which Ahmed painstakingly pieces together *Complaint!* – we offer a series of four fragments, attending to the shattering implications of complaint, in both Ahmed's book and Shakespeare's poem. 'In the book I pick up these pieces not to create the illusion of some unbroken thing', she writes, 'but so that we can learn from the sharpness of each piece, how they fit together' (15). We try to hear these texts together, to take seriously their complaints by listening to them with an avowedly feminist ear, and to see what they collectively have to say about complaint. We want to acknowledge where they 'fit together', and to learn from the places where they don't. By attending to the Young Woman as a complainant, we read Shakespeare's poem as an influential instance of a genre that would eventually become, in Ahmed's hands, a tool for activism as well as poetry. When we listen to these texts together, what can they teach us about how to make a formal complaint?

1. RECORD WHAT YOU DO NOT WISH TO REPRODUCE

To complain is also to create a record. Remember: you have to record what you do not want to reproduce.
(*Complaint!* 288)

To complain is to seek an end to the abuse that prompts the complaint. It is also to relive it. The act of making a complaint requires the person who is its subject to re-experience their trauma for the 'record'. But the purpose of that recording is to end the cycle of repetition by which the object of the complaint enforces his (usually his) will upon the complainant. The aim is to stop the abuse, for both the person bringing the complaint and others who may be suffering at the hands of the same abuser. But one of the grim ironies Ahmed's book makes clear is the way in which the effort of bringing such behaviour to a stop can trigger an ongoing traumatic experience in the person who complains that has repercussions in their own life that are themselves hard to stop. 'Making a complaint is often necessary because of a crisis or trauma', she writes. And, in the next sentence, 'The complaint often becomes part of the crisis or trauma' (13). In an ideal, psychoanalytic world, telling the trauma would help to end the trauma (as in Freud's model of successful, or completed, mourning). But for both the women interviewed for *Complaint!* and the Young Woman of Shakespeare's poem telling leads only to more trauma, a cycle of repeated suffering that threatens to reproduce the pain of the abuse itself (here we

---

[14] 'In *Living a Feminist Life* (2017) [187–212], I described my resignation as a snap, a feminist snap. "Snap" can be what you say when you make the same connection. A snap can also be the sound of something breaking' (8).

catch sight of Freud's melancholic): 'To speak about a past trauma can be to make that trauma present', Ahmed observes (14).[15] '"I want the story to go somewhere (apart from round and round in my head) which is why I am contacting you"', writes an academic whose complaint Ahmed hears. As this prompts Ahmed to observe, 'Telling someone the story of complaint can be how the story goes somewhere. To become a feminist ear is to give complaints somewhere to go' (9).

For Ahmed, listening to the complaints of others recalls her own complaint (auto)biography, supporting a group of students at her former university in making a complaint against a male academic who had been sexually harassing and discriminating against them. The failure of her institution to properly hear their complaint would eventually lead to Ahmed's resignation from her professorial post (8). The complaints narrated by those Ahmed interviews echo her own experiences in ways that threaten to reproduce Ahmed's trauma, even as she seeks to record that of others. This replicates the complex movement Ahmed's book traces between complaint as 'record' – a final version of events that seeks to complete and thereby end them – and complaint as a 'recording' – an ongoing process of telling that may never end but remain trapped in a cycle of traumatic repetition.

This is the landscape in which *A Lover's Complaint* begins:

> From off a hill whose concave womb reworded
> A plaintful story from a sist'ring vale,
> My spirits t'attend this double voice accorded,
> And down I laid to list the sad-tuned tale;
> Ere long espied a fickle maid full pale,
> Tearing of papers, breaking rings a-twain,
> Storming her world with sorrow's wind and rain.
>
> (*LC*, 1–7)

The opening stanza of Shakespeare's poem explores what it might mean to acknowledge – or maybe even to break – the links between recording and reproducing, between compulsion and willed resistance, between suffering and storytelling. In an echoing 'vale' that is explicitly figured as female – metaphorically a 'concave womb' and suggestive of sisterhood ('sist'ring') – a story is heard. Or maybe not heard. Its sound reverberates around the hills and the 'plaintful story' is 'reworded'; it repeats, perhaps unto the point of becoming pure sound. Whether or not he can hear what is actually being said, the speaker of the poem apprehends some resonance between these sounds and his own inner state: his 'spirits' are 'accorded' with what he hears, and to the 'double voice' of complaint is added the further echo of his own personal story. As Ahmed advocates for the conscious adoption of a 'feminist ear', a deliberate effort on the part of the auditor not just to hear the complaint but to fully listen to it, so the speaker here commits to trying to understand what he is hearing. 'And down I laid to list the sad-tuned tale', he says. The reader of *A Lover's Complaint* also hears another echo here, the absent preposition, 'to', which serves to both enhance the archaism of those already aged verbs ('laid' and 'list' are anachronistic by 1609, Colin Burrow notes in his edition of the poem)[16] and, more crucially for our purposes, to elide the experience of listening with that of telling the 'sad-tuned tale'.[17]

That the speaker must physically stop what he is doing and lay down in order to listen to the complaint is also important, as is suggested by the fact this gesture repeats that of the 'reverend' old man, who must also still himself in order to listen, as we have already heard (64). The narrator's request to hear the Young Woman's story is also a plea for her to stop moving (her appearance in the poem up until this point has been characterized by almost constant motion) and, 'being sat', to tell her tale (66).[18] The

---

[15] Sigmund Freud, 'Mourning and melancholia' [1917], in *The Standard Edition of the Complete Psychological Works of Sigmund Freud Volume XIV (1914–1916)*, ed. James Strachey (London, 1957), 243–58.
[16] *Complete Poems*, ed. Burrow, p. 695.
[17] On 'Complaint's echoes', see Sarah C. E. Ross, in *Early Modern Women's Complaint*, ed. Ross and Smith, 183–202.
[18] Prior to this moment, we hear that 'Oft did she heave her napkin to her eyne' (15); 'Laund'ring' the handkerchief (17) that she has 'pelleted in tears' (18); 'shrieking undistinguished woe' (20); her gaze continually moving 'To every place at

relationship between making a complaint and metaphors of movement and stasis is one that Ahmed articulates throughout *Complaint!* A complaint involves both attempting to move through the story contained therein (already hinted at in Ahmed's remarks about it needing 'to go somewhere', quoted above) and also encountering a tendency to get stuck, for a complaint to be 'stalled' (6), and for others to seek to stop the complaint in its tracks. The second chapter of *Complaint!*, 'On being stopped', details 'how blockages and stoppages' threaten to derail the process of a formal complaint, leaving the complainant 'nowhere to go with the complaint' (69). It is not just the complaint process itself that is liable to get 'stuck', however (70). The complaint itself can be '*sticky data*', as Ahmed calls it; 'not only will it stick to you, it will be how you get stuck' (72). A complaint can put a stop to a career (or even an end to a life as it has been lived up until this point).[19] Those within its orbit can be pulled into a seemingly unending process that substitutes the progression of their lives for the endless repetition of trauma.

Informed by Ahmed, Shakespeare's poem emerges as a text that reproduces not just the individual trauma of its Young Woman, but also the collective traumas of all those who have gone before her in the literary genre that came to be identified as complaint poetry (we will return to collectivity in the final section of this article). The Young Woman's complaint is 'reworded' (*LC*, 1) because her voice is amplified by the stories of the other women whose complaints have been heard (if not listened to) before her, as much as by her own cries echoing through hill and vale. The 'papers' that she rends as she goes (6), the numerous 'folded schedules . . . / Which she perused, sighed, tore, and gave the flood', sobbing over them as she rips them to shreds (43–4), the 'yet more letters sadly penned in blood' (47), which 'often she bathed in her fluxive eyes, / And often kissed, and often 'gan to tear' (50–1) (a pun on both the tears she cries and the tearing of these letters as she weeps over them throughout the poem), all embody the pain of which she complains. They also remind us of the long textual prehistory of complaint itself. The poem's often archaic vocabulary reinforces this aspect of its distinctive 'double voice' (*LC*, 3), at once both an instance of the complaint genre and a commentary upon that form. The rhyme royal stanza compounds this effect, evoking a long tradition of female-voiced complaint, and – at a local level – enacting the progress and then stoppages of complaint through its interlinked rhymes and closing couplet.[20]

The Young Woman's description of the Young Man is emblematic of this problem; her attempts to record his charms instead risk reproducing the effect of them. Her impassioned speech struggles to get out of the rhetorical artifice that characterizes his conduct towards her, cycling through his supposedly attractive qualities with a strident insistence on their desirability in a way that mirrors the Young Man's efforts to impose himself upon her. The more the Young Woman repeats the elements of her description of him, the more the reader might doubt its veracity; the effect of this rhetorical *energeia* is to make him seem less, rather than more, life-like. After praising his hair, face, skin, face (again), 'maiden-tongued' speech (100), horse-riding skills, 'real habitude' (114) (whatever that may be) and 'grace' (119), the Young Woman returns to the subject of his speech, and particularly the rhetorical skill that will later be the means by which he deceives and abuses her.

> So on the tip of his subduing tongue
> All kind of arguments and questions deep,
> All replication prompt, and reason strong,
> For his advantage still did wake and sleep.
> To make the weeper laugh, the laugher weep,
> He had the dialect and different skill,
> Catching all passions in his craft of will;

---

once, and nowhere fixed' (27); throwing 'A thousand favours' (36) into the river 'one by one' (38).

[19] One interviewee tells Ahmed: '"He was a known harasser; there were a lot of stories told about him. I had a friend who was very vulnerable. He took advantage of that. She ended up taking her own life"' (*Complaint!* 184).

[20] See Elizabeth Scott-Baumann and Ben Burton, 'Shakespearean stanzas? *Venus and Adonis, Lucrece* and complaint', *English Literary History* 88 (2021), 1–26.

That he did in the general bosom reign
Of young, of old, and sexes both enchanted,
To dwell with him in thoughts, or to remain
In personal duty, following where he haunted.
Consents bewitched, ere he desire, have granted,
And dialogued for him what he would say,
Asked their own wills and made their wills obey.

(*LC*, 120–33)

The Young Man's rhetorical prowess is distinctively that of 'replication', of being able to conjure in his audience the feeling he wants them to experience, to reproduce his desires within their own psyche. 'To make the weeper laugh, the laugher weep', is to invert the emotional life of his interlocutor and to substitute their feelings for that which he would have them feel. Chiasmus appears frequently in the Young Woman's description of the Young Man, in a reflection of this process; the effect of his rhetoric is to entrap those he seeks to persuade within a cycle of suggestion. The final lines quoted above are particularly troubling. Those he targets are so powerfully 'bewitched' that they grant consent before it has been asked for, before even his 'desire' makes their consent a question. The Young Man's interlocutors have so fully internalized his rhetoric that they reproduce (Ahmed's term again) it for him, 'dialogu[ing] for him what he would say', and repeating his script back to him. So estranged are these women from 'their own wills' by the effects of his speech, that they have to consciously stop and ask themselves what they think and feel, and how to fit their thoughts and feelings to what he has suggested they should be.

BE NON-LINEAR

On paper a complaint can appear linear, a straight line. In reality, a complaint is often more circular (round and round rather than in and out).

(*Complaint!* 34)

In recording the actions of her abuser, the Young Woman of *A Lover's Complaint* seeks to tell her own story and thereby to reclaim her abuser's distinctively circular rhetoric – and the repeated suffering brought about by trauma – for herself.[21]

The Young Woman does not seek to impose linearity on her narrative. Rather, the narrative of *A Lover's Complaint* everywhere bears the marks of her abuse. Listening to the Young Woman's story with a feminist ear requires us to recognize this. And – as we'll go on to suggest in this section – Ahmed's work intimates that a non-linear narrative may be the most appropriate way of recording (without reproducing) the characteristic shape of a complaint.

As the Young Woman unfolds her story, we learn that the Young Man who abused her has done this before. 'Many there were that did his picture get', she tells us (*LC*, 134); 'many have that never touched his hand / Sweetly supposed them mistress of his heart' (141–2). Yet knowledge of this 'precedent' is not enough to stop it happening again (155). The Young Woman tells us that she 'knew the patterns of his foul beguiling' (170), the all-too familiar repetitions that characterize the behaviour of a well-practised abuser. In one of the most distressing aspects of Shakespeare's poem, recognizing these 'patterns' does not bring them to a stop. In fact, by a curious rhetorical sleight-of-hand the Young Man calls upon the stories of the 'many' he has abused before in order to license his abuse of the Young Woman. Rather than seeking to conceal his prior actions, as a possible deterrent to the Young Woman he so forcibly seeks to have sex with, the Young Man parades his previous behaviour before her, rehearsing the repeated impositions of his will upon the bodies of other young women as part of his efforts to force her consent. In an age-old rhetorical manoeuvre, the Young Man lists his previous sexual conquests in order to insist to the Young Woman that she, of course, is different: 'Among the many that mine

---

[21] On the ways in which early modern women appropriated the rhetorical techniques their male contemporaries had used against them, 'donning the mask of the logician' to prove 'their rationality at a meta-level', see Hannah Dawson, 'Fighting for my mind: feminist logic at the edge of Enlightenment', *Proceedings of the Aristotelian Society* 118 (2018), 275–306; p. 279.

eyes have seen, / Not one whose flame my heart so much as warmèd' – until, inevitably, now (190–1).

'Look here what tributes wounded fancies sent me', he says, displaying before her the trophies taken from his previous encounters (*LC*, 197). Jewels, locks of hair and even poems are all deployed as evidence of his supposed desirability and offered – bizarrely – to the Young Woman.[22] Worse still, he wants her to touch them.

> O then advance (of yours) that phraseless hand,
> Whose white weighs down the airy scale of praise.
> Take all these similes to your own command,
> Hallowed with sighs that burning lungs did raise
>
> (*LC*, 225–8)

The rhetoric the Young Man employs in his attempt to enforce his will upon the Young Woman has been 'Hallowed' – or made holy – by the violence he has inflicted upon others, by the firestorm that has left them with 'burning lungs', struggling for breath. The 'similes' he employs now operate not just in the comparative mode of their own moment, but also implicitly compare the Young Woman to the 'many' other young women with whom she shares this predicament. He gestures back to the fetishistic objects he has just listed, instructing her to reach for them. And yet in the contorted syntax here, he further withholds any agency from the Young Woman: her hand here is only parenthetically her own and, moreover, cannot be described – 'advance (of yours) that phraseless hand'. We are told only that it is a superlatively 'white', a racializing epithet that the Young Man holds more dear than 'praise', manifesting what Farah Karim-Cooper has called the 'burden of the purity of the white race placed upon white women for centuries'.[23] *Complaint!* documents the myriad ways in which racializing language is complicit in abuse, and the additional burdens that identifying or calling out such language place on the complainant. 'Some words can carry a complaint', Ahmed notes; 'all you have to do is use a word like *race* and you will be heard as complaining' (*Complaint!* 65). Whiteness is valued by the poem and yet also used to silence the Young Woman. Her hand is indescribable because it is so white, 'phraseless' meaning white beyond description. Yet perhaps it also suggests whiteness that does not need description. Brown has discussed the way 'the hypervisibility of unnamed whiteness in the field facilitates the invisibility of Black and brown people'; the narrator's representation of the Young Woman's skin as 'phraseless' in its whiteness, is a statement of both hypervisible and unnamed whiteness.[24] Claiming that her whiteness is 'phraseless', the Young Man inscribes the 'intractability and permanence of whiteness' in Shakespeare's work which scholars including Arthur L. Little Jr, Brown and Ambereen Dadabhoy have exposed.[25] As Dadabhoy notes,

The unmarked and unremarkable nature of these white bodies and white people has resulted in an understanding of the early modern period as race-less or race-free even as technologies to understand cultural, ethnic, and somatic differences (what we might now call race) were being developed in the period[.][26]

The Young Man will repeat his racist gesture shortly thereafter, in stanza 35 of the poem (having just boasted that one of his previous conquests was 'a nun, / A sister sanctified of holiest note' (232–3)). Merging the language of whiteness with the

---

[22] He shows her 'pallid pearls and rubies red as blood' (*LC*, 198); 'talents of their hair' (204); and 'deep-brained sonnets' (209). 'Nature hath charged me that I hoard them not, / But yield them up where I myself must render – / That is to you, my origin and ender' (220–2).

[23] Farah Karim-Cooper, *The Great White Bard: Shakespeare, Race and the Future* (London, 2023), p. 136.

[24] David Sterling Brown, '"Hood feminism": Whiteness and segregated (premodern) scholarly discourse in the post-post-racial era', *Literature Compass* (2020), https://doi.org/10.1111/lic3.12608, p. 7.

[25] Arthur L. Little Jr, 'Is it possible to read Shakespeare through Critical White Studies?' in *The Cambridge Companion to Shakespeare and Race*, ed. Ayanna Thompson (Cambridge, 2021), 268–80. See also David Sterling Brown, *Shakespeare's White Others* (Cambridge, 2023); Ambereen Dadabhoy, 'The unbearable whiteness of being (in) Shakespeare', *Postmedieval: A Journal of Medieval Cultural Studies* 11 (2020), 228–35; Arthur L. Little Jr, ed., *White People in Shakespeare: Essays on Race, Culture and the Elite* (London, 2023).

[26] Dadabhoy, 'Unbearable whiteness', p. 229.

not-so-implicit threat of violence, the Young Man petulantly asks:

> 'But, O, my sweet, what labour is't to leave
> The thing we have not, mastering what not strives,
> Paling the place which did no form receive,
> Playing patient sports in unconstrainèd gyves?'
>
> (*LC*, 239–42)

'Paling' suggests simultaneously an act of enclosure – the shutting up or imprisoning of the imagined, absent, victim of his attentions here – and, perhaps, a process of erasure that is also a whitening out – a blanking of the woman he seeks to subjugate to his will, who is rendered strangely formless by this rhetoric. (Recall that parenthetical 'of yours', a few lines earlier, which likewise sought to instigate a kind of detachment – or breaking off – from her own body.) The racializing aspects of the word 'Paling' are compounded by the language of mastery and that image of the 'unconstrained gyves' – or shackles – which evoke enslavement in a vile inversion of its historical realities; the Young Man metaphorically places himself in a position of subjection, enslaving himself to her, as a means of asserting precisely the opposite, proclaiming his mastery over the Young Woman's body.

'This is an old and primary tool of all oppressors to keep the oppressed occupied with the master's concerns', writes Lorde, in 'The master's tools will never dismantle the master's house' (an essay Ahmed repeatedly engages in *Complaint!*).[27] The Young Man's appropriation of metaphors of enslavement works to reinscribe his own privileged position of mastery upon the poem. 'The justification of violence *is* how that violence is repeated. *The justification of violence is that violence*', Ahmed reminds us (*Complaint!* 134). A complaint that becomes stuck – circling around in the endless repetitions of bureaucracy that mirror the recurrent rhetoric of a racist patriarchy, or the cyclical experience of the trauma that results from abuse – fails because it depends upon the complainant taking up the 'Master's tools' in this way. If circular rhetoric and traumatic repetition characterize the abuse inflicted by the Young Man of Shakespeare's poem, however, Ahmed suggests that reclaiming such patterns might have a role to play in countering racist and sexist abuse.[28] In her fourth chapter, 'Occupied', Ahmed cites Lorde once more:

> When a feminist house is built using the tools of 'racist patriarchy', the same house is being built, a house in which only some are allowed in, or only some are given room. Lorde stresses that those who are resourced by the master's house will find those who try to dismantle that house 'threatening'[.] (*Complaint!* 139)

Occupying the space that others would assert mastery over – taking back possession of one's own body, as the Young Woman tries to recover herself from the formlessness the Young Man imposes upon her – is crucial to the process of complaint, Ahmed shows.

It is important to note the rhetorical method by which Ahmed herself works here. *Complaint!* moves distinctively through its case studies and arguments, circling around particular instances and ideas repeatedly, developing nuance and acuity each time Ahmed revisits them. Certain metaphors recur repeatedly throughout *Complaint!* to the point that they transcend figurative status and become more literal embodiments of meaning. Doors, stoppages, gaps, blockages, blinds and filing cabinets are all subject to Ahmed's cumulative writerly methodology, acquiring metaphorical weight through their repeated invocation in the book and existing somewhere between the concreteness of literal objects and the ephemerality of metaphor. As Shakespeare's Young Woman circles around her description of the Young Man,

---

[27] Lorde, 'The master's tools', p. 43.
[28] Carol Mejia LaPerle has shown us how a similar reclamation is at work in Shakespeare's *Sonnets*, as the 'Black Mistress' (as Jane Kingsley-Smith argues she should be called, in 'Nothing-to-be-glossed-here: race in Shakespeare's Sonnets', in this volume) represents articulate resistance to patriarchy, though in often misogynistic and racist terms. As LaPerle describes it, the *Sonnets* show 'the dark mistress's disruption of male dominance and resistance to passive objectification': Carol Mejia LaPerle, 'The racialized affects of ill-will in the Dark Lady sonnets', in *Race and Affect*, ed. LaPerle, 205–21.

becoming gradually more precise in pinpointing the nature of his abusive rhetoric, so Ahmed's writing amplifies her meaning through each repetition. In neither case is the speaker stuck. But we can see the work going on in this kind of language to resist merely reproducing trauma and instead to give the narrative 'somewhere' to go, to move through the experience that continues to shape the telling of it.

The recurrence of certain photographs throughout Ahmed's book contributes to this effect, by which her rhetorical method adapts the circular logic of complaint (including the repetitions of abuse and trauma) into a form of writing that acknowledges this distinctively cyclical process but also looks to move through and beyond it. Offering us, for instance, the same image of a scribbled doodle, a tangled line-drawing that loops back upon itself, Ahmed captions two figures: '1.4 A drawing of a complaint' (*Complaint!* 36) and '2.2 A Picture of a life' (95). By the latter pages of *Complaint!*, the same image has been recuperated as something useful: '8.2 A queer map' (299). A photograph of a letterbox bearing a Post-it note that reads 'Birds Nesting. Please do not use this Box. Many thanks' appears in three places in the book, captioned '4.2 Queer use: things can be used by those for whom they were not intended' (138); '5.2 Feminism in the academy (letters in the box)' (implicitly going nowhere) (218); and, in an image that offers a variation on this theme – featuring a different letterbox but the same composition, replacing the Post-it with another note that reads 'Birds welcome!' – bearing a caption, '4.4 Diversity as a nonperformative' (172). In repeating the same (or nearly identical) images to illustrate both instances of abuse and the ways in which complaint can speak back to that abuse, Ahmed poses again the question that Lorde articulates so powerfully in her 1984 essay (and which we quoted above): 'What does it mean when the tools of a racist patriarchy are used to examine the fruits of that same patriarchy?' Her answer is subtly different to Lorde's. But this method speaks closely to the attempts by the Young Woman of *A Lover's Complaint* to retell the story of her abuse and its traumatic aftermath.

WITHHOLD YOURSELF

By insisting on our anonymity, we were also insisting that this was not a matter of an individual conflict; this was not a matter of one person in need of resolution with another, not a matter of a dispute between two equal parties. And we were also insisting that we would not be required to place our full trust, and ourselves, again in institutional hands. We withheld ourselves.

(266)

This passionate and moving statement comes in the collaboratively written 'Collective conclusions' to Ahmed's *Complaint!*, written by Leila Whitley, Tiffany Page and Alice Corble, with Heidi Hasbrouck, Chryssa Sdrolia and others. The affirmation of withholding here speaks to a wider feature of the style of Ahmed's book: style as a withholding of self. While Ahmed's study both articulates and evokes strong, heightened emotions (rage, frustration, loss), it often does so through a rhetoric of understatement. Hannah Dawson calls this Ahmed's 'poetic voice'.[29] Ahmed often opens her paragraphs with an apparently simple statement, then amplifies this with another short sentence using similar words. The effect of this apparent simplicity is complex: it draws the reader in through plainly stated and self-evident statements; it sometimes evokes a wry smile through Ahmed's own play on words; yet it also provides critical distance, forcing our close attention to colloquial or idiomatic phrases – especially those used by complainants, harassers or institutions: 'You can become a sore point because of what you need. If you say what you need, a sore point becomes the same point' (*Complaint!* 143). Ahmed combines a wry humour with a flat, almost bathetic, affect, which in turn accumulates to create instead an affective and effective intensity – as the banality of institutional words, or the crass casualness of harassers' words, or the poignant idioms of complainants accrue, example by example. If this is a style of withholding, then, it is also one that generates emotional and political effects.

---

[29] Private correspondence, quoted with permission.

Silence can be a withholding – but it can also be articulate, even a form of complaint. A postgraduate student arrives at a conference and is immediately subjected to unsolicited physical contact and sexist jokes. Everyone seems to laugh along, but she does not, and her silence is heard as complaint. As Ahmed recounts the student's experience:

When people laugh and you do not laugh, you end up stranded, exposed. Being stranded is part of the experience of complaint, a sense that you have been cut off from a group that you had understood yourself to be part of; you come apart; things fall apart. Being cut off can also be a judgment made about the complainer, who can appear as a figure just because she is not laughing, not going along with things, not getting along.

(*Complaint!* 123)

While the complainant's silence is expressive here, there is also something excessive in the way in which she describes (and Ahmed relates) her experience, offering multiple versions of the same phrase and riffing off the rhythms of her own prose. Like the Young Woman of *A Lover's Complaint*, the woman Ahmed interviews here is subjected to others' interpretations of her experience that are inaccurately imposed upon her speech (or lack of it). We watch the Young Woman, through the narrator's eyes, throwing away her lover's tokens:

A thousand favours from a maund she drew,
Of amber crystal and of beaded jet,
Which one by one she in a river threw,
Upon whose weeping margin she was set,
Like usury applying wet to wet,
Or monarch's hands that lets not bounty fall
Where want cries "some", but where excess begs all.

(*LC*, 36–42)

From the exaggeration of the 'thousand favours' she withdraws onwards, the Young Woman's behaviours are seen as somehow too much. The jewels she throws are not only numerous but of high value: amber, crystal, jet. They are also highly crafted: crystal suggesting finely cut glass; 'beaded jet' probably jet that had been made into beads or (following the Quarto's 'bedded') jet embedded in another material – say, metal – as a ring.[30] The richness of the jewels accentuates the richness of language through its alliteratively connected archaisms 'maund' and 'margent' (as the Quarto has 'margin').[31] And the poem's atmosphere is emotionally heightened through the pathetic fallacy of the river itself weeping: 'Upon whose weeping margin she was set'. In this stanza, excess becomes the theme, as the poem's shift into simile signals a reflection on superfluity itself; the Young Woman's weeping and the river's weeping are in turn compared to moneylending and monarchical rule. While 'usury' suggests compounding, or adding more to something, it is not entirely clear whether the Young Woman or the river is the agent here. Is the Young Woman adding water (tears) to water (river), or is the river adding to the Young Woman's tears (as the river itself is described as 'weeping'). What might seem a symbiotically empathetic relation between woman and natural world is pulled uncomfortably into the worlds of self-interest and rule. Is this weeping in fact strategic or self-interested in the way that moneylending is?

Through this fiscal simile, the pathetic fallacy becomes strangely unempathetic (recalling unresponsive, or ambiguously responsive, landscapes elsewhere in the poem, notably the hills 'rewording' the Young Woman's lament at the start). We should recognize here that the comparison of the Young Woman's tears to usury is not one made by the Old Man who hears her complaint, but by the framing narrator.[32] In the powerful assertion of Ahmed's collaborators – 'we withheld ourselves' – it is the complainant who must withhold herself from the infractions of institutions, through mechanisms such as anonymous reporting, with the emotional support of colleagues and fellow complainants, and – perhaps counter-intuitively – by articulating her complaint. In *A Lover's Complaint*, it is the narrator who withholds, however, denying the Young Woman empathy. And he does so

---

[30] *Shake-speares Sonnets Neuer before imprinted* (London, 1609), sig. K2r.
[31] *Shake-speares sonnets*, sig. K2r.
[32] On King James VI and I's accusation that female witches cry fake tears, 'dissemblingly like Crocodiles', see Hannah Dawson's 'Introduction' to *The Penguin Book of Feminist Writing*, ed. Dawson (Milton Keynes, 2021), xix–li; p. xxii.

perhaps precisely because she does not withhold herself; it is the extremity and bodily expression of her emotions that the narrator compares to usury. In a pattern that is also explored in *Venus and Adonis* and *The Rape of Lucrece*, the Young Woman's excess is used to generate a sceptical rather than fully empathetic response to her emotional state and story.

The complaining women of Shakespeare's poems are simultaneously overly eloquent and not eloquent enough. As Ted Tregear argues of Venus and Lucrece, the poems' protagonists are 'women at the fringes of rhetorical training ... who seem at once insufficiently and overabundantly schooled in its lessons'.[33] This is true in different but resonant ways of the archaized and rhetorically emotive Young Woman. And her abundance is expressed in metaphors of flow, the very opposite of withholding or containment:

These often bathed she in her fluxive eyes,
And often kissed, and often gave to tear,
Cried, 'O false blood, thou register of lies.
What unapprovèd witness dost thou bear!
Ink would have seemed more black and damnèd here!'
This said, in top of rage the lies she rents,
Big discontent so breaking their contents.

(*LC*, 50–6)

The unusual and striking term 'fluxive' here implies that her emotions are flowing, in an excessive and bodily display. Joshua Poole's *England's Parnassus* (1657) includes 'fluxive' in a list of synonyms for tears, alongside other increasingly negative terms: 'weeping, rolling, feigned, dissembling, pitied'.[34] The transition from flowing to dissembling here resonates with the way the Young Woman's spontaneous and bodily expressions of overwhelming emotion are denied authenticity, as when her weeping is compared to usury. The Young Woman introduces two further liquid metaphors in the form of blood and ink, comparing these two 'fluxive' writing materials. She mentions 'blood' because we are told, chillingly, that some of the letters are written in blood; yet it also evokes bloodlines, and therefore a kind of fatalism of social position or character. Sterling Brown has argued that focus on bloodlines in early modern drama 'silently pedestalize[s] the domestic subjects' whiteness', drawing on Ariane M. Balizet's observation of the links between blood, class and identity.[35]

Sometimes withholding can be a form of self-protection. One of Ahmed's interviewees had made a complaint about the failure of her university to make reasonable accommodations for her disability. She recounts the bizarre and intrusive requests for data made by her institution, about her medical records, the time it took her to go to the toilet: '"I wouldn't make a complaint about toilets because I feel that being cross-examined about whether I am humiliated by pissing myself in toilets is too much"' (*Complaint!* 144). Of the institutional request that this complainant provide pie charts of how long it took her to go to the toilet, Ahmed wryly comments 'even pee can end up a pie' (144). The experience of complaint, then, is one of being asked to give up details of your body – it can be an intensely bodily experience. And the effects of complaining can, in turn, be felt within – can be legible upon – the body.

The physical effort, you can hear it: the wear and the tear, the groans, the moans. One academic said she could hear herself moaning when she was telling me about the different complaints she had made at different times. She comments, 'I am moaning now, I can feel that whining in my voice [*makes whining sound*]'. (276)

Even some of the Young Woman's most potent articulations are narrated in curiously undermining ways: she is described in one couplet as 'in top of rage' and expressing 'Big discontent' (*LC*, 55–6). To a modern reader, these phrases are strangely deflationary. 'Top' and 'big', while obviously adjectives of magnitude, lack the conviction of related terms, and a certain level of anti-climax here would align with the poem's consciously

---

[33] Ted Tregear, *Anthologizing Shakespeare, 1593–1603* (Oxford, 2023), p. 80.
[34] Joshua Poole, *England's Parnassus* (London, 1657), p. 202.
[35] Brown, 'Hood feminism', p. 4; Ariane M. Balizet, *Blood and Home in Early Modern Drama: Domestic Identity on the Renaissance Stage* (New York, 2014).

ambivalent attitude to its protagonist's experience that we have seen elsewhere.

Such bathos also chimes with Ahmed's depictions of complaint: the deadpan photographic illustrations of office doors and filing cabinets, the mundanity of these ubiquitous and undistinctive features of university spaces contrasting with the destroyed careers, damaged lives and unravelling of mental health caused by the experience of complaint. She describes the importance of these locations and items of furniture, as repositories of complaint:

> To make a complaint is to assemble materials: documents, policies, letters ... Even when the materials end up buried, becoming files, housed in cabinets, they still provide evidence that somebody tried to address a problem. These materials matter wherever they end up. Where they end up also matters. Complaint activism turns the filing cabinet into a political object par excellence. The filing cabinet is another site for complaint.
> (*Complaint!* 291)

Photographs of filing cabinets in *Complaint!* are both bathetic and profound; the cabinets become eloquent political objects – as do the Young Woman's 'thousand favours'. And like the documents of complaint, these favours too are buried:

> Of folded schedules she had many a one,
> Which she perused, sighed, tore, and gave the flood,
> Cracked many a ring of poesied gold and bone,
> Bidding them find their sepulchres in mud;
> Found yet more letters sadly penned in blood;
> With sleided silk feat and affectedly
> Enswathed and sealed to curious secrecy.
> (*LC*, 43–9)

Again, we see the Young Woman's actions framed as excessive ('yet more letters') and writing as embodied (the letters of the Young Woman's predecessors are 'penned in blood'). In burying these other women's letters – complaints, even – the Young Woman does not silence, however, but – in Ahmed's terms – records them. She 'perused, sighed' before burying them, defying their seals and weaving them into her own complaint. Even as she buries these other women's words, she gives them a collective presence in her own complaint. The verb used to describe her actions suggests further dialogue: 'Bidding them find their sepulchres in mud' is an epistolary gesture, commending them to find their way to another recipient or interlocutor, here that of the future reader who might excavate them again. The burial of these love tokens, then, is itself a kind of articulation and re-articulation, a site and repository of complaint, like Ahmed's filing cabinet, or her book itself. Ahmed describes *Complaint!* as 'an unburial':

> A burial of a story can be necessary. A burial is part of the story. To tell the story of a burial is to unbury the story. I could write this book, pull it together, only because complaints did not stay buried ... To tell the story of a complaint is how the complaint comes out from where it has been buried. (*Complaint!* 276)

BE COLLECTIVE

> ... each time I have presented this work, the feeling has been the same, of you being there with me. Maybe to keep doing it, to keep saying it, that is what I needed, for you to be there with me.
> (*Complaint!* 274)

We saw previously how the act of complaining can be felt in the body (just as the originary trauma is). When recording how one of the women interviewed in *Complaint!* says that she can hear herself 'moaning' as she tells her story (as quoted above), Ahmed includes her own response from the interview transcript:

> I reply, 'We have plenty to moan about.' We can hear it in our own voices; we can hear it in each other's voices. We can hear it because we feel it: the sound of how hard we keep having to push. I think of that push as collective, a complaint collective. (276)

Ahmed's reply here, inserting her own voice into the complaint biography in allyship with the complainant, reverses the perceived disempowerment of 'moaning' and 'whining'. Instead, she adds her voice to those of all her interviewees, creating a powerful and articulate collectivity: a complaining 'we'. And in this collectivity lies the power of *Complaint!* Ahmed decisively breaks the cycle of (female-voiced but male-authored) complaint, its perpetuation of the structures of oppression. Instead of the nightmarish version of collectivity instigated by this so-called tradition (as embodied by the Young Man co-opting the voices of his past victims), Ahmed creates an empowered collective by rearticulating complaints in the words of the women she interviews.

We have seen how both the Old Man and narrator introduce scepticism about the Young Woman's account and emotions, suggesting their own erotic self-interest and their distrust of female authority. Moreover, both the narrator and Old Man fail to return at the poem's close. This much-discussed ending might be authorial play with closure (like Sidney's *Arcadia* and Wroth's *Urania*), or incompletion (like *The Faerie Queene*). Critics have debated the gender politics of this lack of final framing, however (as with *The Taming of the Shrew*), and the possibility that it allows the poem to end with the Young Woman's 'own' words.[36] Yet we might also feel the lack of a final frame as the absence of an auditor: the Young Woman's complaint is not heard properly. At the poem's end, her ecphonesis – her successive inarticulate articulations of 'O' – is accompanied by a last attempt to evoke sympathy from her audience:

> O father, what a hell of witchcraft lies
> In the small orb of one particular tear?
> But with the inundation of the eyes
> What rocky heart to water will not wear?
> What breast so cold that is not warmèd here?
> O cleft effect! Cold modesty, hot wrath,
> Both fire from hence and chill extincture hath.
>
> (*LC*, 288–94)

Resuming the liquid metaphors of the Young Woman's earlier sorrow, here she describes how the Young Man's tears 'wear' down her resistance. His artful pretence of passion 'resolved my reason into tears', dissolving (in a sense of 'resolve' we see elsewhere in Shakespeare) her rationality and threatening her sense of self. But to her invocation 'O father', there is no reply. The absence of both the Old Man and the narrator at the end of the poem leaves the Young Woman (in Ahmed's words) 'stranded, exposed', cut off, without any affirmation that she has been heard. The Young Woman's words are left unheard within the poem, without the 'feminist ear' that Ahmed lends to her interviewees.

In the previous section, we saw how the Young Woman of *A Lover's Complaint* finds her story embedded in those of her predecessors, the 'many' other women the Young Man has subjected to his sexual attentions. Having invoked his past conquests in order to convince the Young Woman of his supposed desirability (all those other women want me, why don't you?), the Young Man proceeds to harness their stories to harass the Young Woman into agreeing to have sex with him.

> 'How mighty then you are, O hear me tell:
> The broken bosoms that to me belong
> Have emptied all their fountains in my well,
> And mine I pour your ocean all among.
> I strong o'er them, and you o'er me being strong,
> Must for your victory us all congest,
> As compound love physic to your cold breast.'
>
> (*LC*, 253–9)

Asserting possession of these other women's stories – claiming ownership over the 'broken bosoms' that he has himself caused – and continuing to declare his mastery over them – arrived at through the use of brute force, 'I strong o'er them' – the Young Man seeks to accrue the force of their experiences to his own purpose. His rhetoric here is again appropriative; he would offer the Young Woman a 'compound love' made up not just of his own feelings for her, but also of the feelings these other women have shown towards him (although we might note that at no point – contrary to what the Young Man suggests – are their feelings shown to be

---

[36] Melissa E. Sanchez concludes that the Young Woman's closing words express 'a selfless pity that is precisely the opposite of the pursuit of pleasure' ('The Poetics of Feminine Subjectivity in Shakespeare's Sonnets and "A Lover's Complaint"', in *The Oxford Handbook of Shakespeare's Poetry*, ed. Jonathan F. S. Post (Oxford, 2013), 505–21; p. 514). Sanchez argues against critics such as John Kerrigan and Brian Vickers who have suggested that the woman's assertion that she would do it again is an expression of ongoing desire, or even celebration of desire and its consummation.

those of 'love', rather we learn only of their suffering, 'broken', and 'emptied' of tears). In a particularly coercive gesture, the Young Man tries to implicate the Young Woman retrospectively in his abusive behaviour towards these other women. His physical dominance over them is rhetorically elided with the supposed power she holds over him, again via the figure of chiasmus: 'I strong o'er them, and you o'er me being strong' (257). The tiny word 'and' is doing a lot of work in that sentence, yoking together two sets of experience that are in fact not at all the same (as the imbalance in the chiasmatic logic of these clauses hints; 'I' and 'them' are not straightforwardly transposable to 'you' and 'me'). In a final act of rhetorical manipulation that echoes a familiar gesture instantly recognizable as abusive, the Young Man makes a last-ditch attempt to render the whole thing the Young Woman's fault. Her lack of responsiveness to his evident charms and rhetorical persuasions so far tell the Young Man not (as we might suppose) that she would rather he leave her alone, but rather indicate a pathological behaviour in her; a 'cold breast' can be the only explanation for her apparently unenthusiastic reaction to his efforts. Her failure to reciprocate his lust for her signifies only that she requires 'physic', in the Young Man's myopic view.

After invoking the sad tale of the nun whose commitments to celibacy he violates, her 'vows and consecrations giving place' (263), the Young Man steps up his rhetoric yet further in the poem's fortieth stanza, where he endeavours to render the Young Woman responsible not just for the past harms he has done to other young women, but also for their future happiness, which he frames as dependent wholly on her (specifically, and not surprisingly, her having sex with him).

> 'Now all these hearts that do on mine depend,
> Feeling it break, with bleeding groans they pine,
> And supplicant their sighs to you extend
> To leave the batt'ry that you make 'gainst mine,
> Lending soft audience to my sweet design,
> And credent soul to that strong bonded oath
> That shall prefer and undertake my troth.'
>
> (*LC*, 274–80)

In the concluding lines of his lengthy and highly manipulative speech, the Young Man again evokes the blood in which these women's letters to him are written, the inarticulate groans of their suffering, and the ragged breaths drawn up from burning lungs that we have heard of elsewhere in the poem. A chorus of tragic suppliants joins with the Young Man in his petition to the Young Woman; those he has abused in the past entreat her to consent to her own abuse now. Yet the Young Woman is the one whose behaviour is figured as violent here; the 'batt'ry' – or defences – she has constructed against his assault also hint at her lashing out towards him; his attack on her chastity is momentarily elided with her committing an act of battery upon him. Lest she overestimate the power she holds in this situation, the Young Man ends by reminding her, with more than a hint of threat, that she is 'soft' and credulous, a 'credant soul' that can hardly hope to withstand his 'sweet persuasions' or – failing that – his determination to force what he wants, subject of his 'strong bonded oath' and sworn 'troth'.

That the Young Man seeks to conscript the women he has abused in the past to the cause of the abuse he would effect in the future is a gross misapprehension of the idea of allyship upon which feminist, anti-racist discourse depends. As we have suggested, this rhetorical gesture goes against the idea of collectivity that Ahmed so strongly advocates for in *Complaint!*, while at the same time conjuring its spectral form in order to cynically draw upon the inherent power that adheres to collective action. The Young Man's words seek to make a mockery of the thing that would oppose his predatory intentions. Beyond this, there is something very distinctive about the temporal gesture made by the Young Man here. Drawing upon the past to try and determine the future (a classically Renaissance rhetorical move) disrupts any linear chronology that would allow those he has previously abused to move through (even beyond) their experiences, insisting instead that they relive their trauma at his volition. At the same time, the Young Woman of the present moment is bound into the history of abuse experienced by her predecessors. The Young Man attempts to forestall her future by forcing her to contend with his past. Such a move is entirely characteristic of the abusers encountered in Ahmed's *Complaint!*, who protect their own lives at the cost of those they harm.

A Lover's Complaint ends with the Young Woman listing the rhetorical and bodily forces that the Young Man marshalled against her – tears, blushes, the 'forced thunder' of his speech, his sighs, 'all that borrowed motion' – and reiterating her inability to withstand such an assault, were it to be repeated (323–7). Together, these combined forces, 'Would yet again betray the forebetrayed', she says, 'And new pervert a reconcilèd maid' (328-29). The word 'fore-betrayed' is particularly interesting here, suggesting that the abuse detailed in the poem has already become the stuff of the past, the history underwriting another, impending harassment of her that she is already anticipating. Shakespeare's verse here imagines a future that transforms the past even as it recedes rapidly out of the present. There is an element of inescapability to this. Rather than reading the Young Woman's final words, as many critics have done, as an exultant declaration that she would do the same thing over again, Ahmed's work helps us to hear her closing remarks differently. The couplet rhyme here compounds the effect of finality in these lines, and echoes the ending of the previous stanza, which has been similarly misread. 'Ay me, I fell; and yet do question make / What should I do again for such a sake' (321–2). These lines have often been taken as an indicator that the Young Woman does not in fact feel sorrow or remorse at what has happened, for she would do the same thing again, were the same situation to arise. Such a reading recasts the Young Woman's experiences of the poem, denying her trauma and instead insisting she somehow enjoyed it, an all-too familiar rhetoric still used by abusers and those who enable them today. Listening to the poem – and particularly these two couplets – with a feminist ear, however, such an interpretation seems itself an act of further abuse against the Young Woman. There is nothing in these lines that redeems the Young Man (or Shakespeare's poem) when listened to – and heard – with Ahmed's work in mind. The Young Woman bewails her fate, 'Ay me', in the age-old language of lament. Her simple admission, 'I fell', suggests no pleasure or even any active participation. There is no consent here. Her 'question' (to the Old Man who hears her story, to the narrator of the poem, perhaps, and beyond that maybe to the reader of the poem) is a genuine one: how would one ever avoid such calculated and undermining abusive behaviour? As *Complaint!* makes clear, intimating that women who have experienced abuse are in some way responsible for preventing it from happening, or brought their injuries upon themselves, is a typical marker of the kind of misogyny (frequently, as Ahmed shows, compounded by racism) that seeks to shift the blame for sexual assault onto the women who are subjected to it (and, more broadly, the collective category of 'women' who are often, but not always, its target). 'What should I do again for such a sake' is a bare statement of fact, the simplicity of which attests to underlying complexity and profound pain. The Young Woman withholds herself (in Ahmed's terms here); there is no emotion, no so-called hysteria, just plain-speaking and genuine bewilderment, along with more than a hint of despair. With Ahmed, we are still asking the same question 400 years later: what do we have to do to stop this from happening?

The final paragraph of *Complaint!* hints at a way in which things could be otherwise. Ahmed there suggests that, while we may not 'always perceive the weakening of structures until they collapse', the work of complaint that women (including Ahmed herself) are embarked upon now will have an effect in the future. 'When structures begin to collapse, the impact of past efforts becomes tangible' (*Complaint!* 310). The legibility of actions taken in the past and at the present time may only be apparent to us in the future. Ahmed's closing remarks are perhaps surprisingly early modern in this temporal gesture. Just as *A Lover's Complaint* looks back to the history of complaint poetry as a genre – and, beyond this, to the classical and Medieval texts to which its language alludes – in order to speak to its present moment (and on, into the future we now occupy), so *Complaint!* works to recuperate the past to effect change in the future. As Ahmed states early in her book, 'to make a complaint is to write a history of complaint' (33–4). Such a relation to the past deliberately disrupts attempts by abusers such as the Young Man to shape the future of the women they victimize by mobilizing the weight of history – and its centuries of oppression and inequality – and bringing it to bear upon them. By uniting past experiences of abuse and acting collectively, individual stories accrue the additional power of their predecessors and contemporaries: 'Impact is a slow inheritance', writes Ahmed, in her conclusion (*Complaint!* 310). As we have seen, Ahmed calls this form of action 'collectivity'.

Ahmed ends *Complaint!* with a powerfully counter-intuitive sentence that requires her readers to participate in constructing this collective movement by doing the work of interpretation. 'A complaint can open the door to those who came before', she writes (310). The metaphor of 'open[ing] the door' recurs repeatedly through Ahmed's book (especially in the third part, which is devoted to the literal closed doors behind which abuse so often occurs and the ways in which women who have suffered abuse can hold metaphorical doors of opportunity open to others). But the conclusion of Ahmed's sentence is more unexpected. Complaint opens doors not (as we might imagine) to those still to come, the unknown women of the future whom one would hope might at least benefit from an effective complaints process, but rather (more surprisingly) to those who have come 'before', in the past, including those who have already experienced abuse. The unusual temporal gesture of Ahmed's final sentence suggests that even when complaint is not obviously changing future outcomes (although it may ultimately have this effect), it is still working to change the shared experiences of the collective past. Does *Complaint!* 'open the door to' Shakespeare's Young Woman and the other female speakers of the early modern complaint form? What would it mean if this was the case? We have suggested that reading *A Lover's Complaint* with Ahmed, listening to Shakespeare's Young Woman with a feminist ear, allows us to hear her story afresh, to recognize more fully the Young Man's rhetorical manipulations, and to acknowledge the cycle of trauma that his abuse has forced her into. Reading Ahmed's *Complaint!* changes the experience of reading *A Lover's Complaint* by retrospectively revealing the 'patterns' of the Young Man's 'foul beguiling' (*LC*, 170) that far transcend the poem itself, or the moment in which Shakespeare wrote, and which stretch ahead into a future as yet unimagined in the poem's original lifetime. These 'patterns' are still discernible today, Ahmed's work shows; part of the distinctive nature of abuse is its predictability, its repetitiveness. That a story of abuse written (albeit by a white, middle-class man) in the 1590s remains so recognizable today is perhaps unsurprising. More remarkable is the fact that the ways in which Shakespeare's poem negotiates the conventions of its own complaint genre, and the ways in which Ahmed's book charts the intricacies of the complaints process, collectively show how these conventional forms have failed women across time. And if the Young Woman's efforts to tell her own story (even within the limitations of the poetic form she inhabits, in which her narrative is reproduced by first a male narrator and then by Shakespeare himself) resonate at all with the efforts by the many women Ahmed interviews to have their own stories heard (within the equally oppressive confines of what remains a racist, patriarchal society), we may derive some strength from this instance of collectivity. We may need to. For that may be all we have.

THEY ALSO SERVE WHO ONLY STAND AND WRITE, OR, HOW MILTON READ SHAKESPEARE'S *SONNETS*

AMRITA DHAR

This article is a study of how one poet read another, and of how that reading continues to travel among us. It is about how John Milton, going blind some three decades after Shakespeare's lifetime and caught up in his own tumultuous moment of the English Civil Wars, regicide followed by England's Commonwealth experiment, and the subsequent Restoration of monarchy, continued to read and engage with Shakespeare, and especially Shakespeare's sonnets.[1] Milton went blind over almost a decade: from 1644/5 to 1652/3. In the divide between royalists and republicans in seventeenth-century England, Milton sided decisively with the republicans. He defended the regicide of Charles I, worked hard for the Commonwealth government, and resisted the return of monarchy (in the form of Charles Stuart's coming to the throne as Charles II) until the last possible moment. All this, while steadily going blind and learning how to *be* blind as author and polemicist and poet. For us, today, the most significant poetic outcome of Milton learning to accommodate his blindness through his poetry, and of creating a blind poetics for himself, is *Paradise Lost*. But there were other poetic outputs, namely some remarkable sonnets, as Milton travelled into blindness and taught himself to write blind. All of Milton's lyric poetry from his final blind-going years in the 1650s, with the exception of his verse translations of Psalms 1–8 in 1653, were sonnets, as Milton radically adapted the form in English from lyric statements of love to expressions of political positions, principled statements of ethics, and complex poetic desire. If one constant music accompanied Milton from his sighted days to his blind ones, it was that of poetry. And, as this article will show, Shakespeare remained one of the sustaining poetic companions for Milton on his journey into blindness.

Milton's involvement with Shakespeare went back at least a decade before his first inklings of blindness. Milton's first printed poem was his anonymously published 16-line almost-sonnet, all in couplets, entitled 'An Epitaph on the admirable Dramaticke Poet, W. SHAKESPEARE' as part of the preliminary matter for the 1632 second edition of *Mr. William Shakespeares Comedies, Histories, and Tragedies*.[2] Even then, it was '*my* Shakespeare' (emphasis mine; line 1) whom Milton was ostensibly writing about. The recent identification of Milton's copy of Shakespeare's First Folio has helped bring into more robust conversation than ever Milton's deeply engaged readings of Shakespeare in what would have been some of Milton's last fully sighted days of pleasurably

---

[1] We do not have direct evidence yet about Milton's engagement with Shakespeare's non-dramatic poetry, but given the seriousness of Milton's engagement with Shakespeare's poetry in his dramatic works, and given Milton's own ambitions as a poet, I take it as a given that Milton knew of and engaged with Shakespeare's non-dramatic poetry.

[2] John Milton, 'An Epitaph on the admirable Dramaticke Poet, W. SHAKESPEARE', in *Mr. William Shakespeares Comedies, Histories, and Tragedies*, 2nd edn (London, 1632), sig. πA2r. Further references to this poem will appear in parentheses.

following recent and celebrated literary publications.³ We cannot know precisely how much Milton continued to read his Shakespeare or to have his Shakespeare read to him as he came to rely more and more on the eyes of his companions, amanuenses, caregivers, friends and family – or how and exactly when his actual reading of Shakespeare became a memoried reading of the earlier poet. But somewhere in Milton's intellectual, emotional and poetic journey into blindness, particular ideas, phrases and concepts from Shakespeare's sonnets became, I suggest, incandescent for Milton, and spurred their own Miltonic sonnet engagements.

Without asserting anything like a direct source study and certainly without aiming to be exhaustive, and offering only that Milton takes a Shakespeare-sonnet-music with him into his blindness through the affordances of his own prodigious memory, I want in this article to read mainly two Shakespeare sonnets with two Milton sonnets which demonstrate Milton's active incorporation of his reconstructions, reverberations and syntheses of his sighted and past readings into blind sonnets.⁴ (It is perhaps to be expected that Milton, who decades earlier positioned the 'admirable Dramaticke Poet' Shakespeare as the 'Sonne of Memory' – line 5 of the 'Epitaph' – should later himself by memory follow the earlier poet.)⁵ The Shakespeare sonnets, I submit, remain places for the blind Milton's continued examination of Shakespeare's treatments of time, transience, loss, responsibility and the power of poetry.

In the first section, I read Shakespeare's Sonnet 15, 'When I consider every thing that growes', with Milton's sonnet 'On His Blindness' (a title editorially introduced long after Milton's death; Milton's first line is 'When I consider how my light is spent').⁶ In the following section, I read Shakespeare's Sonnet 43, 'When most I winke then doe mine eyes best see' – with reference also to contemporary poet Imtiaz Dharker's poetic response to Shakespeare's Sonnet 43, 'The Trick' – together with Milton's sonnet 'Methought I saw my late espoused Saint'.

Through my examination of these two Milton sonnets that expressly conjugate his blindness with his poetry, I argue, first, that Milton's engagement with Shakespeare's *Sonnets* gave him a poetic lexicon for discussing the ways and byways of his own visual loss, and, second, that something about the Shakespearian claim of a poet's ability to conjure reality itself (the yearning and the insistence of 'I ingraft you new') shapes Milton's blind reconfirmation of himself into poetic agency, time and purpose.⁷ They also serve, Milton asserts as he stands in the wake of Shakespeare, who only stand and write.

AT WAR AND PEACE WITH TIME

Shake-speares Sonnets Neuer before Imprinted (London, 1609) is full of clusters of poems that pick up particular conceits, concerns and arguments, and interrogate them in sonnet fashion. In the first such cluster, where the narrator of the poems seems to be urging a fair youth towards procreation, Shakespeare's Sonnets 15–18 constitute

---

³ See Claire M. L. Bourne and Jason Scott-Warren, '"Thy unvalued booke": John Milton's copy of the Shakespeare First Folio', *Milton Quarterly* 56 (2022), 1–85.
⁴ See Stephen Guy-Bray, 'Different Samenesses', in this volume.
⁵ See Milton, 'An Epitaph'.
⁶ The naming of Milton's sonnet 'When I consider how my light is spent' as 'On His Blindness' by Thomas Newton in the eighteenth century possibly followed the editorial appellation of another of Milton's poems by another of Milton's editors in the previous century. In 1694, Milton's nephew Edward Phillips had published a translation of Milton's *Literae pseudo-senatûs Anglicani* (published surreptitiously in Amsterdam, 1676) as the *Letters of State, written by Mr. John Milton, to most of the sovereign princes and republicks of Europe. From the year 1649. till the year 1659. To which is added, an account of his life. Together with several of his poems; and a catalogue of his works, never before printed*. This volume published Milton's sonnet beginning 'CYRIAC this Three years day, these Eyes though clear' as 'To Mr. CYRIAC SKINNER Upon his Blindness'.
⁷ Sonnet 15.14. All citations from Shakespeare's sonnets are from the first publication of *Shake-speares Sonnets Neuer before Imprinted* (London, 1609). All citations from Milton's sonnets, unless otherwise mentioned, are from his *Poems, &c. upon Several Occasions* (London, 1673).

a sub-cluster of their own, with the poems breaking explicitly into assertions of poetic agency (albeit not unquestioned ones) and the capacities of poetry to shape reality (again, certainly questioned ones). In this section of my article, I focus mainly on Shakespeare's Sonnet 15 and Milton's Sonnet 19 together, reading for echoes, carryings-over and transcreations of Shakespeare's poems as Milton blindly remakes what he has read and can remember/re-member.

'When I consider', begins Shakespeare's Sonnet 15, likely giving Milton the opening of one of the most beautiful poems ever composed, his own Sonnet XVI (as identified in Milton's 1673 *Poems*; this sonnet is by general editorial practice now identified as Milton's Sonnet 19) on his blindness.[8] Here are the poems:

Shakespeare's Sonnet 15

When I consider every thing that growes
Holds in perfection but a little moment.
That this huge stage presenteth nought but showes
Whereon the Stars in secret influence comment.
When I perceive that men as plants increase,
Cheared and checkt even by the selfe-same skie:
Vaunt in their youthful sap, at height decrease,
And were their brave state out of memory.
Then the conceit of this inconstant stay,
Sets you most rich in youth before my sight,
Where wastfull time debateth with decay
To change your day of youth to sullied night,
   And all in war with Time for love of you
   As he takes from you, I ingraft you new.

Milton's Sonnet 19

When I consider how my light is spent,
  Ere half my days, in this dark world and wide,
  And that one Talent which is death to hide,
Lodg'd with me useless, though my Soul more bent
To serve therewith my Maker, and present
  My true account, least he returning chide,
  Doth God exact day-labour, light deny'd,
I fondly ask; But patience to prevent
That murmur, soon replies, God doth not need
  Either man's work or his own gifts, who best
  Bear his milde yoak, they serve him best, his State
Is Kingly. Thousands at his bidding speed
  And post o're Land and Ocean without rest:
  They also serve who only stand and waite.

'When I consider' and '[w]hen I perceive' the 'little moment' that any 'perfection' holds, says the narrator of Shakespeare's Sonnet 15, 'Then the conceit of this inconstant stay' spurs the poet to write the poems(s) that will remake the loveliness of the person addressed, even as relentless 'Time' takes away from that beloved's life and loveliness. It is almost as though Shakespeare has travelled unreally in time and read his Milton, for the main argument of Shakespeare's Sonnet 15 is: *When I consider how your light is spent, then I, through poetry, engraft you new.* It is no accident that the opening of the later sonnet, Milton's, is a summative reverberation, albeit with a significant reversal, of the earlier Shakespearian one. Milton's 'When I consider' is entirely as preoccupied with time, transience and the coming on of night as Shakespeare's 'When I consider' is – but, in Milton's case, the poem carries the lived resonances of a blind reality. That the first line of Milton's sonnet essentially recapitulates Shakespeare's sonnet, with the poem then widening into a characteristically Miltonic exploration of its adopted Shakespearian themes, is the result of Milton's carrying his Shakespeare with him into poetic probing of his acquired blindness. The poets consider similar matters: intense loveliness and love; poetic talents and the powers thereof; human responsibilities in the face of the ceaseless passage of time. Yet the sonnets are also widely different in mood, tone and preoccupation, and part of the pleasure of considering them together must remain in the intensity of their differences that nevertheless

---

[8] Significantly, several writers-back to Milton have used this opening for their own sonnets. See, for instance, Nuala Watt's 'On her partial blindness', in *Stairs and Whispers: D/deaf and Disabled Poets Write Back*, ed. Sandra Alland, Khairani Barokka and Daniel Sluman (Rugby, 2017), p. 150; and Tyehimba Jess's sonnet 'When I consider how my light is spent' ('Proceedings of the Annual Meeting of the Milton Society of America' booklet, circulated 2017). I have written elsewhere on the sonnets of Milton and Tyehimba Jess together: 'When they consider how their light is spent: intersectional race and disability studies in the classroom', in *Teaching Race in the European Renaissance: A Classroom Guide*, ed. Matthieu Chapman and Anna Wainwright (Tempe, AZ, 2023), 161–86.

also announce their proximities and common grounds through the very words, concepts and figurations they use. As I show below through three remarkable instances of borrowing – or even transcreation – Milton reads and repurposes precisely the obsessions that Shakespeare's poem grapples with.

In Shakespeare's Sonnet 15, the narrator is ostensibly addressing a youth whose splendid 'day' and prime he, the narrator, registers to be at risk of the 'sullied night' of death. This is all perfectly poetically done by Shakespeare. The poet harnesses the vast figurative powers of antitheses such as day/night, light/dark and life/death. But Milton, in his blindness, has the ambiguous privilege of knowing 'night' both as a figuration of death and as the 'darkness' (which is yet another layer of figuration) of visual loss. Critics such as Georgina Kleege and M. Leona Godin point out that blindness is seldom in fact a darkness. Very few blind persons perceive no light at all. Yet the association between blindness and darkness remains a prevailing one, born of the widely used and often mutually reinforcing figurative currencies of the words.[9] If Shakespeare activated the poetics of certain well-established poetic and linguistic dichotomies in his poem, Milton, as a blind poet, re-animates those dichotomies in an exercise also of the recovery of lived and literal meaning alongside the metaphorical.

Similarly, if Shakespeare's narrator is preoccupied with a certain youth of his acquaintance, Milton is, as well: his own. 'When I consider how my light is spent / *Ere half my days*' (emphasis mine), announces a poet who has so far felt old and belated, especially in terms of his poetic career. Until his visual spending of the light, his 'hasting dayes' had flown on with 'full career' while his 'late spring no bud or blossom' showed – even unto the stealing of that youth by that 'suttle theef' called 'time'.[10] Now, as he inhabits 'this dark world and wide' – a world whose disorienting wideness is a *consequence* of its darkness – the poet suddenly feels young, precipitously feels as though it is before even half his days that he has been thus compelled into his present and challenging situation.

Third: if in Shakespeare's sequence it was the narrator who did the chiding – the narrator's chiding of the fair youth towards procreation is less pronounced in Sonnet 15 than in many others, but Sonnet 15 is embedded within a very chain of chides that are the sonnets leading up to and proceeding on from it, and there is no way to quite absolve Sonnet 15 from that chiding – in Milton's sonnet, it is the poet's contemplation of a potential chiding that is the main trigger for the poem. With or without the intention to write 'back' to Shakespeare's poem, Milton's poem both intensifies the matter of chiding and raises the stakes of it for the person potentially being chided. What *if* God exacts 'day-labour' of one thrust into night by in fact being 'light deny'd', he wonders? What *is* one whose 'one Talent' lodges with him 'useless' supposed to do in the onrush of a final expiry of time and a yet more final reckoning about what one did with the time one was given? What if one *wants* to serve one's 'Maker' with their 'one Talent' and 'true account' – but, by circumstance, physically and actionably cannot? It turns out that despite the poet's claims to the contrary, 'patience' cannot quite 'prevent / That murmur' of questions and anxiety in Milton, for a blind poet recalls what he used to be able to do; what abilities (and perhaps perfection) he had worked hard to attain; and what various poets before him (such as the biblical poets and Shakespeare) have had to say about the need to do what one has to do while it is still day. For 'the night cometh, when no man can work'.[11]

Time devours apace in Shakespeare's poem. It appears that there is no relationship that the poet can have with Time that is not adversarial. In love elsewhere, the poet is naturally at war with Time: 'all in war with Time for love of you'. It is also

---

[9] See especially Georgina Kleege's *Sight Unseen* (New Haven, 1999), p. 22, and M. Leona Godin's *There Plant Eyes: A Personal and Cultural History of Blindness* (New York, 2022), p. 80.

[10] See Milton's Sonnet VII (first published in his 1645 *Poems* and reproduced in his 1673 *Poems*), lines 1–4.

[11] See John 9.4: 'I must work the works of him that sent me, while it is day: the night cometh, when no man can work.'

made clear that there is no way to leave one's mark in the relentless passage of time except through poetry. As Time takes away (from the poet's beloved), the poet makes (his beloved) anew through poetry. The poet's work does not brook the passage of time; instead, it *enters* it, meaningfully and monumentally. Being human, Milton too is caught up in that inexorable passage of time. But Milton seems to set himself the peculiar challenge of slowing time down – by the simple means of standing still in it. In his sonnet, something about the condition of being somatically 'light deny'd' arrests the poet's headlong fall into the metaphorics of life versus death, day versus night, light versus dark. Despite the narrator's professed anxieties about the passing of time and the spending of the day (throughout the octet), by the sestet of Milton's sonnet, the pace and rhythm of the poem, and almost time itself, wind down. Time becomes at once an instrument of fulfilment, an agent of a peculiar fruition, and a maturity of thought and purpose.[12] Proto-cinematically, the whole world picks up pace until 'Thousands at his bidding speed / And post o're Land and Ocean without rest'. In the midst of that tumult, velocity and activity, some only stand and take what has been given them to take. They wait. And time stands with them – stands still. With Milton's final line, 'They also serve who only stand and waite', for just a moment, everything holds still. Past the superb enjambments and gathering speed of the first four lines of the sestet, the last two lines, although not in fact a couplet, almost behave like one. The lines are end-stopped, with the 'without rest' at the end of the poem's penultimate line astonishingly uniting both great pace and its utter restraint, and every monosyllabic word in the final line – which is every word save 'also' and 'only' – slowing the poem into completion and quiet at the same time. At the final 'wait', the instant expands. All time, all rest and all endurance belong to these that stand still and carry the particular weight that they have been given to carry. We understand that Milton is one of those who stand, stand still, hold time still, and keep time from drawing into night notwithstanding the spending of the light. On Milton's part, and as Milton has told us without telling us in so many words (for Milton makes no direct reference to eyes or sight or the lack of sight in his poem), it is a blind person's standing still, a blind poet's waiting. What can the blind poet do more than wait? What can the blind poet do less than wait?

Where Milton's poem leaves off is not, however, antithetical to where Shakespeare's does. Even as Shakespeare resorted ultimately to poetry, so has Milton. The narrator in Shakespeare's sonnet is emphatic that he engrafts his beloved new: he writes the beloved into being through and as poetry. Milton does not expressly mention his poetic purpose. We are left to gather that he stands and waits, which is to say, he sits and dictates – and what results is poetry. Thus, there is a peculiar perpendicular resonance between the ends of the two sonnets, as well. What Shakespeare horticulturally and authorially 'ingrafts' new necessarily stands still, as does the final figure in Milton's poem by another necessity. Milton's poem assumes the mood of that last quiet in Shakespeare's poem with his assertion about the standing use of his own talent.

A sustained gift of Shakespeare's sonnets is in their ability to speak to the many moods of love in which human beings find themselves. Shakespeare's most powerful answer to the condition of perfect helplessness that is falling in love, is, of course, poetry itself.[13] To read Milton through Shakespeare today is to understand anew the power of that answer. Milton is a different poet, in need of a different power in poetry – yet Shakespeare makes possible for Milton what he needs in his moment. But to read Shakespeare then back through Milton – namely, through Shakespeare's

---

[12] See also J. K. Barrett, '"Enduring 'injurious time": alternatives to immortality and proleptic loss in Shakespeare's Sonnets', in *The Sonnets: The State of Play*, ed. Hannah Crawforth, Elizabeth Scott-Baumann and Clare Whitehead (London, 2017), 137–56.

[13] I take the phrase 'perfect helplessness' from the title of Robin Coste Lewis's stunning book *To the Realization of Perfect Helplessness* (New York, 2022), in which, too, the response to a fierce and necessary love is in and through poetry.

poetry's percolated involvement in another human life of hard hope and harder writing – is to know the strange truth of Shakespeare's claim of the poet's grafting things new; to know poetry as both a measure of what is impossibly dreamed and unreasonably brought into being; and to grasp poetry as a force that works in compounding potency as it passes through the hands of poets who write as though their lives – and afterlives – depend on their very words.

In my next section, I show through another set of poems how Milton remakes his Shakespeare towards finding language for yet another love: a lost love, an always-love and a present grief that is, nevertheless, poetry.

DARKLY BRIGHT, AND BRIGHT IN DARK DIRECTED

Imtiaz Dharker's gorgeous sonnet 'The Trick' is a poetic response to Shakespeare's Sonnet 43.[14] To me, however, the journey from Shakespeare's poem to Dharker's is marked most luminously by way of Milton's sonnet addressed to his 'late espoused Saint' (Milton's Sonnet XIX as identified in his 1673 *Poems*; this poem is numbered '23' in the Trinity College Manuscript of Milton's poems and thus often referred to as Milton's Sonnet 23).[15] Here are the poems, in chronological order of composition across the decades and centuries.

Shakespeare's Sonnet 43

When most I winke then doe mine eyes best see,
For all the day they view things unrespected;
But when I sleepe, in dreames they looke on thee,
And darkely bright, are bright in darke directed.
Then thou whose shaddow shaddowes doth make bright,
How would thy shadowes forme, forme happy show
To the cleere day with thy much cleerer light,
When to un-seeing eyes thy shade shines so?
How would (I say) mine eyes be blessed made,
By looking on thee in the living day?
When in dead night their faire imperfect shade,
Through heavy sleepe on sightlesse eyes doth stay?
  All dayes are nights to see till I see thee,
  And nights bright daies when dreams do shew thee me.

Milton's Sonnet 23

Methought I saw my late espoused Saint
  Brought to me like *Alcestis* from the grave,
  Whom *Joves* great Son to her glad Husband gave,
  Rescu'd from death by force though pale and faint.
Mine as whom washt from spot of child-bed taint,
  Purification in the old Law did save,
  And such, as yet once more I trust to have
  Full sight of her in Heaven without restraint,
Came vested all in white, pure as her mind:
  Her face was vail'd, yet to my fancied sight,
  Love, sweetness, goodness, in her person shin'd
So clear, as in no face with more delight.
  But O, as to embrace me she enclin'd
  I wak'd, she fled, and day brought back my night.

Dharker's 'The Trick'

In a wasted time, it's only when I sleep
that all my senses come awake. In the wake
of you, let day not break. Let me keep
the scent, the weight, the bright of you, take
the countless hours and count them all night through
till that time comes when you come to the door
of dreams, carrying oranges that cast a glow
up into your face. Greedy for more
than the gift of seeing you, I lean in to taste
the colour, kiss it off your offered mouth.
For this, for this, I fall asleep in haste,
willing to fall for the trick that tells the truth
  that even your shade makes darkest absence bright,
  that shadows live wherever there is light.[16]

We don't know the precise date or circumstance of composition of Milton's Sonnet XIX/23, but it is not surprising that a blind-journeying and still-grieving Milton should find Shakespeare's sonnet treatments of love, sleep, dreams and waking strangely compelling and generative for his sonnet

---

[14] See the context in *On Shakespeare's Sonnets: A Poets' Celebration*, ed. Hannah Crawforth and Elizabeth Scott-Baumann (London, 2016), p. 29.

[15] The Trinity College Manuscript can be viewed online at https://mss-cat.trin.cam.ac.uk/Manuscript/R.3.4; see especially p. 50 of the manuscript for this poem.

[16] See n. 14. Also available online, for example here: https://www.theguardian.com/books/2016/feb/13/wendy-cope-simon-armitage-andrew-motion-shakespeare-love-sonnets-21st-century.

treatment of a vision of his late partner.[17] Again, what Shakespeare experiences and writes as poetry – for poetry is not a luxury, as we know from Audre Lorde, and poetry *is* a witness, as we know from James Baldwin – Milton appropriately, blindly and in perfect reception and remaking, experiences as life and renders back as his own poetry.[18] I again map three connections between Shakespeare's and Milton's sonnets. Every suggestion, in Shakespeare, of what it is to inhabit a state of such longing that one's sleep and waking are confused, that actual sight and wished-for vision become hopelessly (and painfully hopefully) entwined, that absence and presence collide, and that physical shadow and ethereal form become indistinguishable, becomes, in Milton, a touchstone for further expansion of the conceit of such longing while also being a grounding of sense and association in ways that allow words to repeatedly return to their connotations and wander out again into new meanings. I close with a consideration of Dharker's poem, which uses the very energies of longing, dreaming and verbal making and re-making that Shakespeare activates and Milton transfigures.

Shakespeare's poem is expressly addressed to the absent beloved, and also explicitly full of eyes: when the eyes 'winke', they see their best; they view things 'unrespected' (as though not seeing particularly well because not respected, not *seen* very well); they 'looke on thee' in dreams of sleep; they 'un-seeing'-ly register 'thy shade' at night; they long to 'look' 'on thee' in the 'living day'; and they are 'sightlesse' in 'heavy sleepe' save in their perception of the shade/shadow/dream/form of the beloved. Milton's sonnet has no clear addressee – the central figure of/in the poem is referred to in the third person – and has not a single 'eye' in it; it must simply be understood that the eye-less authorial 'I' (the pronoun occurring at beginning, middle and end of the poem, in lines 1, 7 and 14) of the poem, of course, sees differently. The sonnet begins and ends with the poet's non-normative vision: his blindness. There is an absolute ownership of the (non-)visual condition at the heart of the poem, and the poet repeatedly refers to it: '[m]ethought' he saw something,

he says, deliberately skirting actual sight; what or whom he sees is somehow also 'vail'd' to him; 'yet once more' at some point in some future he trusts to have 'full sight' of what he sees; he has but a 'fancied sight' even at his acutest perceptive moment in the poem; and finally, he wakes to have day bring back his figurative night. What in Shakespeare's poem is the contemplation of and longing for an actual vision – an actual presence – is transformed, in Milton's study of his own layered experience of lost sight, companion and quotidian love, into yet another intense amalgamation of both sighted and blind manners of knowing the world and loving in it. 'For all the day they view things unrespected', the everyday blind Milton might say, with eyes that don't see and yet don't *look* like they don't see.[19] 'But when I sleepe, in

---

[17] Critics are still divided even on which late espoused saint Milton is writing about. Some critics have proposed that the subject of the poem is Milton's second wife, Katherine Woodcock: his 'late' or recently espoused wife, whose face had always been 'veiled' to Milton, for they had married in 1656, after he went blind, and whose name, from the Greek *katharos*, 'pure', may have inspired the phrase 'pure as her mind'. Others have proposed his first wife, Mary Powell, who died in 'child-bed', and whom Milton *had* seen in his sighted days, and may therefore 'yet once more ... trust to have / Full sight of' in heaven. What we do know is that the writing of the poem in the Trinity College Manuscript is by one Jeremie Picard, who 'apparently began working as a scribe for Milton in 1658 and also entered the death notice for Katherine into Milton's family bible'. See *The Complete Works of John Milton*, vol. 3, *The Shorter Poems*, ed. Barbara Kiefer Lewalski and Estelle Haan (Oxford, 2012), p. xlviii, n. 75.

[18] See, particularly, Audre Lorde, 'Poetry is not a luxury', in *Sister Outsider: Essays and Speeches* (Berkeley, 2007), 36–9, and James Baldwin, 'Why I stopped hating Shakespeare', in *The Cross of Redemption: Uncollected Writings*, ed. Randall Kenan (New York, 2010), 65–9.

[19] Milton's nephew and early biographer John Phillips described Milton as a man of 'handsom Features; save that his Eyes were none of the quickest. But his blindness, which proceeded from a Gutta Serena, added no further blemish to them.' See Helen Darbishire, *The Early Lives of John Milton* (London, 1932), p. 32. Milton would himself write, in his *Second Defence*: 'And yet they [the eyes] have as much the appearance of being uninjured, and are as clear and bright, without a cloud, as the eyes of men who see most keenly. In

dreames they looke on thee', he might add – for in dreams is now all his looking. Shakespeare's poetic evocation of night and sleep and the time of dreams as the site for charged non-ocular visions is like a gift to Milton: a vocabulary of longing and metaphor and paradox and power that he can renew in his own image.

The second significant gift of Shakespeare's poem for the purposes of Milton's sonnet is its commanding ambiguity. What the narrator in Shakespeare's poem waits for at the deep end of several series of words that are repeated into meaning differently and more ('darkely bright' and 'bright in darke'; 'shaddow shaddowes'; 'forme, forme') is 'a blessing so fiery and fierce it might not be able to be borne'.[20] There is both longing for and a kind of apprehension about the vision that might be, the presence that might be, if and when the beloved appears not merely in dreams but in living and breathing presence. In a not-entirely-idle couplet of questions, the poet asks:

How would (I say) mine eyes be blessed made,
By looking on thee in the living day?
When in dead night their faire imperfect shade,
Through heavy sleepe on sightlesse eyes doth stay?[21]

Would – could – these eyes still see if the beloved in fact appeared before them? What if the sight were blinding bright? If even the imperfect shades (presumably) of the absent beloved's eyes penetrate the narrator's sightless ones through night's heavy sleep, what might the presence of, as it were, 'the real thing' *do* to the viewer/watcher/seer/lover? The particular peril involved here is better understood when we remember the extramission theory regarding the function of the eyes, which was prevalent in Shakespeare's time and place. The extramission theory of eyes' sight proposed that visual perception was accomplished by eye-beams physically emitted by eyes. During Milton's lifetime, and in the course of the seventeenth century, this theory of eyes' sight came to be largely replaced by the intromission theory of eyes' sight, which holds that light enters the eyes to make visual perception possible.[22] In a peculiar withdrawal from the dangers of a profoundly powerful vision,

the final couplet of Shakespeare's poem recedes into the consolations of poetry and the night: 'All days are nights to see till I see thee, / And nights bright daies when dreams do shew thee me.' It is almost best if and that '*dreams* do shew thee me' (emphasis mine).

Milton's sonnet, too, is a record of colossal contradictions.[23] None of Milton's mentions of his absence of regular visual facility is either straightforward joy or simple grief. Instead, delight and sorrow are complexly intertwined in his deeply ambivalent narration of his blindness – especially in his awareness that the intensity of his dream vision is enabled by the reality of his blindness. What or whom the poet sees in the dream is so intensely celebrated because she is in the poet's life doubly absent. The poet cannot see her because she is

---

this respect alone, against my will, do I deceive' (*A Second Defence of the English People*, trans. Helen North, in *The Complete Prose Works of John Milton*, vol. 4 pt 1, ed. Don M. Wolfe (New Haven, 1966), p. 588).

[20] Don Paterson, *Reading Shakespeare's Sonnets, A New Commentary* (London, 2010) p. 129.

[21] Notably, present-day editions of Shakespeare's *Sonnets* prefer the reading, in line 11 of Shakespeare's Sonnet 43, of '*thy* imperfect shade' (emphasis mine) in place of 'their imperfect shade' (as the line appears in the 1609 first appearance of the poems). It makes every sense to read 'thy imperfect shade' – which indubitably better follows the sense of the poem. But, however 'their' got there in that line in the 1609 edition, whether by design or by accident, something about the sheer piercing intensity of what I understand to be the beloved's shade's eyes is lost when we depart from the awkwardness and untidy power of '*their* imperfect shade' (emphasis mine). See, for instance, the editions by: Stephen Booth (*Shakespeare's Sonnets* (New Haven, CT, 1977)); Colin Burrow (*The Complete Sonnets and Poems* (Oxford, 2002)); Barbara Mowat and Paul Werstine (*Shakespeare's Sonnets* (New York, 2006)); and Paul Edmondson and Stanley Wells (*All the Sonnets of Shakespeare* (Cambridge, 2020)).

[22] See Stuart Clark, *Vanities of the Eye: Vision in Early Modern European Culture* (Oxford, 2009).

[23] Contemporary writer Andrew Leland – who, like Milton once did, is going blind gradually and slowly and in mature and writerly adulthood – similarly calls his progressive vision-loss 'a powerful engine of ambiguity'. See his *Country of the Blind: A Memoir at the End of Sight* (New York, 2023), especially p. xx.

departed from life, and the poet cannot see her because he cannot see. (He may never have seen her. Or he may have seen her, but in his blindness felt the loss of her visual presence even when she was around.) An intricate wistfulness thus saturates several levels of consciousness – until the poet gives it expression, leaving accessible the multiple layers of uncertainty and desire. First, his late espoused saint is 'Brought to me like Alcestis from the grave' (by whom?) and 'rescu'd from death by force' (whose force?) – yet she alone and by her own agency 'Came vested all in white' and inclined to embrace her late husband. Second, she came '*as* [one] whom washt from spot of child-bed taint, / Purification in the old Law did save' (emphasis mine) – her actual purification and post-mortal state of redemption by the 'old Law' thus cast into question by the very mention of the once-husband's dream of such salvation for his wife. Third, '[h]er face was vail'd' yet apparent in it *and in* the rest of 'her person' were 'love, sweetness, goodness' – all these, '[s]o clear, as in no face with more delight'. Within the incoherent coherence of the Miltonic dream, these are not contradictions but certitudes and aspirations that the dreamer must nevertheless awake and depart from. Subsequently, in the post-dream wakefulness of the poet, these ostensible paradoxes are owned and inscribed to extend what is already memory. In Milton's poem, sight and the beloved exist together, appear and leave together – and what the dreamer awakes to becomes poetry. By the time Milton composes the sonnet, he is dreaming while awake, dreaming of night, and dreaming of both his last light, of the past, and his last and final light, of the future. Looking to the future – the 'yet once more' that the poet gestures towards – the sonnet records a trust and hope even while it announces that the vision at the heart of it is almost a premonition. *As he has had in his dream*, the poet asserts, there will come a time when he *will* have full sight in heaven without restraint – as though even the fullest of mortal sight was and remains restrained. As in the dream, so in heaven ultimately, Milton trusts: love, sweetness and goodness will be readily apparent (even) through the veiled face of a composite figure of affection, notwithstanding the subject's vision or lack thereof. And just as qualities of goodness will shine through 'her person' – *all* her person, without restraint – so too will the apprehension of these qualities belong to a holistic regard and perceptive faculty that draws from, yet operates beyond, a simple visual register. The love, sweetness and goodness are – and will be – *felt* as much as seen. The (post-)human regard will be as close as possible to the timeless divine regard. Sight will operate in a register that transcends the mortal function of the eyes.[24]

Third: there is a peculiar assonance, again, between the endings of Shakespeare's and Milton's poems. Shakespeare's narrator sought almost a visual self-preservation in their final affirmation of the dream-vision, which was also a withdrawal from what might be brilliantly but perilously available in actual vision. Shakespeare's final lines in Sonnet 43 constitute a genuine couplet, and the poem's mirrored imagery is sustained to the very end, until and into the ambiguity of the sonnet's last words. 'All dayes are nights to see till I see thee, / And nights bright daies when dreams do shew thee me.' There is a strange and risky reciprocity hung in the taut balance of those final words. Who is the seer and who is seen? Do the dreams show 'thee' to 'me', or 'me' to 'thee'? Or do both see both? For what is sight if not the ability to perceive oneself regarded, and to be able to return regard? These questions haunt Milton's poem. The last two lines' almost-couplet (for it feels like a couplet but is not one) in Milton's sonnet XIX/23 is the dénouement of a movement throughout the poem from what can be seen to what cannot, a translation of what may be obtainable in vision to what may not. Liminal though she is, Alcestis, pale and faint and brought to Admetus by Hercules, is intensely and eerily

---

[24] Note also Milton's Samson's intense physical desire for sight to be available 'as feeling [and] through all parts diffus'd', so that one 'might look at will through every pore' (*Samson Agonistes* (London, 1671), p. 14 [lines 97–8]).

visually available.²⁵ The flushed and visceral sadness of a childbed death is chillingly associable with sight, and, indeed, the image almost overpowers the spiritual idea of purification and salvation that is evoked immediately afterwards.²⁶ Even with the assertion of salvation, the persisting memory remains that of death, pain and loss.²⁷ So too is a woman in white, even with her veiled face, entirely amenable to vision. But then we have love, sweetness, goodness and delight. Here, the images end, allowing mnemonic associations to take over. Specialized or 'fancied' sight becomes explicitly a matter of multifactorial sense, emanating from and available to a composite sensibility. 'Love, sweetness, goodness in her person shin'd / So clear, as in no face with more delight.' This is the climax of the dream, and here language too might have stopped, with the dreamer's contentment, allowing the dreamer his embrace, the desired culmination of the dream, the togetherness where language is no longer necessary. But such a culmination is not to be, and this moment of greatest positive sensibility is also the moment directly preceding, and therefore cueing the start of, the dreamer's awakening. Milton records the instant where, alongside the poet's waking consciousness, language must similarly return to carry the weight of wakefulness and its attendant longing. It is almost all stress at the close of Milton's sonnet (as it also was in Shakespeare's sonnet), slowing the poem into awakening and anguish, a dreamer opening his eyes into blindness, which is also poetry: 'But O, as to embrace me she enclin'd / I wak'd, she fled, and day brought back my night.'²⁸

It is this rhythm that Imtiaz Dharker takes up several hundred years later. Dharker's poem heightens in Miltonic terms the stakes of separation that Shakespeare's sonnet invokes. 'In the wake / of you, let day not break', she writes in the twenty-first century, journeying in sonnet with both Shakespeare and Milton. The author of 'The Trick' consciously writes back to and forward from the dreamtime spell of Shakespeare's Sonnet 43. But when 'Greedy for more / than the gift of seeing you, I lean in to taste / the colour, kiss it off your offered mouth', her own response to the Shakespeare sonnet engages with elements not contained in the Shakespeare poem but instead gifted onwards through the synaesthetic unrequitement at the close of the Milton sonnet. What happens after the lover leans in? Do they get to taste the colour – and kiss it off the beloved's offered mouth? We cannot know. 'For this, for this, I fall asleep in haste' – is all that Dharker's narrator tells us. It may be that here, too, just as the one lover inclined to embrace the other, the dreamer waked, the vision fled, and day brought back the dreamer's night. For without naming it as such, Dharker's poem also recalls a desperately and multisensorially unmoored bereavement:

Let me keep
the scent, the weight, the bright of you, take
the countless hours and count them all night through
till that time comes when you come to the door
of dreams.

Like the dreamer in Milton's poem, the dreamer in Dharker's poem has little choice, for in the dream is all the vision they can have of their beloved. They are, they disclose, repeatedly 'willing to fall for the trick that tells the truth'. It is a dual truth that is folded into a final Shakespearian couplet yet bearing a Miltonic message: 'that even your shade makes darkest absence bright, / that shadows live wherever there is light'. By now, we expect that even the beloved's shade makes darkest absence bright. But that shadows live wherever there is light is a peculiarly blind and bereaved and

---

²⁵ In Euripides' play *Alcestis*, Hercules rescues Admetus' wife Alcestis from her grave. The death and resurrection of Alcestis constitute the subject of numerous ancient reliefs and vase paintings.
²⁶ See, particularly, Louis Schwartz, *Milton and Maternal Mortality* (Cambridge, 2009), pp. 15–48.
²⁷ This is a matter of poetic expression precisely because it is a matter of the poet's unresolved memory and hope – because this is about what is greater than a single man's memory. Shakespeare and Milton both write in a world of widespread female death owing to reproductive complications, and simultaneously one of widespread infant mortality.
²⁸ In both Shakespeare's Sonnet 43 and Milton's 'Methought I saw', as well, the final lines are composed of devastatingly simple, monosyllabic words.

Miltonic assertion: it is the blind and visually impaired and blindness-aware that know this truth, and it is the living that have lost someone(s) they love that know this truth. There is nothing about Dharker's poem to explicitly mark its Miltonic route, but four centuries after Shakespeare's sonnets, I suggest, Dharker meditates on Shakespeare through Milton. We might even say that it is Milton's Shakespeare that she responds to. Shakespeare's poems of time, love, longing and dreams allow Milton his explorations of the disconsolate yet profound power of his visual condition, and teach him anew, through memory and desire, how to use poetry to break, and hold, his dreams.

WRITING DELIGHT WITH BEAUTY'S PEN: RESTORING RICHARD BARNFIELD'S LOST CREDIT

WILL TOSH[1]

The title quotation is of course Shakespeare's by way of Lady Capulet, not Richard Barnfield's. Urging her teenage daughter to accept a proposal of marriage from the eligible Paris, Juliet's mother wheels out what in the 1590s was already a hackneyed metaphor: that the young man's face is a 'precious book of love' revealing to the potential buyer his worth, virtue and attractiveness. 'Read o'er the volume of young Paris' face, / And find delight writ there with beauty's pen' (*Romeo* 1.3.89; 83–4): judge – do! – this book by its really extremely handsome cover. Contained within Lady Capulet's cliché is the assumption that male beauty is an uncontroversial topic for a work of literature, as indeed it was in the sixteenth and early seventeenth centuries, in figurations that were both heteroerotic and queer.[2] We might think of Philip Sidney's *Arcadia*, old and new, in which the hero Pyrocles (male-presenting, handsome-identifying) goes undercover as an equally hot Amazon to win the heroine's love. We are sure to think of Shakespeare's *Sonnets*, one of the era's most extended reflections on erotic attraction. But we're much less likely to consider the poems of Richard Barnfield, which represent – along with Shakespeare's – the only collections published in English in the premodern age to structure their celebration of male beauty around an overtly queer male dyad of male speaker and male addressee. What follows serves as a reminder of the obvious, and an expression of critical bewilderment. Given that Barnfield and Shakespeare – who knew each other's poetry – were working on strikingly comparable sequences of queer sonnets within a few years of each other in the 1590s, why is Barnfield still so poorly represented in the scholarship on Shakespeare's *Sonnets*? Part of the answer will be self-evident. Homophobic distaste has kept many critics from engaging with Barnfield's work, even as biographically minded readers of the *Sonnets* have occupied themselves with casting about for the apparently real figures behind the so-called 'fair youth' and 'dark lady'. But Barnfield's continuing neglect prompts further reflection, and I'll close by suggesting that Barnfield's queer sonnets run counter to presently understood histories of sexual subjectivity. We simply don't know what to *do* with Barnfield's queerness, his seemingly categoric assertion of sexual preference in an age which we have been told was innocent of such doctrinaire sexual clarity.

We are now familiar with the combination of literary criticism and wishful thinking that has fashioned the 'fair youth' of Shakespeare's *Sonnets* into the *idée fixe* of Shakespeare biography, and

---

[1] This article was delivered as a plenary lecture at the Twenty-Fifth British Graduate Shakespeare Conference, in association with The Shakespeare Institute in Stratford-upon-Avon, on 15 September 2023 and is adapted from material in Will Tosh, *Straight Acting: The Many Queer Lives of William Shakespeare* (London, 2024). I am grateful to chair Saraya Haddad, and to Jane Addington-May for the invitation. I am also extremely grateful to Sophie Baramidze for working to produce the footnotes and scholarly apparatus to support its appearance in print.

[2] Bruce R. Smith, *Homosexual Desire in Shakespeare's England: A Cultural Poetics* (Chicago, 1994).

the contested locus of conversations about Shakespeare's queerness.³ There is the fertility-shy young gentlemen of Sonnets 1 to 17, whose beauty recalls the 'lovely April' of his mother's young womanhood (3.10), but who needs to marry and head off a slide into onanistic self-abuse (he's been too much given to 'spend[ing] / Upon thyself thy beauty's legacy' (Sonnet 4.1–2)). Shakespeare's speaker urges the young man to redirect his youthful vigour towards an 'uneared', or unploughed, 'womb' (Sonnet 3.5) and reproduce his beauty and gentry status for the next generation. Then there is the flexible 'thou' in Sonnets 18 to 128, a figure that Stanley Wells and Paul Edmondson remind us is unambiguously gendered in only some of the poems.⁴ But many readers have found the speaker's masculinity to carry through the gatherings of thematically linked sonnets, fashioning a stable male love object in their mind's eye even in verses without an identificatory pronoun.⁵

These are the sonnets that explore a sexualized *amicitia perfecta*, the idea that the speaker and his lover harbour a turbo-charged version of Ciceronian perfect friendship, sharing a soul that is divided between two equally ardent bodies.⁶ The speaker preens himself on his handsome lover's 'seemly raiment' (Sonnet 22.6), proud because the younger man's attractive exterior can be understood as the speaker's own, the enclosure of his own heart. He frets that praising his lover is a bit like blowing his own trumpet, asking 'how thy worth with manners may I sing, / When thou art all the better part of me' (Sonnet 39.1–2). The conceit becomes painfully confounding when Shakespeare's speaker confronts the young man about sleeping with his mistress, proclaiming 'here's the joy: my friend and I are one. / Sweet flattery! Then she loves but me alone' (Sonnet 42.13–14). The young man's beauties act on the speaker in powerful and carnal ways. He is the 'master-mistress of [his] passion' (Sonnet 20.2), who occupies the speaker's thoughts and dreams. The lovers thrive, endure separation, turn on each other, part and reunite. The last poem to his 'sweet boy' (Sonnet 108.5) presents a reflection on Time's inexorable power to break through death the most loving of bonds, taking the form of an unusual twelve-line composition where the missing couplet is marked by two sets of empty parentheses. They sit, a pair of cushions stacked on top of each other, at the foot of the poem, perhaps a graphic representation of 'time's fickle glass' (Sonnet 126.2) which counts down the hours till the speaker and the youth must part for ever, or possibly just a pair of buttocks in the left and right margins.

The fair youth appears to take a paratextual form, too, in the lapidary dedication to the 1609 quarto. He is set in what a tabloid subeditor would call 'screamer caps' and pointed with a confetti of full stops, which makes parsing the grammar no small feat of interpretation:

> TO.THE.ONLY.BEGETTER.OF.
> THESE.ENSUING.SONNETS.
> Mr.W.H. ALL.HAPPINESS.
> AND.THAT.ETERNITY.
> PROMISED.
> BY.
> OUR.EVER-LIVING.POET.
> WISHETH.
> THE.WELL-WISHING.
> ADVENTURER.IN.
> SETTING.
> FORTH.
> T.T.⁷

The discreetly anonymized Master 'W.H.' is given credit as the sole begetter, or inspirer, of the *Sonnets*, to whom the 'adventurer', who must be

---

³ Robert Matz, 'The scandals of Shakespeare's *Sonnets*', *ELH* 77 (2010), 477–508; p. 485.
⁴ Paul Edmondson and Stanley Wells, *Shakespeare's Sonnets* (Oxford, 2004), p. 27.
⁵ Sasha Roberts, 'Shakespeare's *Sonnets* and English sonnet sequences', in *Early Modern English Poetry: A Critical Companion*, ed. Patrick Cheney, Andrew Hadfield and Garrett A. Sullivan Jr (New York, 2007), 172–83; p. 179.
⁶ Robert Streiter, 'Cicero on stage: Damon and Pithias and the fate of classical friendship in English Renaissance drama', *Texas Studies in Literature and Language* 47 (2005), 345–65.
⁷ *Shake-speares Sonnets. Never before imprinted* (London, 1609), t. p. Spelling modernized.

the publishing entrepreneur Thomas Thorpe, sends his hopes for literary immortality. The poet – potentially Shakespeare – is 'ever-living' presumably because of the sonnets' invocation of verse that shall 'ever live young' (Sonnet 19.14). What, if anything, connects the Master W.H. of the dedication with the 'fair friend' (Sonnet 104.1) of the *Sonnets*? Not a lot, in truth, beyond a hope (for some a fear) that the 'begetting' for which W. H. is held responsible constitutes an emotional inspiration, making this mysterious individual one of the collection's Lauras to Shakespeare's Petrarch. The *Sonnets*' other alleged Laura, the mistress about whom the majority of the final 28 sonnets are written, is understood not to feature in any of the homosocial networking that constitutes the volume's prefatory matter.

The identity of Master W.H. has been a biographical puzzle for centuries. Was he a boy actor called Willie Hughes, for whom Shakespeare adoringly wrote his chief female dramatic roles, as Oscar Wilde argued?[8] No such person has ever been known to exist. Or is it 'Wriothesley, Henry', Shakespeare's previous literary patron and dedicatee of *Venus and Adonis* and *Lucrece*, the Earl of Southampton, flying under cover?[9] The most popular candidate among present-day sonnetists is William Herbert, who in 1609 hadn't yet ascended to the earldom of Pembroke and was still fourteen years away from receiving the honour of a dedication in the First Folio.[10] Herbert was the son of two important late Elizabethan figures: the author and literary patron Mary Herbert, and her husband the second earl, whose theatre company probably performed two of Shakespeare's *Henry VI* plays.[11] The young Herbert refused matches with four different brides in the late 1590s, a plausible context for the commissioning by his parents of the first seventeen sonnets as persuasory epistles. But even if Shakespeare had been invited to write sonnets for either young man, neither situation explains why Shakespeare took the conceit of a beautiful youth receiving life advice from a wise elder and transformed it into a love story between the two men. Nor does this account for why either high-born nobleman should be referred to with breath-taking insolence as 'Master'.

It's possible, although unlikely, that Shakespeare had a romantic relationship with Southampton or Pembroke. It is almost inconceivable that Shakespeare or Thorpe would see fit to draw attention to it, however obliquely, in print. The queerness wasn't really the issue. It was the cross-class terms of endearment that were social death.

A more plausible but less dramatic interpretation, first offered by Donald Foster and recently developed by Lynne Magnusson, is that 'Master W.H.' is simply a misprint for 'Master W.S.' (or 'W. Sh.').[12] Shakespeare is therefore the 'only begetter,' or author, of the ensuing sonnets, and the 'ever-living poet', or 'ever-living Poet' – the dedication's capitalization makes this ambiguous – is God, maker of all things and provider of an eternal afterlife. This would make Thorpe's dedication, which is the only scrap of prefatory matter in the book, a less exciting affair, but perfectly possible considering other printed sonnet sequences. Edmund Spenser's *Amoretti* also contains a preface by the publisher on the author's behalf.[13] It seems unlikely we'll ever know whether Shakespeare's *Sonnets* were really *poèmes*

---

[8] Oscar Wilde, 'The portrait of Mr. W. H.', in *The Soul of Man under Socialism and Selected Critical Prose*, ed. Linda Dowling (London, 2001), 31–101.

[9] J. A. Fort, 'Thorpe's text of *Shakespeare's Sonnets*', *The Review of English Studies* 2 (1926), 439–45.

[10] Brian O'Farrell, *Shakespeare's Patron: William Herbert, Third Earl of Pembroke, 1580–1630: Politics, Patronage and Power* (London, 2011). Herbert is also the candidate favoured by Katherine Duncan-Jones in her edition of *Shakespeare's Sonnets* (London, 1997), pp. 55–69.

[11] G. M. Pinciss, 'Shakespeare, Her Majesty's Players and Pembroke's Men', in *Shakespeare Survey 27* (Cambridge, 1974), 129–36; Roslyn L. Knutson, 'Pembroke's Men in 1592–3, their repertory and touring schedule', *Early Theatre* 4 (2001), 129–38.

[12] Donald W. Foster, 'Master W. H., R. I. P.', *PMLA* 102 (1987), 42–54; Lynne Magnusson, 'Thomas Thorpe's Shakespeare: "The only begetter"', in *The Sonnets: The State of Play*, ed. Hannah Crawforth, Elizabeth Scott Baumann and Clare Whitehead (London, 2017), 33–54; p. 50.

[13] Edmund Spenser, *Amoretti and Epithalamion* (London, 1595).

à clef relaying a true story, or stories, of passionate adoration and tempestuous sexual jealousy. It's difficult to believe he didn't find some sort of inspiration for his poems in the feelings he experienced throughout his life, but that part of Shakespeare's emotional life is essentially unrecoverable. Any proposed real-life analogues are so hedged as to make the line of enquiry endlessly inconclusive; whether or not our poet was ever-living, Master W.H. certainly shows no signs of dying. Shelves of books and entire provinces of the internet are given over to demonstrating his identity.

But excitable theories about Southampton or Pembroke have obscured another crucial influence on Shakespeare in the 1590s, and prevented a proper consideration of the *Sonnets* as queer literature. It seems to me that we've neglected the queer artist in the hunt for queer biography, and in ignoring queer culture, we've given ourselves fewer opportunities to understand early modern queer experience. Shakespeare's *Sonnets* deserves to be in conversation with something less talked about than the real identity of the fair youth: the single greatest effusion of queer literature that England has ever seen, or would see again until the twentieth century, that took place between 1594 and 1595 – all of it the work of a young writer called Richard Barnfield. In his publications in those years Barnfield did far more than join the ranks of English poets who riffed on classical homoeroticism for a Renaissance audience. He pioneered a new kind of poetry that placed queer desire centre stage, and brought a completely unprecedented candour to depictions of sexual feeling between men while also, not unconnectedly, taking poetic misogyny to new heights. Barnfield's star was to blaze fiercely but briefly, but it shone at its brightest in the years that Shakespeare was fomenting his sequence of sonnets. If we're looking for a fair youth who inspired Shakespeare's *Sonnets*, we need to bring Barnfield into the story of their creation.

Richard Barnfield was baptized on 13 June 1574, born to Midland landowners on both sides. The Barnfields were a Shropshire family with sprawling estates in Edgmond, and a family crest that boasted a crowned lion. His mother's family, the Skrymshers, lived in a formidable, moated grange just over the border in Staffordshire at Norbury. Barnfield's parents, Richard and Mary, were living at Norbury when their son was born, but then moved to the nearby market town of Newport where more children – two boys, Robert and John, and a girl, Dorothy – joined their older brother. As is the way with middling folk four and a half centuries ago, it's not easy to build a biography of Barnfield's life before adulthood, but there's distressing evidence to suggest that, two months after Dorothy's birth and shortly before Richard's seventh birthday, Mary attacked her husband with a knife and then slit her own throat. An uncorroborated contemporary account of the incident and its terrible aftermath exists in a transcript made by a Victorian antiquary and printed in a collection of Shropshire-related notes and queries:

1581. This year and in the month of May one Mistress Barnfield of Newport, being twelve miles from Shrewsbury, killed herself. The cause thereof was that not only she being jealous of her husband, and also not perfect in mind, one night being in bed with her said husband, and holding a naked knife in her hand, would have cut her husband's throat; and missing his weasand pipe [i.e., wind-pipe], [he] awaked upon the same and stayed her fury, and so called for help and locked her in a dark chamber, without any knife about her or anything else to hurt herself. But within a day or two she espied a rusty, broad arrowhead in a privy place and therewith cut her own throat most wickedly.[14]

The judgemental tone of the report belies what may have been postpartum psychosis, another severe mental illness or a response to abuse. But whatever Mary was suffering from, for the

---

[14] *Salopian Shreds and Patches* (1885), cited in Andrew Worrall, 'Biographical introduction: Barnfield's feast of "all varietie"', in *The Affectionate Shepherd: Celebrating Richard Barnfield*, ed. Kenneth Borris and George Klawitter (Selinsgrove, 2001), 25–40; pp. 27–8 (spelling and punctuation modernized). I have relied on Worrall's biographical essay for my account of Barnfield's life.

Elizabethans suicide was a terrible crime. If the account is true, Mary's final days must have been unspeakably wretched, left with her own demons in a dark room – the ordeal experienced by *Twelfth Night*'s Malvolio, and the standard 'treatment' for the mentally ill in the sixteenth century.[15] Unlike Malvolio, Mary wasn't liberated from her captivity, and fear or despair overwhelmed her. If the Mistress Barnfield of the story is Barnfield's mother, Richard senior and the Skrymshers hushed up the scandal, and Mary was buried with all due religious ceremony that spring at Norbury.

The young Barnfield almost certainly remained with his late mother's family in the damp, lowering manor house (when he matriculated at Brasenose College Oxford, he was identified as being from Staffordshire, not Shropshire, the county of his father's estates). Somehow, in the years after his mother's violent death, he put her loss behind him, or pushed it down and away from his everyday thoughts. There's no way to know Barnfield's feelings about his mother's suicide, or whether his later extreme poetic misogyny was in some sense an articulation of unresolved trauma. But it might be relevant that when he came to write a poem on the story of the Trojan princess Cassandra, cursed with unbelieved prophecy by Apollo and regarded as mad by those around her, he diverged from the established myth in which she was killed by Clytemnestra. Instead, his version of Clytemnestra locks Cassandra in a lightless tower where, tormented with grief, she 'ends her fortune with a fatal knife'. Cassandra's 'purest soul' is released from 'endless moan' and transmigrates to Elysium, 'the place for wrongful death and martyrdom'.[16]

Nothing is known of Barnfield's early education, although like Shakespeare's it was evidently thorough. There was plenty of family money to send him to university at fifteen, the standard age for a boy who'd attended a grammar school. Oxford initially suited him. Barnfield graduated in 1592, but swiftly abandoned plans for a Master of Arts, finding eighteen-hour days of theology, Aristotelian philosophy and logic unappealing. Instead, Barnfield cooled his heels until the plague that ravaged London in 1592 and 1593 was beginning to lift, and then made for the capital city. It is likely he was a published poet by the age of twenty. The collection *Greene's Funerals*, published in 1594, which eulogized the current crop of literary celebrities, including Edmund Spenser and the late Robert Greene, is attributed to 'R.B. Gent' and stylometric analysis suggests it is by Barnfield.[17] The volume was dedicated to London's 'gentleman readers',[18] code for the men of the Inns of Court, and perhaps a sign that he had joined an Inn of Court or Chancery himself.

He was an early reader of Shakespeare's brand new *Venus and Adonis* (1593), which he devoured along with the other epyllia that followed in its wake. He got his hands on manuscript copies of Christopher Marlowe's *Hero and Leander* and the wildly popular pastoral lyric, 'The Passionate Shepherd to his Love', which begins 'Come live with me and be my love'. He also leapt on the two plays by Marlowe that appeared in print early in 1594, probably less than a year after the writer's death, *Edward II* and *Dido Queen of Carthage*. All would find themselves echoed or quoted in the work Barnfield wrote at some speed and published in November 1594, a queer erotic fantasy that sensationally lifted the veil on the decorously classicized and Latinized conventions of pastoral romance.[19] This was the book published, anonymously at first, as *The Affectionate Shepherd Containing the Complaint*

---

[15] Theodore Dalrymple, 'Much about madness', *BMJ* 345 (2012), 33.
[16] Richard Barnfield, *Cynthia, with Certain Sonnets and the Legend of Cassandra* (London, 1595), lines 459, 465, 466, 468. Lineation of all of Barnfield's poetry cited in this article is taken from *Poems of Richard Barnfield*, ed. George Klawitter (New York, 2005) – further references in parentheses – although I have modernized the spelling and punctuation in accordance with typical practices when citing Shakespeare's verse.
[17] Wes Folkerth, 'The metamorphosis of Daphnis: the case for Richard Barnfield's Orpheus', in *The Affectionate Shepherd*, ed. Borris and Klawitter, 305–31; Roy Eriksen, 'Marlowe and Company in Barnfield's *Greene's Funeralls* (1594)', *Nordic Journal of English Studies* 12 (2013), 71–80.
[18] 'R.B. Gent', *Greenes Funeralls* (London, 1594), n.p.
[19] Charles Crawford, 'Richard Barnfield, Marlowe, and Shakespeare', in *Collectanea* (Stratford-upon-Avon, 1906), 1–16.

of Daphnis for the Love of Ganymede. It was a miscellany of a kind, but the surrounding material attracted much less attention than the substantial two-part pastoral poem at its heart, 'The tears of an affectionate shepherd sick for love, or The complaint of Daphnis for the love of Ganymede'.

Readers might have expected a familiar rehash of Virgil's short 'Second Eclogue', the hugely influential pastoral poem that told of the love of Corydon for the beautiful, disdainful Alexis.[20] But this new poem was Virgil supersized, sexualized and anglicized into something altogether new. It was in every respect bigger, longer and uncut. The speaker Daphnis – a shepherd but, like all pastoral figures, intimately connected with lordly folk and divine creatures – adores the beautiful young Ganymede. But Ganymede is also beloved by Guendolen, Queen of the Nymphs, who is herself fending off advances from a geriatric suitor and mourning the loss of her first love. Over two parts, or 'lamentation[s]', an increasingly abject Daphnis goes all out to win over Ganymede, and entice him away from Guendolen, whose so-called love, Daphnis argues, is vapid and self-centred.

Never before in English had a poet been so upfront about the bodily reality of queer male desire, a force which frames the poem from its first stanzas and propels the sequence of lures, promises and seductions that Daphnis places before Ganymede to persuade him to 'be my boy, or else my bride' (2.78). In the opening lines Daphnis describes – or perhaps imagines – an early-morning visit to Ganymede's chamber:

Scarce had the morning star hid from the light
Heaven's crimson canopy with stars bespangled,
But I began to rue th'unhappy sight
Of that fair boy that had my heart entangled.
Cursing the time, the place, the sense, the sin,
I came, I saw, I viewed, I slipped in.

If it be sin to love a sweet-faced boy
(Whose amber locks, trussed up in golden trammels,
Dangle adown his lovely cheeks with joy,
When pearl and flowers his fair hair enamels),
If it be sin to love a lovely lad,
Oh then sin I, for whom my soul is sad.
(1.1–12)

The four 'sins' in two stanzas – and the Caesarian implications of conquest in 'I came, I saw, I viewed', to say nothing of the resonance of 'slipped in' – place Daphnis' desires and intentions well beyond anything that could possibly be understood as bloodless poetic yearning.

Part of the romantic deal that Daphnis proposes is transactional: he will reward Ganymede with a wealth of luxuries if the boy sleeps with him. Some are desirable consumer goods such as a golden tennis racquet, or a fan made out of phoenix feathers. But other gifts are succulently edible: ripe-to-bursting cherries, oozing honey and strawberries 'bathed in a melting sugar-candy stream' (2.70). But it is evident that Daphnis conflates the pleasure of these delicacies with the anticipated joy of Ganymede's body: 'O would to God... My lips were honey, and thy mouth a bee', he yearns:

Then shoulds't thou suck my sweet and my fair flower
That now is ripe and full of honey-berries.
Then would I lead thee to my pleasant bower
Filled full of grapes, of mulberries and cherries;
Then shoulds't thou be my wasp or else my bee.
I would thy hive, and thou my honey be.
(1.95–102)

The flower-sucking and honey-depositing stays in Daphnis' imagination. In accordance with the traditions of Petrarchan love poetry or Virgilian pastoral, Ganymede remains unmoved. Daphnis threatens to exile himself to the Caucasus and let 'a vulture gnaw upon my heart' (2.30), but to no avail. He becomes resentful of Ganymede's shining ivory beauty, and his lazy assumption that everyone will fall at his feet in adoration. It's not just white boys, Daphnis hints, who can turn heads: 'We cannot choose, but needs we must confess, / Sable excels milk-white in more or less' (2.275–6). In a society such as Barnfield's, which was developing a growing awareness of racial difference, the possibility that Daphnis might seek

---

[20] Erik Fredericksen, 'Finding another Alexis: pastoral tradition and the reception of Vergil's second eclogue', *Classical Receptions Journal* 7 (2015), 422–41.

love from a man of colour rather than the pale and disdainful Ganymede hovers at the margin of the poem.[21] As 'The tears of an affectionate shepherd' comes to an end, the rueful Daphnis imagines that he has become not just older and wiser but 'age-withered' (2.414) and 'wrinkled' (2.416), his very life-force burnt up by his unrequited passion for Ganymede. He bids 'a thousand-thousand times farewell' to his 'love-hating boy' (2.421–2), and sadly gives up the field, although we never learn if the 'wantoniz[ing]' competitor Guendolen ever gets her man (1.161).

The Affectionate Shepherd targeted the same post-plague readership, hungry for delight, that Shakespeare had served with Venus and Adonis. Barnfield was even more clear-sighted about what he understood his audience to want: an arousingly sexed-up version of the English pastorals that had proved such a hit since Spenser's The Shepherd's Calendar fifteen years before. Barnfield had no intention of sanitizing the form's lush homoeroticism. Spenser's 'January' eclogue sailed close to the wind with its depiction of a homoerotic friendship between Colin and Hobbinol – so much so that Spenser's glossator 'E.K.' assured readers that the shepherds' feelings were free of 'pederastic' 'disorderly love'.[22]

Orderly or otherwise, Daphnis' queer desires were very much the point of Barnfield's poem, and they found instant 'friendly favour' among readers, as the poet later put it in the preface to his next publication, Cynthia, with Certain Sonnets (1595). The Affectionate Shepherd's combination of queer sex appeal and misogynist exclusion – the vampish Guendolen is 'light' and fickle (1.158) – turned out to be popular with the largely young and male readership of erotic lyric verse. More was to come as Barnfield spent the Christmas holidays of 1594–1595 rethinking the destiny he gave to Daphnis and Ganymede at the end of 'The tears of an affectionate shepherd'. Barnfield decided to erase the shepherd's wizened, forlorn end and start his narrative again, reuniting his lovers in a numbered sequence of twenty sonnets. He promoted Daphnis and Ganymede from the established classical setting of the pastoral romance to the as-yet-unqueered territory of the Petrarchan sonnet. He wrote quickly over the vacation, and 'Certain Sonnets' – published as a volume together with his legend of Cassandra and a poem in lavish praise of the queen called 'Cynthia' – appeared, under his own name this time, before Easter.

Daphnis and Ganymede slotted easily into the roles of sonnet speaker and lusted-after love-object (they had, after all, rehearsed the parts extensively in The Affectionate Shepherd). Ganymede still has his 'sin-procuring' body (17.13) and an 'obdurate beauty' (19.4) that rebuffs all seductions; Daphnis vows he'll die unless Ganymede will 'quench [his] thirst' (6.4) with kisses. The mood is alternately keenly voyeuristic and chattily intimate. Daphnis imagines stealing a kiss from the sleeping Ganymede, and watches hungrily from the river-bank as his 'fairest fair' (7.6) swims in the Thames, echoing Marlowe's Hero and Leander when Ganymede attracts aroused interest from Neptune. But Daphnis also settles down beside Ganymede for a revelatory heart to heart, and presents him with a pair of kid gloves, the traditional Elizabethan courtship gift.

Consummation arrives in the form of a vigorous wet dream, as Daphnis dreams that Ganymede's 'Sweet coral lips' (6.1) kiss him into a paroxysm of youthful energy, and he feels from his 'heart a spring of blood' that sends lusty strength coursing through his limbs. Daphnis recognizes that 'in dreaming ... [he] did speed' (6.13), or orgasm in his sleep, and wonders what it would be like to do so with Ganymede 'indeed' (6.14) while wide awake. He doesn't manage to sleep with him in 'deed', but Daphnis achieves something even more astonishing: a declaration to Ganymede that he is and always will be his beloved. In a culture that tried wherever possible to separate the intense

---

[21] Farah Karim-Cooper, The Great White Bard: Shakespeare, Race and the Future (London, 2023).

[22] Edmund Spenser, The Shepheardes Calendar (1579), in The Shorter Poems, ed. Richard McCabe (London, 1999), p. 39.

romantic feelings of male friendship from erotic love, Barnfield collapsed the distinction in a strikingly determined way. Placed in the very middle of the sequence, Daphnis' avowal (Sonnet 11) is worth quoting in full:

> Sighing and sadly sitting by my love,
> He asked the cause of my heart's sorrowing,
> Conjuring me by heaven's eternal king
> To tell the cause which me so much did move.
> 'Compelled,' quoth I, 'to thee I will confess.
> Love is the cause, and only Love it is
> That doth deprive me of my heavenly bliss:
> Love is the pain that doth my heart oppress.'
> 'And what is she,' quoth he, 'whom thou dost love?'
> 'Look in this glass,' quoth I, 'there shalt thou see
> The perfect form of my felicity.'
> When, thinking that it would strange magic prove,
> He opened it; and taking off the cover
> He straight perceived himself to be my lover.

This is queer drama in content and form: Ganymede's sudden realization, delivered by means of a pocket mirror, that he is the cause of Daphnis' heartsickness comes as the *volta* in the sonnet's closing triplet. And although Barnfield's sonnets don't follow a chronological plot, this is a poem that gestures towards what might happen after such a declaration. What does Daphnis hope Ganymede will say? Ganymede might well have struggled to find the words. Barnfield's culture didn't have a language to describe an exclusive bond of erotic love between two men: there was no direct queer equivalent of the romantic and sexual discourse of straight courtly love. In his sonnets, Barnfield was beginning to invent one. By lifting his lovelorn shepherds from classical pastoral and transplanting them into the English love sonnet, he was giving a new vernacular voice to queer desire.

Barnfield continued his run of queer poetic production with yet another highly fashionable contribution in 1595: *Orpheus His Journey to Hell*, also by 'R.B. Gent' and ascribed with some confidence to Barnfield. The story is an Ovidian fantasy that follows the Thracian musician into Hades to rescue his dead wife Eurydice, the failure of which tilts him into fully fledged queer misogyny. He sings 'invective ditties' (655) against 'women's fawning fickle company' (662) in such persuasive tones that he soon attracts interest from other men, who leave their wives and join him in an anti-women, proto-queer commune, 'With which sweet life they seemed so well content, / As made them curse the former time the'ad [they had] spent' (671–2). Unlike in the version of the story in *Metamorphoses*, Barnfield's Orpheus doesn't establish 'stews of males',[23] or boy brothels, to entertain his new followers.[24] The men are enough for one another – until the women of Thrace beat Orpheus to death because 'He was an enemy unto their gender' (696).

The three major homoerotic works of art that Barnfield produced in the year after autumn 1594 constituted the most overt canon of queer literature that had ever been published in English. 'The tears of an affectionate shepherd' and 'Certain Sonnets' made male same-sex desire the central theme in the two most up-to-the-minute genres of 1590s love poetry, the pastoral lyric and the sonnet. In *Orpheus His Journey to Hell* Barnfield had taken the heavily implied homoeroticism, and associated misogyny, of the Ovidian epic, or epyllion, and fashioned those qualities into a mythic origin story for queer male desire predicated on sexist exclusion and conflict: Orpheus is reshaped into the martyred patron of men who turn away from their wives to cavort with one another in a utopic retreat. In my book on Shakespeare's 'many queer lives', I've called this period early modern England's 'queerest year' – and that's not even including Marlowe's *Edward II*, also published in 1594.[25]

---

[23] Ovid, *Metamorphoses*, trans. Arthur Golding, ed. Madeleine Forey (London, 2002), p. 297.

[24] Jennifer Ingleheart, 'The invention of (Thracian) homosexuality: the Ovidian Orpheus in the English Renaissance', in *Ancient Rome and the Construction of Modern Homosexual Identities*, ed. Jennifer Ingleheart (Oxford, 2015), 56–73.

[25] See Tosh, *Straight Acting*.

At this point, let's widen our focus again and consider Shakespeare. The dating of his *Sonnets* is a nightmarish business. There are good arguments for dating one or two of the collection to Shakespeare's schooldays or his courtship of Anne Hathaway in 1582.[26] Others seem to refer to the death of Queen Elizabeth and accession of King James in 1603, while the 1609 volume probably contains poems initiated in one era and progressively worked on over years, if not decades.[27] Francis Meres's reference in 1598 to the 'sugared sonnets' that circulated among Shakespeare's 'private friends' tells us that a collection or poetic album of some sorts was in existence by then;[28] it's reasonable to presume that Shakespeare contemplated a *sequence* of sonnets once he'd read some or all of the numbered collections that appeared after Philip Sidney's *Astrophil and Stella* (1591), such as Samuel Daniel's *Delia* (1592), Michael Drayton's *Idea's Mirror* (1594) and Spenser's *Amoretti* (1595). Most critics place the composition of the majority of Shakespeare's *Sonnets* in bursts after 1595, although dating conclusions are often dependent on which marriage-resistant aristocrat is most favoured as a candidate for Shakespeare's 'fair youth' (Southampton demands an earlier date of composition, and Pembroke a later).[29]

Shedding our attachment to Sotonian or Pembrokian provenances frees us up to look at the much more poetically significant youth who by 1595 had radically intervened in the literary landscape. Barnfield's project of work articulated a new queer sensibility: it was an exclusionary, chauvinistic queerness marked by an elevated celebration of both male beauty and patriarchal privilege, but it was also uncompromising in its honesty and candour about sexual love between men. Most importantly, he reinvented the love sonnet, a form that attracted mockery as often as it prompted emulation. If Shakespeare was already experimenting with the sonnet in plays and stand-alone poetry by 1595, he also has *Love's Labour's Lost*'s Berowne pour scorn on it as 'pure idolatry' (4.3.72).

We need to note the qualities that are unique to Shakespeare's and Barnfield's work in these years. It has sometimes been said that Shakespeare's sonnets to the young man are part of a well-established Elizabethan tradition of love poems between male friends.[30] They're not. Such a tradition didn't exist. Barnfield and Shakespeare are the only poets of the age to write love sonnets between men, and the latter read and knew the former's work, as Barnfield knew Shakespeare's. 'Certain Sonnets' and *Shakespeare's Sonnets* are inextricably connected as unique instances of thematically interlinked queer verse, and Barnfield is well due acknowledgement as a significant influence on Shakespeare.

It was Barnfield's earlier collection that originated the idea, so important to *Shakespeare's Sonnets*, of a male speaker ravished with desire for an exquisite, disdainful young man. Both sequences engage with the same broad narrative arc: the youth has been hand-crafted by the gods for beauty and virtue, and his unattainability compels the speaker to indulge in fantasies of sexual possession. The speaker endures a period of separation from his beloved and comes to realize that the boy is not just coolly uninterested but actively resistant to him. Barnfield's speaker's creative energies wilt by the final sonnet, and he acknowledges that 'these lines, the sons of tears and dole' ('Certain Sonnets', 20.8) – his poems, in other words – will have to stand as witness to his love for the youth, the 'essence' ('Certain Sonnets', 20.5) of his soul. As Shakespeare puts it in his Sonnets 17 and 18, it's his 'verse in time to come' (17.1) that will 'give life' (18.14) to the youth's beauty. Although some of the themes in Barnfield's collection – the pain of unrequited love, the perfection and unreachability of the lover – are conventional in Petrarchan love

---

[26] A. Kent Hieatt, Charles W. Hieatt and Anne Lake Prescott, 'When did Shakespeare write "Sonnets 1609"?' *Studies in Philology* 88 (1991), 69–109.

[27] Helen Hackett, *Shakespeare and Elizabeth: The Meeting of Two Myths* (Princeton, 2021), p. 140.

[28] Francis Meres, *Palladis tamia, Wits treasury* (London, 1598), p. 282.

[29] MacD. P. Jackson, 'Vocabulary and chronology: the case of Shakespeare's *Sonnets*', *The Review of English Studies* 52 (2001), 59–75.

[30] *Shakespeare's Sonnets*, ed. Sidney Lee (Oxford, 1905), p. 10.

poetry, his particular arrangement of homoerotic desire, queer bodily yearning and poetic immortality was not merely strikingly unconventional, but unprecedented in English verse.

Shakespeare didn't just repeat the principal motifs of Barnfield's sequence. He also reworked specific conceits he found in the younger poet's sonnets. These echoes have been studied in detail by Paul Hammond, and I won't rehearse all his findings here.[31] But I will point out that Hammond regards five of Shakespeare's sonnets as adaptations of Barnfield's 'Certain Sonnets', and detects verbal echoes from *The Affectionate Shepherd* across the 1609 collection. What's been less explored is the influence of Barnfield's particularly biting misogyny – extreme even for the 1590s – on the portion of Shakespeare's sonnets that tend to be known as the 'Dark Lady' sequence, despite the racist exoticizing of the term (the sonnets themselves are, it's almost unnecessary to add, themselves racist in the extreme).[32] These poems represent a striking divergence from the norms of Petrarchan love poetry – indeed Margreta de Grazia regards the misogyny of these sonnets as the more scandalous element of the collection, even less acceptable to polite Elizabethan opinion than the homoeroticism of the fair youth poems.[33] The few from the 'Dark Lady' sequence that are widely read today – particularly number 130, the wittily realistic confession that begins 'My mistress' eyes are nothing like the sun' (1) – enjoy their popularity precisely because they are atypically positive in their presentation of the relationship between the speaker and his female lover. More characteristic is Sonnet 147, which takes the Petrarchan conceit of sexual passion as a raging fever and makes it depressingly, insultingly literal: 'I have sworn thee fair, and thought thee bright, / Who art as black as hell, as dark as night' (13–14). Throughout the sequence, the speaker blames the woman for her sexual appetite, for her infidelities (the speaker too is unfaithful), for her unwelcome knack for provoking his lust, and for her disingenuity and deceit. It seems that, as well as revealing to Shakespeare the possibilities in the queered Petrarchan sonnet, Barnfield also demonstrated the cliché-busting capabilities of poisonous misogyny, an innovation to the sonnet form that came at a steep cost to the good taste of Shakespeare's collection. It is perhaps to Shakespeare's credit that he concluded the 1609 quarto with 'A Lover's Complaint', a lyric that sympathetically explores the consequences for an innocent young woman seduced and abandoned by a smooth-talking young man who deploys sonnets as part of his seduction technique. This is assuming that Shakespeare was responsible for the volume's arrangement, which isn't everyone's assumption.

I've titled this piece 'restoring Barnfield's lost credit', which is not to say that he's a new discovery. Thanks to some brilliant work by scholars including George Klawitter, Andrew Worrall, Sam See and others, he's no longer the entirely overlooked figure he was for much of the twentieth and twenty-first centuries.[34] A hundred years ago and more he was a distinctly outré taste: the Victorian socialist and queer rights activist Edward Carpenter treasured Barnfield's sonnets as springing from 'the poet's very heart,' but he was one of a very small number of late nineteenth-century readers of Barnfield.[35] However, as a poet, he remains a minority interest in early modern criticism. The implications of Barnfield and Shakespeare being the *only* writers of the early modern era – the only writers *until* the modern era – to publish openly homoerotic sonnets have not been fully examined. Indeed, Barnfield seems destined to be an eternal surprise. As far back as the 1770s, the literary critic Thomas Warton was

---

[31] Paul Hammond, *Figuring Sex between Men from Shakespeare to Rochester* (Oxford, 2002).
[32] Jane Kingsley-Smith, *The Afterlife of Shakespeare's Sonnets* (Cambridge, 2019), p. 237; Kim F. Hall, *Things of Darkness: Economies of Race and Gender in Early Modern England* (Ithaca, 1996), p. 66.
[33] Margreta de Grazia, 'The scandal of Shakespeare's *Sonnets*', in *Shakespeare Survey 46* (Cambridge, 1994), 35–49.
[34] Sam See, 'Richard Barnfield and the limits of homoerotic literary history', *GLQ: A Journal of Lesbian and Gay Studies* 13 (1993), 63–91.
[35] Recalled by Montague Summers in his *The Poems of Richard Barnfield* (London, 1936), p. xiii.

expressing his astonishment that a writer of Barnfield's 'undoubted genius' should be so little known.[36]

The explanation for his historical neglect is not, of course, far to seek. The 1911 *Encyclopædia Britannica* let its prejudice overtake any bibliographic scruples when it lamented, 'if editors would courageously alter the gender of the pronouns, several of Barnfield's glowing sonnets might take their place in our anthologies'.[37] The Norton brick of Renaissance literature, the handbook to many an introductory undergraduate course, kept Barnfield, emended or otherwise, out of its anthologies until the late 1990s. It says something about the persistence of institutional discomfort that no edition of Barnfield's work is currently in print. If pastoral poems that make little effort to disguise their descriptions of fellatio, or sonnets about wet dreams, were not considered acceptable material in the seventeenth, eighteenth and nineteenth centuries, and most of the twentieth century, it also seems highly likely that Barnfield overstepped the mark in his own time, too.

The slow pace of his critical redemption in the twentieth and twenty-first centuries is slightly harder to explain. I'm sure that anti-queer dislike still remains alive in some quarters: the frequent argument that Shakespeare's sonnets to the young man don't express a sexual passion is harder to maintain when they are put in conversation with Barnfield's more explicitly homoerotic versions. Homophobia is the easy answer: some people have a problem with imagining Shakespeare as a queer artist, just as some people have a problem with queer lives in the present day. But other factors are pertinent, factors which speak to the way we have come to understand the history of sexual subjectivity. Kenneth Borris regards Barnfield's poetry as constituting a form of homoerotic advocacy, 'promoting the legitimacy of same-sex love, and seeking to enhance its social status and currency', presenting an argument that runs counter to established theories about the history of sexual identities.[38] Specifically, Borris resists the notion, based on perhaps over-zealous application of the work of Michel Foucault, that sexual identity had little impact on notions of the self before the modern era.[39] It's difficult to read Barnfield's pronounced commitment to homoeroticism, and his almost equally pronounced exclusionary misogyny, as anything other than an identitarian stand, an assertion of cultural particularity that indexes an emotional and erotic subjectivity. He appears to be a queer poet *avant la lettre*. Perhaps Barnfield is the exception that proves the rule that queer sexual subjectivities had not emerged in the early modern period: and by 'prove', I of course mean 'test'. His poetry asks us to think again about some of our certainties in sexual history, to reopen a Foucauldian can of worms as we reconsider the neglected queer culture of Shakespeare's 1590s.

---

[36] Thomas Warton, *History of English Poetry*, vol. 4 (London, 1871), p. 437.

[37] *Encyclopædia Britannica*, 11th ed., 29 vols. (Cambridge, 1911), vol. 3, p. 415.

[38] Kenneth Borris, '"Ile hang a bag and bottle at thy back": Barnfield's homoerotic advocacy and the construction of homosexuality', in *The Affectionate Shepherd*, ed. Borris and Klawitter, 193–248; p. 194.

[39] David M. Halperin, 'Forgetting Foucault: acts, identities, and the history of sexuality', *Representations* 63 (1998), 93–120.

OCULAR POWER AND FEMALE *FASCINUM* IN SHAKESPEARE'S *VENUS AND ADONIS*

TAMARA MAHADIN

'O, thou didst kill me; kill me once again!
Thy eyes' shrewd tutor, that hard heart of thine,
Hath taught them scornful tricks
                    (*Venus and Adonis*, 499–501)

After Venus faints from Adonis' rejection and he in turn kisses her in Shakespeare's *Venus and Adonis* (1593), Adonis describes her eyes as a 'shrewd tutor'. He accuses Venus' eyes of guiding her heart into committing 'scornful tricks' akin to the cunning of a shrewd woman. Throughout the poem, recurring references to the eyes of both Venus and Adonis play a central role in eliciting bodily responses from both figures. Recognizing this fact not only complicates our understanding of how Venus and Adonis read each other, but also underscores the gendered nature of the gaze, showing how the female gaze has the power to both disrupt and invert the power dynamics and narrative structures within Shakespeare's poem.

In this article, I examine how Shakespeare's metaphors for sight in *Venus and Adonis* create a 'gendered ocular authority', a term I use to describe how gendered discourses of power and influence are linked to the use of sight. My aim is to delve into the profound impact of ocular perception, examining how Venus' character employs her sight as a gendered authoritative influence over Adonis through her feminine gaze. I want to further extend my argument by arguing the reverse: that the gendered nature of Venus' gaze significantly alters the interactions between Venus and Adonis within the narrative structure of the poem.

Venus uses what I will call *fascinum* as a gendered method of control, strategically employing her sight to captivate Adonis. The Latin word *fascinum* refers to the act of bewitching or enchanting, employed as an occult force with the potential to cause harm. In ancient Roman culture, a phallus amulet, known as a *fascinus* charm, was employed at times as a protective measure.[1] The specific notion of *fascinum* I am exploring is intricately linked to, yet distinct from, its association with the concept of a 'divine phallus'. Both the terms *fascinum* and 'fascination' were used in the early modern period; for clarity, in this article, I will use *fascinum* because the meaning of 'fascination' has changed since the twentieth century, and because I intend my use of *fascinum* in this paper to encompass the historical and cultural aspects associated with the evil eye and its connection to the early modern conceptions of fascination.[2] Therefore, my examination will delve into the inherently gendered power dynamic between Venus and Adonis, highlighting how *fascinum*, as a gendered phenomenon, lends Venus

---

[1] David Wray, *Catullus and the Poetics of Roman Manhood* (Cambridge, 2001), pp. 151–2.
[2] Steven Connor writes that fascination has shifted from being the power possessed by certain individuals 'to the power of fascination as it may be lent to or bestowed upon fascinating objects, ideas, or persons'. See Connor, 'Fascination, skin and the screen', *Critical Quarterly* 40 (1998), 9–24; p. 12. On the conceptual history of fascination, including the development of the term, see also Andreas Degen, 'Concepts of fascination, from Democritus to Kant', *Journal of the History of Ideas* 73 (2012), 371–93.

ocular authority in shaping the development of the poem's actions. Venus' sight both creates and challenges the poem's central inversion of gender roles, as Venus' penetrating gaze embodies the full force of her ocular power, ultimately resulting in Adonis' death.

Attention to the function of eyes allows for new insights into Shakespeare's poem, drawing from multiple disciplines, including early modern optical theory, theories of vision and sight, the history of fascination, and the complex intersections of gender and emotions via the prism of the gaze. References to the eyes occur over fifty times in the poem, and throughout the poem imply that Venus' gaze possesses the power to manipulate and alter Adonis' bodily responses. The poem's visual language shows how Venus employs an occult technique of *fascinum*, dominating and controlling Adonis' bodily actions and reactions through her mesmerizing gaze.[3] Venus' gaze enables her to exercise her power and influence over Adonis, shaping the dynamics of their interaction in a way that propels the gender inversion forward.

Early modern scholars have analysed how the poem operates within a conventional Petrarchan framework in which stereotypical gender roles and dynamics are reversed.[4] Peter Hyland, for instance, shows how Venus' assertiveness challenges Elizabethan Petrarchan stereotypes but acknowledges that her character still embodies both maternal and erotic aspects. According to Hyland, 'if there is anything threatening to be found in the Petrarchan gaze it surely derives from the conventions, and not from the way in which Venus is using them'.[5] Rather than limiting my study to an examination of Venus' use of rhetoric and language, my argument centres on an unspoken act – her gaze. My approach differs from that of previous critics by centring the ways in which the power dynamics or potential threats within the Petrarchan gaze are not solely derived from rhetorical conventions but also from the unspoken, nonverbal aspects. For example, I look at instances in which Venus' gaze becomes a destructive force as the poem progresses.[6] Venus demands Adonis look at her 'eyeballs' (119) after he tries consistently to avoid looking at her but fails to do so. From the description of how Venus' 'fiery eyes blaze forth her wrong' (219), because Adonis refuses to give in to her desire, to her eyes becoming 'petitioners' (356) and undergoing a transformation in which they seem to demand that Adonis yield, I argue that the specific mechanisms by which Venus uses her gaze are instrumental to the poem's gender inversion of power dynamics.[7]

Venus and Adonis invokes sight and vision both to establish and to subvert gender-based power dynamics, especially when enacted by Venus' distinctively feminine gaze. As a concept, *fascinum* not only embodies Venus' erotic desire and attraction to Adonis but also encompasses the resistance experienced by him, establishing a framework of power dynamics between them. *Fascinum* has long had negative connotations, particularly related to emotions such as envy and anger. Francis Bacon, for instance, defined 'Fascination' as 'the power and act of imagination intensive upon other bodies'.[8] *Fascinum* is then centred on the mental

---

[3] For instance, Sergei Lobanov-Rostovsky compares the depictions of the intense gaze found in Petrarchan love poetry with the anatomist's introspective capacity to explore the depths of the eye itself. See Lobanov-Rostovsky, 'Taming the basilisk', in *The Body in Parts: Fantasies of Corporeality in Early Modern Europe*, ed. David Hillman and Carla Mazzio (New York, 2013), 195–217.

[4] On gender inversion of the Petrarchan gender roles in Shakespeare's *Venus*, see the introductory chapter in Maurice Evans, *William Shakespeare: The Narrative Poems* (London, 1989), 1–24; Lynn Enterline, 'Psychoanalytic criticisms. Reading: *Venus and Adonis*', in *Shakespeare: An Oxford Guide*, ed. Stanley Wells and Lena Cowen Orlin (Oxford, 2003), 463–71.

[5] Peter Hyland, '*Venus and Adonis*', in *An Introduction to Shakespeare's Poems* (London, 2003), 67–95; p. 87.

[6] On the complex history of Petrarchism and its counterdiscourses, see Heather Dubrow, *Echoes of Desire: English Petrarchism and Its Counterdiscourses* (Ithaca, 1995).

[7] On poetry and its extensive references to the eyes, see Louise Vinge, *The Five Senses: Studies in a Literary Tradition* (Lund, 1975), pp. 71–103; Stuart Clark, *Vanities of the Eye: Vision in Early Modern European Culture* (Oxford, 2007), pp. 22–3.

[8] Francis Bacon, *The Advancement of Learning and The New Atlantis*, ed. Arthur Johnston (Oxford, 1974), p. 115.

projection of one's thoughts, desires and imagination onto something or someone, potentially affecting or influencing those external entities.⁹ Therefore, sight emerges as a significant power in Shakespeare's poem, intricately linked with early modern physiological beliefs concerning the ocular power of *fascinum* (also recognized as the 'evil eye').¹⁰ In early modern understanding, the power of sight thus allows the eyes to influence another person's bodily humoral balance, essentially functioning as a form of hypnosis capable of altering both psychological and physiological responses to cause harm.¹¹ Adonis, the object of Venus' desires, directly experiences this ocular phenomenon. When Venus sees Adonis' lifeless body killed by a boar at the end of the poem, the narrator says: 'Which seen, her eyes, as murdered with the view, / Like stars ashamed of day, themselves withdrew' (1031–2). I contend that the personification of Venus' eyes as being themselves 'murdered with the view' – wounded by the sight of his corpse – draws a powerful parallel between her intense desire for him and the consequences of that desire.

Fascinum has long been linked to women, as people from antiquity onwards believed women possessed the ability to inflict harm through their evil eye.¹² As Sibylle Baumbach points out, 'fascination is highly gendered', and 'narratives of fascination often revolve around an archetype of dangerous female seduction, which also comprises the figure of Medusa: the femme fatale'.¹³ As a goddess of love, Venus has immense power and capacity to use *fascinum* as a potentially destructive force. Jacques Lacan writes: 'The evil eye is the *fascinum*; it is that which has the effect of arresting movement and, literally, of killing life.'¹⁴ Venus' gaze – 'murdered with the view' – experiences the powerful reflection of its own *fascinum*. Venus, being a goddess, strategically employs her gaze, her *fascinum*, as a mechanism contributing to the gender inversion within the poem. A. D. Cousins argues that the Petrarchan language employed by Venus in the poem goes beyond a simple analogy, leading to a form of gender reversal, and that Venus' characteristics become associated with 'a primarily male, human love psychology'.¹⁵ While Cousins emphasizes the role of Petrarchan language in shaping such dynamics within the poem, my analysis of Venus' strategic use of *fascinum* not only highlights her control over Adonis but also emphasizes her divine authority. Such a dynamic elevates Venus above the stereotypical portrayal of women as passive, idealized objects of desire, a common theme in Petrarchan poetry. The poem characterizes Venus as infatuated with Adonis, and her desires are consistently described as overpowering and captivating. Even though Venus attempts to seduce Adonis as she lies besides him early in the poem, Adonis remains 'red for shame, but frosty in desire' (36), failing to reciprocate Venus' passion. After explaining to Adonis that even the 'god of war' yielded to her

---

⁹ See Doina-Cristina Rusu, 'Fascination and action at a distance in Francis Bacon', *Early Science and Medicine* 27 (2022), 403–25; p. 406.

¹⁰ Frederick Thomas Elworthy's book, *The Evil Eye: An Account of This Ancient and Widespread Superstition* (London, 1895), stands as one of the earliest studies on the subject. For a more recent and comprehensive exploration, see John H. Elliott's *Beware the Evil Eye: The Evil Eye in the Bible and the Ancient World*, 4 vols. (Eugene, OR, 2017).

¹¹ On the damaging effect of the eye, see Alan Dundes, ed., *The Evil Eye: A Casebook* (Madison, 1992).

¹² Helmut Schoeck, 'The evil eye: forms and dynamics of a universal superstition', in *The Evil Eye*, ed. Dundes, 192–200; p. 196.

¹³ Sibylle Baumbach, *Literature and Fascination* (Basingstoke, 2015), pp. 43, 114. Baumbach provides a comprehensive study of the history of fascination in the early modern period. On female fascination, see especially the chapter 'Facing the Femme fatale: the poetics of seduction and the fascination with storytelling', 114–47.

¹⁴ Jacques Lacan, *The Four Fundamental Concepts of Psychoanalysis*, trans. Alan Sheridan, ed. Jacques-Alains Miller (New York and London, 1977), pp. 116–17. On Lacanian analysis of Shakespeare's *Venus*, see James Schiffer, 'Shakespeare's *Venus and Adonis*: a Lacanian tragicomedy of desire', in *Venus and Adonis: Critical Essays*, ed. Philip C. Kolin (New York, 1997), 359–76; Catherine Belsey, 'Love as trompe-l'oeil: taxonomies of desire in *Venus and Adonis*', *Shakespeare Quarterly* 46 (1995), 257–76.

¹⁵ A. D. Cousins, 'Venus reconsidered: the goddess of love in *Venus and Adonis*', *Studia Neophilologica* 66 (1994), 197–207; p. 203.

commands, Venus demands that Adonis look her in the eyes, saying: 'What seest thou in the ground? Hold up thy head. / Look in mine eyeballs: there thy beauty lies' (118–19). In this moment, Venus not only asserts her power over his perception of beauty, but also demands that Adonis meet her gaze. Adonis' reluctance to meet her eyes suggests his continued attempt to control not only his physical state but also his emotions and, especially, his sexual desire.[16]

Venus' gaze serves as a powerful driver of the poem's narrative, functioning as a symbol of desire, power and self-reflection that affects Adonis' choices, embodying both her desires and his resistance. Venus is aware of the mesmerizing power her eyes possess, and she believes that gazing into them could entice Adonis to yield to her temptations. While this aligns with the poetic and seductive nature of the gaze within the Petrarchan tradition, the physiological dimension evident in Venus' insistence that Adonis looks at her is unique to Shakespeare's poem.[17] Venus' gesture alludes to this Petrarchan tradition while simultaneously departing from it by using her eyes as a method of control over Adonis. As Pablo Maurette highlights, many distinctive features of Petrarchism, such as *occhi* (eyes), *viso* (face), *raggio* (ray) and *sguardo* (gaze), 'reveal a deep-seated visual fixation'.[18] If Adonis were to look into Venus' eyes and see his own beauty reflected, it might ignite his body's 'heat' (195), as he later mentions in the poem, affecting his bodily reactions. Venus' eyes thus serve as a synecdochical organ, functioning as a mirror in which Adonis can examine his own reflection.[19] They represent not only her physical body but also her attraction and eroticism emitting rays towards Adonis, which she hopes he will perceive as he receives her gaze.

When Venus insists that Adonis look at her, she essentially forces him to engage with her mesmerizing gaze in a way that is comparable to a metaphorical and forceful violation of his autonomy. Venus claims that eyes can also figuratively kiss each other like lips do: 'Then why not lips on lips, since eyes in eyes?' (120). Eye contact creates an intimate and sexual bond, as locking eyes resemble kissing lips. While Richard Rambuss questions interpretations of *Venus and Adonis* that challenge gender stereotypes using terms like 'Inversion, subversion, reversal, androgyny, effeminacy', arguing that they limit reading the poem as an early modern erotic piece, I emphasize the complexities of how Venus' gaze retains its erotic nature.[20] The eyes also possess phallic characteristics, a form of ocular dominance that has historically been gendered male; Venus possessing an erotic gaze inverts power dynamics.[21] Because the phenomenon of fascination inherently carries gender connotations, Venus' erotized ocular gaze plays a dual role in both creating and challenging stereotypical ideas of gender, propelling the poem's inversion, which, in turn, contributes to Adonis' psychological distress and eventual death.

Venus' ocular authority, characterized by its intensity and eroticization, affects Adonis' physical and physiological state, leading to changes in his overall condition and emotional responses. Even though Adonis restrains himself from looking at Venus, his eyes reflect his vulnerability as he

---

[16] See Richard Halpern who examines Adonis' indifference to Venus as a form of sexual impotence, an irony targeted more at Venus than Adonis, in '"Pining their maws": female readers and the erotic ontology of the text in Shakespeare's *Venus and Adonis*', in *Critical Essays*, ed. Kolin, 377–88.

[17] On the Petrarchan tradition and Shakespeare's *Venus*, which both incorporates and challenges this tradition, see Pablo Maurette, 'Shakespeare's *Venus and Adonis* and sixteenth-century kiss poetry', *English Literary Renaissance* 47 (2017), 355–79; Gordon Braden, 'Shakespeare's Petrarchism', in *Shakespeare's Sonnets: Critical Essays*, ed. James Schiffer (New York, 1999), 163–83.

[18] Maurette, 'Shakespeare's *Venus and Adonis*', p. 364.

[19] On the connection between rhetoric and cognition in Shakespeare's dramatic characterization of his characters, see Raphael Lyne, *Shakespeare, Rhetoric and Cognition* (Cambridge, 2011).

[20] Richard Rambuss, 'What it feels like for a boy: Shakespeare's *Venus and Adonis*', in *A Companion to Shakespeare's Works: The Poems, Problem Comedies, Late Plays*, ed. Jean E. Howard and Richard Dutton (Oxford, 2005), 240–58; p. 242.

[21] On ocular 'phallocentrism' in the ancient world, see Catherine Johns, *Sex or Symbol: Erotic Images of Greece and Rome* (London, 1982), pp. 61–7; David Fredrick, *The Roman Gaze: Vision, Power, and the Body* (Baltimore, 2002).

continues to defy her attempts at controlling him, and his language suggests he is acutely aware of the effect of her gaze upon his body. After Venus confesses her love and tries to convince him to reciprocate her feelings, the narrator informs us that Adonis' eyes become 'heavy, dark, disliking' (182), and he wants Venus to stop confessing her love to him, saying that the sun 'doth burn my face; I must remove' (186). Even though distancing himself from Venus does not provide any relief, Adonis makes a distinction between the sun's heat and Venus' eyes, creating a sun-like intensity that is more powerful:

> And, lo, I lie between that sun and thee.
> The heat I have from thence doth little harm;
> Thine eye darts forth the fire that burneth me
> (194–6)

It is Venus' eyes that have the power to harm him, and within the intensity of her gaze, he feels the burn on his skin.[22] Venus' ocular beams become a literal source of heat that ignites a fire within him. Her eyes seem to emit fire towards him, reminiscent of beliefs from antiquity and early modern optical theory, in which the eye was thought to project a beam rather than merely receiving light.[23] The human eye then was not merely seen as a passive receiver of light but was thought to project a focused beam of vision, much like a *camera obscura*; Venus' eyes function similarly as she projects her own desires onto Adonis.[24] This retinal projection, in turn, magnifies her erotic feelings and influences Adonis' affective reactions as we have seen.

Adonis' relentless efforts to avert his gaze from Venus represent a resistance to her visual domination, yet what I term the gendered ocular power of Venus' vision eventually affects Adonis' psychological state nonetheless. When Adonis attempts to move away from Venus, he 'struggles' (227) as she 'locks her lily fingers one in one' (228). Once he escapes her arms, Adonis' horse catches the sight of a female horse. The horse scene, as observed by A. D. Cousins, establishes the conventional power dynamics of the gaze that the poem works so frequently to subvert. Cousins notes that Venus is strategic in using language to create a scenario that stimulates Adonis both visually and sexually as she 'puts before [Adonis] an image of the male gaze and of a consequent intent to enact its sexual power'.[25] However, Venus' gaze not only creates but actively shapes and influences the narrative's unconventional power dynamics. When Adonis' horse sees the female horse, as the narrator describes, 'His eye, which scornfully glisters like fire, / Shows his hot courage, and his high desire' (275–6). The imagery of Venus' eyes, earlier described as emitting fire, is echoed in the description of the horse's eyes. For nine stanzas, the horse becomes what Venus wishes Adonis to be, and Shakespeare's narration of the horse reinforces the conventional gender dynamics that Venus inverts in the main actions of the poem.[26] When Adonis' horse runs after the female one, Adonis sits angrily and attempts again to resist Venus when she reapproaches him:

> He sees her coming, and begins to glow,
> Even as a dying coal revives with wind,

---

[22] Adonis' reference to Venus' eyes creating the sun also illustrates the impact of a sun-like intensity on his skin and its relevance to early modern racecraft. On the racial implications of sun exposure on skin complexions, see Kim F. Hall, *Things of Darkness: Economies of Race and Gender in Early Modern England* (Ithaca, 1995), pp. 62–122.

[23] David C. Lindberg, *Theories of Vision from al-Kindi to Kepler* (Chicago, 1976), pp. 3–6; Eric F. Langley, 'Anatomizing the early-modern eye: a literary case-study', *Renaissance Studies* 20 (2006), 340–55.

[24] On themes of visual perception through the figure of Narcissus in Shakespeare's *Venus*, see Eric Langley, '"And died to kiss his shadow": the narcissistic gaze in Shakespeare's *Venus and Adonis*', *Forum for Modern Language Studies* 44 (2008), 12–26. See also Wendy Beth Hyman, '"Beyond beyond": *Cymbeline*, the camera obscura, and the ontology of elsewhere', *English Literary Renaissance* 52 (2022), 397–412; Anne-Valérie Dulac, 'Shakespeare's Alhazen: *Love's Labors Lost* and the history of optics', in *Spectacular Science, Technology, and Superstition in the Age of Shakespeare*, ed. Sophie Chiari and Mickaël Popelard (Edinburgh, 2017), 133–46.

[25] A. D. Cousins, *Shakespeare's Sonnets and Narrative Poems* (Routledge, 2014), p. 34.

[26] On Petrarchanism and Petrarchan love conventions, see Gordon Braden, *Petrarchan Love and the Continental Renaissance* (New Haven, 1999); Peter Hainsworth, *The Essential Petrarch* (Indianapolis, 2010).

And with his bonnet hides his angry brow,
Looks on the dull earth with disturbèd mind,
Taking no notice that she is so nigh,
For all askance he holds her in his eye.

(337–42)

This simile compares Adonis' physical reaction to that of a 'dying coal', only inflamed by Venus approaching him. Like his body being ignited by fire earlier, the physical proximity of Venus causes Adonis to blaze once again, for, as Baumbach notes, 'in narratives of fascination, the tension of proximity and distance is central for achieving the desired push and pull effect'.[27] Narratives of fascination often rely on a dynamic of bringing the object of fascination closer. In this case, Venus' proximity to Adonis elicits a powerful response. While he decides to control his conflicted emotions by concealing his bodily reactions under his bonnet, Adonis' body grows heated again as she approaches him. His strategy of averting his eyes to the 'dull earth' reveals his internal turmoil, as his 'disturbèd' mind reflects his unsettled emotions in response to Venus' proximity. Adonis' attempt to 'hold her in his eye' suggests that he is attempting to fix or capture her image in his field of vision. Instead, Adonis, with a certain degree of curiosity, observes Venus without engaging in a direct, confrontational gaze.

When Venus and Adonis eventually gaze into each other's eyes, their visual exchange reflects a complex power struggle characterized by both attraction and resistance. So far in the poem, we have seen how Venus' use of *fascinum* has altered Adonis' bodily and affective reactions, despite his resistance from looking into her eyes. This dynamic, however, significantly changes when Venus' earlier plea for meeting 'eyes in eyes' (120) is granted, and Adonis gives in and looks at her. As Venus approaches Adonis, she kneels in front of him and removes his bonnet as they look into each other's eyes. Adonis' defiance continues as he attempts to reject Venus, but when they gaze upon one another their physical proximity instantiates their nonverbal communication:

O, what a war of looks was then between them,
Her eyes petitioners to his eyes suing!

His eyes saw her eyes as they had not seen them;
Her eyes wooed still; his eyes disdained the wooing;
And all this dumb play had his acts made plain
With tears which, chorus-like, her eyes did rain.

(355–60)

The word 'eyes' is used seven times in this stanza, more than any other stanza in the poem, to emphasize the crucial role of sight in the physical encounter between Venus and Adonis. Through the descriptions of their eyes, the poem breaks down the emotional barriers separating Venus and Adonis as they engage in an intense stare. As Eric Langley observes, the 'war of looks' in this stanza describes 'two contrary modes of perception, as Adonis refuses to enter into the extramissive give and take but rather introspects and withdraws'.[28] For Langley, 'Adonis associates himself with intromissive theories of vision which rely upon division between subject and object.'[29] While I agree to some extent with Langley's analysis, the dynamic between Adonis and Venus also shifts, as the personification of 'looks' and 'eyes' illustrates how Adonis' earlier desire in the poem to avert looking at Venus' eyes has failed, leading him to give in to Venus' earlier demand to 'Look in mine eyeballs' (119). Although Adonis eventually looks into her eyes, he simultaneously attempts to resist Venus through his 'disdain[ing]' eyes. Venus' attraction and Adonis' resistance reflect the power of fascination as Baumbach notes that fascination can be achieved through 'intense power of attraction and repulsion.'[30] The tears shed from Venus' eyes are echoed in Adonis' 'disdain[ing]' look, which signifies Adonis' continued attempt at resisting her. While Langley presumes a stable subject/object relation, the dynamic between Adonis and Venus is more complex and shifting than Langley suggests. The use of the phrase 'war of looks' in this context suggests that their visual exchange goes beyond a simple exchange of glances. It

---

[27] Baumbach, *Literature and Fascination*, p. 31.
[28] Langley, 'And died to kiss', p. 15.
[29] Langley, 'And died to kiss', p. 15.
[30] Baumbach, *Literature and Fascination*, p. 68.

underscores the active, emotionally charged nature of what can unfold through the power of the gaze.

The physical closeness of Venus and Adonis not only amplifies the dynamic interplay between them but also draws the reader into the poem's narrative, allowing us to experience the anticipated eye-to-eye interaction. As we engage with the poem, we find our gaze captivated by the visual exchange between them, intensifying the tension between Venus' ocular power and Adonis' resistance.[31] Through the presence of the poem's narrator, who assumes the role of a spectator – or reader – trying to decipher the pair's gazes, discerning their 'war of looks' and the responses of both Venus and Adonis, readers gain insight into the intricate dynamics between Venus and Adonis. Narratives of fascination, according to Baumbach, incorporate several elements, not just limited to the gaze, including narrative structure and pacing.[32] Readers patiently endure over 300 lines before the eye-to-eye interaction between Adonis and Venus takes place. As Maurette points out, not only does each stanza, with its rhythmic sextet and ending rhyming couplets, 'make one dwell and linger in each stanza before passing on to the next', but Venus' intense desire to kiss Adonis also 'functions as a strategy of delay'.[33] The awaited 'war of looks' between Adonis and Venus also showcases the deliberate narrative pacing that is characteristic of *fascinum*. This pacing involves readers in the conflicting forces of attraction and resistance, drawing them deeper into the text while also prolonging the narrative.

Venus' ocular power proves essential in captivating Adonis and exerting dominance over him; without her sight, she would be unable to employ that level of control. She now contends, however, that even in the absence of the ability to see or hear Adonis, her love for him would still have been ignited through touch: 'Though neither eyes nor ears to hear nor see, / Yet should I be in love by touching thee' (437–8). Venus' words illustrate a resurgence of scepticism about sensory experience in the early modern era (a revival of ancient Greek philosophical thought). As Ian Smith notes, the prevailing philosophical traditions of the Renaissance emphasized doubt, particularly challenging the reliability of sensory evidence, especially that which came through visual perception.[34] Historians of science argue that medieval and Renaissance philosophers inherited from antiquity the well-established notion that, in certain situations, all senses can be misleading and may require correction by reason.[35] Among the senses, sight was often deemed the most crucial for acquiring knowledge, and Shakespeare's poem shows how interpreting the gaze presented a complex, and potentially risky, task.[36] Venus' attraction to Adonis strongly ties to the visual aspect of his beauty, to the extent that when she sees him at the beginning of the poem, she declares him 'Thrice fairer than myself' (7), highlighting the sensory nature of her infatuation.

As I have established, metaphors of sight in the poem signify the profound connections between the visual exchange of Venus and Adonis and

---

[31] Chantelle Thauvette points out that Adonis' non-arousal towards Venus shows his power in controlling his physical desires, contrary to the humoral theories of women's supposed lack of such control. See Thauvette, 'Defining early modern pornography: the case of *Venus and Adonis*', *Journal for Early Modern Cultural Studies* 12 (2012), 26–48; p. 42.

[32] Baumbach, *Literature and Fascination*, p. 68.

[33] Maurette, 'Shakespeare's *Venus and Adonis*', pp. 370, 358.

[34] See Ian Smith, 'Racial blind spots: misreading bodies, misreading texts', in *Black Shakespeare: Reading and Misreading Race* (Cambridge, 2022), 53–78; p. 56; Michael Squire, *Sight and the Ancient Senses* (New York, 2015); Mark A. Smith, *From Sight to Light: The Passage from Ancient to Modern Optics* (Chicago, 2019).

[35] David C. Lindberg and Nicholas H. Steneck, 'The sense of vision and the origins of modern science', in *Science, Medicine and Society in the Renaissance: Essays to Honour Walter Pagel*, ed. Allen G. Debus, vol. 1 (New York, 1972), 29–45.

[36] Martin Porter acknowledges the complexity of eye interpretations: 'eyes ... more than any other physical feature, refuse the sort of simple synthesis'. See Porter, *Windows of the Soul: Physiognomy in European Culture 1470–1780* (Oxford, 2005), p. 176. On theories of vision and sight in the Renaissance, see Robert S. Nelson, *Visuality Before and Beyond the Renaissance* (Cambridge, 2000); John Shannon Hendrix and Charles H. Carman, *Renaissance Theories of Vision* (New York, 2016).

their emotions, but sight becomes erotically charged when both lock their eyes. After the pair kiss and Venus opens her eyes, the narrator describes their connected gazes as if they have engaged in a sexual act, with their eyes penetrating each other's bodies: 'Were never four such lamps together mixed, / Had not his clouded with his brow's repine' (489–90). The description of the eyes as 'lamps' aligns with early modern optical theories of how light interacts with surfaces, where the eyes play an active role in the visual process. The comparison of the eyes with 'lamps' shows how, for early moderns, the mechanics of human vision was not limited solely to anatomical components. Instead, the human body's capacity for sight can also be demonstrated or recreated through technologies. As Michael Squire points out, for Kepler and Descartes, 'the science of seeing could not only be explained in relation to the pupil-lens and screen-like retina but also be re-enacted in technological turn'.[37] Like lamps emitting light, the light shines forth from Venus and Adonis' eyes, enabling them to see each other, capturing and processing their visual exchange. I have argued that a more complex meaning also surfaces, particularly within the framework of their erotic exchange. However, Adonis remains reluctant: 'Had not his clouded with his brow's repine; / But hers, which through the crystal tears gave light' (490–1). He experiences erotic suffering, as indicated by the furrowed brow, which momentarily dims the brightness of his gaze – a subtle resistance to Venus' advances.

Venus' gaze thus serves a dual emissive function: conveying her emotions and desires, while simultaneously deceiving Adonis, as her ocular power manipulates his bodily reactions. So far in the poem, Venus has succeeded in controlling Adonis, bending him to her will. Her visual enchantment has influenced his physiological responses in ways I have charted throughout this article. After the kiss, Adonis articulates the idea that a single glance can destroy him. He notes that Venus has figuratively 'killed' him once again, foreshadowing his death at the end of the poem (and I return here to the stanza with which I opened this article):

> 'O, thou didst kill me; kill me once again!
> Thy eyes' shrewd tutor, that hard heart of thine,
> Hath taught them scornful tricks, and such disdain
> That they have murdered this poor heart of mine,
> And these mine eyes, true leaders to their queen,
> But for thy piteous lips no more had seen.
>
> (499–504)

When Adonis refers to Venus' eyes as 'shrewd', he employs a term associated with women's trickery, which he here uses in recognition of the fact that her eyes deploy an ocular enchantment for controlling him. Throughout the first half of the poem, Adonis struggles to interpret the way that Venus uses her sight as well as her true intentions, because she deploys her *fascinum* as a mechanism to control his bodily and affective reactions. Thus, Adonis indirectly characterizes Venus as a goddess who challenges his authority through her powerful gaze, attempting to assert dominance over him. But, as the poem progresses, Adonis comes to understand that Venus' eyes perceive a deceptive character, figuring her as a fascinating woman who has manipulated him into submitting to her. Adonis' eyes also reflect his own self-loathing, as his eyes, which he thought were the most logical part of him, disobeyed him. For Adonis, reading Venus' eyes becomes a difficult task because her true inner self is obstructed by her mesmerizing gaze. Venus' eyes trick him when he gazes at her lips and makes him unable to resist her. She continues to kiss him, even when Adonis explains they must part as nighttime approaches. As she kisses him, the narrator describes 'Her lips conquerors, his lips obey, / Paying what ransom the insulter willeth' (549–50), while Adonis remains 'Hot, faint, and weary with hard embracing' (559). Adonis' surrendering to Venus illustrates that her *fascinum* has worked, as the word 'obey' is echoed

---

[37] Squire, *Sight and the Ancient Senses*, p. 19; Lindberg, *Theories of Vision*, p. 202. On the history of Renaissance vision, see Vincent Ilardi, *Renaissance Vision from Spectacles to Telescopes* (Philadelphia, 2007).

again in the next couple of lines: 'He now obeys, and now no more resisteth' (563). Venus' captivating gaze demonstrates how her *fascinum* draws him towards her desires. Her gaze makes Adonis obedient and unable to resist her, leading to his ultimate submission to her powers.

The interactions between Venus and Adonis, particularly Adonis yielding to Venus' enchantment and their separation in the dark night in the middle of the poem, symbolically foreshadow Adonis' demise. Once Venus decides to let Adonis go, Adonis tells her that he cannot meet with her the following day because he wants to hunt a boar. For over twenty-one stanzas, Venus tries to convince him to not hunt. When Adonis eventually leaves, Venus attempts to run after him, but 'the merciless and pitchy night / Fold in the object that did feed her sight' (821–2). Shakespeare's use of 'merciless' and 'pitchy' night creates a stark contrast between light and darkness. While the absence of light during the pitch-black night may indeed impair Venus' ability to see Adonis (and thus to exercise her powers of fascination), it also symbolically foreshadows his impending death. The night 'Fold[ing] in' the object that fed into Venus' sight highlights how vision relies on external sources of light to illuminate objects for perception. Venus is likewise enveloped in the darkness of the poem's tragedy as the night metaphorically 'Fold[s] in' the object of her affection, Adonis. As readers, we also lose sight of Adonis who no longer is present in the poem's narrative. Like Venus, we are left uncertain of Adonis' fate.

While Adonis is initially captivated by Venus' *fascinum*, his resistance throughout the poem and subsequent separation in the night mark a transformation in their relationship that will ultimately culminate in Adonis' tragic death. When Venus pretends to faint, the narrator informs us about sight as an immense power that possesses the ability to either kill or rekindle one's affection: 'For looks kill love, and love by looks reviveth' (464). This line is fundamental to what I have shown to be the poem's study of the impact of sight within Shakespeare's narrative. His use of chiasmus underscores the idea of a mutual gaze, where each character sees themselves reflected in the other. The depth of Adonis' tragedy lies not solely in its symbolic implications but also in the grim reality of his physical death. Adonis is initially drawn in by Venus' ocular power, but his resistance throughout the poem creates a dynamic in which he is both pulled in and pushed away from her. His death, signifying the end of their 'war of looks' (355), marks the conclusion of this complex interaction.

Venus' witnessing of Adonis' death at the end of the poem intensifies her *fascinum* – a pivotal moment that amplifies the emotional turmoil wrought through sight. The gaze that she has so powerfully used to manipulate Adonis now holds no power to resurrect him: 'Where they resign their office and their light / To the disposing of her troubled brain' (1039–40). Unable to revive him, Venus' eyes now turn inward to her own disturbed mind, disrupting her inner self. The function of Venus' gaze then undergoes a significant metamorphosis as the poem unfolds. The narrator depicts the visual impact when Venus sees Adonis' body: 'Upon his hurt, she looks so steadfastly, / Her sight, dazzling, makes the wound seem three' (1063–4). Venus' emotions upon witnessing Adonis wounded underscore the transformative yet also powerless nature of her gaze. Now, her gaze is turned inward, inflicting harm upon herself. This metamorphosis reveals the profound transformation that takes place within her gendered ocular authority when Venus expresses her loss at Adonis' death, saying: 'Mine eyes are turned to fire, my heart to lead. / Heavy heart's lead, melt at mine eyes' red fire' (1072–3). Venus undergoes a metamorphosis, as the 'fiery eyes' that 'blaze forth her wrong' (219) at the beginning of the poem not only consume Adonis but, by the end of the poem, transform from an outward-looking and harmful influence on Adonis to an inward-looking gaze that reflects Venus' own pain.

As the poem nears its end, Venus attempts to revive Adonis by opening his eyelids but ultimately fails, as she can no longer see her own reflection within:

> She lifts the coffer-lids that close his eyes,
> Where, lo, two lamps, burnt out, in darkness lies;
>
> Two glasses, where herself herself beheld
> A thousand times, and now no more reflect
>
> (1127–30)

Venus' attempt to lift Adonis' eyelids shows how she wants to reignite the power of her gaze and revive the influence and power she once held over him. When Adonis was alive, and both gazed into each other's eyes, their eyes were compared to lamps emitting light. Now, however, Adonis' eyes are burnt out. The sight he once tried to avoid has ultimately contributed to his death, and his lifeless eyes can no longer reflect Venus' gaze. Venus' mesmerizing gaze is no longer mirrored by Adonis. The contrast between Adonis' 'burnt' eyes and Venus' desire to see her reflection in them underscores the irony of the situation. While Venus previously captivated Adonis through her gaze, the eyes in which she seeks her reflection are now lifeless.

Even though Venus cannot revive Adonis, Venus' ocular power and its influence reach their peak with Adonis' demise, and the intensified emotions surrounding his death empower her to wield her gaze once again, completing his metamorphosis. Adonis transforms to a 'purple flower' with the narrator saying: 'By this, the boy that by her side lay killed / Was melted like a vapour from her sight' (1165–6). Scholars have debated Venus' role in transforming Adonis at the end of the poem. Anthony Mortimer reads Adonis' metamorphosis 'as a natural miracle which owes nothing to the intentions or powers of the goddess'.[38] However, Tita French Baumlin asserts that Venus' language 'has the power to change the course of human love and to transform Adonis's flowing blood into an anemone'.[39] I argue that it is the transformative power of her vision that manifests both internally and externally at the poem's end, intensifying her ocular power as Adonis transforms into a flower through the power of her gaze, 'melted like a vapour from her sight'. Beyond Venus' language and rhetoric in the poem, it is through and 'from' Venus' 'sight', I argue, that she can alter Adonis' physical state. As Adonis transforms into a flower, Venus' penetrating gaze once more demonstrates the force of her ocular power.

Attention to sight and vision, I have suggested, reveals how Venus uses *fascinum* as a method of control in Shakespeare's *Venus and Adonis*. This attention to *fascinum* reveals a complex narrative woven through the visual poetic language and metaphors of sight. The poem's frequent references to Venus' gendered gaze as a powerful force underscore its significant role in navigating the complex dynamic between Venus and Adonis. In this intricate interplay, a profound shift occurs in Adonis' material embodiment, as his psychological and physiological states undergo a transformative process under the spell of Venus' gendered practice of *fascinum*. With careful consideration of how the poem uses sight to convey meaning – whether through spoken language or nonverbal embodied communication – I move beyond the conventional Petrarchan approach to challenge our understanding of how ocular narrative techniques shape Venus and Adonis' narrative. From optical theory to the intricate intersections of gender and emotions, my examination of the eyes in Shakespeare's *Venus and Adonis* uncovers the multidimensional implications of analysing sight in this poem. Power dynamics, emotions and gendered fascination converge in the eyes of Venus and Adonis. The

---

[38] See Anthony Mortimer, 'The ending of *Venus and Adonis*', *English Studies* 78 (1997), 334–66; p. 336.

[39] Tita French Baumlin, 'The birth of the bard: *Venus and Adonis* and poetic apotheosis', *Papers on Language and Literature* 26 (1990), 191–211; p. 205. For further readings on Adonis' transformation into a flower, see Pauline Kiernan, 'Death by rhetorical trope: poetry metamorphosed in *Venus and Adonis* and the Sonnets', *The Review of English Studies* 46 (1995), 475–501; Clark S. Hulse, 'Shakespeare's myth of *Venus and Adonis*', *PMLA* 93 (1978), 95–105; Sarah Carter, '"With kissing him I should have killed him first": death in Ovid and Shakespeare's *Venus and Adonis*', *Early Modern Literary Studies* 18 (2015), 1–13.

poem itself becomes a lens through which these intersections are focused, immersing the reader in the complexities of the narrative and the characters' emotions through their gazes. Venus' gaze seizes, captivates and manipulates Adonis' affective responses, culminating in his physical demise by the end of the poem. By gazing through the eyes of Venus and Adonis, Shakespeare's poem itself operates as a kind of *camera obscura*, projecting a reversal of gender power dynamics by revealing the compelling influence of the female gaze and the powers of *fascinum* within its narrative.

PRETTY CREATURES: *A LOVER'S COMPLAINT*, *THE RAPE OF LUCRECE* AND EARLY MODERN WOMEN'S COMPLAINT POETRY

SARAH C. E. ROSS

A pretty while these pretty creatures stand,
Like ivory conduits coral cisterns filling.
One justly weeps, the other takes in hand
No cause but company of her drops' spilling.
Their gentle sex to weep are often willing,
Grieving themselves to guess at others' smarts,
And then they drown their eyes or break their hearts.

(*Lucrece* 1233–9)

At the centre of *The Rape of Lucrece*, Shakespeare positions two weeping women as a 'pretty' tableau of feminine grief. To this point in the poem, Lucrece, violated in the 'false night's abuses', has refused the silence to which Tarquin enjoined her, determining instead that her 'tongue shall utter all' and her 'eyes, like sluices... Shall gush pure streams to purge my impure tale' (1076–8). She delivers a tale of woe that typifies the 'female complaint' in its auxetic and affecting expression of loss and grief, and its recursive focus on the inexpressibility of pain even as pain is expressed. Lucrece is joined in this stanza by her maid, whose 'swift obedience' to the call of her mistress's 'untuned tongue' extends to an emotional reciprocity. Seeing that Lucrece's 'face wore sorrow's livery', the maid is 'enforced by sympathy' and her eyes are wet 'with swelling drops' until the two women together are like ivory fountains, spilling their tears before the witnessing eyes of the implicitly male speaker, who reflects upon the capacity of 'their gentle sex' to weep for each other (1214–37). Like the complaining woman in *A Lover's Complaint* – and in the 'female complaint' subgenre that was fashionable in 1590s English poetry more broadly – Lucrece performs her woe overseen and overheard by male audiences who are, variously, more and less comprehending, this poetic scenario and structure modelling reception and responses to feminine woe.

The most recent discussions of Shakespeare's 'female complaint' poems and those of his male contemporaries have largely moved from questions of the complaining woman's guilt and fame or the authorial impersonation of the feminine to the place of complaint in the early modern construction of sympathy.[1] Literary historians of emotion find in the 'female complaint' poem a form that seems first and foremost designed to move its readers. Katharine Craik describes complaint as 'a unique resource for expressing (and organizing) intense emotion' and identifies the way that 'sympathetic affect is dramatized within the fabric' of Shakespeare's *A Lover's Complaint*, as 'the maiden's double-layered audience' provides the poem's multiple narrative frames.[2] Given the 'female complaint' poem's reliance on voicing female woe,

---

[1] Foundational discussions include Heather Dubrow, 'A mirror for complaints: Shakespeare's *Lucrece* and generic tradition', in *Renaissance Genres: Essays on Theory, History, and Interpretation*, ed. Barbara Kiefer Lewalski (Cambridge, MA, 1986), 399–417; Wendy Wall, *The Imprint of Gender: Authorship and Publication in the English Renaissance* (Ithaca, 1993); Lynn Enterline, *Shakespeare's Schoolroom: Rhetoric, Discipline, Emotion* (Philadelphia, 2011).

[2] Katharine Craik, 'Poetry and compassion in Shakespeare's "A Lover's Complaint"', in *The Oxford Handbook of Shakespeare's Poetry*, ed. Jonathan F. S. Post (Oxford, 2013), p. 525.

such readings inevitably articulate gender as central to its affective structures. Richard Meek argues that in *The Rape of Lucrece* 'Shakespeare implies that female woe is more capable of feeling, and sensitive to the pain of others, than male grief.'[3] Emily Shortslef moves away from exploring 'the nature of sympathy itself' but sees the 'female complaint' poem offering up a model of ethical reading and reception that is 'distinctly feminized', 'modelled on the ideal of an especially impressionable subject ready to mirror or echo another person's demonstrable sorrow'.[4] These are sophisticated readings that relate the depiction of female woe and its sympathetic reception within the text to patterns of response beyond it. They map a concept of feminine sympathy onto the production and circulation of 'female complaint' in a way that extends Wendy Wall's influential 1990s reading of these as 'pseudomorphic' texts, the authors' impersonations underpinning the poems' authority and their reception as 'female' in a male culture of reading, reception and transmission.[5]

While gender is, then, recognized as central to the affective dynamic of Shakespearian 'female complaint' poetry, there is a persistent lacuna in analysis of what gender means in these poems' construction of it: an unwillingness to interrogate the limits of impersonation and to compare Shakespeare's complaint poems to those written by early modern women. It was long thought that only a very few 'female complaint' poems were written by women, and that women are present in the genre only as ventriloquized voices – '[i]nciting prosopopoeia in general, complaint fosters impersonation of the feminine', in the influential words of John Kerrigan.[6] Lynn Enterline has argued, compellingly, that schoolboys voicing 'female complaint' in the humanist schoolroom engaged in 'a labile transfer of feelings' that transgressed 'normative ... gender roles'; her insights destabilize the production of gender and feeling in ways that intimate the potential for trans readings of 'female complaint'.[7] But alongside this scholarship, critical studies of 'female complaint' in Mary Wroth's *Urania* sonnets and her 'Lindamira's Complaint', her aunt Mary Sidney Herbert's *Doleful Lay of Clorinda*, or the political poetry of Hester Pulter have not provoked Shakespearian critics to compare his 'female complaint' poems to women writers' engagement in the form.[8] Of Shakespeare's drama, Dympna Callaghan and others have drawn attention to the absences that the male dramatist's and actors' impersonation of the feminine inscribe, but we continue to explore Shakespeare's 'female complaint' poems as though they were produced in a wholly male-authored tradition.[9] It seems extraordinary that we still need to ask: is it possible to consider the role of gender in complaint's construction of affect and emotion without explicit consideration of women as intra- and extra-textual auditors, readers, writers, transcribers, as consumers and as creators of complaint poetry in early modern

---

[3] Richard Meek, *Sympathy in Early Modern Literature and Culture* (Cambridge, 2023), p. 125.

[4] Emily Shortslef, *The Drama of Complaint: Ethical Provocations in Shakespeare's Tragedy* (Oxford, 2023), p. 136.

[5] Wall, *The Imprint of Gender*, pp. 250–60.

[6] John Kerrigan, ed., *Motives of Woe: Shakespeare and 'Female Complaint'* (Oxford, 1991), p. 2; and see Craik, 'Poetry and compassion', p. 524.

[7] Enterline, *Shakespeare's Schoolroom*, p. 136. For the potential of early modern trans studies to extend further these considerations of gender, voice and body, see, for example, the *Journal for Early Modern Cultural Studies* 19, Special Issue: Early Modern Trans Studies (2019), including Simone Chess, Colby Gordon and Will Fisher's Introduction. Among the numerous revelatory essays in this issue, Julie Crawford's article on 'Transubstantial bodies in *Paradise Lost* and *Order and Disorder*' (75–93) also brings a trans perspective to the work of a seventeenth-century woman poet, finding in her poem the possibility for trans identity within theological and political frameworks that are not usually understood in this way.

[8] See, for example, Danielle Clarke, 'Speaking women: rhetoric and the construction of female talk', in *Rhetoric, Women and Politics in Early Modern England*, ed. Jennifer Richards and Alison Thorne (London, 2007), 70–88; Rosalind Smith, '"I thus goe arm'd to field": Lindamira's Complaint', in *Women Writing 1550–1750*, ed. Jo Wallwork and Paul Salzman (Melbourne, 2001), 73–85; Kate Chedgzoy, *Women's Writing in the British Atlantic World: Memory, Place and History, 1550–1700* (Cambridge, 2007).

[9] Dympna Callaghan, *Shakespeare Without Women: Representing Gender and Race on the Renaissance Stage* (London, 2000).

England? It also seems extraordinary that several decades of nuanced work on early modern women as writers and readers is so infrequently brought to bear on readings of Shakespeare's long poems and on their complaint constructions of gendered affect: too often, we continue to explore gender, sympathy and 'female complaint' without any reference to women and their work.

This article sets out to provide that frame of reference: to consider the limits of gendered sympathy in Shakespeare's poems, and to compare their interrogation of feminine sympathy with early modern women writers' representation of it. Over the last six years, the Early Modern Women's Complaint project I have undertaken with Rosalind Smith and Michelle O'Callaghan has identified an expanded corpus of early modern women's complaint poetry, and as the project comes to fruition, it is providing a new critical framework for discussion of 'female complaint' poetry – by Shakespeare and other male poets as well as by women.[10] Our *Early Modern Women's Complaint Poetry Index* identifies 512 complaint poems authored, transcribed, compiled or performed by women between 1530 and 1680, and our critical work on this corpus reinserts women into consideration of the mode's gendered expression, reception and circulation. My purpose in this article is not to offer a wholescale interrogation of these early modern women's complaint poems – we undertake that elsewhere – but rather to illustrate how the structures of sympathy with which Shakespeare experiments in his complaint poems, and most particularly the role of gender in them, can be understood more fully through comparative consideration of women writers' own experimentation with the form of the framed complaint poem. Shakespeare presents 'pretty creatures' as 'precedents' of intense loss and grief, but the male auditors and witnesses within his poems consistently fail to comprehend that woe or to develop true sympathy for it precisely because it is feminine – and they are not. The potential for sympathy between women is contained within Shakespeare's poems but only ever partially realized, as the poems participate in gendered structures of ekphrasis in which emotion is presented and performed for the consumption of intra- and extra-textual auditors that are distinguished from each other precisely along the lines of gender. I argue here that Shakespeare's 'female complaint' poems persistently interrogate gender as a primary criterion of sympathetic exclusion, and in doing so nuance the affiliations and differences between sympathy, compassion and pity in ways that discussions of these affective responses rarely parse. In the first half of this article, I will consider Shakespeare's *A Lover's Complaint* and then *Lucrece*, exploring the potential they suggest for 'true' sympathy between women, and their use of formal frames and ekphrasis to distance feminine woe from their implicitly male auditors and readers. The second half of this piece compares Shakespeare's framed 'female complaint' poems with those by early modern women to shed light on Shakespeare's structures of differentiation and distance, and their alternative appropriation by women poets for the sympathetic inclusion of intra- and extra-textual auditors, witnesses, respondents, co-complainers, readers and transmitters.

A LOVER'S COMPLAINT: GENDER AND THE LIMITS OF SYMPATHY

One of the clearest insights into 'female complaint' poetry in recent years is the way in which the framed form – where the complaining woman is overheard and described by an implicitly male narrator – not only centres the expression of intense feminine emotion, but models responses to that emotion and the generation of 'sympathetic affect'.[11] The 'fickle maid' (5) in *A Lover's Complaint* sits at the centre of a particularly complex set of frames: she

---

[10] The project's three main outputs are Rosalind Smith, Sarah C. E. Ross, Michelle O'Callaghan, Jake Arthur and Mitchell Whitelaw, *Early Modern Women's Complaint Poetry Index*, https://cems.anu.edu.au/complaintindex (2021); Ross and Smith, eds., *Early Modern Women's Complaint: Gender, Form, and Politics* (Cham, 2020); and Smith, Ross and O'Callaghan, *Early Modern Women and the Poetry of Complaint* (Oxford, forthcoming).

[11] Craik, 'Poetry and compassion', p. 525. I follow John Kerrigan's use of 'female complaint' for poems in the complaint mode that adopt a female voice or persona.

tells her story to a 'reverend man' (57) and this retelling is overheard by the framing narrator typical of the genre, creating a 'double-layered audience'.[12] Her 'clamours' and shrieks of 'undistinguished woe' (20–1) are the poem's centrepiece – but the justness of the maid's complaints and the appropriate readerly response to it are more uncertain, with this moral opacity enacted through the poem's open double frame. The reverend man sits down in an explicit attempt to 'assuage' (69) the maid's grief; he seeks to 'divide' (67) or share the burden of her woes, evoking the proverbial idea that 'fellowship in woe doth woe assuage', as it is articulated in *The Rape of Lucrece* (790). But once the maid begins to recount her tale, she continues to the end of the poem: the reverend man is silent. So too is the framing narrator, who offers no further comment after the opening seventy lines. These opening lines are a third-person ekphrasis, describing in detail the external actions of the maid, and once her tale is delivered through his reported speech, the poem offers no space for him to evaluate that which he initially 'desire[d] to know': 'the grounds and motives of her woe' (62–3).[13] As Craik describes, the silence of the reverend man and the framing narrator after the poem's opening 'makes compassion seem elusive, and, in turn, casts into doubt the degree of sympathy readers themselves feel for the maid's predicament'.[14]

The ambiguous evocation of sympathy in *A Lover's Complaint* is often, as in Craik's detailed analysis, attributed to – or seen to construct – the maid's dubious moral standing or her social class, but I argue here that the principal criterion for the truncations of sympathetic affect that are so marked in the poem is gender. The maid's 'clamours', the extremity of her emotion, are defining postures of the woeful woman in the complaint mode – what we term 'complaint markers' in our *Early Modern Women's Complaint Poetry Index*. Her woe is also, notably, 'undistinguished' only to the male auditors. To the 'fickle maid', its causes are intricately understood and fully documented: there are 'conceited characters' (16), favours, letters, 'folded schedules' (43) whose contents she reads, all documents that she shares with the 'flood', 'Upon whose weeping margin she was set' (44, 39). The river is a feminized and sympathetic fluvial respondent to her female woe. The reverend man's hope that 'from him there may be aught applied' (68) to assuage her grief is unrealized; but in stark contrast, the river returns her grief to her with interest added, 'Like usury applying wet to wet' (40). That the two responses turn on the same verb, a possible application of sympathetic feeling, underscores the contrast. And, like the river, the hill to which the maid cries in the opening lines of the poem also returns her grief to her: its 'concave womb' refracts and 're-word[s]' her story, so that the framing narrator hears it in an echoic 'double voice' (1–3). These feminine correspondences, rewordings and answers in the landscape to the complaining woman's woe provide a stark contrast with the framing narrator who only sees the maid's external gestures and hears the 'clamours' of her emotions, but does not comprehend their causes and is ultimately silent. The incomprehension of the unidentified narrator and the reverend man, in other words, is counterposed in the poem by a shadowy delineation of the possibilities of female sympathy, a series of doubled female voices that return the maiden's woes to her, riverine floods to her 'fluxive' tears (50).

Such possibilities for feminine response and sympathy in the landscape have been recognized in analysis of women writers' engagement in 'female complaint' and the trope of echo. The opening sonnet of Lady Mary Wroth's *Urania* is a frequently cited example, evoking the isolation of the woeful woman in the landscape but realizing more fully the potential for female sympathy suggested in *A Lover's Complaint* and other canonical

---

[12] Craik, 'Poetry and compassion', p. 525.
[13] John Kerrigan describes 'Shakespeare's almost unparalleled refusal to close the frame' (*Motives of Woe*, p. 50). See also Hannah Crawforth and Elizabeth Scott-Baumann, 'How to Make a Formal Complaint: Sara Ahmed's *Complaint!* and William Shakespeare's *A Lover's Complaint*' in this volume.
[14] Craik, 'Poetry and compassion', p. 525.

'female complaint' poems.[15] Urania begins the sonnet 'Unseene, unknowne', 'alone complain[ing] / To Rocks, to Hills, to Meadowes, and to Springs'. Her sorrows return to her in the form of an echo, increasing and doubling her woes, but as the 'monefull voice' of Echo 'second[s] me in miserie', Echo is figured as a 'companion', one who 'answere gives like friend of mine owne choice'. Echo's companionate, sympathetic response prompts Urania to voice the proverbial idea that 'those that grieve, a grieving note doe love'.[16] This echoic female response delivers the female sympathy that is a shadowy possibility in poems such as *A Lover's Complaint*; in doing so, it cuts across the central affective dynamic of male-audited and male-authored 'female complaint' poems like Shakespeare's that are defined by a masculine failure to comprehend women's woe. Wroth's opening *Urania* sonnet suggests that, if attention is turned to the female-voiced, female-audited exchanges embedded within pastoral complaints, we may see women writers taking up sympathetic paradigms and developing them with new emphases. But while these female-authored analogues are occasionally acknowledged, they are rarely afforded detailed literary analysis in discussion of male-authored poems, and so comparative insights and the possibilities of difference are not brought to bear on readings of Shakespeare's poems.[17]

It is important to note that *A Lover's Complaint* experiments in more than one way with failures of sympathy across the lines of gender. Male silence is one contrast with feminine sympathy in the poem; another is its perversion by the unscrupulous lover, who impersonates the capacities for feminine sympathy in order to seduce the maid. She describes him as 'maiden-tongued' (*LC*, 100) – pointing, I suggest, not so much to modesty or innocence in his speech as to the ways in which he crafts, duplicitously, the expression of passion and a feminine reciprocity.[18] He impresses his desires on others and seduces the maid by taking on the postures of sisterly sympathy: he has 'watr'y eyes' that shed tears, 'Each cheek a river running from a fount' (281–3), and he assumes 'burning blushes', 'weeping water' and 'swooning paleness' as disguises that 'he takes and leaves, / In either's aptness, as it best deceives' (304–6). It is through these postures of emotional reciprocity, a performed sympathy entirely at odds with his real purpose, that he convinces the maid to lend him 'soft audience' (278), to 'Have of my suffering youth some feeling pity' (178). Craik is right to observe that 'the maiden is undone by her sympathy for the young man', but I would suggest that she is undone by something more specific than the general 'hazards of compassion' or 'compassion haplessly bestowed'.[19] Rather, the maid is deceived by a crafted performance of a particularly feminine mode of sympathy, a duplicitous impersonation of the feminine in which the unscrupulous lover 'preached pure maid' (315).

THE RAPE OF LUCRECE: SYMPATHY, PITY AND EKPHRASIS

Such differentiation between male and female capacities for sympathy is also central, in different ways, to *The Rape of Lucrece*, where Lucrece's complaint is embedded in multiple structures of reception and response. Tarquin's act of sexual violence is marked by an abject lack of compassion towards the woman he abuses. The 'soft pity' (595) to which Lucrece enjoins him, her plea that he 'Melt at my tears, and be compassionate' (584), evoke those qualities of womanly sympathy which the 'fickle maid' of *A Lover's Complaint* ill-advisedly gave to her unscrupulous lover. Richard Meek has compared Tarquin's lack of compassion

---

[15] See Clarke, 'Speaking women'; and Ross, 'Complaint's echoes', in *Early Modern Women's Complaint*, ed. Ross and Smith, 183–202. This paragraph echoes my argument in that chapter.
[16] Mary Wroth, *The First Part of The Countess of Montgomery's Urania*, ed. Josephine Roberts (Binghamton, NY, 1995), lines 1–2, 6–9, 11.
[17] Shortslef acknowledges Wroth's poem (*The Drama of Complaint*, p. 135).
[18] John Roe glosses 'maiden-tounged' as 'modest or innocent in his speech' in his edition of *The Poems* (Cambridge, 2006), p. 277.
[19] See Craik, 'Poetry and compassion', p. 530.

towards the pleading Lucrece with the tableau of womanly sympathy with which I opened this article, the scene of Lucrece and her maid weeping together as 'pretty creatures'. Meek argues in this comparison that '*Lucrece* is interested in the different ways in which men and women respond to each other's suffering.'[20] Certainly, the poem, like *A Lover's Complaint*, embeds and interrogates the possibilities for feminine sympathy, but at the same time in *Lucrece* these possibilities are most often unrealized. The tears of Lucrece's maid are one in a succession of responses that Lucrece seeks across the poem, and each enacts a relative failure even of feminine sympathetic encounter. 'Frantic with grief' in the immediate aftermath of rape, Lucrece apostrophizes Night in a desperate call for 'co-partners in my pain' (762, 789). She imagines the stars as 'twinkling handmaids' (787) defiled, like her, by Tarquin, and her proverbial declaration that 'fellowship in woe doth woe assuage' can be seen to structure her words and actions across the rest of the poem. But the co-partnership of the stars is only imagined and 'fellowship in woe' is elusive, leaving Lucrece 'alone, alone' to 'sit and pine' (795). Her subsequent attempts to find a grief comparable to her own are equally futile. She is driven 'mad' by the 'sweet melody' of the morning birds and imagines herself singing with Philomel, her own 'deep groans' providing the bass ('diapason') or undersong ('burden') for the melancholy bird's song (1108–34). Here there is potential for concordant co-expression, as Lucrece imagines she and Philomel will 'tune our heart-strings to true languishment' (1141), but her appeal to Philomel is never more than a rhetorical invitation to a mythical female co-complainer and their choric harmony is only imagined. Across her first protracted complaint (747–1211), Lucrece calls for companionate female sympathy, evoking the again proverbial idea that 'Grief best is pleased with grief's society' (1111) – but the sympathy that she seeks, and that the poet-speaker imagines, is elusive.

The difficulties of finding true sympathy are entangled in the poem with the difficulties of expressing the full extremity and quality of woe.

Lucrece calls her maid with an 'untuned tongue' (1214) and when asked by the maid to explain her 'heaviness' she demurs, 'For more it is than I can well express' (1283–6). The maid's sympathy is engendered without any words from Lucrece and without knowing the motive of her complaint; while Lucrece 'justly weeps', the maid 'takes in hand / No cause but company of her drops' spilling' (1235–6), and hers is only a 'poor counterfeit' (1269) of Lucrece's own woe. The description of the maid as a 'counterfeit' is not necessarily itself a negative descriptor, as Meek points out; in sixteenth-century usage, counterfeit could refer to mimesis, 'a representing, counterfeiting, or figuring forth', as Sidney glosses it in the *Defence of Poesy*.[21] In this way, 'counterfeit' could encompass imitation as representation or transformation, as well as intent to deceive; it is also a rhetorical category under which George Puttenham, in the *Art of English Poesy*, lists prosopopoeia or 'impersonation', the device central to the 'female complaint' poem.[22] Lucrece and her maid are both female counterfeits in this sense. More telling is the description of Lucrece's maid as a '*poor* counterfeit' (my emphasis). This could refer to the maid's wretchedness and her own call on her auditors' sympathy or pity: a description of 'poor Philomel' in Hester Pulter's poetry (to which I will turn at the end of this article) carries this sense.[23] But much as Lucrece is able at last to weep with another woman, it is clear in this case that the maid's tears are also 'poor' in the sense of being a lesser or ineffective imitation: as Lucrece describes, the maid's weeping only 'small avails my mood' (1273). And it becomes clear immediately after she dismisses the maid that even Lucrece cannot fully express the extent of her own pain. She attempts to write down the cause and nature of her sorrow but her words are brief and insufficient:

---

[20] Meek, *Sympathy*, p. 116. [21] Meek, *Sympathy*, p. 123.
[22] See Smith, Ross and O'Callaghan, *Early Modern Women and the Poetry of Complaint*.
[23] See below. 'Poor', *OED Online*, sense 5: 'That provokes sympathy, or compassion; that is to be pitied; unfortunate, wretched, hapless'.

'By this short schedule Collatine may know / Her grief, but not her grief's true quality' (1312–13).

It is not until Lucrece encounters the painting of the siege and destruction of Troy that artistic expression – verbal or painterly – is found capable of delineating women's woe and a sympathetic transferral of emotion between women is realized. Lucrece finds in the depiction of 'despairing' Hecuba 'a face where all distress is stelled' (1444–7), and she lends to Hecuba her own words and cries. Realizing the potential in the imagined scene with Philomel, she 'tune[s] thy woes with my lamenting tongue' (1465), lamenting any figures she finds forlorn, from shepherds to swains to Hecuba herself, as 'feelingly she weeps Troy's painted woes' (1492). Lucrece becomes a counterfeit of others' woe, as they are of hers. 'She lends them words, and she their looks doth borrow' (1498); it is only in gazing on the 'well painted piece' (1443) that her own grief is at last assuaged by sharing in that of others, as she is 'from the feeling of her own grief brought / By deep surmise of others' detriment' (1578–9). Lucrece's sympathetic transferral of emotion is realized in an extended ekphrasis, a technique in which, more typically, the silent agonies of a female image are subjected to a male gaze. Marion Wells argues that Shakespearian ekphrasis 'typically stages ... an abjection and appropriation' of the female body, which is 'inscribed and stilled within [its] verbal frame'.[24] Lucrece inverts the gendering of the technique, stepping into what Wells describes as 'the masculine role of the ekphrastic' and performing an ekphrasis of Hecuba and the destruction of Troy that is atypically feminine and sympathetic.[25]

Gazing on others' pain is transformative for Lucrece: her extended ekphrasis of Troy's destruction gives rise in her to the sympathy that she has sought in others. But the complex form of the poem, its own multiple frames, also enacts a commentary on the limits of sympathy not dissimilar to that I have identified in *A Lover's Complaint*. *Lucrece* is not a framed female complaint in the conventional sense, where a male auditor overhears a complaining woman in the landscape; however, its ekphrases perform a comparable function, offering multiple instances and layers of auditing and looking upon, framing and objectification. Lucrece's ekphrastic contemplation of Hecuba and Troy is an embedded set-piece that parallels the poem's ekphrastic contemplation of the woeful Lucrece herself. In the scene with which I opened, Lucrece and her weeping maid are looked upon as static, 'pretty' fountains in the form of statues, 'like ivory conduits coral cisterns filling', and the poetic speaker immediately whirls away into third-person contemplation that enforces deep and absolute differences between the sexes and how they feel. 'Their gentle sex to weep are often willing', the speaker opines: 'men have marble, women waxen minds' (1237, 1240). The speaker is implicitly male, as is the audience and reader he addresses: women are members of *their* sex not *ours*, the third person pronouns instantiating distance, difference and objectification.[26] Having elaborated on differences between 'their gentle sex' and men, the speaker then instructs the reader 'The precedent whereof in Lucrece view' (1261), explicitly inviting the reader to look on Lucrece as the exemplar of his thesis of difference rather than to sympathize or compassionate with her, emotions that are based on a capacity for fellow-feeling.

Ekphrasis, then, typically objectifies women's woe in ways that preclude the transfer of genuine sympathy or compassion across the sexes. Katherine Ibbett has incisively drawn attention to the ways in which compassion in the seventeenth century (as now) is 'a technology that governs social relations, bringing out the structural affiliations of affect', one that 'operat[ed] on a spectrum of inclusion and exclusion' and that tended to

---

[24] Marion Wells, 'Philomela's marks: ekphrasis and gender in Shakespeare's poetry and plays', in *The Oxford Handbook of Shakespeare's Poetry*, ed. Post, 204–24; pp. 206, 223.

[25] Wells, 'Philomela's marks', p. 219. See Tamara Mahadin's article on Venus' deployment of (typically gendered male) rhetorical techniques in this volume.

[26] See William M. Reddy on 'first person, present-tense emotion claims', in *The Navigation of Feeling: A Framework for the History of Emotions* (Cambridge, 2001), p. 104.

reinforce existing social affinities rather than brokering new ones.[27] In Ibbett's analysis, compassion is a 'differentiating and distancing structure', and I suggest that the female quality of Lucrece's (and her maid's) woe is exactly a category of differentiation in Ibbett's terms, inscribing a hierarchical response to her suffering rather than one based on affinity and likeness.[28] Ibbett's precise analysis of sympathy and compassion, and her attention to the cognate term 'pity', also enables a delineation of sympathy's gendered exclusions in *Lucrece*, and the way these exclusions are enacted in the fabric or form of the poem's multiple frames. Ibbett traces the lexical relationships and shifts between 'compassion' and 'pity', noting a slippage between the two terms for much of the seventeenth century which does not at first seem to uphold 'what I took to be a common distinction today, where pity implies a hierarchical relationship and compassion a more companionable sort of fellow-feeling'.[29] But if early modern usage is often mixed, Ibbett shows that 'we can nonetheless distinguish between something like what I would call a pity function and a compassion function: a narrow and hierarchical response or a broader, more generous one'.[30] This distinction is crucial, I would argue, when we consider the representation of sympathy – and the use of that term – in *Lucrece*, where 'sympathy' applies to a feminine co-partnership in pain (the maid is 'enforced by sympathy' (1229)), but the sharing of grief between women does not transfer to an inclusive sharing of grief between women and men. Male responses to Lucrece's woe in the poem remain strictly in the realm of pity, 'narrow and hierarchical', while the ekphrastic description of Lucrece and her maid frames and distances them. The poem provides a feminine alternative, in Lucrece's own sympathetic ekphrasis of the destruction of Troy, just as *A Lover's Complaint* provides a sympathetic, female, double voice alongside the male double frame of the 'reverend man' and the narrator. But this is not matched in the hierarchical, distancing ekphrasis that male witnesses and auditors, within and implicitly without the poem, undertake, as they look on Lucrece as a 'precedent' for an experience and a mode of expression that is distinctly other than their own.

The ekphrastic description of Lucrece and her maid as 'pretty creatures' is mirrored in the poem's ending, as Collatine arrives home and the poem shifts its focus from Lucrece's sympathetic voicing of the complaints of Troy. Collatine is 'sad beholding' as he looks on Lucrece and the outward markers of her woe, a 'tear-distainèd eye' framed by rainbows, 'water-galls' that 'Foretell new storms to those already spent' (1586–90) – all descriptors that echo the 'ivory conduits' of Lucrece and her weeping maid. Collatine's attention to Lucrece's short summary of her rape comes close to sympathy, in a 'speechless woe' (1674) of his own, but on her death, the tone and focus becomes rapidly ekphrastic, as two rivers of blood circle Lucrece's body 'like a late-sacked island' (1740) and the piteous sight gives rise to a contestatory 'emulation' (1808) in her father's and husband's expressions of grief. John Roe aptly describes the scene of Lucrece and her weeping maid as one of the poem's 'distillations of pity', 'asking from the reader a tender awareness of the beauty of pathos', and, as he identifies, these earlier 'distillations of pity' prepare us for the end of the poem, establishing 'the mood intended to be dominant at the end'.[31] 'Pity' and 'pathos' are more accurate terms than sympathy for what this scene, and *Lucrece* as a whole, asks of an audience and a reader who is – crucially – figured as male, modelled in the text's intra-textual audience and its presentation of Lucrece's 'pretty' grief as an exemplar for men to consider. In *Lucrece*, as in *A Lover's Complaint*, gender demarcates who weeps and who watches or listens, who complains and who ekphrasizes; gender matters in these structures of grief and response. Just as Wells argues, compellingly, that Shakespeare himself recognizes the ekphrastic encounter as

---

[27] Katherine Ibbett, *Compassion's Edge: Fellow-Feeling and Its Limits in Early Modern France* (Philadelphia, 2018), pp. 3–4.
[28] Ibbett, *Compassion's Edge*, p. 4.
[29] Ibbett, *Compassion's Edge*, p. 8.
[30] Ibbett, *Compassion's Edge*, pp. 8–9.
[31] *Poems*, ed. Roe, p. 41.

'violently appropriative', I argue that his poems are obsessively interested in feminine sympathy and in its gendered limits, precisely delineating gendered structures of sympathy, differentiation and objectification.[32] In their complex poetic frames and ekphrastic structures, Shakespeare's 'female complaint' poems interrogate the gendered limits of sympathy at the same time as they inscribe them. Suggesting unique possibilities for the sharing of grief between women, as well as the persistent failures of male auditors to comprehend its 'motives', causes or extent, he represents intra-textual limits to feminine sympathy which must be considered to extend to reception and response beyond the text, in an economy of reading and textual exchange implicitly defined as male.

EARLY MODERN WOMEN'S COMPLAINT POETRY: COUNTERFEIT AND COMPASSION

Turning – finally – for comparison to complaint poetry written by early modern women, it is crucial first to note that this corpus is rhetorically complex, comprising ventriloquizations of women's and other voices and engaging extensively in the practices of impersonation and counterfeiture that characterize lyric poetry. Complaint poems written by women, in other words, are not the unmediated 'real' voices of 'real' women: they engage in prosopopoeia to the same extent as complaint poems written by men, even as their rhetorical precedents are eclectic and take us well beyond the prosopopoeic exercises of the humanist schoolroom.[33] Of 512 poems in our *Early Modern Women's Complaint Poetry Index*, 195 have an explicitly female and 145 an implicitly female speaker, but these are not all by any means proxies for the author. Among the explicitly female speakers, for example, are Cleopatra and Diomede, in Mary Sidney Herbert's *The Tragedie of Antonie* (a translation from Robert Garnier's French), Dido in Isabella Whitney's 'Dido to Aeneas', and personifications of nations in Anne Bradstreet's *A Dialogue Between Old England and New*. Even female personae that might seem to have autobiographical elements, such as Lady Mary Wroth's Pamphilia (read by many at the time as a character in a prose-and-sonnet-sequence *roman à clef*), involve considerable rhetorical projection; in Wroth's case, her amatory female complaints are deep engagements in Petrarchanism, the sonnet and pastoral prose romance.[34] Women in the *Index* wrote 95 complaints in explicitly male and 15 in implicitly male voices, from St Peter and Job to shepherds, lovers, foresters and knights; and our designation of the Davidic 'I' of psalmic complaints as a 'multiple' speaker position attests to its openness for occupation by speakers of any gender.[35] Women's complaint poetry, that is, engages in diverse and multiple impersonations across genders; at a fundamental level, 'female complaint' poems authored by women need to be seen as 'inciting prosopopoeia' and 'fostering impersonation of the feminine' as much as the male-authored corpus does.

While women write 'female complaint' prolifically alongside male and open-voiced complaint, however, their use of the complex framed form popular in the 1590s and exemplified in Shakespeare's poems is limited, suggesting that the male-authored corpus's ekphrastic fascination with 'feminine' emotion was of little interest to women writers. Twenty-three poems in the *Index* are tagged as 'framed complaint', but in fact very few of these accord with the emotional and formal dynamics of the male amatory tradition, in which narrators overhear the lament of an unknown

---

[32] Wells, 'Philomela's marks', p. 223.
[33] See Smith, Ross and O'Callaghan, *Early Modern Women and the Poetry of Complaint*; Jennifer Richards, *Voices and Books in the English Renaissance: A New History of Reading* (Oxford, 2019), pp. 112–13; and Sarah C. E. Ross and Rosalind Smith, 'Beyond Ovid: early modern women and the forms of complaint', in *Early Modern Women's Complaint*, ed. Ross and Smith, 1–26.
[34] Rosalind Smith, '"Woman-like complaints": lost love in the first part of "The Countess of Montgomery's Urania"', *Textual Practice* 33 (2019), 1341–62.
[35] *Early Modern Women's Complaint Poetry Index*, https://cems.anu.edu.au/complaintindex/#/discoveries.

female plainant. Some framed complaints in the *Index* are 'framed' only in the sense that they occur in a narrative scenario; for example, Wroth's 'Why do you thus torment my poorest heart?' is a complaint sung by the Prince of Corinth and overheard by Pamphilia and Amphilanthus in the progress of the prose romance *Urania*. Even where narrators frame the complaint within the poem, they often do so in straightforward narrative terms. Wroth's 'The spring now come at last' is delivered by a lovelorn shepherdess who compares the onset of spring to her own psychic darkness; she delivers all of the poem except five lines, when a narrator briefly interjects at the opening of stanza 3:

> A shepherdess thus said
> Who was with grief oppressed
> For truest love betrayed
> Barred her from quiet rest.
> And weeping, thus said she[36]

Such an interjection is a perfunctory framing gesture, providing little more than narrative clarity; it neither develops the narrator as a character nor engages them in the technology – or the 'fabric' – of the poem's emotional expression. Similarly, Sir Robert Ayton's lyric 'When Diophantus knew', transcribed twice in two variant versions in Lady Margaret Wemyss's songbook, opens with a brief narrative frame that locates the complaining male lover, but this frame is straightforwardly factual, telling us that when Diophantus discovered his destiny – that 'he was forced to forgoe / His deare and Lovely sweete' – he wrestled with woe and shame and so delivered the complaint that forms the rest of the poem.[37]

One affecting framed 'female complaint' poem transcribed in Lady Margaret Wemyss's songbook provides an exception that helps to illustrate – through contrast – the emotional and formal affordances of the genre that Shakespeare interrogates, but that are absent in most women writers' use of it.[38] 'When Cynthia with sweet consent' features an implicitly male framing narrator who speaks for the first five of ten stanzas. He rides 'through the wilderness' seeking 'repose' for his spirit; he wearies as he wanders through 'the thickest' of enclosing trees before he hears the voice of a woman who has been 'luckless' in love, abandoned by her 'disdainful deir'. This poetic narrator is far more than the barest of framing presences that we have seen in Wroth's song. He carries emotions of his own and a curiosity about the complaining woman; like the narrator and the reverend man in *A Lover's Complaint*, he desires to know more about the motives and quality of her woe. The poem's frame in this way invokes the possibility of emotional reciprocity, the 'fellowship' or co-partnership in pain, that Shakespeare's framed 'female complaint' poems have reached towards but refused to realize. There is a resonance between his spiritual weariness and the woman's woe and, in contrast to the narrator in *A Lover's Complaint*, he both comprehends her pain and upholds her moral integrity, as he declares her to be 'a lover true and just / Who still did love and gott no trust'. The poem in Wemyss's manuscript is, like Shakespeare's, open-framed – the woeful woman delivers her complaint in the last five stanzas and the narrator provides no concluding comment – but it is possible to see sympathy lightly sketched in its final stanza:

> Will thou not come my deirest deir,
> And ease me of this pain and grief
> Who still doth grieve without relief
> And get na love again.

Because the framing narrator comprehends the woeful woman clearly, and because his weariness has echoed her own from the outset, he implicitly fulfils the role that she asks of her lover, coming to her in the landscape and listening to her pain and grief. And as her auditor within the poem, he

---

[36] *Mary Wroth's Poetry: An Electronic Edition*, ed. Paul Salzman, https://wroth.latrobe.edu.au/all-poems.html.

[37] Lady Margaret Wemyss's songbook, National Library of Scotland, Dep. 314/23, fols 61v–65v and 68v–69v; and *The English and Latin Poems of Sir Robert Ayton*, ed. Charles B. Gullans (Edinburgh, 1963), pp. 110–21.

[38] Wemyss's songbook, fols. 70v–71v; I have lightly modernized and anglicized quotations.

models a response that is available to us as readers or listeners to a framed complaint scenario that is both rich in the utterly typical markers of the framed 'female complaint' genre and, at the same time, an atypical depiction of emotional perspicacity and reciprocity across the genders. The author of the lyric is unknown to us – Wemyss's extensive transcription practices make it unlikely that the poem is her own – but it is entirely possible that she sang the lyric to one of the many tunes transcribed separately in her manuscript, either as a solo voice or perhaps in duet, in a prosopopoeiac voicing of another kind.[39]

Eight framed 'female complaint' poems by Margaret Cavendish identified in the *Index* are a different kind of anomaly: idiosyncratic versions of the genre that also highlight, in departing from them, the framed complaint's more typical interrogations of the possibilities and limits of emotional expression and exchange. Two instances in *Poems, and Fancies* (1653, although later substantially revised) are at first blush the most familiar, opening with male narrators (one explicit, one implicit) who happen upon women destroyed by woe. One comes across a 'mourning beauty' lying 'close by a tomb' in a church where he goes to say his prayers ('On a Melting Beauty'), while the narrator in 'On a Furious Sorrow' observes a personification of Sorrow digging at a grave, her hair loose and her garments undone, shrieking and brandishing a dagger as she lies 'by Death's cold side'.[40] Both poems, however, veer off in unexpected directions. The mourning beauty of the first poem 'congeal[s] to ice', melts, and so seeps as water into her beloved's tomb, in a metamorphic allegory of unification with the deceased. 'On a Furious Sorrow', already allegorical in its personification of Sorrow and Death, stages an exemplary moral reversal that is astonishing not only in its stern denunciation of the auxetic expression of grief that characterizes complaint, but also in its emphasis on clarity of expression and the absolute ability of words to express – and cure – woe. The passing man in this case, 'Pitying her sad condition and her grief, / Did strain by rhet'ric's help, to give relief'; he delivers a rousing speech against complaint, and so:

At last the words like keys unlocked her ears,
And then she straight considers what she hears.
'Pardon you gods', said she, 'my murm'ring crime;
My grief shall ne'er dispute your will divine,
And in sweet life will I take most delight.'
And so went home with that fond carpet-knight.

Sorrow's emotional indulgence is reversed through dialogue with the framing male narrator, as is the woe of a similarly deluded woman in 'A Description of the Passion of Love misplaced', one of six framed complaints in Cavendish's *Natures Picture Drawn by Fancies Pencil to the Life* (1654). The 'weeping Beauty' in this poem is dissuaded of her complaint by a passing gentleman, who tells her to 'grieve and weep no more, / For Nature handsome Men hath more in store'. Convinced, 'she rose, and with great joy, said she, / Farewell, fond Love, and foolish Vanity', in a matter-of-fact denial of the genre in which she participates.[41]

That the framed 'female complaint' poem in Cavendish's hands is so far from the 'unique resource for expressing (and organizing) intense emotion' that Craik identifies in *A Lover's Complaint*, and so far from the Shakespearian interrogation of the limits of sympathy across the sexes that I have explored above, speaks in part to Cavendish's own originality. Her complaints are emotionally spare and incline towards the moral and philosophical, as in 'A Description of the Passion of Love misplaced', in which the weeping woman and the passing gentleman debate the location of virtue and beauty, the body and the soul. All six of the framed complaints in *Natures Picture* eschew the expression of intense emotional experience and instead provide dialogic narratives that

---

[39] For an extended exploration of sung complaints and Wemyss's manuscript, see Smith, Ross and O'Callaghan, *Early Modern Women and the Poetry of Complaint*, ch. 3.

[40] *Margaret Cavendish's 'Poems and Fancies': A Digital Critical Edition*, ed. Liza Blake, https://library2.utm.utoronto.ca/poemsandfancies.

[41] Margaret Cavendish, *Natures Picture Drawn by Fancies Pencil to the Life* (London, 1654), pp. 128–32.

range from allegories and moral philosophies to romance stories of (initially) sad women and their carpet knights. But women poets' more general eschewal or modification of the Shakespearian framed 'female complaint' poem, and its intense and ekphrastic examination of feminine emotion, is notable, and suggests either alternative formal and emotional preoccupations when they frame their woeful speakers or, in rare cases, use of the framed 'female complaint' poems' formal and emotional conventions to alternative ends. In particular, Cavendish's modification of ekphrastic framing towards dialogue is echoed in poems by a number of women in the *Index*, including Wroth, Hester Pulter and Anne Bradstreet, who frequently locate complaint within dialogic structures, where woe is communicated either between women and men or, more frequently, within communities of women. And in the case of Pulter, the framed 'female complaint' poem is fused with the dialogic to the explicit end of representing the transferral of sympathy between women within the text and in an extra-textual community of women readers.

Pulter is the third most prolific poet in our *Index*, the author of thirty-five religious, existential and political complaints; only one of these is a framed 'female complaint' poem, but it is an innovative and extended example that repurposes the technology of the poetic frame for the expression of intense female emotion. 'The Complaint of Thames, 1647', occasioned by the imprisonment of King Charles I in February 1647, features a personified River Thames who delivers a 114-line complaint excoriating the Parliamentarian populace of London and lamenting the state of a nation deprived of its monarch.[42] Pulter's Thames is female – a rarity among the many poetic personifications of the river in seventeenth-century poetry – as is the implicitly female framing narrator who walks upon her banks in the poem's opening four lines, 'Late in an evening' and 'alone'. Like the framing narrator in Wemyss's transcribed lyric, Pulter's proleptically intimates the sadness of the complaints she overhears, and at the end of the poem, understanding the complaints of the Thames completely, she joins the river in her woe: 'I hearing these complaints, though time to sleep, / Sat sadly down and with her 'gan to weep'. Pulter's frame is briefly sketched – four lines at the opening of the poem and two at the end – but the inversion of the framed complaint's typical gendering to provide a female framing narrator, and the inversion of the typical gendering of the Thames to provide a female river, creates the feminized co-partnership in woe for which Shakespeare's Lucrece repeatedly searches. It is matched in a thoroughgoing sympathetic feminization of the county's and the world's rivers, all of whom, Thames tells us, envied her former joys as she carried the queen upon her silver waters. I have written elsewhere of this poem's articulation with another of Pulter's poems, 'The Invitation into the Country', in which the feminized rivers of Hertfordshire weep together in a fluvial sympathy of woes.[43] But for the purposes of this article, my point is that Pulter's reconfiguration of the framed 'female complaint' poem draws our attention – through contrast – to the gendered barriers to sympathy that Shakespeare's poems interrogate and ultimately uphold. 'The Complaint of Thames, 1647' realizes the potential latent in the 'sist'ring vale' and the 'fluxive tears' of the river in *A Lover's Complaint* to reconfigure the relationship of complaining woman and auditor; it displaces altogether the uncomprehending male narrator, and centres instead a sympathetic exchange of woe between women in the landscape – the river and, if you like, a narratorial friend of her own choice. Further, Pulter's framing of her Thames with an implicitly female narrator who is sympathetic and companionate models the possibility of a woman reader's engagement with the poem as an extra-textual 'friend', one who sits down and weeps with the river and the framing speaker, rather than one who is invited, as is the reader of *Lucrece*, to look upon weeping women as

---

[42] Sarah C. E. Ross and Elizabeth Scott-Baumann, eds., *Women Poets of the English Civil War* (Manchester, 2017), pp. 99–103.

[43] Ross, 'Complaint's echoes', pp. 190–8; and Sarah C. E. Ross, *Women, Poetry, and Politics in Seventeenth-Century Britain* (Oxford, 2015), pp. 139–47.

a 'precedent' of 'their gentle sex' and their tendency to woe.

Such dialogic qualities undergird the female sympathy constituted in another of Pulter's complaints, 'A Dialogue Between Two Sisters, Virgins, Bewailing their Solitary Life, P.P., A.P.', a sympathy that models reception and response beyond the text.[44] Pulter ostensibly voices two of her own adult daughters, Penelope and Anne:

> YOUNG ANNE: Come, my dear sister, sit with me a while,
>   That we both Time and Sorrow may beguile;
>   In this sweet shade, by this clear, purling spring,
>   We'll sit and help poor Philomel to sing,
>   And to complete the consort and the choir,
>   I would I had my viol, you your lyre.
> ELDER PEN: Ay me, my sister, Time on restless wheels
>   Doth ever turn with wings upon his heels,
>   Fast as the sand that huddles through his glass,
>   Regardless of our tears, he on doth pass;
>   Yet in the shade of this sad sycamore
>   We'll sit, our wants and losses to deplore,
>   For all things here which do in order rise,
>   Methinks in woe with us do sympathise.
>
> (1–14)

Anne's exhortation to Penelope to 'sit with me a while' and the poem's formal dialogic structure extends the sentiment of the closing frame in 'The Complaint of Thames': the two sisters sit and complain together, sharing their near-identical woes. Anne's suggestion that 'We'll sit and help poor Philomel to sing' echoes Lucrece's desire to do so, a desire to share grief that is here realized as the sisters metaphorically sing with the nightingale, and simultaneously sing with each other, forming part of an imagined complaint consort. The poem explicitly uses the language of sympathy, as the 'sad sycamore' and 'all things' in the landscape around them 'in woe with us do sympathise'. The natural sympathy of the grove in which the sisters sit echoes the dialogue between them, and in turn facilitates a further implied dialogue between the sisters and other audiences. Buoyed by the sharing of their woe, with each other and with 'all things here which do in order rise', the two sisters resolve at the end of the poem to 'cease in vain to make our moan, / And go to our poor mother; she's alone' (53–4). Complaint in Pulter's poems remains affective rather than effectual – there is no remedy or redress, 'no relief' – but as these examples illustrate, its exorbitant grief resounds in a dialogue between women, and between women and a female-voiced landscape, one which constructs a sympathetic, intra- and extra-poetic female community. Complaint creates a community of female voices in Pulter's poems and in turn figures and creates its extra-textual poetic audience, inviting readers and listeners to join, and to become a friend of the speaker's own choice.[45]

CONCLUSION: A SYMPATHY OF WOES

Reading 'female complaint' poems written by early modern women alongside *A Lover's Complaint* and *Lucrece* reveals much about gender and sympathy in these defining examples of the genre. Shakespeare's framed 'female complaint' poems impersonate female grief and seem to be obsessively interested in the limits of those impersonations, as the gender of the complaining women consistently imposes itself as a barrier to male compassion, a limit on the capacity for fellow feeling. *A Lover's Complaint* and *Lucrece* are complex poetic technologies whose narrative and ekphrastic devices 'still' (or 'stell') the expression of 'female' woe and frame their complaining women as objects of pity rather than co-partners in a sympathetic exchange of woe, the potential for sympathy between women only ever lightly traced. Early modern women's 'female complaint' poetry, in contrast, either eschews the narrative frame, uses it sparely or, in the case of Hester Pulter, repurposes the framed form to create a dialogue of sympathy between women, a compassionate co-partnership

---

[44] *The Pulter Project*, gen eds. Wendy Wall and Leah Knight, Amplified Edition, http://pulterproject.northwestern.edu/poems/ae/a-dialogue-between-two-sisters-virgins-bewailing-their-solitary-life.

[45] See my 'Complaint's echoes' for a longer version of this argument, and Smith, Ross and O'Callaghan, *Early Modern Women and the Poetry of Complaint*.

rather than an ekphrastic contemplation of women's 'pretty' pain. Such formal and affective differences between framed 'female complaint' poems suggest ways in which we might consider more precisely the role of gender in Shakespeare's construction of sympathy, the operation of feminine sympathy in his poems, and crucial differences between sympathy and compassion, and pity. Early modern women's complaint poetry offers a new set of texts and approaches alongside that of Shakespeare and his male contemporaries, highlighting the poetic, affective and communal structures in which 'female woe' was exchanged, and showing that it matters who complains and who listens, within the poem and beyond it, and whether auditors and readers are imagined as male or female. Where Shakespeare's poems position feminine sympathy in masculine ekphrastic structures of pity and objectification, women's own complaint poems reveal sympathy exchanged between women and for women, in uniquely dialogic forms that express and organize the transferral of feminine emotion beyond the limits of compassion that Shakespeare imagines.

LYRIC VOICES AND CULTURAL ENCOUNTERS ACROSS TIME AND SPACE: THE POETRY OF WILLIAM SHAKESPEARE AND FAIZ AHMED FAIZ (1911–1984)

JYOTSNA G. SINGH

I

It is remarkable how categories like the 'Global Renaissance' and 'Global Shakespeare' have gained increasing currency in the past few decades, emphasizing new, intercultural, non-European imperatives for early modern scholarship. Scholars have now studied global exchanges of the period from a variety of disciplinary and cultural perspectives: in dramatic texts, travel narratives, cosmographies, material culture, aesthetic artefacts, among others. The discursive terrain of early modern studies now includes the presence of indigenous cultures, peoples and religions within considerations of race, empire and emerging capitalism. This global 'turn' in Shakespeare studies has further brought to the fore important criticism that contextualizes his works, mostly plays, within histories of colonization, racialized enslavement and postcolonial resistance; hence, approaches such as critical race theory and postcolonial theory, among others, have expanded the cultural and political scope of Shakespeare studies, with implications for our own times.[1] Within these wide-ranging studies of trajectories of exchange, however, relatively little attention has been directed towards lyric circulations of poetic, affective voices across the early modern world – or towards contemporary dialogues with earlier lyric voices. Among critics who have observed these lacunae, Ayesha Ramachandran is notable in proposing a new 'Lyric Poetics' for a 'Global Renaissance', directing our attention to the diffusions of lyric elements across cultures:

[T]here has been little attention to lyric – understood as a form, as a process of thinking – amid studies of both early modern globality and an emerging global imaginary.

Yet the lyric wants to travel across time and space, to be smuggled from one cultural context to another via memory and allusion, in snippets of letters, in multi-layered albums, on the fly-leaves of books, in impromptu recitations at court or on the street. Various early modern sources record poetic encounters that seek to confront the experience of a shifting world either through cross-cultural borrowing, topographical evocation, or metaphors of globality.[2]

Highlighting such examples, Ramachandran calls for more 'substantive considerations of lyric poetry', in order to 'usefully expand and deepen

---

[1] Two representative examples are Peter Erickson and Kim F. Hall, '"A new scholarly song": rereading early modern race', *Shakespeare Quarterly* 67 (2016), 1–13, and Jyotsna G. Singh, *Shakespeare and Postcolonial Theory* (London, 2019). Other approaches, such as disability studies, ecocritical studies, sexuality and trans studies have also emerged in conjunction with this globalizing trend.

[2] Ayesha Ramachandran, 'Afterword: lyric poetics for the Global Renaissance', in *A Companion to the Global Renaissance: Literature and Culture in the Era of Expansion, 1500–1700*, ed. Jyotsna G. Singh (Oxford, 2021), 447–56; p. 449.

studies of both the lyric and an early modern experience of globality'.³ In addition, a growing interest in possible Arabic elements in English poetry, for instance, marks a new emphasis on the global cross-pollination of cultural influences in lyric poetry. Within this trend, scholars such as Kamal Abu-Deeb have explored the genealogical links between the European sonnet and earlier Arabic forms,⁴ and Robert Stagg in this volume offers an extensive study of the history of the Arabic lyric and its possible influences on Shakespeare via a variety of cultural formations. The key contribution of such scholarly endeavours, as exemplified in Stagg's article, is their emphasis on the boundary-crossing fluidity of the lyric form, surreptitiously moving from one cultural context to another; overall, they demonstrate how lyric forms and processes can circulate in multiple, divergent directions, in fluid temporalities, and in remaking and unmaking conventions along the way.⁵

My project in this article is to explore an imaginary, global encounter between a Shakespearian sonnet and an Urdu lyric (in English translation) in the nazm form by twentieth-century South Asian-Pakistani poet, Faiz Ahmed Faiz (1911–1984): Shakespeare's Sonnet 57, 'Being your slave, what should I do', and 'Don't Ask Me, My Love, for That Love Again' (1962–1965), by Faiz. The nazm and ghazal are two important, closely related forms of Urdu lyric poetry, generally short or shortish poems. The Urdu ghazal is a traditional, classical form derived from Persianate culture, vocabulary and themes, articulated within a formal metrical structure via a series of couplets. 'Nazm' can describe any short, non-narrative lyric – a later, modern iteration – that deploys similar themes but with some experimentation in form, and sometimes influenced by Western models.⁶ Faiz was deeply immersed in these traditions, and his primary poetic models would have been the earlier Urdu poets of the subcontinent, such as Iqbal and Ghalib, who experimented with a variety of poetic forms, including the nazm and ghazal. But we also know that Faiz had studied Shakespeare in his British education, with graduate degrees in English and Arabic, and he would have been familiar with Western poetic models such as the sonnet.⁷ Overall, as I elaborate in Parts III and IV, an encounter or a dialogue between the two works across a temporal and cultural divide reflects a shared affective investment in feelings of *discontent and consolation* in love which dominates the emotional range and tenor of *both* Faiz's and Shakespeare's poems. In this process, the lyric voices call attention to the human individual in a first-person address, while also evoking and remaking the larger worlds the speakers inhabit, mediating the cultural particularities of individual experience within a contingent world.

As a contextual frame for my analysis of these two poems, I will first briefly examine, in Part II, an *earlier* poetic encounter between Shakespeare and Faiz that has *already* occurred in the popular Indian film *Haider* (2014), a cross-cultural adaptation of *Hamlet* in Hindi/Urdu (with subtitles). Woven into this adaptation at strategic moments are two Urdu lyric poems by Faiz Ahmed Faiz, a ghazal about a lover's call to his absent Beloved to help a garden to bloom and a narrative lament for the nation at the end of the film (sung during the credits), both of which develop the themes of an 'unweeded garden' (*Hamlet*, 1.2.135) and of Denmark/Kashmir as a 'prison' (2.2.246).

For my methodological assumptions in exploring these poetic encounters between Faiz and

---

³ Ramachandran, 'Afterword', p. 449.
⁴ Kamal Abu-Deed, 'The quest for the sonnet: the origins of the sonnet in Arabic poetry', *Critical Survey* 28 (2016), 133–57.
⁵ For a detailed study of the cross-pollination of influences between the early modern sonnet and the Arabic ghazal form, see Robert Stagg, 'Shakespeare's Arabic Sonnets', in this volume.
⁶ See Gopi Chand Narang, 'The tradition and innovation in the poetry of Faiz', *Indian Literature* 28 (1985), 23–34. For additional analysis, see Agha Shahid Ali, 'Introduction', in *The Rebel's Silhouette: Selected Poems, Faiz Ahmed Faiz*, trans. (with a new introduction) Agha Shahid Ali (Amherst, 1991), xvi–xvii.
⁷ For more on the English education system under British rule, see Gauri Vishwanathan, *Masks of Conquest: Literary Study and British Rule in India* (New York, 2014).

Shakespeare, I primarily draw on Ramachandran's concept of 'lyric thinking', which defines her call to revive and deepen our study of the lyric within global contexts in ways articulated above. Following her definition, one can see how each speaker holds a unique perspective, synthesizing different modes of thinking, as she explains:

I want to suggest that the unique conjunction of particular and universalizing modes of thinking in the lyric enable it to articulate a *phenomenology* of worldly experience. In this, the lyric performs the labor of inward abstraction, facilitating forms of thinking that explore what it means for individuals to inhabit a shifting, expanding world. By attending to the philosophical affordances of lyric poetry – what I call 'lyric thinking' – we might discern an alternate means of exploring and expressing the global ... Lyric thinking, in this sense, is the other side of worldmaking: it celebrates the potentials of human fashioning while also embracing the partial, particular view of the individual human.[8]

What particularly resonates in this passage is the critic's emphasis on a '*phenomenology* of worldly experience' (my emphasis) and the 'philosophical affordances' of the lyric in a world that is 'shifting' and 'expanding'. Furthermore, we must also recognize that any merely individual engagement with the individual and personal is not where 'lyric thinking' rests. Rather, while opening up the phenomenological perspectives of the individual speaker, 'lyric thinking' can *also* lead us to think deeply about the larger, often political implications of the experiential in terms of 'a renewed focus on *who speaks and how they speak*'.[9] Expanding on Ramachandran's formulation while pursuing a further understanding of the lyric's place in the world – and in mediating between the universal and particular – I also remain cognizant of Jahan Ramazani's 'transnational poetics', which 'proposes various ways of vivifying circuits of poetic connection and dialogue across political and geographic borders and even hemispheres, of examining cross-cultural and cross-national exchanges, influences, and confluences in poetry'.[10] Such cross-pollinations are evident when we consider how the two poems together serve as a locus for different kinds of mediations and translations between cultures, languages and periods – a 'zone of critical engagement' that resists cultural and national essentialism.[11] Overall, in proposing an interactive reading of the Faiz and Shakespeare pieces – a reading that enables a thematic and affective dialogue or boundary crossing between two lyric voices – in the English sonnet and Urdu nazm (in translation), I expand upon and complicate the intercultural imperatives of recent global Shakespeare scholarship, which has mostly been oriented to performance, adaptation and appropriation on the stage and in different media such as film and digital platforms. Moreover, critics (such as those listed below) have typically focused on the dramatic works and their 'travels' through the world, especially in recent decades.[12]

Acknowledging the impact of these expansive, transnational and cross-cultural imperatives in literary studies, what may be the nature of our 'travels' with and within a lyric poem? The first-person epistemological perspective of the lyric, with its varying effects, draws us to emotional and affective shifts and turns as the speaker also responds to the experiential pull of the world beyond. While the view of the individual or persona who speaks is typically particular and partial, historical references, intertextual borrowings/echoes and varying addressees can *also* open up many worlds 'elsewhere' for the readers of the lyric poem – often

---

[8] Ramachandran, 'Afterword', pp. 449–50.
[9] Ramachandran, 'Afterword', p. 450.
[10] Jahan Ramazani, *A Transnational Poetics* (Chicago, 2019), pp. x–xi. For further analysis, see also Ramazani, 'The local poem in a global age', *Critical Inquiry* 43 (2017), 670–96; p. 696.
[11] Emily Apter, *The Translation Zone: A New Comparative Literature* (Princeton, 2006), p. 5.
[12] Some representative examples of the Global Shakespeare scholarship are as follows: Mark Thornton Burnett, *Shakespeare and World Cinema* (Cambridge, 2013); Carla Della Gatta, *Latinx Shakespeares: Staging US Intracultural Theater* (Amherst, 2023); Craig Dionne and Parmita Kapadia, eds., *Native Shakespeares: Indigenous Appropriations on a Global Stage* (Aldershot, 2008); Jyotsna G. Singh and Abdulhamit Arvas, 'Global Shakespeares, affective histories, cultural memories', in *Shakespeare Survey* 68 (Cambridge, 2015), 183–96.

recognizable worlds of strife and struggle – as we become a part of the 'travels' of the lyric. When viewed through such meaning-making processes, the worlds of Faiz and Shakespeare may be brought closer together. The concerns of Faiz's nazm, 'Don't Ask Me, My Love, for That Love Again', centring on the exigencies of love in a cruel, unstable world, resonate with the poetic vision expressed in Sonnet 57, and more broadly in Shakespeare's sonnet sequence as a whole: 'haunted by the related phenomena of death and change. The poems struggle to find a satisfying answer to the question of what might abide in a world whose only constant is change.'[13] Faiz's speaker laments a love he cannot give 'again' from a lost world that 'was gold, burnished with light' and is now shattered by injustice,[14] while the persona in Shakespeare's Sonnet 57 self-identifies as a 'slave' and despairs of the conditions of his emotional enslavement, bound to 'the hours and times of [his Beloved's] desire' (57.1–2) – conditions that have historical resonances in the slave trade of the period. Overall, a search for love in an intractable world, emerging from both speakers' navigations through their discontents and consolations, can only offer answers that remain tentative and ambiguous, yet their phenomenological struggles with worldly experience constantly lead us to consider *'who speaks and how they speak'* and how different voices are getting heard within larger contexts. Through these explorations, as I demonstrate in Parts III and IV, even though these poems do not connect via any literary genealogies or influences, they bring twentieth-century South Asia and early modern England closer to each other in an interplay of affects and voices.

II

Within this globalizing trend, and as mentioned above, another important poetic encounter between Shakespeare and Faiz has already occurred, in the popular Indian film *Haider* (2014), a creative adaptation of *Hamlet* in Hindi/Urdu (with subtitles). It takes Shakespeare's play (and his audience) into Kashmir – a disputed region, disjunct from the Indian state – during the 1990s militancy and brutal occupation by the Indian military. Woven into this story at strategic moments are two Urdu lyric poems by Faiz Ahmed Faiz, a ghazal about a lover's call to his Beloved to bring the garden to bloom and a narrative lament for a decaying nation that is sung during the credits at the end of the film. The deployment of these poems in *Haider* provides a contextual frame for my imagined encounter between Shakespeare's sonnet and Faiz's nazm in Parts III and IV. Their presence in a Shakespearian adaptation demonstrates the fluidity of the lyric form and how it can unexpectedly travel from one cultural context to another – and from one medium to another. Together they express and synthesize the nostalgia and trauma – both personal and national – underpinning the tragedy of Kashmir, which early in the film (echoing *Hamlet*) is described as a 'prison'. And, as in Shakespeare's play, one brother's betrayal of another overlays the tragedy of Kashmir.

Here, while the director, Vishal Bhardwaj, and the scriptwriter, Basharat Peer, open up Shakespeare's *Hamlet* (and his audience) to local knowledges, voices and experiences of the Kashmiris, what is imaginatively invoked in Shakespeare's *Hamlet* – the 'unweeded garden / That grows to seed; [with] things rank and gross . . . / Possess[ing] it' (1.2.135–7) – is visualized quite literally in the scenes of mass destruction, blasted landscapes and barren gardens in *Haider*. In this disintegrating world, Haider's psychic bearings are disoriented, and he expresses his angst publicly, rather than in the private closeted soliloquies found in *Hamlet*. The two lyric poems by Faiz Ahmed Faiz play a key role here in expressing the pain and trauma of both Haider as a character and Kashmir as a country. The first poem is a ghazal, a short lyric, 'Gulon Mein Rang Bhare' ('The new breeze of

---

[13] Michael Schoenfeldt, 'Introduction', to *A Companion to Shakespeare's Sonnets*, ed. Schoenfeldt (Oxford, 2010), 1–12; p. 4.
[14] Faiz Ahmed Faiz, 'Don't Ask Me, My Love, for That Love Again' ('Mujh se Pehli Si Mohabbat na Maang'), in *The Rebel's Silhouette*, p. 5.

Spring'), a poem structured in couplets. It is a call to a Beloved to come to the garden of Spring, with the opening couplet as follows:

> The new breeze of Spring
> fills blossoms with their hue
> Come now, my love, grant the garden leave
> to go about its business.[15]

The audience first hears this poem in the scene of Haider's bombed-out house, where he recollects in a flashback an occasion with his father singing and quizzing him on an Urdu couplet (with the opening line as its title). Associated with his imprisoned and later dead father, the lyric recurs at two other key moments in the film, stirring in him a nostalgic comfort accompanied by a sense of loss, while the colourful blossoms of the ghazal offer a contrast to the 'unweeded garden' that is now Kashmir. This poem is recited in Urdu (with subtitles), so Western audiences must lose some of the resonances of the figurative language and pathos of the original.

A second, iconic poem by Faiz Ahmed Faiz shapes the final vision of the film, which inflects the Kashmir tragedy within the postcolonial history of the subcontinent. Recited in a poetic narrative epilogue in Urdu (during the credits) and entitled 'Intisaab' ('Dedication'), it was possibly written about Pakistan. As positioned here in the film, it is used to eulogize 'mera desh' ('my country'), thus implying Kashmir.[16]

> (a dedication) to this day And to this day's sorrow ...
> Today's grief that shuns the blooming garden of life,
> To the forest of yellow leaves –
> the forest of yellow (dying) leaves that is my country,
> to the constellation of pain that is my country.[17]

Following this poignant opening about 'the constellation of pain', this poem catalogues the sufferings of people in different professions and personal situations, without offering any hope in the end – keeping a call for social justice alive beyond the final frame of the film. To end the film with this extended lament for the nation is to 'confront the complex history of the region and to bear witness to its on-going conflict and the pain that has resulted'.[18]

It is important to recognize that Faiz was both a revolutionary and a romantic poet – a Pakistani though, more broadly, a figure emblematic of the postcolonial world of South Asia with all its dissonances. According to one critic:

> His poetry exemplifies some of the central dilemmas of Urdu writing in the aftermath of the partition of India at the moment of independence from British rule ... [He attempts] to unhitch literary production from the cultural projects of either postcolonial state in order to make visible meanings that have still not been entirely reified and subsumed within the cultural logic of the nation-state system.[19]

The film represents these disjunctions, but the lyrical voices of the speakers in the two Faiz poems go further in evoking the nostalgia, loss and pathos of these historical struggles in affective, personalized terms, inserting into the political, partly revenge plot of the film 'a *phenomenology*' of worldly (emotional) experience that leads us to give some thought to '*who speaks and how they speak*'. In sum, the 'encounter' between Faiz and Shakespeare does *not* seem arbitrary by the end of *Haider*. As mentioned earlier, a longing for blooming gardens in the ghazal 'Gulon Mein Rang Bhare', associated with Haider's dead father, echo

---

[15] Original poem in Urdu and English translation, 'Gulon Mein Rang Bhare', in *The Rebel's Silhouette*, pp. 34–5. This translation mine.

[16] For a detailed discussion of the deployment of Faiz's poems into the film *Haider*, see Singh, *Shakespeare and Postcolonial Theory*, pp. 177–94. See also Sandra Young, especially her discussion of Faiz's poems in the film, in *Shakespeare in the Global South* (London, 2019), pp. 76–7.

[17] Original poem in Urdu, 'Intisaab', from Ali Madeeh Hashmi and Shoaib Hashmi, *The Way It Was Once: Faiz Ahmed Faiz – His Life, His Poems* (Delhi, 2012), pp. 100–3. The translation is mine. I reference the opening couplet here. It is a long poem, generally considered incomplete, and can be found in varying lengths in different editions. The version sung in *Haider* (during the credits) includes additional stanzas not found in this edition.

[18] Young, *Shakespeare in the Global South*, pp. 77–8. See also Singh, *Shakespeare and Postcolonial Theory*, pp. 185–7.

[19] Aamir Mufti, 'Towards a lyric history of India', *boundary 2* 31 (2004), 245–74; pp. 245–6.

Hamlet's despair at the 'unweeded garden' that Denmark has become. Furthermore, the national mourning of 'Intisaab', coupled with references to Kashmir as a 'prison', reinforces the catastrophic ending of Shakespeare's *Hamlet* with multiple deaths and the conquest of Denmark. In the insertion of these two poems, we can see how lyric forms may travel across time and space. And as Ramazani reminds us, poetry can bridge temporal divides, particularly by 'its inhabiting of multiple spaces and times at once, and its proficiency at straddling discrepant sites, both real and imagined'.[20]

'What is meant by encounter?' Nandini Das asks as she re-considers the 'culture of encounters' recorded in the early modern period, particularly in the travel archive. Instead of focusing on an individual event, she emphasizes 'communal knowledge slowly accreted over a period ... [involving a] negotiation of knowledge, memory, texts, and preconceptions'.[21] The encounter of *Haider* and *Hamlet* via Faiz in one sense moves beyond the early modern period, but its intertextuality is striking in that it reminds us that Shakespeare's play, like the film, involves a 'negotiation of knowledge, memory, texts, and preconceptions' and Faiz's two poems are key to that process. While Shakespeare's poetic palette contributed a new emotional language by which to understand the militaristic Indian state that governed Kashmir during its civil unrest in the 1990s, Faiz's poetry, for its part, harnessed an affective history from the Urdu/Kashmiri milieu, and through 'local knowledges' from 'particular non-metropolitan locations ... offer[s] additional opportunities for thinking about Shakespeare's plays'.[22]

III

In setting up an encounter between the two poems, Faiz's nazm, 'Don't Ask Me, My Love, for That Love Again', and Shakespeare's Sonnet 57, I believe we can access new resonances across a centuries-wide temporal and cultural divide. I approach them through the prism of 'lyric thinking', showing how the speakers fashioning individual selves express a 'phenomenology' of worldly experience, within the constant awareness of their own limits among different kinds of 'worldmaking' within distinct historical contexts.

'Don't Ask Me, My Love, for That Love Again' (c.1962–1965)

That which then was ours, my love,
don't ask me for that love again.
The world then was gold, burnished with light –
and only because of you. That's what I had believed.
How could one weep for sorrows other than yours?
How could one have any sorrow but the one you gave?
So what were these protests, these rumors of injustice?
A glimpse of your face was evidence of springtime.
The sky, wherever I looked, was nothing but your eyes.
If You'd fall into my arms, Fate would be helpless.[23]

In the title and opening stanza of this iconic nazm, Faiz somewhat ambiguously declares it a love poem, using the traditional convention of an address to the Beloved. Here we find the poetic persona torn between the exquisite demands of unrequited love on the one hand, and those of the larger world and its oppressions – 'rumors of injustice' – on the other. The speaker is asking the Beloved not to ask for the kind of love formerly given – 'pahli si mahabbat' – a singular love, alert to nothing but the Beloved's charms and cruelties. But here we also catch a glimpse of the consoling transcendence of this love in which the speaker formerly believed: 'The world then was gold, burnished with light – / and only because of you'. The Beloved is the source of both the sorrows and comforts of love, as he

---

[20] Ramazani, 'The local poem', p. 696.
[21] Nandini Das, 'Encounter as process: England and Japan in the late sixteenth century', *Renaissance Quarterly* 69 (2016), 1343–68; p. 1346.
[22] Martin Orkin, *Local Shakespeares: Proximations and Power* (London, 2005), p. 2. For a further discussion of local and global engagements and negotiations of Shakespearian works and their meanings, see pp. 1–7.
[23] Faiz Ahmed Faiz, 'Mujh se pahli si muhabbat mere mahbub na mang' (Urdu), translated from Urdu by Agha Shahid Ali. Reprinted from *The Rebel's Silhouette*.

nostalgically remembers: a 'glimpse of your face was evidence of springtime'.

Soon thereafter, in the second, closing stanza of the short lyric, we 'travel' with the speaker through visceral scenes of cruelty, injustice and alienation. His sensuous, romantic desire cannot, it seems, coexist with the commodification of bodies in the 'open market'.

> The rich had cast their spell on history:
> dark centuries had been embroidered on brocades and silks.
> Bitter threads began to unravel before me
> as I went into alleys and in open markets
> saw bodies plastered with ash, bathed in blood.
> I saw them sold and bought, again and again.
> This too deserves attention.

The speaker continues to struggle with conflicting emotional and affective responses towards his Beloved:

> And you are still too ravishing – What should I do?
> There are other sorrows in this world,
> Comforts other than love.
> Don't ask me, my love, for my love again.

The speaker circles back to the angst of the opening, and the poem ends where it began.

Approaching Faiz's poem through the lens of 'lyric thinking', we can observe the phenomenology of the speaker's experiences in the immediacy of his psychic and emotional dislocation in a cruel world. He is seeking the embrace of the Beloved, but cannot avail himself of the generic consolations of romance that may be afforded by the love lyric. In the intensity of the speaker's first-person address to the Beloved we get a strong sense of *'who speaks and how they speak'*, but we are led further to consider 'which voices get heard and *how* they get heard' in the world,[24] as the speaker gives a material presence, if not a literal voice, to victims of degradation and particularly of sexual violence, bodies 'bathed in blood' and being 'sold and bought again and again'.

Critical reaction to these fault-lines in the terrain of the poem's world – and of our own habitations – offers a variety of responses to Faiz's poem. While some argue that he merely turns a 'traditional' poetic vocabulary to radical political ends and that we should read the figure of the distant Beloved, for instance, as a figure of the hoped-for revolution, other more nuanced views highlight the tensions between two competing aesthetic and political investments – between Persianate and Arabic influences on poetic form and the socialist, secular forces of his times. Overall, critics have offered many rich insights into Faiz's complex artistic journey – as, for instance, the one below:

> Faiz, in spite of his leftist leanings, is not a rebel poet in the real sense of the word. He is an admirer of the classical image of Urdu Ghazal, and his style bears traces of the language of both [Mirza] Ghalib and [Mohammad] Iqbal [major Urdu poets in the nineteenth and twentieth centuries]. He has accepted and assimilated much that was in the tradition and has used the classical conventions and imagery with such depth and ingenuity that his poetry reflects the heritage of the past and the quest and restlessness of the present.[25]

Another scholar of his poetry describes Faiz's distinct poetic *oeuvre* within the historical experience of the partitioned/disjunct world of the Indian subcontinent: '[Faiz's] poetry exemplifies some of the central dilemmas of Urdu writing in the aftermath of the partition of India at the moment of independence from British rule.... The central drama of his poetry is the dialectic of a collective selfhood at the disjunctures of language, culture, nation, and community.'[26] Faiz's 'lyric voice' was never compromised even when his speakers took head on the forces of history and the cultural logic of the nation-state. 'Don't Ask Me, My Love, for That Love Again' vividly exemplifies this process of the competing pull of contradictory emotions: for instance, he speaks of his Beloved's beauty as 'evidence of springtime' on the one hand, and of 'bodies bathed in blood' on the other. As one critic observes: 'One is calling for love, the other for action. To Faiz, both are dear.... This cleavage between human passions and socialistic obligation,

---

[24] Ramachandran, 'Afterword', p. 450.
[25] Narang, 'Tradition and innovation', p. 24.
[26] Mufti, 'Towards a lyric history', pp. 246-7.

or the division of loyalty between reality and ideal, classical and modern, or love and faith, runs its contradictory course throughout the poetry of Faiz.'[27]

A sketch of Faiz's life reveals the intermixture of influences within the history of empire and postcolonial nationalism in Pakistan. He was born in Sialkot in undivided Punjab, in 1911. He did not have a privileged background, but his father served the royal family of Afghanistan and later studied to become a lawyer in England. 'Faiz did not travel much till later, but he imbibed the spirit of the 1930s from books and pamphlets and went on to earn a master's degree in English literature and another in Arabic.'[28] His continuing left-wing politics led to later conflicts with the Pakistan state, including an imprisonment in his homeland and exile for a few years in Lebanon. But he returned to Pakistan and continued with his complex and compassionate critiques of the repressive nationalism and the plight of nations such as Pakistan, all via the lyric mode.[29]

To return to the nazm (part of his early output), it is among some of Faiz's most iconic poems, widely familiar to large swathes of the population in South Asia through the Hindi–Urdu links – and to parts of the Middle East, where his earlier friendship with Mahmoud Darwish, the noted Palestinian poet and revolutionary, influenced his vision of both poetry and politics. On one level, it is a meta-poetic poem about the social limits of the lyric, but it also represents a 'transnational poetics', demonstrating how a lyric can inhabit multiple sites and temporalities – from the Persianate and Arabic romantic influences on Urdu lyric poetry to socialist, secular politics, yet attuned to the beauties of Islamic culture and languages. Overall, Faiz's constant fluctuations between competing classical/religious traditions and political commitments make him a figure reminiscent of the artistic creators of early modern England such as Shakespeare and his contemporaries. Like them, he hearkens back to classical literary forms, while constantly deviating from them, remaking his cultural legacy and reminding his readers of the limitations of those very forms.

IV

I approach the encounter between Shakespeare's Sonnet 57 and Faiz's nazm within shared phenomenological experiences, while bridging the divide of historical periods and cultures. Recent studies, as mentioned at the outset, have explored genealogical relationships between the sonnet and the ghazal, going back to premodern lyric forms. In this article, I cross a temporal divide and show that a shared affective investment in feelings of *discontent and consolation* in love dominates *both* Faiz's and Shakespeare's lyric poems. Like the inclusion of Faiz's poems in *Hamlet/Haider*, articulating loss and nostalgia in the midst of destruction, an interactive reading of the two poems generates resonances and echoes between them which may not seem obvious in a cursory reading. However, the formal and thematic elements of the classical Urdu lyric – the plaintive complaint, the idealization of the Beloved, the sense of abject vulnerability, and the inability to claim love – all evident in 'Don't Ask Me, My Love, for That Love Again', also shape our travels through the Shakespearian Sonnet 57, 'Being your slave, what should I do but tend'. From the opening quatrain, the sonnet draws us with urgent immediacy into the phenomenological world of an insecure and abject speaker:

> Being your slave, what should I do but tend
> Upon the hours and times of your desire?
> I have no precious time at all to spend,
> Nor services to do, till you require
>
> (57.1–4)

At the outset, the speaker or the persona casts himself as a 'slave', not simply a pleading supplicant, but tending to all the 'hours and times' of the 'desire[s]' of the addressee. On the surface, his enslavement seems to be to a single person, as he

---

[27] Narang, 'Tradition and innovation', p. 31, using a different translation.
[28] Ali, 'Introduction', to *The Rebel's Silhouette*, pp. 34–5.
[29] For a further discussion of Faiz's biography, see Hashmi and Hashmi, *The Way It Was Once*.

incrementally acknowledges his abject subservience to a young friend, both physically and emotionally. One way to view his enslavement then would be only as an individual, not as a general or institutional condition. However, I argue that we can draw out and expand on the social meanings of this lyric self by noting the historical resonances of the word 'slave' in the context of European enslavement practices in the early modern period. One key, recognizable meaning of the word 'slave' at the time would denote a person 'who has the (legal) status of being the property of another, has no personal freedom or rights, and is used as forced labour or as an unpaid servant; an enslaved person'.[30] By self-identifying as a 'slave' throughout the poem, the speaker reveals his helplessness in the face of coercion, while also unsettling the white, identity bonds of English male friendship that provides a throughline for a majority of poems in Shakespeare's sonnet sequence. Critical responses to Sonnet 57 do not touch upon the history of slavery in relation to this poem. Helen Vendler labels the poem as the '"slavery" sonnet 57', but by enclosing the term in scare quotes, she blocks off any historical meanings; instead, she reads it as a 'shadow poem' with an emphasis on the speaker's split motivations, whereby 'one can deduce, from the speaker's actual statements, what he would really like to say to the young man'.[31]

If we explore the implications of Vendler's term, the 'slavery' sonnet, a useful point of entry would be to chart the emotional and affective shifts and turns of the speaker's revelations of the varied conditions of his enslavement. In the quatrain below, the 'slave' reiterates the unrelenting servitude of love without respite, while acknowledging that he must repress any complaint. He generalizes his frustrations as he can only 'chide' the 'world-without-end hour' for his endless servitude. The addressee, the enslaving beloved, is a 'sovereign' (57.6), the centre of power (expanding upon the earlier imagery of the sun with its 'sovereign eye' in Sonnet 33 (2)), intimating a world of hierarchy and domination. An ambiguous comfort seems to be the speaker's fallback, as he refuses to let the 'bitterness of absence sour' him (57.7), once the former has bid him – his 'servant' (8) – adieu.

An absence of the Beloved in the life of the enslaved speaker is a punishment for him, hence his emotional pain is a mark of his service in enthrallment.

> Nor dare I chide the world-without-end hour
> Whilst I, my sovereign, watch the clock for you,
> Nor think the bitterness of absence sour
> When you have bid your servant once adieu.
> (57.5–8)

An aggrieved, though repressed, complaint shadows the final quatrain and couplet. If only the enslaved speaker could disclose his 'jealous thought' (9), then he could confront the Beloved about 'Where [he] may be' (10) and his other possibly erotic attachments or 'affairs' (10). But all remains unspoken, with the acceptance that 'So true a fool is love' (13), accompanied by an effort to think 'no ill' (14) of the Beloved. The sonnet thus has an uneasy, forced closure with the speaker remaining the 'sad slave' (11), implying his failed hopes in love. The breakdown of hope coupled with a sense of the futility of love also informs the emotional angst of Faiz's speaker. As one critic observes, Shakespeare's final 'couplet activates the very suspicions which it claims to suppress'.[32]

> Nor dare I question with my jealous thought
> Where you may be, or your affairs suppose,
> But like a sad slave stay and think of naught
> Save, where you are, how happy you make those.
> So true a fool is love that in your will,
> Though you do anything, he thinks no ill.
> (9–14)

One can also perhaps read the ending as the speaker's distancing himself from his enslavement in a third person – for being a 'fool' for love. But we get no sense that the speaker has overcome – or moved past – his vulnerability and abjection. We

---

[30] *OED Online*, 'slave', sense I.1, revised 2022.
[31] Helen Vendler, 'Formal pleasure in the Sonnets', in *A Companion to Shakespeare's Sonnets*, ed. Schoenfeldt, 27–44; p. 38.
[32] *Shakespeare's Sonnets*, ed. Katherine Duncan-Jones (London, 1997), p. 224.

do not get a social profile or location of Shakespeare's speaker, but, not unlike Faiz's lyric voice, he nonetheless has to mediate his individual experiences in a contingent world, where his own emotional needs and the Beloved's demands – 'hours and times of [his] desire' – produce conditions of instability and deprivation.

While Faiz's nazm clearly references the call for social justice, with concrete images of violence and degradation, I believe that the skilfully constructed argument around the emotional state of the speaker embodied as a 'slave' in Sonnet 57 also invites us to consider larger conditions of slavery and enslavement. Tracking the phenomenology of fashioning a self under duress of rejection, when we consider that it is only the 'slave' who has the speaking voice in the sonnet, then we are prompted to return to the urgent question with which this article opened: who speaks and how do they speak? And are they being heard? Is the 'slave' here just one poetic persona, or can we hear echoes of others in similar conditions? Given that the late sixteenth century was the period of the burgeoning European slave trade, with England joining belatedly, the word, 'slave' would have had historical associations to the early English slave voyages.[33] To consolidate the associations between the enslaved speaker here and the Western slave trade, one has only to further contextualize the poem within the sequence as a whole, specifically in relation to the lyrics addressed to the 'Dark Lady':

[Sonnets] 127 to 154 of Shakespeare's sequence [which depart] from the conventional depiction of the unattainable, virtuous, and fair beauty by attributing to the beloved some rather unflattering attributes: dun breasts, wiry black hair, reeking breath, a heavy tread, and an unrestrained sexual appeal that distempers men to distraction.[34]

Such a contrast between the fair male friend, as in Sonnet 57, and the 'Dark Lady' Beloved reinscribes the racialized dichotomies and hierarchies of the early modern period, thereby inserting race as a defining element in the full sonnet sequence.[35] Thus, drawing on Patricia Akhimie's pedagogical glossing exercise in her article 'Cultivating expertise: glossing Shakespeare and race', we can recognize that while racial dissonance is a familiar theme in Shakespeare's sonnets, particularly in those addressed to the so-called 'Dark Lady', by reading Sonnet 57 in relationship to both those poems, as well as through the lens of enslavement practices and the slave trade, the contextual interconnections of the word 'slave' can be expanded.[36] The sonnets are replete with vocabularies evoking 'darkness' in varying embodiments and references, and the traces of 'dark centuries' evoked by Faiz's lyric, 'Don't Ask Me, My Love, For That Love Again', also haunt Sonnet 57 through and beyond the individual lyric voice of the 'slave'. The erotic and affective investments in both poems partake of this darkness in ways that deepen our phenomenological journey through the two speakers' discontents and consolations of love.

Following the lyric journey of the poems of Faiz and Shakespeare through the different cultural and historical contexts, Vendler's insistence on the seclusion of poetry needs some reconsideration. She rejects the need to study the social contexts of lyric poetry, and argues instead that 'the lyric though it may refer to the social, remains the genre that directs its *mimesis* toward the performance of the mind in solitary speech'.[37] In Vendler's reading of the sonnets, she views political concerns as being antithetical to the aesthetic pleasures of poetry, critiquing those who bring social issues to bear upon what she considers a purely literary analysis. Countering her somewhat narrow view of the affects and social effects of the sonnets, Michael

---

[33] See Jyotsna G. Singh, 'Hakluyt's books and Hawkins' slaving voyages: the transatlantic slave trade in the English imaginary', in *Companion to the Global Renaissance*, ed. Singh, 249–75.

[34] Carol Meija LaPerle, 'The racialized affects of ill-will in the Dark Lady sonnets', in *Race and Affect in Early Modern English Literature*, ed. LaPerle (Tempe, AZ, 2022), 205–21; p. 206.

[35] See Kim Hall's analysis of the dichotomy of dark and fair in *Things of Darkness: Economies of Race and Gender in Early Modern England* (Ithaca, 1995).

[36] Patricia Akhimie, 'Cultivating expertise: glossing Shakespeare and race', *Literature Compass* 18 (2021), n.p.

[37] Helen Vendler, *The Art of Shakespeare's Sonnets* (Cambridge, MA, 1997), pp. 1–2.

Schoenfeldt states that the 'political and aesthetic ... are in these poems absolutely inseparable'.[38] Agreeing with Schoenfeldt, I believe that Vendler's argument imagines the lyric in an impermeable compartment, generating pleasures that are self-referential and implicitly solipsistic. Her reading carries the new critical emphasis on poetic meaning as an intrinsic essence, premised on an eschewing of history and context. Lyric poems want to travel in the world across time and space, and as I have shown in this article on the lyric poems by Faiz and Shakespeare separated by time and space, they are always open to encounters, dialogues and cross-pollinations of cultures.

---

[38] Schoenfeldt, 'Introduction', p. 9.

THE THING ITSELF OR THE IMAGE OF THAT HORROR: FICTIONS, FASCISMS AND *WE THAT ARE YOUNG*

PRETI TANEJA

I was honoured to be invited to give a keynote lecture at the World Shakespeare Congress (WSC), 2021, introduced by Professor Margo Hendricks. It is in Margo's work that my own ideas find concise articulation. She gifts us the courage of her conviction when, in her lecture 'Colouring the past, rewriting our future: RaceB4Race' at the Folger Shakespeare Library's Race and Periodization Symposium 2019, she emphasizes that the 'kinetic importance' of work on premodern critical race studies lies in 'finding ways to destabilise the academy's role in furthering capitalism's use of White supremacy to sustain itself'.[1] For decades, Hendricks has been resolute about this project of expansive recentring, setting the terms but also working to make space for Black, brown and indigenous scholarship; calling for women of colour to see with our own eyes, speak with our own mouths, in our many languages about our multiple histories. When she says she is 'unfiltered', she exhorts us to be as fearless. Taking as given that 'colonialism/ imperialism, capitalism and White supremacy are handfast' and that 'there is a deep connective tissue between the resurgence of white supremacy and fascist discourse'[2] – I take her call seriously; for me it means questioning what people do with *Shakespeare*; and in this I include myself. Self-reflexivity is a critical responsibility, particularly within the privilege of giving a keynote, or indeed when writing a novel. I hope I can do the call some justice here.

In every age fiction writers working in fascist times, where fascism can be understood not as an *appeal* to emotion, but as an emotion itself; and where fascism as named by Toni Morrison is the 'succubus twin'[3] of racism, ask ourselves the same questions. What is the purpose of fiction, the point of making artifice in the face of organized horror? The cult of the individual, of optimism bias as spectacle – where, for example, populism constructs and supports a person and personality who becomes the lightning rod for right-wing ideology by promising to 'make X great again' – are fascism's cornerstones. As Hendricks notes, this 'never allows us to see racism as structural but only as a structural event'.[4] For people of colour, I take this as a definition of trauma.[5] The language of feminist resistance borrows from theatre to deploy the useful term 'gaslighting': putting the burden of

---

[1] Margo Hendricks, 'Colouring the past, rewriting our future: RaceB4Race', Race and Periodization Symposium, Folger Institute and Arizona Center for Medieval Studies, Folger Shakespeare Library, USA, September 2019. For the full transcript, see: www.folger.edu/research/featured-research-projects-and-initiatvies/race-and-periodization/#about-the-symposium.
[2] Hendricks, 'Colouring'.
[3] Toni Morrison, 'Racism and fascism', in *The Source of Self-Regard: Selected Essays, Speeches, and Meditations* (New York, 2019), p. 15.
[4] Hendricks, 'Colouring'.
[5] Preti Taneja, *Aftermath* (Oakland, 2021), p. 13.

'proof' and survival against racism and fascism forever onto the racialized body, not the racist mind and voice. Meanwhile, the real violence that riddles policy, policing, privacy, sexuality and gender, free speech, education and cultural life sinks deeper into our societies and becomes more blatant, murderous and deliberately unaccountable to its citizens. Shakespeare, both as cultural figure and as textual referent is often deployed in such circumstances: we know the great humanist arrives with the arsenal of violent imperialism. In our times this has not changed, though it might have changed form. In the same way, iterations of fascism link Britain to India to the USA – the three locations of three spectacles interpreted through Shakespeare that I explore here. First, in England, as manifest in a xenophobic Brexit and in the COVID-19 pandemic response; then, in India, in the form of the hard-line right-wing Hindu Indian prime minister Narendra Modi and his genocidal, Islamophobic tactics, particularly in evidence in Kashmir; and finally moving to the USA and the rise of the MeToo movement in 2018 when Brett Kavanaugh, a man accused of sexual violence, was nominated to the Supreme Court.

We That Are Young, my novel, published in the UK in 2017 and in the USA the following year, is a translation of Shakespeare's *King Lear* to contemporary India. My use of the term 'translation' draws on critical definitions, including by two women writers – first, Adrienne Rich, who states:

Re-vision – the act of looking back, of seeing with fresh eyes, of entering an old text from a new critical direction – is for us more than a chapter in history: it is an act of survival. Until we can understand the assumptions in which we are drenched, we cannot know ourselves. And this drive to self knowledge for woman, is more than a search for identity, it is part of her refusal of the self-destructiveness of male dominated society.[6]

The writer and translator Kate Briggs offers 'translation' as a way of speaking about working with 'canonical' texts in new forms, languages and contexts, as a feminist act that slightly reframes Rich's 'looking back'. Briggs's contexts (through her use of fragmented form, rather than realist novels where Rich's 're-vision' is often used to theorize Jane Smiley's work on *King Lear*, *A Thousand Acres*[7]) take us forward into writing possible futures before they come about, futures that women writers can anticipate *because* of our 'entering the text' from our own critical direction. Drawing also on *Lear* as a haunting of our language and as a mode of expression but without quotation, as I do in *We That Are Young*, Briggs writes:

I hear this talk of the desire to write the thing itself, only this time by myself, as one possible version – as a very precise way of phrasing my own experience – of the impulse to translate. Translation as a means of writing the other's work out with your own hands, in your own setting, your own time and in your own language with all the attention, thinking and searching, the testing and invention that the task requires. Translation as a laborious way of making the work present to yourself, of finding it again yourself, *for yourself*. Translation as a responsive and appropriative practising of an extant work at the level of the sentence, working it out: a working out on the basis of the desired work whose energy source is the inclusion of a new and different vitality that comes with and from me.[8]

We That Are Young combines my close reading of *King Lear* with Indian epic texts, legal documents on annexation, Partition, the accession of the Princely States, and the abrogation of human rights in Kashmir, accessed in archives and via witness testimony gathered in slum areas and in Kashmir in 2012. I draw on all registers of language, media and experience to make a work of linguistic, thematic and critical engagement with Britain and India's entwined past and its legacies of pain, now meted out in the name of Hindu fascism via tactics inscribed by Imperial Britain into Indian law. I track the language, plot and themes of *King Lear* precisely – Lear's structure is the substructure of *We That Are Young*. I break with form while drawing

---

[6] Adrienne Rich, 'When we dead awaken: writing as re-vision', *College English* 34 Special Issue: Women, Writing and Teaching (Oct. 1972), 18–30; p. 18.
[7] Jane Smiley, *A Thousand Acres* (New York, 1991).
[8] Kate Briggs, *This Little Art* (London, 2017), p. 119 (italics in the original).

on theatre's constructions: the novel is told from the close third-person perspectives of five young people (three sisters and two brothers), who are the inheritors of the damage of colonialism, Partition and the spoils of neo-capitalism. The characters in my novel don't escape the play's rubric. Daughters and fathers die and are blinded: Edgar, or Jit, inherits the kingdom. In my novel he is no prophet of hope, nor do I read him that way in the play. He embodies and predicts a fascist future for India as a means of sounding warning via political fiction, as I read Edgar to do for England. Since Shakespeare wrote, that future has come to be. So, here is my confession: at first, I was uneasy about staying within *King Lear*'s boundaries as generative constraint. What change could come from that?

Arundhati Roy, writing about fiction as a form of resistance to Indian fascism and often from the point of view of others, believes 'fiction has the capaciousness and freedom to hold a universe of infinite complexity'.[9] The same has been argued countless times about Shakespeare's works. True or not, the move is used to justify his relentless centrality, even to shore up a fascist status quo at particular moments of public crisis. As I reckon with the ongoing ravages of our world, I need to think both through that deployment of Shakespeare as cod-analysis of our times, and about the more complex potential that writing fiction within Shakespeare – so, from the point of view of the elite – offered me against the fascisms we face today. As the old idea that Shakespeare's cultural dominance is proof that, somehow, he creates us as humans refuses to die, new forms of fiction, in hybrid cultures often considered subaltern, question what *kinds of humans* arise: from the plays and their dissemination, but also from fusion with 'otherness'.

Though I work in hybrid creative forms primarily, let me borrow the scholarly convention and articulate three key themes that underpin my work. First, my use of 'others'. In *The Hindus: An Alternative History* (which was recalled in India following charges of inciting religious offence and has since been redistributed), Wendy Doniger identifies 'others' as 'People who from the standpoint of most high caste and Hindu males, are alternative in the sense of *otherness*, people of other religions, or cultures, or castes, or species (animals) or gender (women).'[10] In Britain this includes *racialized* people, especially women; it's from that intersectional stance that I see, and explore at the sentence level of my writing, how 'otherness' is punished and pushed towards violent reaction in *King Lear*.

Second, the link between fascism and Shakespeare. In *Racism and Fascism*, Morrison writes a ten-point map to understanding fascism's blueprint, much of which resonates today. The fact that we have seen many of fascism's moves before only tells us that it plays a long game. It is one in which the insistent deployment of Shakespeare as spectacle to shore up spectacle at public moments makes him a synecdoche for the game itself.

Finally, for those who need it, a brief précis of some points in the Partition of India in 1947 that resonate in my work. After over 100 years of colonization by the British, negotiations for Independence between the Nehru-led, majority Hindu Congress Party, the Muslim League led by Muhammed Ali Jinnah and the Imperial power's appointed 'Viceroy', the British king's cousin Lord Mountbatten, resulted in the subcontinent being divided along Hindu/Muslim lines into new nation-states: India, Pakistan and eventually, in 1971, Bangladesh. The forced migration of Hindus to India and Muslims to Pakistan resulted in the biggest mass movement of people the world has seen. Millions were killed, disappeared or died from starvation, thirst, disease. Women's bodies, always analogous for land in feudal societies and in claiming honour for the new nation, were forfeit; many were killed by their own families to avoid them being abducted or raped as they were forced to convert by men of the other faith. In India, princes of independent states now acceded to the new nation of India or chose Pakistan; kings were

---

[9] Arundhati Roy, 'The graveyard talks back', *Lithub* (USA, 2020), https://lithub.com/the-graveyard-talks-back-arundhati-roy-on-fiction-in-the-time-of-fake-news.

[10] Wendy Doniger, *The Hindus: An Alternative History* (Oxford, 2010), p. 1.

effectively left without kingdoms. In Kashmir, the Hindu Dogra ruler administered a majority Muslim population who wanted the right to self-determination. But the maharajah acceded to majority Hindu India, with the promise of a plebiscite to decide the future. Protections for semi-autonomy in Kashmir were enshrined under Article 370 of the Indian constitution, including the provision, set during British rule (so before Partition), that non-Kashmiris cannot own land there. Kashmir became contested territory, split between India and Pakistan, divided by a Line of Control that is the world's most militarized border and which remains in place today.

These broad brushstrokes of Partition, from the division of a kingdom that results in civil war to the fate of women within that, can be traced directly onto the plot of *King Lear* – if one happened to be an immigrant child with a love of reading and an overactive imagination, looking to fill a void of mainstream legitimacy in her own origin story. Though recounted in South Asian homes across the UK, Partition and its harms are not taught in English schools. The curation and erasure of histories is part of a fascist playbook; when taught well, literature can fill such voids. At seventeen years old, *King Lear* became mine in that sense.

But now to switch perspective and move to a story from the recent past. Just imagine – which is the first function of fiction – you are in England. It is March 2020. The seriousness of the COVID-19 pandemic has finally precipitated the ultra-conservative UK government to put the country into its first of a series of overdue lockdowns. And a 'tweet' begins doing the rounds: Shakespeare wrote *King Lear* during quarantine from the plague. The tweet goes viral: it generates a slew of responses in media. In his opening address to the WSC 2021, Peter Holland writes, '[t]he parallels were never quite convincing enough. If it has done nothing else, the pandemic has made us differently conscious of our world.'[11] While you agree that the parallels were not convincing, you respectfully disagree with who is implied by that 'us'. It does not include you. The political function of that collective *we* is what is at stake here: the pandemic has only revealed a world to them which many of us already live in, are all too painfully aware of, incarcerated by.

In the tweet, it feels to you as if Shakespeare is being deployed to fulfil Morrison's ninth point in her ten-point list on how fascism works:

Reward mindlessness and apathy with monumentalized entertainments and with little pleasures, tiny seduction: a few minutes on television, a few lines in the press; a little pseudo-success; the illusion of power and influence; a little fun, a little style, a little consequence.[12]

You scroll further. On your timeline, more Black and brown faces than you have ever seen represented in UK news begin to appear: the first people to die in the UK's pandemic. Later you watch the news and witness the most banal but telling image to sum up those early weeks: people rushing to the supermarket to stockpile toilet rolls. Meanwhile *good* South Asian and Black immigrants are working in every immigration-controlled stratum of Britain's world-famously free national health service as doctors, nurses, hospital porters, or are delivering food, stocking the shelves, working in factories all the way down the food supply chain. The majority are Muslim. Here is the 'we' you recognize. And the part of your brain indelibly occupied by the text of *King Lear* registers why, for us, the pandemic parallel does not work. The *content* of the play is being ignored. The only words you can think of at that moment are:

> So distribution should undo excess,
> And each man have enough
>
> (*Lear* F 4:1.64)

But why should we call on Shakespeare at all to understand this moment? What is the function of that deployment in culture? And what should we make him say to reaffirm, comfortingly, that *Shakespeare told us so*, and re-inscribe the violence of that individual charismatic national genius and

---

[11] Peter Holland, 'Welcome', *11th World Shakespeare Congress: Shakespeare Circuits, 18–24 July 2021, Programme* (Singapore, 2021), p. 1.

[12] Morrison, *The Source*, p. 15.

the singular defence, necessary in his historical context, but not in ours, of the restoration at the end of each play, of a certain status quo? What further damage might our own need for the security of his authority as it meets the prismatic potential of his language do us long term?

The long felt, long silenced sense of racial grief rises as a choking feeling; the lasting indignities of being *generationally* minoritized via the intersections of class, caste, religion and gender in the UK have always been a disproportionate cause of death, and now the pandemic is laying that bare. But it's OK because Shakespeare wrote *King Lear* during a plague, and white people can be sage about this, with him. The first of your friends loses a parent to COVID-19: he was one of the Partition generation. Who experienced colonial rule or its immediate aftermath, and who knew better than most the relationship between imperialism and fascism. Who came to the UK dreaming, soon to realize that colonial stratification informed immigration, but also policing, education and cultural policy in a Britain needing cheap ex-colonial labour to rebuild after the war. This cemented the place and value of Black and South Asian, Hindu and Muslim lives in the essentially still feudal English society now known as late capitalism. Into these losses, we have no words.

But fascism does. The government and the far-right press constantly evoke the 'Spirit of the Blitz' (a reference to the white British public's much-mythologized stoic response to the air raids of World War II), and dub the pandemic workers bearing the life-and-death costs of government policies 'frontline heroes' and 'guards' against COVID-19, deploying the terminology of war and policing to incarcerate workers in place, as the natural sacrificial bodies in the 'fight'.[13]

We clap for the workers even as our government and press, many of them the direct descendants of the elite men of that wartime period, base their 'Leave' arguments on anti-immigrant border control, and on punishing those same 'heroes' – many of them working-class, Muslim people – and sell the potent emptiness of the rhetorical phrase 'Brexit means Brexit' – sounding fury and signifying nothing – to the descendants of that same majority white public.

Rarely coy in showing the dead of other, non-white countries, the press barely reports on the disproportionate deaths, the bodies kept waiting for Muslim burial, in certain parts of our inner cities. The devastation of Black and Asian communities who have worked for decades to live a dignified life in the UK is hidden from public view.

Our xenophobic Brexit comes to pass, and a new era of border imposition begins, directly linked to imperial partitions – Lear's partitions if you like – which run through current Brexit-related disputes over the honouring of the Northern Ireland protocol, signed to protect hard-won freedoms and peace after settler colonization and corresponding violence. And as each lockdown commences, the 'Shakespeare wrote Lear in a plague' tweet does the rounds again, keeping whiteness entertained. How telling that the focus of that tweet's uneasy half-joke shores up the worldview that capitalism, even when it comes to cultural production, requires the sacrifice of a racialized many to keep a more elite and dare I say in Lear's terms, a group who think of themselves as more *naturally* deserving, safe. And you think you are grieving in your country of birth – you don't know yet that not only are your diasporic friends, siblings and families going to be among the hardest hit, but also that, when what was originally called the 'India' COVID variant (changed by the WHO to 'the Delta variant' to avoid racist backlash) begins to take its toll, you cannot join your families in struggle and grief there either.

By the time I gave this keynote over Zoom in July 2021, over 150,000 people had died of COVID-19 and COVID-related causes in the UK, yet the reversals, denials, corruption and bluster of Boris Johnson carried on. Apparently he took the message of the tweet seriously, and was busy working on his book *Shakespeare: the Riddle of Genius*, or trying to get someone else to author it for him. Announced in 2015, the associative wordplay of the title aligns Boris the

---

[13] Jackie Wang, *Carceral Capitalism* (South Pasadena, CA, 2018).

clown through the word *riddle* with Shakespeare's 'genius' in an attempt to confer a statesmanlike gravitas on the politician: here is the Prime Minister on the National Bard. Here is the deployment of Shakespeare as spectacle to endorse power's rhetoric, exactly as Rowan Williams notes, 'We are urged to judge performance in terms of crowd pleasing; we don't want to see our leaders engaged in reflection, or inviting us to look behind and around issues. Fascism is one of the most extreme forms of the triumph of spectacle.'[14] Meanwhile, in the Home Office, UK Home Secretary Priti Patel continued to announce Islamophobic carceral policies, prison expansion, border control. As a British Indian, the daughter of Kenyan-Indian immigrants, she was one of the right wing's most powerful diversity decoys; in 2020, I read her as one of Indian Prime Minister Narendra Modi's true heirs.

I want to go back again now, a year or two to the point I first felt that unease as fiction and life collided. Once again, I begin with a tweet. This time about India, and the erasure of Article 370 of the Indian constitution, which protected the semi-autonomous status of Kashmir in the form of its own flag, constitution and governance; it also promised a plebiscite for Kashmiri self-determination (never enacted through the years). Article 35A sat with this to prohibit non-Kashmiris owning land there – for example, through marriage with Kashmiri women – guarding against that form of settler colonialism in which women's bodies are conduits. Article 370 was widely considered to be inviolable. But in 2019, under the guise of economic development and national 'duty', the Modi government simply swept it away, calling it a 'historical blunder'. The BBC reported that everyone was surprised.[15] A reader in India tweeted and tagged me with a paragraph from my book and this observation: 'Modi's speech about developing Kashmir reminded me of Preti Taneja's *We That Are Young*, a riff on King Lear, where Bapuji, the money-minded patriarch, decides to open his newest, lavish hotel in Kashmir.'[16] He was referring to a passage that correlates to 5.3 of the play, where Cordelia and Kent discuss Lear, and which I wrote at least two years before the actual abrogation of Article 370 took place.

My corresponding characters Sita and Kritik are in a Srinagar garden, eating finger chips before the opening of her father's seven-star hotel – a statement of Hindu Indian arrival through the Trojan horse of development after nearly seven and a half decades of India-imposed sanctions, arrests, disappearances, torture, blindings, floods, internet shutdowns and economic deprivations ... the slow obliteration of Kashmir as is, and of India's Muslims, which is the long game of Hindu-Indian fascism. Sita voices her unease about the ethics of the hotel's existence, and wonders how her father has been able to buy land for the hotel since it was her deceased mother who was Kashmiri, not him. Kritik waves her objections aside:

Do you know how much produce this place can yield? he asks. How much we can benefit from free trade? The land is so fertile; we will sprout money. The West of the East, this place could be. And now is the time for us to make it come good. We will occupy the people with tourism. So what if the old laws prohibit? Time to sweep them away. And you will manage it all.[17]

Writing this passage, I remember feeling like I had crossed a border into that space of liberty that only fiction allows: in which projections and predictions, the culmination of fears and phantasms, can be made – but always only as fiction. When people began to tweet my words back at me while a devastating situation was really unfolding, I was horrified. The real plight of 7 million Kashmiris and the shocking dissolution of a long-standing protection of their right to self-determination, the actual redrawing of the citizenship map during a five-month internet and communications blackout, could not, while happening, be spoken about

---

[14] Rowan Williams, 'Shakespeare in disrupted times', *The New Statesman* (September 2020), www.newstatesman.com/long-reads/2020/09/shakesperean-times-disruption-robert-mccrum.
[15] 'Article 370: what happened with Kashmir and why it matters', *BBC News*, August 2019: www.bbc.co.uk/news/world-asia-india-49234708.
[16] Twitter, 8 August 2019, 5:43 p.m.
[17] Preti Taneja, *We That Are Young* (Norwich, 2017), p. 493.

through the prism of art. The moral void between Shakespeare used as spectacle and fascism's real and murderous harms loomed, and it happened through a tweet about my own work. But I was also thinking, *why was the commentariat surprised?* What was it about the way they were reading the world before this event came to pass that made it so shocking to them when it came?

To move forward, I had to go back: into the grain of what brought that moment about in a complex reality and in the novel. The move to sweep away those protections has a long back story in the power of the saffron-fascist Rashtriya Swayam Sevak Sangh (RSS), the most powerful volunteer organization in India, which arches over its political arm, Modi's party, the BJP. In *We That Are Young* Devraj/Lear is based on a composite of Modi and other Hindu politicians who always have a finger pointing everywhere but at themselves. But my real focus is on their inheritors: the generation who bring the old methods into the new iterations we see today.

I do this through the character of Edgar, whom I conceive as Jit, son of Ranjit/Gloucester. I read Jit/Edgar as perhaps the most selfish, dangerous and amoral of the young characters; he has the greatest tendency towards violence and revenge for being made to feel that core emotion so easy for fascism to harness: a sense of debasement, of threatened dignity, of shame. Jit's Shakespearian blueprint hides behind the performance of poverty and debasement and the construct of chivalry, to excuse his punitive and self-justifying ascent to power (via committing two or – if you include his enabling of his own father – three murders). The least trustworthy person in the play appears to be the most convincing because he keeps saying what we want to hear about who he is. Using powerful symbols, calling on primitive myths and constantly manipulating spectacle, Edgar inherits the kingdom: essentially, he is Lear's shadow. Anyone who might see him well enough to be inclined to stop him – is dead.

Where Edgar becomes Poor Tom, the basest beggar, Jit, a Sikh in the novel, presents himself as an ash-smeared, high-caste Hindu holy man, Rudra, who renounces material modernity, and takes up residence in the nine-circled hell of the basti, or slum. The place lies in a dust bowl between his father's luxury hotel in Amritsar and Napurthala (an imagined place) and Rudra takes refuge there en route to join the annual Hindu Amarnath yatra, or pilgrimage through Muslim-majority Kashmir. But Jit's elite carceral tendencies cannot stay latent. He begins to curate life to suit his ideology. A band of young Muslim boy vigilantes grows up around him; he teaches them yoga to erase their religion and to create fascist solidarity by schooling the male body and mind. He draws on a sense of epic Hindu patriarchal caste entitlement and presents as asexual, deifying this and physical fitness as a manifestation of supreme control. He dreams of re-organizing the basti into caste hierarchies as soon as he gets the chance – or, better still, burning it down. Clearly, Jit's impulses are drawn from RSS practices: from Modi and the RSS's mass yoga movement, and from divisive figures such as the Holy Man cum chief minister of Uttar Pradesh, Yogi Adityanath, and billionaire Ayurvedic guru Baba Ramdev who monetizes and militarizes Hinduism under Modi's gaze to command huge audiences as voters. Jit's contradictions and lies were born out of a combination of their methods and harms, the dangerous Islamophobic rhetoric in public life that, coming from a similar awareness in the UK, I felt igniting around me on the ground as I conducted my research for *We That Are Young* in India in 2012.

My view of Edgar goes against the grain, which understands the context of his decisions within the boundaries of the early modern period: treason against his own father would be punishable by death. The contemporary moment largely forgives his capacity to dissemble, believes in his moralizing of it; and in the scale of epic tragedy allows and even traditionally applauds his rationale of pushing his father over the edge of a fake cliff, precipitating his 'fall' as a reverse back to grace: to effect his salvation. Scholars have worried and worked away on this performance of shame in the Christian context of sin and redemption. I've often wondered: is this reading of Edgar as a symbol of an uneasy and hopeful potential future after the blasted heath comforting in the way of Christian forgiveness, or in the way that millions keep voting for fascism perhaps because they are trained to feel its punishment as love, and be comforted that the natural order of things is restored at the end of the play, that evil, stinking daughters – or any daughters in fact – can never inherit this earth?

Moving the context to India allows me to think through shame and how it performs in masculinity and power and via religious fascism without Christianity; without having to try to keep the myth of Edgar's essential goodness intact. Instead, shame in *this* context is absolutely projected onto 'others' as a means to claiming personal divinity on earth. Edgar deploys shame as a spectacle of feminized bodies, naked bodies – as Lear puts it: 'poor, bare, forked animal' (*Lear* F 3.4.102) bodies. With this in mind, my novel situates Jit in a culture that forces him to hide his homosexuality, his truth.

Imperial policy modelled on the English 'Buggery Act' of 1533, passed by Henry VIII, made sexual activities 'against the order of nature' illegal via Section 377 of the Indian penal code. The law remained in place in independent India for over sixty years. After decades of campaigning, it was revoked, and then reinstated under Modi – until it was finally revoked for good in 2018. A brief legal history cannot voice the trauma this deligitimizing/legitimizing has imposed on millions. Jit might be one of them. For most of his life his true nature has been illegitimate; shame is his driving emotion. He performs and projects it as a masquerade of *otherness* to re-establish the old, feudal, patriarchal and Hindu world order which he longs to be loved by. What am I saying and seeing? That *shame* as *power* needs to swallow, speak as and submerge *others* to sustain its fictions of self. Toxic masculinity enabled by sacred right is Jit's mode; much of this foundation exists in *King Lear* – I simply look at it from an other's point of view.

Jit's love for his boyfriend Vik seems his only true emotion in the novel until we realize Vik is not his real name. He has been given it by Jit, to mask the fact that he is a working-class Kashmiri, a Shi'a Muslim – placing him only slightly higher in the objectification of beauty as possession than the Kashmiri artefacts that Jit uses his privilege to trade illegally in. The Preservation of Beauty by a higher culture is his excuse. The extraction of artefacts as a right can be traced back to the British looting of priceless treasures from lands it colonized, or simply took from. It was in constructing Jit that my sense of fascism's long and breathtaking unaccountability, its lack of shame, was able to project forwards into a terrible future for Kashmir, one which pointed to the sweeping away of long-standing constitutional protections and promises by a Hindu political administration reliant on manipulating myth as spectacle, backed and encouraged by the super-rich in search of coveted land, wealth, water, oil, beauty, at the expense of generations of Muslim lives.

It was with the same focus on toxic masculinity that I understood fascism's manipulation of shame as performance in the case of Dr Christine Blasey Ford's testimony against Trump's nominee Brett Kavanaugh to the Supreme Court of the USA in 2018. This was the height of the MeToo movement begun by the work of Black American activist Tarana Burke and inspired the campaign message: Times Up. Dr Ford came forward after decades to say that she had been sexually abused by Kavanaugh while they were at college. Kavanaugh's reputation, his future on the Bench and President Trump's symbolic power were at stake. Trump, also accused of sexual harassment during his Presidential campaign, at first called Ford 'a fine woman' and said her testimony 'seemed credible'. Then Kavanaugh gave his evidence, and nearly cried.

Later in the *New Yorker* magazine, Michael Lista described the moment, writing that Kavanaugh was in what Othello called 'the melting mood'.[18] Kavanaugh as Othello? Or as an Othello *mood*? Lista quotes a line from one of the most highly charged racial speeches in the play – the one that

---

[18] Michael Lista, 'The tears of Brett Kavanaugh', *The New Yorker* (4 October 2018), www.newyorker.com/culture/culture-desk/the-tears-of-brett-kavanaugh.

Othello makes to reckon with his whiteness (*Othello*, 5.2.346–65) which I read to be the 'token' racialized 'successful' body's moment of awakening: to self-betrayal, to internalized racial shame finally untenable as existence. I wonder what Lista was thinking in making that highly inappropriate analogy, that takes in early modern Blackness, masculinity and stereotypical tropes of violence and duplicity as innate, and expresses a deep psychic trauma, when his conclusion about Kavanaugh's tears is, rightly, that they were entirely in self-pity and self-interest. Clearly, we cannot take Lista seriously, but not everyone will know the text. Lista wants to find a mythic literary precedent to dignify the moment but must condemn what was essentially #whitemaletears and uses Shakespeare out of context to do it.

Since then, the ways Shakespeare has been utilized to make sense of this moment, from versions of *Measure for Measure* to analogies with *Merchant of Venice* as Portia goes to Washington, make a similar categorical error of perspective: one which Hendricks identifies when she talks about whiteness constantly sustaining white supremacist ideology by thinking only of Othello's emasculation or Caliban's de-humanization or Aaron's vengeful turns, 'instead of considering such men through the lens of anti-whiteness'[19]– from the inside out. In this case, we need to consider them through the lens of intersectionality of class, race and gender. To me it felt the Kavanaugh case would best be read through the men of Shakespeare's most misogynistic play, *King Lear*.

To illustrate this briefly, we recall the scene in which Lear struggles not to cry when confronted with his own needs by women: 'And let not women's weapons, water-drops / Stain my man's cheeks' (*Lear* F 2.4.451–2), he pleads. The speech is usually played and understood as a moment of great pathos, almost elevated to godliness even as we watch this man, this King, slut-shame (to use the contemporary language) the daughters he has raised, while struggling not to cry. He begs the heavens give him the strength to hold back: while *his* tears are legitimate, he believes *women* cry performatively to spark pity and he does not want to be accused of that. His shame-as-outrage spikes as his daughters take each other's hands in solidarity against him. The gesture threatens his very core.

While Lear is not wrong (and 'white-women-tears' are a thing), the point I make here is about cults of power that sustain themselves and pacify their audiences by taking language and gesture from those *less powerful*, whose real feelings, when expressed, threaten the status quo. Lista gets it right in this context, when he notes that Kavanaugh 'has no avenue of appeal, except his own hurt feelings. He is in touch with them, as he was taught to be. And so, he has seemingly weaponized crying, the way a little boy does when he's in trouble.'[20] Who taught him? I'd say *Lear*, not *Othello*, and certainly not *women* coming forward about abuse.

All of this coalesces in Shakespeare's absurd fake trial scene, in which Lear and his faithful men sit in a hovel turned courtroom: they are judge and jury while joint stools stand for women. They 'anatomise' and 'arraign' women as unnatural monsters, no better than wooden parts or animals. They must be exposed, shamed and punished for their existence, which shames men. The scene gained terrible resonance as the Kavanaugh hearings began to feel like a fake trial in which women who speak out are cast as perpetrators for having done so. Where was the storm of reckoning in those weeks? It raged on social media as people rallied behind the bravery of Dr Blasey Ford. It also raged against her. The most powerful outrage came from Trump, standing on a podium at a full rally, mocking Dr Ford as judge and jury, as if *she* was on trial, already guilty. At the end of the play, Shakespeare invites his audience to forgive Lear and Edgar. After Kavanaugh's confirmation took place, Trump apologized to Kavanaugh publicly for *his* ordeal.

Overarching all of this is the question of justice: who seeks it and how, who gets it, who deserves it, who metes it out and who rigs it. And what role spectacle plays in convincing us that the performance of justice is enough. *King Lear* covers this ground and presents a dismal, dangerous future that Edgar inherits. In this moment, I saw the

---

[19] Hendricks, 'Coloring'. [20] Lista, 'The tears'.

camera itself as Edgar via the close-up on Kavanaugh and on Trump, showing us the performance while titillating us with it. I think of white men, some ex-military perhaps, young and old and disaffected, watching at home. Usually, our sympathy stays with Edgar because we know he was wronged. But also because he is authoritative: completely consistent in his individualistic ideology, his gaze solely on one goal – to avenge himself by working back to his naturally appointed place as favoured godson, as sure as a man enabled by Trump's spectacle, media, commentariat and decades of righteousness might one day storm the Capitol. We know what happened next.

A year on, Dr Ford described her reluctance to go public, saying, 'Why suffer through the annihilation if it's not going to matter?' She did it anyway, shifting the focus onto women's authority, not victimhood or fallibility. Her example in its context tells us that a different kind of justice might finally be done: one that does not beget more violence, set women against each other, absolve tyrants or support the world that enables them. Even if onstage the women die, in life in this crucial moment, the overarching message of *Lear* in *my reading* is: Times Up. Also, perhaps, that Shakespeare understood the trap carceral capitalism wants us to remain in, wishing like children for art to 'comfort and not burn' us (*Lear* F 2.2.346). In the challenge to traditional readings, we might 'see better' (*Lear* F 1.1.167). But *is* this other reading in itself, as activism, enough?

We are not children. We cognitively know that the spectacle of appealing to myths to maintain power is an everyday function of rhetoric. Are we blasé enough about it to think knowing that it is happening is enough, however, to avoid being duped by it – or, worse, colluding with it? That retweeting is enough? That producing work in the academy or in literary culture is enough? When we write with or through Shakespeare, is it enough to ground ourselves in his culturally endorsed authority for purpose, while placing the burden of trust on our readers, students, random twitter followers to do something after, with our words?

As Richard Seymour, author of *The Twitter Machine*, notes: 'Fascism consolidates through experimentation, learning the ropes through episodes that, at first, appear amateurish and thuggish, from the beer hall putsch to the demolition of the *Babri Masjid*. First as farce, then as tragedy.'[21] Evidence shows us we have not done enough, with consequences we call *tragic*, as if to say – inevitable. I agree with Seymour, but also want to argue that it might be a reliance on tragedy as structure for *individual* redemption that we need to address when we try to think with and through Shakespeare.

On some level we are all deeply primed to embrace that top-down hierarchy and, almost despite ourselves, be comforted by gestural politics, the spectacle of the patriarch and his coterie as singular event. We need a better understanding of collectivity to organize any meaningful resistance. As Priya Satiya argues,

Analogizing Trumpism to fascism abnormalizes Trump as an aberration in American history only if we understand 'fascism' as a unique evil unrelated to other troubling pasts. With a clear grasp of fascism's connection to empire, the comparison of Trumpism to fascism might inspire us to challenge the myths of liberal exceptionalism that blind so many to the realities of American and British imperialism.[22]

In similar vein, I want to ask that we continue to challenge the use of Shakespeare to shore up the spectacle of fascist events in mainstream culture, because that feeds into a status quo that can no longer be viable. Perhaps we need a different model from tragedy in the Western sense too: it gives us imaginative insight into questions of causation and agency but its focus on a singular hero

---

[21] Richard Seymour, 'A return to civility will not begin to quell the threat of fascism in the US', *The Guardian* (8 January 2021), www.theguardian.com/commentisfree/2021/jan/08/threat-fascism-us-storming-capitol-far-right-trump.

[22] Priya Satiya, 'Fascism and analogies – British and American, past and present', *LA Review of Books* (16 March 2021), https://lareviewofbooks.org/article/fascism-analogies-british-american-past-present.

gives us no way forward. Its form does cathartic rehabilitative work that keeps 'Shakespeare' as spectacle intact. We need instead a collective eye and voice to see and speak better how we might combat the inexorable entitlement and dehumanization of *others* that capital brings those who amass it.

Certain strategies offer aesthetic and political solutions to fiction writers. I first dislocate Lear as primary narrator in favour of polyvocality, portioning the story between the young people of the play. To avoid reinscribing the idea of Shakespeare's primacy, I weave the language of *King Lear* with phrases and ideas from Hinduism's core texts, which have the high-caste male at their centre and set the terms for social life in extreme forms today. So fascism is *also* articulated in my adaptations of Doniger's translations of the Manusmriti, which Jit as Rudra, or Poor Tom the beggar, uses to ground himself within ancient caste hierarchies that are the skeleton of Hindutva. Jit teaches them to the next generation of young men, some Muslim, in the basti as a form of conversion therapy: an awful pattern, since this would have been his father's preferred method to deal with his son's own homosexuality. This is not simply to say: *look, Indian texts are as bad as Shakespeare*. I also call on *other* interpretations of texts from the Upanisads to the *Mahabharata*, again in translation by Doniger,[23] adapting these for Nanu's / the Fool's speech, to undercut Jit's aspirations towards a conservative vision of (Hindu) 'India Shining' (a popular nationalistic slogan). *The Yoga Sutras of Patanjali* begin with the Sanskrit sutra 'citta vritti nirodha', which I quote in the novel: that yoga is the cessation of the fluctuation of the mind – the detachment of ego, not the blueprint for creating a new model army based on a fascism of the body around the cult of an individual. The syncretic voice of Kabir, the fifteenth-century Indian mystic poet known for being critical of both Hinduism and Islam, is also present. Kabir was threatened by both faiths for his views – though, when he died, he was claimed by both. My use of Kabir – who was born in Varanasi, Uttar Pradesh, now Yogi Adityanath's state – presents revolutionary poetics against Indian fascism and Imperial legacies, and frames this resistance as unexclusive to one world poet (Shakespeare) but, instead, creates a conversation between equals. It's also a political citational practice: chronologically, Kabir is premodern to Shakespeare.

The key moment comes when Jit huddles in the storm, framed by Kabir and by the *Bhagavad Gita* to speak the Fool's prophecy. Kabir sets up the hypocrisy of the world, while the *Gita* reminds us that time's revolution means men can be *more* than the present makes them. 'Never was a time that I was not, nor thou, nor these lords of men, nor will there ever be a time hereafter when we all shall cease to be.'[24] There is still a chance for *us* – in a different world, as long as this is true. The *Chandogya Upanisad*'s affirmation, 'tat tvam asi', or *that thou art*,[25] is at the core of Hinduism's construction of ideas of self as ineffable: not attached to a body or individual identity – it is deeply anti-fascist in that sense, theologizing unity, and it haunts Jit's conscience. He thinks he hears Devraj/Lear say it, just as Lear questions Edgar's trick: is Poor Tom *the thing itself* – unaccommodated man or the *image* of that horror? Recognition of what and who *we* are is at stake here: a moment as significant as a joining of hands with sisters, heeding unsilenced women in a country not made for 'us'.

The last years have shown much. Has the time come worldwide when, as the Fool prophesies, 'going shall be used with feet' (*Lear* F 3.2.103) – and I'm not talking small steps – when we not only demand, but achieve, equality in our institutional and cultural life? From Black Lives Matter, to farmers' tax in India, to women's fight against police brutality in the UK, to the toppling of the Colston statue in Bristol, we want to think so. But power understands that the threat falls into three main categories: freedom of the press, of speech and of assembly of the masses – criteria outlined as early as 1938 in

---

[23] Doniger, *The Hindus*.
[24] *Bhagavad Gita*, 2.12, trans. S. Radhakrishnan (Delhi, 1993), p. 103. The popular translation (used in *We That Are Young*) reads, 'Never was a time I did not exist, nor you, nor all these kings. Nor in the future shall any of us cease to be.'
[25] *Chandogya Upanisad* 6.12–14 (translation author's own).

a pamphlet, *Fascism in the Colonies*; the context was Trinidad. The state solution is to strengthen carcerality. Among other indignities, Britain's Police Crime, Sentencing and Courts Act 2022 criminalizes protest by British citizens, and disproportionately affects Black and brown people; in America, federal forces are sent into US cities against peaceful protests for racial justice. In India, journalists, poets and protestors are labelled anti-national or terrorists and imprisoned; Muslim areas are burned and people made homeless; the state has legislated to access private WhatsApp messages – activists using such media to organize, beware.

What does this mean for Shakespeare? Abolitionist scholar and poet Jackie Wang exhorts us to tune into 'a mode of thinking that does not capitulate to the realism of the Present'.[26] To counter carcerality via what Black American prison abolitionist Mariame Kaba calls 'a jailbreak of the imagination',[27] calls for more than the creative writer's ability to imagine and make a new world into being through art. It means going further, as Kaba does, into action. To manifest the intertextual dailiness of our world, the decolonization of our minds, cities, education and justice systems, our texts, styles (and textual style guides).[28] Towards a seeing better, hearing better, a reading and writing better, towards a doing better: instead of finding false refuge in trusted narratives, to de-trust them enough to de-make them, to de-legitimize them for the sake of formal equality, and so to make anew in the compact between art and the person who encounters it. To promise that, even if *we don't live so long*, we can set the terms via a reformation of culture itself. Whiteness, even in brown bodies, cannot plead innocence; nor can individuals. As soon as *I* lay down any claim to singularity as universality, *we* begin. The road is full of false starts and outright failures, but is propelled by determination and hope, whether for full revolution, or harm reduction *now*. Revolutionary activists know that their struggle is a small piece of a larger contest for freedom and dignity: we never forget that what can be imagined can be realized. I can imagine a world in which Shakespeare is just one referent of many, which will lessen the potency of his deployment as Imperial stooge. As collective voices, we can find new forms to recognize, articulate and support a hybrid culturality. I see it happening all around me: that keeps me hopeful still.

---

[26] Wang, *Carceral Capitalism*.
[27] Mariame Kaba, *We Do This 'Til We Free Us, Abolitionist Organising and Transformative Justice* (Chicago, 2021), p. 25.
[28] See the choice of example used for the 'Quotations' section in the Bloomsbury *House Style Guidelines for Authors and Editors* (2013), https://media.bloomsbury.com/rep/files/ba-house-style-for-authors-and-editors.pdf.

SHAKESPEARE'S REFUGEES

DENNIS KENNEDY[1]

More than half of Shakespeare's plays involve the exile of a major character. Exactly how many depends on the definition of major, but by my reckoning at least twenty of the thirty-eight plays present some significant form of banishment, self-exile or separation from homeland by shipwreck. In Joyce's *Ulysses*, Stephen Dedalus claims that exile is central to the canon: 'The notes of banishment', he says in a disquisition on Shakespeare, 'banishment from the heart, banishment from the home, sounds uninterruptedly from *The Two Gentlemen of Verona* onward till Prospero breaks his staff.' Starting with Nicholas Rowe in 1709, Shakespeare's own departure from Stratford to London has often been seen as a parallel to his banished characters, until he breaks his quill and returns home, where every third thought will be his grave. Considering how few years remained to him, perhaps every second thought. Though there is little evidence to support this biographical view, its appeal is perennial. Two recent fictional works continue the tradition: Kenneth Branagh's film *All Is True* of 2018, and Maggie O'Farrell's novel *Hamnet* of 2020.

Of course, exile is a common theme in European literature, just as it is in classical Chinese poetry. The foundational texts of the Western tradition are based on the fact or fear of exile: the banishments of Adam and Eve, Cain, Joseph, the Egyptian enslavement of the Israelites and their wanderings in the desert. Cain's case is enlightening in that he deserves death for killing his brother, but banishment is considered a worse punishment; in Genesis (4.15), Yahweh puts a 'mark' on Cain that prevents anyone from killing him, so that he must live out his sentence of wandering without early release. Thus, in the origin story claimed by the three Abrahamic religions, the first three humans offend the creator and are punished by exile. To move from Genesis to recorded Jewish history, the Babylonian captivity after the destruction of Jerusalem around 600 BCE fostered a rich exilic literature, including parts of Jeremiah, Ezra and Daniel, as well as the final redaction of the Torah, and holiness became equated with exile. In the Christian Greek scriptures, we can add Paul's letters and the Acts of the Apostles, works that assume that expatriation and shipwreck are necessary components of proselytizing. In secular Greek, both in the archaic and classical eras, we find a surfeit of examples: *The Odyssey*, *The Oresteia*, the Oedipus tragedies of Sophocles and about half the surviving plays of Euripides are centred on exile. And in the grand epic of Rome's formation, the *Aeneid*, Virgil proposes that exile from Ilium was the foundation of later glory in Latium, defeat and banishment leading to a new and greater home.

It's hard to find a period in world history when exile was not a significant motif. The biblical instances echoed loudly into the Elizabethan era, and were supplemented by the number of poets and artists who were themselves exiled for displeasing a ruler. In Italy alone, the catalogue includes

---

[1] This article is adapted from the opening address to the World Shakespeare Congress, 2021.

Ovid, Dante, Petrarch, Michelangelo and Caravaggio, examples that are part of the heroic tradition of exile, in which the banished figure achieves a kind of sanctity as a result of expulsion, as a figure of resistance.

Shakespeare had much to draw on, directly and indirectly, when he worked the theme. Given its large implication for his plots and their melodies, the subject could easily overwhelm if we let it loose, touching as it does on the biographical, the psychological, the historical, the literary, the theatrical, the religious and the philosophical. Yet little attention has been paid to the topic. Is it remarkable that so little Shakespeare criticism has focused on expulsion? Jane Kingsley-Smith thinks so; happily, her book *Shakespeare's Drama of Exile*[2] is a study worth its pages. Kingsley-Smith's purpose is different from mine, however, in that I'm interested less in the dramatization of banishment and more in what I see as a complicated concern for performance, the problem of the exile's return.

The return: another common theme. If we ask what happens after exile, the dramatic purpose of deportation seems less clear. A taxonomy of Shakespearian exile would notice that returning from banishment in the tragedies leads almost always to catastrophe. When Romeo, Hamlet and Cordelia come home, they spark the terminal bloodshed. On the other hand, the tragicomedies obviously point to reconciliation. The plots of both *Cymbeline* and *The Winter's Tale* are based on exile and return, banishment ultimately leading to atonement and clemency. The years of exile of Belarius, Guiderius and Arviragus are expunged in general absolution at the end of the play, or so King Cymbeline seems to think. But, of course, those years cannot be recovered, any more than years of imprisonment can be erased by a convict's exoneration, or the life of a refugee compensated by achieving asylum. Unlike King Cymbeline, King Leontes knows this, and for sixteen years has polished his guilt over the disasters his blind jealousy caused. He cannot restore what has been lost by Perdita's banishment and Hermione's hidden exile, not to mention the deaths of Mamillius and Antigonus. When forgiveness is granted in the final scene, it is seen as uncanny, dangerously magical, treading on the supernatural.

Hemmings and Condell were unsettled by *Cymbeline* and placed it as the final play in the First Folio, in the tragedy section, as if it didn't quite belong anywhere, despite their having set *The Winter's Tale* among the comedies, and despite the numerous examples of Fletcherian tragicomedies that had been staged and printed by 1623. It's a good reminder that generic definitions are at best partial, as anyone knows who has tried to choose a film on Netflix. Wells and Taylor, our modern Hemmings and Condell, agree about *Cymbeline*. 'The play as a whole is a fantasy', they write in the Oxford edition, 'an experimental exercise in virtuosity' (p. 1275).

When considering Shakespeare's use of exile, then, we might as well try a different set of categories, focused on homecoming. I suggest there are four types of return:

- Disastrous (*Romeo, Richard II, Hamlet, Lear*)
- Beneficent (*Two Gentlemen, Dream, Cymbeline, Winter's Tale*)
- Neglected (*Errors, Twelfth Night*)
- Projected (*As You Like It, Pericles, The Tempest*)

What intrigues me is the last group, and that's where I'm heading.

But first. The last hundred years have seen an explosion of writing by exiles and about exile. This is hardly surprising. The twentieth century – the worst so far, Brecht said, and he lived through only half of it – witnessed an unprecedented dislocation of peoples around the globe through conflict, ethnic cleansing, political expulsion, climate change or economic migration. Brecht wrote his best plays in exile, including his four greatest ones, on the run in Europe and unsettled in Los Angeles. Los Angeles, he said, was a place much like hell, though he had

---

[2] Jane Kingsley-Smith, *Shakespeare's Drama of Exile* (London, 2003). Her book was preceded by Leslie A. Fielder's *The Stranger in Shakespeare* (New York, 1972) and Jeanette Dillon's *Shakespeare and the Solitary Man* (London, 1981), though both are about alienation in general and do not deal with banishment and exile as separate themes.

plenty of compatriot exiles there, from Thomas Mann to Marlene Dietrich.

For refugees, the new century has not improved. To take a notorious example, a dozen years of the Syrian civil war have dislocated almost half the pre-war population of 22 million, and about 6 million have fled abroad, taking long and tortuous routes in the hope of European resettlement. The Russian war in Ukraine displaced more than 6 million in less than two years. In about the same period, a million people from Central America have been uprooted by violence and insecurity. The dislocation of Palestinians intensified in 2023 after the Israeli invasion of Gaza. According to the UN High Commissioner for Refugees, in the middle of 2023 about 42 million people worldwide were refugees or asylum seekers, and a further 62 million were internally displaced.[3] This is a global problem without a realistic global solution.

Refugee camps and immigrant detention centres are now an expected part of the world disorder. Unable or unwilling to return to their original lands, untold millions will live out their lives stateless, homeless and without rights. And have children so condemned. The exilic surge has prompted repressive action against migrants of all types, as the liberal democracies re-examine their principles and push away boats over-crowded with desperation, or build stunning walls at their southern borders. Overwhelmed by numbers, the concept of exile has lost all of its earlier sense of the heroic. Already in 1944, the refugee Hannah Arendt wrote that 'Everywhere the word "exile," which once had an undertone of almost sacred awe, now provokes the idea of something simultaneously suspicious and unfortunate.'[4]

Alienation and exile are the grand themes of the literature of modernism and beyond, running from Kafka, Joyce and Pound through Camus, Nabokov and Beckett to W. G. Sebald, Gao Xingjian, Roberto Bolaño, Margaret Atwood and Kazuo Ishiguro. Exile wins Nobel prizes. Beckett is central, with his uncanny enactments of absence as a presence, making what is not here more felt than what is, which is one way to describe the psyche of the displaced person. Edward Said, another illustrious exile, might have been thinking of Brecht when he wrote that whatever a person might achieve in exile is 'permanently undermined by the loss of something left behind for ever'.[5]

***

Such a large and powerful movement naturally has prompted a range of commentary about exile literature in general, especially in German studies. There is even an *Oxford Book of Exile*.[6] It puzzled me that so little has been written on exile in Shakespeare until I remembered that I had not thought about the topic myself until I directed *As You Like It*. One of the best-known of the exile plays, it is set in motion by three sets of banishments: Duke Senior and train, Rosalind with Celia and Touchstone, and Orlando with Adam. Yet it leaves out all the returns and feels unfinished.

It isn't only the ending that feels incomplete, since much of the action of *As You Like It* is perfunctory. Most of the plot is revealed before

---

[3] www.unhcr.org/refugee-statistics.
[4] Hannah Arendt, *The Jewish Writings*, ed. Jerome Kohn and Ron H. Feldman (New York, 2007), p. 211.
[5] Edward Said, *Reflections on Exile and Other Essays* (Cambridge, MA, 2000), p. 173.
[6] John Simpson, ed., *The Oxford Book of Exile* (Oxford, 1995). Recent treatments of Shakespearian exile include Margaret Tudeau-Clayton, *Shakespeare's Englishes: Against Englishness* (Cambridge, 2020) on the Elizabethan context of the stranger or foreigner in the early plays, and David Schalkwyk, 'Storms and drops, bonds and chains: exile in *King Lear* and *The Comedy of Errors*', *Shakespeare Jahrbuch* 155 (2019), 59–77. A number of scholars have drawn on the contemporary refugee crisis to illuminate texts and performances. Examples include Stephen O'Neill, 'Shakespeare's hand, or the stranger's case', *The Journal of Shakespeare and Appropriation* 13 (2020, online), n.p.; *Shakespeare's Others in 21st-Century European Performance*, ed. Boika Sokolova and Janice Valls-Russell (London, 2022); a section on Shakespeare and refugees edited by Ton Hoenselaars and Stephen O'Neill in *The Shakespeare International Yearbook* 19 (London, 2022); and *Global Shakespeare and Social Injustice*, ed. Chris Thurman and Sandra Young (London, 2023). A more general treatment of value is *The Palgrave Handbook of Theatre and Migration*, ed. Yana Meerzon and Stephen Elliot Wilmer (Basingstoke, 2023).

the end of the second act, and the long middle section in acts 3 and 4 is dedicated to Rosalind toying with her identity and teasing Orlando about his, in a charming but perverse test of his love. Then a cursory coupling of eight lovers, united without explanation by a mythical creature, and a messenger announcing the conversion of the young Duke, to get fast to a comic-book ending. Complaints about the plotting have been frequent since Samuel Johnson in 1765: 'By hastening to the end of his work Shakespeare supressed the dialogue between the usurper and the hermit, and lost the opportunity of exhibiting a moral lesson in which he might have found matter worthy of his highest powers.'[7]

Shakespeare's haste arose from how closely he followed his source. Thomas Lodge's *Rosalynde or Euphues' Golden Legacy*, printed in 1590, about a decade before the play, gave Shakespeare the court, the major characters, the usurpation, the wrestling match, the banishments, the forest, the lioness, Rosalind's disguise, the wooings, the marriages, and even prompted the play's title. Shakespeare's Touchstone and Jaques are critical additions, lending irony to the sylvan sanctuary, and some rough edges are smoothed: Orlando is made much softer and the deaths in the source, including that of the wrestler and the usurper, do not occur. Though Lodge brings the exiles back to their court in Paris, he deals with the return in a single short paragraph. Like its model, the play is primarily an eclogue or pastoral romance, more interested in sexual politics than exile politics. Its stage history, especially in English, is the history of the players of Rosalind and of what the Forest of Arden looked like. The lack of an onstage resolution of the banishments that incite the action has been of little concern.

Shakespeare keyed the ending to the fantasy of the forest and added a titillating epilogue from a boy actor to conjure applause. Onstage, banishment is inherently dramatic, coming home is not. A scene of return can be tedious, whether enacted as in *Cymbeline* or narrated as in *Winter's Tale*. But to omit it entirely, to leave it at the level of a project, opens a narrative and theatrical gap. The gap is emphasized by the conversion of Duke Frederick, who trades places with Duke Senior, town for country. It's a conclusion in keeping with the idyll of the greenwood tree but it weakens the overplot or arc of the play.

Duke Senior and his courtiers arrive in the Forest of Arden seeking refuge; they are, in the literal sense, refugees. They camp out because they own no place; they create their own refugee centre. And though the old Duke *was* the state when at court, in Arden he becomes stateless. With his kin and familiars, he is reduced to the condition of naked humanity, that poor bare, forked animal, without rights, without protection, without social status. And when he returns to the court, what will he be? Exile should change him, as it changes Rosalind, Celia, Orlando, Oliver, Touchstone and Jaques. But while we see how the lovers have been transformed, we do not see how the old Duke has been. The exiles lost their social identities when banished and two of them lost their genders. Back in the city, will their old selves be restored, or somehow renovated?

The question is outside the text but reasonable because the depredations of the civilized world have not been repaired in the forest. Life there has not been idyllic. It is cold, there is little shelter, there are snakes and man-eating lions, starvation is real, an army invades, death not far away. *Et in Arcadia ego*. We don't know why the young Duke usurped his brother, but something led to a *coup d'état*. Why would we think that Duke Senior's reinstatement will be untroubled?

You may have noticed that these questions are similar to those asked by Jan Kott. 'The kingdom of nature', he wrote, 'is equally ruthless and egotistic as the world of civilization.' That's from 'Shakespeare's bitter Arcadia', Kott's essay on the sonnets, *Twelfth Night* and *As You Like It*, included in *Shakespeare Our Contemporary*, a book first published sixty years ago that now stands as the chief monument to the Cold War interpretation of

---

[7] *Johnson on Shakespeare*, ed. Arthur Sherbo, 2 vols. (New Haven, 1968), vol. 1, p. 265.

Shakespeare.[8] Heavily influenced by Beckett, Kott thought Shakespeare's green world both impossible and necessary: 'He takes us into the Forest of Arden in order to show that one must try to escape, though there is no escape; that the Forest of Arden does not exist, but those who do not run away will be murdered.' Kott's book, with its insistence that Shakespeare portrayed the cruelty and absurdity of human life, affected a large number of productions, particularly in the two decades after its publication.

One of the most notable was Peter Stein's *As You Like It* in Berlin in 1977, which signalled its position by reprinting 'Shakespeare's Bitter Arcadia' in the production programme. Starting in 1970, Stein had led the Berlin Schaubühne as a socialist collective. The company prepared for their first Shakespeare production by studying and workshopping material relating to the Elizabethan period, which was presented publicly in December 1976 as *Shakespeare's Memory* – the title was in English – a two-evening performance of scenes, lectures, readings and visual delights based on material that might have been in Shakespeare's memory or the collective memory of his time. The staging was environmental with elaborate scenography, and took place in the CCC Film Studios in the West Berlin district of Spandau, not far from the prison where the strangest of Nazi exiles, Rudolf Hess, was the sole remaining prisoner.

As You Like It opened the following September, using the same location and some of the same costumes and built pieces. At first Stein was hesitant about the choice of play, which he thought 'totally foreign ... so full of ideas, so complex and lacking in consistency' that he had difficulty finding a starting point.[9] His solution was to emphasize the difference between the prison of city and the liberty of forest, while agreeing with Kott that escape from civilization was impossible. The performance began with the 300 spectators standing crowded around a small platform with rising steps in a white space with cold blue lighting. All the court scenes occurred there without interruption, and the acting was as stiff and artificial as the black Elizabethan costumes. Actors gave lines extracted from different spots in the text, sometimes speaking in the midst of the audience, shifting the focus in an unsettled manner. In making the court such a formal and threatening place, the performance risked alienating the spectators in order to achieve its larger goal.

The court scenes ended with Duke Frederick commanding Oliver to arrest Orlando (Shakespeare's 3.1). Oliver and servants left through a door in one of the white walls, and the audience followed, single file, into a cramped tunnel covered by plastic ivy, damp with dripping water, lit in a green glow. There they encountered mysterious items from *Shakespeare's Memory* set into niches – unexplained displays, often uncomfortable in nature, a little like a circus freak show. The spectators were taking the same journey as the exiles, banished from an unwelcome court to an uncertain otherness. 'The conception was brilliant', Michael Patterson wrote, 'to pass from the formality and brutality of the court through an underground labyrinth to the freedom and innocence of the forest was like being born anew'.[10]

Spectators arrived one by one out of the tunnel into a magnificent artificial Arden, created by the company's designer Kart-Ernst Hermann. Birdsong, a bathing pool, craftsmen at work, houses, a farm, a rowboat, curios in cases, things needed and not needed, constructed inside a vast sound stage, inhabited by actors occupied with pastoral life – a unity made out of miscellany, all visible from the raised seating surrounding the great space in a U-shape. The arrangement allowed

---

[8] *Shakespeare Our Contemporary* was published in two Polish editions, in 1961 and 1962, in a French translation in 1963 (which Peter Brook read), and in English in 1964, translated by Bolesław Taborski, with an introduction by Brook. The two quotations are from the revised English edition (London, 1967), p. 224 and pp. 226–7. On Kott in history, see 'Shakespeare and the Cold War' in Dennis Kennedy, *The Spectator and the Spectacle* (Cambridge, 2009). W. B. Worthen's 'Jan Kott, *Shakespeare Our Contemporary*' historicizes Kott through Worthen's personal encounters with the book, in *Forum Modernes Theater* 25 (2010), 91–7.

[9] Schaubühne Rehearsal Protocol 444 of 2 January 1975, quoted in Michael Patterson, *Peter Stein: Germany's Leading Theatre Director* (Cambridge, 1981), p. 133.

[10] Patterson, *Peter Stein*, pp. 137–8.

multiple scenes to occur at once, some from the text, some reported in the text, some invented, giving an illusion of life in the forest, and at the same time ironically undercutting the illusion. The old Duke sat huddled with his shivering courtiers under a canvas cloth for the uses of adversity speech, and the second set of exiles arrived pulling a wooden cart, dressed in twentieth-century costumes, looking like refugees from one of the world wars.

To get to my point, we can skip to the end.[11] The wedding scene was conducted on a wagon or rolling platform, Hymen suspended in a tree. Most of the main characters were in court dress; others threw off their rough country cloaks to reveal Elizabethan costumes underneath. Thus, when Jaques de Bois appeared with the message of Frederick's conversion, they were already prepared to leave Arden, abandoning the illusion of a sylvan escape. De Bois had left the door to the tunnel open, and light from beyond it intensified – not the fertile green light of the mysterious passage, but the cold blue-white light of the court from the first scenes. The wagon began to roll towards that light, but it would not fit through the door and came to a halt with a bump. The courtiers jumped or were knocked off the platform and staggered towards the door, dazed, caught between a desire to return to civilization and an almost drunken illusion of the Eden they were leaving.

Spectators were left looking at an Arden stripped of dream, a set of artificial scenes in an artificial space, a mechanical arcadia, like an abandoned holiday camp. To underline the company's Marxist analysis of the text, Corin began clearing up the mess the sophisticated revellers left behind. Just as the production had shown the attack by the lioness on Oliver, and the arrival in Arden of Duke Frederick with his invading army, Stein used the gap at the end in Shakespeare's text to stage – if only in part – the missing scene of the return of the exiles.

Patterson points out that the fantasy of escape had particular relevance for the West Berlin audience in 1977, caught as they were in an artificial capitalist city surrounded by a hostile socialist country and divided from their friends and family in East Berlin by what the GDR called the Antifascist Protection Barrier, otherwise known as the Berlin Wall. Though there were urban green spaces in the western part of the city, and rivers and lakes as well, to get to anything like a complete natural environment its citizens would have to drive over 300 kilometres non-stop to the border of West Germany. They were exiles in their own city, trapped by geopolitics, fantasizing a return.

Stein's *As You Like It* was not perfect. It was sometimes confusing in intent; it sometimes departed from Shakespeare's text without effect. It was overwhelmed by its ambition, and sometimes its visuals looked like a rigorous Marxist Disneyland. But no other production of the play that I know managed to suggest so well the dream of escape and the problem of an exile's return.

***

Expulsion is punishment to the degree that the excluded figure remembers what he or she has lost. Shakespeare's banishment plays dramatize the precarious psychology of exile, the necessity of recalling the old while adapting to the new. Duke Senior claims he's happier in the forest than at court but cannot avoid remembering the court, and when he can return, he goes.

Of all the banishment plays, *The Tempest* deals most extensively with the condition of exile, and does so by suggesting that its meaning is constructed by the exiled. Banishment is pain to Prospero but not to Miranda, who has only fleeting recollections of Milan and her deportation by water. Prospero is a refugee, Miranda an assimilator. Notoriously retrospective, the piece is exceptional in dramatizing neither the banishment nor the return. In the long second scene, Prospero's

---

[11] Aside from Patterson, the production is discussed in English by Peter Lackner, 'Stein's path to Shakespeare', *TDR* 21 (1977), 80–102, and Wilhelm Hortmann, *Shakespeare on the German Stage: The Twentieth Century* (Cambridge, 1998). My treatment from a visual perspective is in Dennis Kennedy, *Looking at Shakespeare* (Cambridge, 2001), pp. 260–5.

task is to transplant his memory to his daughter; to participate in the procedure of return, she must understand what has been taken from her. Prospero's restoration means unseating the usurper, his brother Antonio, but, parallel to *As You Like It*, the finale prefers reconciliation to revenge. Though reparations are agreed, when we get to the point where retribution is in order, Prospero shuts down the reprisal machine. He says to Alonzo:

> There, sir, stop.
> Let us not burden our remembrance with
> A heaviness that's gone.
> (*Tempest*, 5.1.201–3)

And he moves briskly to the epilogue.

The most remarkable detail in the last scene is Antonio's silence. The younger brother defied primogeniture and deposed Prospero, as Frederick deposed Duke Senior. But in this scene, Antonio says nothing, not when Prospero reveals the plot against him, not when Prospero forgives the noble offenders and invites them to dinner. When Antonio is unmasked, he is revealed to be empty, like one of Ben Jonson's deflated humour characters. If we find the conversion of Frederick abrupt and implausible, what are we to make of the ending of *The Tempest* where the villain is neither converted nor punished?

The tradition of interpreting the play as Shakespeare's farewell to the stage blunts its political force and gives Prospero more credit than he deserves. It romanticizes the work as a paean to freedom, foregrounding the liberation of the four main characters. But Prospero admits he is partly responsible for his banishment, and for a dozen years has been that deeply troubling and highly anomalous figure, a slaveholding refugee. He is not an explorer seeking trade, not a settler or planter interested in civilizing and commercializing the island. What Kingsley-Smith calls the shame of exile has suspended him between his noble past and his uncertain future: the time of exile is a no-time.[12]

These matters unsettled Ninagawa Yukio when he came to direct the play in 1987. He'd never seen a production and the text did not strike him as a masterpiece. He was disappointed with the narrative and the lack of an arresting dramatic action,[13] much as Stein had been put off by the multiplicity of ideas in *As You Like It*. Ninagawa felt distant from the concerns of *The Tempest*, thinking himself a 'listener' to a foreign culture, not a participant.[14] During the London run he said that *The Tempest* 'was about how people made peace with the world',[15] but in Tokyo he felt that a drama so European in style and conception would strike a Japanese audience as false. He overcame his hesitations by a process of japanning, adding blended elements of nō, kabuki and kyōgen, and a generalized Japanese look. But he did it overtly, by setting the performance inside the device of a rehearsal. Using this method, he said, 'we would be signaling our pretence. We wouldn't need blond hair ... We could remain Japanese.'[16]

Additionally, Prospero's isle would not be Malta or the Bermudas or unlocated, but a very specific prison island well known in Japanese culture and identified in the production's title, *The Tempest: A Sadoshima Nō Rehearsal*. Sadoshima, or Sado Island, off the west coast of Honshu, had been a site for political banishment since about the year 1200. One of its most famous exiles was Zeami, the founding actor and writer of nō drama, who'd been banished there by the emperor for unknown reasons in 1434, at the age of seventy-two. Zeami built a nō theatre, and thereafter the practice of nō was taken up by islanders as part of regular folk festivals. At one time, there were some 200

---

[12] Kingsley-Smith, *Shakespeare's Drama of Exile*, p. 170.
[13] Hisao Oshima, '*The Tempest* and Japanese theatrical traditions: noh, kabuki and bunraku', *Critical and Cultural Transformations: Shakespeare's The Tempest – 1611 to the Present (REAL – Yearbook of Research in English and American Literature)* 29, ed. Tobias Döring and Virginia Mason Vaughan (2013), 153.
[14] 'Tempesto: Sadoshima nō rehasuru', Japanese interview in *Marie Claire* (Tokyo), January 1987, before rehearsals began.
[15] *The Times* (London), 1 Dec. 1992, quoted in Virginia Mason Vaughan, *The Tempest* (Manchester, 2011), p. 153.
[16] Interview in Minami Ryuta, Ian Carruthers and John Gilles, eds., *Performing Shakespeare in Japan* (Cambridge, 2001), p. 213.

outdoor *nō* theatres on the island; about 30 remain, often used by amateur players. When Ninagawa visited, he was astonished by how weather-beaten the stages were, lovely and magical, he said, 'as though the dead were looking down at me from the sky'.

The Tokyo audience saw a rustic version of an outdoor dilapidated *nō* theatre, built inside the proscenium of the indoor Nissei Theatre, with villagers and schoolchildren arriving on stage to prepare for a folk festival, supervised by a village elder. They chose *The Tempest* to perform in *nō* style, making the elder first the director of the rehearsal, and then the player of Prospero – an actor playing an elder playing a director playing Prospero, who implied the exiled Zeami, in a play within a play, in a playhouse within a playhouse, Shakespeare's exiled characters set on an actual island of exiles. It was a recursive artificiality, a *mise-en-abyme* of exilic commentary.

The Tempest, with the script of a masque inside the script, invites reflexiveness, and a number of productions have used metatheatrical devices. Ninagawa's did something else as well: it placed the play within Japanese memory, in the way that Stein's Forest of Arden evoked the little island of West Berlin in the rough sea of East Germany. Both lent local habitation to what in the texts are amorphous settings, and it's not surprising that in Edinburgh and London Ninagawa's context was lost and the production received as exotic Orientalism.[17]

In any performance of *The Tempest*, the elements of magic, music and fantasy tend to overtake its political pulse, as pastoralism does in *As You Like It*. Instead of dramatizing Prospero's return, Shakespeare sends him downstage like Rosalind to beg for applause. In Ninagawa's version, however, in the epilogue it was not clear who this Prospero was. A village elder, the character of the magus, a stage director, Zeami, a stand-in for Ninagawa, or Hira Mikijirō, the actor underneath it all? After the last line, he broke free of whatever he was playing, patted a fellow actor on the back, congratulated another and casually walked offstage. 'My production of *The Tempest* this year', Ninagawa said, 'can be likened to the crossing and intermingling reflections of a shattered mirror.'[18] He did not stage Prospero's homecoming, but with quaint devices evoked Japanese cultural memory to fill the space Shakespeare left vacant. It was not a magic isle but a real isle, a prison, and a Japanese one.

In these two texts, then, instead of restorations Shakespeare wrote celebrations. He forecast the return of the exiles without having to deal with tiresome matters of reconstruction or repair. While dramatically appropriate, I still find it unsettling. When I directed *As You Like It* in Beijing, I was so bothered by the omission that I invented a silent scene at the end in which the usurper Duke Frederick, hands tied behind his back, was brought before Duke Senior to face reprisal. That was a stretch, deliberately out of keeping with the spirit of absolution in the finale, but it rounded out the politics of banishment, if you squinted.[19]

I don't know of any productions of *The Tempest* that staged Prospero's re-entry to Naples or Milan, but in London both Charles Kean in 1857 and Herbert Beerbohm Tree in 1904 ended with the sentimental image of Alonzo's ship sailing away in the distance. Kean had Ariel elevated on a wire watching it go, while Tree, playing a hairy-ape Caliban himself, reached out for the receding vessel in what his edition of the play calls 'mute despair'. That's one way to fill the narrative void, to concentrate on the two figures left behind. Even Jonathan Miller's production of 1970 did this, albeit in a harsh postcolonial mode: a black Ariel mended the broken pieces of the white Prospero's magic staff, then held it aloft over the black Caliban.[20] 'Ban, 'ban, Cacaliban, has a new master, indeed.

---

[17] See chapter 6 of Dennis Kennedy, *The Spectator and the Spectacle* (Cambridge, 2009).
[18] Quoted in Miyashita Nobuo, 'Ninagawa Yukio, theatrical pacesetter', *Japan Quarterly* 34 (1987), 404.
[19] The production was in Mandarin and used the play's standard (though unfortunate) translated title, *Everybody's Happy* – Beijing, 2005.
[20] The three productions are briefly discussed in Vaughan, *The Tempest*, pp. 40–3, 58–63 and 105–10.

The postcolonial approach to *The Tempest* has become so entirely naturalized that we can hardly think of Prospero, Ariel or Caliban in terms other than those outlined in Aimé Césaire's revision of 1969, *Une tempête*. It is now difficult for critics to imagine Shakespeare's original as anything other than a proto-imperialist text. Yet theatres continue to mount productions that ignore or downplay the issues of conquest, subordination and reparation that many commentators find central. No doubt this is a result of the text's deep ambiguity about its own themes of exploration and exploitation. Surely Prospero is one of Shakespeare's most abstruse characters, an all-commanding protagonist who is both subjugator and liberator and whose propulsion goes from repression and reprisal to release and retirement. Given the retrospective narrative, it is easy to forget that Prospero did not arrive on the island voluntarily.

For almost three decades, I have lived in a postcolonial country. The island of Ireland was England's first colony, and its northern six counties may well be its last. When the Irish Free State was established in 1922, after a bloody war of rebellion that led in turn to a bitter civil war, the detachment from the British Empire was incomplete and economically convoluted. In the eyes of some commentators it remains so, complicated anew by Brexit. In Dublin I have hosted a number of British academics and artists who seemed surprised that the post boxes in the Republic of Ireland, some still embossed with *VR* for Victoria Regina, are painted not red but green, and that the currency is not the pound but the euro. Was Shakespeare thinking of Ireland when he set Prospero down on his shadowy and forbidding island, the ultimate location of otherness, that place that had to be invented, in Declan Kiberd's terms, in order to define what England was not?[21]

Thinking of the island setting leads me to a final suggestion. Of course, it's not necessary to pinpoint the magic isle in the real world as Ninagawa did, but Milan, Naples and Tunis were actual cities in the seventeenth century and remain so in the twenty-first. If I were to choose a logical spot, I'd not make it Ireland but one of the Pelagie Islands of Italy. There are three of them, lying between Tunisia and Sicily, uninhabited in Shakespeare's day, safe anchorage for a ship blown off course in sailing between Tunis and Naples. The largest is called Lampedusa. For over twenty years, Lampedusa has been the preferred entry point for hundreds of small boats, mostly from Libya, packed with Syrians and Libyans and sub-Saharan Africans seeking asylum in the European Union. What better place for Prospero to have landed a dozen years before, in an open boat from the open sea? A banished exile himself, a widower carrying his infant daughter, expelled from his city by politics and foreign intervention, a homeless refugee.

---

[21] Declan Kiberd, *Inventing Ireland: The Literature of the Modern Nation* (London, 1995).

SHAKESPEARE AS A SOURCE OF DRAMATURGICAL RECONSTRUCTION

TANG SHU-WING

Before I go into the concrete content of dramaturgical reconstruction, I would like to talk a little bit about certain generic issues regarding myself and also my creative process, so that you know why I picked this topic tonight.

First is the meaning of art for me. I suppose for many artists, art represents truth and beauty. For some, the two go hand in hand; for some, they may be separated; but for me, I think if truth appears, beauty will come along. Beauty here does not refer only to physical beauty, like shapes, colour, rhythm, etc., but is a kind of transcendency in your spirit. That is for me a very important research and pursuit in my artistic creation. In particular, performing art, be it drama, dance, music or multimedia expression, is about a representation of life – representational elements expressed in terms of visual and audio ingredients, including the performers as human beings.

For performing artists, art is about feeling and expression – that is, how a performer expresses his or her sentiment through a certain artistic expression. In between feeling and expression, there is an auto-transformation inside this person, which is indeed very hard to see. But from the way this performer expresses himself or herself, we can feel their impulse behind their expression. So performing artists are a very particular form of expression compared to other arts like visual arts, for example, or literature, because human beings are involved in the form of the art. What does it mean if we have a personal style as an artist? I think it means that we have not only the capacity of imagination, curiosity, passion and craft, but also vision. Vision is fundamental for an artist to have a personal style, or indeed to exert a certain impact on the artistic profession and community.

And for me, there is also the last thing, which is to have a corresponding attitude in life. What do I mean by an attitude in life? I express mine in this way: 'Every step counts in life.' If we really understand that, we would not be afraid anymore of time and failure. We would know why we create and what the relationship between our creations and their environment is. Only at this point can our works become transparent. Maybe for each individual the notion of an attitude of life is very different. But for me, this attitude of 'every step counts in life' is very important. That means there is no waste at all. It's just a different direction you will go if you turn to the left, or you turn to the right. I have taken various formative steps, like my studies in law and physical cultures such as dance, Chinese opera, mime and martial arts, and also spiritual practice. All of these formative steps add up together and all seem to point to certain phenomena, which is to say that they arise from a common origin: that is, the beingness of all these things which are external to every individual; like the interplay between rational and irrational, body and mind, movement and language, in which movement is very often abstract, but language, words, are very precise, and we need both.[1]

---

[1] Tang Shu-wing, in a private conversation, explained that the directionality of language is strong compared to movement, as the meaning of movements can be elusive and hard to pin

Then, there's also a necessity of self-enquiry, to ask questions such as: Why do I live here on this planet? What do I like? What do I dislike? What is the relationship between like and dislike? In this aspect, 'like' and 'dislike' generate a very, very important thought in my mind: that is, there could never be a definite answer to any problem. Supposing I specify three things as 'A', 'B' and 'C'. If we say something is 'A', very often we would neglect everything that is not 'A'. But my creative process is always to the contrary. If I say something is 'A', then I would explore what is 'B', which is the complete opposite of 'A'. In travelling between 'A' and 'B', I would try to discover 'C', which could be something in between, or may be something totally different from the nature of 'A' and 'B', and that is very fascinating. I have developed a sort of structured and systematic methodology regarding this 'A', 'B', 'C' which I will talk about later on.

Regarding the various cultural backgrounds that I have been exposed to, like Chinese, British, French and Indian, many people ask me how these cultures affect me, how they influence me. Every person's cultural existence is formed through a process of initiation involving certain teachings like books, certain dealings with the people, the architecture, the soil, the landscape, and also artistic creations like cinema, books, performing arts, paintings, etc. These are all created out of an individual's enquiry between himself or herself and something larger than him or her, which he or she may not be able to understand or grasp. In doing so, this person is trying to establish a communication with others. For a real communication to take place, there must be a self-assertion or self which arises so that you have the distinction between you and non-you. That enquiry can then start to take place. So I would say that these cultures are platforms, enabling me to jump to another level. That level is solitude, or to be able to place yourself before real solitude. A real solitude can generate a real connection to humanity. And only a real connection can give birth to a real concern for humanity. For me, this is a fundamental belief.

Then, on the creative process that is closely related to tonight's topic, the dramaturgical reconstruction of Shakespeare, I believe, from all my various formative steps and also my cultural background, less is more. This is not just a generic axiom of minimalism. It is a two-way or two-level process of thought that I would call Level One and Level Two. Level One is the fundamental things that I need to create a work. For every individual, it is different. For you it might be this, and for me it might be that. But each has to locate and identify the fundamental things that serve as pillars of our creation. Without them, our creation will not stand or will collapse. That is Level One, and it is very difficult to arrive at because I need to go through the process many, many times, not only inside me, but also with my collaborators, and we have to build up the common consensus: what is the most important thing which holds up the work that we're going to create?

Level Two is very tricky. It's something that we can have in a creation or we can take it away. That is a very difficult question. For me, if we can take it away, then it is better to take it away and not incorporate it into our creation. Because once you incorporate that into your creation, you have to make it Level One. Otherwise, you'll be running into great troubles in your creation when you incorporate something which you are not sure belongs to Level One. Let me give a concrete example from my work on *Macbeth*: the monologue of Lady Macbeth, 'Un-sex me'. That is fundamental. I cannot take it away. If I take it away, there's a strong gap in the dramaturgy, because that particular monologue reflects my interpretation or my feeling towards this character and also her relationship with Macbeth, her husband, in that particular context. She is talking to herself, but she is also talking to something else beyond herself. The important thing is to let the audience hear the text, the poetry and power of the text. In my treatment of this particular scene, I later eliminated all the movements that I had created for the premiere of the show at the Globe. At the premiere, in that

---

down whereas language leaves much less room for interpretation. [Note provided by Yong Li Lan.]

scene the performer moves a lot, which I thought might help. But in the end, I think that it does not help. You had better move as little as possible so that you generate a strong relationship with time. If you move slowly, that means fewer things will happen, and people would hear more what you are saying. Then, hearing what you are saying, combined with the slowness or fewer movements in your action, would inject another imagery that is spiritual, which I hope can jump to the soul of the audience.

I will say more about imagery shortly, but first let me address the question: why Shakespeare? For me, Shakespeare is a very intriguing dramatist. His way of constructing drama is very particular. It falls basically into the generic or traditional narrative form or aesthetics according to Aristotle – that is, there's a beginning, there's a middle and there's an end. But his poetics of language is so powerful that the readers or audience are naturally captivated by his use of language. Of course, the second layer is the issues of humanity Shakespeare has touched upon, which are universal, and regardless of which culture we belong to we have a certain echo. Some may be further than others, but we have some echoes. So he is very special in the history of theatre. No other playwright can singly occupy such a position.

Then, for me as a theatre-maker, Shakespeare is a great platform for experimentation on form, on the art of narration, on language, and also on movement, and many, many things. That is why I believe that not only for theatre-makers, but also for artists in other mediums like painters or musicians, we should have a basic knowledge of Shakespeare. Of course, we can criticize his work because critical thinking about it is important for a really personal and authentic creation that is particular to a certain team of creators. This is because every production belongs to that particular team working in a particular time, in a particular moment in history. After working on several Shakespeare pieces – including *Hamlet*, when I was still in the Academy of Performing Arts in Hong Kong, three versions of *Titus Andronicus*, and *Macbeth*, with five years of ongoing creation and re-examination of the piece – I have come to a conclusion regarding Shakespeare: that is, life is never as simple as you think, but life can be very simple if you know about it. So I would say that if we know more about Shakespeare, we could know more about the here and now.

Moving on to the concrete examples of my dramaturgical reconstruction, many people would ask: why do I, as it were, reconstruct the dramaturgy? I think for every theatre-maker working with Shakespeare, it is very tempting to juggle around the tension between subjective and objective forces. Subjectively speaking, we want to input our personal feelings and sentiments regarding the dramaturgy of Shakespeare and also the dramatic action and the characters, to draw Shakespeare towards a contemporary audience, or, vice versa, to let the contemporary audience go towards the innermost universe of Shakespeare – not just the words, and not just the scenes.

Secondly, which is difficult, there is an objective framework laid down by the writing of Shakespeare. And Shakespeare only uses words to create drama, to create tension and to touch upon the psychology of every individual character in his plays, no matter whether it is the main character or just a minor character. So everything counts in his words. Of course, if we want to cut certain passages or cut certain characters, we need specific reasons for doing so. Where does that reason come from? I would say that it comes from another question, which is, what are we going to represent if we are going to tackle a text of Shakespeare's?

For me, we have to represent visual elements and audio elements. Visual elements include human beings, costumes, the scenography, lighting, and the audio elements are music, sound. Lighting is very interesting: it can be an element of time as well, not only an element of space, through the notion of rhythm. Rhythm is the number of things that happen in a fixed duration. If you have many things happening in this fixed duration, the rhythm must be quick. If you have fewer things happening, then the rhythm will be slower. Rhythm takes place on stage through the movement of the actors or performers, and especially the conflict between the floor, which is concrete, solid, and the apparent soul, the body of the performers, which comes into contact with the floor. Lighting has two elements: timing and intensity. Once it hits the bodies of the performers, either stationary or in movement, it will generate another dimension of rhythm that is very particular to lighting. At the Globe, where there is no artificial lighting, everything had to be delivered with twice as much energy as when we perform in a conventional theatre.

However, representing visual and audio elements is not the primary aim or the fundamental pursuit. The fundamental pursuit is to create suitable images, or ideal images, through a particular work. Images induce imagery. Imagery is something not tangible. I would roughly divide imagery into three categories. The first category is the imagery that is being formed when a dramatic action is being executed. The second imagery is seen after its execution: there is still something left behind in your mind but it might not be directly related to the imagery felt during the execution of the dramatic action. And the third layer of imagery is something between the first one and the second one. Sometimes when you look at an action being executed, you will associate it with something else. That is very intriguing. As a theatre-maker, I am always concerned about these three levels of imagery. That is the fundamental and ultimate pursuit of representing visual and audio elements.

Let me elaborate on my creative concepts using photos from two versions of *Titus Andronicus*. Figure 11 is taken from the work that we presented at the Globe in 2012. This is the scene at the Roman Square, when both of Lavinia's hands and her tongue have just been mutilated, and Titus is on the edge of becoming insane. Marcus at the left and Lucius at the right are trying to comfort Titus and proposing other solutions. As you see, this is drama, this is a dramatic action: we have characters, we have costumes, we have make-up, we have all those visual elements that are necessary to create the illusion of a dramatic experience.

This work, presented in 2012, was originally created in 2008 for the Hong Kong Arts Festival.[2] I am not very satisfied with it because I have always been constrained by drama: characters, time, space.

No matter how minimalistic the poses that I had the performers adopt, still there are certain boundaries which I can't break through to enable them to fully express themselves through the holistic use of their bodies, including everything available with just their bodies, without any external elements.

So, about nine months later in 2009, I created *Titus 2.0*. The idea for that came one day during meditation in the morning, when I heard a voice inside me saying 'storytelling'. I immediately phoned a playwright to ask him to change the dramatic text to a storytelling text, where I engaged seven narrators to narrate the whole story: sometimes they would stand outside the action as pure narrators and sometimes they would go into the action to act as the characters. But they all are dressed in black and we only have seven chairs.

Figure 12 shows the same scene in *Titus 2.0*, the scene at the Roman Square. There are two women and five men in this work. We have only seven chairs on stage because, during our work in progress and workshopping, I only allowed them to use seven chairs, nothing else. They dressed in black, so I used black costumes as their performing costumes. Once we adopted the approach of storytelling and narration, the whole dramaturgical structure is being reconstructed minute by minute during the performance. We didn't have a pre-conceived concept of what we were going to do. We had only one aim: to explore how a human being can narrate a story with the full use of his or her body without the help of external elements.

What are these expressions? I call them pre-verbal after this show.[3] First, the pre-verbal is physical displacement in space without doing any particular gesture, just very neutral displacement with different rhythms. Second, it is gestures,

---

[2] The full video-recordings of *Titus Andronicus* (2008) and *Titus 2.0* (2009) are archived with translations in the Asian Shakespeare Intercultural Archive (A|S|I|A), http://.a-s-i-a-web.org.

[3] Tang comments further on the pre-verbal in Yong Li Lan, 'Tang Shu-wing's *Titus* and the acting of violence', in *Shakespeare Beyond English: A Global Experiment*, ed. Susan Bennett and Christie Carson (Cambridge, 2013), 115–20.

11 *Titus Andronicus* performed in Cantonese by Tang Shu-wing Theatre Studio, Hong Kong Jockey Club Amphitheatre, The Hong Kong Academy for Performing Arts, 2012.

12 *Titus 2.0* performed in Cantonese by Tang Shu-wing Theatre Studio, Hong Kong City Hall Theatre, 2009.

SHAKESPEARE AND DRAMATURGICAL RECONSTRUCTION

either when you are displacing yourself or when you are stationed immobile; facial expressions; eyesight; voice, whether vocal (that is, from the vocal cord) or non-vocal; and also breathing. This is very simple. You can try it yourself without the use of any objects, like drumming, or with an object like a pen. The chairs in this case have several functions. They can serve as seats for the performers, but they can also serve as practicals [a unit on stage], so that we can move them along to generate different symbols or symbolic meaning, and create different levels. But they are never intended to be something like a prop or set in a traditional sense. So this scene is a dramaturgical reconstruction of the original drama. And with the help of lighting, we create tableaux of images, which can generate, hopefully, the three different layers of imagery.

Figure 13, from the 2012 *Titus* performed at the Globe, is the scene of Tamora disguising herself as the Goddess of Revenge, with her two sons, visiting Titus whom they believe to be insane. As you see, the performers' make-up, their costumes, and also their gestures point to a coherent representation of a dramatic character working in a particular chosen dramatic moment of the text. But again, even though they act very well, they are conditioned by the dramatic situation; they could not free themselves totally.

Figure 14 shows the same scene in *Titus Andronicus 2.0*. The six chairs at the far left serve as a barrier between Titus, whose chair is at first on the other side (stage right side) of the chairs, and the other characters, who basically become a tableau, not doing anything; they just sit there. Those characters include Tamora, performed by a man, and her two sons, also performed by two men. And then there's a messenger running between Tamora's group and Titus sitting alone on the far side of the chairs.

Titus was represented by a woman. It is after the crossing of the messenger and then the delivery of lines that this woman representing Titus moved the chair on which she was sitting to the other side or

13 *Titus Andronicus* performed in Cantonese by Tang Shu-wing Theatre Studio, Hong Kong Jockey Club Amphitheatre, The Hong Kong Academy for Performing Arts, 2012.

14 Act 5, scene 2 of *Titus 2.0* performed in Cantonese by Tang Shu-wing Theatre Studio, Hong Kong City Hall Theatre, 2009.

the other space belonging to Tamora's group. Then she literally inverted herself for about one minute while this group just looked at her, as Figure 14 shows. Finally, this group will look at the audience without saying anything. All these actions take place in complete silence.

The moment when the actor representing Titus inverts herself is an intuitive interpretation or association with that particular scene, the visit of the Goddess of Revenge. In this scene it seems that everything is playing on the double: what appears on the surface is not the true nature of the things that each character wants. The inversion physically or formally expresses the idea of double alienation in a particular manner, constructed under such circumstances. This scene, I think, carries the most daring step in constructing *Titus 2.0* as a grammar of dramaturgical reconstruction, which I hope can generate another imagery in the mind and spirit of the audience. Since imagery is something hard to define, it really depends on the perception of each individual member of the audience.

Turning again to the 2012 *Titus* performed at the Globe, Figure 15 shows the very sad, tragic scene after Lavinia was raped, when Marcus discovers her in the countryside. Even without watching the whole enactment, you can see from this photo that it's again drama: Marcus is crying hysterically at seeing such a creature in front of him. And that scene, on the Globe stage, is very powerful. I remember that, during the rape scene and after the rape scene, some members of the audience fainted; they were so shocked by this scene that they literally fainted. This is not the first time that has happened at the Globe:

SHAKESPEARE AND DRAMATURGICAL RECONSTRUCTION

15 *Titus Andronicus* performed in Cantonese by Tang Shu-wing Theatre Studio, Hong Kong Jockey Club Amphitheatre, The Hong Kong Academy for Performing Arts, 2012.

whenever *Titus Andronicus* is being performed, there are some audience members who faint and fall to the ground.

Figure 16 shows the same scene in *Titus 2.0*.[4] We have seven narrators who are sitting on seven chairs with a live musician [not seen at stage right]. I'm trying to balance the objective side and the subjective side of the performance and also the overall aesthetic treatment, where I create a sort of black in colour in which the flesh of the performers – the two arms, the neck, the face and the lower part of the legs and the feet – is visible. That creates a complete contrast between a dark environment and the organic components of a human being.

The grammar of navigating between a narrator and the construction of character is somehow similar to the alienation aesthetics of Bertolt Brecht. But it is not totally the same, because storytelling is the first performing language of every culture: storytelling before drama. In this scene an actress who is representing Lavinia uses a simple gesture to create a mutilated body. Then, she does something with the displacement of her body. As you all know, in that particular scene only Marcus speaks. But I divide the speech between the narrator who is acting or representing Marcus and the actress who is representing Lavinia. Both of them speak part of the text of Marcus so as to create what I would call a double dimension of alienation. Finally, after the actor representing Lavinia leaves the stage, I also wish to evoke some internal feelings through the imagery created by the bodily actions of the narrator who is representing Marcus.

To conclude, I would like to use two quotes from different plays by Shakespeare. The first

---

[4] At this point in his live keynote speech delivered at the WSC 2021, Tang played a video clip of act 2, scene 4 of *Titus 2.0*, from which Figure 16 is taken. The video clip can be viewed at A|S|I|A (http://a-s-i-a-web.org), 0:44:40–0:49:30.

16 Act 2, scene 4 of *Titus Andronicus 2.0* performed in Cantonese by Tang Shu-wing Theatre Studio, Hong Kong City Hall Theatre, 2009.

quote is from *As You Like It*: 'All the world's a stage, And all the men and women merely players'; the second is 'To be or not to be, that is the question' from *Hamlet*. In placing these two quotes together, I often reflect on their maybe coherent meanings. That is, for a theatre-maker, we have to act. To act is very important. Once we understand and fully utilize acting, then we can make something onstage which can realize what we are thinking in the mind with a team of people going in the same direction. In this situation, there's no right or wrong. It's just whether we carry a full energy and conviction going in our direction.

SHAKESPEARE, RACE, POSTCOLONIALITY: THE STATE OF THE FIELDS

JYOTSNA G. SINGH (CHAIR), JESSICA CHIBA, AMRITA DHAR AND CHRISTOPHER THURMAN

INTRODUCTION[1]

Our charge for the roundtable 'Race and Postcoloniality: The State of the Fields', at the 11th World Shakespeare Congress was to define and produce a 'conversation' between two related yet distinct fields within Shakespeare studies: postcolonial theory/criticism and critical race theory. Both fields emanate from shared, and often overlapping, histories of Western colonization, global capitalism, enslavement practices and the European slave trade. Both aim to 'decolonize' Shakespeare and his associations with 'whiteness', and, instead, contextualize his work within contemporary ideological and cultural struggles for justice and inclusion. Yet these fields often seem to veer far apart, with directives from distinct national political and cultural agendas. Put simply, they come from different places with different originating investments and concerns. Why does this chasm persist? Does it reflect fault-lines between the local and global – between the familiar and foreign/alien? Does this gap push different parties towards inward-looking self-preservation? To address these questions in the venue of the World Shakespeare Congress (WSC), we began with historically inflected definitions of both fields, the movements from which they originated and some particular challenges they have faced.

Postcolonial Theory/Criticism

Initially, Shakespearian postcolonial studies developed out of critical observations about emerging colonial paradigms in early modern English culture and literature. We saw an interest in figures such as Othello, Caliban or Shylock, as well as in Shakespearian representations of regions and lands far afield, covering racial, multi-ethnic terrains from the Mediterranean to the Americas and lands to the east. Thus, the idea of a European Renaissance was displaced by a view of the period as an era of expansion, cross-cultural encounters and emerging colonization. Overall, a postcolonial approach performs a proleptic function in revealing England's expansionist role, while providing a critical vocabulary to work through the relationship between the past and present. Here it is also important to recall that the genesis of postcolonial Shakespeare studies/approaches lay in the freedom movements beyond Europe. Figures at the vanguard of decolonizing Shakespeare, such as Frantz Fanon, Aimé Césaire, George Lamming, Ngũgĩ wa Thiong'o and Roberto Fernandez Retamar led the way by deconstructing the white canonical Shakespeare in Africa, in Latin America and in the Caribbean.

While absorbing early anti-colonial legacies, postcolonial Shakespeare studies today have given way to a polyphony of voices – beyond the binary of colonized and colonizer – which are recognized

---

[1] Jyotsna G. Singh.

to have evolved into what is broadly defined as the *global Shakespeare movement*.² The programming of the WSC gave a vivid sense of this global 'turn' in Shakespeare studies, telling stories about diverse lives and experiences, and tracking Shakespeare's interactions with local knowledge, as well as with Indigenous, non-metropolitan cultures on the stage and the screen, including different kinds of performance traditions.

Shakespeare and Critical Race Studies

While responding to shared histories of colonization with postcolonial approaches, critical race studies as a field has also made contributions that are unique and distinct.³ Emerging in the US, it has expanded its generative influence across global manifestations such as 'Black Lives Matter' and anti-slavery activism, including a call for reparations and for removing memorial statues and other commemorations of racialized enslavement. While it has demonstrated the need for new archives and scholarly modes of inquiry about why 'race' should be central to literary and cultural studies, critical race theory has come under attack in the US through our legislatures. These attacks caricature the field, and more importantly wish to erase the history of enslavement, the Reconstruction, the Jim Crow laws, along with their lingering effects. Such a repression of history in terms of race, ethnicity and religion reflects a familiar and long-standing impulse of repressive societies. For instance, one can find echoes in the Modi government's marginalization of Mughal/Islamic history in India, identifying their ethnic and religious lineage as foreign, since it is not Hindu.

Keeping these historical struggles in mind, let us consider how the burgeoning early modern race scholarship has expanded and enriched Shakespeare studies. For example, by deploying race as a viable lens of investigation in literary studies, while emphasizing topics such as race thinking, and racial biopolitics, it has produced a new, more inclusive, scholarly paradigm. The 'Introduction' to the special issue of *Shakespeare Quarterly* 'A "New Scholarly Song": Rereading Early Modern Race' (2016) brilliantly sums up the significance of early modern race studies,

pursuing historically specific definitions of race, while exploring topics such as visual culture, stagecraft, performance and hitherto unknown archives to produce new methodologies.⁴ Early modern race studies' most unique contribution – not directly articulated by postcolonial studies – is their promotion of 'whiteness studies', already an important subfield within critical race theory. As they argue, the 'use of the term "race" to mean only black or "of color" is unsatisfactory even in the Renaissance. The full complexity of the term [only] becomes accessible when whiteness as a racial category is examined.'⁵ Thus, 'whiteness studies' is crucial in challenging the 'universal' Shakespeare, with its assumptions about immutable human nature and a timeless English canon for and about white people.⁶

More closely echoing the goals of postcolonial theory, Hall and Erickson also assert that 'race scholarship needs to continue to expand beyond the limits of England and its colonies, providing a wider European purview that combines different linguistic and national traditions'.⁷ Here we can see overlapping interests of the two fields in globalizing Shakespeare studies. Thus, on reflection, one can recognize that the gap between the two fields is not substantive or unbridgeable, and they could come together in a *global conversation*. The presentations at

---

² Jyotsna G. Singh, *Shakespeare and Postcolonial Theory* (London, 2019). Information about the history and contemporary iterations of postcolonial theory and criticism is drawn from pp. 1–55, 149–94.
³ We owe a large debt to the RaceB4Race movement for promoting premodern critical race studies. It defines itself as 'an ongoing conference series and professional network community by and for scholars of color working on issues of race in premodern literature, history, and culture': https://acmrs.asu.edu/RaceB4Race.
⁴ Peter Erickson and Kim F. Hall, 'A "new scholarly song": rereading early modern race', *Shakespeare Quarterly* 67 (Spring 2016), 1–13.
⁵ Erickson and Hall, 'A "new scholarly song"', p. 7.
⁶ Arthur L. Little Jr, ed., *White People in Shakespeare: Essays on Race, Culture, and the Elite* (London, 2023). Recognized by Hall and Erickson (in 'A "new scholarly song"') and others, Little has provided a valuable conceptualization of 'whiteness' as a racial category, especially as applicable to early works.
⁷ Erickson and Hall, 'A "new scholarly song"', p. 6.

this WSC roundtable addressed in a variety of ways the concerns of postcolonial and critical race studies, often within parameters in which the two fields converge. And a particular unifying factor was that all the arguments, summarized below, address from varying perspectives how to read the past in terms of the present.

In addition to the summaries below, it is important to acknowledge Ato Quayson, who was a part of the live roundtable at the WSC, though his summary is not included in this article. Quayson's presentation offered key reflections on the conversation between the two fields with a reading of *Othello* through anti-colonial race theories, in this case through the specific lens on the Black body provided by Frantz Fanon in his chapter 'The fact of Blackness', in *Black Skin, White Masks*. His argument was contextualized via a comparison between W. E. B. DuBois's notion of double consciousness and Fanon's idea of the discombobulation of the Black bodily schema – not as opposing modalities, but ultimately as dialectical aspects of the same instances of (mis)recognition from the standpoint of the racialized body. Finally, he expanded his discussion of racial embodiment by referring to the *Othello* morphology in Tayib Salih's novel *Season of Migration to the North*.[8]

The three summaries, and the conversation they generate, elaborate on the possibilities and challenges faced by the two fields as they navigate the critical and cultural terrains of early modern studies in our fraught, contemporary times. We learn from them – as we did in the live WSC roundtable – that enabling and listening to a polyphony of voices can open the way to solidarities across difference.

TOWARDS GLOBAL CONVERSATIONS BETWEEN SHAKESPEARE STUDIES, CRITICAL RACE STUDIES AND POSTCOLONIAL STUDIES[9]

As an early-career scholar, I spent all my graduate years wishing for greater dialogue between critical race studies and postcolonial studies. How could I not wish such a thing? I grew up in Calcutta, in the east of India, and I was studying in the American Midwest while spending time in India and greater North America. My presentation is on what I see as the relationship between critical race studies and postcolonial studies, especially as it pertains to Shakespeare studies in the twenty-first century – and where I should like to see us going in these fields of study.

Critical race theory – as it is current in the most influential axis of scholarship in English literary studies today, which is the US–UK axis – is a product of scholarly, legal and activist resistance to racism in the US and the UK, especially resistance to anti-Black racism in these geographies. Critical race studies has also provided key leverage for resistance to anti-Hispanic and anti-Indigenous systemic racisms in these geographies. As Jyotsna Singh mentions in her Introduction, it is precisely because critical race theory calls the matter as it is that it is currently under attack in the US from right-wing factions. It is impossible to overstate the practical indebtedness that someone like me, an early-career scholar of colour working in the academy in the global North, has to the towering energies of this Black – and, to a significant extent, specifically Black feminist – intellectual movement. (It is important to mark that critical race theory is not actually very new. It is several decades old, potentially even centuries old – even though its inception in the form we most readily recognize today may be dated to 1989 with the 'New Developments in Critical Race Theory' Conference organized by Kimberlé Crenshaw and Mari Matsuda.) I simply could not do the work that I do today without the foundations laid by intersectional Black feminist scholars in my profession. Critical race theory, then, is very much a product of particular social, cultural and legal situations in the global North.

Postcolonial theory, on the other hand, especially as it is practised by literary and cultural critics in and of the post-colonial global South is a product of analytics, scholarship, solidarities, and political

---

[8] For a fuller discussion, see Ato Quayson, *Tragedy and Postcolonial Literature* (Cambridge, 2021).
[9] Amrita Dhar.

and cultural situations most widely pertaining to and recognizable in the global South. Here I make a distinction between 'post-colonial' with the hyphen, denoting a state of erstwhile political colonization, and 'postcolonial' without the hyphen, denoting a capacious analytic that critiques all forms of colonial thinking, irrespective of temporal linearity or colonial/erstwhile-colonial status of any given polity.

Broadly speaking, therefore, there is perhaps a North–South difference in terms of where critical race theory and postcolonial theory come from. But there is another way in which I could mark the distinction between critical race theory and postcolonial theory – and in so doing, I might also point out how things become rather more entangled. That brings me to the main thrust of this piece, which is that critical race theory and postcolonial theory urgently, widely, coalitionally, multilingually and collaboratively need to be in dialogue with one another.

The key point that I wish to make is that critical race theory was born in a geography under continued settler colonialism, the US. To this day, the US is the most powerful settler colony of Europe. We must also remember that the US is itself a terrible colonizing and imperial force in the world today. US imperialism – as fuelled by its superlative and advanced capitalism, its military spending and over-reach, and its continuous profiteering war in many parts of the world – is part of US policy.

Postcolonial theory, on the other hand, largely arose in geographies that are today facing – and in many pockets trying to resist – the reality of what comes post- or after colonialism, which is in fact the terrible situation of neo-colonialism. The most disenfranchised have only ever changed masters upon any political post-colonialism. The reality of post-colonialism is neo-colonialism in so many parts of the world. Think of governments attacking their own poorest and most disenfranchised people in so many post-colonial polities today, from Brazil to India. Who needs colonizers with governments such as these, governments that have learnt the lessons of the colonial so well that they now better the instruction?

The best of postcolonial studies succeeds in imagining something like justice, something like genuine equity, even in the aftermath of being colonized. Urvashi Chakravarty, writing about 'The state of Renaissance studies', picks up on that peculiar word, 'state', and wonders about the topics, concerns and engagements that are seen to be natural, naturalized and naturalizable in the field of Renaissance studies.[10] Here I, too, want to flag that word: state. Given this North–South division that I have been marking: are there topics, concerns and engagements that are intrinsically not naturalizable within the fields of Shakespeare studies, critical race studies and postcolonial studies? Can, for instance, critical race studies and post-colonial studies afford to not talk to one another because they 'come from' different places – because they have different originating investments and concerns? I believe that in the interest of progressive global realignments of shared interests, critical race studies and postcolonial studies must talk to one another.

Where postcolonial studies and critical race studies have been in conversation through early modern studies and Shakespeare studies, new and generative directions of study, such as eco-critical early modernisms, transnational early modernisms, borderland and migration studies, global performance studies, food studies, critical book history, Chicanx studies, critical caste studies, Indigenous studies and critical disability studies have found a substrate on which to grow and build. From the intersection of critical race studies and postcolonial studies, we can learn about originary rhetoric surrounding European identity, which in the pre-modern period was being solidified as white and Christian. We can also learn about European 'superiority' – as considered by Europeans – over non-European peoples. Third, we can learn about

---

[10] Urvashi Chakravarty, 'The state of Renaissance studies II: the Renaissance of race and the future of early modern race studies', *English Literary Renaissance* 50 (2020), 17–24.

the fashioning of institutions and policies that make it easy to render 'new' worlds and geographies useful by potential for extraction and settlement. Fourth: this also is where we learn about historical continuities of the very lines of discriminatory and disqualifying-from-complete-human-subjecthood thought that persist to our own day. For examples of work emerging from this intersection, we might mark the scholarship coming out of the RaceB4Race initiative.[11] Assuredly, RaceB4Race is yet another initiative in the global North, and yet another English-language-centred enterprise. But going by the initiative's past work and ongoing commitments, it appears that RaceB4Race is trying to shape a global and political conversation centring all matters of racial thinking while placing the premodern in dialogue with the contemporary.

The violent age of empire necessarily also saw profound solidarities and cosmopolitanisms between colonized peoples. Today, in our time of extreme capitalist-colonialist oppressions, our moment of so many mechanisms of disenfranchizement in the world, and of peculiar estrangements and detentions and separations as results of lines drawn on/as maps, we cannot afford not to use that past model of coalitional dialogue, group effort, community-building and justice-making.[12]

LISTENING TO INDIGENOUS VOICES: WHAT COUNTS AS KNOWLEDGE IN *THE TEMPEST*[13]

Postcolonialism is a crucial part of Shakespeare studies, and as Jyotsna Singh has pointed out, increasingly involves 'a polyphony of voices beyond binaries of colonizer/colonized'.[14] Often extending into 'Global Shakespeares', it is a broad field, encompassing performances, adaptations, reception, translation and analysis from around the world. At the same time, postcolonialism and 'Global Shakespeares' are often treated as marginal to textual, historical scholarship in Anglo-American studies. The global does not constitute the centre in Shakespeare studies. But Shakespeare's works undeniably represent global culture, and the ways they came to be so – the focus of many postcolonial readings – must be acknowledged not just as a marginal enterprise, but as a central part of what it means to study Shakespeare today. This is not simply a question of colonialism and the centralized cultural imperialism of the past, but the future of academic thinking in our discipline and what counts as knowledge. I focus here on 'acceptable knowledge': what is epistemically privileged in Western academic thinking. If *The Tempest* is the quintessential colonial text of exploitation, linguistic dominance and sexual control, Prospero's relationship with Ariel and his spirits might also offer a different approach to other forms of knowledge.

Shakespeare presents Prospero as a scholar of 'the liberal arts' (1.2.73)[15] whose chief source of knowledge is his books. Shakespeare places much emphasis on these books in Prospero's narration, where he claims that 'my library / Was dukedom large enough' (1.2.109–10), that 'I loved my books' and that on his exile Gonzalo provided him 'From mine own library with volumes that / I prize above my dukedom' (1.2.166–7). Prospero loses his dukedom because of his bookish obsession, and his attempt to educate Caliban becomes a form of enslavement in language. However, if it is only a question of language, there would be no need for this repeated focus on physical books that represent the form of Prospero's knowledge: the kind of knowledge that can be written in books.

The power that Prospero wields and that allows him to control Caliban and the spirits on the island evidently derives from these books. Thus, Caliban

---

[11] See RaceB4Race, https://acmrs.asu.edu/RaceB4Race.
[12] For a discussion of why Shakespeare is a particularly apt site for such intersectional work and coalitional dialogue, see Amrita Dhar, '*The Invention of Race* and the postcolonial Renaissance', *The Cambridge Journal of Postcolonial Literary Inquiry* 9 (2022), 132–8.
[13] Jessica Chiba.
[14] Singh, *Shakespeare and Postcolonial Theory*, p. 3.
[15] William Shakespeare, *The Tempest,* from *William Shakespeare: The Complete Works,* 2nd ed., ed. Stanley Wells, Gary Taylor, John Jowett and William Montgomery (Oxford, 2005). All subsequent parenthetical references are to this edition.

tells Stephano repeatedly to 'possess his books; for without them / He's but a sot' (3.2.85–6); to 'Burn but his books' (3.2.88). There appears to be only one *magic* book – the book that Prospero will drown at the end of the play, but the plural form used by Caliban suggests that his other books also have power. Notably, Prospero dictates the shape that the spirits take based on the kind of knowledge contained in his books: nymphs, harpies and the Roman gods are 'respectable' pagan figures of classical learning.

Prospero commands his spirits from an assumed position of greater knowledge. There is no exchange of ideas – for instance, almost everything Ariel says refers to the tasks Prospero has set for him. At one point, Ariel even expresses fear about telling Prospero anything he doesn't explicitly ask for: 'I thought to have told thee of it, but I feared / Lest I might anger thee' (4.1.168–9). A difference in knowledge is implied, for knowing how to control the spirits is not the same as sharing the spirits' knowledge. However, there is one moment in this relationship when Prospero actively listens to Ariel and is inspired to change his mind. This is when Ariel describes to Prospero the torments to which the nobles have been subjected, telling him, 'if you now beheld them, your affections / Would become tender' (5.1.18–19). For the first time in the play, Prospero is interested in what Ariel thinks – 'Dost thou think so, spirit?' – and Ariel's reply, 'Mine would, sir, were I human' (5.1.19–20), changes Prospero's reaction entirely. Primarily motivated by revenge, Prospero always refers to his brother and the Neapolitans as his 'enemies', but in response to Ariel's words, says he will be 'kindlier moved' (5.1.24), concluding that 'The rarer action is / In virtue than in vengeance' (5.1.27–8). Although this same commonplace notion could have come from any Renaissance humanist text or Christianity, it is crucial that, in this instance, it does *not* come from his books. Prospero is inspired to think so because of Ariel. It is also significant that Ariel is a spirit that is never Christianized. Even though what he says here is not astoundingly different from many European spiritual notions, the insight of this native spirit suggests the possibility of alternative spiritualities that do not come from a book or Western academic and religious practices. It may be fanciful to claim that Prospero says 'I'll drown my book' (5.1.57) in response to this interaction, but Prospero does appear to be freed from his obsession with book learning by the end of the play. In saying of Caliban, 'this thing of darkness / I acknowledge mine' (5.1.274–5), he seems to name a relationship that is not based on knowledge and control: Caliban can remain undefinable, a thing not fully understood – in the early modern sense of 'dark' – but still be acknowledged.

We ought to recognize what is Prospero-like about our approaches to knowledge. What Prospero does can alert us to the potential tyranny and limitations of a particular kind of knowledge, but also show the beginnings of a better ethical relation with the world through the choice to listen to a source of wisdom that is not book-learning, not Western, not even human. Ariel can represent local knowledge, alternative spiritual understandings and the possibility of a world that is not anthropocentric. Global views and positions outside what is ordinarily accepted as knowledge might reinvigorate research by challenging preconceptions.

This is not a defence of Prospero or a suggestion that native knowledge requires recognition from colonial thinking. Such binaries do not serve either side, and indeed *create* sides in what could instead be an enlightening exchange of knowledge. Our postcolonial world cannot just be about blame and recognition. Reparation may be impossible, the subaltern may be barred from expression, and many voices have been lost in colonial epistemicide, but it is never too late to listen. A listening ear might be the best and most ethical way to keep an open mind about what counts as knowledge.

SHAKESPEARE, RACE AND SOUTH–SOUTH/SOUTH–NORTH SOLIDARITY[16]

Observing what can only be described as belatedly widespread recognition of the scholars whose

---

[16] Christopher Thurman.

pioneering work on race in early modern studies continues to speak powerfully to the present historical moment – Kim F. Hall's *Things of Darkness* (1995) is a prime example, and another is Margo Hendricks and Patricia Parker's *Women, Race and Writing in the Early Modern Period* (1994), to which the convenor of this roundtable, Jyotsna Singh, contributed – I can't help wondering whether these leading lights and guiding spirits of what has now become a burgeoning field look across the decades between then and now and ask of their peers: what took you so long? Why is it only in the past few years that race has become one of the most prominent lenses, if not now the most prominent lens, through which a field such as Shakespeare studies conducts its analytical work? (The answer, in places like America and Britain, is in one sense obvious: the advent of #blacklivesmatter and the zeitgeist that lent this movement its urgency.)

Likewise, postcolonial Shakespeare scholars – or scholars in and of the global South, broadly construed – might be inclined to turn to their colleagues from the US and the UK, asking: what took you so long? We've been doing this for ages! In fact, in a postcolonial / global South context, it was never possible (or never convincing) to undertake any form of engagement with early modern European or English literature and drama without foregrounding histories of race and racism along with their contemporary legacies. *Postcolonial Shakespeares* (1998), edited by Ania Loomba and Martin Orkin, came at the tail end of decades of postcolonial scholarly and creative engagement with Shakespeare. In Loomba's *Gender, Race and Renaissance Drama* (1989) and Orkin's *Shakespeare against Apartheid* (1987) we have two books marked by their authors' Indian and South African perspectives. They could be seen as applying to Shakespeare/Renaissance studies what Ngũgĩ had called *Decolonising the Mind* (1986), which again was the culmination of postcolonial, decolonial and anti-colonial responses to a European literary canon dating back thirty years and more.

The desire to declare 'We've been doing it' is arguably what lies beneath a perceived friction between, on the one hand, US/UK scholars whose approach to race in the early modern period is filtered through – or expressed through an academic discourse on – race and racism in the global North, and, on the other hand, scholars of the global South who might feel that their analysis of – and, indeed, experience of – race and racism in early modern studies is once again being marginalized by an imperial centre. We might conceive of this, broadly, as the challenge of sustaining North–South solidarity when it comes to race in/ and early modern studies.

Thinking about the problem in this way – the declaration 'We've been doing it!' – I couldn't help but call to mind a popular South African TV commercial promoting mobile phone company Vodacom's introduction of smartphone functionality some years ago.[17] Dubbed 'We've been having it!', the advert drew not only on Western caricatures of the African dictator, but also on familiar South African tropes regarding 'other' African countries that are continually spurred by (and in turn used to justify) xenophobia and a general superiority complex. This is, of course, a problem of South–South solidarity. What does it mean for Shakespeare studies? For one thing, we need to be attuned to the risks attached to African stereotyping of Africa – as one instance, I have in mind Brett Bailey and Third World Bunfight's version of Verdi's *Macbeth* (2013), which was conceived by a company from the global South but which has been performed primarily for audiences in the global North, reproducing similar 'African dictator' imagery.[18]

If we want to consider the grounds for South–South solidarity via Shakespeare, Sandra Young's *Shakespeare and the Global South* (2019) is a key point of reference. Young's book, however, also

---

[17] See Vodacom, 'We've been having it!', https://youtu.be/-ILE6yUEyyQ?si=t4fq3Y7QpE7D9AdL.

[18] During the full presentation of which this text is a summary, I briefly discussed other examples that might 'test' South–South solidarity via Shakespeare: the relationship between South Africa, India and the Indian South African community; Janet Suzman's 2009 production of *Hamlet*; and recent South African / Indian Shakespearian collaborations.

gestures towards the ways in which the global South might not hold together as a concept, never mind a geography. Here Dilip Menon's *Changing Theory: Concepts from the Global South* (2022) offers an alternative paradigm; the volume contains essays that explore these concepts specifically as they are contained within or expressed by certain languages. Insofar as these concepts may be seen as shared despite linguistic barriers, or shared across various languages in/of the global South other than English, another means of approaching South–South solidarity presents itself. This is not an argument against translation so much as against remaining bound within, or beholden to, the Anglosphere.

It is within the English language, however, that I want to return to the question of South–North solidarity, for such instances of solidarity require a recognition not only of what is shared but also what is different. Slippages in racial terminology are telling; to write about Shakespeare and race requires careful navigation across different national and cultural contexts. An example is 'colored', a pejorative term in the US that doesn't mean the same as 'coloured' in South Africa, where it was an apartheid-era racial category but remains in the post-apartheid period as an accepted racial or cultural descriptor. BIPOC, as employed in America, doesn't transplant well to South Africa. The phrase 'people of colour' is an attempt to be more inclusive, but is rejected by many black South Africans as an alien import into our already dense lexicon of race. Likewise, while 'Indigenous' has come to replace 'Native American' as a descriptor in the US, 'native' in South Africa has a very specific colonial- and apartheid-era stigma, and the discourse of indigeneity is dangerous because it has been invoked to suggest that black people and white people were equal migrants to (and therefore settlers in) a geographical region from which the first peoples were expelled. So 'Indigenous' or 'native' Shakespeares would carry a stigma in South Africa, in the same way that analysis of 'coloured' characters in a South African Shakespeare production requires extensive footnoting for American readers. All of this assumes English as lingua franca; as Menon's collection demonstrates, however, trans- or interlingual movement of concepts is both richer and more fraught.

When it comes to race in/and early modern studies, and Shakespeare in particular, it is evident that 'We've been doing it!' in our respective national and regional contexts. Perhaps a closer attention to the language(s) in which we have been doing it will help to achieve greater levels of both South–South and South–North solidarity.

CONCLUSION[19]

In conclusion, in following these conversations emanating from our WSC roundtable, I believe our voices have come together via shared concerns and guideposts of the two fields. These interactions have occurred not in terms of universals or grand narratives where colonialism or race are static, unchanging categories, but rather by taking us on varied journeys through landscapes of premodern and contemporary connected histories. I use the term 'connected histories' as coined by the historian Sanjay Subrahmanyam; it enables a way of bringing together historical phenomena that are disparate, diverse and multi-vocal – phenomena that are often artificially separated by historiographical convention.[20] If we contextualize postcolonial studies and critical race studies within global networks, we can witness an interplay of connections and echoes as both fields are invested in expanding their topics of inquiry, in working across disciplines, in including more local, Indigenous voices, and in questioning our notions of 'knowledge'. Thus, I believe, as these summaries show, race struggles in early modern England and in the contemporary US–UK nexus are connected cross-culturally with the postcoloniality of the global South, spanning regions, subjects and archives.

---

[19] Jyotsna G. Singh.
[20] For a general description and analysis of Sanjay Subrahmanyam's theory of 'connected histories', see Sanjay Subrahmanyam's *Connected Histories: Essays and Arguments* (London, 2022). This is one among a series of publications that use this lens to study encounters and engagements of various cultures and polities.

For my final vision of collaboration and affiliation between the two fields and their engagements with the global North and South, I wish to evoke the idea of an 'affective community' shaped by a 'politics of friendship' between persons and groups with disparate origins and identities. Drawing on Derrida's theory of friendship, Leela Gandhi puts forth a powerful new model of the political in friendship as an important resource for anti-imperial and transnational collaboration. She coins the term 'affective community', based on solidarities across transnational, cross-racial and cross-religious boundaries.[21] In contemporary critical terrains, as groups seek equity and justice, they are often led to close ranks around particular identities. Given that postcolonial and race scholars have shared interests, a new politics of friendship can only bring them closer in ways that are empowering for both.

---

[21] Leela Gandhi, *Affective Communities: Anticolonial Thought, Fin-de-Siècle Radicalism and the Politics of Friendship* (Durham, NC, 2006), 1–15.

ASIAN SHAKESPEARES ONLINE FROM SINGAPORE

YONG LI LAN, MICHAEL DOBSON, MIKA EGLINTON, LEE HYON-U, BI-QI BEATRICE LEI, ALVIN ENG HUI LIM AND ELEINE NG-GAGNEUX

INTRODUCTION: THE WSC 2021 DIGITAL ASIAN SHAKESPEARE FESTIVAL[1]

Originally, the 11th World Shakespeare Congress (WSC) in 2021 was to have been held in Singapore. A small island entrepôt, Singapore was a key node on maritime trade routes – the 'Silk Road of the sea'[2] – that connected Southeast Asia with India and China. It had been a site of convergence and exchange among peoples, goods, languages and cultures for several centuries when Stamford Raffles made it part of the British Empire. Shakespeare, too, then entered circulation through Singapore in travelling performances, English-medium education, translations into local languages and adaptations for Asian theatres. Situated along such a historical trajectory of trade, and in the context of Singapore society's present constitution as a multiracial, multicultural nation, the WSC 2021 was planned with a performance programme of several Shakespeare productions from South, Southeast and East Asia. When in 2020 the COVID-19 pandemic brought international travel to a halt and recourse to a virtual conferencing platform, the artistic communities in Asia who create performance work with Shakespeare and the international academic community of Shakespeare scholars lost the experience of coming together in the theatre. These two communities do not often find occasion to meet. With this in mind, the organizing committee re-designed the performance programme to treat the online medium as another kind of trade route, in what was renamed the *Digital* Asian Shakespeare Festival.

The Festival hosted full-length video-recordings of Asian Shakespeare performances, not as substitutes for live events but as the basis for different events. The Congress duration was extended by pre-and post-Congress periods to a month, during which the videos, subtitled in English, were accessible online. In the week before the Congress proper, informal watch parties were held nightly (or daily depending on your time-zone) when a director showed a selection of clips from the video of their work and commented in detail upon their artistic process, choices and intentions, followed by conversation with the attendees. The watch parties supported In-Conversation sessions and keynote presentations during the main Congress with several of the directors. Having engaged their audience about one work in detail, directors became more comfortable speaking broadly about how their creative strategies relate Shakespeare's work to their own political and artistic contexts. In the course of these different events, the engagement between theatre practitioners and scholars shifted ground from the

---

[1] Yong Li Lan.
[2] John Miksic, *Singapore and the Silk Road of the Sea, 1300–1800* (Singapore, 2013).

meeting point of production and reception in the theatre to an unusual discursive middle ground of shared watching and discussion.

A major opportunity of the Congress's online medium was that it enabled a greater number and diversity of performances to be watched over a stretched conference period than the funds, organization or compressed time of an on-site Congress would have allowed. The Festival presented nine video-recordings of performances and an animation: The Actors Studio's *Mak Yong Titis Sakti* (2009, Malaysia); the Royal Shakespeare Company and Shanghai Dramatic Arts Center's *Henry V* (2019, UK/China); the Annette Leday / Keli Company's *Kathakali-King Lear* (2019, France/India); Contemporary Legend Theatre's *The Tempest* (2004, Taiwan); Nine Years Theatre's *Lear Is Dead* (2018, Singapore); Shizuoka Performing Arts Centre's *Miyagi Noh Othello ~Phantom Love~* (2018, Japan); Cake Theatrical Productions' *Ophelia* (2016, Singapore); Yohangza Theatre Company's *Pericles* (2016, South Korea); Tang Shu-wing Theatre Studio's *The Tragedy of Macbeth* (2019, Hong Kong); and the animation *As You Like It*, directed by Hannes Rall (2020, Singapore). The curation aimed to showcase works by major directors that had toured internationally as well as works led by younger directors that were local in attention and reference. None except the RSC/SDAC *Henry V* used a translation of Shakespeare's play, the others employing instead an original script adapted to serve the director's and company's particular artistic objectives, style and approach to Shakespeare.

The following summaries of the directors' work with Shakespeare and the performances they presented are by scholars in Asian Shakespeare who were members of the WSC organizing committee and were closely involved in the directors' events. The authors provide contexts for relating the work to the director's career, to the audience reception, theatre forms and languages of its own locale, and, in the case of *Kathakali-King Lear*, to the history of its own long life. They are all also members of the Asian Shakespeare Intercultural Archive (A|S|I|A), a collaborative project in archiving East and Southeast Asian Shakespeare performance, which

I have led since 2009. To a considerable extent the design and delivery of the WSC 2021 Digital Asian Shakespeare Festival drew upon our experience in preparing, translating and working together across languages and countries, our working protocols for the digital archiving of performance and, most importantly, our friendships with the directors. The wiring of circuits along a digital trade route was already in place, but had yet to be live in a collective event.

NELSON CHIA AND NINE YEARS THEATRE'S *LEAR IS DEAD*[3]

Nine Years Theatre's *Lear Is Dead* (2018), directed by Nelson Chia, is the Singaporean theatre company's first staging of a Shakespeare play. Co-founded in 2012 by Nelson Chia and Mia Chee, the company's work ranges from 're-imaginations of classics and adaptations of literary works, to original plays as well as interdisciplinary and international collaborations'.[4] *Lear Is Dead* epitomizes the company's 're-imagination' of Western plays. For the Mandarin-language theatre company, Mandarin translations of Western plays are an opportunity to re-introduce realist theatre to Singaporean audiences, as Chia explained in his Director In-Conversation session during the WSC in 2021.

For Chia, these adaptations also test what it means to stage a Singaporean play. Referencing the history of Singapore theatre and the search for a national theatre in the late twentieth century, Chia pointed out that there is a 'conflation of what is local and what is Singaporean'.[5] Staging a foreign play in Mandarin represents an alternative realization of a Singaporean identity that is not based on localized or hybridized identity markers

---

[3] Alvin Eng Hui Lim.
[4] 'About Nine Years Theatre', www.nineyearstheatre.com/en/about.php.
[5] 'Director In-Conversation: Nelson Chia', 11th World Shakespeare Congress, Singapore: Shakespeare Circuits, International Shakespeare Association, Singapore, 19 July 2021.

that Singapore is internationally known for: local food, mixed ethnicities or mixed heritage Singaporeans (such as Peranakans) and Singlish, a colloquial form of English. Singapore's identity as a multilingual, multicultural, multireligious and relatively young country means that identity formations which exist within and beyond the island-nation are complex and nuanced. Staging Shakespeare in this context must go beyond mere tokenism of multicultural Singapore, as well as resist essentializing a particular culture or ethnicity. Chia's stagings of Western plays translated into Mandarin constitute one part of Singapore's pluralism.

Singapore's many engagements with Shakespeare can be partly understood as a product of the British colonial era, when, as Philip Smith describes, Shakespeare served as 'a civilising agent'.[6] Later, adaptations of Shakespeare in postwar Singapore suggested that the desire to present a localized and multicultural version of Shakespeare's plays often resulted in unsuccessful endeavours. Smith reports that 'Singapore audiences, and Europeans particularly, had developed a specific idea of how Shakespeare should look and sound' (p. 92). That said, multicultural casting and staging elements drawn from non-English traditions and cultures were attempts to bridge the cultural divide. For instance, Emily Soon points out that:

[f]or English-medium schools to feature the *wayang* [the local Malay term for Chinese street theatre], traditionally the preserve of the Chinese-speaking community, shows that . . . at least some individuals in the English education system actively created opportunities for ethnically Chinese students in English schools to reconnect with their cultural heritage, and for their non-Chinese classmates to learn more about this art form too.[7]

Situated within the historical context of Shakespeare in Singapore, Nine Years Theatre's first adaptation of Shakespeare reflects the complex negotiation needed to translate Shakespeare within a multifaceted context. In a context where cultural identities are often delineated into neat racial categories, *Lear Is Dead* is an attempt to provoke an active reflection of what it means to translate Shakespeare's language into Mandarin, itself a language borrowed to distil diverse diasporic Chinese communities (Cantonese, Hokkien, Teochew, Hainanese, to name a few) into one homogeneous identity. Instead of drawing from an overtly Chinese tradition, the production gestures towards several identity markers, made possible because of the company's unique process of intercultural mixing.

Chia's identity as a theatremaker crosses boundaries. He is an acting coach, director, performer, playwright and lecturer. Bilingual in English and Mandarin, he has translated Western plays into Mandarin. He began directing professionally in 2003 as Associate Artistic Director of Toy Factory Productions (2003–2013), but his career as a director must be understood alongside his journey as a performer. Since 2008, he has trained in the Suzuki Method of Actor Training and Viewpoints, both of which he learned with SITI Company in New York. Further, he trained with Suzuki Company of Toga (SCOT) in Japan. From 2014 to 2021, Chia formed and led the NYT Ensemble (NYTE), 'a company of actors who train regularly in a systematic way and create work together over an extended period of time'.[8] Nine Years Theatre also holds Mandarin diction classes for the general public and classes for actors to learn Mandarin speech techniques. While it identifies itself as a Mandarin theatre company, its ensemble model is based on SITI's model and training methods.

With *Lear Is Dead*, the company's early realist style of performance has been replaced by a heightened style in which the performance conveys a constant sense of self-awareness – gesturing that it is a Shakespearian adaptation, a contemporary take on Shakespearian foolery, and a morality play infused

---

[6] Philip Smith, *Shakespeare in Singapore: Performance, Education, and Culture* (Abingdon, 2020), p. 57.
[7] Emily Soon, 'Cultural inclusivity and student Shakespeare performances in late-colonial Singapore, 1950–1959', in *Shakespeare Survey 74* (Cambridge, 2021), 167–79; p. 177.
[8] 'Our team', www.nineyearstheatre.com/en/team.php#Nelson.

17 Lear and the Fools, Nine Years Theatre, *Lear Is Dead*, Singapore, 2018. Photo: The Pond Photography, courtesy of Nine Years Theatre.

with the belief system that the afterlife is a place of nothingness: all grace and grievances no longer mean anything. The fools in the production wear bowler hats and dress in an attire reminiscent of Charlie Chaplin. They also change into highly stylized costumes that are a cross between *xiqu* (Chinese opera) costumes and abstract representations of noble characters in Lear's court.

The performance begins with a pre-show dialogue, echoing and reversing the company's practice of holding post-show dialogues with the audience members (often over Chinese tea). The NYT Ensemble forms the chorus, and each performer plays two or more characters. The metatheatrical frame is introduced in the pre-show dialogue: a pseudo-organization called the Fools' Society is staging the tragedy of Lear (Figure 17). This Society effectively replicates the NYTE model, where each production casts the same Ensemble members.

These performative elements constantly signal a play-within-a-play framework. Chia's edited script, in which key *Lear* scenes are spliced with interview dialogues between an interviewer and members of the Fools' Society, also heightens this metatheatricality. Moreover, going beyond the fictional plot, King Lear and all the main characters are also depicted as dead, returning from the afterlife to re-enact their previous lives. In effect, the performance becomes an episodic exploration of how authority is constructed and deconstructed, and who gets to tell the story of (the rise and fall of) an authority figure. The passing of the nation's former prime minister, Lee Kuan Yew, in 2015 was followed by a public family dispute over the fate of Lee's house. In 2018, when the production of *Lear Is Dead* was staged, the family feud between Lee's children was still fresh in the consciousness of local audiences as Lear's own family feud played out onstage.[9] At once viewed as a serious

---

[9] See 'The rift in Singapore's first family turns even nastier', *The Economist*, 29 March 2023, www.economist.com/asia/2023/03/09/the-rift-in-singapores-first-family-turns-even-nastier.

political commentary on the political drama that ensues when a leader of a nation dies, and a comedic retelling of a foreign and fictional kingdom, this posthumous retelling of *Lear* reflects the status of Shakespeare in Singapore – one that simultaneously emphasizes a colonial legacy which still haunts the nation, as well as its departure from Shakespeare. At the heart of Shakespearian adaptation in Singapore is the freedom with which theatremakers reimagine the language, the performance style and the politics, creating a space for reflecting on Singapore's cultural diversity and divisions.

MIYAGI NOH OTHELLO ~PHANTOM LOVE~ (2018)[10]

Miyagi Satoshi founded Ku Na'uka Theatre Company in 1990, and since 2007 he has been the Artistic Director of the Shizuoka Performing Arts Centre (SPAC). Over the course of his career, Miyagi has gained a reputation for bold reinterpretations of classic plays from East and West, including adaptations of Shakespeare's *Hamlet*, *Macbeth*, *Othello*, *A Midsummer Night's Dream* and *The Winter's Tale*.

Drawing on Asian theatre traditions and aesthetics, Miyagi's productions are known for the dual performance of a single character shared between two performers, a 'mover' and 'a speaker', where one enacts the character's movements and another speaks the character's lines, thus separating words and action. This device was used in his production of *Mugen Noh Othello*, originally staged by Ku Na'uka in 2005 and revived at SPAC in 2018. As part of the World Shakespeare Congress 2021 in Singapore, I invited Miyagi to discuss the core themes of this production by viewing six pivotal scenes as part of an online 'Watch party' with Congress attendees.

Miyagi had always felt that the original character of the chaste Desdemona murdered by her husband as a whore was too idealistic, passive and even parasitic on her husband's power, and this made him reluctant to direct *Othello*. Yet he found the possibility of conceiving and directing the piece from the heroine's perspective after reading an essay[11] by a Japanese scholar of comparative literature, Sukehiro Hirakawa, and subsequently he asked Hirakawa to adapt the entire play. In the essay, Hirakawa writes on the life and accomplishment of Arthur David Waley, a British scholar of Oriental classic literature who adapted John Webster's *The Duchess of Malfi* into a *noh* dream play around the 1910s.

Traditional *noh* dream plays consist of two parts. In the first half, called the *maeba*, the *shite* or primary performer, who plays the main character (often a ghost), enters with companions called *tsure*, and they interact with the *waki* or secondary actor, who is often a travelling monk with the function of a mediator between the *shite* and the audience, the world of the dead and the world of the living. There is then a short *kyogen* performance, a comical and conversational interlude, between the more serious and musical *noh* scenes. In the latter half, called the *nochiba*, the *shite* reveals the identity of the ghost and re-enacts the most critical and final moment in his or her life in front of the *waki*. By re-enacting and re-living the past in the present time, the ghost-*shite* achieves redemption and finally leaves this world. What the *shite* and the audience witness can be read as a mere dream vision of the *waki*, inspired by the memory of the land or a local tragic story.

In Hirakawa's adaptation, the *shite* is the ghost of Desdemona. Thus, the tragedy of the interracial marriage emerges from the vision of the marginalized white Venetian wife and not that of the jealous husband. The play is set in Cyprus, now under the control of Turkish Muslims, reflecting the shifting history of the fortress at the intersection of Arab, African and European worlds. A female performer, Honda Maki, both verbally and physically played a travelling monk from Venice. The cross-gendered male priest took the position of

---

[10] Mika Eglinton.
[11] Hirakawa Sukehiro, 'The parting of lovers in the morning: the magical world in *Tales of Genji* explored by eccentric Arthur Waley', *Bungakukai* (August 2004), 190–256.

the *waki* and encountered a group of abandoned Venetian women. These women functioned both as the movers of the *tsure* as well as the *hayashi*: musicians who sit at the back of the stage. The poor women have been abandoned by their fellow Venetians and have survived as prostitutes and slaves under the Turkish occupation.

In the course of narrating their misery, one of them turned out to be the ghost of Desdemona. The *shite* sought the priest for her redemption. The *maeba* ended with the *nanori* by the *shite*, the self-introduction of the ghost, and she exited through the *hashigakari* or bridge-way between the *noh* stage and the offstage. The most notable part of the *maeba* was the physicalization of Desdemona by the mover of the *shite*, played by Micari, whose lines were mainly articulated by the *jiutai*, the chorus seated at the side of the stage. The *jiutai* then even performed the masked comical interlude known as *ai-kyogen* on the central stage, while the monk *waki* fell asleep.

After the third *kyogen* scene, the *shite* returned to the stage and faced the awoken *waki*. The *shite* showed an attitude of indignation towards the *waki* and *jiutai* who accused Desdemona of betraying the Christian Venetians in a conspiracy with the Black Muslim Moor and the Turks, and also of committing adultery with Cassio. In order to disclose the bitter truth, in front of the *shite* and the *waki*, the most formidable moment of Othello's deception by Iago was enacted as the fourth *ai-kyogen* scene. As if the past were revived in the present, Iago and Othello, who had removed the primitive masks they had previously worn, re-performed act 3, scene 3 of Shakespeare's play, which Desdemona in life had never known. Furthermore, Desdemona's most critical moment – and yet her closest to Othello – her own murder, was re-enacted by herself. Not only the movement and narration of Desdemona, but also that of Othello, were integrated into the body and voice of Micari; her white hand wore Othello's black armour-clad hand and in a symbolic gesture she seemed to choke herself. While the *jiutai* sang 'The chrysanthemum whiter than snow / The chrysanthemum whiter than snow / I hesitate for a while', quoted from Natsume Soseki's *haiku* on *Othello*, 'siragiku ni sibasi tamerau hasami kana' ('a pair of scissors hesitates for a short while at the white chrysanthemum'),[12] Desdemona's *hitamen* – literally meaning 'a direct mask', or a mask that resembles a white face – evoked a variety of emotions, which shifted between disturbance and determination, grotesqueness and grace, sanity and insanity, and love and hate. Her white hand and black hand fought, struggled and danced together. After a while, the white and black hands folded and overlapped and strangled the *shite* (Figure 18). As the boundary between the black man and the white woman dissolved, Desdemona's hesitation and agony were resolved in the song of the *jiutai*, 'The light of life is put out / and it's gone / and it's gone.' With the help of the monk's prayer, Desdemona was released from this world and earthly desires and departed for the next with a mysterious smile. Miyagi draws a parallel between Micari's Desdemona and the Virgin Mary, as well as Miroku Bosatsu (Maitreya), who in Buddhist eschatology is viewed as the future Buddha, a direct successor of Gautama Buddha. In the Japanese Buddhist tradition, Miroku Bosatsu is regarded as a female figure, whose unconditional love will save all souls.

Miyagi's *noh* dream play opened the possibility of defusing binaries such as black and white, masculinity and femininity, to murder and to be murdered, to forgive and to be forgiven, the East and the West, and tradition and contemporaneity. In addition, while deviating from *noh*'s prescribed tradition, this production redefined Miyagi's own method in practical terms. For example, to suit the acoustics and rhythms that a contemporary audience may be used to, the slow articulation and movement of *noh* was altered and speeded up by the speakers and the musicians. The mixed use of Asian and African instruments, especially Indonesian *gamelan*, was effective in describing the pitches of the characters' emotions, while avoiding the evocation of overt Japaneseness. The costumes were a mixture of pseudo-Western,

---

[12] Published in the preface to Takeji Komatsu, trans., *Sao Monogatari Shu* ('Charles Lamb's Tales from Shakespeare') (Tokyo, 1904).

18 Micari as the ghost of Desdemona, Shizuoka Performing Arts Center, *Miyagi Noh Othello ~Phantom Love~*, Shizuoka, 2018. Photo: K. Miura.

Islamic, African and Japanese styles, reflecting the melting pot of race and religion in Hirakawa's version of the play: Christianity, Islam, Buddhism and Shamanism.

WU HSING-KUO: FROM INNOVATIVE *JINGJU* TO WORLD THEATRE[13]

Wu Hsing-kuo is the Artistic Director of the Contemporary Legend Theatre (CLT) and a holistic performing artist traversing the fields of traditional Chinese theatre, modern theatre, dance, film, television and multimedia. His works have been performed in over twenty countries and screened worldwide, winning him multiple awards and honours, including the Golden Statue Awards for Literature and Art (1985, 1986, 1987), the Hong Kong Film Award (1994), the Taipei Culture Awards (2005), the Ordre des Arts et des Lettres-Chevalier (2011), the National Literary and Art Award (2014) and the Grand Cordon Order of Brilliant Star (2015).

Wu began his rigorous training in *jingju* at an early age. Also known as Beijing Opera or Peking Opera, *jingju* is a total theatre, combining drama, opera, mime, dance, acrobatics and martial arts. It emerged centuries ago and was once a favourite court entertainment. After its popularity peaked in the early twentieth century, *jingju* went into gradual decline, superseded by imported forms of entertainment including Western music, realist drama, films and television. Born and raised in Taiwan, Wu faced a double challenge – with the rise of nativism in the 1970s, *jingju* lost its status as the national theatre and became politically incorrect as an alien genre. Many practitioners were forced to leave the field, and the overall artistic standards and morale sank. Desperately trying to

---

[13] Bi-qi Beatrice Lei.

invigorate a dying tradition and to attract young audiences, Wu summoned Shakespeare. Based on *Macbeth*, *The Kingdom of Desire* premiered in 1986 rocked Taiwan's stage as a groundbreaking *jingju* production. Formally, it featured innovative music, exquisite set and costume designs, and film-like *mise en scène*. Thematically, it departed significantly from the convention of traditional Chinese theatre validating Confucian values by presenting the regicides as three-dimensional, sympathetic figures despite their moral corruption. The production was no less refreshing as a Shakespearian adaptation, with its infusion of Eastern aesthetics and its hyper-theatricality. Wu's initial ambition was only local, but the production turned out to be a huge success on the international market.

Between producing traditional *jingju* titles and original plays based on Chinese stories, Wu continued to experiment with Western classics. Known for his brilliant fusion of East and West, ancient and modern, he became a frequent visitor at international arts festivals and is often compared to other theatrical interculturalists such as Ninagawa Yukio and Eugenio Barba. Shakespeare has occupied a unique position in his creative career: after *Macbeth*, he adapted *Hamlet* (1990), *King Lear* (2001), *The Tempest* (in collaboration with Tsui Hark, 2004), *A Midsummer Night's Dream* (2016) and *Julius Caesar* (2024). Reset in premodern China and costumed in period dress, these productions were nonetheless endowed with local and contemporary meanings. In addition, Wu tackled a wide range of Western literature, including Euripides' *Medea* (1993) and Aeschylus' *Oresteia* (in collaboration with Richard Schechner, 1995); Beckett's *Waiting for Godot* (2006); Chekhov's short stories (*Run! Chekhov!* 2010); Kafka's novella, novels and letters (*Metamorphosis*, 2013); and Goethe's *Faust* (2017). Beyond *jingju*, he also incorporated performance elements from other traditional Chinese genres, Western opera, ethnic music, Taiwan's Indigenous culture, popular and rock music, dance, multimedia and immersive theatre.

One of Wu's most celebrated works is the monumental solo *King Lear*. His ingenious and personal approach to his source, as well as his stunning virtuosity in playing all ten roles, won standing ovations around the world. Wu disrupted Shakespeare's linear plotlines and interwove his own experience as an abject artist struggling to save *jingju* into the familial and political tragedy, repeatedly asking 'Who am I?' and finding himself in the stubborn and despairing king, the blind Gloucester, the ambitious discontent Edmund, the blunt Kent, and the unjustly wronged Edgar and Cordelia. Wu's Buddhist realization of emptiness led not to nihilism but to humility and boundless compassion. His reworkings of Shakespeare, as well as Beckett, Chekhov, Kafka and Goethe, went far beyond the so-called hegemonic intercultural theatre, or HIT.[14] *Jingju* was not utilized to adorn and endorse Western classics and to prove their timelessness and universality; instead, it offered different intellectual and philosophical lenses and served to deconstruct, cross-examine and even modernize the old texts. Indeed, Wu's productions can no longer be viewed as mere adaptations, localizations or transplantations, but are original works with contemporary relevance.

Ariane Mnouchkine once said: 'All these years, Le Théâtre du Soleil has been experimenting a theatre form that could encompass all art elements. What we have been pursuing, I see that it has been achieved by the CLT. From the CLT, I see the dream of the theatre of the world.'[15] Wu confessed that it was from Mnouchkine that he heard the phrase 'theatre of the world' for the first time. His understanding of the concept is performance that transcends the barriers between languages, geographies, races, religions and cultures, and can touch and move people from all backgrounds. While he resonates with the idea of a theatre for all audiences and enjoys global acclaim, he does not compromise to please overseas critics or pander to the taste of international festivals. For him, the top

---

[14] Daphne P. Lei, 'Interruption, intervention, interculturalism: Robert Wilson's HIT productions in Taiwan', *Theatre Journal* 63 (2011), 571–86.

[15] Ariane Mnouchkine's remarks after watching Wu Hsing-kuo's *Metamorphosis* performed at Le Théâtre du Soleil in 2022.

priority is always to make sincere, high-quality performance that addresses humanist issues and touches people's hearts. Empathy and compassion are the core of his art. In *The Tempest*, for example, he employed an Indigenous actor to play Caliban (Figure 19), so each performance painfully re-enacted the historical trauma of the native Taiwanese, colonized by Han Chinese, the Dutch, the Spanish, the British, the French and the Japanese in turn. *Julius Caesar*, his latest creation, relates to those frustrated by today's depraved politics, often bordering on chaos, populism and tyranny.

Keenly aware of the changing time, Wu believes that *jingju* must continue to update, innovate and rejuvenize. To cultivate young talents, he founded the Legend Academy in 2011 at his own expense. The Hsing Legend Youth Theatre, an offshoot of the CLT, now regularly performs traditional *jingju* titles and experimental pieces and has embarked on international festivals and collaboration. Having turned seventy, Wu may need to discontinue performing his signature backflip off an 8-foot platform, the highlight of *The Kingdom of Desire*. Notwithstanding, his creative energy is as high as ever, and his legacy will carry on.

KATHAKALI *KING LEAR* / *KATHAKALI-KING LEAR*[16]

Is the name of this production, first scripted by David McRuvie, translated into Malayalam by K. Marumakan Raja, and directed and choreographed by Annette Leday in 1988, Kathakali *King Lear* or *Kathakali-King Lear*? This has been one of the most influential and long-lived of all Asian intercultural Shakespeares, comparable in its lifespan and impact only with Ninagawa's *Macbeth*. Its original production toured much of the world between 1988 and 1999, and a revival toured through India and beyond in 2018–2019. The screening of a video-recording of this more recent iteration of the show at the 2021 World Shakespeare Congress, accompanied by live interviews with Leday, provided the occasion for reflections on the nature of this enduring production, and whether it is best understood as a *kathakali* adaptation of Shakespeare's *King Lear* ('Kathakali *King Lear*') or as a *kathakali* performance which happens to have King Lear as its protagonist ('*Kathakali King Lear*').[17]

Leday herself is very clear that the production arose from her immersion in the culture of *kathakali* in Kerala rather than from any particular specialism in Shakespeare, and claims, remarkably, that before the 2021 Congress she had little or no contact with the world of Shakespearian scholarship. *King Lear*, she explained, simply struck her as a play that

19 Wu Hsing-kuo as Prospero (right), with Shih Hung-Chun as Caliban (left), Contemporary Legend Theatre, *The Tempest*, National Theatre of Korea, Seoul, 2009. Photo: Kuo Cheng Chang.

---

[16] Michael Dobson.
[17] The title of this production in the WSC programme was *Kathakali-King Lear*; this italicization reflects the production's acquired status as a landmark, comparable to the way in which Ninagawa's *Macbeth* had already become *Ninagawa Macbeth* within its director's lifetime.

would suit the conventions of *kathakali* and would resonate strongly with Indian audiences, partly because it seemed to be at core a parable, like an Indian folk-tale, operating as forcefully at the level of plot and emblem as at the level of motivation. (*Hamlet*, she suggested, wouldn't do for *kathakali* at all.)[18] As she and McRuvie worked on their adaptation, they were guided throughout by the responses of the *kathakali* performers with whom they were working (primarily Leday's 'master', Kalamandalam Padmanabhan Nair, one of a number of experienced performers who took it in turns to play Lear), and they were much more tentative about modifying the inherited conventions of *kathakali* in order to incorporate the *Lear* material (notably, by the importation of a Fool figure) than about altering the plot of *Lear* to make it work better as *kathakali*. Hence, in their version, the elder two sisters compete for France's hand as well as for larger shares of their father's kingdom, so that France, counterpointing the standard 'flawed king' role in which Lear is cast, can become a much larger figure in the play, a 'righteous warrior king' who eventually kills the two elder sisters to avenge the death of Cordelia (Figure 20).

This careful collaboration with established *kathakali* artists did not save the production's first performances in Kerala from considerable criticism. *Kathakali*, though it was never a sacred, temple theatre-form but offered a kind of larger-than-life performance (like *kabuki* in Japan) that was always aimed at a wide public, is a very conservative genre, and there is always a hyper-traditionalist element in its audiences. Although more warmly applauded outside India, the show was at first received by some Western audience members who were attracted primarily by the idea that they were coming to see a *King Lear* in a manner which mirrored its reception in Kerala: while in India *kathakali* fans were liable to object that this wasn't authentically *kathakali* because it was too busy being *King Lear*, in Europe Shakespeare fans were liable to object that this wasn't authentically *King Lear* because it was too busy being *kathakali*.

20 Padmanabhan Nair as King Lear and Annette Leday as the dead Cordelia, Annette Leday / Keli Company, *Kathakali-King Lear*, Kerala Kalamandalam Institution, Cheruthuruthy, Kerala, 1989. Photo: Keli Paris.

Within the academy, a good deal of thought about the nature of intercultural theatre had supervened by the time of the 2018 revival, and beyond it attitudes had changed too, since in 2018 *Kathakali-King Lear* was able to draw eager crowds in Kerala, its other Indian venues even including a large cricket stadium in Poona. As Leday observed at the World Shakespeare Congress, different audiences with different acculturations and positionalities understand and respond to different aspects of the show, and in

---

[18] 'Watch party: *Kathakali King Lear*', 11th World Shakespeare Congress, Singapore: Shakespeare Circuits, International Shakespeare Association, Singapore, 13 July 2021.

her experience many audiences globally are nowadays much more willing than they were in the last century to accept the idea that they may find themselves in front of performances whose signifiers they may only partially be able to decode.[19] Her attitude to her own performers (this is the 'Annette Leday / Keli Company', after all) is exemplary here. Asked why the Fool's body make-up included a symmetrical pattern of red spots, and why his costume included a skirt oddly lifted up at the back, and why some of the performers had metallically elaborated fingernails on the fingers of one hand only, she simply replied that, despite having asked her cast about these details from time to time, she didn't really know. Similarly, asked whether the attempts by Goneril and Regan to seduce France were drawn from *kathakali* convention, imitated from other, traditional playscripts, she replied that this sequence was in *Kathakali-King Lear* mainly because everyone enjoyed it. She had challenged the all-male conventions of *kathakali* by casting herself as Cordelia in the original production largely for her own convenience as a director, she suggested, and the casting of a male performer in the 2018 revival was not so much a surrender as a rueful acknowledgement that she was no longer young.[20]

Seen again on screen, twenty years and more since it came to the stage of Shakespeare's Globe in London, one of the aspects of *Kathakali-King Lear* which seemed most striking was its elaborate musicality. *Kathakali* suits this most tragic of Shakespearian tragedies because it is not actor-led but music-driven: the performers are primarily dancers, following an inexorable choreography at a speed dictated by percussionists. While some of those percussionists are watching the dancers' incidental gestures and facial expressions minutely so as to be able to comment on them and underline them in sound, most are playing a pre-ordained score which the actor-dancers can only obey, dancing onwards to the tragic denouement. As Leday said at the Congress, the music of this production has by now successfully communicated with audiences from a huge range of different cultures, across three decades, and the death of Cordelia in her production has continued to make them cry. Perhaps rhythm and death are more intercultural than we have sometimes allowed ourselves to admit.

ONG KENG SEN: INTERCULTURALIZING SHAKESPEARE THROUGH ASIAN THEATRE[21]

Ong Keng Sen is a leading Singaporean director who is recognized internationally for his cross-cultural and multi-genre theatrical works that mix creative media, performance cultures, languages and styles. Ong is the Artistic Director of the Singapore-based theatre company, T:>Works (formerly TheatreWorks, established in 1985), and has won numerous awards for his achievements in developing local and Asian theatre.[22] As an artist-curator, Ong has led major curatorial and discursive projects at local and international festivals and art institutions. He established the In-Transit Festival in Berlin (2001), and was the founding director of the Singapore International Festival of Arts (2013–2017).[23] The seminal *The*

---

[19] Leday, 'Watch party'. On this change of attitude among audiences of intercultural Shakespeare, see also Michael Dobson, 'Shakespearean comedy and the boundaries of Europe', in *The Text, the Play, and the Globe: Essays on Literary Influence in Shakespeare's World and His Work in Honor of Charles R. Forker*, ed. Joseph Candido (Madison and Teaneck, 2016), 251–64.

[20] 'Director In-Conversation: Annette Leday', 11th World Shakespeare Congress, Singapore: Shakespeare Circuits, International Shakespeare Association, Singapore, 20 July 2021.

[21] Eleine Ng-Gagneux.

[22] Ong won the Singapore Young Artist Award for Theatre in 1993 and the Singapore Youth Award (Arts & Culture) in 2000; in 2003, he received the International Society of Performing Arts Distinguished Artist Award, the Excellence for Singapore Award and the Cultural Medallion (theatre). He won the *Life!* Theatre Award for Best Director in 2007, and the Fukuoka Arts and Culture Prize in 2010.

[23] Ong also conceptualized the International Curators Academy in Singapore, and the Young Curators Academy in Maxim Gorki Theatre, Berlin. See T:>Works' website: www.72-13.com/copy-of-72-13.

Flying Circus Project (FCP), conceived and curated by Ong in eight editions from 1996 to 2013, cemented his commitment to connecting and expanding the aesthetic practices in both Asian theatre and contemporary performance. FCP was an artist laboratory that brought together practitioners and specialists from diverse creative fields and backgrounds (e.g. visual arts, performing arts, literature, new media); '[the artists] are not unlike a flash mob that comes together and travels through a city of Asia for two weeks'.[24] This concept of theatre practice as an exploratory and discursive forum for artist-sharing and artistic collaboration formed the basis for Ong's *Lear*, and informs his overarching approach to working with Shakespeare.

Since the late 1990s, Ong has directed five productions that adapt Shakespeare's plays: *Lear* (1997, 1999), *Desdemona* (2000), *Search:Hamlet* (2002), *Lear Dreaming* (2012) and *Sandaime Richard* (2016, 2023).[25] His adaptations are characterized by the experimental reimagination of Shakespeare's plots and characters through a collaborative method, which simultaneously transforms Shakespeare's text and the contemporary and traditional performance practices employed through trans- and intercultural negotiations. In his keynote speech at the 11th World Shakespeare Congress, Singapore: Shakespeare Circuits, Ong traced his experience of adapting Shakespeare, focusing in particular on *Sandaime Richard*. Explaining the decade-long gap between *Lear Dreaming* and his earlier Shakespearian adaptations, Ong recalled that 'the urgent political purposes of appropriating Shakespeare' he once had felt had faded.[26] However, in 2012 he felt the desire to revisit his first work, *Lear*, and recast it as *Lear Dreaming*. The question of identity that underpinned *Lear* continued to haunt him. Reflecting on his journey as a practitioner moving into his fifties, *Lear Dreaming* expressed Ong's self-reflexive examination of his own position within the arts scene as he was 'becoming the older generation that stood in the way of [the] emerging, constantly restless, New Asia'.[27]

As *Lear Dreaming* shows, in many ways Ong's encounters with Shakespeare addressed his exploration of creating contemporary Asian theatre and the complexities of intercultural practice. The collaborative underpinning of *Lear* probed the nature of current theatre in (New) Asia and its future developments. As a response to *Lear*, which was criticized by some as an overly polished production that erased the economic and cultural inequities that plagued theatrical interculturalism,[28] *Desdemona* conversely showcased the discordance that could arise during artistic collaboration. *Desdemona* staged the complicated process of theatrical interculturalism by representing the divergences between multiple aesthetics, performance cultures and languages on a single stage. His next production, the site-specific *Search:Hamlet*, which was held at Kronborg Castle in Denmark but with its titular character physically absent from the stage, continued Ong's interrogation of international collaboration, the topic of cultural ownership and the assumptions that reduced intercultural theatre to a vehicle of cultural identity. Ong's latest Shakespeare work, *Sandaime Richard* (Figure 21), routed his reimagining of Shakespeare's *Richard III* through the work of a Japanese playwright and director, Noda Hideki, similar to his reworking of Kishida Rio's adaptation of *King Lear* for his *Lear*.

In Noda's satirical play, Shakespeare is on trial for misrepresenting history, maligning the reputation of Sandaime Richard, the Grand Master of an Ikebana clan, and is being prosecuted by Maachan of Venice (a tongue-in-cheek allusion to Shakespeare's Shylock).[29] The fictionalized William Shakespeare is transported to a Japanese

---

[24] Flying Circus Project 2013, https://flyingcircusproject2013.wordpress.com/directors-message.

[25] The performance recordings of *Lear*, *Desdemona*, *Search:Hamlet* and *Lear Dreaming* are available on the Asian Shakespeare Intercultural Archive (A|S|I|A), http://a-s-i-a-web.org.

[26] Ong Keng Sen, 'The queering of Shakespeare's *Richard III*', 11th World Shakespeare Congress, Singapore: Shakespeare Circuits, International Shakespeare Association, 20 July 2021, online, keynote speech.

[27] See Rustom Bharucha, 'Consumed in Singapore: the intercultural spectacle of *Lear*', *Theater* 31 (2001), 107–27.

[28] Ong, 'Queering'.

[29] Singapore International Festival of Arts website, www.sifa.sg/archive-programmes/sandaime-richard-advisory.

21 Nakamura Kazutaro as Sandaime Richard (Richard III), *Sandaime Richard* (2016), written by Noda Hideki, directed by Ong Keng Sen. Image courtesy of Jun Ishikawa for World Theatre Festival Shizuoka, Singapore International Festival of Arts and Tokyo Metropolitan Theatre.

context, and the plot of *Richard III* is reframed as infighting within a clan. In fact, Noda's adaptation of Shakespeare's play takes inspiration from Yushi Odashima's translation of *Richard III*, and maps the Wars of the Roses (1455–1487) against a warring clan in Japan.

Using Noda's script, Ong transfigured the iconic character of Richard III by casting a famed *kabuki onnagata* (female impersonator), Nakamura Kazutaro, as Sandaime Richard. Although Ong had employed cross-dressing and female impersonation in his adaptations of Shakespeare's plays, his purpose for casting Kazutaro was decidedly to queer Richard III, interlacing Shakespeare's play and Noda's cross-cultural revision with 'histories of the unhappy queer'.[30] Ong felt that Richard III was a unique subject for queering as the Shakespearian character was not a typical figure for discussions of sexual and gender identities. Again, Shakespeare becomes, for Ong, a way to layer current topical themes onto interweaving texts and Asian performance practices. Like his preceding intercultural adaptations of Shakespeare, *Sandaime Richard* included an international cast, a multilingual script (in Japanese, English and Indonesian) and integrated traditional art forms (e.g. *wayang kulit* and *noh*) with modern performance styles (e.g. the Takarazuka Revue).[31]

In his keynote speech, Ong recounts that reworking Shakespeare's *Richard III* through Noda's script was to 'approach Shakespeare through a double adaptation – an adaptation upon an adaptation', engendering a creative space for him to 'ruminate on the double refractions of Shakespeare's work'.[32] To Ong, his *Sandaime Richard* is his 'counter-appropriation of Noda's appropriation' – a means to demystify and challenge the value and authority attached to canonical classics through creative variation. Citing Roland's Barthes's *Mythologies*, Ong notes that the act of counter-appropriation 'brings up the whole process of myth-making',[33] and allows Shakespeare and his significance to be rewritten by a new generation of theatremakers for contemporary audiences. Ong's *Sandaime Richard*, as such, belongs to a long tradition of reimagining and recontextualizing Shakespeare's corpus within the Asian region. The bold experimentation of intermingling tradition with modernity in *Sandaime Richard*, a hallmark of Ong's productions of Shakespeare, continues to push the boundaries of

---

[30] Ong, 'Queering'.
[31] The Takarazuka Revue Company is an all-female musical theatre troupe that was formed in 1914 and is based in Japan. For more information, see the company's website: https://kageki.hankyu.co.jp/english/index.html. Also see Lorie Brau, 'The women's theatre of Takarazuka', *TDR* 34 (1990), 79–95.
[32] Ong, 'Queering'.
[33] Roland Barthes, *Mythologies*, trans. Annette Lavers (New York, 1984).

how Asian theatre is defined. *Sandaime Richard* is scheduled to be restaged with the Sydney National Institute of Dramatic Arts (NIDA), attesting to the continued relevance of Ong's adaptations, which pluralize the understanding of creating Shakespeare in the Asia Pacific.

YANG JUNG-UNG'S SHAKESPEARE AND *PERICLES*[34]

It is his Koreanized *A Midsummer Night's Dream* that made Yang Jung-ung internationally famous. This production by Yohangza Theatre Company has toured to more than twenty countries. It was performed not only at the Barbican Centre in 2005 but also at Shakespeare's Globe as part of the Globe to Globe Festival for the 2012 London Olympic Games. Numerous reviews and articles have acclaimed it highly, in Korea and abroad. With this and other Shakespearian works such as *Hwan (illusion): Macbeth* (2004), *Hamlet* (2009) and *Twelfth Night* (2011), Yang has built a strong reputation for Koreanized Shakespeare.

However, it can be said that Yang Jung-ung is a cosmopolitan director who does not hesitate to incorporate and synthesize exotic cultural or artistic elements. While he has a wide knowledge of traditional Korean performance such as *gut* (Korean shamanic ritual) and *pansori* (traditional Korean narrative song), and has used these forms in his performances, his *Romeo and Juliet* (2014), *Coriolanus* (2021), *Peer Gynt* (2009) and *Faust* (2013) show contemporary postmodern styles. Even his representative Koreanized Shakespeare performances reveal traces of foreign cultures and cinematic techniques. Yang's versatility and interest in Western(ized) genres can be seen in his direction of musical, opera and ballet performances as well as dramas, and his recent directorial debut in movies with *The Box* (2021).

An unchanging characteristic of his theatre directing is that he is an imagist. He directs a scene as if he were painting a canvas or composing a cinematic frame, by harmonizing traditional styles, colours, costumes and actors' movements. His production of *Pericles* (2015) most vividly shows the characteristics of his theatre.

What most caught the audience's eye in Yang Jung-ung's *Pericles* is the 30-metre deep stage covered with 50 tons of sand, which creates the overwhelming images of sea, seashore, island and the meaninglessness of life. The 4-metre-tall statue of Diana's head, lying sideways on the sand, symbolizes the precarious or indifferent god. A chandelier lying on the sand implies an unpredictable fate that can suddenly change drastically. A grand piano and a double bass case express the thematic importance of music in bringing new life. The huge images of a compass and a moon, which are alternately projected on the back screen of the stage, provide an appropriate backdrop for Pericles, who wanders from place to place. The compass directs Pericles where he should go, and the moon symbolizes his longing for his family. This play shows Pericles' long journey to his family reunion, which takes place before the huge moon in the last scene. A half-submerged boat, located at the opposite side of the stage from the chandelier, expresses Pericles' arduous adventure, in contrast with his luxurious court life. These images, which Im Il-jin designed on the huge sand canvas, are harmoniously positioned to create a painting on a grand scale.

While imagism is Yang Jung-ung's hallmark in scenography, there are always actors' dynamic movements in the images. Their dynamism is maximized through playing, the basic mode of traditional Korean theatre, in the *madang* (yard), the performing space where traditional Korean theatre such as *talchum* (mask dance) or *talnnori* (mask play) is performed, without a spatial distinction between the audience area and the stage. The enormous sandy stage of *Pericles* reminds me of the *madang*. The first scene, in which Pericles solves Antiochus' riddle, is transformed into 'an almost contemporary game show-like' wrestling match.[35] This manner of playing in the *madang* is reminiscent

---

[34] Lee Hyon-u.
[35] Julie Jackson, 'Shakespeare's *Pericles* gets modernist twist', *Korea Herald*, 14 May 2015, www.koreaherald.com/common/newsprint.php?ud=20150514000994.

22 Nam Yoon-ho as young Pericles and Yoo In-chon as Gower, Yohangza Theatre Company, *Pericles*, Seoul, 2015. Photo: Park Gyeong-bok.

of the performing mode of traditional Korean theatre. The mode of playing in the *madang* is repeated in the competition for Thaisa's hand in marriage, which is staged like a comic race; in the sea-storm scene that uses chairs, tables and water spray to express shipwreck in a metatheatrical way; in Cerimon and his acolytes' comic philosophy class and their rescue of Thaisa's body in the double bass case; in the comic, acrobatic mime of rescuing Marina from the water; and in Tarsus' famine scene, where Cleon and Dionyza struggle in the tank pool.

As Peter Kirwan points out, '[l]ocation and action are ... generated by the bodies of the actors themselves, who frequently adopt a choric function to represent the transient movements of humans within this cavernous set of fixed locations'.[36] Changes of location, from Antioch through Tyre, Pentapolis, Tarsus to Mytilene, are mainly expressed by actors' choric movements and their forming of scenery. These scene-changing strategies, also found in Yang Jung-ung's other Koreanized Shakespeare works, such as *A Midsummer Night's Dream*, are part of the performance style that traditional Korean theatre, such as *Hahoe Byeolsin Gut Talnori*, often employs.

One of the notable unique features in Yang Jung-ung's productions is the utilization of the narrator. Yoo In-chon plays the role of Gower in part 1, and takes on the role of the elderly Pericles in part 2. Nam Yoon-ho (real name Yoo Dae-sik), who portrays the young Pericles,

---

[36] Peter Kirwan, 'Pericles (Yohangza) @ Seoul Arts Centre', The Bardathon, 3 August 2021, https://blogs.nottingham.ac.uk/bardathon/2021/08/03/pericles-yohangza-seoul-arts-centre.

is Yoo In-chon's son. In the 2015 run (shown in Figure 22), Nam alone played the role of young Pericles, but in the 2016 run, Nam only provided the vocal performance while Kim Do-wan, a dancer, acted the role physically. While this was an emergency measure because Nam suffered a leg fracture on the first day of the run, the outcome was highly effective. Kim's choreographic movements presented Pericles' body as a poetic form, extending and expressing his inner emotions of joy, sadness, desire and fear. In contrast, Pericles as the narrator, sitting beside the grand piano and delivering lines while maintaining a distance from the dramatic situations, strengthened the narrative structure of the play as a story told by Gower. Moreover, this narrative structure is further enhanced as Gower, while playing the elderly Pericles himself, blends into his own story. The transformation of the narrator into a character actor in an instant is a typical pattern found in *pansori* performances, where a solo performer takes on various roles and creates a theatrical story. Yang Jung-ung's *Pericles* is dressed in exotic clothing, but it seamlessly incorporates various characteristics of traditional Korean theatre, making the performance a unique blend of styles.

On the other hand, the stage of *Pericles* looks like a movie studio in that each scene is performed along an axis of images on the vast stage. Actors in blue raincoats represent the sea-storm and shipwreck by pushing and pulling a table from upstage to downstage while creating rain with water spray. The family reunion under the giant image of the moon in the final scene can also be considered highly cinematic. As Sarah Olive points out, the expression of Korean sentiment in the audience's emotional response to the last reunion scene, which she personally found slow-paced and even boring compared to most other *Pericles* performances she had seen in the UK,[37] demonstrates that Yang Jung-ung successfully combines Shakespeare and Korean emotions. Even though his *Pericles* performs elements of Western theatrical styles, it fills the interior with traditional Korean theatrical style and emotions, showing him to be a synthesis of Korean and cosmopolitan modes.

CONCLUSION[38]

The discussions above point to the performances' back stories, which shape their engagements with Shakespeare. In Wu's *Tempest*, Ong's *Sandaime Richard*, Miyagi's *Miyagi Noh Othello* and Yang's *Pericles*, marked stylistic differences from the director's other Shakespeare work illuminate not only his own artistic shifts, but also the changing purchase Shakespeare offers in the fast-moving field of intercultural performance practice. *Sandaime Richard* and *Miyagi Noh Othello* also reach back to pivotal moments in the one-and-a-quarter centuries of performing Shakespeare in Asia. Re-making or re-thinking an earlier playwright's strategy, these two productions use performative encounters between theatrical forms onstage to actively historicize their approaches to Shakespeare. *Kathakali-King Lear* and *Lear Is Dead* on the other hand display barely any joins between Shakespeare and their performance form or style, instead making a point of their aesthetic unity. It hardly seems a coincidence that both productions – their directors' only Shakespeare work – are based on *King Lear* and both were made in ex-British colonies (Ong's first production too was *Lear*). *King Lear* is particularly apt for dealing metatheatrically with the change of authority. The Annette Leday / Keli Company emphasizes the continuity of authority in their re-mounted *Kathakali-King Lear* as 'a new approach and a new team which includes a core of artists who participated in the first production in their youth and have now reached the full maturity of their art.

---

[37] Sarah Olive, 'Pericles, Yohangza, dir. Yang Jung-ung, CJ Towol, Seoul Arts Centre, Korea', 23 November 2016, https://bloggingshakespeare.com/reviewing-shakespeare/pericles-yohangza-dir-yang-jung-ung-tj-towol-theatre-seoul-arts-centre-korea-november-2016. Olive states, 'As my ears registered the sound of sniffles around me in the house, it belatedly occurred to me that, in this moment, I was dwelling among Koreans' living memories and on-going experiences of physical division; cherished dreams of reunions, familial and national; something of the emotional disorientation and brand of sorrow unique to Koreans caused by sustained foreign invasions – "*han*".'

[38] Yong Li Lan.

Young artists have also been selected to ensure the transmission between generations.'[39] Here the notion of transmission balances between the old and the new authority: a wider advocacy among contemporary traditional Indian dance practitioners for a more intercultural training regularly cites the aesthetic principles of Phillip Zarrilli,[40] who discussed the first *Kathakali-King Lear* thirty years earlier in 'For whom is the king a king?'[41] A similar precarious preserving of shifted authority can be seen in the interview sections of *Lear Is Dead*, which resonate with the issues of legacy and succession in Singapore's political leadership. Even as the transmission of performance knowledge in the traditional forms is an urgent concern in many Asian theatres, reinforced by discourses of mastery and lineage, the common and collective note struck by these performances is the daring experimentation of both the performers and the artistic concept. Paradoxically enough, traditional authorities (including Shakespeare's) embodied in specific performance skills, aesthetic principles and plots continue to exert their force, however reimagined, in productions that are at the same time unique, of the moment and unrepeatable.

---

[39] Company information document.
[40] See, for example, Arjun Raina, 'Intercultural Kathakali actor training', *Indian Theatre Journal* 3 (Apr.–Oct. 2019), 31–46.
[41] Phillip Zarrilli, 'For whom is the king a king? Issues of intercultural production, perception, and reception in a Kathakali *King Lear*', in *Critical Theory and Performance*, ed. Joseph Roach and Janelle Reinelt (Ann Arbor, 1992), 86–108.

STRANGE SHADOWS: TRANSLATING SHAKESPEARE – THE STATE OF THE FIELD

SHOICHIRO KAWAI, TIMOTHY BILLINGS, JEAN-MICHEL DÉPRATS, KIM TAI-WON AND SHEN LIN

INTRODUCTION[1]

For the World Shakespeare Congress 2021 round-table 'Translation: The State of the Field', held on 23 July 2021, we had prepared ourselves for months, exchanging papers and ideas via Zoom meetings. Our discussion on translating Shakespeare began by picking up the points made by Professor Alessandro Serpieri's Seminar on Translation and Performance at Stratford-upon-Avon, more than twenty years before, as follows:

a. since drama is both voice and action in space, any dramatic translation should first of all be faithful to the performative aspect of speech;
b. a certain amount of literalness in Shakespeare translation proves to be functional to its theatrical implications;
c. the original semantics and rhetoric should be preserved even when this may mean a little forcing or overstretching of the semantic import in the target language; and
d. rhythm (which is part of the prosodic pattern, but is also strictly related to syntax and rhetoric) is no less important than semantics.[2]

We then went on to argue that in order for translators to reproduce Shakespeare's drama in a target language, they have to take care not only of the semantic import of the text but also of its intended dramatic effects (according to the translator's understanding), including rhythms, tones, connotations, inflections and many other elements, so that the audience in a target language could appreciate Shakespeare's drama regardless of the language barrier. This is an ideal. Because of the differences in language structures, translated Shakespeares may look like 'translated' Bottom (*A Midsummer Night's Dream* 3.2.113), monstrously different from the original. However, just as the 'translated' Bottom with his ass-head would reveal what he really is, so translations of Shakespeare may help our better understanding of his drama, not least because Shakespeare's texts are fraught with difficulties. As Serpieri puts it, 'translating any play by Shakespeare necessarily implies editing it'.[3] Textual cruxes must be smoothed over and erased before translating the text. Naturally, the translated version would be more lucid than the original. Thus, any translation could demonstrate another way of holding a mirror up to the original.

The five translators making up this roundtable, who have rendered Shakespeare's texts in French, Chinese, Korean and Japanese, all agree that a translator has to be not only an editor but a lot more, as is evident in the following summaries. And Timothy Billings brilliantly points to the significance of multiple readings of Shakespeare.

Let me briefly introduce our members. Timothy Billings is a professor at Middlebury College in the US, where he teaches Shakespeare and Chinese poetry. He has translated and annotated three multilingual editions of poetry by Victor Segalen,

---

[1] Shoichiro Kawai.
[2] Alessandro Serpieri, 'Translation and performance': https://shine.unibas.ch/translationserpieriprint.htm.
[3] Alessandro Serpieri, 'The translator as editor: the quartos of *Hamlet*', in *Shakespeare and the Language of Translation*, ed. Ton Hoenselaars (London, 2012),167–83; p. 167.

Matteo Ricci and Ezra Pound, in English, French and Chinese. He has also published in *Shakespeare Quarterly* and edited *Love's Labour's Lost* for the Internet Shakespeare Editions.

Shen Lin, a professor at China's Central Academy of Drama, is also a writer, translator and theatre curator. He has held visiting professorships at universities in Europe and North America. His publications span intercultural performance, Shakespeare and contemporary theatre. He has created a number of acclaimed productions in China since the early 1990s.

Professor Jean-Michel Déprats is well known for his French translation of more than thirty plays by Shakespeare. He was Senior Lecturer in the Department of English and the Department of Theatre Studies in Nanterre for forty years. Gallimard has published his translations in eight bilingual volumes. All his translations have been staged by major European directors. His translation of *Henry V* was staged at the Festival d'Avignon in 1999, directed by Jean-Louis Benoît.

Kim Tai-Won, Professor of English at Sogang University, Seoul, teaches Shakespeare and early modern English drama. He translated *King Lear* into Korean (2010) and published an introductory book on Shakespeare's authorship, *Was Shakespeare a Fraud? The Authorship Controversy in the Age of Conspiracy* (2015). His most recent publications include 'Beyond the 100 Year history of Shakespeare translations in Korea', in *Shakespeare Review* 55 (2019).

Shoichiro Kawai, a professor at the University of Tokyo, is also a translator, director and playwright. He has translated sixteen of Shakespeare's plays and worked with such directors as Yukio Ninagawa, Gregory Doran, Jonathan Kent and Simon Godwin. He has recently contributed to *The Routledge Handbook of Shakespeare and Interface* (2022) and *The Cambridge Guide to the Worlds of Shakespeare* (2019).

THE MUSHRUMP NETWORK[4]

The first translation of Shakespeare into French was done in the 1740s by Pierre-Antoine de La Place, a tranche of ten plays, some merely summarized, including *Macbeth*. Of special note is the stage direction for the ghostly dumbshow in 4.1: 'ced*A shew of eight Kings, and Banquo last, with a glasse in his hand*' (TLN 1657–8). A decade earlier, Lewis Theobald had suggested this may have been a masque-like device to flatter King James by showing him his own image in the succession of future Scottish kings. But in La Place the ghostly figure '*tient un verre qu'il porte aux yeux de Macbeth*'.[5] That is, he holds before the king's eyes a *verre* – not a looking glass, but a drinking glass – as if about to toast him with a fine Burgundy. La Place had read Theobald, but his Macbeth nevertheless sees his *veritas in vino*. (Stephen Orgel once told me there is an engraving of this moment, wine glass and all, but I haven't seen it.)

So, what do we do with that? Well, we could say it's wrong. In the critical language of the last century: it reveals a failure in the transmission of semantic content from source text to target text. (And yet that failure perfectly replicates the experience of most American students on a first reading.) Or, considering the 'cultural turn' in translation studies in the 1990s, we could say: it reveals the filtering of a guest text as reinvented in the host language and culture of eighteenth-century France. (And yet, Gallic oenophilia notwithstanding, anyone who has ever read a fairy tale knows that drinking to a king's health is far more sensible than holding up a mirror to his face.) But the truth is, I love this moment in *Macbeth* so much more because of this translation. It teaches me nothing about the play itself, of course, but that is no longer the only measure of value for me. As the realization of a potentiality, it thickens and enriches the text. It's a tickly little tendril stretching out from an ever growing play.

Over the past two decades, there has been a convergence of ideas – including those from object-oriented ontology and ecocriticism (from the likes of Graham Harman, Quentin Meillassoux, Bruno Latour, Timothy Morton and

---

[4] Timothy Billings.
[5] Pierre-Antoine de La Place, *Le Théâtre Anglois*, 8 vols. (London, 1746–1749), vol. 2, p. 478.

STRANGE SHADOWS: TRANSLATING SHAKESPEARE

Jane Bennett) – combined with the assumptions of poststructuralism and late twentieth-century commitments to cultural relativism, resulting in what feels like an emergent episteme, a sort of 'rhizome 2.0'. Half a century ago now, Gilles Deleuze and Félix Guattari proposed the *rhizome* as a metaphor for the reconfigurations of discourse under postmodernism. Against the 'arboreal' (tree-like) model of classical hierarchies ramifying upward and outward from a central trunk, they proposed the 'rhizomatic' (root-like) model of postmodern networks spreading horizontally in every direction. But what has recently captured the imagination of so many ecological writers and *Star Trek* fans alike is the subterranean mesh of mycorrhizae, the mycelial filaments connecting all the trees in the forest in a vast mycorrhizal network. Or, to give it a Shakespearian habitation and a name, the mushrump network.

Like the term 'myco-rrhizal' itself, the mushrump network of texts and translations includes both the mycelium and the rhizome, intertwined and interdependent. Biologists believe that 'mother' trees provide most of the nourishment in the network, but everything contributes what it can. The episteme is reflected in Morton's ecological vision of Harman's 'flat ontology', in which everything *exists* as *objects* on the same ontological plane, sometimes even with a kind of agency, but with no other judgement of value: the vital microbiome of bacteria and fungi in my body *exists* in the same way the rest of me does – along with toads, tigers, flying rivers and all the lithium in Bolivia. It's a radical vision not all of us may be ready to accept, but this 'ecological thought', as Morton calls it, is potentially transformative in shifting the anthropocentric worldview that continues to create ecological disasters.

All this seems far away from our little field, but I recognize it when I hear Peter Holland say that perhaps it's time to drop the 'Global' from Global Shakespeares. What we call 'Shakespeare' is a vast network of texts, translations, adaptations, tradaptations and appropriations, interconnected and ever growing. We need no longer begin in London, or even in English, then work our way outward. We snuffle up mushrumps wherever we dig.

During our roundtable, Shen Lin suggested that the upstart translator of Shakespeare in the twenty-first century must perform four roles: editor, director, actor and poet. Perhaps no translator has been more explicit about the first of these than the late Alessandro Serpieri who 'felt obliged more often than not to construct a virtual edition' of his own when translating a play.[6] Consider Serpieri's approach to the famous crux in Hamlet's soliloquy in 1.2 (all italics mine). Q2 reads: 'Oh, that this too too *sallied* [sullied] flesh would melt, / Thaw, and resolve itself into a dew!'. Q1 agrees. But F reads '*solid* flesh' (TLN 313). The conflating editor can choose only one, and shunt the other into a note. But Serpieri – who, as an editor-translator, is changing all the words anyway – chooses both: 'O se questa *lurida solida* [sullied solid] carne. . . .' There is no simple source-to-target semantic transfer here, or even cultural filtering. Serpieri is literally translating a text that does not exist, except as what we might call a virtual translingual epiphenomenon of the multiple texts of *Hamlet* (which, as a 'source', has always been a moving target). In other words, a mushrump. The crux here may be nothing more than a pun or a compositor's error, but its potentialities are realized in Italian and woven into the mesh.

In the mushrump network, we value translations not merely because they make Shakespeare accessible to non-English speakers, but because they activate potentialities, because they contain and carry nutrients, and because they enmesh themselves with and continue to expand the web of texts we already love. Dig anywhere.

---

[6] Alessandro Serpieri, 'Translating Shakespeare: a brief survey of some problematic areas', in *Translating Shakespeare for the Twenty-First Century*, ed. Ton Hoenselaars and Rui Carvalho Homem (New York, 2004), p. 32.

SHAKESPEARE TRANSLATOR AS EDITOR, DIRECTOR, ADAPTER AND POET[7]

Recently, the RSC has sponsored a new Chinese translation of Shakespeare's plays aiming to be theatrically viable, actor-friendly and audience-accessible. To try to achieve this three-fold goal, the translator faces some challenges, which in turn will impose on him a multifaceted role.

Two and a half centuries ago, the Bishop of Rochester confided to Pope his difficulty in reading Shakespeare's plays: 'The hardest parts of Chaucer are more intelligible to me than some of those Scenes, not merely thro the faults of the edition, but the obscurity of the writer.'[8] Equipped with an unprecedented knowledge of the Elizabethan language from his work on the *Dictionary*, Dr Johnson set about tackling the Bard's obscurity. About this endeavour, Gary Taylor was to observe grimly: 'Shakespeare, like Chaucer, like Sophocles, will have to be translated for his own countrymen.'[9] The translator bent on rendering Shakespeare accessible to target audiences has to face the additional labour of first explicating and even emending the early modern English before proceeding to the next phase of his work. A Shakespeare translator here assumes the role approximating that of a Shakespeare editor. For instance, when Lady Macbeth chides her husband for having scrupled to carry out their murderous plan:

> Was the hope drunk
> Wherein you dressed yourself? Hath it slept since?
> And wakes it now to look green and pale
> At what it did so freely?
>
> (*Macbeth*, 1.7.35–8)

Samuel Bailey, annoyed by the 'harsh' image of 'dressed', complained that 'surely it is on the confines, at least, of absurdity to speak of dressing yourself in what may become intoxicated', before emending 'dressed' to 'blessed'.[10] The Chinese translator Zhu Shenghao's choice of 'immersed' was a de facto emendation too:

> Was the hope wherein you were immersed
> Nothing but wine-induced vagary?
> And wakes it now to look ashen and regretful
> In realization of its audacity.[11]

The theatrical viability of the translation of a dramatic text relies on the apt transformation of words into actions. Words of dramatic texts supposedly have the power of calling for action besides giving out information. Dramatic actions are often implied, not by words per se, but between lines of the playtext, and the question a Shakespeare translator often has to answer is 'What's the action of it?', besides 'What's the meaning of it?' By taking lines beyond their face value, he will have to imagine entailed scenes. By this assertion, he comes close to being a stage director. For instance, in the scene after Anthony's departure, between Cleopatra, her ladies-in-waiting and the eunuch:

> Enter Cleopatra, Charmian, Iras, and Mardian.
> CLEOPATRA Charmian!
> CHARMIAN Madam?
> CLEOPATRA *(yawning)* Ha, ha. Give me to drink mandragora.
> CHARMIAN Why, madam?
> CLEOPATRA That I might sleep out this great gap of time My Antony is away.
> CHARMIAN   You think of him too much.
> CLEOPATRA O, 'tis treason!
> CHARMIAN   Madam, I trust not so.
> CLEOPATRA Thou, eunuch Mardian!
> MARDIAN   What's your highness' pleasure?
>
> (*Antony and Cleopatra*, 1.5.1–8)

What is it that constitutes 'treason' in the above exchange? The question, perhaps too simple, never bothers scholarly editors. Still, suppose the line

---

[7] Shen Lin.
[8] Alexander Pope, *The Correspondence of Alexander Pope*, ed. George Sherburn, 5 vols. (Oxford, 1956), vol. 2, pp. 78–9.
[9] Gary Taylor, 'The Bard stripped bare', review of *Reinventing Shakespeare, The Sunday Times*, 14 January 1990.
[10] William Shakespeare, *A New Variorum Edition of Shakespeare*, ed. Horace Howard Furness (Philadelphia, 1878), vol. 2, p. 75.
[11] William Shakespeare, *The Complete Works of Shakespeare*, trans. Zhu Shenghao and others, 11 vols. (Beijing, 1978), vol. 8, p. 325. The English translation is mine.

responds to the one preceding 'you think of him too much', could it mean then that 'not to think of him too much' would be a betrayal of the great love between Anthony and Cleopatra? Suppose it answers to a perceived insinuation at the Queen's self-indulgence – could it be tantamount to repudiating the subordinate's impudence? Suppose it reflects on the Queen's movement of thought still fixated on her absent lover (his having left me thus amounts to treason!) – could Charmian's reply read 'that he would not have dared, Ma'am'? Faced with these possibilities, the translator finds himself virtually in the position of a director deciding on the directions of the stage action.

A theatrically viable translation of Shakespeare by definition needs to command instantaneous audience response. For instance, success in translating the comic, that stage effect for which instantaneous response is vital, depends on how successfully dramatic and histrionic traditions overcome cultural barriers, and substitution proves to be the translator's favoured stratagem. In choosing appropriate theatrical and verbal equivalents to the original, the translator's role approximates that of an adapter. For example, Cao Yu substituted 'peach',[12] a Chinese classical allusion to feminine beauty, for the original 'open-arse' (medley), and 'banana', a common fruit of easily recognizable phallic resemblance, for the rarely seen but same-looking 'popp'rin' pear' in Mercutio's original bawdy lines:

> O, Romeo, that she were, O that she were
> An open-arse, and thou a popp'rin' pear.
> (*Romeo and Juliet* 2.1.37–8)

The translator of Shakespeare's dramatic texts, like all translators of dramatic texts, needs to pay attention to the sound of lines, even more so as he is dealing with a measured sound. Chinese translations of Shakespeare's original iambic pentameters without regard to cadence often sound pedestrian and tedious. The question naturally arises of how iambic pentameters will sound to today's English audiences and, by extension, would have sounded to Elizabethan audiences. The answer would probably prompt the Shakespeare translator to emulate instead of simulate the poet's original metres. In fact, the driving force behind the RSC project of re-translating the Bard is the will to fight time's corroding force, which has affected adversely the effectiveness of Shakespeare's language. Chinese, the target language, has been similarly doomed to vicissitudes of age. The RSC-sponsored translator would be hard put to find Shakespeare a voice for today's Chinese audiences. His new translating effort should try to attain a musicality both pleasing the ears and touching the hearts of target audiences, and this would turn him into a kind of poet.

INTERLINGUISTIC AND INTERSEMIOTIC TRANSLATION[13]

I wish to broach two topics: a very general one about the similarities and differences between translating Shakespeare's plays for the stage and translating Shakespeare's *Sonnets* for the page, and a very specific one about the partial untranslatability in *Henry V* of the scenes comprising passages in dialects and passages in 'Shakespeare's French'. Confronted with those linguistic impossibilities, the French translator has to become an adapter, a rewriter, if not a director.

After having spent thirty years (re)translating Shakespeare's plays for specific theatre productions, and recently commissioned by Gallimard to translate the *Sonnets*, I was faced with the question of whether my main options for translating for the stage[14] could apply to translating the *Sonnets*. Now, the intricate interweaving of the poetic and the theatrical in Shakespeare's work is evident. Nobody would claim that Shakespeare is more of a poet in his *Sonnets* than in his plays. The plays indeed comprise countless lyrical forms. Conversely, the *Sonnets* are theatrical. They display a dramatized development, and even a clearly

---

[12] William Shakespeare, *Romeo and Juliet*, trans. Cao Yu (Beijing, 1956), p. 58.
[13] Jean-Michel Déprats.
[14] For the presentation of those translating principles and procedures, see Jean-Michel Déprats, 'The "Shakespearian gap" in French', in *Shakespeare Survey 50* (Cambridge, 1997), 125–33.

definable plot. *Orality*, and even *vocality*, impregnate Shakespeare's poetics in his *Sonnets* as much as in his dramatic work. In other words, Shakespeare's *Sonnets* are texts meant to be *spoken* and *breathed* as much as texts to be *read*.

In my view, the modern translator is confronted with two main antithetical options, both dangerous traps: either he reproduces all the formal characteristics of the original, in particular the rhyming scheme, or he chooses a freer adaptation. The exclusive fascination for the initial forms – in particular, the rhymes and the rhyming pattern – asserts the primacy of versification. Words are chosen for their rhyming properties, not for their semantic accuracy. But those who are suspicious of rigid formality also run a risk – the risk of transforming the poem into a mere narrative in rhythmical prose. I chose a form of synthesis of the two approaches by translating the *Sonnets* in blank (unrhymed) Alexandrines, thus giving primacy to sound patterns. Assonances, alliterations, internal echoes, inner rhymes and global rhythm present just as powerful a principle of structuration as rhyming verse.

My second topic is about three particularly problematic scenes in *Henry V*. The first one in chronological order (3.3) is the scene written in stylized dialects, in which three Captains – the Welsh Fluellen, the Irish Macmorris and the Scot Jamy – discuss with the English Captain Gower the conduct of the war and the merits of their respective 'nations' on the battlefield. The second one (3.4) is the scene of the English lesson famous for its licentious innuendoes. The enumeration of equivalents in English of the French words for the various parts of the body leads to the exhilarated and falsely offended discovery by Katherine and Alice that the English words *foot* and *gown* – pronounced as those words were in the sixteenth century – sound like the French words *foutre* and *con*. The third problematic scene is the wooing scene between King Henry and Princess Katherine in act 5.

Henry V is by far Shakespeare's most polyglot play. As a result, it is the one that most defies translation, especially translation into French since three scenes (in fact four, since we have to add 4.4, the scene between Pistol and a French soldier) are written in 'Shakespearian French', strange and in part grammatically incorrect French (probably Anglo-Norman).[15] Any French translation, even if it retains the slight shift that the quaint Shakespearian French presents, by definition erases the bilingualism. In those cases, the operation of translation – in the usual sense of seeking equivalencies – goes off course. These language situations oblige the translator to invent other strategies, to find transposition methods other than word-by-word rendering. In those scenes featuring French characters, the French translator has the choice between two antithetical options. Preserving this strange French – which lacks neither charm nor flavour – leads to the absurdity of French characters expressing themselves in chaotic and old French while English characters, the King first, express themselves – a convention of translation – in correct and modern French. For the subtitles and dubbing of Kenneth Branagh's film, *Henry V*, it is the option I chose, but Branagh's film is an English film interpreted by English actors and actresses. For Jean-Louis Benoît's theatre production at the 1999 Festival d'Avignon, I translated this 'Shakespearian French' into modern French.

As Ton Hoenselaars notes,[16] it is impossible to offer a completely convincing and satisfying translation of a macaronic and Babelian text.

The most acute translation problems stem from the scene in dialects. Most of the time, French translators try to transpose those English local ways of speech into French supposed equivalents (Breton or Alsatian, for instance), ignoring the fact that vernaculars are geographically specific and

---

[15] See Anny Crunelle Vanrigh, '"Fause Frenche enough": Kate's French in Shakespeare's *Henry V*', *English Text Construction* 6, Special Issue: Multilingualism in the Drama of Shakespeare and His Contemporaries, ed. Dirk Delabastita and Ton Hoenselaars (2013), 60–88.

[16] Author of a very interesting article on François-Victor Hugo, translator of *Henry V*: ' Shakespeare for the "people". François-Victor Hugo translates Henry V', *Documenta* 13 (1995), 243–52.

cannot be transposed. It is up to the actors to find the pronunciation specificities which will particularize their characters. So the solution is not a written one but an oral one. In the theatre, there is no valid purely linguistic translation of regional accents, only a temporary, individualized and always to be reinvented oral solution.

To use Roman Jakobson's terms, the scenic transposition (or intersemiotic translation) takes over the interlinguistic translation. In other words, the interlinguistic translation is relayed by the intersemiotic translation. The theatre production or scenic transposition can not only make up for the shortcomings of the interlinguistic translation but also increase its effect, provided we think in terms of transposition, adaptation and recreation and not exclusively in terms of translation.

SHAKESPEARE TRANSLATOR AS EDITOR AND COLLABORATOR[17]

The year 2023 marks the 100th anniversary of the first appearance of Shakespeare's plays in Korea with the first Korean translation of *Hamlet* by Hyeon-cheol in 1923. Koreans can now boast of five different complete editions as well as numerous individual plays available as separate volumes. Despite the 100-year history of Shakespeare translation in Korea, however, I regretfully must report that many new translations in the 2000s are barely informed by the most recent textual and editorial achievements in Shakespeare studies. The new millennial Korean Shakespeares seem to rarely echo or incorporate the breathtaking transformation of Shakespeare scholarship, particularly in the textual criticism. While implicitly taking 'Shakespeare' as a unified, fixed and consistent corpus of texts, the majority of Korean translators in the past two decades have turned a blind eye to most of the textual problems. They seem negligent in dealing with textual variances of Shakespeare and often uncritical of the traditional positions and interpretations.

As mentioned before, the late Alessandro Serpieri persuasively argued that 'translating any play by Shakespeare necessarily implies editing it' (167).[18] In this sense, I would claim that any serious Shakespeare translator must be attentive to the issues of textual problems and be acquainted with the new development in the field. Such an awareness of textual complexities should enable the translator to discover a new venue through which to move beyond familiar polemical topics in translation studies such as target-oriented versus source-oriented, foreignizing versus domesticating, literal versus figural, literary versus theatrical, historicizing versus modernizing, interlinguistic versus intersemiotic versus intercultural, and so on.

Since the 1980s, textual scholarship in Shakespeare studies has offered many inspirational new approaches and has even resulted in publications of several innovative editions with reformed editorial policies and practices.[19] While stirring up many controversies, for example, the appearance of *The Oxford Shakespeare* in 1986 and *The New Oxford Shakespeare* in 2017 have certainly compelled many scholars to reevaluate the established status of the Bard's texts, overhaul the sense of his works and authorship, and even rethink the idea of the text itself. In the wake of the recent development and discoveries in textual studies, Shakespeare translators are being asked to thoroughly reconsider what it means to translate Shakespeare, as well as how we can do it in keeping with the state of the art.

For a typical case of nonchalance to textual matters in Korean Shakespeare, I may point to a 2008 single-volume translation of *King Lear* which claims to be based upon the version from *The Riverside Shakespeare*, with a few stage directions imported from the Arden third series edition of the play. According to the translator, the choice of the source text was made simply because *The Riverside Shakespeare* was most frequently cited in scholarly

---

[17] Kim Tai-Won.
[18] Serpieri, 'The translator as editor', p. 167.
[19] On the various fronts in post-New Bibliographical textual studies, see, for example, Gary Taylor and Gabriel Egan, eds., *The New Oxford Shakespeare: Authorship Companion* (Oxford, 2017).

articles. This statement was not even true in 2008, though it might have been the case in the 1980s. Another translation of *King Lear* published in 2004 refers to the Arden third series edition as its source-text, but does not care to spell out a justification of its textual choice. These translations of *King Lear* do not show any sign that they have tried to engage seriously with the well-known textual problems of *King Lear*'s folio and quarto versions.

Many recent Korean translations do not state which version or edition was used for translation and, if they do state the source edition, tend to avoid explaining the reasons for their choice. The new complete Shakespeare translation by Lee Sangsup in 2016 is symptomatic. It claims to have adopted the 1986 *Oxford Shakespeare* for its source-text but substitutes the Oxford *King Lear* with the Arden third series edition instead. The translator does not offer any rationale for his surprising replacement of the Oxford edition with the Arden one. My reasonable guess would be that he simply tried to sidestep the thorny textual controversies of *King Lear*, which I believe were exactly what the 1986 *Oxford Shakespeare* editors wanted to provoke.

In order to advance the current state of Korean Shakespeare translation, I draw upon Lukas Erne's insight about the role of modern editors. In *Shakespeare's Modern Collaborators*, Erne claims that Shakespeare's works were made possible by the aid of three levels of contemporary collaboration: (1) with his fellow playwrights; (2) with his fellow actors and theatre workers; and (3) with his printers. Erne then adds to the list the modern editors as Shakespeare's fourth collaborator: 'What we read as "Shakespeare" is decisively shaped by the collaboration between Shakespeare and his modern editor.'[20] While agreeing with Erne's assertion on the significance of editorship in our experience of Shakespeare's works, I would add that Shakespeare's translator must be seen as his fifth collaborator. Needless to say, Shakespeare would come to non-English speakers almost always as a translation, in translation, by translation.

Translation is not only a linguistic labour to mediate between a source-text and the target language but also a cultural, historical endeavour to transpose the original story into the new terrain for the target readers. With the varied, layered and fluid texts, however, the Shakespearian translator should take up one more responsibility of editorship to sort out the textual and editorial matters. In this sense, Shakespeare's translator deserves to be seen as a modern, translinguistic co-author of his works. A Shakespeare translator is not just a ventriloquist, but rather a conjurer who should be ready to bring the dead writer's letters back to life or, in a Benjaminian sense, an afterlife – and even a completely new life. The ghost of Shakespeare or Shakespearian ghosts should be called back and revitalized by the conjuration of the translator, who would encourage spectators and readers to confront those ghosts, however benign or malign, and attend to their voices for improved understanding. The knowledge of textual complexities is a necessary and indispensable magic-spell for the conjurer-translator to bring the dead back to life. This is why a Shakespearian translator had better learn, and even have expertise on, how to speak with the dead, to borrow Stephen Greenblatt's well-known phrase.

CONCLUSION[21]

The act of translating has two dimensions: first, the original text must be 'correctly' interpreted, and in this procedure, a translator has to work as an editor to solve textual cruxes, and a director to determine the dramatic function of the scene; and when expressing it in the target language, a translator must be creative, sometimes substituting original puns, dialects and other untranslatable matters with comparable expressions in their own culture, or re-creating some dramatic effects akin to the original, thus playing the parts of adapter and poet (dramatist).

Our roundtable was fecund, and it is regrettable that only its gist is recorded here. I was especially fascinated with a charming point made by Timothy Billings, which he had to leave out from his concise

---

[20] Lukas Erne, *Shakespeare's Modern Collaborators* (London, 2008), p. 3.
[21] Shoichiro Kawai.

summary above. It is about the enigmatic 'sea-mews' that Caliban offers to 'get' 'from the rock' for Trinculo and Stephano in *The Tempest* (2.2.170–1). The word is printed as 'Scamels' in the First Folio, which seems to be a compositor's error, but Timothy calls it his 'favorite filament in the mycorrhizal mesh'. It would be a great pity if we didn't share Timothy's brilliant and extremely pregnant argument on it as follows:

Editors have been wondering since the eighteenth century whether the word might be a corruption of 'seamels', an alternative spelling of 'seamews', which is a kind of gull, like a seagull. This is why Zhu Shenghao and Liang Shiqiu both render it as 海鷗 (seagull), and most other translators do likewise in their own languages. In translation, the paratext congeals in the text itself. Part of the editorial work of the critical apparatus, representing collective knowledge drawn from the mycelium, becomes 'Shakespeare'. This has profound implications for performance texts where the audience doesn't have access to footnotes. In this way, audiences of foreign language Shakespeares may sometimes apprehend a sense that is actually closer to what Shakespeare's original audiences may have understood – which is not to say that it is necessarily better, as I have already stressed, or even always true. Indeed, because Lewis Theobald (1733) in the eighteenth century proposed that scamels may have been a corruption of 'shamois' or little goat-like antelopes, sometimes translators render that. Or, because John Holt (1749) a little later in the eighteenth century proposed that a 'scamel' was a kind of 'limpet', a shellfish, some translations give that. So, just looking at the French translations from the eighteenth to the twentieth centuries, Caliban apparently likes to eat all three: mouettes (seagulls), chamois (goats), and coquillages (shellfish). And in François Guizot's memorable translation of 1864: *quelquefois je t'apporterai du rocher jeunes pingouins* (sometimes I'll get thee young penguins from the rock). Yes, among the wonders of the Mushrump Network is also to be found a penguin-ivorous Caliban. What's not to love about that.[22]

In many Japanese translations too, like Chinese ones, 'seagulls' is usually adopted, except one which renders it as 'bar-tailed godwits', based on Joseph Wright's *The English Dialect Dictionary* (1898–1905), which probably relied on Henry Stevenson's *Birds of Norfolk* (1866). H. H. Furness cites this definition and adds:

But as this bird is not a rock-breeder, it cannot be the one intended in the present passage if we regard it as an accurate description from a naturalist's point of view. We must suppose therefore either that the description is not strictly accurate, or that in Shakespeare's time the word 'scamel' may have had a wider application.[23]

The idea of the mushrump network is attractive, simply because the application seems quite wide. When the original text itself is so resonant in different meanings, translated Shakespeares should be more resonant.

---

[22] *The Works of Shakespeare*, ed. Lewis Theobald, 7 vols. (London, 1733), vol. 1, p. 39; John Holt, *An Attempte to Rescue that Aunciente English Poet, and Play-Wrighte, Maister Williaume Shakespere, from the Maney Errours, faulsely charged on him* (London, 1749), p. 57.

[23] William Shakespeare, *The Tempest: A New Variorum Edition of Shakespeare*, ed. Horace Howard Furness (Philadelphia, 1892), p. 140.

GENDER AND SEXUALITY: THE STATE OF THE FIELDS

MARJORIE RUBRIGHT AND VALERIE TRAUB (CHAIRS), KUMIKO HILBERDINK-SAKAMOTO, JUDY ICK, ALEXA ALICE JOUBIN AND MADHAVI MENON

INTRODUCTION[1]

This roundtable highlighted various approaches currently animating studies of gender and sexuality in performance studies, queer philology, trans theory and queer history. Our session had a prehistory, born of opposition, particularly in the US and the UK, to holding the Congress in Singapore. This opposition was spearheaded by queer people and our allies, who advocated a boycott of the Congress in response to Singapore's state-authorized homophobia. Singapore's law, Section 377A, which was only lately repealed in December 2022, specifically criminalized consensual sexual acts between men. It read: 'Any male person who, in public or private, commits, or abets the commission of, or procures or attempts to procure the commission by any male person of, any act of gross indecency with another male person, shall be punished with imprisonment for a term which may extend to 2 years.' This law, while not routinely enforced, survived multiple legal challenges in recent years, including a 2007 amendment that deleted references in the statute to oral and anal sex between heterosexuals, and a High Court opinion issued in March 2020 that found criminalizing homosexual sex to be constitutional. In addition, the government had until recently censured positive media or public LGBTQ depictions, and LGBTQ people, who were unable to legally marry, were implicitly discriminated against by public housing policies (recently rescinded) that restricted individuals from purchasing larger apartments.

After I, Valerie, heard of the boycott, I investigated the International Shakespeare Association's reasons for choosing Singapore, the status of prosecutions in Singapore, forms of LGBTQ discrimination, and local queer political activism such as the annual event Pink Dot SG. I also consulted with friends and colleagues in the field, whose responses varied. Several queer friends indicated support for the boycott; others indicated that, while they would not publicly support the boycott, they also would not travel to Singapore. Some colleagues living outside of North America countered that Singapore should not be singled out; they would be just as loath to travel to the US because of the toxic policies of the then-current president. Meanwhile, gay men who live in or regularly travel to Singapore thought it important for queers to be publicly present and vocal within Singapore's borders. And some Asian colleagues articulated the view that the Western-generated boycott was colonial in effect, if not intention. Although I remained ambivalent, it was these latter voices that I chose to privilege, particularly because of the tensions that had emerged between US and Asian perspectives. I issued my invitations to panelists, while also making sure they knew about the controversy. Not everyone I invited chose to participate.

I narrate this prehistory because the issues it raises are complex and demand candid dialogue.

---

[1] Marjorie Rubright and Valerie Traub.

GENDER AND SEXUALITY

Furthermore, there is an early modern connection here. Section 377A, like the sixteenth-century anti-sodomy law upon which it was based, specifically criminalized sexual acts between men while remaining silent on female–female sex. It was this law that the British imported into the colony in 1938, via the Indian penal code, and it is this history that enabled people today to think of Section 377A as simply an outmoded and insignificant 'relic' of colonial power. The role of colonization in disrupting indigenous sexual systems around the globe is a history that early modernists are particularly well suited to explore, especially given the ways in which queer scholarship over the past thirty years has nuanced our perspective on the complex ways in which the past informs the present. Moreover, this issue speaks to the meanings we attach to sexual freedom, as well as to the way our lived differences of location, citizenship, race, gender and religion affect our capacities to attain such freedom.

I thus want to make it clear that it is *as a lesbian* – that is, as someone who would be deemed as such by any government on earth – *and as a queer* – that is, as someone who resists normative taxonomies, including those that seek to narrow the possibilities of sexual and gender expression – *and as a feminist Shakespearian* – dedicated to thinking about the gendered histories of sexuality, past *and* present – that I reach out in solidarity with anyone present who feels the force of oppression due to their gender, gender expression and/or sexual practices or sexual identity. I invite you to contact me if there is any way that you think I can aid your aspirations for freedom.

The roundtable presentations summarized below represent a snapshot of the more expansive conversations that ensued leading up to this roundtable and during its Q&A. They nonetheless provide rich perspectives on the role of language in designating bodies and desires; the affordances that a trans analytic brings to the study of gender and sexuality; the import of cross-cultural differences and similarities in embodied performance experiences and traditions; and the impact of cultural differences and convergences in feminist, trans and queer studies as they travel around the globe. While our roundtable was historically, geographically and politically situated in the context of the 2021 Singapore World Shakespeare Congress, and while much headway has been made in the intervening years, we hope that the topics explored and questions raised will serve to animate ongoing debates and collaborations in our fields.

LESS ABOUT, MORE WITH: GENDER AND SEXUALITY IN ASIAN SHAKESPEARE[2]

Let me start by highlighting two illustrative moments during the Watch parties organized as part of the Asian Shakespeare Digital Festival which was a prequel to this Congress. The first moment comes from the Q&A session with Norzizi Zulkifli, the director of *Mak Yong Titis Sakti* (2009), a traditional Malay adaptation of *A Midsummer Night's Dream*. Despite modernizing certain aspects of the production, when questioned about keeping to the traditional gender of actors in the *mak yong* (an all-female Kelantanese theatre form where only the clowns are male), the director was quick to dismiss the dangers of being called out by authorities for inadvertently representing same-sex desire with a ready-made argument of keeping to 'Islamic values'. In other words, she aimed to maintain an expectation of modesty in representing expressions of desire between members of the opposite sex by having them represented by same-sex actors. That same-sex desire may possibly surface in keeping to traditional casting did not seem to occur to her at all.

The second moment revolves around Miyagi Satoshi's annotations to his production, *Mugen Noh Othello* (2005). In this adaptation of *Othello* to the *Mugen Noh* style, a Venetian Pilgrim played by the *waki* (secondary performer of a *noh* play), who is cross-dressed to boot, encounters the spirit of Desdemona played by the *shite* (principal performer of a *noh* play). The director defuses the

---

[2] Judy Ick.

radical potentials of his Desdemona-centred interpretation, by reading Desdemona's liberation as symbolic of the liberation of all oppressed individuals, rather than as a particularly gender-bound reading. He interprets the play as a triumph for Desdemona by suggesting that, in reliving her trauma as the *shite* (spirit of Desdemona), she then frees herself from all attachments to this world and crosses over to the next. The fact that her gender was at the root of her fate in this world did not seem to matter at all.

In some ways, these moments illuminate the difficulties of gender criticism in the field of Asian Shakespeare: its complex entanglements that often lead to the diffusion or even dissolution of gender as a primary category of critique, and its slipperiness, and tendency to dissolve into other equally weighty categories. In the first example, 'Islamic values' presents a site for potential, cheeky subversions when worldviews collide; in the second, gender is subsumed under a cosmography of redemption difficult to ignore. After all, who can argue with reaching the status of a Buddha and achieving Nirvana?

Being a feminist Asian Shakespearian critic is undoubtedly complicated. The paradigms or theoretical frameworks developed in Anglo-American Shakespearian scholarship on gender and sexuality are of necessarily limited use, having arisen from a different history and having as their object of study Shakespearian origins firmly rooted in Western, Judaeo-Christian traditions. To examine sexuality and gender in Shakespeare in Asia is always to begin from a position of incommensurability – or at the very least, a crippling hyperawareness of nuance. Let me illustrate by posing some deliberately provocative questions: does Asian Shakespeare have a pronoun? The ubiquitous pronoun question just doesn't ring true or bear asking because what do pronouns matter in the many ungendered languages of Asia? Or, further, what value would Judith Butler's breakthrough theory about the performativity of gender have to bring to the study of Asian theatre traditions that have employed masks, costumes, movements, voice and other technologies to create various representations of the gendered body – in several instances crossing gender lines, and both ways too, for centuries?

The rise of Global Shakespeare may have also partially helped to obscure gender studies in Asian Shakespeare by focusing on a national label as a point of entry. The strategic use of the national as an adjective – as in Philippine Shakespeare or Chinese Shakespeare – guaranteed a quicker entrance into global academic discourse. Often, doing Global Shakespeare also includes providing copious descriptions and backgrounds for unknown forms for which there is no mutually intelligible critical shorthand. The space for critical theorizing becomes restricted. No wonder gender is not a stronger presence in the critical landscape of Asian Shakespeare. While there are a few fine examples, there are not nearly enough.

The less-than-robust engagement with critical gender studies in Asian Shakespeare is a puzzling deficiency given that there is no shortage of fascinating examples of Asian Shakespeare performances or cultural reproductions that provoke critical analysis of the categories of sex and gender. For example, the androgynous aesthetics of many types of Asian Shakespeare performance traditions, as well as in popular cultural forms (like Japanese *manga*), serve to disrupt gender codes and compel a reassessment of gender and its fluidities as a force in analysis. It is almost as if we 'do gender' very well in Asia; we just don't speak or write about it enough. If I might use myself as an example, feminism deeply informs my teaching and theatre work, but I don't write about gender, not anymore. The lack of a critical language or the incommensurability of the paradigms developed in mainstream Shakespearian feminist criticism is perhaps one reason. A second is exhaustion (or conference time limits or publication word counts). The labour expended to explain, provide background, and describe Shakespearian incarnations in my local culture is considerable and often leaves little room for much else.

Clearly, there is a pressing need to develop not so much separate as more capacious theories of and critical frameworks for issues of gender and sexuality in Shakespeare that can accommodate its Asian incarnations. The work may well begin by looking deeply at Shakespearian productions and reproductions from Asia as sites of both convergence and crucial critical differences that feminists – from both inside and outside Asia – might explore. More than simply producing scholarship on gender and sexuality *about* Asian Shakespeare, we ought to think of developing critical frameworks and theories on gender and sexuality *with* Asian Shakespeare and other Shakespeares around the world. This roundtable represents a significant step in that direction.

CRITICAL RACE AND TRANS STUDIES[3]

How might we parse Banquo's and Macbeth's question to the witches: 'You should be woman, / And yet your beards forbid me to interpret that you are so' (1.3.43–4) and 'what are you' (1.3.45)? How does a cisgender woman of colour's performance of a trans feminine white male character diminish anti-trans violence or trivialize trans life, as in the case of Belinda Sullivan's 'doubled drag' performance of Falstaff as the Witch of Brentford in the 2013 African-American Shakespeare Company production of *Merry Wives of Windsor*? How do we make sense of singer Joni Mitchell's 1976 blackface acts and later insistence that she is a 'Black man trapped in a white woman's body', telling the *New York Times* in 1998 that she was 'the only Black man at the [Halloween] party'?[4] In what ways are similar narratives complicated by pandemic-era hate crimes, such as the mistreatment of, and protests against, Darren Merager who identifies as a woman, in a Korean spa in Los Angeles in 2021? To answer these questions, we need to bring performance theories to critical race and trans studies.

Gendering and race-making practices share analogous logics as processes through which people shape and contest their embodied experiences. Gender and race are as much nouns (identity categories) as they are verbs (actions and social practices). Gender and race are often intertwined, because racialized imaginaries often delimit gender practices, and gender-based exclusions help racial prejudices 'perform' discriminatory acts. At our roundtable, we have spoken at length on words that are not on the page, words that post-date Shakespeare, and speculative philology. Here, I would like to add performance studies methods – critical tools that capture transformative cultural practices – to the conversation, because performance produces synchronous layers of social meanings of race and gender. Performance, both as an artistic form and as a critical concept, adds nuance to the artifices of race and gender by illuminating the ways race and gender evolve over time and in different social spaces.

Performativity (how language tacitly or overtly affects social actions) is the core of imaginative literature. Characters and readers behave in particular ways to fit into or deviate from social norms, and socially structured speech acts and nonverbal communication become key components of our cultural life. Performance dislodges the idea that text alone can encompass everything the words connote. For example, cisgender textual interpretations of *Twelfth Night* typically regard Viola's Cesario as a temporary act to score personal gains in a patriarchal society. The gender nonconformity is assumed to be a pragmatic plot twist rather than embodied trans experience. In performance studies terms, gendering and race-making are technologies of representation that can restructure social expectations. Further, the playing space itself is a transitory space through which actors and characters traverse.

Actors' offstage racial identification adds nuance to the picture. British-Indian actor Shubham Saraf's trans performance of Ophelia, against Michelle Terry's cross-cast white Hamlet, traverses gender and racial lines in Federay Holmes and Elle While's 'post gender' production of *Hamlet* at the Globe in 2018. British-Ugandan actress Sheila

---

[3] Alexa Alice Joubin.
[4] Neil Strauss, 'The hissing of a living legend', *New York Times*, 4 October 1998.

Atim's trans-masculine performance of Cesario in Adam Smethurst's film *Twelfth Night* (2018) complicates class aspirations and embodiment of genders.

Trans-inclusive and anti-racist campaigns have a lot more in common beyond their shared agenda of social justice. Trans studies, with its critical tools to understand gender variance and atypical bodies, can amplify critical race studies' efforts to support minority life experiences. In fact, race and trans studies are both born out of the necessity for everyone to live a livable life. What one sees correlates to how one sees. Whether one is truly seen (by having one's presence properly acknowledged) hinges on whether a society can tackle the epistemic invisibility of minorities. In honour of our host city, Singapore, I would like to offer case studies that keep our conversation focused on global sites.

Naturalistic acting, for instance, sometimes makes cross-gender enactment 'invisible' because it often defaults to a cisgender-centric position, as is the case with Trevor Nunn's 1996 film *Twelfth Night*. There are exceptions. The 2021 Taiwanese film *As We Like It* directed by Chen Hung-i and Muni Wei uses Franco-Taiwanese mixed-race actress Camile Chalons's cross-gender and bilingual performance of Celia and two openly trans actresses' 'backpassing' acts to queer *As You Like It*, which has traditionally been read as a cisgender narrative. The film does away with such binary gender accessories as moustaches or wigs. It presents characters of all genders – played by actors identifying as women – matter-of-factly, without apology or additional justification.

In contrast, heavy stylization of the presentations of characters, such as those in Richard Eyre's 2004 film *Stage Beauty* and Akira Kurosawa's 1957 samurai film adaptation of *Macbeth*, *Throne of Blood*, draws attention to the gendering and race-making practices themselves. In *Stage Beauty*, the seventeenth-century adult boy actor Ned Kynaston performs Desdemona's vulnerable white femininity in cross-gender acts. Kynaston presents as female in his romantic life offstage, before eventually playing Othello in blackface in trans-racial enactments of violent masculinity onstage. In *Throne of Blood*, the significance of gendered pronouns is obscured by English subtitles, though the film's witch figure resides in a non-binary space, by way of their stylized *noh* acting and vocal work. Appearing in a translucent robe and with a halo around them, the genderqueer witch spins yarn in a bamboo hut in a dense forest. They appear to be turning a double-spooled spinning wheel, but the fibre is simply spun from the smaller wheel onto the larger one without producing yarn. By moving a domestic chore into nature, the witch queers the otherwise quotidian act, signalling that they reside in a social space between different worlds. Both Kynaston and the witch can be interpreted as trans.

Artists have used our historical 'safe' distance from the early modern period as a screen for engaging contemporary gender issues. This trend is a version of what Jack Halberstam has called 'perverse presentism', a methodology that uses history to denaturalize contemporary articulations of gender and sexuality.[5] It is my belief that, with critical race and trans methodologies, we can and should use a trans lens to read so-called 'non-trans' films. The trans lens enables us to attend to racialization and gender-play, particularly the liminal paths to gender expression and characters' indeterminate state of being. Performance can reveal that gender variance is more than just a dramatic device or the replaying of the early modern theatre practice of boy actors playing female characters who transform into pageboys. Since film and theatre are technologies of gendering and race-making, films that feature casts of the same race can be read as 'race films' or films about race, just as films starring cisgender actors should be read through a trans lens to uncover cisgender sexism and tacit transness in their characters.

Combined with performance theories, the trans lens helps us assess the artifice of, and tensions between, gendered experiences. Encompassing all practices that cut across binary identities, trans theory is useful in furthering our understanding of gender-play in Shakespeare,

---

[5] Jack Halberstam, *Female Masculinity* (Durham, 1998), pp. 50–9.

THE TROUBLE WITH PRONOUNS[6]

With the change of voice came the change of name. For a little while, I wanted my feminine first name to be treated as masculine. I wanted to keep calling myself Beatriz and to be treated, according to the rules of grammar, with masculine pronouns and adjectives. But this grammatical torsion was even more difficult than the corporeal fluidity of gender. So I [had] to look for a masculine first name.[7]

(Paul B. Preciado, *An Apartment on Uranus*)

Queer theory in general, and trans* theory in particular, has emphasized the close relation between words and desires, names and things, language and ontology. What has seemed clear, well before Juliet's rhetorical question about 'what's in a name' (*Romeo* 2.2.47) is the extent to which language and sexuality are mutually intertwined. And this is perhaps nowhere more pronounced than in the grammatical unit known as the pronoun. Several of our most current academic and social debates on sexuality revolve around the use and abuse of pronouns. What pronouns might best describe which persons? How do languages other than English do gender and desire and sexuality? Do different languages produce different desires, and therefore provide different fodder for queer theorization?

Brad Epps reminds us that '[g]ender trouble, in a global frame, needs to be at once supplemented (in the deconstructive sense) and recast as "translation trouble" or, better yet, "language trouble"'.[8] Thus, Bulleh Shah shows us how Preciado's dream had already come true in a Gurmukhi poem written in eighteenth-century Punjab:

You have raised your veil and made me wander, like Zulaikha in Egypt. With a burqa on his head, lord, Bullha has been made to dance by your love.

(Lyric #5; *c*.1730)[9]

Bulleh Shah keeps his (masculine) pronoun, but dresses it in feminine attire. His pronoun of choice is 'his', and that 'his' wears a burqa and dances in the desert. A gendered pronoun yields more than one gender, regardless of the pronoun, and Bulleh Shah easily transitions across those borders, not allowing his gender or sexuality to be contained in or reflected by a pronoun. In an earlier vocabulary of geopolitics, this is what might be termed non-alignment.

Bulleh Shah's poem is written in gendered Gurmukhi, but follows the style of Sufi poetry, much of which was written in Persian, which, like English, is an ungendered language. In both Persian and English, nouns and verbs are not marked by gender. But Persian is even more radical than English because its pronouns are ungendered while modern English retains its associations with Old English in its use of he/his/she/her. Urdu and Hindi – the languages in which Sufi poetry was written on the Indian subcontinent – are fiercely gendered languages despite their affiliation with Persian. They have gendered nouns, verbs and adjectives, but, interestingly, they do not have gendered pronouns. And even their gendered nouns and adjectives are not always 'properly' placed. For instance, the word for masculinity (*mardangi*) is feminine, while the term for vagina-owner (*bhosdi-wala*) is masculine – indeed, the feminine version does not even exist.

So, there is really no such thing as a fully ungendered language, and no such thing as a fully gendered language: all languages seem to hover betwixt and between. Gurmukhi is a gendered language with no gendered pronouns, while English is an ungendered language with gendered pronouns. Even as ungendered languages like Persian offer interesting insights into pronouns that are not easily mappable onto genders, seemingly fully gendered languages like Gurmukhi and

---

[6] Madhavi Menon.
[7] Paul B. Preciado, *An Apartment on Uranus: Chronicles of the Crossing* (South Pasadena, CA, 2000), p. 34.
[8] Brad Epps, unpublished remarks quoted in Afsaneh Najmabadi, *Professing Selves: Transsexuality and Same-Sex Desire in Contemporary Iran* (Durham, 2023), p. 8.
[9] All references to Bulleh Shah are from the Murty Library edition of his *Sufi Lyrics*, trans. and ed. Cristopher Shackle (Cambridge, MA, 2015).

partly gendered languages like English can be transgendered in important ways, creating schisms in the supposedly transparent relation between pronoun and sexuality.

Modern English, the language that Shakespeare played a key role in creating, is an excellent example of an ungendered language that can do clever things with desire despite having gendered pronouns. A look at the famous Sonnet 20, the subject of much impassioned sexual and editorial debate, illustrates this complex play of gender and sexuality.

There is no 'he' or 'she' used for human beings in this poem, even though it is a poem about men and women. But it is precisely because it is about the confusion of man and woman, the profusion of master and mistress, the intrusion of the one into the other into the many, that this Sonnet allows us to theorize the multiple relations among pronoun and gender and sexuality. The subject of the Sonnet is a master-mistress, whose sex and gender are never disambiguated. Several stereotypes about women and men are trotted out in a vain bid to separate the one from the other. And the single instance of a gendered pronoun in this poem – 'A man in hue, all hues in *his* controlling' (7) – makes apparent Shakespeare's complication of pronomial accuracy.

Starting with Samuel Johnson, criticism has often remarked on Shakespeare's fondness for the pun – his 'fatal Cleopatra'.[10] The pun, of course, is that which encodes more than one thing – a master and a mistress. The puns in Sonnet 20 on 'you', 'yew', 'hue', 'Hugh', 'use', all cluster together next to the poem's single human use of 'his'. The poem's recipient's pronouns of choice, we might say, are you/his, in which the indeterminacy of 'you' is use(d) to colour (hue) his pronoun. After all, the poem's master-mistress is both he and she and they and you. And even as this line might seem to suggest 'his' as a universal pronoun, we are told two lines later, 'And for a woman wert thou first created' (9), the fuzzy phrasing of which makes it unclear whether the man was first created *as* a woman, or whether he was made for the use *of* women. Puns seem to replace pronouns in Sonnet 20.

Shakespeare's Sonnet 20 is the country cousin of Bulleh Shah's poem in challenging the belief that pronouns can be accurate indicators of gender and sexuality. Just as the ghazal is the precursor of the sonnet form, so too do Shakespeare and the Sufis breathe the same air of multi-gendering. What we and they get by getting pronouns 'wrong' is a world of sexual possibility that does justice to language's inability to speak the truth.

SPECULATIVE PHILOLOGY FOR NON-BINARY FUTURES[11]

Inside the word 'philology' lives a love story, one that conjoins a desire for language with desires arising from language. Philology's love story is born in the tensions between transitive and intransitive desires. New work in queer philology orients us to the powers of intransitive-thinking: attending to desires, actions and affects that exist without a set object, predetermined direction or destination. To be a philologist, in this sense, is to recognize that one shares in the epistemological project of transgender studies: a field that attends to proliferating modes of gender non-conformity, plurality and expansiveness – in both the past and present – and does so, to borrow Jack Halberstam's formulation, by way of 'refusing to situate transition in relation to a destination, a final form, a specific shape, or an established configuration of desire and identity'.[12]

From the start, the field of transgender studies in North America has been a philological affair. Susan Stryker's 2008 *Transgender History* opens with a sex and gender lexicon that invites readers to invent new words and to delete others that are outmoded or un-affirming. The inaugural issue of *Transgender*

---

[10] Samuel Johnson, *Preface to Shakespeare* (Cambridge, MA, 1909–14), para 44.
[11] Marjorie Rubright.
[12] Jack Halberstam, *Trans* A Quick and Quirky Account of Gender Variability* (Oakland, 2018), p. 4.

Studies Quarterly, published in 2014, offers two volumes of keywords for trans studies, each term authored by different contributors. Like a living language, the philological work of transgender studies is collective and continuously in the making. In 'Toward a Trans Philology', Joseph Gamble underscores that:

> trans people, both inside and outside the academy, are practicing a form of philology when they generate new pronouns like ze and hir, or when they produce new gender identity labels like genderqueer, genderfluid, nonbinary, [and trans] .... Emending, glossing, bracketing, and collating various visions of the relationship between gender and bodies, trans people are, in many ways, gender's editors.[13]

Pivoting focus onto cultures of the past, Jeffrey Masten, in *Queer Philologies*, contends that 'the study of sex and gender in historically distant cultures is necessarily a *philological* investigation'.[14] In *Thinking Sex with the Early Moderns*, Valerie Traub proposes that such philological investigations involve thinking 'like a queer concordance, locating words in a thick associational web of linguistic, textual and social contexts'.[15]

How will these new philologies reshape our critical, editorial, and pedagogical practices? I am, I should declare, primarily a reader of Shakespeare – and so my thinking about transformations of identity, identification, and desire often begins with an encounter with the multivalence of a single word, the inter- and intra-linguistic density of Shakespeare's English, and the scenes of translation and metamorphosis that give rise to transformations of identity, identification, and desire. Given this textual focus, I am especially interested in discussing with my colleagues how philological questions can expand our thinking about possibilities for gender non-binary performance on stage and in film. How might the philologist's contemplation of a single word or cluster of terms translate to and inform performance? In thinking with new philologies across diverse cultural traditions, languages, and time periods – as our panel attempts today – when might we discover that Shakespeare is too small to think with?

I would like to propose three ways that queer and trans★ philology can reshape our critical, editorial and pedagogical practices. First, this new work tasks us with exploring how our own naturalized critical practices, such as using singular names and gender markers for characters who resist those restrictions, conditions us to be less critically kaleidoscopic than we might otherwise be in our engagements with gender-expansive figurations in the drama of Shakespeare and his contemporaries. Simply put, we must attend to how cis-sexism gets reproduced through our critical lexicon, and therefore perpetuated in our critical practice. In both our scholarly criticism and our classrooms, we ought to engage the 'transgender capacity' of words and phrases in an effort to raise questions that recognize and grapple with the productive opacities of gender nonconformity.[16] Second, as Valerie Traub has entreated editors who gloss sexual language, 'be candid about what you don't know, allow the ongoing production of sexual knowledge to be on display, including its opacities'.[17] Once and for all, let us say *good riddance!* to that deliberately obfuscating gloss, 'a bawdy pun', which often baffles students into silence concerning questions of embodiment and desire, and *welcome!* to more epistemologically attuned glossing practices that make 'available to readers as many meanings as possible', and allow 'readers to adjudicate between them'.[18] Finally, in our classrooms, I propose that we practice what

---

[13] Joseph Gamble, 'Toward a Trans Philology', *Journal for Early Modern Cultural Studies*, Special Issue: Early Modern Trans Studies, ed. Simone Chess, Colby Gordon and Will Fisher, 19.4 (2019), 26–44; p. 36.

[14] Jeffrey Masten, *Queer Philologies: Sex, Language, and Affect in Shakespeare's Time* (Philadelphia, 2016), p. 15.

[15] Valerie Traub, *Thinking Sex with the Early Moderns* (Philadelphia, 2016), p. 213.

[16] On 'transgender capacity', see David J. Getsy, 'Capacity', *TSQ: Transgender Studies Quarterly* 1 (2014), 47–9. As it operates in early modern drama, cf. Marjorie Rubright, 'Transgender capacity in Thomas Dekker and Thomas Middleton's *The Roaring Girl* (1611)', *Journal for Early Modern Cultural Studies* 19, Special Issue: Early Modern Trans Studies, ed. Chess, Gordon and Fisher, 45–74.

[17] Traub, *Thinking Sex*, p. 214.

[18] Traub, *Thinking Sex*, p. 213.

I characterize as 'speculative philology': on the one hand, invite students to mobilize etymological inquiry for how it opens rather than resolves questions, exploring how it activates a series of if–then propositions about identity, identification and desire; on the other hand, encourage students to operate counter-intuitively, working against the grain of history to ask questions about words that are not on the page. These might include: words that never were (neologisms they invent), words we use today that post-date Shakespeare, or words culled from other languages. Taken together, these strategies may further open our imaginations to the queer and transgender capacities alive in Shakespeare's works, then and now.

THOUGHTS ON GENDER AND CASTING[19]

In theatre, we see many sorts of bodies onstage, all of which were chosen for their role in the performance. *The Oxford Encyclopedia of Theatre and Performance* states, '[c]asting is often based on the theory that certain actors are "right" for certain roles. This sense of "rightness" may derive from culturally determined attitudes toward character types and their physical attributes.'[20] Cross-gender casting is therefore construed as against-the-type casting, and is one of the interesting theatrical devices using the body. Onstage, the bodies work as signifiers, involving the creation of extratextual meanings, and hold a mirror up to society, illuminating social and political attitudes towards gender.

What I would like to reconsider here is gender-blind casting, which along with other blind and against-the-type casting has become a new feature in British theatre. We are living in an age of diversity and inclusivity, where the theatrical representation of diverse bodies is now apparently normalized. So, does this mean we are supposed to forget the gender of a performer and conclude that he/she is just brilliant in the role? This has been a common compliment paid to gender-bending performances. But how can such praise be really positive if gender ceases to be relevant to it?

What does it mean to be blind to gender? Does it mean we ignore the body present (the real body) and see the character (the fictional body) embodied by it? Aren't we treating the body of a performer like a transparent vessel then? Antoine Vitez observes, 'Even if, hypothetically, it [casting] were done blindly, it would find its own balance; everything always takes on (or produces) meanings.'[21] Therefore, there is no blind casting and the body of a performer always signifies something as part of the material realities of a performance situation.

I have reservations about gender blindness or gender-blind approaches towards cross-gender casting. We cannot ignore the 'affective presence' of the body present, or the effect that the body has upon us even before we are conscious of feeling it. The awareness that makes us 'forget' or 'ignore' the gender of the body present may obscure sensations or visceral perceptions we experience in theatre. The female body needs to be recognized rather than neutralized behind a male character in cross-gender casting. As in linguistic obscuring, bodily obscuring only makes it harder to acknowledge more complex and rich meanings animated by the body.

Let me turn to my favourite all-female production series, the Donmar Shakespeare Trilogy, the first instalment of which in 2012 brought a change to the scene of all-female productions in the UK. Lyn Gardner in her *Guardian* article entitled 'All-female Shakespeare? It's about time', writes, 'when you have Shakespeare as your national dramatist, it's harder to separate the plays from 400 years of performance history – a performance history dominated by penises and poetry'.[22] As a feminist, I shared her sentiment and was overjoyed at the production's success. However, as I observed what followed this emancipating development, I came to wonder

---

[19] Kumiko Hilberdink-Sakamoto.
[20] Rosemary Malague, 'Casting', in *Oxford Encyclopedia of Theatre and Performance*, ed. Dennis Kennedy, 2 vols. (Oxford, 2003), vol. 1, p. 231.
[21] Patrice Pavis, *Dictionary of the Theatre: Terms, Concepts, and Analysis* (Toronto, 1998), p. 44.
[22] *The Guardian*, 4 September 2012, www.theguardian.com/stage/theatreblog/2012/sep/04/theatre-shakespeare.

whether the situation has really changed that much, or is simply mirroring the trend in society?

The Donmar Shakespeare Trilogy is a unique example of gender bending without really bending gender. By using a female prison as the framing device, the Trilogy invites the audience to acknowledge the female body, a prison character played by a woman, behind the male body of Shakespeare's masculine character. This way, it is not a work of gender-blind casting; rather, the audience is encouraged, before, after and throughout the performance, to witness gender fluidity with constant reminders of the female body playing both genders.

I would be very happy to see more women playing Shakespeare's male roles and I believe there is no more solid proof of gender performativity than cross-gender casting. In such instances, it is the performer's own empathy with the character and the other gender that constitutes their embodied and therefore lived experience of another person's life. And this emotional response to her own body performing the male gender is a key to explain empowerment through cross-gender acting. For instance, Cush Jumbo expresses her sensory response while playing Antony in *Julius Caesar*: 'You're free, you feel you're transcending something. It made the hairs on the back of my neck stand on end when I did "Friends, Romans, countrymen".'[23]

However, to return to the audience's or a critic's side of the story, being blind to gender could generalize or stabilize perception rather than destabilizing it to explore an interplay of genders. Instead, we should be free to feel the sensations and visceral perception we receive from the body which lives both genders on stage.

Since I spoke at the WSC Roundtable in 2021, cross-gender theatre has changed a great deal. In 2022, Shakespeare's Globe staged a new play, *I, Joan*, which depicted the eponymous character as non-binary. It was labelled 'controversial' even before its opening, but was received well for its high-spirited performance once onstage. Theatrical performance has become a site of struggle, as gender can now be binary or non-binary even in a cross-gender production. Another example of productions that move beyond the traditional binary was the Globe's 'all-female and non-binary' *Titus Andronicus* early in 2023, which offered a unique take on this notoriously violent play. Thus, gender-related casting remains a great eye-opener to us.

We cannot underestimate the impact of theatrical enactment and embodiment on society, existing cultures and individuals, whether performers or audience. Speaking from Japan, where male or female gender-specific acting is a very well-established art form, to the extent that it can be called 'super-binary', too much emphasis on gender stereotypes, I wonder how non-binary approaches will interact with, transform or enrich Japan's existing theatrical traditions.

OPEN-ENDED QUESTIONS[24]

Animated by speculations, provocations and open-ended questions for the fields of gender and sexuality, our roundtable opened onto a Q&A that – while grounded in the specificity of the intersections represented by the panelists – identified topics and pressed questions that continue to animate debate as well as much-needed collaboration in the fields.

First, regarding the capacities of language and its relationship to trans desire and embodiment, to what extent are there resonances or common cause in the panelists' varied approaches to language, especially to pronouns, and how is translation across cultures implicated in these different approaches?

Second, to what extent are we committed to always problematizing or troubling gender? The kind of trans studies practised by Alexa, Marjorie and Madhavi refuses teleological, linear models of gender which would find their fulfilment in

---

[23] 'Cush Jumbo: "There was no makeup, no boys to kiss – all we had was the text and we rocked it"', interviewed by David Jays, *The Guardian*, 23 May 2016, www.theguardian.com/stage/2016/may/23/cush-jumbo-on-an-all-female-julius-caesar-phyllida-lloyd-production.

[24] Marjorie Rubright and Valerie Traub.

relationship to a fixed destination or configuration of desire and identity. What about trans people for whom claiming a specific gender is crucial to a sense of self and who see gender transition as providing a fixed, even essential, identity? How do the appeals of instability, change and transition get balanced with the needs for material or psychological stability, continuity or coherence?

Third, does this issue of our attachment to gender have anything to do with tensions among feminist and trans studies? Kumiko highlights how gender-blind casting is a problematic strategy for advancing feminist goals precisely because it unproblematizes gender. What are the theoretical, methodological and political convergences and divergences across feminist and trans studies that come to light when we explore gender inside Shakespeare studies and performance – and what's lost or occluded when we do so?

Fourth, Judy points to the incommensurability of Western feminist theory with Asian Shakespeare. In precirculated questions, she wondered how the other panelists reconcile Western feminist/queer Shakespearian theory with Asian or Global Shakespeare productions or production cultures? What do you do when the paradigms just don't fit? What accommodations or adjustments can or should be made? Is this even a desirable move? Must or can sisterhood, like Shakespeare, be global?

Fifth, given the imperative within the Anglo-American context to treat gender and sexuality in connection with race, it is interesting that race has not really come up in these short presentations. Does the issue of race seem particularly exigent to feminist, queer and trans work? How has the Black feminist concept of intersectionality travelled within global Shakespeare?

SHAKESPEARE PERFORMANCES IN ENGLAND, 2022–2023

LOIS POTTER, London Productions, 2023

This is my last Shakespeare review for this journal, and a good thing too. Most of the Shakespeare productions I saw this year were really adaptations. Almost all were 'presentist'. This does not mean that I didn't enjoy many of them, just that my particular kind of expertise was largely useless: their ideal reviewer would be a social historian or an expert on popular culture. Because the collective tendency seemed to me significant, I am covering more productions than usual, and, because they were dominated by a directorial vision, I am naming only directors. This is of course unfair to the actors, but the abundance of online reviews means that anyone can supplement my accounts. Directors often seemed to rely on their audience's previous experience or expectations of the plays, which is presumably why they mostly confined themselves to the same small group that everyone already knows.

HISTORICAL PERSPECTIVES: NEOLITHIC LEAR, 1936 MERCHANT, TWELFTH NIGHT FROM CUE SCRIPTS

The programme for Kenneth Branagh's *King Lear*, which he directed and starred in, offered a psychologist's take on the dysfunctional family issues in the play, but also gave some facts about the neolithic period in which the play was supposedly taking place. My heart always sinks when I see that Stonehenge is to be the setting for a play in which the characters are constantly reading, writing and intercepting letters. The actors, in their shaggy, furry clothes, were mostly indistinguishable; we were obviously in a world of very basic human emotions. The more poetic aspects were suggested by the cosmic circle above the stage, where a giant eye looked down indifferently at the human suffering on the circular stage beneath. The play began with Lear encircled by his subjects, banging their wooden staves on the floor in some sort of warrior ceremony. It ended with Edgar, now king of Britain, banging his staff on the floor, as if to say that the entire story might be starting again.

Branagh cast the production entirely from RADA graduates, many of them quite recent ones, as a gesture of thanks to his old drama school. These actors were perfectly competent, but the choppy rhythm of the heavily cut text (two hours, with no interval) gave them too little room in which to develop their roles. Stage time replaced story time: Kent, having supposedly spent an entire night hanging by the wrists, seemed to have suffered no ill effects.

Naturally, what most of the audience wanted to see was Branagh himself as Lear. His decision to play Lear as a man of his own age (sixty-two) made him a more credible father of such young daughters; it may also have been prompted by a fear that impersonating someone 'fourscore and upward' might be seen as a form of 'cripping up' (the term now used, on an analogy with 'blacking up', for impersonating disability). When his daughters reminded him that he was old, we were presumably meant to remember that sixty was indeed old in warrior societies, but many of his lines sounded odd coming from someone so obviously energetic. In *Beginnings*, his 1989 autobiography, he comments on the work of his speech teachers; from the way he stressed some of his final consonants, it sounded as if he was trying to show how well he had learned their lessons. But, if his choices removed much that normally makes the play feel relevant to our own ageing society, the play's most moving scenes were still moving in this production; it may have felt less truncated, and more interesting, to spectators who were less well acquainted with it than an academic reviewer.

The other history-based production was the RSC's *The Merchant of Venice 1936*, which, as its title indicates, was set in the East End of London during the most dangerous period of British fascism. Brigid Larmour adapted and directed it, with Tracy Ann Oberman, who also played a female Shylock. Both women were determined to save the play from its own anti-semitism, and their two-hour, small-cast version made Shylock's story run parallel with the rise of British fascism, as seen in projections of 1930s films and headlines from the British press. There were extensive cuts, especially of the comedy: Launcelot became an Irish, anti-semitic Mary Gobbo. By the time of the trial scene, the Christian characters were wearing black armbands and giving Nazi salutes, and Portia's famous 'mercy' speech was played so harshly as to have no chance of converting Shylock. Whereas some productions with a 1930s setting might have ended with Shylock on his/her way to a concentration camp, this one offered an alternative ending. Judging from the reviews, this touring production was played somewhat differently in different venues, but there was a special frisson for those who saw it at Wilton's Music Hall in London. After her courtroom defeat, and the perfunctory winding-up of the 'ring' plot, Shylock came forward and, joined by the rest of the cast, unrolled a long banner saying 'They shall not pass'; projections depicted the famous battle of Cable Street, just round the corner from Wilton's, in which Oswald Mosley's British blackshirt march was routed by collective anti-fascist action.

Stepping outside the play, Oberman described the role that Wilton's – and her own grandmother – had played in the events of 1936. The effect was to replace an unsatisfactory ending with one that suggested hope of better outcomes through community activism.

Two plays dramatized theatre history of the recent past, both focused on the playing of Hamlet (the character, not the play). Though Jack Thorne's *The Motive and the Cue* (directed by Sam Mendes) gave a number of the actors a chance to speak lines from Shakespeare, it was less concerned with the play than with the uneasy relationship between John Gielgud and Richard Burton, whom Gielgud directed in the role in 1964. Dickie Beau's one-man show, *Re-member Me*, used the recorded voices of a number of *Hamlet* actors (including Gielgud), lip-synched with their photographs, as the actor tried to reassemble a dismembered mannequin, an objective correlative for his recreation of a composite Hamlet. The show, however, was chiefly a celebration of Ian Charleson, who died of AIDS in January 1990 after playing Hamlet for only a few performances in Richard Eyre's National Theatre production. Those who saw him said that he was brilliant; tragically, his performance was never recorded, and his brief life in the role has consequently become part of the Hamlet mythology.

The Globe's *Twelfth Night for One Night*, a single, high-priced performance on 18 September 2023, claimed to be showing us how the play would have been given in 1602 – except that it had a Director (Blanche McIntyre) and women played roles originally written for boys. The actors had learned their lines in isolation from cue scripts, followed by a couple of sessions with the director; there had been 'virtual calls' for the music and jigs, but the company had met together only at 10 a.m. on the day of performance. The music by Tim Sutton had apparently been composed specially for this production and the programme also credits a choreographer.

The result (given in Elizabethan costumes and without scenery apart from a box tree) was not all that different from an ordinary performance, except for the presence of an onstage prompter in costume who played several small parts and was amusingly worked into the action (e.g., Olivia told him, in his servant role, to leave, and he insisted, in his prompter role, on staying). There was surprisingly little need for him. Like their Elizabethan counterparts, many of the actors had worked together before and probably knew the play (moreover, the text had been fairly heavily cut). The rapturous spectators around me in the yard loved the moments when actors asked for a prompt or ad-libbed, and wondered aloud whether most other productions weren't over-rehearsed. It was a welcome return to the spontanteity that used to characterize the late lamented 'Read Not Dead': staged readings of non-Shakespearian drama which stopped during lockdown and, at the time of writing, have still not been restarted.

THE WANAMAKER PLAYHOUSE: *TITUS ANDRONICUS* AND *THE WINTER'S TALE*

Both the Globe and the Wanamaker can generally count on full houses, as they attract people who simply want to see the theatre. The Wanamaker's two winter productions were, however, a challenge for much of their audience. The most enjoyable part of *Titus Andronicus* (directed by Jude Christian) were the songs by Bourgeois & Maurice, which made fun of the appetite for horror and bloodshed that had supposedly brought us to see the play in the first place. The production did its best to disappoint us: a play notorious for depicting the rape and mutilation of a woman was staged by an all-female cast; the violence was staged as make-believe, with visible sound effects, and each character's death was indicated by the snuffing out of a candle, a good use of the theatre's most distinctive feature. Characters announced their identity when they entered, a necessary help to spectators, because the doubling of so many roles and the pyjama costumes of the cast made them look virtually identical. Even so, I doubt that most spectators knew what was going on.

Sean Holmes's *Winter's Tale* took the word 'tragicomedy' apart, recognizing that the play juxtaposes rather than harmonizes its two genres. The Sicilia scenes took place in the Wanamaker Playhouse and were given a stripped-down, modernist production which never acknowledged the presence of its audience. The play opened with Leontes's family at a very regimented dinner, placing napkins over their heads in order (as I learned from other reviews) to experience the full fragrance of a dish of ortolans. All the action took place around that table and Leontes remained onstage throughout. The first three acts were so heavily cut that the trial scene had none of its usual power. It looked as if the director wanted to get out of Sicilia as soon as possible.

Bohemia was located in the Globe Theatre. Of course, this meant that the audience had to move between the two theatres and, as the Wanamaker's capacity is only 353, as opposed to the Globe's potential 1,570, this logistical nightmare threatened to dominate the production itself. Thus, the Bohemia scenes came as even more of a relief than usual, with plenty of audience participation. Autolycus gave something of a comic tour de force, speaking and singing a mixture of his own lines and Shakespeare's, and doing his best to achieve rapport with an uncomfortable, chilly audience, some of whom were even persuaded to join in the sheepshearing dance. He also managed the transition to Sicilia (and to the Wanamaker), where he was given a monologue incorporating (some of) the lines of the three Gentlemen who describe the reunion of Perdita with her father. The statue scene took place in near-darkness, making it hard to know whether one was looking at a statue or a living person, and it lacked its usual mystery and emotion. Instead, the emphasis was on the precariousness of the comic ending. Leontes's puzzling line 'What? Look on my brother!' was played as a sudden flare-up of jealousy, and for a moment it looked as if the whole story might start again. The play ended with a song, whose last line – 'When that I wander far and near / I then do go most right' – struck me as a possible rationale for the whole production.

THE GLOBE SEASON

The Globe's *Comedy of Errors* and *A Midsummer Night's Dream*, though aimed at a mainstream audience at the height of summer, were not dully predictable crowd-pleasers. Sean Holmes's *Errors* provided plenty of opportunities for audience interaction – as in the dialogue about hair and wit, with glances at specific spectators – and boats 'sailed' through the groundlings to reach the stage. The play began with almost too much of a bang: as Aegeon waited his turn to be executed, another prisoner tried to bolt for freedom, was dragged back and realistically decapitated; the head was tossed into the yard, from which someone hastily tossed it back. Not surprisingly, the audience reaction drowned out Aegeon's opening lines. This, and the melee that followed Aegeon's one-day reprieve, set the tone of the play: awareness of its darker side – the beatings, the dysfunctional marriage – was accompanied, and sometimes undercut, by metatheatrical jokes. For spectators who had noticed that Philip Cumbus was doubling the role of the Duke with that of Dr Pinch, one such joke came when, as the Duke, he listened with increasing annoyance to the Ephesian Antipholus's grotesque description of the doctor, his other self.

Elle While's *A Midsummer Night's Dream* will probably be remembered for one of its casting choices. Hermia was played by Francesca Mills, an excellent actor who has a form of dwarfism. This naturally meant that Lysander's cruel lines to her in the climactic forest scene ('Get you gone, you dwarf!') drew gasps of horror from the audience. The other striking performance was the sinister, green-faced Puck: when Hermia briefly woke up and saw this creature bending over her, she screamed, and Puck, putting her back to sleep, told her to 'wake *when I am gone*'. The amateur actors, all female, were dominated by Bottom (or *Botome*, as she prefers it pronounced), furious that her death scene got laughs from its audience. The child over whom Oberon and Titania squabble (a baby wrapped in white) was present in all her early scenes, tenderly looked after by the fairy queen and her followers until, spellbound by Bottom, they all apparently forgot about it. When Puck came on at the end he appeared to be carrying the child, but on 'I am sent with broom before', he unrolled the bundle, which now became a broom. All along, it had been an empty pretext for a plot that no longer mattered.

At the end of the summer the theatre brought on two more innovative, and hence controversial, productions. An outdoor theatre is obviously unable to create the sinister darkness which *Macbeth* seems to require, but Abigail Graham's *Macbeth* went out of its way to deny the audience any sense of atmosphere or the supernatural. In a sort of prologue, Lady Macbeth and her husband came downstage carrying a bundle that seemed to be a baby. As an upside-down tree rose from the middle of the stage, the couple turned away, letting the empty cloth waft in the air. They were expressionless throughout, but a chorus had meanwhile been singing words from *Richard III* ('Sorrow breaks seasons and reposing hours, / Makes the night morning and the noontide night') that explained the inversion of the natural order and the horror of what follows as the result of the loss of a child. As if to add to the couple's pain, children were more visible than usual in the play: the act 1 messenger was replaced by a pregnant Lady Macduff, who arrived with her son to tell Lady Macbeth of Duncan's approach; Siward's son, the last person Macbeth kills, was played as very young. All three children became apparitions in the cauldron scene.

The smallness of the cast meant that there was virtually no court for Duncan (played as female), apart from Ross (also female). Macduff was the sergeant who had saved Malcolm from captivity; Donalbain was omitted, so Malcolm told the audience of his plan to escape to England. As in many productions before the twentieth century, the witches were played by male comedians. Sometimes they wore yellow hazmat suits and wheeled gurneys with bodies on them, sometimes long-nosed masks (Figure 23). In a particularly obvious bit of Grand Guignol, their 'cauldron' was a blender into which one of them put disgustingly realistic items while another was busy eviscerating a corpse and a third read out directions

23 *Macbeth*, dir. Abigail Graham. Ben Caplan, Calum Callaghan and Ferdy Roberts as Witches, Max Bennett as Macbeth. Photo: Johan Persson / ArenaPAL. www.arenapal.com.

from a recipe book. (In one performance, the blender needed some persuasion to work and the witch muttered, 'Technology!') Sometimes they became characters in the play, as in the harrowing sleepwalking scene where they spoke the lines of the Doctor, the Lady in waiting, and Seyton. The Doctor's 'infected minds / To their deaf pillows will discharge their secrets', far from being a compassionate reaction to his patient's misery, was a warning that she needed to be kept from saying too much; putting on rubber gloves, the others followed her offstage. We knew that Malcolm's later report of her suicide was a convenient fiction.

The absence of the supernatural also meant an absence of grandeur. Graham did not want 'great' performances, even from the Macbeth couple. Banquo's pleasant remarks about the habits of the 'temple-haunting martlet' were an attempt to fill the awkward silence while Duncan and her court waited for their host and hostess to appear, with the further embarrassment that only the Lady arrived (hastily pulling on the jacket of her hideous trouser suit), giving no explanation of Macbeth's absence. The utter lack of sympathy with the play's notions of good and evil was evident in Macduff's reaction to Malcolm's assurances of his chastity: a muttered 'Wierdo!' It was the singing of the Chorus, between scenes and sometimes as commentary, that provided most of the emotion, but located it in a past that had nothing to do with the world we saw.

Theatres now give 'trigger-warnings' about the content of their plays; in the case of Shakespeare, it would make more sense to warn them about the productions. *Macbeth* offered a genuinely new take on the play, which was interesting but not very appealing to an audience. *As You Like It*, directed by Ellen McDougall, was positively divisive. There were some walk-outs at every performance, and the theatre website had to tell spectators that it was recommended only for age fifteen and above, probably because of its unabashed celebration of queerness. The scenes between the female Orlando, in her painted moustache, and the non-binary Rosalind (who later sported a similar, obviously fake, moustache) were delightful, while the transgender Celia was possibly the best I have ever seen – in fact, too good for a role that peters out at the end (Figure 24). However, McDougall seemed

24 *As You Like It*, dir. Ellen McDougall. Nina Bowers as Rosalind and Macy-Jacob Seelochan as Celia. Photo: Ellie Kurttz / ArenaPAL. www.arenapal.com.

to have left the rest of the play for the actors (mostly men) to do what they liked. The Forest of Arden was a commune, a place of unlimited (sexual) possibilities. The songs (led by Emanuel Akwafo, who played Amiens as a Lord of Misrule) were modern pop numbers, with only a tangential relation to the play. They were noisy and the dancing went on for a long time. For some reason, Jaques, despite his supposed misanthropy, hugged everyone he talked to and, having said farewell to the cast at the end, came back as soon as he could to join the dance. In place of the Second Brother, the wicked Duke himself described his conversion and was embraced by his brother. Love was apparently the solution to all problems. In both *As You Like It* productions this year (and in the 2022 production by Northern Broadsides), the play ended with Rosalind still not restored to her 'real' female identity. At the end, she performed a short balletic sequence which, like the epilogue it replaced, depended on confusing actor and role. Who or what did Orlando think he was marrying?

TRAGEDIES

Rather surprisingly, the emails from the Rose Theatre, Kingston, urged us to 'Celebrate the arrival of May with maypoles and Morris dancing in *Richard III*!' But, yes, it was sort of celebratory. Adjoa Andoh, who directed as well as playing Richard, set this story of tyranny, treachery and revenge not in the usual dystopia, medieval or modern, but in the timeless world of lovely rural England, warm, tree-shaded and very, very white. All the cast, apart from Andoh, were white, and the basic costume was the white tunic and trousers worn by Morris dancers. The extensive cuts to the text included many of the lines about Richard's deformity, since Andoh thinks that blackness in a white society is equivalent to deformity. Richard began his opening soliloquy under a tree, but when Morris dancers appeared, singing part of his lines, they put a pig mask on him and imprisoned him within the ribbons of their maypole dance. The ghosts were Green Men.

Though reviewers generally seemed to want the production to be more obviously dark and political than it was, it's clear that Andoh wanted her *Richard III* to be the enjoyable crowd-pleaser that it always used to be. It was often funny and it never became bloody. In place of the brutal onstage violence of most recent *Richard*s, executions took place in shadow play behind a screen, followed by the sounds of cawing crows. In the midst of Richmond's sincerely delivered final speech, the dead Richard started to rise, saying, 'There is no creature loves me', and, left alone, he looked upward at a beam of light, rather as Olivier's Richard, in the film, looked up at his cross-shaped sword hilt. The play was not obviously 'anti-racist' – yet it gave a visual equivalent for something that dominated this year's productions: a basic clash between the idealized, homogenized England of the past and the multiple kinds of diversity now demanding to be given their place in the modern one.

Rebekah Frecknall, who had played Juliet two years earlier at the Globe, directed the Almeida's *Romeo and Juliet* as a synthesis of the best-known moments in the play and its afterlife in other genres (Prokofiev's music, *West Side Story*, the Baz Luhrmann film), omitting nearly everything else. The prologue, which makes the tragic ending a foregone conclusion, was projected, one line at a time, onto a wall while the actors came on, one by one, to beat against it until it collapsed, perhaps offering the hope that, this time, the story might end differently. The production was even more focused than usual on the lovers, who were often onstage during other characters' scenes. Mercutio played with Juliet's hair as he spoke the Queen Mab speech. The Friar, Nurse and even the parents, were all younger than usual and sympathetically portrayed, though their roles were minimal in this version. The most famous lines remained (with a surprising amount of wordplay), beautifully spoken. By contrast with the Globe production, which had emphasized the awfulness of Romeo's death, Frecknall ended the play with Juliet's still more horrible one: she clutched at the dead Romeo, screamed, ran around the monument, desperately tried to find how to use the dagger, and died in agony. The very real power of this production came from the fact that it gave audiences the essence of the play: the *Romeo and Juliet* that they remember, or imagine, not the one that they may or may not have read.

Many of the other productions of tragedies came from small, experimental theatre companies. When I saw Frantic Assembly's *Othello* (dir. Scott Graham) at the Lyric Hammersmith, its mainly young audience was audibly shocked at a lot of what went on. The play, heavily cut, was set in a bar with a pool table, scoreboards and a juke box, which spewed out loud music and pounding noises for at least 20 minutes before the start. Much of the story was told through dance sequences: Brabantio, apparently a mafioso, introduced Othello to the club and then vanished from the play. Characters conversed while playing pool. Iago often eavesdropped on other characters. The frank conversation between Desdemona and Emilia took place – where many such conversations probably do take place – in the toilet cubicles. Othello finally killed himself (offstage) with broken glass from the toilet window; Iago was killed not by Othello but by the other men, whose macho code he had offended. Though I found the loudness hard to take and could not always follow the adaptation, it struck me as a powerful retelling, which somehow managed to make the words something that these barely educated characters might plausibly say; Desdemona, in particular, turned out to be genuinely moving as she tried to retain some sort of integrity in a bewildering situation.

How small-scale can a production be and still be recognizable? Most current productions of *Macbeth* make as much as they can of the relationship between the central couple; in *Macbeth / Partners in Greatness*, directed by Mark Leipacher for The Faction, they were the only characters in the play and the scenes that took place before Macbeth returned to his wife were dealt with through letters between them, while projections explained the action further with Brechtian titles to each scene. As at the Globe, the couple's childlessness was stressed. Even on the battlefield, Macbeth was carrying a small teddy bear. The murder of Banquo was symbolized by Macbeth's multiple stabbing of a teddy bear, and Banquo's ghost took the form of an enormous robotic teddy, invisible to everyone else, which came straight towards him with its paws reaching for his neck. (The audience found this hilarious.) The line of kings that stretches to the crack of doom was a series of small teddies. Lady Macbeth (here called Bellona because of the reference to 'Bellona's bridegroom') fought beside her husband in the final scenes. Her last line, before she shot herself, was 'We have no children.'

Flabbergast Theatre performed *Macbeth* at Southwark Playhouse with a cast of eight. The Macbeths (Henry Maynard – who was also director and designer – and Briony O'Callaghan) were part of an ensemble of muddy-looking figures from which characters and puppets occasionally emerged. They had discovered some new puns: Duncan said that praising Macbeth was 'a banquet to me', punning on Banquo's name, to the obsequious laughter of the court; Lady Macbeth, welcoming the banquet guests, found a pun on 'meat' and 'meet'. Despite these local effects (the Porter was also given a great deal of space), I could not find the theme announced in the publicity – male fear of female power. The production felt more like an experiment with different theories of acting (the company had worked with Grotowski) that did not quite add up.

Lazarus Theatre Company (dir. Ricky Dukes) gave '*Hamlet* without the adults'. It opened with its cast of damaged young people, in a group therapy session, taking it in turn to explain what they had been made to do (on orders, we realized, from an adult): for example, Guildenstern pointed out that he had had to betray his best friend. Claudius, Gertrude and Polonius were godlike voices from above the stage; only the Ghost was visible, though his words were voiced by a number of different actors. This production was meant particularly for schools, where Laertes's final cry – not 'The king's to blame' but 'The adult's to blame!' – must have been particularly well received. And in fact the adaptation, though too long, did bring out the extent to which the play's adults use their children for their own ends. The guiltiest adult was, of course, Shakespeare himself.

COMEDIES

As with some of the tragedies, two comedies this year were virtually new plays, yet with their Shakespearian originals still clearly recognizable. The National Youth Theatre's *Much Ado About Nothing* (dir. Josie Daxter) was cleverly adapted by Debris Stevenson as a version of the TV show *Love Island*, in which the participants are constantly being manipulated by the producer (a conflation of Leonato and Don Pedro – and, potentially, the author) for the sake of audience ratings. Like the show (which I know only from this parody), the stage production was designed to show off its performers, so lines were redistributed to allow more people to have decent speaking parts. The adaptation provided a good explanation for the behaviour of Don John, a female contestant in attention-seeking bright pink: having realized that she had been cast as the villain of the show, she was determined to get herself as much publicity as possible. Dogberry was an incompetent psychiatrist attached to the programme. Projections of the 'chat', meanwhile, showed the hilariously moronic reactions of a fictitious online audience.

Taming Who?, a production of the Intermission Youth Theatre (dir. Stevie Basuala), was equally delightful. The adaptation, by Darren Raymond, made Petruchio a Nigerian student in London who is so determined not to return home to his mother that he tells her he's married; she promptly announces that she's coming to London to meet his wife, so he's desperate enough to marry the girl that everyone else dislikes. Most of the language was modern and racy, though a few Shakespearian lines were heard from time to time, usually greeted with bewilderment by the person to whom they were addressed. The basic characters and situations of the play could still be recognized and the cultural differences helped make sense of the ending, especially when the formidable African mother acted as the mouthpiece for the idea that wives must be totally submissive.

SHAKESPEARE PERFORMANCES IN ENGLAND, 2022–2023

CONCLUSION: ADAPTATION, TRANSLATION OR . . . ?

The rules of casting seem to have been much the same this year as last: no one should play a disability that is not theirs and no white actor should play a member of a different race; there is an increasing insistence that everyone should share the sexual orientation of the character they play, except when women are playing men (I saw my third female Kent this year; Adam in both versions of *As You Like It* was female; so was the entire company of *Pyramus and Thisbe* in the *Dream*). Emphasis on inclusivity does not apply to the employment of child actors, who were present only in the Globe *Macbeth* and in the Wanamaker *Winter's Tale*. Elsewhere, adults usually took their roles. In the Flabbergast *Macbeth*, all the children were played by puppets, as was young York in the Kingston *Richard III* (the production's least good idea).

What struck me most about this year's productions, however, was their uneasiness with the plays' language in the mouths of characters so obviously modern. Ironically, given the Globe's earlier reputation for historicism, most of its productions were quite free with the texts. *As You Like It* had what it called a prologue, in which Jaques told the audience that he would be delivering one of the most famous speeches in Shakespeare. When the time came, he stood centre stage and played it straight out front, like a sixth-former at a school assembly, and got applause at the end. (Interestingly, when I saw the production again a month later, he made the speech less presentational and there was no applause.) As with the Wanamaker's *Titus Andronicus*, which commented on the play through its songs, this *As You Like It* was literally 'in your face', with messages sent, word by word, on a wire across the theatre: 'You are wild pretending to be tame', 'There are more kinds of love than you know'. The play's original songs had been replaced by modern equivalents, pop songs with explicit words and a message that must have been even clearer to those who, unlike me, recognized the sources.

The point of all these directorial choices seemed to be that much of the play's language no longer belonged to its characters or to its original context. Rosalind and Celia didn't like the line 'I am a woman: when I think, I must speak', and were clearly holding it at arm's length. The characters in *Macbeth* often seemed uncomfortable with their own language: Malcolm wondered ineffectually whether he should say something when he was made prince of Cumberland; Banquo, hearing Queen Duncan say 'Let me enfold thee to my heart', was obviously unsure whether he should take this literally. The *Midsummer Night's Dream* treated Theseus's famous lines about 'the lunatic, the lover, and the poet' as a drunken attempt at profundity, and Hippolyta, equally drunk, giggled in response.

Given this uneasiness about language, it was appropriate that one of the Globe's 'Research in Action' sessions was devoted to the work of Play On Shakespeare, a project (based at the Oregon Shakespeare Festival) to produce performable translations of Shakespeare into modern English. We were given some idea of the effect through performances of some bits of dialogue, first in the original, then in translation. They were not fully modernized, since the verse form was retained and, in some cases, even the grammar. I would have to hear a complete performance to judge the success of this enterprise. Responses to the samples were predictably split. Some people enjoy watching a Shakespeare production precisely because they know that they are hearing 400-year-old language; others find that language a barrier. I am reminded of what Hugh Quarshie said with regard to his production of *Othello*: 'the plays are not timeless; the stories are timeless'.

Yet there are other ways of looking at the language. I have already noted that Intermission Youth Theatre used some Shakespeare lines as part of the generally modern text of *Taming Who?* (my difficulty with the London slang of the black swingers was the counterpart of their difficulty with Shakespeare). Even more interesting was the

Shakespearian infiltration in a production by teenage members of this theatre company. *Excluded*, described as 'devised by the company, based on the world of Shakespeare', is set in a classroom where students from appallingly difficult backgrounds (Hamlet, Othello, Romeo, Beatrice, Isabella, etc.) are trying to study for crucial exams. Though most of the dialogue is modern, the characters occasionally speak lines from the play to which they belong. In the talkback afterwards, the actors were asked how they felt about this, given their lack of any earlier study of the texts, and I got the impression that simply learning to say the words had helped break down a barrier. The Folger Shakespeare Library, on Shakespeare's birthday, always used to have an event where schoolchildren took it in turn to stand on the reproduction Elizabethan stage and speak five memorized lines of Shakespeare.

Another possibility was suggested by the production I have kept for last, which, for me, was the most satisfying one of the year (in fact, it opened in December 2022, just too late for my last review): Josie Rourke's production/adaptation of *As You Like It* at the new @Sohoplace theatre (Figure 25). Last year's *Henry V* at the Donmar Warehouse provided surtitles translating the French dialogue, but this *As You Like It* was, to my knowledge, the first production to give surtitles (on screens at gallery level) for the entire text of the play. Though these were obviously intended for the hearing-impaired, this was not their only use. Many people, even when not hearing-impaired, have difficulty in taking in information given orally, especially when it is in an unfamiliar idiom. The surtitles translated the lines that were signed in British Sign Language (BSL) by Celia, a deaf performer; they described sound effects (telling us, for instance, when the piano was playing the 'Forest of Arden theme'); and when Orlando, instead of hanging his verses on the trees, threw them into the air, they miraculously appeared on the screens.

The production thematized the use of signing even more than the 2018 one at the Globe: Celia's father forced her to communicate by speech in her desperate attempts to protest against Rosalind's banishment, whereas Oliver, almost at once after meeting her, attempted to learn to communicate by signing. Rourke also allowed the play to communicate through music. This new theatre's technologically sophisticated space allowed designer Robert Jones to have multiple trap doors, including one large enough to take a piano, the only thing onstage apart from the mat for the wrestling match. Actors stood and lay on it. Adam got his secret stash from inside it. Visible in the opening scenes as part of a glitzy court, it later sank partway through the floor and became part of the forest of Arden, covered with leaves and flowers. The Composer/Pianist (Michael Bruce) was very much part of the action. Characters, especially Touchstone, sometimes addressed him or strummed the piano themselves or urged him to play, but he was given only one syllable, sung as the final beat of one of Touchstone's songs.

'Blow, blow, thou winter wind', which the cast sang at the beginning, set the tone for the play with its refrain combining cynicism ('Most friendship is feigning, most loving mere folly') with the conclusion that, nevertheless, 'this life is most jolly'. Jaques (female) seemed to live in a perpetual autumn, under a localized fall of leaves, and a localized snowfall accompanied Adam's death. (Both of this year's productions assumed that Adam died and was then 'reborn' as Corin, though this means delaying Corin's first appearance.) The adaptation did all the current 'trendy' things – cut and telescoped scenes and characters, was 'inclusive' in its casting, and added music wherever possible. But these choices felt part of the production's imaginative world. The heavy cutting brought out striking effects: Celia was at her lowest point, realizing that she was going to lose the person she loved most, just before the arrival of Oliver. There was a particularly brilliant transition from Touchstone's 'much virtue in if' to Rosalind's own speech with all the 'if's in it, as if Touchstone somehow knew what she had in mind and, moreover, understood Stanislavsky's

25 *As You Like It*, dir. Josie Rourke. Nathan Queeley-Dennis as Silvius, Tom Edden as Duke Frederick, Dickon Gough as Charles, Alfred Enoch as Orlando, Allie Daniel as Amiens, Michael Bruce as Pianist, Syakira Moeladi as Hisperia, and Martha Plimpton as Jaques.
Photo: Johan Persson / ArenaPAL. www.arenapal.com.

'magic if'. This *As You Like It* gave audiences the visual and aural beauty that they wanted from this comedy, while offering new takes on its gender-fluidity and its varying textures of light and shade. It was inclusive not only of its diverse cast but of its entire audience, an achievement that eluded many other productions in 2023.

ELEANOR RYCROFT, *Productions Outside London, 2022–2023*

COVID-19 seemed like a distant memory as theatres re-opened in 2022; faces went unmasked, and houses seemed fairly full as I began travelling the country for performances of Shakespeare. Perhaps surprisingly, few performances focused on or even contained traces of the pandemic. Instead, other pressing social concerns came to the fore, including the climate emergency, intergenerational conflict – recalling the supposed disparities between Boomers, Gen X, Millennials and Gen Z – as well as questions of representation and identity, especially regional and national identity. I saw plays in pairs in the hope that productive comparisons would ensue, and common themes did emerge. The two *Midsummer Night's Dream*s were focused on issues of language and translation, while the two *Hamlet*s shared a concern with child and adult dynamics. Both *Tempest*s interrogated issues of ecology and climate change, while the *Macbeth*s foregrounded the contemporary through their aesthetics and appeal to new audiences. Despite this attempt at balance, however, much of this review will be weighted towards my stand-out production of the year, Deborah Warner's visionary *Tempest* at the Ustinov Studio, a production delivering an urgent message about climate crisis that demanded to be both heard and heeded.

TWO TEMPESTS

The Tempest, *Dir. Deborah Warner, Ustinov Studio,*
20 July 2022

It is something of a mystery as to why Deborah Warner, one of the world's preeminent directors, has taken up artistic directorship of the Ustinov Studio, the experimental wing of the Theatre Royal Bath. Coming directly from the most magnificent theatres and opera houses of Europe to a tiny space in the south-west of England, Warner pledged to revive 'major classics alongside the development of new plays / theatre work', and set out her stall with an inaugural production of *The Tempest*.[1] She brought with her some of the most accomplished theatremakers in the world, including the designer Christof Hetzer who co-created her German translation of the play, *Der Sturm*, at the Salzburg Festival in 2016. The Ustinov *Tempest* seems to be a revival of this production, aesthetically at least.

When first entering the space, a stage manager walked around with a dustpan and brush doing some last-minute clearing of a stage littered with stuff, notably the slabs of wood, copper and stone piled up against the walls. This sweeping of the stage immediately focused attention on the debris and detritus of existence – a reading that would be elaborately developed in a performance which explored and excoriated the Anthropocene. Above the stage, a cloud was suspended. On the floor a pile of what looked like junk was carefully placed at the front of the stage – a bottle of water, a jug, a plastic bowl, some driftwood that would become a staff – not rubbish at all, in fact, but Prospero's treasured possessions. But possessions are always inextricable from possession, and in

---

[1] www.whatsonstage.com/bath-theatre/news/the-tempest-deborah-warner-ustinov-studio_56309.html.

addition to *The Tempest*'s usual questions about power, rightful rule and tyranny, Warner also examined ideas of ownership through an ecocritical lens.

The scenography was determined by natural elements – there was a pool of mud, or possibly a cesspit, stage left, and a small pit of rocks at the back of the stage. Suggestions of nature were disrupted by the stark modernity of a video screen at the back of the stage which displayed exquisite HD images. Across this screen a pristine parade of strange creatures danced and revelled as we waited for the play to begin, like medieval mummers at the top of an illuminated manuscript. It would become clear over the course of the performance that these were the island spirits, who, like Ariel, were near-omnipresent throughout.

Ariel was also onstage as we entered the venue, a film of static projected onto his back and wearing a T-shirt which told us in an unmistakably concrete way that he was 'Invisible'. His very presence communicated a concern with the material and the immaterial, the substantial and insubstantial, that was threaded throughout the performance. The static that accompanied his every stage appearance insinuated that Ariel was a ghost-in-the-machine, a glitch. And this idea was brilliantly furthered through harnessing Dickie Beau's sublime powers of lip-synching: Ariel's dialogue was entirely delivered through the mouthing of a pre-recorded performance by his mentor, Fiona Shaw. Invoking another dimension to the concept of 'possession' in the play, Shaw's disembodied voice was always strange and alien to Beau's body. The precision of his lip-synching was matched by an uncanny precision of movement: nothing was wasted in Beau's performance, every gesture and look fraught with significance.

Beau's lip-synching helped to establish a fascinating and fundamental tension between the corporeal and the ethereal in the play. All of the visions of the isle were shown to be unreal – the masque was a model box in which the previous mummer-spirits were revealed as puppets manipulated by Ariel. Elsewhere, these spirits only ever manifested as mannequins, as characters on-screen, or were – in a truly magical bit of theatrical creation – glimpsed via the delighted reactions of the shipwrecked Italians, lying on their fronts to marvel at the spirits' smurf-like antics. Ariel, too, was only ever caught through reflection and refraction, summoned by Prospero (Nicholas Woodeson) through a backwards mirror, a mere trick of the light. Such moments emphasized *The Tempest*'s well-known interest in artifice and nature.

In this way, Warner's was at times quite an 'old-fashioned' *Tempest* in that it explored theatricality, truth and representation. As the model box was flown out of the space during the masque sequence, Ferdinand and Miranda (Piero Neel-Mee and Tanvi Virmani) covered their eyes with their hands to continue watching it, a theatrical invocation of VR sets that moved us from early modern to 21st-century modes of entertainment in an instant. Equally remarkable was the play's staging, and the implications of space and place that Warner and the performers were able to suggest through ingenious blocking and proxemics – the tiny stage variously becoming jungle or a bog or Prospero's cell, depending on the deft positioning of slabs and bodies.

Warner's major innovation of *The Tempest*, however, was to press questions about fiction and reality into the service of environmental critique. The Lilliputian spirits of the isle may delight the Italians with their minute antics, but everything that is joyful and magical in the play is only invisible or imagined. That everything kept on vanishing became difficult to divorce from the various incarnations of plastic that appeared during the performance – a perished piece aloft a stick to spellbind Ferdinand; the single-use bottle of water which Prospero drank from; the shower curtain which acted as the door to his cell; a disposable rain cape which functioned as an especially rubbish 'magic garment'. And then there was Ariel's Harpy with a face wrapped in clingfilm, fighting to free itself from suffocation. *The Tempest*'s preoccupation with man-made interventions, with the art of representation and anthropocentric privilege to produce particular versions of the world, were plagued by these recurrences of plastic and waste. Plastic was simultaneously a magical prop – a 'baseless fabric' (4.1.168) – and a very real and poisonous substance which clogs up the oceans and kills delicate spirits like Ariel, as well as the creatures of the sea.

This mutability of plastic led to a reassessment of the other 'natural' materials on the stage and, sure enough, the wood proved to be plywood, the stone merely a painted veneer, and the copper bore the smears of human touch. The onstage mud was contained in a neat square, and the pebbles and rocks were in fact the decorative kind that you might find in a garden centre. The staging of the island's natural environment was therefore thoroughly artificial – another man-made production – and the fact that the stage was absolutely littered took on ecocritical force. There was stuff everywhere, too much stuff, reminding me of Jonah Hill's satirical elegy at the end of the apocalyptic film *Don't Look Up*: 'There's dope stuff, like material stuff, like sick apartments and watches, and cars, um, and clothes and shit that could all go away, and I don't wanna see that stuff go away.' We might be such stuff as dreams are made on, but we also harbour our dreams in stuff – stuff that will destroy the very planet whose resources we plunder to make it. Humans were decidedly less than dreamy-stuff in Warner's vision – they became part of the litter, the dirty detritus of existence; they were sweaty, leaky, wholly natural animals who constantly extruded beyond themselves to make the world that little bit filthier and more cluttered.

Warner's deep and multifaceted investment in what is natural and unnatural also shone new light on the relationships in the play. Miranda and Ferdinand's courtship was a sweet and simple encounter, during which Miranda – not knowing the rules – made them up as she went along. This resulted in their betrothal occurring while both lay face-down on the floor, head-to-head, awkwardly reaching for each other's hands. Ferdinand, enthralled by this guileless woman, mirrored her, relinquishing stale, heteronormative European frameworks to let her take the lead on what love should look like. Miranda was always more powerful in the relationship, playful, sensual, earthy and devoid of affectation. And yet this was a very male-dominated production. The fact that Miranda lacked awareness of her inferiority only threw European misogyny into sharp relief. In the same way as Ferdinand argues that she is a foil for womankind, her lack of socialization commented on other strange 'civil' structures too, and the throwaway sexism of the play rang out like a bell when viewed alongside Miranda's clear-eyed certainty that she has a place in this 'brave new world' (5.1.217). Miranda's physicality of crawling on the floor, sitting cross-legged or slouching while everyone else stood – brilliantly animated by Virmani – indicated something bestial and childish which distanced her from European standards of decorum. So you feared for Miranda in Italy – for how her indoctrination into feminine standards would strip her of bodily freedom, how her open-armed love of mankind would be replaced by the demand for her subordination to them.

Male domination was not only a European phenomenon though. In this production Caliban (Edward Hogg) was just a man, and one in filthy vest and underpants that barely concealed the outline of his genitals. That he represented a clear sexual threat to Miranda was intensified by the proximity to performers that the Ustinov affords. While scared of Caliban, however, Miranda didn't think herself lesser, and continued to show care towards her tormentor by, for instance, tying his shoelace, demonstrating that it is kindness rather than strength which elevates us. Yet this was a distinction that Prospero himself straddled uneasily, and, in using physical force to protect his daughter, he brutalized Miranda as well as Caliban by making her witness to his violence, reactions that demonstrated that political power is maintained through acts of aggression.

The production therefore explored ideas of kindness and unkindness. While Prospero and Miranda were shown to largely control the island, they were also both shown acting with parental care, for instance when Prospero wrapped his own clothes around Caliban's waist as he acknowledged the 'thing of darkness' to be his (5.1.330). By covering Caliban's soiled underpants with his shirt, Prospero demonstrated a paternal duty towards an unacculturated being. However, this reading also produces problems because, if Miranda is inherently kind and Prospero merely a domineering parent, then Caliban is placed in the position of savage native who does not share the nobility and civility of Europeans. This seems like a retrogressive reading given the critical responses to Caliban in recent decades, particularly those emerging from the field of premodern critical race studies. It was telling, then, that at the moment of Caliban's 'This Isle is full o'noises' speech (3.2.148), he seemed to be temporarily possessed by the spirit of Ariel, Hogg channelling Fiona Shaw's clipped tones in his delivery. It was a subtle, easily missed choice, but a challenging one. Taking away even his poetry situates Caliban decisively in the barbaric, rapacious, inhumane mould of prior responses to the character. And – while this was very much *not* an 'American' reading of the play – the haunting of Warner's production by such versions nevertheless indirectly endorsed a throwback idea that native inhabitants are in need of the civilizing force of colonialism. While the fact that Shakespeare's closest representation of an Indigenous person is also a rapist is a crux which every director must deal with – ignoring the problem doesn't make it go away.

At the same time, the political dynamics were not monolithic, and there was a sustained depiction of the shipwrecked Italians as being equally malicious and unkind, their tuxedos belying their impropriety as they spitefully sniped at each other as if at a dinner party rather than marooned on an island. It was not long before the sniping turned to violence between Sebastian and the King (Luke Mullins and Derek Hutchison), revealing again the masculine force that underpins the veneer of politesse. Antonio (Finbar Lynch) and Sebastian stalked the edges of the stage during these scenes, suave and malignant, ever ready to mock sincerity, drip poison or puncture idealization, with Lynch, in particular, giving a superb performance as an Iago-like Antonio. Their malevolence destroyed total redemption and forgiveness up until the very last moments of the play – Sebastian noisily walking over the rocks to show his lack of joy at the union of Miranda and Ferdinand, with the last laugh given literally to Antonio, who sniggered scornfully in Prospero's face before his prologue. The poison remained in the system.

In this toxic playworld, Ariel's cleanliness and freedom from a speck of dirt was absolute – even his tattoos seemed colourful and sharp when compared with the courtiers' increasing dishevelment, and the castaways' drab costume. He was placed outside and above the inevitable degradation of the material; you could hear his preternatural disgust at the clowns dancing in a 'foul lake' that '[o]'erstunk their feet' (4.1.204–5). In direct opposition to immaculate Ariel was Caliban's dirty underwear, but also Stephano's and Trinculo's (Gary Sefton and Stephen Kennedy) equally repellent sweat-stained, muddied and shabby appearance – as if they had been on the island for three years instead of three hours. The scenes between the trio were among the most startling of the whole production insofar as they took the brutal systems that underlie power relationships to their extreme. This approach was encapsulated in Caliban's sordid licking of Stephano's filthy shoe – and later his foot – made all the more disgusting by the extreme close-ups enabled by the tiny venue. Every appearance by the trio contained grotesque sequences dominated by bodily and non-bodily fluids, urine and wine, as well as their befouled bodies – muddy knees and filthy fingernails and dubious stains. While, again, there were problems produced by the animalistic representation of Caliban – who lapped at alcohol from a dish like a cat and monkied around the stage – Warner's direction brilliantly weighted the subplot with exactly the same amount of time, respect and detail as those involving the elite characters. Because these scenes were seen as equally important, they were able to enter into a dialogue with the main concerns of this production – civility/incivility, kindness/unkindness, materiality/immateriality, humanity/animality, natural/unnatural – in a way which mutually illuminated both. Lines which are usually glossed over were suddenly imperative, and the relationships between

Stephano, Trinculo and Caliban were shown to be integral to understanding the whole.

In manifold and complex ways, this was a *Tempest* deeply invested in the question of what makes us human, with the corporeality of being alive, and with the beast that lurks just beneath the surface. At one moment the impeccable Antonio removed his shoes and socks to deal with a toe injury in a precise, blink-and-you'd-miss-it performance at the side of the stage. In doing so he exposed the animality that we attempt and fail to disavow. The thinness of the covering that separates fleshy, fallible, hairy humans from beasts resonated with the repeated appearances of plastic in the performance and, in Warner's typically nuanced approach to this issue, the depiction of what makes us (in)human connected plastic to the other translucent veils that are produced by bodies. There was *always* a sheen of sweat on the faces of the courtiers despite their 'fresh' tuxedos, for instance. And, in a truly stunning moment, when Beau finally broke out of his ventriloquism to speak in his real voice on the line 'Mine would, sir, were I human' (5.1.26), his eyes slowly and rheumily filled with tears.

Despite his blindness to his spirit's suffering, the relationship between Prospero and Ariel was nevertheless one in which, nominally, the latter was dominant. Prospero was nothing without Ariel (Figure 26) – calling needily upon him to appear – and it was apparent that the master was a conduit for the slave's supernatural powers rather than the other way round. The question of why he would be enslaved when he is the source of most of Prospero's power was answered by Ariel's extraordinary and shocking physical transformation when he was made to relive his year knotted in the pine; the taut and dainty movements of Ariel were overtaken by jerks, wracking and red-faced shaking as he appeared to suffocate before us, his eyes eventually rolling back as he nearly passed out with the pain. It was a remarkable reproduction of Ariel's tortures by Beau. The usual undecidability around whether theirs is a loving or oppressive relationship was decisively answered at the end of the play when, at the very point of freedom – static clouds projected onto the back wall – Prospero smashed

26 Nicholas Woodeson as Prospero in *The Tempest*. Photo: Hugo Glendinning.

his mirror to the ground, and Ariel dropped to the floor, murdered, destroyed, of no use to the magus anymore.

And so Ariel, and his skyscapes, disappeared, concluding Warner's other brilliant intervention: the aforementioned scenic cloud. At the very centre of the 'stuff-ness' of the production was this little fluffy cloud (made of kapok? – or cotton wool?) which looked, at times, a bit naff, moving awkwardly across the rig during the first half. However, its significance became apparent after the interval, as it returned us conceptually to the performance's obsession with materiality and immateriality, substance and nothingness, stuff and dreams. Concentrating ideas about the 'baseless fabric' of man's vision, this prop cloud invoked the question of what it would ultimately become. Would it join a performance archive, or be moved to some storage facility? Or, more likely, would it become just another bit of rubbish in the world – a piece of disposable scenery representing our great, natural recycler of water, which may or may not be recycled. The reason behind the occasional clumsiness of this 'cloud-capped' stage seemed to be that the scenic cloud served as a foil for real clouds (4.1.169). For directors, usually, *The Tempest* poses the problem of how you can possibly create a storm onstage, but for Warner, the question was how you could possibly represent a cloud. And, indeed, why you would bother, when actual clouds in all of their spectacular, vanishing magnificence exist. Both there and not there – wisps in the air – clouds elude materialization.

And this seemed to be precisely Warner and Hetzer's point. Like baseless fabrics, clouds may melt 'into air, into thin air' every day (4.1.167), but unless humans mend their ways, they will vanish permanently, and so shall everything else in this 'great globe ... dissolve' (4.1.170). The presence of this cloud-like stuff, alongside Prospero's destruction of Ariel, became a powerful comment on climate change – unlike Ariel's, Prospero's 'pulse/ Beats' (5.1.125–6); he is an arrogant human at the apex of the Anthropocene. And as the human animals in this play sweat, bleed and urinate their way through the performance, everything, *everything*, is infected to some degree by their selfishness. Warner's urgent, crystal-clear production of *The Tempest* thus examined whether human luxuries such as theatre are necessary at all at this historical moment, while using its incomparably dense and layered semiotics to raise issues that are undoubtedly so.

The Tempest, *Dir. Elizabeth Freestone, Royal Shakespeare Theatre, 23 February 2023*

A second ecologically themed *Tempest* was produced at the Royal Shakespeare Theatre in the following year, with an accomplished performance by Alex Kingston as Prospera at its heart. The decision to stage a matriarchal protagonist was productive, at the beginning especially, as Prospera clutched a newborn daughter to her chest while a tempest whirled around her. It was impossible to divorce the image from the terrible stories about migrant boats that have dominated the news headlines, and the danger for Miranda (Jessica Rhodes) that resulted from her mother's usurpation felt more insistent in this version. The gender swap also produced some deeply touching moments, such as Prospera holding up Miranda's monster-faced toddler T-shirt or passing her childhood fluffy toy: the stage was littered with sippy cups and old fruit shoot bottles as remnants of a fast-disappearing childhood. Nevertheless, the difficulty of trying to raise a child from infant to teen in such deprived circumstances was strongly communicated; the cluttered, domestic, new-age-traveller aesthetic of their cell – washing line strung across the stage – expressed life's continued toil in near-impossible conditions, however magical the isle.

In such circumstances, a slightly fractious mother–daughter relationship rang true as Prospera demanded Miranda heed her backstory in act 1, scene 1. While some of the earlier subtleties around maternality lost momentum as the play progressed, they returned forcefully at the end of the play when Prospera allowed her various 'children' to fly the nest. Ariel (Heledd Gwynn) was another daughter figure, but the pressure placed on this child to perform 'goodness' contrasted sharply and uncomfortably with Miranda's freedom. Prospera's parenting was therefore peppered with errors, such as successfully reasoning Ariel into a loving compliance only to gainsay her advantage with the disproportionate threat to peg her into a tree. No wonder Ariel displayed delayed emotional development by putting a bucket on her head as Prospera once again lectured her on why she should be grateful.

While petulant daughters might require persuading and cajoling, the wayward Caliban (Tommy Sim'aan) was in need of a sterner hand, and the rapacious threat that he presented was intensified on the feminocentric island. Male aggression was echoed in the dynamic between a female Trinculo (Cath Whitefield) and male Stephano (Simon Startin) whose brandishing of a fist against her irrevocably altered their friendship into a gendered hierarchy. Caliban's own snarling, hissing malice was barely kept in check by the boundary of Prospera's staff. And yet, baring his back in later scenes, we were witnesses to his healed but deep scars, raising the spectre of who exactly had mistreated him – Sycorax or Prospera? – with a wider implication concerning how little boys become violent men.

However dysfunctional the parent/child relationships in this version, their losses were still keenly felt and the emancipation of her three 'children' added a new dimension to the magi's resignation from life in the final scene: with Prospera's sustaining maternal role now over, she was shown to be heading into a new, but concluding, phase of life. Indeed, what sustains us was placed at the forefront of the production. The narrating of stories onstage – Prospera's usurpation, Antonio's proposed plot – was achieved by deploying plastic objects as stand-ins for characters, reminiscent of Forced Entertainment's 'Tabletop Shakespeare' performances. In this instance, however, the technique was connected to the ecological emphasis of the production and, while this might be the stuff on which dreams are made and stories told, the trash also threatened to overwhelm the stage. As in Warner's production, it was a wonder where it all came from and why there is so much of it. Tellingly, one of Ferdinand's labours involved litter-picking, but also questioned the difference between rubbish and belongings, especially when that litter included the ice cream tub of an audience member.

Like Warner's then, Freestone's *Tempest* chose to focus on climate crisis, though more unevenly than the meticulous and cohesive version of the play at the Ustinov. The RSC production also fell short in other ways: the actual tempest was underpowered, the comic scenes were not particularly funny, and those involving the shipwrecked Italians never quite found purchase. However, while Warner's *Tempest* unsettled in its apocalyptic worldview, Freestone's was redemptive and hopeful. Its most spectacular piece of scenery – an entire forest which sprang from Ceres' tiny shoot – was discovered behind a curtain during the masque. It had been there all along. It would also be the only thing that remained once the settlers had departed, suggesting that nature would ultimately reclaim the island. A sense of the world continuing after our little lives are rounded with a sleep functioned as a palate cleanser after Warner's depressing and disturbing vision.

The ecological commitment of the RSC's *Tempest* was embedded at all levels of production, guided by the principles of the 'Theatre Green Book' which include the remaking, repurposing and recycling of old scenery and rubbish at the venue. Thus the gaberdine was a net in which Trinculo and Caliban became tangled up like dolphins, overskirts and peplums were made of rubbish, while the harpy formed by Ariel and the island spirits was constructed through black bin bags. The forest itself was created through trees sourced from a recently thinned local wood, their added leaves made of either compostable canvas or reusable plastic. These pledges of sustainable theatre-making were signs of environmental hope, and were paralleled by an ultimately positive take on the play. Unlike Warner's murderous ending, this *Tempest*'s Ariel and Caliban were freed, and their liberation was affiliated with their reclamation of native languages.

There were some delightful moments, such as when the gawky masque transformed into a joyous barn dance (Figure 27), and it was also a *Tempest* energized from its core by Kingston's expert performance. There was nothing weak about this female Prospera: hilariously casual movements of her staff could fling Ferdinand (Joseph Payne) into physical paroxysms about the stage, but she could also unintentionally hurt others – including her own daughter – with the intensity of her power too. Such moments served to underscore the production's concern with parenthood and responsibility. In the end – like the forest which remained onstage after all the clutter had been cleared – both children and the world will survive and thrive, despite the damage that we, as adults, may inflict.

TWO *DREAMS*

A Midsummer Night's Dream, *Dir. Matthew Dunster and Jimmy Fairhurst, Cockpit Theatre at the Shakespeare North Playhouse, 1 October 2022*

A new-car-smell pervaded the Cockpit Theatre for its opening production – or rather a new-reconstructed-theatre-smell. The main space at the Shakespeare North Playhouse in Prescot was presented as an octagonal theatre in the round (but has the capacity to be configured in different ways) and sported several trap doors, chandeliers and galleried seating (Figure 28). The Cockpit had, therefore, many hallmarks of an indoor playhouse, modelled as it is on Inigo Jones's seventeenth-century cockpit-in-court theatre. It also enjoyed plenty of electric lighting, amplified and recorded sound, and a flexibility of space – including gangways for entrances and exits – so that reconstruction was very much a loosely applied term.

With the aroma of carpentry in the air, *A Midsummer Night's Dream* began, although in fact the performance had already started half an hour before in the foyer as a host of micro-dramas played out between the bar and gift shop. We heard tannoy announcements that members of the cast were missing, for instance; we saw a couple presenting as members of the 'audience' who were clearly plants, and we witnessed some sort of theft perpetrated by the person who would go on to be Puck (Monique Johnson) who had seemingly wandered in off the street. Indeed, this connection between the new playhouse and its immediate context, between Shakespearian 'insiders' and 'outsiders' – realized through costumes which mixed trainers with ruffs – was central to the production.

Purple graffiti adorning the building told it (or us) to 'Get Pucked' and 'Puck Off'; this same spray would later become the 'love-in-idleness' of the play. The night before the performance I asked a friendly woman in a restaurant what Prescotians thought of the enormous new theatre in their midst, and she told me that, while schoolchildren and the middle-aged and elderly were enthusiastic, those in between were not so sure. The producers of this show – a co-production between

27 The betrothal masque as barn dance in *The Tempest*, dir. Elizabeth Freestone. Photo: Ikin Yum © RSC.

28 The Cockpit Theatre at The Shakespeare North Playhouse: Photo: Andrew P. Brooks.

Shakespeare North Playhouse, Northern Stage and Not Too Tame – seemed acutely aware of that tension. Matthew Dunster writes in the programme that this *Dream* would be about 'reframing things', about being 'an antidote to the poison of the tedious introductions to Shakespeare ... that some people might have had in the past', while Natalie Ibu of Northern Stage told us it was directed at people 'who think Shakespeare isn't for them'. In many of these aims, the production succeeded, but its anxiety to achieve them also detracted from total success.

Judging by the outward appearance of the audience, the Playhouse hasn't – yet – triumphed in engaging the kinds of people and communities who think that Shakespeare isn't for them, but one of their major strategies for doing so was to include a festival of northern accents on the stage. From Lancashire to Yorkshire to Scotland, Manchester to Liverpool to Newcastle – there wasn't a single RP vowel to be heard, and the performance became a celebration of northern voices. This was connected to the desired audience in that members of the stage crew and plants in the audience had to step in to take up various roles for the show – the casting process hastily taking place onstage in a mirror of the mechanicals' own production process a little later on – highlighting the involvement of community in the space.

The performance thus relied upon a number of complex interrelationships, interpretations and interventions that, unfortunately, neither the micro-dramas nor the main performance had the time or space to fully explicate. Offstage relations coloured what was happening onstage: Lysander (Dexter Williams) and Demetrius (Tyler Dobbs) seemed to have 'real-life' beef with each other which bled into their performance, a similar dynamic appeared to inform Helena (Siobhan O'Flynn) and Demetrius's offstage relationship as 'Kate' and . . . I didn't catch his name. There was also something going on about flatmates and jealousy and drama school when it came to the interactions between Hermia (Rebecca Hesketh Smith) and 'Helena' and 'Demetrius'. However, access to the pre-show metadrama depended so much upon chance that the degree to which it was woven into the actual performance proved confusing. For instance, questions about Puck's relationship to the performance remained opaque; in jeans, hi-tops and a green parka, it wasn't clear whether they were homeless, a tourist or an interloper, or even whether the whole show was their drug-induced fantasy. They were certainly an outsider, but a Scot rather than from Prescot, so their 'Get Pucked' resistance to the Playhouse – if indeed they were the graffiti artist – needed more context. "I'm invisible!" they seemed to discover after the interval, but we had already witnessed them filming Hermia and Lysander's escape plot on a tablet right at the beginning of the show – did they not know that they were invisible then? The numerous half-realized or unresolved ideas in the production affected the logic of a playworld which was overloaded with concepts, and a bit chaotic.

The gendered reading of the play was absolutely clear, however, and it was one incensed with the regressive politics of the text. Hippolyta (Natasha Clarke) simmered with repressed rage, a bodice applied over her T-shirt as a material sign of the constraints of enforced wifeliness. Standing up for Hermia throughout Egeus's complaints in 1.1, Theseus was interrupted by his wife-to-be's ad-libs – 'She's a child!' – as well as her evident unhappiness when he weighed in on the side of paternal authority. With Hippolyta ripping off her bodice and offering Hermia silent comfort at the end of the scene, the production showed its concern to dismantle Athenian patriarchy. Book-ending this interpretation were the radical final moments of the performance. While the other couples – touches of purple in their cream-toned wedding garb to suggest the ongoing influence of the woods – joyfully danced across the space, Hippolyta – bodiced again – moved solemnly and rejected Theseus's kiss. Justice was around the corner though. In place of an epilogue, a new scene was staged, in which Titania and Hippolyta joined forces to throw Theseus down one of the trap doors – 'You've just been cut, mate!' they jeered. Meanwhile Oberon, represented here as a red circle of light above the stage and voiced by a recording of David Morrissey, was cut off mid-sentence – his punishment for the humiliating violation of Titania.

In the article 'Thou Art Translated', Ayanna Thompson argues that *A Midsummer Night's Dream* is a play 'deeply invested in exploring what happens when situations, locations, people, plots, and objects change, move, migrate'.[2] The Shakespeare North Playhouse is a prime example of just such a translation, a brave and bold attempt to reclaim Shakespeare from London for the North, premised on the putative links between Shakespeare, Lord Strange and Strange's troupe of players. The concept of translation was crucial for this version of *Dream*, especially the idea of relocating Shakespeare for different communities. These included D/deaf audience members and their onstage representative, Tyler Dobbs in the role of Demetrius. Jill Bradbury has written brilliantly on how the trend for signed Shakespeare performance can obscure as much as it clarifies for D/deaf spectators when the actors are not skilled signers themselves. I cannot speak to the competence of the hearing performers' use of British Sign Language (BSL) in this production, but was pleased to see that entire swathes of Dobb's dialogue were delivered without audio interpretation at all; his signing was allowed to speak for itself. Indeed, the fact that the

---

[2] Ayanna Thompson, https://bridgetheatre.co.uk/thou-art-translated.

premium on 'translating' him occurred in Athens served as a comment upon the repressive nature of the city, as well as hearing Shakespeare audience members more widely. In the woods, Demetrius was free to communicate without mediation.

Translating from one community to another thus became a metaphor for what is not understood in Shakespeare. Where this idea of translation became less useful was when it came to textual revision and modernization, however. While it was common under Emma Rice's tenure at the Globe (where Dunster enjoyed great success with *Imogen*) to insert contemporary references and swearing into Shakespeare to make it 'relevant', I consider this a condescending and problematic way to update Shakespeare. It patronizes potential Shakespearian audiences to suggest that they can only 'get' his plays if they contain couplets like 'If we can be wooed / then we can fucking woo'. My concern isn't prurient, or about the sacredness of 'the text', but that it actually reinforces the binary between those with knowledge superior enough to 'translate' Shakespeare, and those who need to have him translated. In order to get – and keep – audiences, it is probably better to make drastic cuts to plays and reduce their playing time than to add 'relatable' material. The textual interventions exposed a squeamishness about Shakespeare that was made more egregious by the fact that many changes were fairly pointless – 'calendar' for 'almanac', for instance.

Other attempts to engage the audience were more effective and more direct. Metatheatrical ad-libs repeatedly called attention to absurd realities – the actor playing Flute exclaiming, 'I'm 53 years old man!', for example – and a major feature of the performance was the co-opting of a member of the audience, whom they called 'Brian', into the role of Lion, 'Brian the Lion'. His continual hauling up onstage was a vibrant and often funny attempt to break down boundaries between actor and audience. The audience were also taught a dance by the mechanicals, which Bottom (Johnny Sinclair) would make them perform every time the mechanicals met, and which would become a final jig for us all to join in. In terms of comic engagement,

Bottom's own translation worked especially well, his baseball cap sprouting ass ears, UV light revealing green gnashers, and a phallus of donkey-sized proportions painted onto his trousers, his T-shirt telling us that 'I've Been Pucked' and – if we were in any doubt – 'Totally Pucked' on the back.

There were therefore in evidence a number of playful strategies for countering the potential pomposity of 'The Bard'. Also effective was the imagining of the woods, very much in the mode of Robert Le Page or Peter Brook's dark vision rather than a space of bucolic loveliness. In contrast to Titania (Nadine Shah)'s spotless Elizabethan dress, the strange, black-costumed fairies wore gas masks or eye patches, while emitting strange screeches, or adopting grotesque postures – strings of fungus, or possibly viscera, hanging around their necks like horrid garlands. Bottom's seduction was weird and disturbing; Titania's insistent desire revealed the perversity of a lust uncoupled from emotion, her sexual hunger unbridled even as Bottom's tongue was tied up with a ball gag. Demetrius and Lysander were also infected too with this unhinged desire, following Helena around the stage like a couple of creepy love zombies.

Dunster and Fairhurst revelled in the possibilities of the space, inventively layering up its contemporary and classical affordances so that the performance benefitted from trapdoors and candles at the same time as UV light and sound distortion (Figure 29). While this meant that the use of production techniques felt somewhat indiscriminate, it also meant that this first play at the Cockpit Theatre was a showcase for what the Shakespeare North Playhouse can do, in a performance which made an admirable statement about its aspiration to be as inclusive as possible. If it can come to less anxious terms with its environs, the Playhouse has the potential to have a hugely positive impact outside the theatre, as well as within.

A Midsummer Night's Dream, Dir. Joe Murphy, Sherman Theatre, 22 October 2022

The idea of translation took on different and more choate resonances in another exploration of *Dream*

Nicholas Hytner's 2020 production at the Bridge Theatre, it swapped their roles so that it was Theseus/Oberon who fell in love with Bottom (Sion Pritchard). Much like the Bridge *Dream*, this enabled Hippolyta to teach Oberon a lesson about enforcement and consent; however, Murphy managed the potential homophobia of this production choice better than Hytner, through focusing on the romance between Bottom and Oberon rather than the sex. The laughs therefore stemmed from Oberon's hopelessly doting and devoted attitude to a guileless, albeit increasingly enamoured donkey – a hilarious performance from Pritchard – encapsulated in an overly sentimental version of the power ballad 'I want to know what love is' before the interval. Nevertheless, the danger remained that the audience were laughing at the notion of same-sex rather than cross-species desire, which seems an almost inevitable consequence of this gender swap.

The Sherman's likeable production was particularly insightful about identity and difference and how these can illuminate the play's conflicts. In the depiction of the same-sex coupling of Hermia and Lysanna (Lauren Morais), sexuality proved less significant than class in terms of the Athenian condemnation of their relationship. While Hermia, Helena (Rebecca Wilson) and Demetrius (Tom Mumford) sported preppy twin sets, golf socks, and jumpers casually flung around the shoulders, Lysanna wore a baggy hoodie and jeans. When Hermia brought an exaggeratedly heavy suitcase to the woods, Lysanna bought a four-pack of beer and some Doritos. In Morais's first professional and very assured performance, Lysanna's Welsh accent was broader, her body language more relaxed. She seemed to be from a different age to her uptight peers – a millennial, rather than a relic of the twentieth century, secure in herself and her sexuality and her love.

Elin Steel's deceptively simple set design of art deco geometric panels along the edges of the stage in green and gold magically became the trunks of multiple trees when the lights were dimmed in the woods. The forest, inhabited by fairies in pagan masks, was instantly rougher and more natural

29 Candlelight meets electric light in *A Midsummer Night's Dream* at Shakespeare North Playhouse, dir. Matthew Dunster and Jimmy Fairhurst. Photo: Patch Dolan.

at the Sherman Theatre in Cardiff. The play's oppressive gender politics were again examined, with Hippolyta (Nia Roberts) a similarly reluctant bride and supporter of Hermia (Dena Davies) as the play opened. Despite observing a happy Hippolyta take in the morning air in its first moments, we quickly realized that her freedom was compromised as ranks of heavies closed threateningly around her. That she had no agency in her marriage was highlighted when Theseus (Sion Ifan) delivered his verdict on Hermia directly to his future wife. Hippolyta fought back at the end of the scene, though, by refusing to take his proffered hand.

In line with this opening, the performance centred its exploration of gender dynamics in the play by having Roberts and Ifan also play Titania and Oberon. However, in the same way as than the smoothed surfaces and frosted glass of Athens; the aesthetic transformation all the more remarkable for the fact that it depended solely on lighting changes. Costume was also used to register the distinction between city and woods. Dressed in leather jacket and DMs, a graffitied dress, and a Mohican of antlers, Leah Gaffey embodied an eclectic Puck, her aesthetic part Alice in Wonderland, part Wicker Man, part grunge, part punk. The language of the woods was marked by hybridity too. As soon as Puck came onstage to deliver her lines – not only in Welsh, but also in an updated and rewritten version of the text by Mari Izzard and Nia Morais – it was clear that the forest was associated with linguistic freedom and colloquialism as well as a departure from Athenian restrictions. In this way, translation was used to speak back to hegemonic Shakespearian practice.

Bilingualism produced a number of cogent and meaningful effects in performance. That Bottom spoke in Welsh after his conversion to an ass manifested the idea that he had been translated in more ways than one; that the deceived lovers spoke in Welsh after being touched by Puck's magic reinforced the sense that they had undergone a fundamental identity shift. Welsh lucidly registered who was a forest creature, and who had been spellbound. But the real revelation of the production's polyglotism was its critique of the cultural authority of Shakespeare. The Welsh woods emerged as a space for expanded boundaries rather than narrow interpretations, realized theatrically as Puck increasingly used the spaces beyond the stage to make her entrances and exits. Welsh freed up restricted identities and stage conventions, it structured the questioning of power relations both onstage and beyond, and interrogated the authority and centrality of the sacred Shakespearian 'text' in the English performance tradition.

As such, it was a shame that – in a similar way to Shakespeare North's *Dream* – the performance betrayed anxieties about audience comprehension through frequent and unwarranted ad-libs. Demetrius was particularly guilty of seeking cheap laughs through extra bits of dialogue – 'My what?', 'Relax', 'You're too much right now', etc. Given that the translated sections of text provided both the frame and freedom to rewrite the play for a contemporary Welsh audience, this 'answering back' to Shakespeare during the English-language scenes actually muddied the clarity of that message. If the issue is that Shakespearian language is problematically elitist for a modern Welsh audience, then the text needed to be adhered to during the English scenes for the point to obtain.

Where bilingualism worked especially well in this production was in its resolution of the Hippolyta/Theseus dynamic. In act 5, scene 1, Theseus continually shut Hippolyta down while the lovers relayed their adventures. Then, in a mirror of the first scene, he held out his hand to lead her off, at which point Puck suddenly crossed the stage. Empowered by the wanderer of the night, Hippolyta asserted 'Theseus, I overbear your will', and began to speak in Welsh herself, as she would for the rest of the performance. Puck's sudden irruption into the space evidently reminded her of Titania's rapprochement with Oberon/Theseus in the forest, so that this time she held out *her* hand to him. At this moment, comically, Bottom also crossed the stage. Also reminded of his double's disgrace and the fairy rulers' promise to be loyal, Theseus took Hippolyta's hand and they left the stage together, power rebalanced.

For the remainder of the play, all the lovers spoke in Welsh, irrevocably changed by the linguistic and emotional freedoms of the forest. An amalgamation of languages conveyed the lessons that had been learned and the success of the lovers' evasion of Athenian (and English) supremacy. It also marked the performance's casting off of Shakespearian imperialism. This was emphasized by a performance of 'Pyramus and Thisbe' which seemed to have accrued all the baggage of centuries of bad Shakespearian practice: in an engagingly ludicrous version of the play-within-the-play, Bottom's performance of Pyramus hit new heights of mannered, cod-Shakespearian declamation. The anti-colonialism of the Sherman *Dream*'s climax culminated in a stupendously silly jig, showing with aplomb how bilingual Shakespeare can enact critique while remaining theatrically compelling.

SHAKESPEARE PERFORMANCES IN ENGLAND, 2022–2023

TWO *MACBETHS*

Macbeth, Dir. Andrew Quick and Pete Brooks, The Dukes Lancaster, 3 March 2023

In early 2023, imitating the dog (itd) applied their successful mediatized theatre approach to *Macbeth*, creating a moody, modern adaptation for a nationwide tour. Secondary-school teachers must have rejoiced upon news of this updated and gritty version of a core English text, recontextualized in a metropolitan gangland called 'Estuary City'. Known primarily for their real-time camera work and large-scale digital projections, the company's technically sophisticated work appeals to younger audiences, and their 'neon-noir' *Macbeth* was specifically geared towards a 14+ age group. It was defined by the youthful coupling of Macbeth and Lady Macbeth (Benjamin Westerby and Maia Tamraker), both of whom had grown up in care, bonded together by psychological damage and class abjection. The motivating factor for the play's violence was Lady Macbeth's trauma resulting from childhood sexual abuse and Macbeth's subsequent protection of her at all costs. Indeed, the first murder happens outside of the realm of the play through Macbeth's spontaneous killing of the last in a long line of Lady Macbeth's rapists. This was a plausible trigger for their murderousness, though meant that Lady Macbeth lost her agency to be unaccountably evil as a consequence.

In Quick and Brooks' adaptation, ambition was replaced with survival, Lady Macbeth pushing her husband to kill Duncan so as to stop the cycle of abuse – or, as the play has it, 'They simply wanted their lives to be a little less shit.' But, because blood must have blood, a new cycle of violence begins nonetheless, this time governed by the logic of remaining top dog. Macbeth's change was exhibited sexually as much as socially, his former impotence replaced by a sudden priapic virility. He also began brutalizing Lady Macbeth himself. In fact, one of the adaptation's major interventions was for Lady Macbeth to escape at the end, albeit on a promise to return and wreak revenge in the future.

The programme informs us that both financial constraints and conceptual design aligned when choosing to stage the play with only five actors. All of the other parts were performed by the demonic witches (Laura Atherton, Stefan Chanyaem and Matt Prendergast), who were Heath-Ledgerlike-Joker-tricksters, a strategy, according to the programme, which 'allows the witches to comment upon and drive the narrative'. Their choric function was cogently handled, although there was an inevitable streamlining of minor roles to fit the circumstances. The witches' interpolated dialogue was clever and contemporary, with knowing cultural references made to Ledger and Kurosawa, Michael Fassbender and Denzel Washington, as well as the Jacobean political context for which the play was originally written.

itd's version of the play was thus liberally and profanely rewritten for an underworld of shooters and sexual exploitation. The central crime organization itself was mutable, sliding from London gangsters to the Japanese *yakuza*, revealed in the switch of titles from thane to *oyabun*, for example. Scottishness was confined to some costume kilts, and Shakespearian text jostled alongside interpolated speech with refreshing irreverence. There was often a certain numbness in the delivery, Westerby's especially – whose laissez-faire soliloquies were another way in which the production established its youth-focused approach and aversion to conventional Shakespeare. Such understatement did produce moments of litotic humour, as when Macbeth pronounced after Duncan's murder – 'It was a rough night' (2.3.70) – a nearly original line which sounded entirely new. The gangland setting also helpfully sharpened the play's focus on and disruption of obligation and service: what it means to be dutiful, and the consequences of not knowing your place, were keenly expressed.

Facilitated by Simon Wainwright, Davi Callanan and Andrew Croft's stunning projections onto an enormous screen at the back of the stage, the action moved swiftly from dingy club, to back alley, to twinkling cityscape, settings which were sometimes definitely English – Epsom recurred as a location at the climax – others which could have been any dystopian, rain-sodden metropolis. Nokia flip-phones and fruit machines seemed at times to place 'Estuary City' at the turn of the twenty-first century, but we were also flung into neon-drenched, futuristic, *Blade Runner*-like topographies. Japanese manga scenes and Korean Tonto characters juxtaposed the onstage violence to dissonant effect. The shifts were thus both sophisticated and disorienting, articulated through a constant interface between projection, real-time camerawork and stage action. Live streamed video created loci such as car interiors, but was primarily used for close-ups of Macbeth and Lady Macbeth speaking or reacting, allowing us access to their interiority without sacrificing the panorama of staged action.

While this aesthetic busyness generally worked well, the adapted script was busy in a less useful way with much of the plot conveyed through telling as much as showing. This perhaps reflected the frenetic pace of the target youthful audience's supposed imaginations, their multiple cognitive engagements, but it left little space for interpretation. There was also a disconnection between the volume of screen work and the intensity of what could be built onstage. The primacy of actors' faces on-screen sometimes pulled focus from staged action, and this was emphasized at moments where the timescapes of long soliloquies misaligned with streamed close-ups, leaving actors feeling a little marooned on camera.

I would also have liked to have seen more care taken around the intersection of criminality, race and ethnicity in the adaptation. With both Macbeth and Lady Macbeth performed by mixed-race actors, the production's focus on bling, guns and street violence was at risk of an uncritical and negative racialization. Given all of the space for metatheatrical commentary and critique afforded by the production style, some acknowledgement of this potential cliché would have been welcome, particularly in light of the fact that this 'gritty, urban' *Macbeth* was being consumed primarily by a white audience in the north-west of England. These problems were intersectional; there was also a related danger of the production sliding into 'poverty porn' and class appropriation at times.

Overall, however, this was an aesthetically impressive *Macbeth* buoyed by an invigorating interpretation. As the company website tells us, school 'test audiences ... have found the production to be very exciting and accessible as a way into understanding *Macbeth* and a unique introduction to Shakespeare', and this was endorsed by anecdotal reports I received from teenagers who attended the performance. Whatever its dramaturgical issues or cultural assumptions, there is no doubt that this *Macbeth* was an imaginative and technically dazzling effort to invest new audiences in Shakespeare and, given that young adults were the target audience, itd's success in animating *Macbeth* for Generation Z should be seen as their key achievement.

Macbeth, Dir. Wils Wilson, Royal Shakespeare Theatre, 29 September 2023

Wils Wilson's *Macbeth*, the concluding play of Daniel Evans and Tamara Harvey's first season as incoming Artistic Directors of the RSC, was a cacophony of conceits. The one which received the most press attention was the rewriting of the Porter's monologue by Stewart Lee, performed by a typically brilliant Alison Peebles. The monologue itself was fun: knowledgeable about its source, pleasingly anti-Tory, taking knowing swipes at the insincerity of a Stratford audience filled with GCSE students and middle-class snobs. However, it was only a small aspect of a very long version of the play which was stuffed with ideas both enduring and baffling.

The production contained moments of spectacular effectiveness, as when the witches (Amber Sylvia Edwards, Eilidh Loan and Dylan Read) bubbled up from the trap door like hairy, human magma, or, later, when one spoke to Macbeth whilst straining against a film of opaque, stretchy plastic – as if prophesying from behind the membrane of another world. At times they would strike tableaux that quickly dissolved, and Julia Cheng as the Movement Director found postures and stances that were truly weird – an arm suddenly jerked above the head like a twisted flamenco dancer from *The Evil Dead*, for instance. But these feats of theatricality were measured against the many ideas which should have been left in the rehearsal room: a tiny red light shining through the sleeve of Gruach, Lady Macbeth (Eilidh Loan, understudying for Valene Kane), during her sleepwalk, for some reason; or the attempted *coup de théâtre* of hoisting the witches aerially over the Macduff family massacre which, somehow, barely registered in the general overwhelm. Nevertheless, the production succeeded in creating an unholy and peculiar atmosphere. Dead crows plummeted intermittently from the sky, and our senses were unexpectedly stimulated by the smell of woodsmoke from a letter burned by Gruach (the production reinvested *Macbeth*'s women with agency by giving them first names), which wafted across the rocky stage towards us while drizzle fell vastly behind her. Earth, air, water, fire thus converged on her first entrance to demonstrate that elemental forces were at play.

Accents told us this was Scotland, as did the bagpipes among a musical ensemble creatively fundamental to production. However, the stage was also strangely placeless, a desolate hinterland suggested by a few rocks and occasional mists, inhabited by witches constructed mostly of matted hair and grass and feathers (Figure 30). The witches were always present at the worst moments, silently powering the most foul action such as the murders of Banquo (Anna Russell-Martin) or Anne, Lady Macduff (Emma King). However, wildness was not limited to them. Lady Macbeth's flashes of armpit hair, the slightly outgrown beard of Macbeth (Reuben Joseph), the shagginess and the afros and the loose locks across the cast were redolent of the Picts, especially the blue costume and

30 Amber Sylvia Edwards, Dylan Read and Eilidh Loan as the three witches in *Macbeth*, dir. Wils Wilson. Photo: Marc Brenner © RSC.

face markings which signified regal power in the play. A general hirsutism brought resonance to lines such as Siward's assertion, 'If I had as many sons as I have hairs / I would not wish them a fairer death' (5.8.56–7), engaging interestingly with the early modern connection between beards and masculinity, as well as the play's own equivocation on hairs and heirs.

For all of the media emphasis on Lee's rewriting of the Porter scene, the production was largely devoid of humour. In fact, it was brutal, the murderers revelling in the deaths of the tiny Macduff children, and the final showdown between Macduff (George Anton) and Macbeth consisting of a bloody and prolonged fight to the death which finally culminated in the tyrant's braining with a rock. Macbeth himself was riven almost immediately by the murder of Duncan (Thérèse Bradley), tapping and clawing at his tortured skull for comfort, while manhandling his wife around the stage like a mannequin. Loan was an excellent understudy for Kane on the night we saw the play, focused and powerful in the role of Lady Macbeth.

Still, it was difficult to grasp on to anything that centrally defined this production, either interpretatively or aesthetically. The blue touches and the jabs of red on clothing and on bodies interrupted the largely neutral costume palette, but the costumes themselves were from all time periods, and little seemed to locate Georgia McGuiness's set design in what the programme tells us is 'the near future'. In terms of its performance languages, the production is situated in the programme as a 'thriller', and leant towards melodrama, though invoked stand-up for the Porter's monologue. Dance theatre materialized the Battle of Dunsinane, followed by an experimental theatre approach to the climax when the Porter's mic reappeared for Macbeth's final speeches. While such formal heterogeneity is not by definition a problem, it was symptomatic of a wider issue with this production, characterized by an overabundance of ideas, and in need of editing. It was unclear whether this was a play driven by a couple's psychological devastation following child loss, or supernatural forces and evil possession; if it was a commentary on Scotland, or a critique of English bardolatry. It was all of these things, but none clearly – messy in terms of the 'big picture' but precise in terms of details. As such, it was not in any way an ineffective *Macbeth*, just an uncontrolled and overlong one, in need of dramaturgical support to draw out its core story, rather than the time it took to tell it. At the same time, it was successfully impressionistic, and I have no doubt that its weirder moments will unexpectedly bubble up in my memory, like those uncanny witches from beneath the stage.

TWO *HAMLETS*

Hamlet, Dir. John Haidar, Bristol Old Vic, 19 October 2022

As *Hamlet* clanged into being at the Bristol Old Vic, a home video of the boy prince projected against the set morphed into a televised speech in which Claudius (Finbar Lynch) informed us of the trouble brewing between Denmark and Norway. Hamlet (Billy Howle), however, was only interested in an instant caught on his cassette player: Claudius saying 'Therefore our sometime sister, now our Queen' (1.2.08), which he stopped, rewound and played again; stopped, rewound and played again. By opening with act 1, scene 2, rather than Horatio's ghostly encounter with King Hamlet's spirit, and by completely excising Fortinbras thereafter, the production announced its intention to focus on *Hamlet's* psycho-drama. Hamlet's mental anguish was examined with especial rigour by Howle, whose prince was devastated by his mother's incestuous remarriage. However, the confrontation with his father's Ghost (Firdous Bamji) seemed to initiate a more serious psychic rupture and breakdown of reason for Hamlet, who became lucid and frantic by turns, his brain and body increasingly erratic.

This was very much a Hamlet-centred *Hamlet* then, framed by home videos of the prince as a boy, and an acute sense of familial loss. You could see that Gertrude (Niamh Cusack) really did live 'almost by his looks' (4.7.12) and was bewildered by her son's faltering mental health. That he was a troubled youth was evident from the outset, however, with Howle wearing an inky cloak of black double denim and an 'Unknown Pleasures' T-shirt. The time was definitely out of joint for this Hamlet, with Howle demonstrating an almost uncanny ability to slide between phases and ages. At points, he seemed to change before our eyes from a troubled teen into a grown man. At others, time went backwards and he crouched like a terrified toddler before the Ghost's commands.

Elsinore was dominated by an Edward Gordon Craig-like ridged, black and massive rectangle: a tardis of hidden staircases, corridors and levels, swivelling and opening to reveal its scenographic secrets. It was a resourceful piece of set from Alex Eales which generated some theatrical thrills, such as the trippy moment that the ridges, in combination with the lighting design of Malcolm Rippeth, became wavy as Ghost Hamlet retreated back into its walls, evoking the bending of the fabric of space and time. Otherwise, the lighting was monochrome and stark, exposing rather than concealing the action. For much of the performance, a minuscule amount of dry ice would curl across the stage, a *memento mori* which became more reality than a reminder when Hamlet dug his hands into his father's ashes, holding them hopelessly out to his horrified mother in the closet as the remains of King Hamlet also wisped and dissipated in the air. This design motif, sustained throughout the production, was suggestive of the permeability of life and our eventual, inexorable journey into a 'quintessence of dust' (2.2.332).

In a similar vein, alongside the home videos and cassette players, a dictaphone served for Hamlet's 'tables', as if committing something to tape might shore up the unreliability of memory and the tricks that it plays. Recordings served as evidence of what has definitely been, but also of the eruptive haunting of past trauma and how it fractures the present. By contrast, and though his face was hidden by a huge monk's cowl, there was a corporeality to Bamji's voice when he first appeared as the Ghost, which disturbingly invoked the very recent, very material loss of a father. However, as Hamlet's disintegrating mind became more obvious, the Ghost's voice became more echoey, and the fact that no one but he could ultimately see his father suggested that he was fully delusional by the second half.

The performance thus played with what was real and what was fantasy, enshrined in a shocking moment when – Ghost at his shoulder – Hamlet suddenly took action and shot Claudius at the end of the first half, before the lights went down. When they came back up after the interval, however, the Ghost was gone, and Claudius was still very much alive. Unfortunately, the well-paced first half was not matched by the second. While Claudius was calculating and watchful before the interval, he was rushed and mannered after it, and the culmination of the various plots involving Rosencrantz and Guildenstern, Polonius, Ophelia and Laertes were more functional than affecting. The dragging second half was thankfully lifted by a final scene which included Bret Yount's excellently choreographed fencing match, in which the various deadly exchanges were distinct and the murders bloody.

The production utilized a reorganized text, a hybrid of 1603 and 1604 quartos, as well as folios of 1623 and 1685. Haidar writes in the programme that he was 'most concerned with those editions most likely gathered together from actors' drafts of the play's first performances'. Without opening the can of worms that is memorial reconstruction, this was unarguably a production perched on the *platea*, Hamlet more often than not on the edge of the stage, eyeballing the audience who sat in the pit as he poured out the contents of his brain. Jason Barnett unearthed every potential laugh as a wonderfully funny Polonius through direct audience address, while Laertes (Taheen Modak) very nearly fell off the stage's precipice during the final fray. There was a nice gesture towards the ghosting of Hamlet by a history of performance during the rehearsals for The Mousetrap, Howle holding a 'Practical Handbook for the Actor' and appearing to channel the ghosts of Olivier and Burton as he read aloud its 'Advice for Actors' at the boundary of the stage. Despite the issues with its second half, the many intelligent production choices in evidence, and the immediacy of Howle's performance, meant that this particular iteration illuminated the play's concerns with life and death, family and memory, with what we lose, and with what remains.

NT Schools, Directed by Tinuke Craig (2022) and Ellie Hurt (2023)

The second *Hamlet* was also concerned with the dynamics of childhood and adulthood: however, a few caveats are needed to frame this review. This National Theatre (NT) schools' tour of *Hamlet* was originally adapted by Jude Christian and directed by Tinuke Craig in 2022, then by Ellie Hurt in a remounted production in 2023. I was unable to catch the remount so reviewed the production via a video-recording, kindly provided by the NT's Learning Department. This initial version went on tour across the UK for four weeks, to Liverpool, Wolverhampton, Essex and Sunderland, alongside a three-week run at the Dorfman Theatre. The remount toured for six weeks to Knowsley, Tameside, Blackpool, Blackburn with Darwen, Lincolnshire and Havering, before a two-week run at the Dorfman between February and March 2023.

Despite the limitations of a video-recording of the 2023 production, I was able to attain a keen impression of Hurt's remount of Craig's deft, energetic production, one which opened with a sequence which telescoped the death of King Hamlet, the succession of Claudius (Vedi Roy) and the remarriage of Gertrude (Claire Redcliffe), all while the cast sang a song composed of excerpts from the play's early scenes. 'Mum!' was the first spoken line of the production – an angry, incredulous Prince Hamlet (Kiren Kebaili-Dwyer) calling out after his mother and uncle as they exited the stage like giddy sweethearts. The affective experience of childhood emerged as one of the most fruitful ideas in the production; the frustrations of restricted autonomy, and youthful antagonism towards the hypocrisy of the adult world, were driving forces behind Hamlet's malcontent. The actual wedding – MC'd by Rosencrantz and Guildenstern (Efé Agwele and Curtis Callier) – ended abruptly when Hamlet shouted at all the guests to get out. Whether this was the act of a man or the throwing of a tantrum hung in the air.

Perhaps predictably, the young audience responded more vocally to the moments when Hamlet was infantilized and patronized by a father-uncle goading his lack of maturity. Christian's heavily abridged text refocused the performance onto themes which are sometimes subsumed in longer productions but whose appeal to teenagers is clear – Hamlet and Ophelia's love, the curbing of Ophelia's freedom, her betrayal, her broken heart. In the adaptation, the nightwatch was edited out, as were the travelling players, alongside much of Hamlet's soliloquies. Because of this reweighting of the play, the normally marginalized Ophelia (Jessica Alade) was able to take up more stage space, and the performance felt more connected at points to *Romeo and Juliet* than the post-1600 tragedies – a canny decision given the target audience.

Christian's nimble adaptation also homed in on the idealistic hope and potential of youth in contrast to adult corruption, displacing Hamlet's 'insanity' onto the dishonest, unequal and exploitative nature of the dominant order. While his version was necessarily heavily edited, Christian still found space for additions to augment this idea: Hamlet's disbelief at his uncle's villainous murder – 'this madness' – was emphasized through such couplets as 'They teach us right and wrong in school / When outside the ones in charge don't follow the rules'. Christian's rejuvenation of a character who can be viewed as the pinnacle of Shakespearian cultural capital into an evangelist for youthful rebellion, encouraging his audience not to 'stay in your lane', was well pitched, and welcome.

Kebaili-Dwyer's Prince (Figure 31) used both this old and new text to carve out an engaged and authentic relationship with his audience: 'You wanna see something cool?' he asked them before The Mousetrap; 'Yeah!' several schoolkids enthusiastically answered. With tie knotted around his head, Hamlet looked like nothing more than a pupil on the last day of summer term rather than a madman, using both direct address and ad-libs to make his Hamlet assuredly 'one of them'. His 'antic disposition'

(1.5.192) was defined by an increasing childishness, blowing a raspberry at Polonius (David Ahmad) to garner the biggest laugh of the performance. Such immaturity seemed like a reasonable response to the debased and dismissive adults of the play.

Craig repeatedly produced a great deal theatrically from very little materially, and the small cast and lower production stakes befitting a school tour gave the performance a DIY aesthetic. The performers were corralled into backing vocals for example, or impressed into acting the roles of The Mousetrap, alongside the audience themselves – who were split into sections to serve as wind, rain and animal sound effects, before coming together to chant 'Murderer! Murderer!' as Claudius went to pour poison into Polonius's ear. The imperatives of touring meant the play used sparse, almost Brechtian props, Hamlet initially entering with a flower wreath which spelled out 'DAD' for instance. The audience were particularly delighted by the ingenious Ghost, a classic white-sheet affair but one rendered unnaturally tall by the actor holding a puppet head on a stick beneath the billowing chiffon. The Ghost was therefore prone to uncanny, sudden growth, which – when combined with abnormally paced movement in the tiny space – produced squeals of delight when it suddenly rushed the stage diagonally to get in Hamlet's face.

Dom Coyote's sound design was characterized by music and song, the action in early scenes moving seamlessly between spoken dialogue and R'n'B-inspired musical numbers that flashbacked, for example, to Hamlet and Ophelia's initial romance. For all of the gains of such an abridged version, there were inevitable dramaturgical losses though. The closet scene provided too little an opportunity for Gertrude to move through the phases of loving wife, grieving widow and terrified mother, while the last third of the performance was too compressed to navigate some of the wilder narrative jolts of acts 4 and 5, such as Ophelia's suicide and the court's reaction. Great fun was had by bringing the offstage English scenes onstage however, which were depicted as a childhood imaginary game interrupted by real-world adult deadliness.

The initial question of whether Hamlet was responding to events as a man or a child was one that was never resolved, although it became increasingly clear that he was inhabiting a man's body as the play turned violent in its final act. At the same time as Kebaili-Dwyer's characterization and physicality became increasingly infantile, the sheer fact of his strength in comparison to a female Laertes (Channel Waddock) registered as brutishness at Ophelia's graveside. That a production of little over an hour was able to keep these ambiguities in play during a performance which never flagged is a sign of both Craig and Christian's dexterity, as well as the benefits that abridgement and interpretative focus can bestow on this difficult play.

31 Kiren Kebaili-Dwyer as Hamlet and Claire Redcliffe as Gertrude in *Hamlet*, dir. Tinuke Craig (2022) and Ellie Hurt (2023). Photo: Harry Elletson.

PROFESSIONAL SHAKESPEARE PRODUCTIONS IN THE UK, JANUARY–DECEMBER 2022

JAMES SHAW

Most of the productions listed are by professional companies, but some amateur productions are included. The information is taken from listings, company publicity and published reviews. The websites provided for theatre companies were accurate at the time of going to press.

ALL'S WELL THAT ENDS WELL

Royal Shakespeare Company. Royal Shakespeare Theatre, Stratford-upon-Avon, 16 August–8 October.
www.rsc.org.uk
Director: Blanche McIntyre

AS YOU LIKE IT

Northern Broadsides. New Vic Theatre, Newcastle-under-Lyme, 4-26 February and tour to 2 July.
Director: Laurie Sansom
Northern Broadsides 30th anniversary production.

The Lord Chamberlain's Men. Stonor Park, Henley-on-Thames, 9 June and tour to 23 August.
https://tlcm.co.uk
Director: Peter Stickney

Apricity Theatre. Elmgrove Centre, Bristol, 15–16 July and tour to 28 July.
https://apricitytheatre.com
Director: Matilda Dickinson
Feminist interpretation with all women and non-binary cast.

@Sohoplace, London, 6 December to 28 January 2023.
https://sohoplace.org

Director: Josie Rourke
Rosalind: Leah Harvey
Celia: Rose Ayling-Ellis
Rosalind and Celia communicated primarily using sign language with surtitles.

Adaptation

As You Like It with CBeebies
BBC CBeebies. Shakespeare's Globe Theatre, London, 9–10 August.
Directors: Geoff Coward and Ellie White
Adaptation for young people, filmed and later shown on BBC iPlayer.

THE COMEDY OF ERRORS

Mercury Theatre, Colchester, 13–28 May.
www.mercurytheatre.co.uk
Director: Ryan McBryde

Citizens Theatre. Beacon Arts Centre, Greenock, 19-22 August and tour to 17 September.
www.citz.co.uk
Director: Dominic Hill

HAMLET

Shakespeare's Globe. Sam Wanamaker Playhouse, London, 21 January–9 April.
www.shakespearesglobe.com
Director: Sean Holmes
Hamlet: George Fouracres

Guildford Shakespeare Company. Holy Trinity Church, Guildford, 29 January–23 February.

PROFESSIONAL SHAKESPEARE PRODUCTIONS 2022

www.guildford-shakespeare-company.co.uk
Director: Tom Littler

Bristol Old Vic Bristol, 13 October–12 November.
Director: John Haidar
Hamlet: Billy Howle
Gertrude: Niamh Cusack

Adaptation

Hamlet – Reimagined for Young Audiences
National Theatre. Dorfman Theatre, London, 4–6 April.
www.nationaltheatre.org.uk
Director: Tinuke Craig

Hamlet
The Wardrobe Theatre, Bristol, 5–7 May.
Director: Yuxuan Liu
1-hour adaptation with text, music, and movement.

Waiting for Hamlet
Smokescreen Productions. The Quay at Sudbury, 8 June; theSpaceUK, Edinburgh, 6–26 August.
www.smokescreenprods.com
Playwright: David Visick
The ghost of Yorick persuades the ghost of Hamlet's father not to appear to Hamlet.

Hamlet the Comedy
Oddsocks. Belgrade Theatre, Coventry, 14–16 June and tour to 13 July.

The Hamlet Voyage
Re:Verse Theatre. Bristol Harbour Festival, 16-17 July; Bridewell Theatre, London, 19–23 July.
www.re-versetheatre.com
Director: Ben Prusiner
Playwright: Rex Obano
In 1607 *Hamlet* is performed for West African dignitaries by sailors on board ship.

St Stephen's Theatre, Edinburgh, 3–28 August.
Hamlet: Ian McKellen
Director: Peter Schaufuss
75-minute narrative ballet with McKellen's spoken extracts accompanied by dance and mime company.

HENRY V

Donmar Warehouse, London, 11 February–9 April.
www.donmarwarehouse.com
Director: Max Webster
Henry V: Kit Harington

Antic Disposition. Bath Abbey, 9–14 May; Temple Church, London, 27 May–4 June. Revival of 2015 production.
www.anticdisposition.co.uk
Director: Ben Horslen and John Risebero
In 1915 wounded soldiers decide to stage *Henry V*. With songs adapted from A. E. Housman.

Cambridge Shakespeare Festival, Trinity College Gardens, 1–20 August.

Shakespeare's Globe Theatre and Headlong. Sam Wanamaker Playhouse, London, 20 December–4 February 2023.
www.shakespearesglobe.com
Director: Holly Race Roughan

Adaptation

Into the Breach
Giles Shenton Productions. Brighton Open Air Theatre, 13 April.
George joins the village drama group hoping for panto and ends up playing Henry V.

HENRY VI

Henry VI Rebellion / Wars of the Roses
Royal Shakespeare Company. Royal Shakespeare Theatre, Stratford-upon-Avon, 1 April–4 June.
www.rsc.org.uk
Director: Owen Horsley and Gregory Doran

HENRY VIII

Shakespeare's Globe. Sam Wanamaker Playhouse, London, 19 May–21 October.
www.shakespearesglobe.com
Director: Amy Hodge

JAMES SHAW

Adapted to include additional female voices such as Katharine's daughter Mary, Henry's four later wives, and adult Elizabeth I.

JULIUS CAESAR

Company of Wolves. Cumbernauld Theatre, Cumbernauld, 17–18 March and on tour to 20 May.
https://companyofwolves.org
Director: Ewan Downie
Gender-blind production.

Shakespeare's Globe. The Globe Theatre, London, 11 May–10 September.
www.shakespearesglobe.com
Director: Diane Page
Brutus and Cassius played by and as women.

KING LEAR

Shakespeare's Globe. Globe Theatre, 10 June–24 July.
www.shakespearesglobe.com
Director: Helena Kaut-Howson
Lear: Kathryn Hunter
Foor/Cordelia: Michelle Terry
Kaut-Howson and Hunter first staged *King Lear* for the Young Vic in 1997.

Cambridge Shakespeare Festival, King's College Gardens, 11–30 July.

Miracle Theatre. Penlee Park Open Air Theatre, Penzance, 15 July and tour to 7 August.
https://miracletheatre.co.uk
Outdoor Shakespeare with cast of five.

The Extraordinary Theatre Company and Brownsea Open Air Theatre. Bournemouth Little Theatre, Bournemouth, 25–29 October and tour to 18 November.
Director: Tim Fearon

Adaptation

King Lear: The Musical
Bristol Shakespeare Festival. The Mission Theatre, Bath, 10–12 November.
Playwright: Shina Rachel Waterhouse
Musical with re-worked pop songs.

MACBETH

Leeds Playhouse, Leeds, 26 February–19 March.
https://leedsplayhouse.org.uk
Director: Amy Leach

Rough Cast Theatre, UK tour March–April. Original 2021 production delayed due to pandemic.
www.roughcast.co.uk
Director: Mark Burridge

Tread the Boards Theatre Company. The Attic Theatre, Stratford-upon-Avon, 24 March–24 April.
www.theattictheatre.co.uk
Director: John-Robert Partridge

Flabbergast Theatre. Theatre Royal, Winchester, 14 April and touring through to 2023.
www.flabbergasttheatre.co.uk
Incorporating puppetry, clown, mask, ensemble and physical theatre.

Daniel Taylor Productions. Epstein Theatre, Liverpool, 4–9 October.
https://danieltaylorproductions.co.uk
Director: Daniel Taylor

Adaptation

Handlebards. Ventnor Exchange, Ventnor, 20 January and tour to 6 March.
www.handlebards.com
Comic abridged version.

The Blue Apple Macbeth
Blue Apple Theatre Company. Theatre Royal, Winchester, 7–9 July.
https://blueappletheatre.com
Director: Richard Conlon
Company for people with learning disabilities.

Macbeth the Musical
Bristol Shakespeare Festival. The Mission Theatre, Bath, 8–9 June and Edinburgh Festival, 11–13 August.
Writer: Shona Rachel Waterhouse
Comic version with re-worked pop songs.

PROFESSIONAL SHAKESPEARE PRODUCTIONS 2022

Don't Say Macbeth
GOYA Theatre Company. Edinburgh Fringe Festival, Zoo Playground, 18–28 August.
www.theatregoya.com
Director and writer: Sam Woof
Comedy musical: the first night of *Hubble Bubble: The Musical* goes wrong.

The Macbeth Project
Bright Umbrella. The Sanctuary Theatre, Belfast, 27–29 October.
https://brightumbrella.co.uk
Director: Trevor Gill
75-minute version aimed at younger audiences.

Macbeth – Partners of Greatness
The Faction. Northcott Theatre, Exeter, 2–5 November.
www.thefaction.org.uk
Director: Mark Leipacher
Two-hander focusing on the main couple, Macbeth and Bellona.

MEASURE FOR MEASURE

Shakespeare's Globe. Sam Wanamaker Playhouse, London, 2 December 2021–15 January.
www.shakespearesglobe.com
Director: Blanche McIntyre

Drayton Arms Theatre, London, 1–5 March.
www.thedraytonarmstheatre.co.uk
Director: Sacha Duchamp

THE MERCHANT OF VENICE

Shakespeare's Globe. Sam Wanamaker Playhouse, London, 18 February–9 April.
www.shakespearesglobe.com
Director: Abigail Graham

A MIDSUMMER NIGHT'S DREAM

Reading Rep Theatre, Reading, 11 May–5 June.
www.readingrep.com
Director: Paul Stacey
Cast of six.

Guildford Shakespeare Company. Racks Close, Guildford, 16 June–2 July.
www.guildford-shakespeare-company.co.uk
Director: Abigail Anderson

Bard in the Botanics. Glasgow Botanical Gardens, 22 June–9 July.
www.bardinthebotanics.co.uk
Director: Jennifer Dick

Lakeside Arts Centre, Nottingham, 25–26 June; Nottingham Playhouse, 16 July.
www.lakesidearts.org.uk
Director: Martin Berry

Festival Players. Penlee Park Open Air Theatre, Penzance, 28 June and tour to 29 July.
www.thefestivalplayers.co.uk
All-male company.

Iris Theatre. St Paul's Church (The Actors Church), London, 29 June–13 August.
https://actorschurch.org
Director: Sara Aniqah Malik
Outdoor promenade production.

The Duke's Theatre Company. BOAT (Brighton Open Air Theatre), Brighton, 29 June–2 July and outdoor tour to 24 August.
www.thedukestheatrecompany.co.uk

Ultraviolet Productions. Chapel Down Vineyard, Tenterden, 2 July and tour 25 June–2 July.
www.ultravioletproductions.com

Hull Truck Theatre Company. Hull Truck Theatre, Hull, 2–9 July.
www.hulltruck.co.uk
Director: Tom Saunders
Community production with a cast of over forty.

Illyria Theatre Company. Penlee Park Open Air Theatre, Penzance, 22 July and outdoor tour to 26 August.
www.illyria.co.uk

SEDOS. Bridewell Theatre, London, 14–24 September.
www.sedos.co.uk
Director: Matt Hudson
Billed as a queer re-telling.

Sherman Theatre Company. Shakespeare North Playhouse, Knowsley, 22 September–22 October; Sherman Theatre, Cardiff, 14–29 October.

Director: Joe Murphy
Lysander gender swapped to Lysanna and Oberon falls in love with Bottom. The fairies speak Welsh in a multi-language adaptation with both English and Welsh surtitles.

Not Too Tame. Cockpit Theatre, Shakespeare North Playhouse, Prescot, 27 September–22 October; Epic Space, Northern Stage, Newcastle, 29 October–12 November.
www.nottootame.com
Director: Matthew Dunster
Lysander signed by deaf actor.

Adaptation

OVO. The Roman Theatre of Verulamium, St Albans, 24 May–11 June.
https://ovo.org.uk
Director: Adam Nichols
70s disco musical.

Midsummer Mechanicals
Splendid Productions and Shakespeare's Globe. Sam Wanamaker Playhouse, London, 28 July–21 August.
https://splendidproductions.co.uk
The mechanicals stage another play.

Opera

Scottish Opera. Theatre Royal, Glasgow, 22–26 February.
Composer: Benjamin Britten

MUCH ADO ABOUT NOTHING

Royal Shakespeare Company. Royal Shakespeare Theatre, Stratford-upon-Avon, 4 February–12 March.
www.rsc.org.uk
Director: Indra Bhose and Roy Alexander Weise

Shakespeare's Globe. Sam Wanamaker Playhouse, London, 22 April–23 October.
www.shakespearesglobe.com
Director: Lucy Bailey

Bear in the Air Productions. UK tour June–September.
www.bearintheairproductions.com
Director: Heather Simpkin

Sun & Moon Theatre. Poltimore House and Grounds, Poltimore, 4 June and tour to 27 August.
https://sunandmoontheatreuk.com

Bard in the Botanics. Glasgow Botanical Gardens, 14–30 July.
www.bardinthebotanics.co.uk
Director: Gordon Barr

National Theatre. Lyttelton Theatre, London, 17 July–10 September.
www.nationaltheatre.org.uk
Director: Simon Godwin

Folksy Theatre. Martineau Gardens, Birmingham, 19 July and tour to 18 August.
https://folksytheatre.co.uk

HER Productions, Unseemly Women and Girl Gang Manchester. Shakespeare North Playhouse, Knowsley, 30 August–4 September.
www.herproductions.co.uk
Director: Kayleigh Hawkins
All-female company.

Ramps on the Moon and Sheffield Theatres. Crucible Theatre, Sheffield Theatre, 9–24 September.
https://rampsonthemoon.co.uk
Director: Robert Hastie
Company aiming to elevate the presence of deaf and disabled people both onstage and offstage. Integrated sign language, audio description and captioning.

OTHELLO

Changeling Theatre Company. Open air tour July–August.
https://changeling-theatre.com
Director: Robert Forknall

Watermill Ensemble. The Watermill Theatre, Newbury, 16 September–15 October.
www.watermill.org.uk
Director: Paul Hart and Anjali Mehra
Iago: Sophie Stone

Frantic Assembly. Curve Theatre, Leicester, 19 September–1 October and tour to 11 February 2023.
www.franticassembly.co.uk
Director: Scott Graham

PROFESSIONAL SHAKESPEARE PRODUCTIONS 2022

National Theatre. Lyttelton Theatre, London, 23 November–21 January 2023.
www.nationaltheatre.org.uk
Director: Clint Dyer
Othello: Giles Terera
Iago: Paul Hilton
First black director to stage *Othello* at a major British theatre.

Adaptation

Nothello
Belgrade Theatre, Coventry, 7–21 May.
www.belgrade.co.uk
Director: Justine Themen
Issues of race and gender addressed by actors stepping out of character and planted interjections from the audience.

Opera

Otello
Grange Park Opera, West Horsley, 21 June–9 July.
https://grangeparkopera.co.uk

PERICLES

Flute Theatre. Riverside Studios, London, 8–13 November.
www.flutetheatre.co.uk
Director: Kelly Hunter
Includes specially devised performances billed as *Pericles for Autistic Individuals*.

RICHARD II

We Are Animate. Jack Studio Theatre, London, 22 February–5 March.
Director: Lewis Brown

Quandary Collective. The Vaults, London, 6 April–8 May. Revival of 2021 production.
www.quandarycollective.com
Director: Annie McKenzie
Richard played as a woman posing as a man in order to retain the crown.

RICHARD III

Royal Shakespeare Company. Royal Shakespeare Theatre, Stratford-upon-Avon, 23 June–8 October.
www.rsc.org.uk
Director: Gregory Doran
Richard III: Arthur Hughes

Adaptation

Boris the Third
Something for the Weekend. Edinburgh Festival Fringe, Pleasance Courtyard, 3–29 August.
www.sftw.info
Director: Adam Meggido
Boris Johnson plays the lead in an Eton school production of *Richard III*.

ROMEO AND JULIET

Southwark Playhouse, London, 14 January–5 February.
www.southwarkplayhouse.co.uk
Director: Nicky Allpress

Chapterhouse Theatre Company. UK tour 18 June–1 September.
www.chapterhouse.org

Stafford Gatehouse Theatre. Stafford Castle, 24 June–9 July.
www.gatehousetheatre.co.uk
Director: Tim Ford

Grosvenor Park Theatre, Chester, 25 July–28 August.
www.grosvenorparkopenairtheatre.co.uk
Director: John Young

Stamford Shakespeare Company. Tolethorpe Hall, Stamford, 1–15 August.

Adaptation

Romeo & Juliet!
Teater Asterions Hus. Edinburgh Festival Fringe, Dance Base, Studio 3, Edinburgh, 11–14 August; and on tour. Revival of Teater Møn, Borre, Denmark, 2013.
www.asterionshus.com
Director: Emil Hansen and Peter Kirk
Dance adaptation.

Ballet

Royal Ballet. Royal Opera House, London, 5 Oct 2021–25 February.
Choreographer: Kenneth MacMillan
Composer: Prokofiev

JAMES SHAW

Russian State Ballet and Orchestra of Siberia. St David's Hall, Cardiff, 31 December 2021–2 January; and tour to 28 January.
Choreographer: Kenneth MacMillan
Composer: Prokofiev

THE TAMING OF THE SHREW

Cambridge Shakespeare Festival, King's College Gardens, 1–27 August.

THE TEMPEST

Wildcard Theatre. Main House Cabaret, Pleasance, London, 11 March–3 April.
www.wildcardtheatre.co.uk
Director: James Meteyard

Ustinov Studio, Theatre Royal, Bath, 1 July–6 August.
Director: Deborah Warner
Prospero: Nicholas Woodeson
Deborah Warner's inaugural production as Artistic Director of Theatre Royal, Bath's Ustinov Studio.

Bard in the Botanics. Glasgow Botanical Gardens, 14–30 July.
www.bardinthebotanics.co.uk
Director: Nicole Cooper

Guildford Shakespeare Company. Stoke Park, Guildford, 15-30 July.
Director: Caroline Devlin

Shakespeare's Globe. Sam Wanamaker Playhouse, London, 22 July–22 October.
www.shakespearesglobe.com
Director: Sean Holmes

TITUS ANDRONICUS

Cream Faced Loons. King's Arms, Salford, 18–21 October.
www.creamfacedloons.co.uk
Director: Abey Bradbury
Audience offered free ponchos and ear plugs. Aaron's lines given to Tamara.

TWELFTH NIGHT

Tower Theatre Company. Tower Theatre, Stoke Newington, 18–28 May.
https://towertheatre.org.uk
Female Malvolio.

East London Shakespeare Festival. Higham Hill Hub, London, 16 June and tour to 7 August.
www.elsf.uk
Director: Scott Le Crass

Players Theatre Company. Drayton Arms Theatre, Inner London, 21–25 June and tour to July.
All-female company.

Troubadour Stageworks. Penlee Park Open Air Theatre, Penzance, 5 July.
https://troubadourstageworks.com

Heartbreak Productions. Riverside Theatre, Coleraine, 5 July and tour to 22 August.
www.heartbreakproductions.co.uk

Cambridge Shakespeare Festival, Downing College Gardens, Cambridge, 11–30 July.

Sixteenfeet Productions. Kew Gardens, London, 29 July–28 August.
Director: Peter Hamilton Dyer
www.sixteenfeet.co.uk

Three Inch Fools. Tour July–September.
www.threeinchfools.com

First Encounters: Twelfth Night
Royal Shakespeare Company. The Other Place, Stratford-upon-Avon, 10–12 November and tour.
Director: Robin Belfield
90-minute version aimed at 7–13-year-olds.

Adaptation

The HandleBards. Berrybank Amphitheatre, Upper Oddington, 19 July and tour to October.
www.handlebards.com

12th Night Lite
Evoke Productions. Edinburgh Festival Fringe, Paradise in Augustines, The Studio, 10–11 August.
www.evokeproduction.co.uk
Abridged version with cast of three.

MISCELLANEOUS

47th
Old Vic Theatre, London, 12 April–28 May.
Playwright: Mike Bartlett
Director: Rupert Goold
Satire on Donald Trump written in Shakespearian blank verse with allusions to several plays.

PROFESSIONAL SHAKESPEARE PRODUCTIONS 2022

Doctor Who: Time Fracture
Immersive Everywhere. Immersive LDN, London, 16 June–11 March 2022.
Director: Tom Maller
Multiple actors interact in multiple rooms, including Shakespeare composing a play for Elizabeth I.

Shake'd Up
IK Productions. Brighton Fringe, Brighton Open Air Theatre, 19 May.
Improvised show with the audience suggesting genre, characters and performance style.

Shakespeare in Love
Brighton Little Theatre. Brighton Open Air Theatre, 17–19 August.
www.brightonlittletheatre.com

The Shark is Broken
GFour Productions. Ambassadors Theatre, London, 21 October–15 January 2022.
Director: Guy Masterson
The filming of *Jaws*. Includes recitation of Sonnet 29 by Robert Shaw's character.

THE YEAR'S CONTRIBUTION TO SHAKESPEARE STUDIES

1. CRITICAL STUDIES

REVIEWED BY EZRA HORBURY

These are books filled with uncertainty. This theme is explicit and central to Lauren Robertson's *Entertaining Uncertainty in the Early Modern Theater*, but uncertainty features throughout 2023's Shakespeare studies in sometimes surprising ways. Questions of knowing and unknowing, the uncertainty of sound, and the slippery unknowability of identities, categories and physical phenomena present a world of unstable knowledge and fraught attempts to fix sense and meaning upon it. Questioning, deconstructing and rendering deliberately obscure emerge as key critical methods, and much seems productively indeterminate.

To begin with those texts tied more closely to questions of performance, Laura Jayne Wright's *Sound Effects: Hearing the Early Modern Stage* considers 'the shifting and malleable sonic world' of early modern drama (2). This is a work concerned more with the semantics than the mechanics of sound effects, though audience response is a key preoccupation. The book nicely complements ongoing work on recreating the soundscapes of early modern London, as explored by such large projects as Early Modern Soundscapes and the English Broadside Ballad Archive, providing here an attentive interpretation of the meanings of sounds in early modern drama. We come to understand audiences as both makers and receivers of sound, the importance of becoming 'sound-aware readers' (20) and the mix of deliberate and accidental sounds that comprise the theatrical backdrop.

The book includes four chapters that chart soundgrams, nocturnal sounds, Ben Jonson's use of sound, and Shakespeare's use of sound, and in doing so analyse four ways to 'read' those sounds: as allusive, as acousmatic, as invasive and as imagined. We begin with the instability of sound effects, and the ways in which playwrights can deploy sounds allusively. This shows how 'Sound effects are caught between their capacity to signify and their capacity to contain subjective meanings' (33). The semantic ambiguity of thunder, trumpets, guns and bells is explored here, with the analysis of bells and trumpets proving particularly rich. Trumpets as a 'signal of beginnings' (42) and bells as markers of specificity – 'a sonic dissonance between *here* and *there*, *this bell* and *those bells*' (58) – facilitate compelling ways of reading these sonic moments. As intriguing as the allusive use of sound to recall specific uses of sounds in other plays might be, our only major example is in William Rowley's *A New Wonder*; if this is a widespread feature of early modern drama, it would be fascinating to hear more about it. The broader allusive use of soundgrams considers how sounds such as gunfire, trumpets and bells can refer to environments, experiences and situations, 'dependent on memory', and can subvert meanings just as much as they communicate them (64).

In chapter 2, the subject of nocturnal soundscapes is shown to 'interrogate... contemporary spiritual and philosophical concerns over the veracity of the senses' (73). Sounds can be sourceless and disorientating: nocturnal, indefinable yet meaningful, liminal and unseen; and they can be 'acousmatic', sounds without known sources. Such sounds are uncertain and unrecognized by players, which means 'To listen becomes an act of theatrical faith that trusts in the evidence of things not seen' (108). Chapters 3 and 4 turn to Ben Jonson and William Shakespeare respectively, considering Jonson's use of bodies and sound and Shakespeare's use of potential sounds. Jonson is a critic and modifier of sounds, first drawing a clear distinction between sound and speech before positioning the body as, 'like the playhouse, ... the producer, the receiver, and the container of sound' (116). The windy nonsense of speech is treated here, and there are unexplored opportunities to engage with other windy concepts – Falstaffian air, Bakhtinian belching – though we remain attentively textually engaged. This chapter provides frequently useful axioms for thinking with, such as the tenuousness between 'meaningful speech and meaningless sound' (119–20) and how 'The body both made sound and suffered from sound' (124). There is definitely potential for more theoretical extension of these ideas, but this is a strong textual foundation. This includes a stimulating reading of *Volpone*, where Morose figures as 'a megaphone, magnifying the sound he would contain' (147–8). The possibility for comparative readings is tantalizing here: in Jonson, 'dangerous speech and sounds are not merely frivolous; they are infectious, and the act of listening can make one vulnerable' (148) – how might these readings of sonic infection apply to 'breathier' texts such as *Coriolanus*?

On Shakespeare, the subject is the unheard and the untold, where 'sound onstage can be a fallacy, as much of an error that might drive ears amiss as speech can be' (156). This centres on the question of how audiences are always also 'auditors' who construct their own forms of sound in their mind, and thus all produce sound as individual experiences – essentially a question of qualia. This chapter raises a wide variety of fascinating avenues to consider: the absence of sound always invoked in its description, the 'phonographic ekphrasis' (164) of comparing sounds to painting, and how 'verbal descriptions of sound are ... subject to the manipulation of their speakers. What is spoken can be false; and what is heard can also be misheard' (173). Sounds serve to mark doubt, with unreliable descriptions creating soundscapes 'mediated by unreliable listeners who infect audiences with their own sense of doubt' (181). This emphasis on the audience as active listeners and thus participants in the creation of plays' auditory worlds is especially promising.

Wright's book is a strong complement to ongoing research in early modern soundscapes, perhaps most notable for its wide-ranging textual readings which rove from the familiar to the obscure. Wright identifies sonic tropes across a vast selection of plays to assemble these first two chapters, and indeed a minor complaint might be that the density of these comparisons makes the latter two author-focused chapters a little less compelling. There is a great deal of theoretical potential in further pursuing some of the ideas raised in this book that can hopefully be taken up in future, or by other scholars. For anyone interested in sound on the early modern stage, Wright's book is a very worthy addition to the corpus.

In contrast to Wright's exploration of the listening audience of early modern drama, Hannah August's *Playbooks and Their Readers in Early Modern England* provides a look into its reading audience. This book treats the early readers of early modern printed plays, examining what playbooks 'imply about their readers – textually, paratextually, and materially' (3). This is an excellently written and particularly accessible text; while audiences as readers are less commonly covered in the teaching of early modern drama, this is a perfectly understandable text for strong undergraduates and would make a good choice for courses teaching about audiences beyond the playhouse.

Its first chapter asks who read plays, and explores a diverse demographic of readers, considering particularly the dynamics of purchasing and ways to motivate and manipulate consumer habits. Attention is paid to fine details of paratextual materials which are found to express the common anxiety of playwrights that their plays will not suit the tastes of a consumer public, while navigating difficulties including readers' lack of education and the phenomenon of printers' profits conflicting with playwrights' desires for a more elite demographic of readers. These studies shore up work on the consumer impact of paratexts, where it appears that excessive paratexts are similarly used to appeal to buyers in plays as well as biblical texts. Other playwrights, August demonstrates, particularly Thomas Heywood, seek to court a less specific readership, encompassing lower-class and women readers. But attempts to specifically court a female readership 'do so by stressing the propriety of their subject matter, in order to combat the non-dramatic discourses that view women's playreading as an incitement to immodest thoughts or behaviour' (56). As August emphasizes, however, it 'is not that playbooks were marketed to women: it is clear from the examples Levin gives that they weren't. It is that they weren't *not* marketed to women' (59). This, too, contributes well to ongoing scholarship on women readers. August's explorations into how playwrights manipulate readers, inviting their judgements and thus allowing them 'to imaginatively self-identify as intellectually and/or socially superior', are especially stimulating (62).

Chapter 2 asks the straightforward question of why plays were read, and expands on the paratextual discussion of chapter 1 to consider how these paratexts affected readings. August's argument here is that readers developed a more sophisticated understanding of generic taxonomy, and that paratexts subsequently heightened the poetic nature of plays in order to interact with that growing understanding. There is an important argument here about complicating assumptions that playtexts aimed to convey the original performance; as August demonstrates, subsequent editions of plays were expected to reflect the most recent productions and thus would change appropriately to remain updated. The chapter then turns to the question of the market value of author identity, asking exactly what the name of an author signified and arguing that it served a 'generic' purpose, indicating to readers what a play might contain by its authors. Tragedies and histories are accompanied by generic indicators, whereas comedies were not: for Shakespeare's work, it is the specific inclusion of his name that indicates their comic structure. We see how attempts to advertise playbooks' poetic nature are fraught with difficulty: playbooks printed with 'paratexts that reached out to those readers who were sufficiently educated to appreciate the genre's pedigree ... ran the risk that those same readers would be familiar with the precepts regarding the ideal form and content of that genre' (92). The importance of paratexts is clearly paramount, as they come to emphasize the bawdiness and originality of their works to sell them. Divorced from the overall content of the book, these arguments as to the influence of paratexts fit well within the growing scope of paratextual scholarship.

The final two chapters turn to the process of reading plays, examining 'extractive reading' in the commonplace books of Edward Pudsey, William Drummond and Abraham Wright, as well as analysing the manuscript additions made to plays themselves. First, August emphasizes how gentlemen readers organized commonplace books against the means of organization recommended by theorists: these readers develop their own, esoteric systems of organization. For example, Pudsey excludes Shakespeare's name as a header because of his familiarity with him, employing a 'method of organisation [that] enables the use of his notebook as a reference tool ... structured through his privileging of the early modern author and its classificatory function' (134). By contrast, 'For Pudsey, what is important is the playbook as a locus of extractable text, not performed or performable text' (141). It is extremely rewarding to see these gulfs between the prescriptive or intended purposes of organizational systems or paratexts and their actual use. For Drummond, his own selections of quotations and their arrangement reveal 'a prurient fixation upon erotic subject matter' (141), including the recontextualizing of quotations to suit his personal interests and heightening or introducing misogynistic senses as he does so. This is an interesting practice to compare with a work such as Thomas Bentley's *The Monument of Matrones* (1582), which offers similar recontextualizations of non-dramatic works for misogynistic purposes. By contrast, Abraham Wright 'retains a sense of plays as performable wholes, even as he reshapes them into groups of textual fragments' and 'collapses the distinction between plays and another early modern genre that existed in both oral and textual form: the sermon' (153). These are rich, complementary case studies with obvious application beyond their immediate context of playbooks.

In the final chapter, August considers the use of books in the sense of both manuscript additions (e.g., underlining) and the 'book-ness' of books. August considers how 'the marks and marginalia ... point to moments of "use", to "acts of reading", to shared and individual reading practices, and (occasionally, if not often) to "readings"' (178). The actual process of early modern reading, of course, remains mostly lost to us, but through such marginalia August is able to consider responses to the playbook as material object, how marginalia function as an aid to reading, what we can learn from them about the ways in which readers categorized their playbooks, and their use of recordkeeping. August demonstrates conclusively that 'it is by no means certain that performance was at the forefront of readers' minds when they annotated these books ... their sense seems largely to have been of these material objects as books that resembled other books, containing texts that invoked other texts – rather than the performances of those playtexts that were historic, contemporaneous, or virtual' (219). This is convincingly and thoroughly argued.

August's book is an exceptional work with relevance not just to its immediate topic of playbooks and readers but to wider interests in reading practices and paratexts outside of the world of drama. Eminently readable and excellently structured, it is a very strong contribution to the field.

My personal interests and research on early modern financial ethics led me to Anne Enderwitz's *Economies of Early Modern Drama: Shakespeare, Jonson, and Middleton*, which considers household management and commerce on the early modern stage, and the socio-economic contexts of plays grappling with the new implications of exchange in an increasingly mercantile world. Chapter 1 discusses household management and oeconomy, with thorough consideration given to both classical and early modern perspectives on these themes. It argues that 'The sheer amount of verbal instructions in the prescriptive literature of the time indicates the household's political significance, but also its lack of transparency and the anxieties this produced' (41). We are told the plays' 'dynamic network structure is clearly at odds with the discrete, governable space of prescriptive literature' (85); however, what these differences are, how they occur, and why they are of interest could be more clearly considered, given the weight of household management in the first chapter and that this is a book on early modern drama. These relationships are made clearer in chapter 3, which considers master–servant relationships in *Othello* and *The Alchemist* and contrasts 'the instrumental use of business skills as villainous' in the former and such skills 'as object of satire' in the latter, 'yet both plays highlight the entrepreneurial efficiency of "wisdom of business", persuasive speech, theatrical self-display, and the manipulation of credit and desire' (175).

Chapter 4 offers some of the most interesting ideas in the book, which build on Craig Muldrew's foundational research to consider the dynamics of lending in *Volpone* and *Timon of Athens*. Here, Enderwitz argues, 'In a culture of credit and investment, the interval between an initial act of lending, borrowing, or investing and its recompense is particularly precarious because it leaves time enough for all kinds of complications' (176). The book emerges here as deeply concerned with moments of tension and uncertain futurity, a subtextual thread through much of its discussion, and an untapped cohesive theme. The reading of gifts in *Volpone* is strong: here, 'The gift shares the structural delay of a reciprocal action with credit. It is thus ideal for an exploration of the asynchronous temporality of profitable lending and investing' (181). I am less convinced by the author's reading of *Timon of Athens*, which focuses almost exclusively on the first acts of the play and is very brief on Timon's discovery of the gold. I agree with Enderwitz in saying this has 'an important structural function', but the reading glosses too easily over Timon's use of this gold (221). His intentions are not merely destructive, but rely on the excessive nature of sexual disease as parallel for excessive spending in order to reap syphilitic profit.

There are some structural components of the book that seem questionable. The prose is extremely dense and some of the author's syntax can stymy clarity (e.g., 'the chapter seeks to put a finger on the ethical drift' and 'seeks to identify neuralgic points': 26–7). Chapters are lengthy, yet tend to advance relatively discrete theses for different plays without much justification for their combination into single long chapters. For a book ostensibly on early modern drama, there is no substantial discussion of the plays until one-third of the way through, at page 79 of a 237-page book (excluding postfatory material). The choice of play pairings is certainly striking and intriguing – *A Chaste Maid in Cheapside* with *Macbeth*, *Othello* with *The Alchemist*, *Volpone* and *Timon of Athens* – but it is rarely made clear why such works have been placed in tandem, as there is extremely little comparison. This is primarily a concern in its discussion of *A Chaste Maid in Cheapside* and *Macbeth*, which focuses on oeconomy and 'the exploits of practical rationality beyond the limits of virtue ethics', and how 'they contribute to the revaluation of private interest in commercial society' (82). There is surprisingly little attention given to the extremely diverse settings of seventeenth-century London streets and the castle and heath of medieval Scotland, given this chapter's discussion of 'the intersection of the domestic and the political' (81).

The book is replete with extremely rigorous, contextually informed and textually supported readings of its plays, and it will doubtless prove an excellent resource for any reader interested in oeconomy as it relates to the individual plays. While the book is overall thoroughly researched, particularly in early modern and classical contexts, there are some notable gaps in its engagement with early modern scholarship. The author's analysis of gift theory à la Maus and Derrida would have benefitted greatly from engagement with Sean Lawrence's *Forgiving the Gift: The Philosophy of Generosity in Shakespeare and Marlowe* (Penn, 2012). A couple of pages of Joshua Scodel's *Excess and the Mean in Early Modern English Literature* (2002) are cited, but this foundational text ought to have more thoroughly informed Enderwitz's discussions of Aristotelian excess and moderation. However, its first chapter, with its extensive analysis of husbandry manuals, conduct books and other writings on household management, is an excellent overview of the subject. Its sum is weaker than its parts, and this is perhaps a book best encountered in pieces rather than totality.

Daniel Blank's *Shakespeare and University Drama in Early Modern England* brings new attention to early modern university plays, arguing for their influence on Shakespeare and early modern drama in general, as well as considering the role of drama in transforming Oxford and Cambridge into 'more outward-facing universities' (43). This work explores many lesser-known plays, recovering the details of plays whose ephemerality and limited audience have necessarily precluded them from more extended study, but grants them new significance in this reevaluation of the landscape of early modern university drama and popular theatre.

Chapter 1 focuses on Thomas Legge and William Gager, presenting a rich portrait of university drama at its most lavish, considering 'the university stage's large-scale, festive activities in the years when the commercial stage – along with its most prominent generation of playwrights – was still finding its footing' (15). These are men, Blank argues, who were considered comparable to professional playwrights, and there was a greater affinity between the academic and commercial stages than is conventionally assumed. The chapter offers a reevaluation of Legge's *Richardus Tertius*, contrasting its language and dramaturgy with Shakespeare's *Richard III*, and examines the appeal of Gager's own plays beyond the university. The importance of the university press is brought into relief: this allowed for a reach beyond immediate audiences, and facilitated the broader influence of university drama. Blank acknowledges that the comparisons between these playwrights and Shakespeare are purposed to 'illuminate' the latter rather than establish influence, and its conclusion is more that academic performances 'may have alerted him to the impressive productions of the university stage', rather than demonstrating any concrete impact (37).

Chapter 2 is rooted in compelling close readings of academic and commercial plays, considering the university's reaction to concerns about academic insularity and the impact of the threatening intrusion of the town on students' moral and academic standing. It treats particularly the concern of love as a threat to scholarship, an idea 'being expressed with particular vehemence at the end of the sixteenth century in England' (41). This provides a strong framework for a stimulating reading of *Love Labour's Lost*, wherein, Blank argues, 'Shakespeare explores the impracticality and unsustainability of this exclusionary model' (42). As above, Blank eschews any argument for the direct influence of academic plays on Shakespeare, and considers instead the potential of parallel readings. This includes a persuasive reading of *Doctor Faustus*, arguing 'that Faustus' global inclinations signify not only a rejection of Reformation theology and the philosophical learning it entailed; they also signify a rejection of academic isolation, of the inward-facing space of scholarship itself' (52–3). The conception of the university in drama, Blank argues, is marked by 'porousness': 'It is an institution from which scholars can come and go, and upon which outside forces can freely intrude' (61). This provides a stimulating context through which to consider commercial drama, and makes a convincing case that 'In addition to depicting the collision between the universities and the outside world, theatrical performance – both academic and commercial – was doing a great deal to facilitate it' (62).

Chapter 3 considers the ultimate exemplar of the Shakespearian scholar, Hamlet. While Hamlet's background as a university player has long been considered, Blank is specifically interested in the culture of university drama that informs Hamlet's own dramaturgy: 'that university concerns [...] constitute an unnoticed dimension of the play – a dimension that is quite separate from power politics or familial turmoil, and one that relates specifically to the misogynistic and antitheatrical elements of the tragedy' (72). This is an extremely intriguing reappraisal of the metatheatre of *Hamlet*, bringing new attention not only to how the criticisms of John Rainolds et al. impacted university drama but their role, too, in commercial drama. Hamlet's speech to the players, Blank suggests, 'simultaneously recreates a university performance while imposing upon it the "modesty" that Rainolds had so fervently demanded' (86). Blank also pays consistent attention to the misogynistic theme in the criticisms of love, female sexuality and the outside world, and offers a convincing argument for Hamlet's worldview as a product of the university drama concerns about insularity and antitheatricalism.

Chapter 4 turns to disputed prophecies in *Macbeth*, centring Shakespeare's encounter with *Tres Sibyllae* and his departures from Matthew Gwinne's play, considering Shakespeare's play as a 'subtle commentary upon the relationship between kingship and intellectual culture' (98). As with Blank's reading of Hamlet and university culture, this offers a nuanced and productive reevaluation of the themes of Shakespeare's works, and perhaps results in a more successful argument than earlier chapters' more speculative theses. This discussion includes a particularly impressive reading of the witches as 'imperfect speakers', emphasizing the overlooked grammatical sense of the imperfect tense and Macbeth's desire for 'the temporal position heralded by *Tres Sibyllae*. While *Macbeth* (and Macbeth) looks anxiously toward an uncertain future, *Tres Sibyllae* looks triumphantly back at the past, with the uncertainty of a vague prophesy now safely lodged in history, rendered "perfect"' (108). The chapter is also notable for connecting *Macbeth* to Edmund Leigh's university notebook, which transcribes a disputation whose debates, Blank suggests, reflect the concerns of Shakespeare's play and may suggest Shakespeare's own encounter with this notebook.

Finally, Blank considers Ben Jonson as a commercial playwright whose desire to be part of university culture is embedded with the complexly changing world of academic insularity. Blank finds Jonson's pull to the universities 'based upon an outmoded conception of the university stage' (133). By the time at which Jonson took up his residency at Christ Church, the inward nature of the university had so much transformed and university drama had shifted so much to the concerns of the public stage that Jonson's conception of the old university stage no longer existed. Blank offers another excellent close reading, this time of *Volpone*, and considers its questioning of university drama as the very means by which Jonson was able to access the university stage. Ultimately, Blank convincingly demonstrates, 'the academic theater scene that Jonson was expecting – teeming with Latinate, erudite, neoclassical stage-poetry – may well have been quite different from the one that he found' (151).

Blank's study is a thorough and consistently convincing analysis of the relationship between university and commercial drama, which presents a useful and carefully painted portrait of an overlooked dynamic in early modern theatrical culture. Readers might find chapters rooted in specifically evidenced arguments for influences more compelling than those that more modestly consider potential illumination, but this is overall a strong contribution to our understanding of the early modern theatre.

One of the strongest works this year, and one engaging uncertainty most explicitly, is Lauren Robertson's *Entertaining Uncertainty in the Early Modern Theater: Stage Spectacle and Audience Response*. This is an outstanding and incisive examination of the ways in which the early modern theatre explores and experiments with uncertainty, particularly the sense of presenting a specifically *entertaining* uncertainty, where uncertainty is defined by theatrical effect rather than emotional affect. This is against an epistemological background of discomfiting uncertainty: in addition to commonly recognized factors driving uncertainty – including the Reformation, emergence of Baconian scepticism, crisis of succession, and massive changes in London – Robertson advances a 'cultural circulation of uncertainty' (13). The book opens with the familiar sight of Old Hamlet's ghost, yet emphasizes that an early modern viewer would not be able to immediately identify him as such. Subjected to such uncertainty, audiences could thus participate in performance through their own imaginative engagement with that staged uncertainty. The book treats an incremental increase of the effect of uncertainty, as playgoers develop an ever increasing context for staged uncertainties, and theatre appropriately responds and adapts. With a lucid and productive focus on bodies, time, props, space and audience, Robertson expertly recontextualizes many familiar and unfamiliar moments in early modern drama through the highly rewarding lens of entertaining uncertainty. We see how tragicomedy emerges from staging bodies that reveal themselves to not necessarily be dead, how history plays offer the invitation to '*unknow*' (17) the past and create pleasure from a crisis of succession, how the 'ephemerality of theatrical spectacle' exists as 'alternative to the permanence of partial knowledge' (17), how communities share a 'mutual recognition of their opacity' (18) and, finally, that changes in Caroline drama meant that the most certain playgoers were the most open to uncertainty.

Chapter 1 addresses bodies, contextualizing the semiotic ambiguity of actors pretending to be dead alongside the spiritual ambiguity of the line between life and death, and the importance of the resurrection. The connection between sleep and death renders the process of reading breath highly uncertain, a fact exploited by the *Henry IV*s with both Hal mistaking his father for dead and Falstaff's comic resurrection, as well as Falstaff's stabbing of Hotspur's body. Such moments 'looked forward to a theatrical reality in which onstage corpses universally reverberated with the possibility of their own animation' (47). In chapter 2, on time, the book investigates the achievement of uncertainty in the history play. Such works encourage spectators to unknow history, 'cultivat[ing] conditional thinking by giving spectators a truthful baseline from which their minds were encouraged to wander; they were training grounds in speculation' (75).

Through manifesting foreclosed possibilities, plays exploring succession crises such as *Edward II*, *Richard II* and *Macbeth* explore the possibility of speculative thinking.

The third chapter addresses props, particularly minuscule objects and the theatre's struggle to represent not only the very large (battles, countries, storms) but also the very small, thus inviting its spectators to look on things that they cannot see. It is striking that such obscure props 'are deployed as evidence intended to resolve the epistemological and erotic crises produced by the perceived inscrutability of women's bodies' (115), as is explored through Thomas Massinger's *The Picture*. This includes a rich reading of *Cymbeline* and Iachimo's dynamics of squinting, as well as treating Antony and Cleopatra's final 'paradoxical display of what is lost when only probably knowledge remains' (135). In considering space, the subject of chapter 4, Robertson considers how 'playgoers' emerged as a new category of identity, one that persisted beyond the conclusion of the play to which such spectators were going. This raises the question of how spectators identified one another at a time 'when the theater was still actively deciding what its plays looked like' (150). This follows into a rich analysis of how playwrights utilize the physicality of the playhouse to contextualize plots of mistaken identity, where 'the bifurcated structure of the enclosed playhouse' becomes crucial to the entertainment of uncertainty (151). The unseen worlds beyond the theatre doors are crucial to these entertainments. The chapter also explores Impersonation as a spatial trope, where Portia must navigate space as well as costume, and *The Roaring Girl* signals the impossibility of pinpointing imposters among spectators. Such uses of space all serve to 'remind … spectators of their interpretive limitations and partial knowledge' (160).

Finally, the book turns to the subject of audience in relation to the Caroline theatre, by which point it was not just knowledge of the theatre but also the limits of that knowledge that constructed this idea of audience of community. Focusing on *The Spanish Tragedy* and *The Roman Actor*, Robertson explores how 'The dramatic arc of *The Roman Actor* thus encourages spectators to make sense of the world of the play with the interpretive tools so crucially withheld from them in *The Spanish Tragedy*, only to thwart, ultimately, precisely that attempt' (206). Such forms of intertheatricality situate uncertainty in the allusions between texts, and link interestingly with similar points about subversive allusions in sound made in Wright's work. Knowing a play meant one also had to be 'open to its next unpredictable, transformed appearance on the stage', and so such uncertainty became central to changes in early modern epistemology (207). In gesturing to the Restoration theatre's inability to manage the uncertainty that had defined its forebears, Robertson concludes that 'Uncertainty was the definitive mode of early modern theatrical phenomenology' (208). These theses are all brilliantly argued, creating an overall excellent, stimulating work, fluently written, that offers new insights into early modern theatre and epistemology.

This is not a year that saw a great deal of theological or religious studies treatment, but Roberta Kwan's *Shakespeare, the Reformation and the Interpreting Self* is worth noting. It is unfortunate that this book must suffer from the medium of its publication. Edinburgh University Press now exclusively supplies review copies through their Edinburgh University Press ebook application. This ereader app provides no functionality for highlighting or note-taking, while attempting to copy text will crash the app. This is an extremely poor way to read and review books and I urge Edinburgh University Press to consider alternatives.

Kwan's book presents an exploration into Reformation hermeneutics which 'juxtaposes early modern theological hermeneutics with modern-day philosophical hermeneutics', thus 'bring[ing] together two overlapping (rather than remote) ways of apprehending human being' (170). Kwan explores Shakespeare's 'interpreting selves' (2) through the plays – those conventionally categorized as problem plays. Knowing God and knowing the self is central to early modern

Reformation understanding, Kwan argues, and this can be traced through Shakespeare's works. Readings are, at their best, deep and subtle, tightly interweaving early modern and modern philosophical approaches, though this means it won't have much broader appeal. After an initial chapter mapping out Reformation hermeneutics, which is somewhat unoriginal and syntopic, we move on to *Hamlet* and the titular prince as an interpreting self; chapter 3 considers *Troilus and Cressida* alongside the unreliability of our own self-interpretation, 'and the potential that this flawed knowledge has to corrode the self as a moral agent' (24–5). Chapter 4 turns to *Measure for Measure* and interrogates the effect of justice and individual agency on modern selfhood. Chapter 5 concludes with *All's Well That Ends Well* and its 'eschatological hermeneutic which directed early modern English people's attention to the next life' (25).

Some of the strongest moments in this volume are those with the narrowest of focus: the Friar's response to the slander against Hero, where he is positioned as an interpreter and not receiver of truth; or the shared inability of the Duke and Angelo to see themselves and their failure to enact genuine mercy. Its modern philosophical method may make this appeal more to those of a similar school rather than Reformation or Shakespeare scholars more generally, but the book thoroughly treats the question of self-interpretation through a mixed early modern and modern philosophical framework.

Turning to more identitarian themes, Victoria L. McMahon's *Shakespeare, Tragedy and Menopause: The Anxious Womb* provides a historically sweeping and textually vigorous account of menopause in early modern England, and how Shakespearian tragedy engages with its major ideas. McMahon takes a carefully anti-presentist approach, arguing that '"Menopause" did not exist medically or culturally until the early nineteenth century when it was recognized as a holistic condition' (1). McMahon instead presents a history of a 'proto-menopause', assembled from an array of different medical, cultural and philosophical ideas circulating at this time (5). The five main themes addressed include petrification (both in the womb and through the eyes), botanical conceptions of female reproduction, animalistic comparisons and the vagina as mouth, humoral envy and the cyborg womb.

It is a great credit to McMahon's work that the central characters of this study – *Hamlet*'s Gertrude, *Titus Andronicus*'s Tamora, *Coriolanus*'s Volumnia, *Macbeth*'s Lady Macbeth, *Antony and Cleopatra*'s Cleopatra – emerge, despite their familiar and canonical nature, as such new and exciting figures through these readings. McMahon has assembled a stunning selection of ideas and methods through which these plays are read, and the interpretations that emerge are exciting and stimulating. A definition of the early modern menopause is both badly needed and timely, and makes an excellent companion to Sara Read's 2013 *Menstruation and the Female Body in Early Modern England*, also published by Palgrave Macmillan, with which McMahon engages. Its wide thematic explorations are also laudable: this is a book that mediates between concerns of witchcraft, motherhood, midwifery and humoral theory, and ranges through animal studies, cyborg studies and plant studies. It is also a deeply generous book in terms of its engagement with other scholarship. McMahon consistently acknowledges the strengths of previous scholarship and defines her own departures from them without ever demeaning earlier work. It thoroughly footnotes its influences and references, and will thus provide a very useful work for undergraduates who are keen to learn more about these subjects. While I cannot say I am always convinced by the readings, they certainly offer some dazzling new perspectives on the texts.

The book is structured across six chapters and a conclusion, lacking an introduction and providing instead a contextual overview of 'Uterine pathologies and menopausal ambiguities' (1). These are long, rich chapters, helpfully divided into subsections that are each separately listed in the contents. Although it is a dense work, McMahon's prose is extremely readable and she writes engagingly and feelingly of both the plays themselves and the real individuals on whom various medical studies were conducted that inform her readings. The first chapters define McMahon's methods for approaching menopause, with a study that 'doesn't intend to exclusively medicalize early modern "menopause"' but rather 'embraces the recognition that conceptions of the female body were informed by differing belief systems – not only of how that body was physiologically constituted, but also how that body was expected to perform in social space' (2). At 66 pages, this is a complex exploration, but well worth the time even for readers who might be less interested in the literary applications themselves.

Hamlet and Gertrude is the first literary subject, in which McMahon 'explore[s] the specific implications of a drying womb and its corollary influence upon the female sex drive, the pathology of which caused the desiccating body to emanate deadly, petrifying toxins, both within and without the body proper' (71). Two of the main themes here are the idea of the petrifying womb which could literally transform foetuses into stone, as in the case of *lithopedia*, and the eye as the site of emanating ossifying toxins. McMahon's combination of such stimulating material and innovative readings is both the strength and the weakness of this book. This chapter offers new perspectives on Gertrude and her son, and the parallels between the medical contexts and the plays can be striking, though the relationship between the context and text could be more convincing. McMahon does not seem to argue that Shakespeare would have encountered accounts of some of these medical phenomena (other than the *lithopedia*'s fame being sufficient for Charles I to hope to purchase a specimen), and so there may be some limited utility to considering them as necessarily informing the texts. Nonetheless, McMahon's lack of concern for establishing empirical influences in favour of generating parallel readings allows for some of the most intriguing interpretations in this book, so this methodological quibble may not be a concern to all.

Tamora and her 'invasive vegetable womb' provides the next subject matter (109). This chapter provides a botanical understanding of her reproductive capabilities, considered alongside plants and those animals that were believed to generate spontaneously in earthy environments, such as flies and tadpoles. McMahon argues, 'as a subject of the ageing process, Tamora's "invisible" pregnancy speaks to how changes within the womb's microclimate transpiring under certain environmental conditions were perceived as pathological and likely to result in unnatural conception' (115). These are strong readings and position Tamora's pregnancy and the 'blackamoor' child in a new and productive framework.

We then turn to Volumnia, connecting proto-menopause with 'uterine afflictions' and 'their metaphorical connection to the bestial' (156). This considers both the role of blood in the play, covering Coriolanus and connecting him with Volumnia's own body, as well as the double 'mouths' of the female body. Both the reproductive power of the uterus and the rhetorical power of the mouth are silenced in this play, as a means to 'tame' 'the proto-menopausal woman's many "mouths"' (156). Valeria is absent in this analysis, and Virgilia appears only fleetingly. McMahon's focus on the most overtly proto-menopausal characters is obviously sensible, but I wonder – especially given McMahon's troubling of the category of 'old' for women – if there is opportunity, too, to consider those characters less overtly considered menopausal. Virgilia's single son has been variably attributed to her husband's lengthy warring or to his aversion to marital sex, but could these readings lead us to challenge the conventional 'age coding' of other female characters?

Lady Macbeth is read alongside Invidia, the figuration of envy whose dried body and monstrous form provide a parallel for her own unsexing and greed. Here, McMahon argues, 'Shakespeare presents us with an early modern body in the throes of a particular pathology that mimics many aspects of contemporary menopause: changes to the quantity and consistency of menstrual flow; irrational thought and behaviours; and manic depression' (198). This is one of the most specific and conventionally convincing interpretations in the book, though also the least exciting, and it reflects many similar ideas about witchcraft and the female body particularly generated by Lyndal Roper's work. Finally, in the most theoretically distinct chapter, McMahon tackles Cleopatra as a mechanical cyborg. Cleopatra 'challenges the boundaries of what her ageing body can do within the play ... playing with themes of power and control housed within a radically reconfigured body – a body informed by systems of emergent scientific thought' (243). Alongside readings of Cleopatra's self-fashioning and her use of prostheses, perhaps the strongest idea is the simple reconceptualization of Enobarbus' infamous description of Cleopatra's barge. Here, the barge is imagined as a mechanical metonymy, extending Cleopatra's flesh into a cyborg: here, 'The fans, bellows, oars, flutes, and sails are aerial instruments that represent the hidden ventricles, arteries, ducts, and alveoli of the female body' (256). Like almost all of the female characters discussed in this book, Cleopatra must ultimately meet in failure. Given McMahon's own focus on statues and self-fashioning, perhaps there is opportunity for a more positive reading here, in Cleopatra's self-sequestering within her monument, and the architectural extension of her body.

This is a consistently excellent piece of literary scholarship, with frequently sparkling readings. Beyond presenting a definition of the early modern proto-menopause, some of its strongest ideas include an emphasis on the irrelevance of the cessation of menses to early modern ideas about reproductivity, as well as the surprisingly late points at which women were believed able to reproduce. As a caveat, alongside the lack of attention to clear influential strains between these contextual writings and Shakespeare, it would have been helpful to gain a greater understanding of the extent to which some of these ideas about reproduction were rare exceptions versus commonplaces. I must register an objection to McMahon's forward-looking conclusion, which unhelpfully compares mastectomies and hysterectomies as though these are two singular procedures rather than two categories of different procedures. The conclusion then emphasizes hysterectomies as 'dangerous, risky and debilitating': this is not necessarily the case, and rather unhelpful given the incredible difficulty people with uteruses have with accessing the procedure (289).

This final blip aside, the book is especially commendable for challenging the very category of 'old age' for women at this time: 'Not only was biological "age" an inconsistent early modern marker of senescence, but one would be unable to find a homologous ontological understanding of what it means to be "old" today', McMahon emphasizes (27). This opens some intriguing potential for challenging exactly how old we assume dramatic characters to be, and rethinking the categories of middle and later age.

Also on identitarian themes, *Intersectionalities of Class in Early Modern English Drama* provides an edited collection by Ronda Arab and Laurie Ellinghausen containing fourteen essays plus an introduction that seek to 'take intersectionalities of class as the primary lens of analysis in the study of early modern English literature' (11). Class is examined through a range of lenses, including race, gender and sexuality, and overall the work makes a very useful contribution to scholarship's increasing interest in the role of class in early modern culture. This is the first essay collection on the subject of class, and it aims to unpack 'inequality; stratification; privilege and marginalization; social, cultural, and economic change and stasis' (11).

If it is not too counter to the essential intersectionality of the book, the work can be loosely divided into four chapters on race, two eco-critical essays, three on women, three more on gender, and two on war and servants. These are all relatively short essays and, with such a wide ground covered, there is certainly a sense that there is much more to be said on any of these topics, but altogether this is a sparkling and varied collection of essays.

Emily MacLeod's reading of 'Blackness, race, and class in George Chapman's May Day', which considers how the frequent comparison between racial blackness and chimney sweeps gave rise to a permanent association between race and class, even if sootiness is customarily associated with removability. Peter Lewis's and Timothy Francisco's chapters both consider contemporary adaptations, with Francisco particularly considering 'the cultural politics of white working-class Iago', who has become common in modern performances, arguing that this is 'classing racism in ways that ultimately do little to dislodge the status quo' (72).

Juan Pedro Lamata provides a useful comparative reading of two of the most notorious early modern trans figures, Antonio de Erauso and Mary/Jack Frith. Lamata treats the important question of 'why, in the seventeenth century, did the English and Spanish-speaking worlds concurrently develop separate fascinations with two trans figures who also happened to be both "rogues" and royalists?' (93). This is a strong and timely reading of figures who are becoming increasingly entrenched in early modern trans studies and teaching, and provides a very useful comparative colonial reading. Ronda Arab's work, too, considers gender and class in the context of sexual violence, investigating the use of sexual violence as a 'tool used by lower-class men against their social superiors' (263); this is also a useful study.

Paul Budra's chapter on servants, jesters and fools is another highlight, which considers how the lower classes employed performance in interacting with upper classes: how did class structure require them 'to adopt affective strategies that became crucial features of their lived experience' (150)? Its focus on disassociating affect is part of growing work on this topic and it is interesting to see applied here. On a similar note, Christi Spain-Savage's work on women's shop labour considers how such figures 'were active, invested, and vital participants in the commercial world of early modern London', and contributes usefully to our understanding of women in city comedy (232). Relatedly, Kimberly Huth's work on mixed-estate marriages is a strong, historicist piece and a useful complement to popular teaching plays such as *Arden of Faversham* and *The Duchess of Malfi*, considering how such marriage might 'expose the period's conceptions of class and gentility as cultural constructions' while rubbing up against conservative ideology (198).

Considered with the other essays in this volume, *Intersectionalities of Class in Early Modern English Drama* is a welcome and rewarding – if somewhat diffuse – selection of essays that are perhaps more useful in isolation than the collection is in its entirety, but which contribute many useful perspectives.

Finally, in the field of critical race and whiteness studies, David Sterling Brown's *Shakespeare's White Others* engages seriously with constructions of whiteness as alterity in Shakespeare. This book centrally advances the concept of the 'intraracial color-line', which 'delineates distinctions among early modern English white people that rely on the devaluing of somatically similar white folks' (2). The book interrogates the invisibility of whiteness and 'reveal[s] how anti-Black racism, anti-Black violence, and general, harmful anti-Black sentiments were and are integral to white identity formation and white ideology construction', specifically in the absence of Black characters (7). This is another strong entry in the growing field of Shakespearian critical whiteness studies, and extremely worthwhile.

It is a short but compelling work, primarily considering *Titus Andronicus*, *Antony and Cleopatra*, *Hamlet* and *Othello*. In *Titus Andronicus*, Brown examines those scenes and moments in which Aaron – the usual centre of race studies in this play – is absent, positioning him instead as a distraction from white-on-white violence between the Romans and Goths. Brown's chapter on *Hamlet*, which considered Hamlet's blackened masculinity and the play's striving for the restoration of white masculinity, makes excellent companion reading with Ian Smith's chapter on Hamlet's appropriation of black identity in *Black Shakespeare*. In *Antony and Cleopatra*, Cleopatra emerges very intriguingly as a 'racially hybrid scapegoat', with her 'tawny' body bearing a 'white hand' (100). Brown focuses on the whitening of Cleopatra through Antony's rhetoric, though there is an untreated question about Cleopatra's similar blackening. If Antony's rhetoric makes her white, do 'Phoebus' amorous pinches' partake in a similarly transformative blackening role or is this blackness assumed as essential and primary (1.5.33)?

Turning finally to *Othello*, Brown offers an ambitious and whirlwind reading of 'Iago's mind-fuck game' and the unacknowledged sexual violence inflicted against black characters, which Brown affectingly contextualizes alongside contemporary sexual assault (137). In stressing the importance of listening to black voices and paying attention to black pain, Brown productively contributes to the ongoing, transformative relevance of the text. Tamora's sexual violence against Aaron is also usefully highlighted, an element of *Titus Andronicus* often overlooked (despite its influence on William Heminges's more violent sexual assault scene in *The Fatal Contract*). Incisive, often fascinating, it is an excellent addition to Shakespeare and critical whiteness studies.

On the subject of Shakespeare's plays themselves, *Hamlet*, *Othello* and *Macbeth* emerge as the frontrunners of critical studies. *Antony and Cleopatra* also recurs, but in this particular crop there is little to be said of the histories, and almost nothing of the comedies. Driving questions of the uncertainty of identity and engagement make the tragedies particularly suitable vehicles for such concerns (although *King Lear* features surprisingly little this year), but it will be interesting to see how these epistemological questions figure when posed of more comic works.

WORKS REVIEWED

Arab, Ronda, and Laurie Ellinghausen, eds., *Intersectionalities of Class in Early Modern English Drama* (London, 2023)

August, Hannah, *Playbooks and Their Readers in Early Modern England* (London, 2022)

Blank, Daniel, *Shakespeare and University Drama in Early Modern England* (Oxford, 2023)

Brown, David Sterling, *Shakespeare's White Others* (Cambridge, 2023)

Enderwitz, Anne, *Economies of Early Modern Drama: Shakespeare, Jonson, and Middleton* (Oxford, 2023)

Kwan, Roberta, *Shakespeare, the Reformation and the Interpreting Self* (Edinburgh, 2023)

McMahon, Victoria L., *Shakespeare, Tragedy and Menopause: The Anxious Womb* (New York, 2023)

Robertson, Lauren, *Entertaining Uncertainty in the Early Modern Theater: Stage Spectacle and Audience Response* (Cambridge, 2023)

Wright, Laura Jayne, *Sound Effects: Hearing the Early Modern Stage* (Manchester, 2023)

2. EDITIONS AND TEXTUAL STUDIES
reviewed by EMMA DEPLEDGE

2023 saw the release of an updated edition of the New Cambridge *Romeo and Juliet*, featuring a new Introduction by Hester Lees-Jeffries; engaging minigraphs on *Shakespeare, Malone and the Problems of Chronology* and *Facsimiles and the History of Shakespeare Editing*, written by Tiffany Stern and Paul Salzman, respectively; and Heidi Craig's and Sarah Ledwidge's studies which offered exciting new evidence to revise our understanding of the status of Shakespeare's works in the book trade between the 1640s and early 1660s. 2023 was, of course, the quatercentenary of the Shakespeare 'First Folio', a milestone marked by an 'Anniversary' special issue of *Shakespeare Quarterly* entitled 'On Shakespeare's First Folio and Early Modern Critical Race Studies', guest edited by Noémie Ndiaye. The special issue called for scholars to reflect on 'the kinds of shifts and destabilizations that we want the quatercentenary celebrations to orchestrate' (185), and this was responded to in book-historical terms by contributors Brandi K. Adams and Emily Weissbourd, and by Emma Smith in the new preface added to the second ('400th anniversary') edition of her *First Folio: Four Centuries of an Iconic Book*.

The third edition of the New Cambridge Shakespeare *Romeo and Juliet* retains G. Blakemore Evans's text – based on the second quarto – but adds a brand new Introduction and other fresh paratexts by Lees-Jeffries. The second edition, published twenty years ago, still featured Blakemore Evans's Introduction, with an updated performance history provided by Thomas Moisan. The new Introduction supersedes Moisan's work, analysing productions and adaptations from the Restoration period through to screenings taking place during COVID-19 lockdowns. It also offers numerous fresh ways of thinking about one of Shakespeare's most popular plays. An updated 'Reading list' features works from as recent as 2023, and a new 'Note' has been added to frame Blakemore Evans's discussion of textual matters. The note provides a (very necessary) nod to the most relevant work by textual scholars, particularly that which moved us beyond notions of 'bad' quartos, and studies that undermined arguments based on 'memorial reconstruction', but it does so whilst trying not to overly emphasize the fact that Blakemore Evans's work is now over forty years old, a fact which is impossible to overlook. The text and its collational notes remain products of the period in and for which they were first produced, but Lees-Jeffries's additions do a good job of bringing the rest of the edition up to date in terms of both performance history and scholarly debates.

She presents the case for reading *Romeo and Juliet* as part of a 'cluster of Shakespeare's works' which were 'part of the same extended, mutually informative creative process as Shakespeare read and wrote both poetry and drama' (2). Drawing on new findings in dramatic history, she argues that the theatre closures of 1592–1594 should be read not simply as a moment when Shakespeare turned his attention to writing narrative poems but also as a time that may have helped to bring about the significant increase in new writing recorded in the years that followed. Throughout the Introduction, *Romeo and Juliet* is placed in the rich context of Shakespeare's other writings and the wider world of Elizabethan poetry and theatre as Lees-Jeffries draws attention to allusions, in addition to the sources usually discussed in introductions to the play, but rightly refrains from trying to push arguments about directions of influence. She specifically analyses echoes between lines of *Romeo and Juliet* and contemporary sonnets and epithalamiums, and between the play's scenes and spatial dynamics and those found in plays thought to have been performed around the same time. A key example given is the so-called 'balcony scene' of *Romeo and Juliet* and the deposition scene of *Richard II*. A section entitled 'Body Language' features skilful close readings of Romeo and Juliet's shared sonnet and Juliet's 'Gallop apace' soliloquy.

In her reflections on the 'practical, theatrical considerations that shaped Shakespeare's writing' of the play, Lees-Jeffries sets out the evidence on which 'best guesses' can be made about the actors who may have performed the play's different roles and then offers responses to scholarly debates about famous staging cruxes. It has long been assumed, thanks to Capulet referring to his serving-man as 'Will' in Q1 and the presence of his full name in a stage direction of Q2, that Will Kemp played Peter, but Lees-Jeffries adds to this the perceptive suggestion that Alexander Cooke or Robert Gough probably embodied Juliet in early productions, and the hypothesis that, rather than playing Romeo, Richard Burbage might have played Mercutio. Her logic – that a company's leading actor cannot have always played the lead as he would need to balance major roles with lesser roles, or at least less physically demanding ones, in order to cope with the workload – seems sound in itself, but Lees-Jeffries also reminds us that Mercutio is a bigger speaking part than one might assume. He only appears in four scenes but nonetheless has 'the sixth largest speaking part' and 'the largest share of the text of any sixth-largest role in a surviving 1590s play' (13).

The answers Lees-Jeffries provides to staging questions that 'may have been overthought' by her predecessors – such as the question of what happens to Juliet's bed in 4.4 – are delivered with the aplomb and common sense of an editor well versed in theatre history and dramaturgy. The idea of Romeo and Paris fighting with rapiers seems to her 'hideously dangerous for tired actors', and the overall take-home point is that most things become straightforward once we let go of expectations of spatial coherency and anything else that is 'unduly realist'; 'it might be assumed that what Quince and his amateurs regarded as essential (a real wall; some representation of the moon) is the opposite to the conventions of the professional stage' (17).

The Introduction also provides new thinking about the play's relationship to Italy and Italian(s), its portrayal of 'Dancing and Duelling', and its treatment of relations between men. However, the most notable strength is Lees-Jeffries's meticulous exploration of the play's enduring legacy, spanning from the seventeenth century to recent productions for different media. Her comprehensive analysis updates the play for a new generation through insightful examinations of film versions 'Beyond Zeffirelli' – including *Gnomio and Juliet* (directed by Kelly Asbury, 2011), which features star-crossed garden gnomes from Stratford-upon-Avon – and observations about the late twentieth-century tendency to present the lovers in productions and adaptations as divided along lines of class, race, religion and nationality (70–1). The survey of productions and adaptations, which takes a Global approach, illustrates this observation with examples such as francophone Capulets and anglophone Montagues in a Canadian production (1989–1990); an Iraqi Theatre Company production (in Stratford and London, 2012), entitled *Romeo and Juliet in Baghdad*, in which Capulet is Sunni and Montague Shia; and examples of the play's appropriation within young adult fiction, such as Pamela Laskin's verse novel *Ronit and Jamil* (2017), which depicts Israeli Ronit and Palestinian Jamil. Also discussed is the popular recent musical *& Juliet* (London 2019, Broadway 2022) which features Max Martin pop songs such as Britney Spears's 'Baby one more time', a Juliet who does not die but instead goes to Paris with her friends (the Nurse, Anne Hathaway and best friend May), and production merchandise with the slogan 'Romeo Who?'.

A final section entitled 'Love in the Time of Coronavirus' then takes us through the 'rush' of productions of *Romeo and Juliet* that appeared in the UK in 2021 – some postponed, some born-digital, others adapted for new platforms as a result of theatre closures – each responding in different ways to the context of the COVID-19 pandemic and the theatres/platforms in and for which they were (and were not) envisioned. This is a fantastic aspect of the play's afterlife with which to end as it enables Lees-Jeffries to demonstrate the crucial role the play continues to play as theatre and Shakespeare performances are reinvented across different media.

Discussion of Juliet's age is a necessary and expected inclusion in an introduction to the play and the contextual analysis of how the age of 13–14 was treated in contemporary epitaphs / poetry of mourning is sensitive and insightful, but the conversation gains nothing from the words of John Sutherland (one of the authors of *Henry V, War Criminal? And Other Shakespeare Puzzles*), whom Lees-Jeffries cites even as she reflects herself that it is 'hard to know what to say in response' to both his 'tone and opinion' (33). It is a shame his misogynist remarks were given such a platform and it is out of keeping with what is otherwise a work of scholarship that is as sensitive to the poetry of the play and the moment in and for which it was produced as it is to the needs and interests of a great variety of readers. Indeed, the Introduction is followed by a page entitled 'Advice and support', a wonderful inclusion that provides phone numbers for and links to services offering assistance for those struggling with their mental health, suicidal thoughts, or faced with the threat of forced marriage. Many of us provide trigger warnings before teaching some of Shakespeare's plays and it would be great to see versions of this page added to more editions of the plays, and not simply to plays renowned for their use in high schools, as the issues raised in Shakespeare's plays can impact readers at any point in their lives.

Lees-Jeffries is less concerned with 'tying the play to a specific date', which she 'broadly' assumes to be 1595, than she is with mapping out the kinds of conversations 'Shakespeare's play might be having with other texts around that moment' (3). The methods used to discuss chronology in single volumes and complete works of Shakespeare is the subject of Stern's new study, *Shakespeare, Malone and the Problems of Chronology*, which also traces the legacy of Edmund Malone (1741–1812) – an Irish lawyer cum literary scholar – and the development of his quest to date Shakespeare's plays in *An Attempt to Ascertain the order in Which the Plays Attributed to Shakespeare Were Written* (1778) and the subsequent versions of *An Attempt* published in 1790 and (posthumously, completed by James Boswell the Younger) in 1821. Malone, whose notes were originally produced to accompany George Steevens's edition of 1778 (known as the Johnson–Steevens Shakespeare because it updated Samuel Johnson's edition of Shakespeare's works), pioneered the fields of theatre history and literary chronology and, as Stern notes, his legacy is felt in the chronological methodology we continue to use.

By ordering plays chronologically, we risk, Stern reminds us, contributing to the fallacy that it is possible to accurately date when a play was written or the order in which Shakespeare's plays were written, whilst also reinforcing the canonization of Shakespeare and belief in the supposed development and progress of his 'genius'.[1] Stern's minigraph joins a string of recent revisionist readings of the work and impact of early scholars whose names and claims have dominated the world of Shakespeare editing and textual studies, but it is neither an attack on nor a defence of Malone. Stern questions Malone's correctness and methods but does so while paying homage to his perceptiveness, perseverance and achievements, especially at a time when access to early editions of Shakespeare's plays was so restricted, even for a man of Malone's wealth and connections. She suggests that Malone suffers from unfair representation in modern scholarship, particularly because it is his findings in the first version of the *Account* that tend to be cited and not his revised ideas. She thus outlines developments in Malone's thinking across time and reminds us of the fact that he called his work an *Attempt* (i.e. he never claimed to be offering the final word on chronology), but also highlights the many times when he simply rejected or ignored 'evidence' that did not fit the chronologies he wished to propose.

Stern's study is full of common-sense observations and prompts for us to reflect on why it is that we think we know what we think we know about when different Shakespeare plays were written. First and foremost, she notes that Malone, and a number of editors who followed him, ask the

---

[1] One notable exception, that Stern rightly praises, is the New Oxford Shakespeare, which replaced an order based on (supposed) times of composition with one based on the order in which plays were published, distinguishing between those published during and those published after Shakespeare's lifetime.

wrong question as it simply is not possible to pin the composition of a play down to one moment in time: 'most plays are palimpsests containing additions and revisions from different periods of time' (86). The second and third sections of her study are dedicated to the problems of using external and internal information, respectively, to try to produce chronologies or date plays. External evidence draws on information found on title pages and in Stationers' Register entries and documents recording performances. External evidence can only really provide a date by when something existed, and recorded performances do not necessarily record premieres. *Au contraire*, Stern suggests that the presence of lists of court or other performances that Malone uncovered make it more likely that these plays were modified for special events, thus further undermining his quest to pinpoint a single moment of writing. She also posits that it could be that Shakespeare's plays were revised not only for court performances, as Richard Dutton has argued, but also to make amphitheatre plays fit the staging requirements of the indoor Blackfriars theatre.

Internal evidence is that which is found within playtexts, be it references to other texts, topical allusions, the use of what might be deemed time-specific words and phrases, or patterns in the ways in which Shakespeare used verse, to take one formal feature, across groups of plays. Although particularly appealing when there is nothing else to guide us, internal evidence requires a 'higher level of interpretation than external information' and 'on further consideration, [often] proves to be slight and untrustworthy' (39). Stern illustrates the latter point by drawing attention to examples where Malone 'force[d], and invent[ed] dates for lexical or historical habits' and proposed far-fetched contemporary allusions instead of simply assuming that Shakespeare, as a writer of fiction, might have made things up.

As she notes, even when not repeating Malone's proposed allusions, modern editors often suggest their own readings of newly identified topical allusions. Further, Stern implies that, like Malone, modern critics tend to ignore how texts in the Folio – especially those first published within the 1623 collection – 'tend to have a date range that extends from during to beyond Shakespeare's lifetime' and probably date 'at least in certain aspects from the 1620s' (11). Especially misleading, Stern suggests, are chronological lists that merge dates based on external with dating based on internal evidence, and misguided assumptions that Shakespeare finished one play before beginning the next. Indeed, there may 'be a great deal of overlap, not just between plays that – in our chronologies – are placed side by side but also between plays that are far apart; an earlier play may be being revised while a later one is being written' (84). It is important to return to the questions of what we mean when we speak of a play's date of composition and to pause to reflect on the validity of such approaches because the 'single chronology that has dictated our method of thinking about Shakespeare for so long has brought about conclusions and sequences that may not be there' (86). This may be true, but the oft-repeated single chronologies are so crisp and have become so entrenched in the collective consciousness that it will be hard to dislodge them. It should also be remembered that arguments over a play's supposed date of composition, like new claims about internal evidence, are part and parcel of the rhetoric used to promote and sell Shakespeare editions within a saturated market.

Having identified a problem in our handling of Shakespeare chronology, Stern ends with a proposed solution. Labels used could be 'The Work, to make clear that it is about the play of that name, not about the surviving text' and 'The Text', which would refer to 'the extant text(s), considering issues of lateness and revision as well as adaptation', and could include all surviving texts, listed more than once if there are multiple versions in different formats. She further suggests that all dates on the list would potentially be date ranges, reflecting the different (somewhat) datable passages found in the text (with the heavy proviso that dating from a vague word or historical event is itself contentious, and that all the dates on the list are therefore open to question). A further proposal is that '"early" information be separated from "late" information, and "external" from "internal"' (86). As the description and the sample table containing only two plays (provided in the closing pages) suggests, Stern's idea is wonderfully liberating in theory but would likely be unwieldy in practice, not to mention hard to compile, and potentially undermined by its reliance on stylometric information from sources (Gary Taylor's and Rory Loughnane's work) which are by no means without detractors. The solution may not be perfect, but it is a start and, like Malone in the different versions of *An Account*, one imagines that Stern will continue to reflect on the best way to represent chronological uncertainty when presenting different types of evidence.

That this study is a generous contribution to human knowledge is in no doubt: Stern has read Malone across three editions, meaning that future editors can write with greater accuracy about his findings without having to re-read Malone's (pedantic) prose themselves.[2] Stern's account of the 'story that brought Shakespeare's chronology into being' is a thoroughly enjoyable read and it will appeal to scholars who find the idea of chronological instability liberating. In its questioning of the methodologies we use, and its sobering reminders about just 'how hard chronological certainty is to come by' (86), it ought to be required reading for anyone with an interest or investment in the question of when 'Shakespeare's plays were written' and what that question really means (1).

In *Facsimiles and the History of Shakespeare Editing* – another exciting study published this year as part of the Cambridge Elements in Shakespeare and Text series,[3] overseen by Claire M. L. Bourne and Rory Loughnane – Salzman considers the history of facsimiles produced using different techniques, ranging from what he terms 'artisanal facsimiles' – those that are drawn or traced by hand ('pen-facsimiles') or printed using either old type or 'pseudo-old type' – through to facsimiles made using photographic and digital technologies. His study covers various developments, not just in the techniques used to produce facsimiles but also in their perceived use for textual studies, as reflected in the debates of New Bibliographers and New Textualists, as well as in contemporary discussions about the attractions and detractions of digital facsimiles and websites offering users the opportunity to read specific copies of plays alongside one another, such as the British Library's Shakespeare in Quarto site and the new First Folios Compared website.[4]

The story told by his study is that of the mutual rise and intertwined history of scholarly editing and facsimiles, an important chapter that has until now been largely overlooked in accounts of Shakespeare's afterlife. It is argued that eighteenth-century editions of Shakespeare and other early modern writers, such as Francis Beaumont and John Fletcher and John Milton, helped to prepare the ground for the production of an increasing number of facsimile books. As Salzman explains, 'this is because the editions became further removed from the physical appearance of the original texts, while at the same time, the textually sensitive approach of editors made more people aware of how significant the early editions were' (33). This was coupled with an antiquarian 'interest in, and at times obsession with, collecting old and often rare volumes' and, when such volumes were hard to come by, 'or were imperfect, facsimiles stepped in to make up the gap', either by providing substitute copies or else by supplying missing leaves needed to complete or 'perfect' individual copies (33).

It is a riveting read, particularly the section on type-facsimiles, such as Joseph Smeaton's 1805 reproduction of Thomas Kyd's *Soliman and*

---

[2] There is even a helpful summary in the form of a table recording 'Malone's dates per *Attempt*', which are presented alongside dates proposed by the second edition of the 2022 RSC Complete Works because it is 'the most recent complete works to come out', but this is slightly misleading as it is really a 2007 edition in this respect because, like much of the second edition of Jonathan Bate and Eric Rasmussen's RSC *Works*, the 'Conjectural chronology' has not been revisited since the publication of the first edition.

[3] At *c.*30,000 words, 'Elements' fall between the scope of a long essay and that of a full monograph.

[4] See www.bl.uk/treasures and https://firstfolios.com, respectively.

Perseda, which was made by setting pieces of type 'that closely resemble' the original type used (6). Smeaton's facsimile resembles material copies of the 1599 edition of Kyd's play so well that it has fooled many into thinking it is a genuine early modern edition. Smeaton signed his work, but did so in the bottom corner of the verso of the title page. Lukas Erne, who edited a facsimile of the British Library copy of the play for the Malone Society Reprints, argued that the presence of the signature suggests that Smeaton 'intended no deception', i.e. he was not trying to pass his work off as genuine copies of the 1599 edition (8), but Salzman counters that the placement of Smeaton's signature 'allows for plausible deniability' (9). He explains that the signature placement may have been chosen with the aim of enabling owners to simply cut it out, should they so wish, as is the case in the British Library copy. I find Salzman's argument persuasive and thought-provoking and, whilst I appreciate his detailed analysis of a wide range of examples from the eighteenth century to the present day, it is a shame he did not offer more sustained discussion of how facsimiles were marketed and sold to consumers, and their status (as facsimiles) in the contemporary rare book market.

The example of the Smeaton signature and its removability, like other examples Salzman brings to light, reflects the delicate balance that existed between a desire for access and demands for authenticity, or else just a desire to learn more about Renaissance texts and the early modern book trade. R. B. McKerrow, A. W. Pollard and W. W. Greg drew extensively on facsimiles and founded the Malone Society editions (1907), which continue to be of great value to students and scholars of early modern drama. Students and scholars were their target audience from the outset and, rather than the material verisimilitude of Smeaton's work, the Malone editions aimed to be 'truer to content than form'. As Salzman notes, facsimile techniques developed across the time covered by his study, but newer was not always seen as better. Greg and his colleagues saw facsimiles as valuable, we are told, for both access and textual studies, particularly collation work, and Charlton Hinman took the learning value a step further when he produced his print facsimile, the Norton Facsimile of the First Folio of Shakespeare, in 1968. Hinman's is arguably the best-known example of a Shakespeare facsimile and, yet, it is not really a facsimile. Hinman reproduced pages from numerous Folger copies of the First Folio in a bid to produce – and thereby better understand – what might be considered 'an "ideal" [printer's] copy' of the First Folio (69–70). The examples discussed in these sections, like the (re)setting of old or pseudo-old type in type facsimiles, indeed raise important questions about whether or not a facsimile can be thought of as an edition.

The latter part of Salzman's study offers clear, sensitive histories of well-known (but often misunderstood) projects to produce microfilm and digital facsimiles in the twentieth and twenty-first centuries, and makes a strong case for the vital role they played both in widening access to the field of early modern studies and in broadening the focus of early modern scholarship. He details the history of the 'microfilm revolution', the aims of Eugene Power (founder of University Microfilms), and the relationship between microfilm facsimiles, the Short Title Catalogue (STC), Wing and the development of Early English Books Online (EEBO). As he rightly states, facsimiles based on the contents of the STC and Wing did not just give more people access to the works of canonical writers of literary texts but also encouraged the study of lesser-known writers, especially female authors, and of non-fiction texts and genres seldom found in the kinds of curated anthologies offered for sale in contemporary bookshops.

He draws attention to concerns over preservation at the heart of Power's microfilm project, which was awarded funding so as to enable his team to work faster at a time when wartime bombings threatened to destroy rare books held in institutions like the British Museum. Equally, in debating the pros and cons of the increasing number of digital facsimiles 'that can be added to EEBO as resources not just for scholarship, but also for teaching and as windows for the general public into the rich diversity of early modern books and manuscripts' (95), Salzman again reflects on issues of preservation and the often limited lifespans of digital platforms, like that which used to allow users to compare and contrast digital copies of quarto playbooks held at different libraries, a platform that does not appear to have been maintained.

Salzman ends with a Coda dedicated to issues of access and scholarship during the COVID-19 pandemic, the time when his study was produced, and issues of access remain incredibly relevant in late 2023. One cannot help but wonder if the cyberattack on the British Library, which (as I write in December 2023) continues to make most of its collections of rare books inaccessible to readers, has helped to drive sales for their '400th Anniversary Facsimile', which is said to 'reproduce one of the finest copies' of the First Folio 'held in the British Library collections', and which retails for £85. In sum, Salzman convincingly demonstrates how facsimiles can be used to gauge both 'reverence accorded to an authentic Shakespeare text' and demand for copies of his texts across time, be they in 'original' form or in the form of convincing reproductions. It is a vital addition to our knowledge of the history of Shakespeare editing and it also demonstrates the importance of facsimiles to the wider history of early modern literary studies.

This minigraph, which has so much to say about the importance of widening access, practises what it preaches: Salzman invites readers to consult images of facsimiles alongside images of the copies the facsimiles were designed to reproduce. *Facsimiles and the History of Shakespeare Editing* is richly illustrated with images of books predominantly housed in different institutions across the world, thereby allowing readers to admire the handiwork of a range of artisans across time but with the caveat that differences are only easy to spot when you have both copies side by side. In other words, we are given privileged access that was not available to most owners of facsimiles. It is to be hoped that this charming, easily digestible study will help to inspire additional work on the different, fascinating facsimile projects introduced by Salzman.

Ledwidge provides fascinating new insight into an earlier period of Shakespeare's print afterlife, that of the second half of the seventeenth century, in 'From boards to books: the circulation of Shakespearean songs in manuscript and print during the Interregnum', the opening chapter of *Performing Restoration Shakespeare*, a volume which, as its title suggests, predominantly focuses on performance. Ledwidge provides important data on one of the least-studied aspects of Shakespeare's print history: the circulation of Shakespeare's songs in manuscript and print. The essay details occasions when 'any song performed in part or full in a Shakespeare play' circulated in manuscript or print, and records whether the song's music, text or both were included in the publication. Ledwidge delivers a learned account of musical practice and the status of music during the theatre closures of 1642–1659, arguing that 'the manuscript and printed sources which have survived from this period indicate that certain theatrical and musical practices survived the suppression of public performances and that dramatic song remained popular, though it may have found alternative contexts for performance' (15). She further contends that the continued circulation of Shakespearian song may have contributed to his plays remaining 'fresh in public memory throughout the years of theatrical curtailment' (16); she identifies among the most popular songs in circulation across the period surveyed 'Take, o take those lips away' from *Measure for Measure*, and 'Full fathom five' and 'Where the bee sucks' from *The Tempest*. She also notes that music to the plays is more often found published in manuscript form and that song lyrics are most often found preserved in printed form.

Ledwidge offers a publication history for Shakespeare's songs and an account of their appearance, omission or modification in Restoration adaptations of Shakespeare and in plays by other pre-1642 writers. The examples of Shakespeare songs in manuscript and print from the 1630s to the 1660s are organized into a helpful table with individual songs listed under the title of the play in which they appear. Shakespeare's poems were almost completely absent from the print market of the period 1640–1700, with only John Benson's *Poems* (1640), John Stafford's *Lucrece* (1655) and an edition of *Venus and Adonis* (1675) published in this sixty-year period, but this short list grows if, as some have suggested we ought, we include songs in our lists of Shakespeare's poetic output. Ledwidge's table includes the imprints of printed texts and it is illuminating to note that, alongside John Playford, a publisher one would expect to see as he dominated the publication of music at the time, one also finds the names of stationers associated with the publication of Shakespeare's poems. The names in the 1675 *Adonis* imprint also crop up in Ledwidge's table, as does John Benson – the stationer behind the 1640 edition of Shakespeare's *Poems* – who (with Playford) published both the music and the text of 'What shall he have that killed the deer' from *As You Like It* in 1652. Ledwidge's table thus suggests that some of the stationers behind the limited number of poetry books also published Shakespeare songs, making it a wonderful resource for those interested in stationers' engagement with different types of Shakespeare texts and alternate ways of charting Shakespeare's print afterlife in the second half of the seventeenth century.

Craig's monograph, *Theatre Closure and the Paradoxical Rise of English Renaissance Drama in the Civil Wars* focuses on the same period of history and argues that the Civil War and Interregnum marked a crucial turning point in English dramatic history. The closure of the theatres, Craig argues, was described by contemporaries as a form of cultural death and offered an opportunity for reflection, 'enabl[ing] them to take stock of their own theatrical past', and resulting, she suggests, in pre-1642 drama being viewed as a 'distinct genre' (3). Major developments explored in the study – firsts which for Craig mark these years as the watershed moment in English dramatic history – include the 'surge in first editions of professional plays' which reversed publication trends observed in the previous four decades; the increased frequency with which paratexts offering commentary appeared in printed drama (a development linked to the stationer Humphrey Moseley); the first dramatic anthology (John Cotgrave's *English Treasury of Wit and Language* of 1655); and the first serialized play collection and first 'comprehensive bibliography of English plays in print' (3). Craig does not, therefore, just offer an account of the afterlife of English Renaissance theatre during the ban on acting in place between 1642 and 1659, but also argues that the posthumous history of pre-1642 drama was both shaped by and made possible as a result of theatre closure.

Craig's chapters skilfully balance theatre history with book history and cover a range of authors, including Shakespeare (discussed below) and Beaumont and Fletcher, as well as the way in which 'English drama as a whole acquired a comparable literary status only after the theatres closed' (38). She offers a corrective to studies that see the origins of English dramatic criticism as beginning during the Restoration, with figures such as Dryden (chapter 5), and instead locates its origins earlier, arguing that 'theatre history begins after 1642 because that is when theatre became history' before defining different strands of criticism that emerged in the 1640s and 1650s: 'theatre history, dramatic criticism, and bibliography' (40).

Other notable contributions of Craig's monograph include the important (and too often missed) point she makes about how 'the effects of theatrical prohibition continued to shape dramatic afterlives and discourse even after the theatres reopened' (40). As Craig rightly insists, through a sensitive and detailed discussion of the plight of 'theatre professionals who continued to be marginalised from the industry' when Charles II imposed a theatre duopoly and prohibited performance without a licence, 1660 did not mark a 'fresh start'. The kinds of dramatic conditions enjoyed by performers and audiences before the theatre ban in 1642 were by no means 'restored' either, and it is hoped that Craig's study will help to inspire more revisionist histories of the understudied decades of the 1640s and 1650s and the (often) misrepresented decades of the 1660s, 1670s and 1680s.

Craig's first chapter explores playbooks as '"relics" of the dead theatre' and notes a transition in the ways in which playbooks were marketed at the start of the acting ban and later on, when 'the ban dragged on' (38). Whereas early publications sought to distance plays from their theatrical origins to 'assert their cultural value' (in the same way theatre flops tended to be marketed in print prior to the ban), later playbooks instead stressed theatrical origins as a way of garnering respectability for their contents. One of the most exciting and original chapters (chapter 3) considers Beaumont and Fletcher and the reasons why they were so popular in (surreptitious) performance during the theatre ban and in print during the Civil Wars and Interregnum. Craig here offers a fresh appraisal of *A King and No King* and argues against readings that suggest that the playwrights' popularity at this time was merely down to the political valances of their plays.

Craig posits that Shakespeare's popularity in the middle of the seventeenth century was more theoretical than practical as, despite the (mis)attribution of a number of works to him, only a few of his plays were reprinted during the 1640s and 1650s. As she puts it, his 'name and image had considerable cachet in this period', but 'the publication of texts by Shakespeare plunged' (79). What is strikingly original about Craig's approach to Shakespeare's print afterlife is that she does not only focus on occasions when Shakespeare's texts and characters and name circulated, but also offers deep reflection as to why it might be that more of Shakespeare's plays were not published in these decades.

In charting the presence of Shakespeare's works and characters in commonplace books, anthologies, collections of abbreviated plays known as 'drolls', and the titles of his plays in book-list catalogues, Craig surmises that Shakespeare had acquired 'flexible cultural associations'; he was 'an emblem of royalism and republicanism, classical high culture and working-class English entertainments' and 'celebrated as the author of indelible dramatic characters at the same time that his plays were mined for decontextualised fragments' (80). Craig also observes how 'various play titles were misassigned to him because they sounded "Shakespearean," an increasingly stable category of dramatic organisation' (80).

Craig does a particularly good job of illuminating the complicated history of rights in copy to Shakespeare's plays at the time and offers possible reasons why those who owned the rights to his plays did not publish new Shakespeare editions. She has painstakingly detangled decades' worth of transfers in the rights to Shakespeare's plays, be they due to sales or to inheritance and, in doing so, returns to the question of disputes over ownership potentially delaying the publication of the third folio. She also ponders whether a desire to avoid rocking the boat politically accounts for why Richard Coates – who inherited from his brother Shakespeare titles once owned by Jaggard and Pavier – published republican closet plays but no Shakespeare plays.

The most illuminating and convincing of her arguments relates to Moseley's relationship to Shakespeare. In 1653 Moseley entered into the Stationers' Register four plays that he attributed to Shakespeare. These were: '*The merry Devill of Edmonton*'; '*Henry ye. First & Hen: ye 2nd*', which was co-attributed to 'Davenport'; and '*The History of Cardenio. By Mr Fletcher. And Mr Shakespeare*'. In 1660, Moseley registered another three plays that he again assigned to Shakespeare: '*The History of King Stephen*', '*Duke Humphrey*' and '*Iphis & Iantha, a marriage without a man*'. That he went to the expense of entering these plays suggests that he had considered publishing them, but he did not do so and this fact has continued to puzzle critics. None of the plays are part of the Shakespeare canon but, according to Craig's line of argument, this may have been precisely what appealed to Moseley, who is the stationer who was 'largely responsible for the Interregnum playbook market's reorientation towards first editions' (80). It could be, she posits, that demand for dramatic novelty accounts for why plays that are now established parts of the Shakespeare canon were not published alongside others in Moseley's New Plays series – because they were already available in print. Paratextual notes within Moseley's publications, as she states, highlighted his desire to not reprint that which had already been released onto the print market, so Moseley's 'inaction with the 1653 entries, and his acquisition of more Shakespeare titles in 1660, might reflect his desire to acquire more titles before going to press ... but Moseley died in 1661, thwarting yet another potential Shakespeare publication' (96). It is a very plausible thesis and the study as a whole is field reshaping in its suggestions about the posthumous histories of canonical playwrights such as Shakespeare and Beaumont and Fletcher, and in the alternate accounts of theatre history it provides for both the 1640s and 1650s and the post-1660 period. Craig's account of Shakespeare's posthumous reputation and its links to the book trade is a topic also taken up by Adams in an essay published in *Shakespeare Quarterly*.

Adams's essay, '"Whither are you bound": the publication and shaping of Shakespeare in 1623 and 1923', published in the journal's Folio anniversary issue, analyses 'structures of silent whiteness in the early modern English book trade' and how 'John Heminge and Henry Condell (in conjunction with the publishing syndicate) helped establish the 1623 Shakespeare Folio as a part of white English racial formation' (192, 193). The essay opens with an eye-opening discussion of how members of the Stationers' Company sought to alienate the poet George Wither 'from the larger English community through sustained dehumanization' as a way to justify their exclusion of his *Psalms, Hymns and Songs of the Church* (1623) from the English Psalter. Concerned that physical changes to the publication would impact their profit margins, the stationers (and an anonymous defender of their conduct) used 'calculated and rhetorical moves', undermining both his qualifications and his Englishness, whilst labelling some of his hymns 'popish' (191). Adams sees the example as 'a sharp analogue to what Margo Hendricks, Patricia Parker, and Kim F. Hall have each identified as the expanding and contracting notions of whiteness in early modern England through careful race-making strategies that are tied to and dependent upon various rhetorical, political, and economic situations' (191).

In his response to what he (understandably) considered his unjust treatment at the hands of the publisher-booksellers, Withers wrote a rebuke which, as Adams demonstrates, shows his awareness of just how much power publisher-booksellers wielded over the book trade, 'discourses of reading' and the wider community by extension (192). He used metaphors of slavery and bondage to describe the treatment of tradespeople and authors by bookseller-publishers. 'And instead of invoking metaphors of Blackness in early modern England in his use of slavery and bondage, he maps out discourses of whiteness in what Karen E. Fields and Barbara J. Fields term "racecraft" – a system of thinking that Ayanna Thompson summarizes ... as "the underlying imaginative horizon, belief system, or individual and collective mental landscape that seeks to divide humans along unequal lines"' (193). The example – of Withers's treatment and the language used by him, and against him to dismiss his claims for inclusion in the volume – offers a useful backdrop for reflections on the figures and the industry that 'memorialized Shakespeare, through the publication of the First Folio, and that helped to create the most formidable representation of white Englishness across history and throughout the world' (193).

Adams's essay, like that by Weissbourd, which follows it in the same volume, urges us to think afresh about the Folio's well-known paratexts. She argues that Heminge and Condell played an important role in the 'longue durée of white English racial formation and Shakespeare' (194), citing their Epistle Dedicatorie imploring the earls of Pembroke and Montgomery to act as guardians to Shakespeare's 'orphan' plays as 'a declaration of their ambition for the volume to become a relative and property belonging to the earls' (195). Further, she suggests it should be considered a move that helped to associate the volume, and Shakespeare by extension, with 'the aristocracy, which comprised individuals belonging to a distinct kind of English whiteness that did not necessarily engage with a multiracial London that Imtiaz Habib' has recovered in historical archives of the early modern period (195).

EDITIONS AND TEXTUAL STUDIES

Weissbourd, in 'Shakespeare from the bottom: transnationalism, unfounded whiteness, and the First Folio', concurs that 'the editorial apparatus that frames Shakespeare's First Folio ... emphasizes Shakespeare's English whiteness, erecting a fantasy of singular native genius belied by the texts' foundation in a transnational literary and cultural tradition' (205). She provides thought-provoking analysis of the construction of Shakespeare found in the volume's paratexts. Shakespeare, she writes, is in the dedication 'linked not only with nature and the native but [also] with milk, cream, and swans – all terms associated with racialized whiteness' (208). In Ben Jonson's exclamation in 'To the memory of my beloued, the Avthor, Mr. William Shakespeare: And what he hath left vs', Jonson tells 'Britaine' to triumph in having '*one to showe, / To whom all scenes of* Europe *homage owe*', a form of jingoism which is carried yet further, Weissbourd argues, by Hugh Holland who, in the following poem, urges '*Britaines* braue' to emphatically mourn Shakespeare's death (208). Together, the paratexts 'reveal a persistent rhetoric of English triumphalism specifically at the expense of other European countries' (210). The Folio paratexts' contribution to the damaging and long-lasting portrayal of Shakespeare and the first collected edition of his plays as white, British property is made abundantly clear in these excellent essays.

Adams goes on to trace the same kind of rhetoric and troping of Shakespeare and the Folio in the vocabulary 'of capture, prize-winning, and conquest' used on both sides of the Atlantic at around the time of the Folio's tercentenary, be it to lament or to celebrate the large-scale purchase by wealthy American businessmen of copies of the Shakespeare First Folio. She notes how such investment both underlined and undermined notions of Shakespeare as English cultural property and argues that the extraction of the Folio from 'its historical home' and its insertion 'into a country that was simultaneously erasing and shaping its own history' resulted in 'readership and curiosity about the material book becoming a topic of interest for traditionally marginalized readers', such as Black Americans whose 'connection to Shakespeare, his writing, and the material book' is reflected in his 'persistent cultural imprint' in late nineteenth- and early twentieth-century Black newspapers, 'which also occasionally featured stories concerning the sales of 1623 Shakespeare Folios' (202). She rightly insists that it is high time we recognize such legacies and make concerted efforts to consider 'the relevance that Shakespeare had to circles outside of white, wealthy English and American people' because 'the First Folio should not just be for all time, but should also be a part of as many histories of people, however complicated, as possible' (203).

In the new preface added to the second edition of *First Folio: Four Centuries of an Iconic Book* (first published in 2016), Emma Smith also reflects on legacies of white ownership of the Folio. She considers the title she gave to her study and the moment when the first collected edition of Shakespeare's plays stopped being merely *Mr. William Shakespeares Comedies, Histories, & Tragedies* (1623) and instead became the 'First Folio', 'a newly hyperbolic consumer object'. The Folio achieved its status as a luxury item in large part, Smith tells us, due to the increased money circulating in late eighteenth-century England as a result of 'slave-produced goods, especially sugar' (xi, xiv). Describing the discovery of two new copies and the infamous resale of the Mills College copy of F1 (for $20 million) in the years since the publication of the first edition of her study, Smith draws attention to the biographies of early recorded owners of F1, men who made the fortunes that enabled them to buy and drive up the price of the collection through the ownership of enslaved people. These same figures, she reveals, were also intimately linked with elite societies of bibliophiles, such as the Roxbourghe Club. The new preface added to this 'anniversary' issue thus ends on the sobering point that slave ownership did not simply accompany but also 'enabled the rising value of the First Folio copies in the decades before abolition', and urges us to recognize the fact that the rare book libraries we visit and the field in which we work have yet to make 'a proper reckoning with their complex economic histories ... and foundational legacies' (xix).

As the Folio moves into a new era, it is important that we embrace Adams's and Weissbourd's encouragement to recognize the legacy of the Folio paratexts and the book trade more generally in shaping structures of whiteness, and to look beyond the hold of the white and the wealthy on Shakespeare and the First Folio to explore alternate archives and engagements. It is also vital for scholars of book history and bibliography to respond to Smith's call to formulate ways to acknowledge in 'contemporary academic practice and citation' the histories and legacies of the institutions on which much of our research relies (xix).

WORKS REVIEWED

Adams, Brandi K., '"Whither are you bound": the publication and shaping of Shakespeare in 1623 and 1923', *Shakespeare Quarterly* 74 (2023), 190–203

Craig, Heidi, *Theatre Closure and the Paradoxical Rise of English Renaissance Drama in the Civil Wars* (Cambridge, 2023)

Ledwidge, Sarah, 'From boards to books: the circulation of Shakespearean songs in manuscript and print during the Interregnum', in *Performing Restoration Shakespeare*, ed. Amanda Eubanks Winkler, Claude Fretz and Richard Schoch (Cambridge, 2023), 15–37

Lees-Jeffries, Hester, and G. Blakemore Evans, eds., *Romeo and Juliet*, 3rd ed. (Cambridge, 2023)

Ndiaye, Noémie, guest ed., *Shakespeare Quarterly* 74, 'Anniversary' Special Issue: On Shakespeare's First Folio and Early Modern Critical Race Studies (2023)

Salzman, Paul, *Facsimiles and the History of Shakespeare Editing* (Cambridge, 2023)

Smith, Emma, *Shakespeare's First Folio: Four Centuries of an Iconic Book*, 2nd ed. (Oxford, 2023)

Stern, Tiffany, *Shakespeare, Malone and the Problems of Chronology* (Cambridge, 2023)

Weissbourd, Emily, 'Shakespeare from the bottom: transnationalism, unfounded whiteness, and the First Folio', *Shakespeare Quarterly* 74 (2023), 204–16

ABSTRACTS OF ARTICLES IN *SHAKESPEARE SURVEY 77*

KATHARINE A. CRAIK

'Persuasion by Similitude': Finding Likeness in Shakespeare's *A Lover's Complaint*
This article considers questions of control and consent in *A Lover's Complaint* through an exploration of the Renaissance 'figure of similitude'. Shakespeare's poem works through patterns of likeness and unlikeness, exploring the chilling risks involved for women when they – or their lovers – are taken to resemble something they are not.

HANNAH CRAWFORTH AND ELIZABETH SCOTT-BAUMANN

How to make a Formal Complaint: Sara Ahmed's *Complaint!* and William Shakespeare's *A Lover's Complaint*
This article reads Shakespeare's *A Lover's Complaint* alongside Sara Ahmed's *Complaint!* It makes prominent the differences in identities and circumstances between Ahmed's complainants and Shakespeare's. It analyses Ahmed's style and the hope for change that her writerly activism offers, alongside the Young Woman's use of objects, tears and other women's voices to make her complaint heard.

AMRITA DHAR

They Also Serve Who Only Stand and Write, or, How Milton Read Shakespeare's *Sonnets*
This article studies how John Milton, going blind some three decades after Shakespeare's lifetime and caught in his own tumultuous historical moment, engaged with Shakespeare's sonnets. Reading two pairs of sonnets by the two poets, it shows that Shakespeare remained a sustaining poetic companion for Milton's journey into blindness.

STEPHEN GUY-BRAY

Different Samenesses
In discussions of adaptations of Shakespeare's texts, the focus is generally on how much the later writer has changed. This article, however, looks at a number of recent adaptations of some of Shakespeare's sonnets,

ABSTRACTS OF ARTICLES

with a focus on adaptations that retain many of the original features of the poems. The poets who write these adaptations demonstrate how what we might see as repetition is also difference.

MIRIAM JACOBSON

The Poetics of Antiquarian Accumulation in *A Lover's Complaint*

This article argues that, as much as Shakespeare's poem *A Lover's Complaint* stages unavoidable love and betrayal, it also interrogates antiquarianism, a uniquely sensory approach to history. Referencing Spenser's *The Ruines of Time* alongside Ovid's Narcissus, *A Lover's Complaint* stages both the attractions and dangers of interacting with the past in an antiquarian way.

SHOICHIRO KAWAI,
TIMOTHY BILLINGS,
JEAN-MICHEL DÉPRATS,
KIM TAI-WON AND
SHEN LIN

Strange Shadows: Translating Shakespeare – The State of the Field

A translator of Shakespeare in the twenty-first century must perform many roles: editor to solve textual cruxes; director to determine the dramatic function of the scene; and adapter and poet to recreate the drama in a target language. Translations activate potentialities of Shakespeare's text, which is resonant in different meanings.

DENNIS KENNEDY

Shakespeare's Refugees

Shakespeare's treatment of banishment, exile and exclusion in his comedies and late plays is explored in the context of recent performances and current patterns of migration.

JANE KINGSLEY-SMITH

'Nothing-to-Be-Glossed-Here': Race in Shakespeare's *Sonnets*

This article argues for the replacement of that nineteenth-century euphemism 'Dark Lady' with a Black Mistress. The more we examine the language that creates this figure, the more the so-called Fair Youth and even the speaker of the *Sonnets* become less 'fair', thereby exposing the instability of whiteness. This article will also examine some of the reasons for our racial blindspots when it comes to the *Sonnets*.

JOYCE MACDONALD

Remembering Shakespeare's *Sonnets* in *Lucy Negro, Redux*

Caroline Randall Williams's 2019 collection reorients the biographical speculation surrounding the 'Dark Lady' sonnets towards the woman who has been advanced as their inspiration, focusing on her instead of on Shakespeare, to help embody black women's often-obscured history in the West.

ABSTRACTS OF ARTICLES

TAMARA MAHADIN

Ocular Power and Female *Fascinum* in Shakespeare's *Venus and Adonis*
This article argues that, in Shakespeare's *Venus and Adonis*, Venus employs her penetrating gaze as ocular power to influence Adonis. Utilizing *fascinum*, a gendered phenomenon, Venus' gaze disrupts the gender power dynamics, ultimately causing Adonis psychological distress and leading to his tragic demise.

MADHAVI MENON

Allegorical Desire, or, The Sufi 'Phoenix and the Turtle'
Two bird poems – William Shakespeare's 'The Phoenix and the Turtle' and Farid ud-din Attar's *Mantiq-al-Tayr* – allegorize the Sufi idea of non-possession in desire. Sufism's absolute goal is desire, and desire's absolute condition is death: 'I long for death; what use is "I" to me', says Attar, as he ventriloquizes Shakespeare's dead lovers.

FEISAL G. MOHAMED

***Lucrece*, Letters and the Moment of Lipsius**
This essay focuses on Lucrece's letter-writing on the morning after being raped by young Tarquin, placing it in the context of Justus Lipsius's *Epistolica institutio* (1591) and of the 1590s vogue for Tacitism and *raison d'état*. An association with Lipsius may further be signalled by the 'anchora spei' device appearing on the title page of the first edition of *Lucrece*.

AYESHA RAMACHANDRAN

The Poetics of Shakespearian Erasure: Lyric Thinking with Bhanu Kapil and Preti Taneja
This article will focus on Shakespeare's poetry and its refractions in the work of Bhanu Kapil and Preti Taneja, asking how forms of lyric thinking emerge in a prose-poetry of lament. Examining how and why Shakespeare's poetry resonates (differently) for these two postcolonial writers, I consider how lyric's distinctive ontological perspective makes uniquely legible the imbrications of race and poetic form.

COLLEEN RUTH ROSENFELD

Shakespeare's Canvas
This article reads Shakespeare's Sonnet 128 alongside Picasso's studies of Diego Velázquez's *Las Meninas* to argue for the critical value of the discursive practice of variation in literary studies.

ABSTRACTS OF ARTICLES

Sarah C. E. Ross

Pretty Creatures: *A Lover's Complaint*, *The Rape of Lucrece* and Early Modern Women's Complaint Poetry
This article reexamines Shakespeare's *A Lover's Complaint* and *The Rape of Lucrece* in light of recent work on early modern women's complaint poetry. It explores the limits of feminine sympathy in Shakespeare's framed 'female complaint' poems and, in comparison, women writers' distinctive use of the form to eschew the ekphrastic contemplation of women's 'pretty' pain.

Marjorie Rubright and Valerie Traub, Kumiko Hilberdink-Sakamoto, Judy Ick, Alexa Alice Joubin and Madhavi Menon

Gender and Sexuality: The State of the Fields
A roundtable from the World Shakespeare Congress of 2021, discussing the state of play around gender and sexuality in Shakespeare studies.

Jyotsna G. Singh

Lyric Voices and Cultural Encounters across Time and Space: The Poetry of William Shakespeare and Faiz Ahmed Faiz (1911–1984)
This article explores an encounter between a Shakespearian sonnet and an Urdu lyric (in English translation) in the nazm form by twentieth-century South Asian-Pakistani poet, Faiz Ahmed Faiz (1911–1984): Shakespeare's Sonnet 57, 'Being your slave, what should I do', and 'Don't Ask Me, My Love, for That Love Again' (1962–1965), by Faiz.

Jyotsna G. Singh, Amrita Dhar, Jessica Chiba and Christopher Thurman

Shakespeare, Race, Postcoloniality: The State of the Fields
A roundtable from the World Shakespeare Congress of 2021, discussing the state of play around race and postcoloniality in Shakespeare studies.

Robert Stagg

Shakespeare's Arabic Sonnets
This article makes a new case for the worldly character of Shakespeare's sonnets, first by tracking the sonnet form to its possible origins in Arabic literature and then by asking whether Shakespeare could have known about such Middle Eastern poetry.

Preti Taneja

The Thing Itself or the Image of That Horror: Fictions, Fascisms and *We That Are Young*
When Shakespeare is deployed to endorse fascist spectacle, can fiction spark resistance to structural violence? Through recent political crises in Britain, India and America, and via Taneja's novel *We That Are Young*, this article interrogates racism, misogyny and

ABSTRACTS OF ARTICLES

media artifice, and calls for activism through collective narrative and the writer–reader bond.

TANG SHU-WING

Shakespeare as a Source of Dramaturgical Reconstruction
A practitioner's account of Shakespeare's dramaturgy, and his importance for theatremakers and other artists.

WILL TOSH

Writing Delight with Beauty's Pen: Restoring Richard Barnfield's Lost Credit
Twin explanations are offered for the historic lack of scholarly interest in Richard Barnfield, now acknowledged as a significant influence on Shakespeare: a homophobia inherited from the nineteenth century; and a more recent critical bewilderment occasioned by Barnfield's seemingly self-evident queerness, which runs counter to presently understood histories of sexual subjectivity.

YONG LI LAN, MICHAEL DOBSON, MIKA EGLINTON, LEE HYON-U, BI-QI BEATRICE LEI, ALVIN ENG HUI LIM AND ELEINE NG-GAGNEUX

Asian Shakespeares Online from Singapore
A roundtable from the World Shakespeare Congress of 2021, discussing Asian Shakespearian theatre.

INDEX

Footnotes are indicated by 'n.' after the page number, and figures by 'fig.'. Unless otherwise stated, the works cited in the index are by (or are attributed to) Shakespeare.

& *Juliet* (musical), 334

Abu Dhaqn, Yusuf ibn, Copt, 122
Abu-Deeb, Kamal, 118, 119, 195
Adams, Brandi K., 342, 343–4
adaptation studies, 24
'Aethiopissa' (Herbert), 71
Affectionate Shepherd, The (Barnfield), 162–4
Aftermath (Taneja), 91–3, 94, 96, 99, 103, 216
Agnew, Vanessa, 14–15
Ahmed, Sara. *See Complaint!* (Ahmed) and *A Lover's Complaint*
Akhimie, Patricia, 203
Alcestis (Euripides), 156n.25
Alchemist, The (Jonson), 323
Ali, Agha Shahid, 99, 101, 102–3, 201
All for Money (Lupton), 75
All Is True (Branagh film), 217
Allison, Sophia Nahli, 5
All's Well That Ends Well, 328
Altman, Toby, 49n.68, 71
Amari, Michele, 118
Amoretti (Spenser), 160, 166
'anchora spei' (printer's device), 106, 113–15, 114 fig.9, 10
Andoh, Adjoa, 286–7
Antipodes, The (Brome), 117
antiquarianism of *A Lover's Complaint*
  amplification motif and reenactments, 22–3, 140
  introduction to study, 12–13
  Spenserian echoes, 15–19
  the Young Woman as antiquarian interpreter, 19–22
Antony and Cleopatra, 264–5, 327, 330, 331
Apology for Poetry, An (Sidney), 15, 61, 116, 123, 185
Arab, Ronda, 330–1
Arabic influence on Shakespearian sonnet
  cultural exchange over time, 120–1, 195
  Daniel's alternative history of feminine rhyme, 126–9
  introduction to study, 116–17
  Middle Eastern literature in early modern England, 121–5, 126–7
  Sonnet 20's feminine rhymes, 128–9
  Sonnet 126 as pattern poem, 125–6
  via Sicily, 117–20
Arcadia (Sidney), 143, 158
Archdeacon, Anthony, 18
Aristotle, 17, 228
Arte of English Poesie, The (Puttenham)
  on 'figures of similitude', 51–2, 56–8, 185
  on pattern poetry, 124–5, 126
  title page, 113
As We Like It (Chen and Muni), 274
As You Like It, 129, 233–4, 340
  exile and return in, 219–22
  Taneja's 'Aliena' pseudonym, 92
  UK productions (2022–2023), 285–6, 286 fig.24, 289, 290–1, 291 fig.25
Asbury, Kelly, 334
Asian Shakespeares
  Asian language translations. *See* translating Shakespeare
  gender and sexuality in, 271–3
  introduction to roundtable, 244–5
  Kathakali – King Lear (Leday), 252–4, 253 fig.20, 259–60
  Lear Is Dead (Chia), 245–8, 247 fig.17, 259–60
  Mugen Noh Othello (Miyagi), 248–50, 250 fig.18, 259, 271–2
  Ninagawa's 1987 production of *The Tempest*, 223–5
  Ong's interculturalizing productions, 254–7, 256 fig.21, 259
  Titus Andronicus, Tang Shu-wing productions, 229–33
  Wu's *jingju*-based productions, 250–2, 252 fig.19, 259
  Yang's *Pericles*, 257–9, 258 fig.22
Astrophil and Stella (Sidney), 70
Atim, Sheila, 273–4
al-Atrabanishi, Abi l-cAbbās, 118
Attar, Farid ud-Din. *See Mantiq al-Tayr* (Attar)
Atterbury, Francis, Bishop of Rochester, 264
Atwood, Margaret, 92–3, 103
Aubrey, John, 14
August, Hannah, 321–3
Augustine, Saint, 113–14
Ayton, Robert, 189

Bacon, Anthony, 107–8
Bacon, Francis, 14, 170
Bailey, Brett, 241
Baker, J.M.R., 128–9
Baldwin, James, 153
Balizet, Ariane M., 141
banished characters in Shakespeare. *See* exile and return theme
Barba, Eugenio, 251
Barbieri, Giammaria, 118
Barkan, Leonard, 15
Barnes, Barnabe, 38, 40, 43
Barnfield, Richard
  Affectionate Shepherd, The, 162–4
  Certain Sonnets, 164–5, 166–7
  critical neglect, 158, 167–8
  early life and writings, 161–2
  Orpheus His Journey to Hell, 165
Barroll, Leeds, 127
Barthes, Roland, 256
Basuala, Stevie, 288
Bates, Catherine
  on love tokens in *A Lover's Complaint*, 17n.24, 20, 22, 54n.17

350

INDEX

on *A Lover's Complaint* generally, 12, 17, 60, 61
Baumbach, Sibylle, 171, 174, 175
Baumlin, Tita French, 178
Baynham, Luce. *See* Negro, Lucy
Bearden, Elizabeth, 47
Beau, Dickie, 282, 293, 296
Beaumont, Francis, 341
Beckett, Samuel, 219, 221
Bedwell, William, 129
Bell, Ilona, 67
Benjamin, Walter, 99
Benoît, Jean-Louis, 266
Benson, John, 340
Bentley, Thomas, 323
Berg, Sara van den, 41
Bervin, Jen, 25, 49n.68, 71
Best, Stephen, 36, 49
Betts, Gregory, 47–9, 48 fig.8
Bhardwaj, Vishal, 197
Billings, Timothy, 261–2
black lives in early modern England, 3, 66–8
Black Luce. *See* Negro, Lucy
'Black Mistress' sonnets. *See* 'Dark Lady' sonnets
black women's archival invisibility, 5, 7, 9
blackface performances, 72, 75, 76–7
#blacklivesmatter movement, 241
Blank, Daniel, 324–6
Blount, Edward, 129
Blount, Henry, 123
Blount, Thomas, 123
Booth, Stephen
  editorial decisions regarding *The Sonnets*, 12–13, 69n.51
  on Sonnet 50, 44
  on Sonnet 128, 42, 48, 49
  on 'unharnessed potential' of *The Sonnets*, 39–40
Borris, Kenneth, 168
Botero, Giovanni, 107
Bovilsky, Lara, 57, 65
Bradstreet, Anne, 188, 191
Branagh, Kenneth, 217, 266, 281–2
Brathwaite, Kamau, 93
Brecht, Bertolt, 218–19
Brett, Richard, 122
Brexit, 209, 225
Bridewell Hospital, London, 1
Briggs, Kate, 206
Brinkema, Eugenie, 49, 50
British Library cyber attack (2023), 339
British Sign Language, 290, 301–2
Brome, Richard, 117
Brooks, Pete, 305–6
Brown, David Sterling, 74n.80, 76n.91, 132, 137, 141, 331–2
'Brown Sugar' (The Rolling Stones), 10
Browne, Laynie, 26, 27

Browne, Thomas, 13, 14, 76–7
Bruijn, J.T.P. de, 87
Budra, Paul, 331
Bulleh Shah, 83, 275, 276
Bulwer, John, 74
Burbage, Richard, 334
Burrow, Colin, 18, 23, 63, 69n.51, 78, 134
Burton, Ben, 45n.57
Burton, Jonathan, 63n.5
Butler, Judith, 272

Cain, exile of, 217
Callaghan, Dympna, 181
Camden, William, 14, 20
Campion, Thomas, 126, 129
Cano-Echevarría, Berta, 124–5
Cao Yu, 265
Carpenter, Edward, 167
Carr, Morwenna, 75
Cavendish, Margaret, 190–1
Certain Sonnets (Barnfield), 164–5, 166–7
Césaire, Aimé, 93, 225, 235
Chakravarty, Urvashi, 3, 68n.39, 238
Chapman, George, 84
Charles II, 340
Charleson, Ian, 282
Chaste Maid in Cheapside, A (Middleton), 324
Chaucer, Geoffrey, 80n.6
Chen Hung-i, 274
Chia, Nelson, 245–8, 259–60
Christian, Jude, 283
Chu, Andrea Long, 35
Church, Margaret, 125
Cicero, 106–7, 108, 110, 159
Clark, T.J., 44
Clarke, Samuel, 122
class, intersectionalities of, 330–1
Coates, Richard, 341
Cohen, Sharmila. *See Sonnets: Translating and Rewriting Shakespeare* (Cohen and Legault)
Cohen, Walter, 79, 81
Comedy of Errors, The, 2, 284
Complaint! (Ahmed) and *A Lover's Complaint*
  articulate collectivity, 142–6
  introduction to study, 130–3
  non-linearity reclaimed, 136–9
  trauma of telling, 133–6
  withholding of self, 139–42
Complaint of Rosamund (Daniel), 18–19
'Complaint of Thames, 1647, The' (Pulter), 191–2
complaint poems. *See Complaint!* (Ahmed) and *A Lover's Complaint*; gendered sympathy in 'female complaint' poems
Complaints (Spenser), 15–7, 18–20, 22, 23
Condell, Henry, 218, 342

Conference of the Birds The (Attar). *See Mantiq al-Tayr* (Attar)
Connor, Steven, 169n.2
Conrad, Joseph, 6, 10
Cooke, Alexander, 334
Coriolanus, 57, 329
Cotgrave, John, 340
Cottrell, Robert D., 89
Courbet, Gustave, 6
Cousins, A.D., 171, 173
COVID-19 pandemic, 208–10, 273, 292, 334, 339
Craig, Heidi, 340–2
Craig, Tinuke, 310–11, 311 fig.31
Craik, Katharine, 180, 183, 190
Crawford, Julie, 181n.7
Crawforth, Hannah, 48n.64, 53n.12
Creation (Coventry mystery play), 75
critical race theory. *See also* race; slavery
  key concerns, 63, 66, 131
  and postcolonial studies. *See* postcolonial and critical race studies, global conversations
  RaceB4Race movement, 205, 236n.3, 239
  recent critical work, 331–2, 333
  and trans studies, 273–5
critical works (2023). *See also* editions and textual studies (2023)
  on household management and oeconomy depictions, 323–4
  on identitarian themes, 328–32
  on playbooks and their readers, 321–3
  on Reformation hermeneutics, 327–8
  on staging and performance, 320–1, 326–7
  on university drama, 324–6
Crowe, Ben, 99
Cumbie, Jimmie, 30n.9
Cymbeline, 218, 220, 327

Da, Nan Z., 37n.14
Dadabhoy, Ambereen, 137
Daniel, Samuel, 18–19, 126–9, 166
'Dark Lady' sonnets. *See also individual discussions of Sonnets* 127–152
  black beauty depictions, 68–72
  black lives in early modern England, 3, 66–8
  'black' suggestive of immorality, 62, 65–6, 67–8, 73–5, 77–8, 203
  'Dark Lady' term, 63, 65, 167
  Mary Fitton identification, 8
  introduction to study, 62–4
  Lucy Negro identification. *See* Negro, Lucy
Darwish, Mahmoud, 201
Das, Nandini, 121, 199
Davis, Dick, 82, 83–4
Dawson, Hannah, 139
Daxter, Josie, 288

351

INDEX

Daybell, James, 112
Defence of Poetry, A (Sidney), 15, 61, 116, 123, 185
Defence of Rhyme (Daniel), 126–9
Deleuze, Gilles, 263
Delia (Daniel), 127–8, 166
Déprats, Jean-Michel, 262
Derrida, Jacques, 1, 16, 243
Desdemona (Ong), 255
Devereux, Robert, Earl of Essex, 107–8
Dharker, Imtiaz, 152, 156–7
'Dialogue Between Two Sisters, Virgins, Bewailing their Solitary Life, P.P., A.P., A' (Pulter), 192
Dieterling, Averyl, 77
Dimock, Wai Chee, 120
Dixon, Willie, 10
Doctor Faustus (Marlowe), 62, 325
Doniger, Wendy, 207, 215
Donne, John, 13, 14
'Don't Ask Me, My Love, for That Love Again' (Faiz). *See* Faiz, Faiz Ahmad, encounters with Shakespeare
Doty, Mark, 50n.78
dramaturgical reconstruction of Shakespeare
 performance art, meaning of, 226–7, 233–4
 Shakespeare as medium for experimentation, 228–9
 thought levels of creative process, 227–8
 versions of *Titus Andronicus*, 229–33
Draper, John W., 129
Drayton, Michael, 62, 166
Dreaming Gave Us Wings (Allison short film), 5
Drummond, William, 322–3
Dryden, John, 340
DuBois, W.E.B., 237
Dubrow, Heather, 73n.13, 22, 63n.10, 73
Dudley, Robert, Earl of Leicester, 19–20, 23
Duncan-Jones, Katherine, 67, 69n.51, 70
Dunster, Matthew, 298–302, 303 fig.29
Dutton, Richard, 336
dwarfs, 41
Dworkin, Craig, 26

Earle, John, 14
East, Gilbert, 6, 10
Eastern and Middle Eastern lyric thinking and Shakespeare
 Aftermath (Taneja), 91–3, 94, 96, 99, 103, 216
 'Aliena's' poetry (Taneja), 92, 99–103
 How to Wash a Heart (Kapil), 98–9
 lyric thinking concept, 93–4, 194–6, 199
 philological interpretations of, 94
 Sonnet 57 encountered by Faiz. *See* Faiz, Faiz Ahmad, encounters with Shakespeare
 Sonnet 91 rewritten by Kapil, 96–8
 Threads (Parmar, Kapil and Ramayya), 94–6
Eastern and Middle Eastern poetic forms. *See also* Arabic influence on Shakespearian sonnet
 ghazal, 101, 102, 120, 195
 hui-wen (Chinese palindromes), 124
 nazm, 195
 pattern poetry, 124–6
 Persian poetry, 275
 Sufi poetry, Shakespearian parallels, 83–4, 85, 88, 275–6. *See also* 'Phoenix and the Turtle, The'
Echo (Ovidian character), 17–18, 19, 183–4
Eckhart, Meister, 87
Eckstine, Billy, 5
editions and textual studies (2023). *See also* critical works (2023)
 on facsimiles, 337–9
 on First Folio publication and legacy, 342–4
 on Malone's influence on dating of works, 335
 on pre-1642 plays in Civil War and Interregnum, 340–2
 on publication of Shakespeare's songs, 339–40
 Romeo and Juliet, New Cambridge Shakespeare 3rd edition, 333–5
Edmondson, Paul, 63n.7, 69n.49, 159
Edward II (Marlowe), 165, 327
Edwards, Dennis, 67–8
Ellinghausen, Laurie, 330–1
Enderwitz, Anne, 323–4
'English' sonnet form, 116–17, 120, 121. *See also* Arabic influence on Shakespearian sonnet
Enterline, Lynn, 181
Epistolica institutio (Lipsius), 106, 107–8, 115
Epps, Brad, 275
Erasmus, Desiderius, 106–7, 108n.22, 110
Erauso, Antonio de, 331
Erickson, Peter, 236
Erne, Lukas, 268, 338
Erpenius, Thomas, 121
Essex, Robert Devereux, Earl of, 107–8
Euripides, 156n.25, 217
Evans, G. Blakemore, 333
Excluded! (Intermission Youth Theatre), 289
exile and return theme
 in *As You Like It*, 219–22, 224
 exile literature, 219
 introduction to study, 217–19
 in *The Tempest*, 222–5

Fabricius, Johann, 122
facsimiles, 337–9
Faerie Queene, The (Spenser), 143
'Fair Youth' sonnets. *See* 'Young Man' sonnets
Fairhurst, Jimmy, 298–302, 303 fig.29
Faiz, Faiz Ahmad, encounters with Shakespeare. *See also* Eastern and Middle Eastern lyric thinking and Shakespeare
 'Don't Ask Me, My Love, for That Love Again', 199–201
 Sonnet 57 compared, 201–4
 in *Haider* (Bhardwaj film), 195, 197–9
 introduction to study, 194–7
 via Taneja, 92, 103
Fanon, Frantz, 95, 235, 237
fascism, contemporary manifestations, 205–6, 207, 208–10, 212–16
Fasti (Ovid), 105
Feerick, Jean E., 53
female complaint poems. *See Complaint!* (Ahmed) and *A Lover's Complaint*; gendered sympathy in 'female complaint' poems
Field, Richard, 106, 107, 113, 114–15, 114 fig.9, 129
Fields, Barbara J., 342
Fields, Karen E., 342
Fineman, Joel, 45, 49, 86
First Folio, 338, 339, 342–4
Fitton, Mary, 8
Fleissner, Robert, 69n.46
Fletcher, John, 67, 71–2, 341
Florman, Lisa, 43–4
Floyd-Wilson, Mary, 17n.24, 20, 61
Ford, Christine Blasey, 212, 213, 214
Foster, Donald, 160
Foucault, Michel, 35–6, 39n.27, 44, 168
Fowre Hymnes (Spenser), 113
Francisco, Timothy, 331
Fraunce, Abraham, 53
Frecknall, Rebekah, 287
Frederick II of Sicily, 117–19
Freestone, Elizabeth, 297–8, 299 fig.27
French-language translations of Shakespeare, 265–7
Freud, Sigmund, 88, 133
Frith, Mary/Jack, 331
Fryer, Peter, 2n.7
Furness, H.H., 269

Gager, William, 324–5
Galassi, Susan Grace, 36
Gamble, Joseph, 277
Gandhi, Leela, 243
Gardner, Lyn, 278
Gascoigne, George, 123–4
gender and sexuality studies. *See also* critical race theory; women

INDEX

Asian Shakespeare productions, gender and sexuality in, 271–3
critical race and trans studies, 273–5
gender and casting, 278–9, 289
introduction to roundtable, 270–1
non-binary philologies, 276–8
open-ended questions, 279–80
pronouns, 275–6, 277
gender dynamics in *Venus and Adonis*. *See* Venus' *fascinum* gaze
gendered sympathy in 'female complaint' poems
introduction to study, 180–2
male silence and responsive landscape in *A Lover's Complaint*, 182–4
reciprocal tears in *A Lover's Complaint*, 18, 22, 23, 51, 57, 184
sympathy, pity and ekphrasis in *The Rape of Lucrece*, 184–8
women's complaint poetry compared, 188–93
Georgievitz, Bartholomaeus, 126–7
Gesta Grayorum (account of 1594 Christmas revels at Gray's Inn), 2, 3, 66
ghazal-form poetry, 101, 102, 120, 195
Ghost of Lucrece, The (Middleton), 18–19
Giacomo da Lentini, 117, 118, 119
Giddens, Rhiannon, 9
'Global Shakespeare', 116, 194–5, 196–7, 235–6, 272, *See also* Arabic influence on Shakespearian sonnet; Asian Shakespeares; Eastern and Middle Eastern lyric thinking and Shakespeare; Eastern and Middle Eastern poetic forms; Faiz, Faiz Ahmad, encounters with Shakespeare; postcolonial and critical race studies, global conversations; translating Shakespeare
Gnomio and Juliet (Asbury film), 334
Godin, M. Leona, 150
Golding, Arthur, 18
Goldsmyth, Margaret, 6
Golius, Jacobus, 122
Gordon, Colby, 29–30
Gordon Burn Prize, 91
Gough, Robert, 334
Grafton, Anthony, 14
Graham, Abigail, 284–5, 285 fig.23
Graham, Scott, 287
Grant, Rosa, 4–5
Grazia, Margreta de, 63n.9, 12, 23, 54, 167
Greenblatt, Stephen, 15n.15, 67, 268
Greg, W.W., 338
Guattari, Félix, 263
Guernica (Picasso), 44
Guicciardini, Francesco, 107
Guizot, François, 269

Gurmukhi language, 275–6
Gwinne, Matthew, 325

Habib, Imtiaz, 3, 63n.9, 64, 66, 67–8, 75, 342
Hadfield, Andrew, 107
Hagseed (Atwood), 92–3, 103
Haider (Bhardwaj film), 195, 197–9
Haider, John, 308–10
Halberstam, Jack, 274, 276
Hall, Kim F.
on poetics and politics of race, 3, 29, 65, 68, 72, 240–1, 342
on race studies, 62n.3, 236
Halpern, Richard, 172n.16
Hamlet, 59, 99, 218, 233–4, 326, 328, 331
cross-race and cross-gender productions, 273
Gertrude as menopausal woman, 329
Haider (Bhardwaj film adaptation), 195, 197–9
metatheatre in, 325
Ong's reimagining (*Search:Hamlet*), 255
Serpieri's Italian translation, 263
UK productions (2022–2023), 282, 308–11, 311 fig.31
Hammond, Paul, 65, 167
Hamnet (O'Farrell), 217
Hampton, Lionel, 5
Harington, John, 117
Harris, Jonathan Gil, 16–17, 83n.18
Harrison, G.B., 2
Hartman, Saidiya, 1, 7
Hatclyffe, William, 7–8
Hayden, Robert, 5
Heart of Darkness (Conrad), 6, 10
Heminges, John, 218, 342
Heminges, William, 332
Hendricks, Margo, 131, 205, 213, 241, 342
Henry IV plays, 326
Henry V, 11, 266–7
Henslowe, Philip, 10
Herbert, George, 71
Herbert, Mary Sidney, 181, 188
Herbert, William, Earl of Pembroke, 160, 166
Hermann, Karl-Ernst, 221
Hero and Leander (Marlowe), 62, 164
Hetzer, Christof, 292
Heywood, Thomas, 75, 105–6, 109, 322
Higgins, Dick, 126
Hinman, Charlton, 338
Hirakawa Sukehiro, 248
Hoenselaars, Ton, 266
Hofer, Johannes, 4
Holland, Hugh, 343
Holland, Peter, 208, 263
Holmes, Federay, 273
Holmes, Sean, 283–4
Holt, John, 269

Hooks, Adam, 113
hooks, bell, 131, 132
Hoover, Paul, 30–2, 33–4
Horace, 105, 106–7
Hotson, Leslie, 3, 7, 8
How to Wash a Heart (Kapil), 98–9
Howard, Henry, Earl of Surrey, 117
Hubert, Étienne, 123
hui-wen (Chinese palindromes), 124
Huth, Kimberly, 331
Hydriotaphia, Urne Burial, or a Discourse of the Sepulchrall Urnes Lately Found in Norfolk (Browne), 13, 14
Hyland, Peter, 170
Hyman, Wendy Beth, 55, 60
Hypnerotomachia Poliphili (Colonna), 17
Hytner, Nicholas, 303

I, Joan (Josephine), 279
Ibbett, Katherine, 186–7
Ibn Arabi, 87
Ibn al-Farid, 120
Ibn Hamdis, 118, 119
Ibn Qalaqis, 118
Ibn Sab'in, 119
Idea: The Shepherd's Garland (Drayton), 62
Idea's Mirror (Drayton), 166
India. *See also* Kashmir
carceral policies in, 216
law on homosexuality in, 212
non-Hindu history marginalized, 236
Partition, 207–8
poetic forms in. *See* Eastern and Middle Eastern poetic forms
Ingram, W.G., 70n.51
Ireland, 225
Irwin, Robert, 120, 122
al-Isfahani, Imad ad-Din, 118, 119
'Italian' sonnet form, 117, 120, *See also* Arabic influence on Shakespearian sonnet

Jacobson, Miriam, 124
Jakobson, Roman, 267
James, Etta, 10
James, Heather, 37n.14
jingju theatre, 250–2, 252 fig.19
Johns, Jeremy, 118
Johnson, Boris, 209–10
Johnson, Samuel, 220, 264, 276
Jonson, Ben, 84, 107, 223, 343
Alchemist, The, 323
bodily sounds, use of, 321
Masque of Blackness, The, 71, 72
as university dramatist, 325–6
Volpone, 323, 325–6
Joyce, James, 217
Julius Caesar, 108
Jumbo, Cush, 279

353

INDEX

Kaba, Mariame, 216
Kalas, Rayna, 40, 49n.72
Kapil, Bhanu, 94, 96–9
Kapoor, Sweety, 99
Karim-Cooper, Farah, 29, 76, 137
Kashmir. *See also* India
   background to conflict, 208
   in *Haider* (Bhardwaj film), 195, 197–9
   Modi's policies in, 206, 210–11
   in *We That Are Young*. *See We That Are Young* (Taneja)
Kathakali King Lear (Leday), 252–4, 253 fig.20, 259–60
Kauffmann, Miranda, 3, 66
Kavanaugh, Brett, 206, 212–14
Kawai, Shoichiro, 262
Kean, Charles, 224
Keats, John, 128, 129
Kemp, Will, 66, 334
Kendall, Mikki, 132
Kerrigan, John, 55, 56n.25, 143n.36, 181, 183n.13
Khusrau, Amir, 83–4, 86
Al-Khwarizmi, Muhammad ibn Musa, 81
Kiberd, Declan, 225
Kim Tai-Won, 262
King and No King, A (Beaumont and Fletcher), 341
King Lear
   Branagh's 2023 production, 281–2
   Chia's reimagining (*Lear Is Dead*), 245–8, 247 fig.17, 259–60
   evoked in COVID-19 pandemic, 208–10
   Korean-language translations, 267–8
   Leday's 1988 production, 252–4, 253 fig.20, 259–60
   misogyny of, 213–14
   Ong's reimagining (*Lear Dreaming*), 255
   resistance and redemption in, 214–15, 218
   'translated' by Taneja. *See We That Are Young* (Taneja)
   Wu's 2001 production, 251
Kingdom of Desire, The (Wu), 251, 252
Kingsley-Smith, Jane, 138n.28, 116, 218, 223
Kirkman, Elizabeth, 6
Kirwan, Peter, 258
Kiséry, András, 109, 115
Klawitter, George, 167
Kleege, Georgina, 150
Knight of Malta, The (Fletcher and collaborators), 67, 71–2
Knolles, Richard, 123
Korean-language translations of Shakespeare, 267–8
Korn, A.L., 124
Kott, Jan, 220–1
Kunin, Aaron, 49
Kurosawa, Akira, 79, 274

Kwan, Roberta, 327–8
Kyd, Thomas, 327, 337–8

La Disparition (Perec), 24
La Place, Pierre-Antoine de, 262
Lacan, Jacques, 171
Ladha, Hassanaly, 118, 119, 120
Lamarta, Juan Pedro, 331
Lamb, Charles and Mary, 116
Lamb, Jonathan, 14–15
Lamming, George, 235
Langley, Eric, 174
language of Shakespeare. *See* translating Shakespeare
LaPerle, Carol Mejia, 64, 75n.89, 131, 138n.28, 203
Larmour, Brigid, 282
Las Meninas (Velázquez), 35–6, 47
Las Meninas (After Velázquez) (Picasso)
   Variation 1, 36–7, 37 fig.3, 40, 41
   Variation 13, 41–2, 41 fig.4
   Variation 28, 46–7, 46 fig.5
   Variation 40, 47, 47 fig.6
   Variation 41, 47, 48 fig.7
Laskin, Pamela, 334
Lawrence, Sean, 324
Lear Dreaming (Ong), 255
Lear Is Dead (Chia), 245–8, 247 fig.17, 259–60
Leday, Annette, 252–4, 253 fig.20, 259–60
Ledwidge, Sarah, 339–40
Lee, Stewart, 306
Lee Kuan Yew, 247–8
Lee Sangsup, 268
Lees-Jeffries, Hester, 333–5
Legault, Paul. *See Sonnets: Translating and Rewriting Shakespeare* (Cohen and Legault)
Legge, Thomas, 324–5
Leicester, Robert Dudley, Earl of, 19–20, 23
Leigh, Edmund, 325
Leipacher, Mark, 287–8
Leland, Andrew, 154n.23
Leland, John, 14
Leo Africanus (al-Hasan ibn Muhammad al-Wazzan), 122–3
letters in Shakespeare's plays, 104. *See also* Lucrece's letter-writing
Levine, Caroline, 49–50
Lewis, Peter, 331
Liang Shiqiu, 269
Liceti, Fortunio, 14
Lings, Martin, 79n.2
lipograms, 24
Lipsius, Justus
   letter-writing manuals, 106, 107–8, 114 fig.10, 115
   and *The Rape of Lucrece*. *See* Lucrece's letter-writing
Lista, Michael, 212–13

Little, Arthur L., 66, 76, 137
Liu, Timothy, 30n.9
Livy, 104–5
Lobanov-Rostovsky, Sergei, 170n.3
Lodge, Thomas, 220
Loomba, Ania, 63n.5, 241
Lorde, Audre, 132, 138, 139, 153
Losensky, Paul E., 86
Loughnane, Rory, 337
Lover's Complaint, A
   antiquarianism of. *See* antiquarianism of *A Lover's Complaint*
   gendered sympathy in. *See* gendered sympathy in 'female complaint' poems
   similitude and dissonance in. *See* similitude and dissonance in *A Lover's Complaint*
   The Sonnets, relationship with, 12, 22, 23, 52, 60, 167
Love's Labours Lost, 69n.51, 69, 166, 325
Love's Martyr: or, Rosalin's Complaint (various poets), 84. *See also* 'Phoenix and the Turtle, The'
Love's Mistress (Heywood), 75
Lucrece's letter-writing
   Erasmus on politics of letter-writing, 106–7, 108n.22, 110
   introduction to study, 104–6
   Lipsius on politics of letter-writing, 106, 107–8
   Lucrece as Lipsian actor, 109–13, 115
   Tarquin's use of Lipsian maxims, 109
   title page with 'anchora spei' seal device, 106, 113–15, 114 fig.9,10
Lucy Negro, Redux (Vasterling ballet), 2n.4, 9
Lucy Negro, Redux (Randall Williams)
   archival sources and gap-filling, 1–2, 3, 7–8, 10, 11
   Lucy's sexuality, 6–7, 8, 10–11
   slave experiences, 4, 5, 8–10
Lupton, Thomas, 75
lyric poetry, 121. *See also* Eastern and Middle Eastern lyric thinking and Shakespeare

Macbeth, 324
   Kurosawa's film adaptation (*Throne of Blood*), 274
   Lady Macbeth as menopausal woman, 329–30
   prophecies in, 325
   Tang Shu-wing's production, 227–8
   translations of, 262, 264
   UK productions (2022–2023), 284–5, 287–8, 289, 305–8
   Wu's reimagining (*The Kingdom of Desire*), 251, 252
Macbeth (Verdi), 241
MacDonald, Joyce Green, 67, 68–9

354

INDEX

MacLeod, Emily, 330
Magnusson, Lynne, 75n.87, 104, 160
Mak Yong Titis Sakti (Zulkifli), 271
Malone, Edmond, 15, 64, 128, 335–7
Man, Paul de, 89
Mann, Jenny, 58
Mann, Randall, 30–1, 32–4
Mantiq al-Tayr (Attar). *See also* 'Phoenix and the Turtle, The'
    allegorical mode, 82–3, 89–90
    desire and death in, 84, 85, 89
    self and other in, 82–3, 85–6
Marcus, Leah, 74
Marcus, Sharon, 36, 49
Marlowe, Christopher
    Barnfield, influence on, 162
    Doctor Faustus, 62, 325
    Edward II, 165, 327
    Hero and Leander, 62, 164
Marston, John, 84
Masque of Blackness, The (Jonson), 71, 72
Massey, Gerald, 65n.18
Massinger, Philip, 327
Masten, Jeffrey, 277
Maurette, Pablo, 172, 175
Maynard, Henry, 288
Mayo, John, 115
McDougall, Ellen, 285–6, 286 fig.24
McIntyre, Blanche, 282–3
McKerrow, R.B., 338
McMahon, Victoria L., 328–30
McMillan, Scott, 85, 88
McRuvie, David, 252, 253
Measure for Measure, 213, 328, 339
Meek, Richard, 181, 184–5
Mekyns, William, 6
memory, slavery and, 1, 3–5, 7
Mendes, Sam, 282
Menocal, Maria Rosa, 120
'menograms', 25, 34
Menon, Dilip, 242
menopausal characters, 328–30
Merager, Darren, 273
Merchant of Venice, The, 66, 111, 213, 282, 327
Meres, Francis, 166
Metamorphoses (Ovid)
    Echo in 'female complaint' poems, 17–18, 19, 183–4
    influence on Shakespeare's poetry generally, 38
    Niobe's tears, 20, 57
    Orpheus His Journey to Hell (Barnfield), 165
    Picasso's illustrations for Skira's edition, 43–4
    Pythagoras' doctrines, 17, 19, 38–9
'Methought I saw my late espoused Saint' (Milton, Sonnet 23), 148, 152–7
#MeToo movement, 206, 212

Middle Eastern poetry. *See* Arabic influence on Shakespearian sonnet; Eastern and Middle Eastern poetic forms
Middleton, Thomas, 18–19, 324
Midsummer Night's Dream, A, 65, 218
    UK productions (2022–23), 284, 289, 298–304
    Yang Jung-ung's 2005/2012 production, 257, 258
    Zulkifli's reimagining (*Mak Yong Titis Sakti*), 271
Miller, Jonathan, 224
Milton's reading of *The Sonnets*
    introduction to study, 147–8
    Sonnet 15 and Milton's Sonnet 19 compared, 148–52
    Sonnet 43 and Milton's Sonnet 23 compared (via Dharkar), 148, 152–7
Mitchell, Joni, 273
Miyagi Satoshi, 248–50, 250 fig.18, 259, 271–2
Mnouchkine, Ariane, 251
Modi, Narendra, 206, 210, 211, 212, 236
Moisan, Thomas, 333
Morgan, Jennifer L., 3
Morrison, Toni, 5, 205, 207, 208
Mortimer, Anthony, 178
Morton, Timothy, 263
Moseley, Humphrey, 340, 341–2
Motive and the Cue, The (Thorne), 282
Mr Moore's Revels (Oxford masque), 76
'Mr. W. H.' identity, 8, 159–61, 166
Much Ado About Nothing, 11, 100, 288, 328
Mufti, Aamir, 198, 200
Mugen Noh Othello (Miyagi), 248–50, 250 fig.18, 259, 271–2
Muldrew, Craig, 323
Muni Wei, 274
Murphy, Joe, 302–4

Narang, Gopi Chand, 200–1
Nardizzi, Vin, 53
Nashe, Thomas, 14
nazm-form poetry, 195
Ndiaye, Noémie, 333
Negro, Lucy
    as brothel keeper/prostitute, 5–6, 10, 66, 67–8
    Gesta Grayorum performance description, 2, 3, 66
    Randall Williams's depiction. *See Lucy Negro, Redux* (Randall Williams)
    Shakespeare's lover theory, 2–3, 7–8
Nelson, Jennifer, 37n.14
neo-colonialism, 238
neoplatonism, 87, 90
Nets (Bervin), 25, 49n.68, 71
Newton, Thomas, 148n.6
Ngũgĩ wa Thiong'o, 235, 241

Nietzsche, Friedrich, 94n.12
Ninagawa Yukio, 223–4, 251, 252
nostalgia, 4–5, 197
Nunn, Trevor, 274

'O Daedalus, Fly Away Home' (Hayden), 5
Odyssey (Homer), 217
O'Farrell, Maggie, 217
Ogden, Emily, 50
Ogunnaike, Oludamini, 89
'Oh that I were sly *Proteus*' (Tofte), 43
Olive, Sarah, 259
'On His Blindness' (Milton, Sonnet 19), 148–52
Ong Keng Sen, 254–7, 256 fig.21, 259
Oresteia (Aeschylus), 217
Orkin, Martin, 241
Orpheus His Journey to Hell (Barnfield), 165
Othello, 11, 60, 99, 123, 212–13, 323, 332
    Eyre's film adaptation (*Stage Beauty*), 274
    Graham's 2022 production, 287
    Miyagi's reimagining (*Mugen Noh Othello*), 248–50, 250 fig.18, 259, 271–2
    morality and immorality tropes, 57, 65, 77–8
    Ong's reimagining (*Desdemona*), 255
    Quarto and Folio editions compared, 74
    Quayson on, 237
OuLiPo movement, 24
Ovid
    Fasti, 105
    Metamorphoses. *See Metamorphoses* (Ovid)

Paradise Lost (Milton), 147
Park, Julie, 15
Parker, Patricia, 241, 342
Parliament of Fowls (Chaucer), 80n.6
Parmar, Sandeep, 94–6
Partheniades (Puttenham), 55
Parthenophil and Parthenophe (Barnes), 38, 40, 43
Passionate Pilgrim, The, 74
Patel, Priti, 210
pattern poetry, 124–6
Patterson, Michael, 221, 222
Paul, Saint, 217
Peer, Basharat, 197
Pembroke, William Herbert, Earl of, 160, 166
Perec, Georges, 24
Pérez-Gómez, Alberto, 17
Pericles, Yang's 2015 production, 257–9, 258 fig.22
Persian poetry, 275
Petrarch, 120
Petrarchan tropes and vocabulary
    applications of, 19, 33, 51, 68, 71, 83
    Sonnet 128 rewritten using, 44–5

INDEX

Petrarchan tropes and vocabulary (cont.)
  subversions of, 6, 12, 18, 21, 68–9, 167
  in *Venus and Adonis*, 170, 171, 172
Pettus, Edmund, 9
Philip, M. NourbeSe, 92
Phillips, Edward, 148n.6
Phillips, John, 153n.19
'Phoenix and the Turtle, The'
  allegory versus algebra, 80–3
  death of the phoenix (without rebirth), 84–5, 88–90
  desire and death in Sufi poetry, 83–4, 85, 86–90
  introduction to study, 79–80
  phoenix and turtledove reflected in each other, 85–7
Picasso, Pablo
  Guernica, 44
  illustrations for *Les Métamorphoses de Ovide* (ed. Skira), 43–4
  Las Meninas (After Velázquez). See *Las Meninas (After Velázquez)* (Picasso)
  on *Tête de Taureau*, 43
Picture, The (Massinger), 327
Piggott, Stuart, 14
Pitcher, John, 128
Place, Vanessa, 29–30
Plautus, 108
playbooks and their readers, 321–3
Playford, John, 340
Pococke, Edward, 122
Politicorum libri sex (Lipsius), 106, 107, 114 fig.10
Pollard, A.W., 338
Pollock, Sheldon, 94
Pompanio Leto, Giulio, 14
Poole, Joshua, 141
Pope's Parliament (Mayo), 115
Porter, Martin, 175n.36
postcolonial and critical race studies, global conversations. *See also* critical race theory
  indigenous voices and knowledge in *The Tempest*, 239–40
  introduction to study, 235–7
  need for, 237–9
  tensions, solidarity and friendship, 240–3
postcolonial reception of Shakespeare. *See* Asian Shakespeares; Eastern and Middle Eastern lyric thinking and Shakespeare; Faiz, Faiz Ahmad, encounters with Shakespeare; *Lucy Negro, Redux* (Randall Williams); *Sonnets: Translating and Rewriting Shakespeare*
Pound, Ezra, 25
Power, Eugene, 338
Pratt, Mary Louise, 120
Preciado, Paul B., 275

pronouns, 275–6, 277
Pudsey, Edward, 322
Pulter, Hester, 181, 185, 191–3
Puttenham, George
  Arte of English Poesie, The. *See Arte of English Poesie, The* (Puttenham)
  Partheniades, 55

Quarshie, Hugh, 289
Quarterman, Wallace, 4
Quayson, Ato, 237
queer literature. *See* Barnfield, Richard; 'Young Man' sonnets
queer studies. *See* gender and sexuality studies
Quick, Andrew, 305–6

race. *See also* slavery
  black lives in early modern England, 3, 66–8
  complaints and racialized language, 137–8
  contemporary fascism, racist forms, 205–6, 207, 208–10, 215–16
  First Folio's racialized whiteness, 342–3
  Shakespeare studies engaging with. *See* critical race theory; postcolonial and critical race studies, global conversations
  in *The Sonnets*. *See* 'Dark Lady' sonnets; 'Young Man' sonnets
RaceB4Race movement, 205, 236n.3, 239
Rainolds, John, 325
Ramachandran, Ayesha, 194–6, 200
Raman, Shankar, 81n.10
Ramazani, Jahan, 196, 199
Rambuss, Richard, 172
Rancière, Jacques, 39
Rankine, Claudia, 92, 103
Rape of Lucrece, The
  gendered sympathy in. *See* gendered sympathy in 'female complaint' poems
  A Lover's Complaint compared, 21–2, 141
  Lucrece's letter-writing. *See* Lucrece's letter-writing
Rape of Lucrece, The (Heywood), 105–6, 109
Read, Sara, 328
readers of playbooks, 321–3
Redpath, Theodore, 70n.51
refugee crises, contemporary, 219, 225, *See also* exile and return theme
Re-member Me (Beau), 282
Reson(able), John, 66
Rice, Emma, 302
Rich, Adrienne, 91, 92, 103, 206
Richard II, 83, 85, 88, 107, 327, 333

Richard III, 255–7, 256 fig.21, 259, 286–7, 324
Robbins, Bruce, 49
Robertson, Lauren, 320, 326–7
Roe, John, 187
Rohy, Valerie, 37, 94
Rollins, Hyder, 3, 7
Roman Actor, The (Massinger), 327
Romeo and Juliet, 83, 89, 158, 218, 275
  Cao Yu's Chinese-language translation, 265
  Frecknall's 2023 production, 287
  'jewel in an Ethiope's ear' image, 62, 69
  New Cambridge Shakespeare 3rd edition (2023), 333–5
Ronit and Jamil (Laskin), 334
Roper, Lyndal, 329–30
Rosenberg, Jessica, 40
Rosenfeld, Colleen, 53
Rourke, Josie, 290–1, 291 fig.25
Rowe, Nicholas, 217
Rowley, William, 320
Rowser, Kayla, 9
Roy, Arundhati, 207
Rubens, Peter Paul, 43–4
'Ruines of Time, The' (Spenser), 16–17, 18–20, 22, 23
Rūmī, Jalāl al-Din, 92

Said, Edward, 219
Salih, Tayib, 237
Salkeld, Duncan, 1, 7, 66, 69n.46
Sallust, 108
Salzman, Paul, 337–9
Sanchez, Melissa E., 46, 143n.36
Sandaime Richard (Ong), 255–7, 256 fig.21, 259
Sanford, Hugh, 127
Sappho, 99
Saraf, Shubham, 273
Satiya, Priya, 214
Savile, Henry, 107
Sawyer, Daniel, 121
Schalkwyk, David, 73n.75
Schimmel, Annemarie, 80, 84
Schneider, Rebecca, 15
Schoenbaum, Samuel, 67
Schoenfeldt, Michael, 197, 203–4
Schwab, Lisa, 14
Scodel, Joshua, 324
Scott, Clive, 119
Scott-Baumann, Elizabeth, 45n.57, 53n.12
Search:Hamlet (Ong), 255
Sedgwick, Mark, 87, 167, *See* Sam
Selim I, Ottoman sultan, 123
Seneca, 107, 108
Serpieri, Alessandro, 261, 263, 267
sexuality and gender studies. *See* gender and sexuality studies

356

INDEX

Seymour, Richard, 214
Shakespeare productions (2022–2023). *See* UK Shakespeare productions (2022–2023)
Shakespeare studies. *See* critical race theory; critical works (2023); gender and sexuality studies; postcolonial and critical race studies, global conversations
'Shakespeare's Alphabet' (Betts), 47–9, 48 fig.8
Shake-speares Sonnets (Thorpe's 1609 quarto edition)
  ordering of, 63–4, 67, 128, 148–9, 167
  Sonnet 43 in, 154n.21
  Sonnet 126 in, 125
  Sonnet 128 in, 41, 42
  title page and dedication, 8, 13, 125–6, 159–61
Shakespeare's works. *See* editions and textual studies (2023); *titles of works*
Shaw, Fiona, 293
Shaw, George Bernard, 65n.18
Shen Lin, 262
Shepherd's Calendar, The (Spenser), 164
Shortslef, Emily, 181
Sicily, sonnet form in. *See* Arabic influence on Shakespearian sonnet
Sidney, Philip
  Apology for Poetry, An, 15, 61, 116, 123, 185
  Arcadia, 143, 158
  Astrophil and Stella, 70
  memorialized by Spenser, 19–20, 23
  similitude and dissonance in *A Lover's Complaint*
    introduction to study, 51–4
    love tokens likened to women, 20–1, 54–7, 61, 137
    protagonists' reciprocal tears, 18, 22, 23, 51, 57, 184
    rhetoric of persuasion, 57–61, 135–6, 143–5
Sinclair, Safiya, 93
Singapore, 244, 245–6, 247–8, 270–1
Singh, Jyotsna, 239, 241
Sixe Bookes of Politickes (Lipsius), 106, 107, 114 fig.10
slavery. *See also* critical race theory; race in early modern England, 68, 202
  and First Folio sales, 343
  transatlantic slave trade, 1, 3–5, 7, 203
Smeaton, Joseph, 337–8
Smiley, Jane, 206
Smith, Bruce R., 59
Smith, Emma, 343–4
Smith, Ian, 72, 73n.72, 175, 331
Smith, Philip, 246
social class, intersectionalities of, 330–1
songs, publication history, 339–40
Sonnet 1, 23, 72, 75, 76
Sonnet 2, 25
Sonnet 3, 159
Sonnet 4, 75, 159
Sonnet 5, 31
Sonnet 7, 129
Sonnet 15, 148–52
Sonnet 17, 166
Sonnet 19 (Milton), 148–52
Sonnet 20, 29–30, 128–9, 159, 276
Sonnet 21, 56
Sonnet 22, 159
Sonnet 23 (Milton), 148, 152–7
Sonnet 27, 69
Sonnet 29, 45
Sonnet 30, 26
Sonnet 35, 73
Sonnet 36, 81
Sonnet 39, 159
Sonnet 40, 66–7
Sonnet 42, 159
Sonnet 43, 27–9, 28 fig.2, 148, 152–7
Sonnet 50, 44
Sonnet 57, 201–4
Sonnet 60, 38–9
Sonnet 63, 76
Sonnet 64, 38–9
Sonnet 65, 76
Sonnet 82, 77–8
Sonnet 87, 128
Sonnet 106, 27
Sonnet 108, 159
Sonnet 111, 76
Sonnet 112, 40
Sonnet 113, 59
Sonnet 116, 32
Sonnet 124, 32
Sonnet 126, 40, 125–6
Sonnet 127, 68–72
Sonnet 128
  'accidental overtones' in, 46
  fantasy of transformation in, 37–8, 40–1, 42–3
  rewritings of, 44–6, 47–9
Sonnet 129, 100
Sonnet 130, 21, 56, 167
Sonnet 131, 78
Sonnet 132, 7, 10, 72n.66, 74
Sonnet 133, 68
Sonnet 135, 46, 67, 76
Sonnet 136, 46, 100
Sonnet 137, 67n.37, 67, 70
Sonnet 144, 62–3, 73–5
Sonnet 147, 73, 167
Sonnet 148, 70
Sonnets, The
  Arabic influence on sonnet form. *See* Arabic influence on Shakespearian sonnet
  'Dark Lady' sonnets. *See* 'Dark Lady' Sonnets
  dating of, 166
  Déprats's French language translation, 265–6
  'Global'/postcolonial reimaginings. *See* Faiz, Faiz Ahmad, encounters with Shakespeare; *Lucy Negro, Redux* (Randall Williams); *Sonnets: Translating and Rewriting Shakespeare*
  interpretative approaches to, 93
  A Lover's Complaint, relationship with, 12, 22, 23, 52, 60, 167
  Milton's reading of. *See* Milton's reading of *The Sonnets*
  Ovidian influence. *See Metamorphoses* (Ovid)
  particular Sonnets. *See* Sonnet numbers above
  quarto edition. *See Shake-speares Sonnets* (Thorpe's 1609 quarto edition)
  Sufi poetry compared, 83
  'vagueness'/'unharnessed' potential of, 37–8, 39–40, 49–50
    Picasso's variations compared. *See Las Meninas (After Velázquez)* (Picasso)
  Sonnet 128 illustrating. *See* Sonnet 128
  'Young Man' sonnets. *See* 'Young Man' sonnets
Sonnets: Translating and Rewriting Shakespeare (Cohen and Legault)
  introduction to study, 24–5
  Sonnet 2 by Bervin, 25
  Sonnet 5 by Hoover, 30–2, 33–4
  Sonnet 20 by Place, 29–30
  Sonnet 26 by Browne, 26, 27
  Sonnet 30 by Zboya, 25–6, 26 fig.1, 27–8
  Sonnet 43 by Tiffany, 27–9, 28 fig.2, 31
  Sonnet 91 by Kapil, 96–8
  Sonnet 106 by Wier, 27
  Sonnet 124 by Mann, 30–1, 32–4
  Sonnet 128 by Betts, 47–9, 48 fig.8
Sontag, Susan, 36
Soon, Emily, 246
Sophocles, 217
sound, use in early modern theatre productions, 320–1
Soussloff, Catherine M., 44
Southampton, Henry Wriothesley, Earl of, 107, 160, 166
Spain-Savage, Christi, 331
Spanish Tragedy, The (Kyd), 327
Spenser, Edmund
  Amoretti, 160, 166
  Complaints, 15–17, 18–20, 22, 23
  Faerie Queene, The, 143
  Fowre Hymnes, 113
  Shepherd's Calendar, The, 164
Spicer, Jack, 8
Squire, Michael, 176
Stafford, John, 340

INDEX

Stage Beauty (Eyre), 274
Starks, Lisa, 19
Steevens, George, 335
Stein, Peter, 221–2
Stenhouse, William, 14
Stern, Tiffany, 335–7
Stevens, Andrea, 72
Stewart, Alan, 104, 108n.22
Stow, John, 14
Stryker, Susan, 276
Subrahmanyam, Sanjay, 242
Suetonius, 108
Sufi poetry
    Shakespearian parallels generally, 83–4, 85, 88, 275–6
    and 'The Phoenix and the Turtle'. *See* 'Phoenix and the Turtle, The'
Sullivan, Brenda, 273
Surrey, Henry Howard, Earl of, 117
Sutherland, John, 335

Tacitus, 107–8
Tales from Shakespeare (Lamb and Lamb), 116
Talib, Adam, 119
Taming of the Shrew, The, 143
Taming Who? (Raymond), 288, 289
Taneja, Preti
    Aftermath, 91–3, 94, 96, 99, 103, 216
    'Aliena's' poetry, 92, 99–103
    on contemporary fascism and creative resistance, 205–6, 207, 208–10, 212–16
    Margo Hendricks's influence on, 205
    We That Are Young. *See We That Are Young* (Taneja)
Taylor, Gary, 218, 264, 337
Tempest, The, 99, 339
    Atwood's reimagining in *Hagseed*, 92–3, 103
    indigenous voices and knowledge in, 239–40
    Ninagawa's 1987 production, 222–5
    Taneja inspired by, 102, 103
    translation controversy, 268–9
    UK productions (2022–23), 299 fig.27, 292–8
    Wu's 2009 production, 252 fig.19, 259
Terence, 108
Terry, Michelle, 273
Tête de Taureau (Picasso), 43
textual studies. *See* editions and textual studies (2023)
Thauvette, Chantelle, 175n.31
Theobald, Lewis, 262, 269
Thompson, Ayanna, 62, 301, 342
Thornber, Karen Laura, 120
Thorne, Jack, 282
Thorpe, Thomas. *See Shake-speares Sonnets* (Thorpe's 1609 quarto edition)

Threads (Parmar, Kapil and Ramayya), 94–6
Throne of Blood (Kurosawa), 274
TIDE (Travel, Transculturality and Identity in England) project, 92, 99–103
Tiffany, Daniel, 27–9, 28 fig.2, 31
Timon of Athens, 323–4
Titus Andronicus, 67, 72, 279, 331, 332
    Christian's 2023 production, 283
    Tamora as menopausal woman, 329
    Tang Shu-wing productions, 229–33
Tofte, Robert, 43
Tomann, Juliane, 14–15
Toomer, G.J., 121
trans studies. *See* gender and sexuality studies
transatlantic slave trade, 1, 3–5, 7, 203
translating Shakespeare
    into British Sign Language, 290, 301–2
    interlinguistic and intersemiotic translations, 265–7
    introduction to roundtable, 261–2
    mushrump network of texts and translations, 262–3, 268–9
    into 'relatable' language, 289, 302
    Taneja on, 206
    translator's multifaceted role, 264–5, 267–8
    into Welsh, 304
Traub, Valerie, 277
Travel, Transculturality and Identity in England (TIDE) project, 92, 99–103
Tree, Herbert Beerbohm, 224
Tregear, Ted, 141
Tres Sibyllae (Gwinne), 325
'Trick, The' (Dharker), 152, 156–7
Trillini, Regula Hohl, 42n.42
Troilus and Cressida, 328
Trump, Donald, 212, 213–14
Tuck, Richard, 107–8
Tuke, Thomas, 73–4
Tullett, William, 14
Turkish poetry in early modern England, 123–5, 126–7
Twelfth Night, 162, 273–4, 282–3
Tylman, Edward, 74

UK Shakespeare productions (2022–2023)
    of *A Midsummer Night's Dream*, 284, 289, 298–304, 300 fig.28, 303 fig.29
    of *As You Like It*, 285–6, 286 fig.24, 289, 290–1, 291 fig.25
    of *The Comedy of Errors*, 284
    of *Hamlet* (and *Hamlet*-inspired productions), 282, 288, 308–11, 311 fig.31
    of *King Lear*, 281–2
    list of, 312–19

    of *Macbeth*, 284–5, 285 fig.23, 287–8, 289, 305–8, 307 fig.30
    of *The Merchant of Venice*, 282
    of *Much Ado About Nothing*, 288
    of *Othello*, 287
    overview by reviewers, 281, 289–90, 292
    of *Richard III*, 286–7
    of *Romeo and Juliet*, 287
    of *The Taming of the Shrew* (*Taming Who?*, Raymond), 288, 289
    of *The Tempest*, 292–8, 299 fig.27
    of *Titus Andronicus*, 283
    of *Twelfth Night*, 282–3
    of *The Winter's Tale*, 283
Ulysses (Joyce), 217
university drama, early modern, 324–6
Urania (Wroth), 143, 181, 183–4, 189
Urdu poetry. *See* Eastern and Middle Eastern poetic forms
Urn Burial (Browne), 13, 14

Valentine, Gerald, 5
Valerga, Pietro, 120
Vasterling, Paul, 2n.4, 9
Vaughan, Virginia Mason, 75
Vautrollier, Thomas, 113, 114
Velázquez, Diego. *See Las Meninas* entries
Vendler, Helen, 64, 70, 202, 203–4
Venus and Adonis, 93, 141, 162, 164, 340
    gendered ocular authority in. *See* Venus's *fascinum* gaze
    title page, 113, 115
Venus' *fascinum* gaze
    after Adonis' death, 177–8
    divine control exerted by, 170–2, 178–9
    effect on Adonis, 172–4
    introduction to study, 169–70
    'war of looks' between protagonists, 174–7
Vickers, Brian, 143n.36
Vickers, Nancy J., 30, 55–6
Virgil, 217
Vitez, Antoine, 278
Volpone (Jonson), 323, 325–6

'W. H.' identity, 8, 159–61, 166
Waley, Arthur David, 248
Wall, Wendy, 65, 181
Wang, Jackie, 209, 216
Warner, Deborah, 292–7, 296 fig.26, 298
Warner, William, 14
Warton, Thomas, 167–8
Waszink, Jan, 107
al-Wazzan, al-Hasan ibn Muhammad (Leo Africanus), 122–3
We That Are Young (Taneja), 92, 95, 216
    Edgar/Jit's toxic masculinity, 211–12

INDEX

Hindu texts used in, 215
    as response to Partition of India and Kashmir conflict, 206–8, 210–11
    as 'translation' of *King Lear*, 206
Webster, John, 67
Weissbourd, Emily, 343–4
Wells, Marion, 186, 187–8
Wells, Stanley, 63n.7, 69n.49, 159, 218
Wemyss, Margaret, 189–90
'When I consider how my light is spent' (Milton), 148–52
While, Elle, 273, 284
White Devil, The (Webster), 67
whiteness studies. *See* critical race theory
Whitney, Isabella, 188
Whitworth, Stephen, 52n.10
Wier, Dara, 27
Wilde, Oscar, 160
Willes, Richard, 124–5
Williams, Caroline Randall, 9, *See also Lucy Negro, Redux* (Randall Williams)
Williams, Rowan, 210
Wilson, Wils, 306–8, 307 fig.30
Winter's Tale, The, 218, 220, 283
Wither, George, 342
women. *See also* gender and sexuality studies
    'black' immorality of, 62, 65–6, 67–8, 73–5, 77–8, 203, 331
    black women's archival invisibility, 5, 7, 9
    complaints by. *See Complaint!* (Ahmed) and *A Lover's Complaint*; gendered sympathy in 'female complaint' poems
    love tokens likened to, 20–1, 54–7, 61, 137
    menopausal characters, 328–30
    as playbook readers, 322
    poetic depictions generally, 30
Wood, Anthony, 14
Woolf, Virginia, 93
Worrall, Andrew, 167
Wright, Abraham, 322, 323
Wright, Joseph, 269
Wright, Laura Jayne, 320–1
Wriothesley, Henry, Earl of Southampton, 107, 160, 166
Wroth, Mary, 143, 181, 183–4, 188, 189, 191
Wu Hsing-kuo, 250–2, 252 fig.19, 259
Wyatt, Thomas, 117

Yang Jung-ung, 257–9, 258 fig.22
Young, Sandra, 241–2
'Young Man' sonnets. *See also individual discussions of Sonnets 1–126*
    'blackness' of Poet, 76–7, 203
    'blackness' of Young Man, 63–4, 66–7, 72–5, 77–8
    'Mr. W. H.' identity, 8, 159–61, 166
    'The Phoenix and the Turtle' compared with, 81
    as queer literature, 29–30, 158–9, 161, 166–7
    Barnfield's work compared. *See* Barnfield, Richard
    'sweet' term used in, 70n.55
Yushi Odashima, 256

Zarrilli, Phillip, 260
Zboya, Eric, 25–6, 26 fig.1, 27–8
Zeami, 223, 224
Zhu Shenghao, 269
Zulkifli, Norzizi, 271